Tips on Becoming a Better Presenter

Visually Speaking

The world is composed of a growing number of visual creatures. Th[...] from a visual source called television. This medium provides two cri[...] tures crave—action and eye contact. On TV, the images move and t[...] or directly at the camera. Planned movements and timely eye conta[...] Presenting is no different.

Many studies have been done about the way we communicate in various situations. The statistics may shock you. Some studies suggest that 55% of everything you say is seen and understood from what you look like when you speak. Another 38% is conveyed by how you actually deliver the information and only 7% is from what you say. Some may argue that the percentages are different, but most agree that the delivery style of the messenger can surely affect the interpretation of the message.

The three components of a presentation are the message (script), the media (visual support), and the mechanics (delivery). Because 93% of the communication is physical, the actions of the presenter, from a physical delivery standpoint, affect the value derived from the event. Actions speak louder than words and in many cases, poor delivery skills become the noticeable distractions that an audience translates into a waste of time. If you want to master the skill of presenting, you will need to concentrate mostly on your delivery mechanics. Here are some simple actions to take for more effective delivery.

Conquer the Fear

There are four main reasons why people fear public speaking: looking foolish, being judged, appearing boring, and wasting the listener's time. Possibly hundreds of other reasons exist, but these four usually cover most people's fears. All of the reasons have one thing in common: Each is a result of being self-conscious. The focus of the problem is both internal and self-directed. It becomes a question of, "What will they think of me?" Whenever the problem is internal, the solution is external. You need to concentrate on things outside of yourself in order to remove the doubt.

Establish an Anchor

When presenting with visual support, you need to set an anchor for the audience. Anchor your body to the same side as the language is normally scanned (left-to-right or right-to-left). For presentations in English (or similarly patterned languages), you must stand on the left side of the room—that is, the left side from the audience's point of view. In the English language, words are read from left-to-right. The eye is less distracted if it sees the presenter speaking from the left, glances slightly to the right to read the visual (left-to-right), and then returns to view the speaker again. If you stand on the opposite side of the room (the audience's right), the audience has to look at your face, then navigate backward and across the visual just to find the reading anchor, and then "read" just to get back to you again.

Build a Triangle

Visual creatures demand action and, as a visual presenter, you must provide that action by moving your body. The only way to know how or when to move is to know where to move first. To do this, create an area in front of the audience in which you can move. This imaginary area is called the *Presenter's Triangle*™.

While standing at a fixed distance from the display equipment, draw an imaginary line from the eyes of the person sitting on your far right to the screen. This becomes the long side of the triangle and an angled wall you can't penetrate. From each end of this line, draw two lines meeting at a 90° angle to complete the shape behind you. This puts you inside a large triangle. Using the "angled-wall" as a boundary, you simply play along the wall without ever penetrating it. If you step through it, people on your right will not be able to see the screen.

There are only three positions of the triangle: the front, closer to the audience; the middle, where you should be most of the time; and the back, closer to the screen. The reason for the three positions is because you have to move! You need to change the position of your body every so often or people won't watch you. Visual creatures demand action, and if your body is not adding value for the audience, then your audience has less reason to watch you present the information.

Play an Angle

There are only two body positions: rest and power. For most of your talk, you should be at a 45° angle to the room. This is a rest position. It establishes a non-threatening stance for the audience and opens your body to the screen when you need to gesture or move. To create the angle, point your shoulders to the opposite corner of the room.

When you square your shoulders to the back of the room, you move into the power position. It's a signal that the information being communicated is of greater importance. But don't stay in that stance too long or the effectiveness of your words and actions will diminish.

Lend a Hand

Most presenters just don't know what to do with their hands. Don't put your hands together for more than three seconds. Don't keep your arms locked at your sides as if your elbows were sewn to your ribcage. Be careful about folding your arms in front of you. With your hands locked under your arms, your gestures will be completely limited. Don't clasp your hands together behind your back, since your hands must always be in view of the audience.

The best gesture is a "reaching out" gesture. When the palm faces up as the arm extends out to the audience, it is a very friendly move. By gesturing with your left hand to the screen, you can help guide the eyes of the audience to specific points in your content. If you move away from the audience in your triangle, use your left hand and gesture to the screen. If you don't gesture when backing up, your retreat will appear distrustful or insecure and your words will have less impact. By using your gestures logically and correctly, you can orchestrate your content in a more visual manner.

Shift the Weight

Gestures won't look good if your weight is evenly balanced. If your heels are both touching the floor, you can't make gestures that look natural. Instead, they appear stiff. Consider the theater principle called "off-balance perspective." This approach is very effective. The weight must be on one foot or the other for the gesture to look smooth.

The easiest way to know if you are shifting your weight properly is to keep the base of your neck lined up with the same foot you're placing your weight on (you could also line your chin up with your knee). Now you can gesture and it will look natural. If the nape of your neck is not lined up with one of your feet, then your weight is probably evenly distributed and you are most likely resting on both heels. If you gesture from this position, it will look unnatural.

These are just some of the physical ways that your body plays a role in the delivery of your presentation. There are a number of other elements that add to your effectiveness, including your voice, your mind, and your heart. Acquiring the mechanics of form and function allows you to deliver the details of your quality message using the support from your well-designed visual media from PowerPoint 2002. All that information and more waits for you in this *Special Edition Using Microsoft PowerPoint 2002*.

Special Edition
Using
Microsoft®
PowerPoint®
2002

Patrice-Anne Rutledge

and Tom Mucciolo

A Division of Pearson Education
201 W. 103rd Street
Indianapolis, Indiana 46290

CONTENTS AT A GLANCE

SPECIAL EDITION USING MICROSOFT® POWERPOINT® 2002

COPYRIGHT© 2001 BY QUE

International Standard Book Number: 0-7897-2519-3

Library of Congress Catalog Card Number: 20-010-87730

Printed in the United States of America

First Printing: June 2001

04 03 02 01   4 3 2 1

TRADEMARKS

WARNING AND DISCLAIMER

Associate Publisher
Greg Wiegand

Acquisitions Editor
Stephanie J. McComb

Development Editor
Susan Hobbs

Managing Editor
Thomas F. Hayes

Project Editor
Karen S. Shields

Copy Editors
Kay Hoskins
Gene Redding

Indexer
Sheila Schroeder

Proofreader
Jeanne Clark

Technical Editor
Jim Grey

Team Coordinator
Sharry Lee Gregory

Interior Designer
Ruth Lewis

Cover Designers
Ruth Lewis
Dan Armstrong

Page Layout
Stacey Richwine-DeRome

TABLE OF CONTENTS

ABOUT THE AUTHORS

Patrice-Anne Rutledge is the best-selling author of more than 20 computer and business books. In addition, Patrice has contributed to numerous international publications, developed the columns "Global Business Today" and "eCommunicate," and currently manages a large global communications department for a leading Internet software company near San Francisco. She has used—and has trained others to use—PowerPoint for many years, designing presentations for meetings, seminars, trade shows, and worldwide audiences. She can be reached at patrice@patricerutledge.com or through her Web site (www.patricerutledge.com).

Tom Mucciolo, founder and president of MediaNet, is an accountant turned actor turned author and an acclaimed speaker on presentation skills. He is an expert at enhancing the key components of communication, including the message (scripting), the media (visual design), and the mechanics (delivery). His seminars and workshops have been rated as "exceptional" and "entertaining," and many consider Tom one of the country's top presentation specialists. His one-to-one coaching sessions, ranging from basic to advanced, develop individual style and prepare a person for presenting in a very visual world.

DEDICATION

To my family with thanks for their love and support.

—PR

To my wife, Joan, and my son, Peter. They tolerate my travel, inspire my creativity, and motivate my performance. Their love, their patience, and their willingness to let me spend valuable weekend hours writing made my efforts on this book so much easier.

—TM

ACKNOWLEDGMENTS

PATRICE-ANNE RUTLEDGE'S ACKNOWLEDGMENTS

I'd like to thank everyone who contributed to the creation of *Special Edition Using Microsoft PowerPoint 2002*: Stephanie McComb, Susan Hobbs, Nick Goetz, and Jim Grey for their organizational and editorial contributions and Tom Mucciolo for creating many great chapters on real-world presentation techniques. And special thanks to my mom, Phyllis Rutledge, for both her editorial expertise and her encouragement throughout the creation of this book.

TOM MUCCIOLO'S ACKNOWLEDGMENTS

I'd like to thank my brother, Rich, for his support and advice, along with his creative talents in designing, capturing, and printing all the figures used in my chapters. My thanks to Patrice-Anne Rutledge for shaping the main content of this book and to the editorial team, from copy to technical to production, in being so adept at bringing this project to fruition.

On the personal side, I want to thank my mom and dad for always supporting everything I attempted, regardless of success or failure. On the technical side, I owe a debt of gratitude to my notebook computer for accepting every keystroke throughout the entire project without complaint. A really important thank you goes to my friend, the Backspace key, without which my words would loofk ljke thyss. Oh, and finally, I want to thank everyone on the island of Crete, mainly because no one ever thanks those people for anything, and this has to stop right now!

TELL US WHAT YOU THINK!

As the reader of this book, *you* are our most important critic and commentator. We value your opinion and want to know what we're doing right, what we could do better, what areas you'd like to see us publish in, and any other words of wisdom you're willing to pass our way.

As an associate publisher for Que, I welcome your comments. You can fax, e-mail, or write me directly to let me know what you did or didn't like about this book—as well as what we can do to make our books stronger.

Please note that I cannot help you with technical problems related to the topic of this book, and that due to the high volume of mail I receive, I might not be able to reply to every message.

When you write, please be sure to include this book's title and author as well as your name and phone or fax number. I will carefully review your comments and share them with the author and editors who worked on the book.

Fax: 317-581-4666

E-mail: feedback@quepublishing.com

Mail: Greg Wiegand
            Associate Publisher
            Que
            201 West 103rd Street
            Indianapolis, IN 46290 USA

INTRODUCTION

In this introduction

Microsoft PowerPoint 2002 is the latest version of this powerful presentation graphics software program and is part of the Microsoft Office XP family. Using PowerPoint, you can create a basic slideshow quickly or you can delve into sophisticated features to create a customized presentation. Because it's part of the Microsoft Office suite of products, you'll find PowerPoint intuitive and very familiar if you already use any other Office applications, such as Word or Excel.

Because creating a successful presentation is more than just becoming a PowerPoint power user, we've included a special section in this book on presentation skills. After you master PowerPoint, you can master presentation techniques, such as creating a script, evaluating the use of multimedia and color, reaching your audience, rehearsing your speech, speaking in public, and dealing with the technicalities of presentation. This information combines with a thorough discussion of all PowerPoint's many features to create a complete reference manual for anyone who makes presentations using PowerPoint.

WHY YOU SHOULD USE THIS BOOK

Special Edition Using Microsoft PowerPoint 2002 is for experienced computer users who want to be able to use PowerPoint's more sophisticated features, as well as its basic ones. The focus of this book is to get you up and running quickly and then spend more time exploring the advanced features PowerPoint has to offer—customization, Web interface, animation, and multimedia. If you want to become a PowerPoint power user, this book is for you.

HOW THIS BOOK IS ORGANIZED

Special Edition Using Microsoft PowerPoint 2002 is divided into seven parts and includes two appendixes.

Part I, "PowerPoint Basics," introduces the fundamentals of using PowerPoint, such as navigating, using views, getting help, creating a basic presentation, and saving and opening files. If you're an experienced computer user but are new to PowerPoint, these chapters will get you up and running quickly. If you've used PowerPoint extensively in the past, they can serve as a quick review and introduce you to the new, exciting features of PowerPoint 2002.

In Part II, "Editing and Formatting Presentations," you continue on to the most essential, and universally used, features of PowerPoint—formatting, organizing, and adding content to your slides. You'll learn to work with text and tables, organize with Outline view, and customize and format your presentation. PowerPoint's new collaboration and speech tools are also introduced.

Part III, "Making Presentations," takes you to the logical next step—the actual delivery of a presentation. You'll learn how to easily set up a slideshow, customize it to work with a particular projector, create timings and narrations, preview your work, and even create portable PowerPoint presentations to display from another computer. Finally, you'll learn how to create a variety of printed material, such as notes and handouts, to go with your slideshow.

Next, you can start exploring some of PowerPoint's more advanced capabilities. Part IV, "Working with Graphics, Charts, and Multimedia," introduces you to techniques that can add a creative flair to your slideshows. For example, you can add charts—including organization charts—to provide additional information in a presentation. Or you can add clip art, photos, movies, sounds, and animation for a complete multimedia effect. For a finishing touch, you can format, customize, and add a variety of special effects to these multimedia objects.

From here, you can check out PowerPoint's Web capabilities in Part V, "Working with PowerPoint on the Web." Many of these are new to PowerPoint 2002. From saving PowerPoint presentations as Web pages to designing Web scripts to creating online broadcasts and meetings, you can integrate all the latest Web technologies with your PowerPoint presentation.

Part VI, "Advanced PowerPoint," explores other sophisticated uses of PowerPoint. You can embed and link Office objects, create macros to automate procedures, utilize the power of VBA (the programming language Visual Basic for Applications), and extensively customize PowerPoint's features and interface.

Part VII, "From Concept to Delivery," takes you out of PowerPoint and into the world of presentation design. Written by a presentations expert, this section offers detailed information and advice about actually creating a presentation specifically for PowerPoint. It covers topics such as scripting a concept, choosing a visual design, developing presentation skills, and using technology in your presentation.

And finally, the appendixes cover areas such as troubleshooting and using PowerPoint 2002's foreign language features.

CONVENTIONS USED IN THIS BOOK

Special Edition Using Microsoft PowerPoint 2002 uses a number of conventions to provide you with special information. These include the following elements.

Tip from
Patrice-Anne Rutledge

Tips offer suggestions for making things easier or provide alternative ways to do a particular task.

Note

Notes provide additional, more detailed information about a specific PowerPoint feature.

Caution

Cautions warn you about potential problems that might occur and offer advice on how to avoid these problems.

Cross-references refer you to other sections of the book in which you find more detailed explanations of a particular function, such as the following.

→ To learn more about preparing yourself to present, **see** Chapter 25, "The Mechanics of Function—Developing Internal Presentation Skills."

Most chapters end with two specific elements: "Troubleshooting" and "Design Corner." The "Troubleshooting" section provides tips on common problems you may encounter using the PowerPoint features presented in the chapter. "Design Corner" provides a before-and-after look at a specific feature explained in that chapter. "Design Corner" takes you one step further than the typical example in this book by showing you common design tasks you might perform and their end results.

PART I

POWERPOINT BASICS

CHAPTER 1

Introducing PowerPoint 2002

In this chapter

POWERPOINT OVERVIEW

PowerPoint is a powerful, easy-to-use presentation software package that is part of the Microsoft Office XP suite of products. You can use PowerPoint to create presentations for a wide variety of audiences and for a wide variety of purposes. A presentation communicates information, and a good presentation can truly convince, motivate, inspire, and educate its audience. PowerPoint offers the tools both to create a basic presentation and to enhance and customize it to truly meet its goals.

UNDERSTANDING WHAT POWERPOINT CAN DO

One of PowerPoint's strengths is its flexibility. Using wizards and other automated features, you can quickly create a basic presentation even if you have little or no design skills. And if you are a designer, PowerPoint's advanced features and customization options enable you to have complete creative control. With PowerPoint you can

- Create a presentation using a wizard, using a design template, or from scratch.
- Add content to your presentation with text and tables.
- Use task panes to create new presentations; search for documents and clip art; and apply design templates, layouts, transitions, and animation.
- Format a presentation by customizing color schemes, background, and templates.
- Make a presentation onscreen using a computer, with overheads and a projector, or via the Web.
- Create and print notes and handouts for you and your audience.
- Add content with charts, pictures, clip art, and other shapes or objects.
- Bring multimedia into the picture through the use of sound, video, and animation.
- Use PowerPoint's powerful Web features to create online broadcasts, Web discussions, online meetings, Web scripts, and even complete Web pages.
- Explore advanced features such as linking, embedding, and macros to create customized PowerPoint applications.

EXPLORING NEW POWERPOINT 2002 FEATURES

PowerPoint 2002 includes many new features that users of previous versions will enjoy. This new version of PowerPoint focuses particularly on user productivity and integration with the Web. Some new features that may interest you include the following:

- **A user interface redesigned with task panes**   Office XP's new task panes put the most commonly used features and functions at your fingertips, occupying the same screen as the presentation you're creating.

→ For detailed information on using the new PowerPoint task panes, **see** "Using PowerPoint Task Panes" in this chapter.

■ **Additional slide layouts**   PowerPoint 2002 now offers 31 different layout options through the Slide Layout task pane. With the new content palette available for content-based slides, there are even more options and flexibility.

→ To learn more about slide layouts and content palettes, **see** "Understanding Slide Layouts" in Chapter 2, "Creating a Basic Presentation."

■ **Enhanced animation features**   Animation functionality is available through several task panes with even more choices and options than PowerPoint 2000.

→ For more information on animation features, **see** Chapter 15, "Working with Animation."

■ **Integrated organization chart creation**   You can now create organization charts directly in PowerPoint without having to rely on Microsoft Organization Chart 2.0. The new org chart functionality enables you to use the formatting power of PowerPoint itself (rather than the limited formatting options of Organization Chart 2.0) and also offers the ability to create diagrams.

→ To learn how to use the new organization chart and diagram features, **see** Chapter 12, "Working with Diagrams and Organization Charts."

■ **Speech and handwriting recognition**   You can now dictate text and issue voice commands within PowerPoint as well as "write" text with your mouse and have PowerPoint convert it to computerized text. A special training wizard makes it easier for PowerPoint to recognize your voice and speech patterns.

→ To see if speech and handwriting recognition will work for you, **see** Chapter 8, "Working with Speech and Handwriting Tools."

■ **Reviewing and collaboration**   The new Revisions pane lets you evaluate, compare, and consolidate the color-coded reviews of multiple reviewers. E-mail routing and review make the process even easier.

→ For more details on reviewing and collaborating on PowerPoint presentations, **see** Chapter 7, "Collaborating on Presentations."

Other new PowerPoint features and enhancements include the following:

■ Print preview

■ Password protection

■ Digital signatures

■ The ability to control AutoCorrect, AutoFit, and Paste options

■ Help functionality on the menu bar with the Ask a Question box

■ Enhanced multilingual presentation features including full Unicode support

■ A Clipboard that holds 24 objects

■ Enhanced search functionality

■ Enhanced clip art functionality via the new Clip Organizer

■ Easier object rotation

■ GDI+ technology to reduce jagged edges and improve transparency and blending

USING MENUS AND SHORTCUT MENUS

You use PowerPoint menus to perform specific actions. The PowerPoint menu bar includes nine menu categories, each displaying a list of related commands. Figure 1.1 illustrates the menu bar.

Menu bar

Figure 1.1
Use menus to navigate PowerPoint.

In PowerPoint, only the most commonly used menu commands are displayed when you first install the program. To see additional menu commands, click the double down arrows at the bottom of the list. After you use a menu command, it becomes part of the regular menu, and you don't need to select the down arrows to locate it.

To open a menu using the keyboard, press the Alt key plus the underlined letter in the menu category you want to open. For example, pressing Alt+D opens the Slide Show menu. This is called a *hotkey*.

To customize how menu commands display on menus, choose Tools, Customize and go to the Options tab of the Customize dialog box (see Figure 1.2).

Figure 1.2
Choose how to display menu commands.

Select the Always Show Full Menus check box to display all menu commands rather than personalized menus. If you select this option in PowerPoint, it also affects menus in other Office programs.

Select Show Full Menus After a Short Delay to display the entire menu after you hover the mouse over an open menu for a few seconds.

→ To learn how to add, delete, and modify menu commands as well as create your own menu, **see** "Customizing Menu Commands" in Chapter 21, "Customizing PowerPoint."

Several PowerPoint menus include submenus, identified with a right arrow next to the menu command itself. Figure 1.3 illustrates a submenu.

Figure 1.3
A submenu is a second-menu level of navigation in PowerPoint.

PowerPoint also includes shortcut menus, specific menus that are context sensitive and relate to a selected object. To view a shortcut menu, right-click the mouse. Figure 1.4 displays a shortcut menu.

Figure 1.4
To see specific menu options, right-click the mouse.

USING TOOLBARS

A toolbar is similar to a menu because it categorizes related commands to make it easier for you to perform a specific task. Toolbars use a graphical representation, or button, rather than a menu-based text representation. Even though toolbars use buttons rather than text, you can still display a text description of what the button does by pausing the mouse over it. A *ScreenTip* appears, identifying the button's function. Figure 1.5 illustrates a ScreenTip.

Toolbar

Figure 1.5
ScreenTips identify
toolbar buttons.

ScreenTip

⚠ ***ScreenTips don't appear?*** *See the "Troubleshooting" section near the end of the chapter.*

The Standard and Formatting toolbars are the two most commonly used PowerPoint toolbars. Table 1.1 describes the buttons on the Standard toolbar, which you'll use frequently in PowerPoint.

Note

You can switch between displaying the Standard and Formatting toolbars on either two rows or one with the Show Standard and Formatting Toolbars on Two Rows check box on the Options tab of the Customize dialog box. Open this dialog box by selecting Tools, Customize. Although it's usually easier having access to all these buttons on two rows, you might want to combine these toolbars if you want to save screen space.

→ To view a table of the buttons on the Formatting toolbar, **see** "Using the Formatting Toolbar" in Chapter 3, "Working with Text."

TABLE 1.1 STANDARD TOOLBAR BUTTONS

Button	Name	Description
	New	Creates a new presentation and opens the New Slide dialog box, in which you can choose from a variety of slide layouts.
	Open	Opens the Open dialog box from which you can open an existing presentation.
	Save	Opens the Save As dialog box in which you can save your open presentation.
	E-mail	Displays fields in which you can enter an e-mail recipient to whom you want to send the open presentation.
	Search	Opens the Advanced Search task pane where you can search your computer or a network drive.
	Print	Prints the presentation on the default printer.
	Print Preview	Displays the current presentation in Print Preview.

TABLE 1.1 CONTINUED

Button	Name	Description
	Spelling	Checks the spelling and style of the open presentation.
	Cut	Cuts the selected text or object, which is deleted from the presentation, and places it on the Clipboard.
	Copy	Copies the selected text or object, which remains on the presentation, and places it on the Clipboard.
	Paste	Pastes the selected Clipboard object into the location in the presentation you specify. If you haven't selected an object, the most recently cut or copied object is pasted.
	Format Painter	Copies the format of the selected text or object and applies this formatting to the next object you click.
	Undo	Undoes the last action.
	Redo	Does the previous action again.
	Insert Hyperlink	Opens the Insert Hyperlink dialog box, from which you can insert a hyperlink to a Web page, e-mail address, or another document or presentation.
	Tables and Borders	Displays the Tables and Borders toolbar.
	Insert Table	Displays a palette in which you can choose the size of table you want to insert.
	Insert Chart	Activates Microsoft Graph, with which you can insert a chart in your presentation.
	Expand All	Expands the content of the Outline tab in Normal view to display all titles and body text for each slide. This button acts as a toggle; click again to contract the outline.
	Show Formatting	Displays text formatting in the outline pane.
	Show/Hide Grid	Acts as a toggle for displaying a grid on your presentation, which you can use to more accurately position objects on your slides.
	Color/Grayscale	Displays a menu that enables you to preview your presentation in Color, Grayscale, or Pure Black and White.
37%	Zoom	Enables you to select a zoom percentage from the drop-down list from 25% to 400%, or enter your own percentage from 10% to 400%.
	Microsoft PowerPoint Help	Activates the Office Assistant.

DISPLAYING TOOLBARS

To open and close toolbars manually, choose View, Toolbars and then select or deselect toolbars from the list of available options. Figure 1.6 illustrates this menu and the available toolbars.

Figure 1.6
Select a toolbar from this menu to display it.

→ To learn how to customize and modify PowerPoint toolbars to fit your needs, **see** "Customizing Toolbars" in Chapter 21.

MOVING TOOLBARS

You can easily move a toolbar to a new location. How you do this depends on whether the toolbar is *docked* or is *floating*. Figure 1.7 illustrates both types of toolbars.

Move handle

Docked toolbar

Figure 1.7
You can move PowerPoint toolbars to make the program easier to use.

Floating toolbar

To move a docked toolbar, drag the move handle on its left side to a new location. To move a floating toolbar, drag its title bar. You can easily switch a toolbar from docked to floating and vice versa. Drag a docked toolbar to another location on the screen to float it. Drag a floating toolbar to the edge of the window to dock it.

Tip from
Patrice-Anne
Rutledge

You can resize a floating toolbar by dragging on any side. This way you can display the buttons straight across in one row or in several rows, depending on which way it's easier to view your presentation.

 Can't find a toolbar button you've used before? See the "Troubleshooting" section near the end of the chapter.

USING POWERPOINT TASK PANES

PowerPoint 2002 introduces a new user interface tool—the task pane. PowerPoint has eight main task panes that are readily accessible, as well as several others that appear only under certain conditions (such as the Revisions pane for reviewing and collaborating). These task panes are

- **New Presentation**   Enables you to create a new presentation in a variety of ways or open an existing presentation. Choose File, New from the menu bar to open this task pane, seen in Figure 1.8.

Click to switch to another task pane.

Figure 1.8
The New Presentation task pane is one of many new task panes in PowerPoint 2002.

 To learn how to use the New Presentation task pane, **see** Chapter 2.

- **Clipboard**   Offers the ability to collect and paste up to 24 different items. Choose Edit, Clipboard from the menu bar to open this task pane.

- **Search**   Provides both basic and advanced search capability on both your own computer and a network. Choose File, Search from the menu bar to open this task pane.

- **Insert Clip Art**   Displays search functionality for locating clip art images as well as links to the Clip Organizer. Choose Insert, Picture, Clip Art from the menu bar to open this task pane.

→ For more information about using clip art and the Media Gallery, **see** Chapter 13, "Working with Media Clips and the Clip Organizer."

- **Slide Layout**   Enables you to apply up to 31 different layouts, each with its own additional design flexibility. Choose Format, Slide Layout from the menu bar or click the New Slide button on the Formatting toolbar to open this task pane.

- **Slide Design**   Offers three sections of design functionality: Design Templates, Color Schemes, and Animation Schemes. Choose Format, Slide Design from the menu bar or click the Design button on the Formatting toolbar to open this task pane.

→ For more information about slide layouts and design, **see** Chapter 2.

- **Custom Animation**   Enables you to apply sophisticated animations to your slides or objects on your slides. Choose Slide Show, Custom Animation from the menu bar to open this task pane.

- **Slide Transition**   Offers the ability to apply animated transitions as you move from slide to slide. Choose Slide Show, Slide Transition from the menu bar to open this task pane.

→ For more information about the Custom Animation and Slide Transition task panes, **see** Chapter 15.

You can also choose View, Task Pane from the menu bar to open the task pane. The most recently viewed pane opens, but you can easily change to a different task pane. To do so, click the down arrow on the upper-right side of the task pane to open a menu of all available panes.

The upper-left corner of the task pane contains back and forward arrows that you can click to go back to the previously viewed task panes in the order in which you opened them and forward again. To close a task pane, click the Close button in the upper-right corner or choose View, Task Pane again.

To customize when task panes appear, choose Tools, Options and go to the View tab of the Options dialog box (see Figure 1.9).

Remove the check mark by the Startup Task Pane check box if you don't want a task pane to appear upon startup. Remove the check mark by the Slide Layout Task Pane When Inserting New Slides check box if you don't want the Slide Layout task pane to open when you click the New Slide button.

You can also resize the task pane if you want to make it horizontally bigger or smaller. To do so, pause the mouse pointer over the left edge of the pane until the pointer displays as a two-headed arrow. Click the mouse and drag the left edge to either the left or right, depending on whether you want to increase or decrease the amount of screen space the task pane occupies.

Figure 1.9
Customize how to
display task panes
in PowerPoint.

USING THE CLIPBOARD TASK PANE

The Clipboard task pane is new to PowerPoint 2002 and is shared with other Office XP applications such as Word and Excel. This collect-and-paste feature enables you to copy multiple items and then paste them selectively, rather than simply copying and pasting a single item. In Office XP, you can collect up to 24 items—text, objects, graphics, documents, Web pages, and so forth—and then selectively paste these as needed. The Clipboard task pane enables you to view and manage the 24 items you have most recently copied. To open this task pane, choose Edit, Office Clipboard. If you already have a task pane open, click the down arrow in the upper-right corner and choose Clipboard from the menu that appears. Figure 1.10 illustrates this task pane.

Click an item on the Clipboard task pane to paste it on the current slide (where the cursor is active). On this task pane you also can

- Click the Paste All button to paste all collected objects into the open presentation or document.
- Click the Clear All button to delete all collected items from the Clipboard.
- Right-click on a selected item and choose Delete from the menu that appears to delete the individual item only.
- Click the Options button for four additional options:
  - **Show Office Clipboard Automatically** Automatically displays the Clipboard when you copy or cut an object.

Figure 1.10
You can easily manage and share information using the Clipboard task pane.

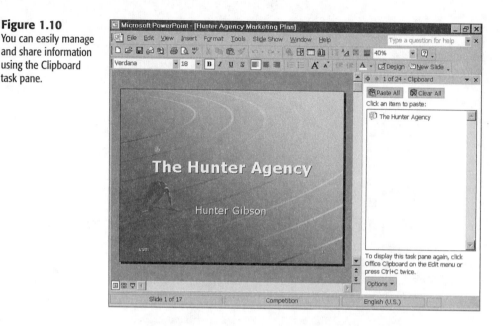

- **Collect Without Showing Office Clipboard** Enables you to copy and cut text and objects without displaying the Clipboard.
- **Show Office Clipboard Icon on Taskbar** Displays a Clipboard icon on the taskbar in the lower-right corner of your screen when the Clipboard task pane is open.
- **Show Status Near Taskbar When Copying** Displays the Clipboard's status (such as 6 of 24 collected) next to the Clipboard icon in the taskbar when you copy text or an object.

USING THE SEARCH TASK PANE

Sometimes you won't be able immediately to find a presentation you want to open. You might have so many saved presentations that it's difficult to find files whose names you've forgotten. Or you might have saved the file you're looking for in another folder and can't locate it. Using the Search task pane, you can conduct sophisticated searches based on text found in a particular presentation, as well as on specific presentation properties, to help you find the exact file you need. Basic Search is the default PowerPoint task pane, but you can click the Advanced Search hyperlink on this task pane to open the Advanced Search pane, where you can do more detailed searches based on file properties.

PERFORMING A BASIC SEARCH

To open the Search task pane, choose File, Search from the menu bar. If you already have a task pane open, click the down arrow in the upper-right corner and choose Search from the menu that appears. The Basic Search task pane opens by default (see Figure 1.11).

Figure 1.11
To search for specific text in a presentation, use the Basic Search task pane.

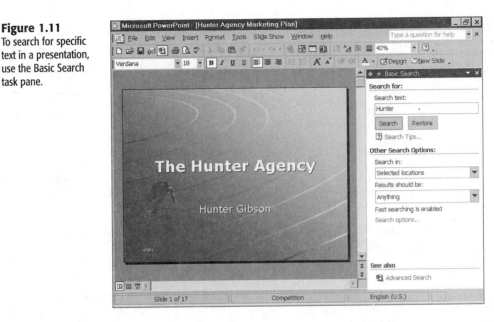

To perform a basic search, follow these steps:

1. Enter the specific text you want to search for in the Search Text field. This can be any text included in the presentation you want to find.

2. In the Search In field, select the folder or folders you want to search from the drop-down list. These can be folders on your computer, on a connected network drive, or on a Web folder. To expand a folder, click the plus (+) sign; to collapse it, click the minus (-) sign. When you find the folder you want, place a check mark in the box that precedes it.

Tip from
Patrice-Anne Rutledge

If you have no idea where the file is located, choose Everywhere to search in all locations. Be aware, however, that it takes longer to search all folders rather than to focus on specific folders.

3. Select the type of files to look for in the Results Should Be drop-down list. Options include a variety of Office file types (PowerPoint, Word, or Excel files, for example) or Web pages.

Tip from
Patrice-Anne Rutledge

If you want to enable PowerPoint's Indexing Service, click the Search Options hyperlink to open the Indexing Service Settings dialog box (see Figure 1.12). Enabling Indexing Service directs PowerPoint to index your files when your computer is idle so that searches are faster and more accurate. If Fast Search isn't installed, you'll first need to click the Install hyperlink to install it before you can see the Search Options hyperlink.

Figure 1.12
Indexing speeds up searching a large collection of files.

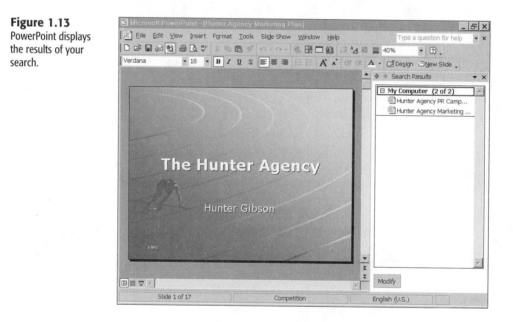

4. Click the Search button to begin the search process. PowerPoint finds matching presentations and displays them in the task pane, which is renamed Search Results (see Figure 1.13).

Figure 1.13
PowerPoint displays the results of your search.

5. Double-click the file you want to open.

Note

For additional options, click the down arrow next to the selected file. From the menu that appears, you can edit the file, create a new file from this file, copy the link to the Clipboard, or view the file's properties.

Click the Stop button to stop a search in progress. Click Modify to return to the Basic Search task pane.

PERFORMING AN ADVANCED SEARCH

If you want to search on specific presentation properties, you'll need to use the Advanced Search task pane. These properties align to the information you see in the Properties dialog box. To access Advanced Search functionality, click the Advanced Search hyperlink at the bottom of the Basic Search task pane. Figure 1.14 illustrates the Advanced Search task pane.

Figure 1.14
You can search on the properties in the Advanced Search task pane.

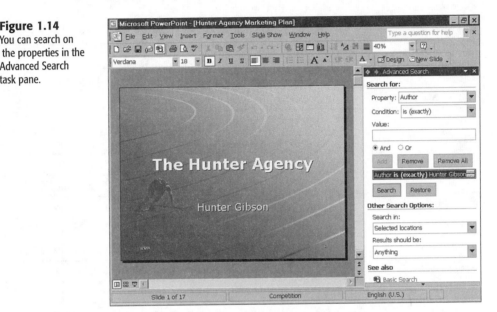

→ If you want to know the exact definition of each file property, **see** "Setting Presentation Properties" in Chapter 21.

Table 1.2 lists all the properties you can search on the Advanced Search task pane as well as the conditions available for each, which fall into three main categories: text, numbers, and dates.

TABLE 1.2 ADVANCED SEARCH PROPERTIES AND CONDITIONS

Property	Available Conditions
Application Name	Is (exactly), includes
Author	Is (exactly), includes
Category	Is (exactly), includes
Comments	Is (exactly), includes
Company	Is (exactly), includes
Contents	Is (exactly), includes
Creation Date	On, on or after, on or before, today, tomorrow, yesterday, this week, next week, last week, this month, next month, last month
Description	Is (exactly), includes

TABLE 1.2   CONTINUED

Property	Available Conditions
File Name	Is (exactly), includes
Format	Is (exactly), includes
Keywords	Is (exactly), includes
Last Modified	On, on or after, on or before, today, tomorrow, yesterday, this week, next week, last week, this month, next month, last month
Last Printed	On, on or after, on or before, today, tomorrow, yesterday, this week, next week, last week, this month, next month, last month
Last Saved By	Is (exactly), includes
Manager	Is (exactly), includes
Number of Characters	Equals, not equal to, more than, less than, at least, at most
Number of Characters + Spaces	Equals, not equal to, more than, less than, at least, at most
Number of Hidden Slides	Equals, not equal to, more than, less than, at least, at most
Number of Lines	Equals, not equal to, more than, less than, at least, at most
Number of Multimedia Clips	Equals, not equal to, more than, less than, at least, at most
Number of Notes	Equals, not equal to, more than, less than, at least, at most
Number of Pages	Equals, not equal to, more than, less than, at least, at most
Number of Paragraphs	Equals, not equal to, more than, less than, at least, at most
Number of Slides	Equals, not equal to, more than, less than, at least, at most
Number of Words	Equals, not equal to, more than, less than, at least, at most
Revision	Is (exactly), includes
Size	Equals, not equal to, more than, less than, at least, at most
Subject	Is (exactly), includes
Template	Is (exactly), includes
Text or Property	Includes
Title	Is (exactly), includes
Total Editing Time	Equals, not equal to, more than, less than, at least, at most

Depending on your selection in the Condition field, the Value field may activate. For example, if you search the Last Printed property and choose Yesterday as your condition, no further value is required. However, if you search the Title property and select Includes Words as the condition, you have to enter a value to indicate the exact words to include.

As another example, let's say you want to find a specific presentation whose filename you've forgotten. You do remember, however, that you created the presentation sometime last week. To find this file, you could search the Creation Date property for the Last Week condition. Based on this information, you can locate all presentations created within the past week, which should narrow your search considerably.

To use the Advanced Search task pane, follow these steps:

1. Select a property from the drop-down list.
2. Select a condition from the available choices for the chosen property.
3. If required, enter a value that matches the criterion for which you're searching.
4. Click the Add button to add this criterion to the search list.
5. Continue adding search criteria as needed. As you add criteria, choose either the And or Or option button to specify whether the search should look for this criterion *and* other specified criteria or whether it should look for this criterion *or* other specified criteria.

 Note To remove a search, select it in the list and click Remove. To remove all searches, click Remove All.

6. Continue with steps 2 through 5 described in "Performing a Basic Search," earlier in this chapter.

UNDERSTANDING POWERPOINT VIEWS

PowerPoint 2002 includes three different views. A *view* is a way you see and work with the software; which one you use depends on what you're doing at any particular time. To display a particular view, click its View button in the lower-left portion of the PowerPoint window.

PowerPoint's three views are

- **Normal view** This is the default view and displays three panes: the Normal View pane, which includes the Outline and Slides tabs, the slide pane in the center, and the notes pane beneath it. Figure 1.15 illustrates Normal view.

  Note that your screen might also display a task pane. This is a separate pane and isn't connected to your choice of view. If you have a task pane open, it will appear in both Normal view and Slide Sorter view, but it won't appear if you present a slideshow.

  The three Normal view panes are

  - The slide pane, which is the largest of the three panes. You can add text, graphics, tables, charts, and other objects to your presentation on the slide pane.

Note You can also use the scrollbar on the right side of the slide pane to navigate between presentation slides. The Page Up and Page Down keys also enable you to navigate.

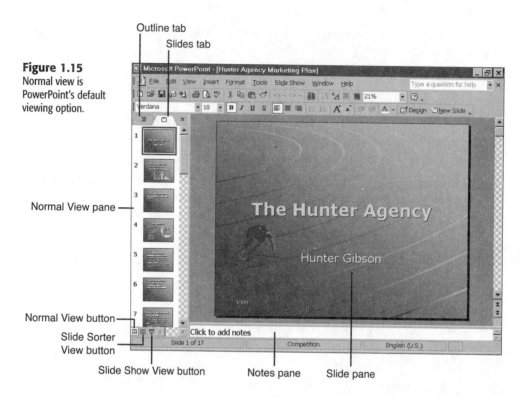

Outline tab

Slides tab

Figure 1.15
Normal view is
PowerPoint's default
viewing option.

Normal View pane

Normal View button

Slide Sorter
View button

Slide Show View button   Notes pane   Slide pane

- The Normal View pane, on the left side of the screen. This pane offers an Outline tab, which displays an outline of your presentation, including the initial text of each slide. It also offers a Slides tab, which displays a thumbnail of your slides. You can use this pane to rearrange and organize slides or to move to another slide. On the Outline tab you can also enter content. Note that when you click the Outline tab, text labels are displayed (Outline and Slides). When you click the Slides tab, an icon appears as a label.

- The notes pane includes space for you to write speaker's notes or notes to yourself about your presentation.

→ For suggestions on creating effective speaker's notes, **see** "Creating Notes and Handouts" in Chapter 10, "Creating and Printing Presentation Materials."

   You can easily resize the panes in Normal view. To do so, drag the border between panes to a new location. If you want to hide the Normal View pane, click its Close button. You can always reopen it later by choosing View, Normal (Restore Panes).

   ■ **Slide Sorter view**   This view, shown in Figure 1.16, displays miniature previews of all the slides in your presentation, making it easier for you to organize them.

→ To learn how to use this view, **see** "Using the Slide Sorter View" in Chapter 6, "Formatting Slides and Presentations."

   ■ **Slide Show view**   Slide Show view displays your slides as they would appear in a slideshow, full-screen without any PowerPoint menus, toolbars, or other features. Figure 1.17 illustrates this view.

Figure 1.16
Seeing miniature versions of your slides can help you rearrange them.

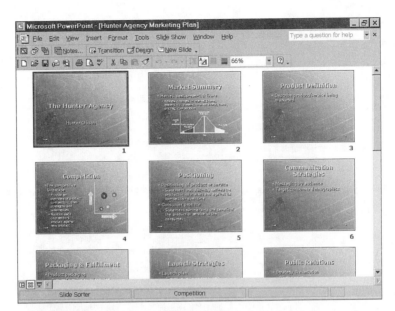

Figure 1.17
Slide Show view demonstrates how your presentation will look when you present it.

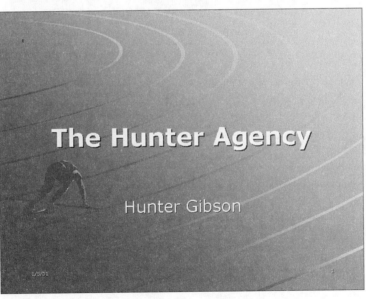

→ For details on viewing slideshows, **see** Chapter 9, "Presenting a Slideshow."

PowerPoint's default view is Normal view with the Outline tab selected. If you want to change this, choose Tools, Options and go to the View tab on the Options dialog box, as shown in Figure 1.18.

Figure 1.18
You can alter
PowerPoint's defaults
in the Options dialog
box.

On this tab, you can specify your default view from the Open All Documents Using This View drop-down list.

GETTING HELP

PowerPoint includes a wide variety of help options, one of which should suit your needs and the way you use information. Options include the Ask a Question box, Office Assistant, a full-search Help window, and help on the Web.

> **Note**
>
> At times, PowerPoint might not behave as expected, or it might deliver an error message when none is needed. To find and repair these problems automatically, choose Help, Detect and Repair.

USING THE ASK A QUESTION BOX

The Ask a Question box (see Figure 1.19) puts help at your fingertips, always available on the menu bar.

To use this new feature, simply enter a question or keyword in the box, press Enter, and choose from a menu of help topics. The Microsoft PowerPoint Help window opens with specific information on the topic you chose, shown in Figure 1.20.

Figure 1.19
Use the Ask a
Question box for fast
and easy help.

Figure 1.20
The Help window
displays detailed help
on your selected topic.

→ To learn more about the Microsoft PowerPoint Help window, **see** "Using Microsoft PowerPoint Help" in this chapter.

USING THE OFFICE ASSISTANT

The *Office Assistant* lets you ask natural language questions, such as "How do I insert WordArt?" It provides help topics that answer these questions. If the Office Assistant doesn't already appear on your screen, click the Microsoft PowerPoint Help button on the Standard toolbar or press F1. Click the Assistant when you need help, and a balloon appears that asks you what you want to do (see Figure 1.21).

Enter your question—or just a word or phrase if you like—and click the Search button. The balloon offers a list of topics related to the question. Click the most relevant topic to open the Microsoft PowerPoint Help window.

Note

Click See More at the bottom of the Help caption to view additional help topics.

Office Assistant

Figure 1.21
The Office Assistant can answer your PowerPoint questions.

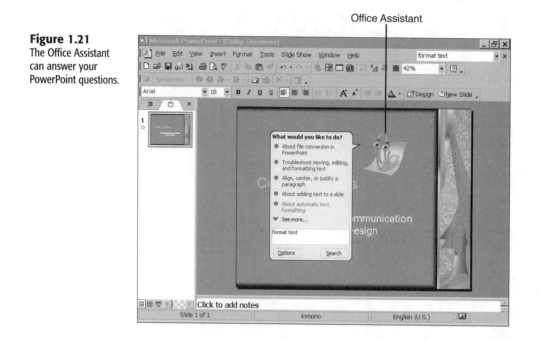

You can change to a different Office Assistant if you don't like the default. Click the Options button in the Assistant balloon and choose the Gallery tab on the Office Assistant dialog box, shown in Figure 1.22.

Figure 1.22
Make Rocky your Office Assistant, if you like.

The Gallery offers alternative Assistant images, including Rocky, Mother Nature, and the Dot.

Temporarily hide the Office Assistant by choosing Help, Hide the Office Assistant. This isn't the same as turning off the Assistant because it's temporary. The Assistant returns again the next time you ask for help by clicking the Microsoft PowerPoint Help button or another dialog box help button. You can also temporarily hide the Office Assistant by right-clicking on the Assistant and choosing Hide.

If you really don't like the Office Assistant at all and want to turn it off, click the Options tab on the Office Assistant dialog box and remove the check mark from the Use the Office Assistant check box.

The next time you press F1 for help, the Microsoft PowerPoint Help window will open directly, bypassing the Office Assistant. If you decide to give the Office Assistant another try, just choose Help, Show the Office Assistant and it will reappear.

PART

I

CH

1

> **Note**
>
> The Office Assistant settings you make in PowerPoint, or another application such as Word or Excel, are used in all Office applications.

USING MICROSOFT POWERPOINT HELP

You can access the Microsoft PowerPoint Help window through the Ask a Question box, through the Office Assistant, or directly from F1 (or the Microsoft PowerPoint Help button) if the Assistant is turned off. The Microsoft PowerPoint Help window includes three main tabs, as seen in Figure 1.23.

The Contents tab lists a table of contents for the help system based on specific tasks you might want to perform.

The Answer Wizard enables you to ask a question in plain English, much like the Office Assistant.

Figure 1.23
This screen lets you search Microsoft PowerPoint Help by keyword.

The Index includes a list of words and phrases you can search to find the appropriate help topic.

From each help topic, you can click the Back button to return to the previous screen, click the Print button to print the topic, or click the Hide button to display the help topic windows without the search tabs.

GETTING HELP FROM THE WEB

You can also search for the latest tips, information, downloads, and news about PowerPoint on Microsoft's Office XP Web site. To access it, select Help, Office on the Web.

TROUBLESHOOTING

DISPLAYING SCREENTIPS

A ScreenTip doesn't appear when I pause the mouse over a toolbar button.

Verify that the Show ScreenTips on Toolbars check box is checked on the Options tab of the Customize dialog box. Access this dialog box by selecting Tools, Customize.

DISPLAYING HIDDEN TOOLBAR BUTTONS

I can't find a button I need on the toolbar.

If you've moved your toolbars or placed two toolbars on the same row, not all buttons might be visible. Click the Toolbar Options button (it looks like a small down arrow) at the far right of the toolbar to display additional buttons.

HIDING THE OFFICE ASSISTANT

The Office Assistant is in the way. How do I get rid of it?

Temporarily hide the Office Assistant by choosing Help, Hide the Office Assistant. To turn off the Assistant, click the Options button in the Office Assistant balloon and remove the check mark by the Use the Office Assistant check box on the Options tab.

DESIGN CORNER: REARRANGING TOOLBARS

One of the nice things about PowerPoint is its flexibility. Even if you don't yet have strong knowledge of how to customize PowerPoint, you can still rearrange your basic work tools to better suit your needs—in just a few seconds. For example, you can easily arrange toolbars to make working with PowerPoint easier. Let's say that the Standard and Formatting toolbars currently appear on two separate lines at the top of your screen and the Drawing toolbar appears at the bottom. You'd like to have more screen space and make the drawing tools accessible in another location on the screen. To accomplish this quickly, follow these steps:

1. Choose Tools, Customize and select the Options tab.

2. Remove the checkmark from the Show Standard and Formatting Toolbars on Two Rows check box.

3. Click the Close button.

4. Drag the move handle on the left side of the Drawing toolbar to place it in a new location on the screen; it becomes a floating toolbar.

5. To resize the toolbar to appear as a square or rectangle, pause the mouse pointer over the left or right edge of the toolbar and drag the toolbar edge when the pointer becomes a two-headed arrow.

BEFORE

Figure 1.24

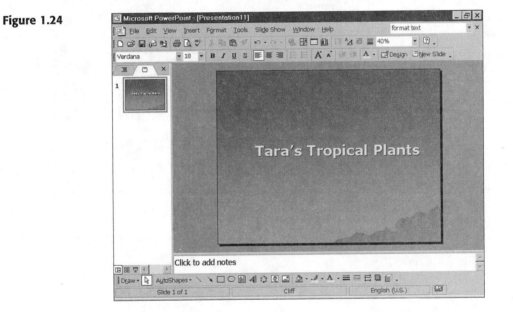

AFTER

Standard and Formatting toolbars on the same row

Figure 1.25

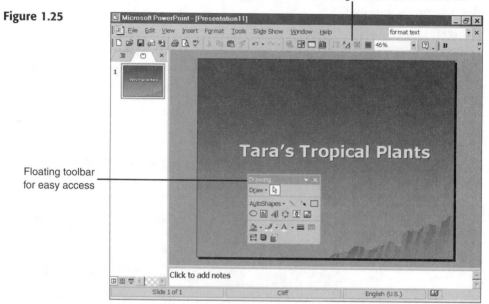

Floating toolbar
for easy access

CHAPTER 2

CREATING A BASIC PRESENTATION

In this chapter

UNDERSTANDING POWERPOINT PRESENTATIONS

Once you learn—or refresh your memory of—how to navigate PowerPoint, you can create a basic presentation. This chapter gets you up and running on presentation basics so that you can quickly move forward to more advanced and sophisticated PowerPoint techniques.

In PowerPoint, you can create a presentation in several different ways, depending on the amount of content and design assistance you require. You can create

- **A presentation using the AutoContent Wizard**   The wizard selects a design template that matches your presentation type and creates a series of slides with content and slide layout suggestions. Using the AutoContent Wizard can help you save time and provide detailed design assistance if you aren't yet design savvy.

- **A presentation using a design template**   This lets you add your own slides and content and still have a consistent design scheme (layout, colors, fonts, and so on). You also can create a presentation using your own template on a Web server or computer. Downloading a template from Microsoft's Web site is another option.

- **A new presentation from an existing presentation**   This option enables you to create a new presentation that you can edit and modify by copying an existing one. The existing presentation remains as is.

- **A blank presentation**   This type of presentation includes no preset design, colors, or content suggestions. Create a blank presentation only when you are very experienced with PowerPoint and know you want to create a custom design rather than use one of PowerPoint's existing designs.

Tip from
Patrice-Anne Rutledge

> Even if you want to create a custom presentation, it often saves you time to start with a similar existing design and then customize it.

UNDERSTANDING DESIGN TEMPLATES

A *design template* includes preformatted fonts, colors, and styles that blend together to create a consistent look and feel for your presentation. You apply design templates using the Slide Design task pane. It's usually a good idea to apply a single design template to a presentation for consistency, but you can apply multiple design templates to a single presentation if you want. Figure 2.1 illustrates a sample design template.

The AutoContent Wizard automatically selects a design template that is suited to the type of presentation you want to make. If you don't use the AutoContent Wizard and instead select your own design template, be sure that the template you select matches your audience and fits the message you want to convey.

Figure 2.1
An artsy design is great for an artistic crowd but not something you would use for a corporate audience.

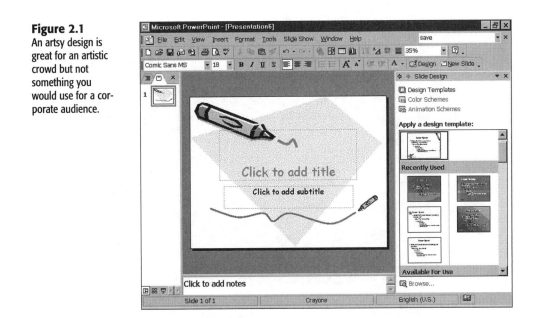

Depending on which method you use to create a new presentation, your presentation may already contain a design template. If you want to view the templates ahead of time, apply one directly to a presentation, or change to a different template, you can do so directly by clicking the Design button on the Formatting toolbar to open the Slide Design task pane.

UNDERSTANDING SLIDE LAYOUTS

In addition to a design template, the other important design feature you need to consider is a slide layout. A slide layout helps you add specific types of content to your slides, such as text, tables, charts, and pictures.

Even though PowerPoint provides a multitude of layout combinations from which to choose, these layouts contain a total of only seven different elements. They are

- **Text** Inserts a placeholder on a slide in which you can add the desired text, such as a title or bulleted list.

→ To explore the ways you can add desired text, such as a title or bulleted list, **see** Chapter 3, "Working with Text."

- **Tables** Inserts a table that you can format and customize.

→ To explore the ways you can work with tables even more, **see** Chapter 4, "Working with Tables."

- **Charts** Inserts a chart such as a bar, column, or pie chart in your presentation. Charts offer a visual means for showing relative sizes. Charts are excellent when showing cost allocation or percentages of sales figures. Figure 2.2 illustrates a chart.

Figure 2.2
Charts can add visual punch to a presentation.

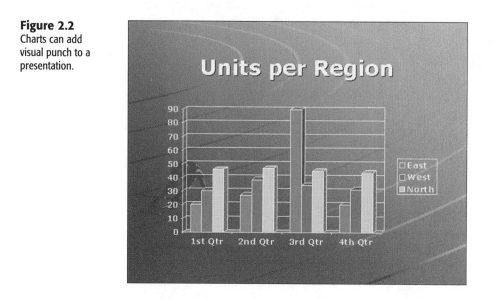

→ For more information about using charts in PowerPoint, **see** Chapter 11, "Working with Charts."

■ **Diagrams or Organization Charts**   Opens the Diagram Gallery, from which you can create a variety of diagrams and organization charts. Figure 2.3 illustrates such a chart.

Figure 2.3
Use an organization chart to help present your organization to new team members.

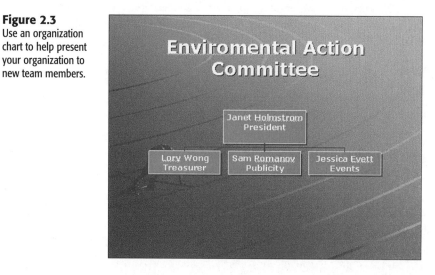

Note

PowerPoint 2002 includes totally revised organization chart capabilities directly in PowerPoint, rather than relying on an external charting program. This new feature also includes the capability to create diagrams such as cycle, radial, pyramid, venn, and target diagrams.

→ To learn more about diagrams and org charts, **see** Chapter 12, "Working with Diagrams and Organization Charts."

■ **Clip Art**   Inserts a clip art image in your presentation, either from Office's vast collection of ready-made graphic images or from your own computer or network. Figure 2.4 illustrates a slide that contains clip art.

Figure 2.4
Clip art provides numerous ways to illustrate the basic concepts of your presentation.

PART
I
CH
2

→ To learn more about working with clip art in PowerPoint, **see** Chapter 13, "Working with Media Clips and the Clip Organizer."

■ **Media Clips**   Inserts a media clip, such as a sound or movie file, enabling you to add musical effects to your presentation or display a video within it.

→ To learn more about inserting media clips, **see** Chapter 13.

■ **Pictures**   Opens the Insert Picture dialog box, from which you can insert graphic files such as GIFs or JPEGs. A picture is very similar to clip art, except that you use the Insert Picture dialog box to find your own graphic images rather than insert one from the gallery.

→ To learn more about inserting pictures, **see** Chapter 14, "Creating and Formatting Objects."

You add each of these elements to a PowerPoint slide using the Slide Layout task pane. On this task pane, PowerPoint offers 27 different types of slide layouts divided into four categories:

Text Layout   A text layout contains only text. The slide may contain a title, one- or two-column text, or a combination of the two.

Content Layout   Content layout slides offer the option of one, two, three, or four pieces of content in several arrangements. Content is defined as a graph, photo, organization chart, or other visual element.

Text and Content Layout   The seven text and content layouts offer various options of placing both text and pieces of content on a slide.

Other Layout   This section includes layouts that don't fit the other categories. Options include the capability to create a slide with a single table, diagram, or organization chart or to create combinations with text, media clips, clip art, and charts.

> **Note**
>
> If none of these predefined layouts is what you want, you can modify a blank slide or customize one of the existing layouts by adding, moving, or deleting objects.

Depending on which method you use to create a new presentation, it might already contain slide layouts. If you want to view these layouts before you create a presentation, apply them directly to a slide, or change a layout, you can do so directly by choosing Format, Slide Layout to open the Slide Layout task pane.

Many of PowerPoint's slide layouts include an option for inserting content. For example, if you choose any of the layouts under Content Layout or Text and Content Layout in the Slide Layout task pane, a content palette will appear as a placeholder. This content palette includes six buttons:

Insert Table

Insert Chart

Insert Clip Art

Insert Picture

Insert Diagram or Organization Chart

Insert Media Clip

You'll note that, with the exception of pictures, PowerPoint also includes separate layouts specifically for adding the other content types. For example, you can also insert a table using the Title and Table slide layout or a chart using the Title and Chart; Title, Text, and Chart; or Title, Chart, and Text slide layout. What's the difference? Mainly, it's a choice of location on the slide, formatting, and content combinations. You should experiment with the available slide layouts in PowerPoint 2002 to determine exactly which work best for your presentation.

USING THE AUTOCONTENT WIZARD

The AutoContent Wizard guides you step-by-step through the creation of a PowerPoint presentation and is the option that provides the most assistance and automation. You answer a few basic questions about the type of presentation you need to make, and PowerPoint does the rest. The result is a complete series of slides with content suggestions based on the presentation type you chose. In addition to creating your presentation based on a content template, PowerPoint also applies a design template suitable to the type of presentation you want and applies a slide layout to each individual slide.

→ To learn techniques for adding dynamic content to your presentations, **see** Chapter 22, "The Message—Scripting the Concept."

From here, revise the content suggestions with your own information, and you'll be ready to present. As an alternative, you can modify the appearance of your presentation by applying a different design template, modifying the design, adding or removing slides, and so forth.

To start the AutoContent Wizard, follow these steps:

1. Select File, New to display the New Presentation task pane if it isn't already displayed.

2. Click From AutoContent Wizard on the New Presentation task pane. The wizard appears (see Figure 2.5).

PART

I

CH

2

Figure 2.5
The AutoContent Wizard offers detailed guidance on creating a presentation.

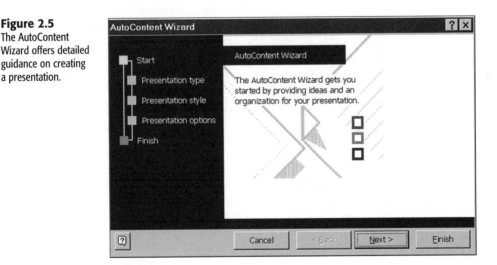

3. Click Next to continue to the next step, shown in Figure 2.6.

4. Click the category button that represents the type of presentation you want to create. The adjacent box displays the available presentations.

Tip from
Patrice-Anne Rutledge

To add your own presentation to the AutoContent Wizard, click the Add button. To remove a presentation, click Remove.

Figure 2.6
You can choose from a variety of presentations in specific category groups.

5. Select the presentation you want to use and click Next.

⚠ ***Having trouble finding a design template to fit your recurring needs?*** *See "Creating Your Own Template" in the "Troubleshooting" section near the end of this chapter.*

Caution

Not all presentations are installed initially. PowerPoint lets you know if you choose a presentation that isn't currently installed and asks if you want to install it. You must have your Office XP installation CD in the CD-ROM drive to do this.

6. Select the type of output to use. Choices include the following:

- **Onscreen presentation** The standard PowerPoint presentation format, delivered on a computer screen
- **Web presentation** For presentations delivered via the Web
- **Black-and-white overheads** Useful as a backup or as a cost-effective alternative to full-color overheads
- **Color overheads** For full-color transparencies
- **35mm slides** Formatted for delivery to a service bureau for conversion to 35mm slides

PowerPoint chooses a background and color scheme suited to the output you select. Press Next.

Tip from
Patrice-Anne
Rutledge

To change the background after you've created your presentation, click Color Schemes on the Slide Design task pane and choose from the available options.

7. Enter a presentation title.

8. If you want to include a footer on each slide, enter it. For example, you could enter your company name or a copyright statement in the Footer field.

9. Select the Date Last Updated check box or Slide Number check box to include this information in the presentation.

10. Click Finish.

PowerPoint displays a presentation with sample content that you can replace. You can also delete images and slides that you don't need, change the design of your presentation, and otherwise modify it to your satisfaction. Figure 2.7 illustrates a sample presentation for facilitating a meeting.

PART
I

CH
2

Figure 2.7
The AutoContent
Wizard includes content suggestions for
facilitating a meeting.

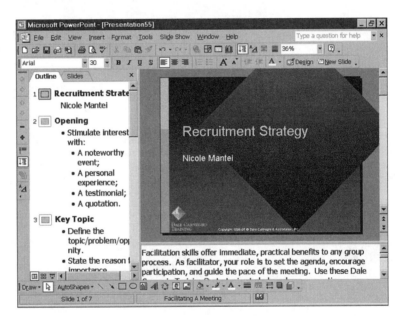

CREATING A PRESENTATION USING A DESIGN TEMPLATE

If you don't want the assistance of the AutoContent Wizard to create sample slides and content, you can start with a design template and then add your own slides and content.

To create a new presentation from a design template, follow these steps:

1. Select File, New to display the New Presentation task pane if it doesn't already appear.

2. Click From Design Template on the New Presentation task pane. The Slide Design task pane appears, displaying all available design templates in preview format (see Figure 2.8). The design template used in the current presentation (if there is one) appears at the top, followed by the most recently used templates (only if you've previously applied a template), and then all other available templates.

Figure 2.8
PowerPoint includes numerous design templates from which to choose.

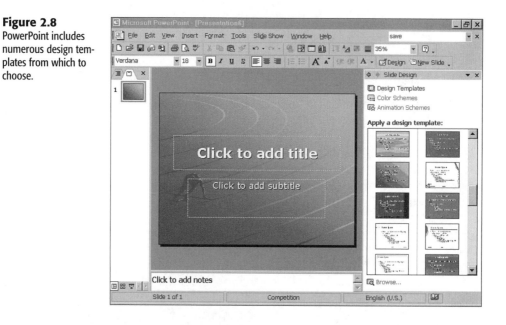

Tip from
Patrice-Anne Rutledge

If you want larger previews of the design templates, click the down arrow that appears to the right of any template preview when you hover the mouse over it. Then, choose Show Large Previews from the shortcut menu that appears. The preview templates will increase in size. To go back to normal-size previews, simply select this option again to remove the check mark.

Caution

Not all design templates are already installed. If PowerPoint displays a warning that you need to install a template, be sure to have the program CD-ROM in your CD-ROM drive and follow the installation instructions in the warning.

3. Select the template you want to use. PowerPoint applies this design to your new presentation and displays an empty slide with the Title Slide layout.

From here, you can add content to your presentation, format it, and insert additional slides.

→ To learn how to add more slides and apply slide layouts to them, **see** "Adding Slides" in Chapter 6, "Formatting Slides and Presentations."

→ To learn how to apply a new design template to a presentation you've created or use multiple design templates in a single presentation, **see** "Applying a New Design Template" in Chapter 6.

CREATING A NEW PRESENTATION FROM A TEMPLATE

You've already seen how you can create a PowerPoint presentation using a content template (with the AutoContent Wizard) or a design template. You can also directly attach an existing template located on your computer, a Web server, or the Microsoft.com site:

1. Select File, New to display the New Presentation task pane if it doesn't already display.

   From the New from Template section of the New Presentation task pane, choose one of the following options:

   - A recently used template, whose name appears at the top.
   - General Templates, which opens the Templates dialog box where you can search for a template stored on your computer or network.
   - Templates on My Web Sites, which opens the New from Templates on My Web Sites dialog box (see Figure 2.9), where you can select a template on a Web server.

Figure 2.9
Alternatively, you can use a template on a Web server.

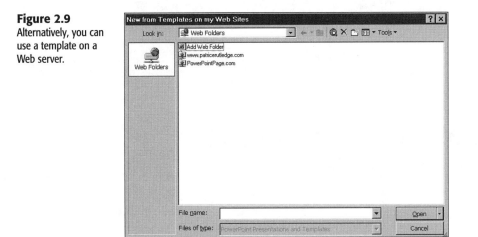

   - Templates on Microsoft.com, which opens the Microsoft.com Web site where you can choose a template from the Template Gallery. You can either browse through the available categories, such as Marketing or Legal, or perform a search on a keyword (like "PowerPoint").

CREATING A NEW PRESENTATION FROM AN EXISTING ONE

Another way to create a new presentation is simply to copy an existing presentation whose content and format are similar to what you want to create:

1. Select File, New to display the New Presentation task pane if it doesn't already appear.

2. Click Choose Presentation on the New Presentation task pane. The New from Existing Presentation dialog box opens, seen in Figure 2.10.

Figure 2.10
Creating from an existing presentation can save you lots of time.

3. Select the existing presentation on which you want to base the new one.

4. Click the Create New button. PowerPoint creates a copy of the original presentation, which you can modify.

CREATING A BLANK PRESENTATION

You can create a blank presentation by following these steps:

1. Select File, New to display the New Presentation task pane if it doesn't already appear.

2. Click Blank Presentation on the New Presentation task pane. A blank presentation appears, and the Slide Layout task pane opens.

3. Choose the slide layout you want to use in your presentation; it will be applied automatically.

Figure 2.11 illustrates a sample blank presentation.

Remember that a blank presentation doesn't include a design template unless you attach one manually.

Caution

Be sure that none of the existing design templates suit your needs before starting with a blank presentation.

Figure 2.11
To have complete
design control, you
can use a blank pre-
sentation.

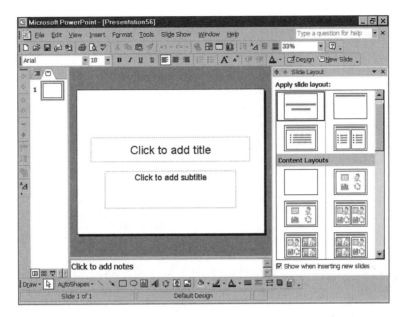

SAVING A PRESENTATION

After you create a presentation, you'll want to save it. PowerPoint enables you to save a presentation in a variety of ways, including as

- A regular presentation readable by either the current or previous version of PowerPoint
- A Web page as a folder or a Web archive as a single file
- A design template
- A PowerPoint show, ready to run on its own
- A graphic image, enabling you to display a slide as a graphic on a Web page, for example
- An outline, which you can format later in Word or another program

To save a PowerPoint presentation you created, follow these steps:

1. Click the Save button on the Standard toolbar or press Ctrl+S. If this is a new presentation, the Save As dialog box appears, shown in Figure 2.12.
2. From the Save In drop-down list, select the folder in which you want to save your presentation.

Tip from
*Patrice-Anne
Rutledge*

The default folder in which to save your presentations is My Documents. You can customize the default folder on the Save tab in the Options dialog box (Tools, Options).

⚠ ***Your presentation doesn't get saved in the right location?*** *See "Choosing a Save Location" in the
"Troubleshooting" section near the end of this chapter.*

Figure 2.12
Specify Save As
parameters in this
dialog box.

3. Enter a name for the presentation in the File Name field.

Caution

The drop-down list in the File Name field includes previously saved presentations. Be sure that you don't choose one of these filenames and accidentally overwrite an existing presentation. PowerPoint will warn you if you try to do this.

4. Choose the file format from the Save As Type drop-down list.

Presentation is the default file type, but you can also save your PowerPoint presentation as a Web page, as a design template, or in a previous PowerPoint version format such as PowerPoint 2000 or 97. Table 2.1 lists the available options for saving your presentation.

5. Click Save to save the file.

TABLE 2.1   POWERPOINT FILE TYPES

File Type	Extension	Result
Presentation	PPT	Saves as a regular PowerPoint presentation
Web Page	HTM, HTML	Saves as a Web page in a folder
Web Archive	MHT, MHTML	Saves as a Web page in a single file
PowerPoint 95	PPT	Saves in this previous version of PowerPoint
PowerPoint 97-2002 & 95	PPT	Saves as a Presentation presentation you can open in PowerPoint 95, 97, 2000, or 2002
Design Template	POT	Saves as a design template that you can use for future presentations

TABLE 2.1   CONTINUED

File Type	Extension	Result
PowerPoint Show	PPS	Enables you to run the presentation directly as a slideshow
PowerPoint Add-In	PPA	Saves as a custom add-in
GIF Graphical Interchange Format	GIF	Saves as a graphic for use on the Web
JPEG File Interchange Format	JPG	Saves as a graphic for use on the Web
PNG Portable Network Graphics Format	PNG	Saves as a graphic for use on the Web
Tag Image File Format	TIF	Saves as a TIFF graphic image
Device Independent Bitmap	BMP	Saves as a bitmap graphic image
Windows Metafile	WMF	Saves as a graphic image
Enhanced Windows Metafile	WMF	Saves as a graphic image
Outline/RTF	RTF	Saves as an outline

→ To learn more about saving a presentation as a Web page, **see** "Saving a Presentation as a Web Page" in Chapter 16, "Using PowerPoint's Web Features."

Tip from
Patrice-Anne Rutledge

After you've saved a presentation, clicking the Save button on the toolbar once saves your changes without opening the Save As dialog box.

Note

To set and modify Save options such as fast saves and AutoRecovery, choose Tools, Options and go to the Save tab of the Options dialog box.

→ To learn more about advanced save options, **see** "Setting Save Options" in Chapter 21, "Customizing PowerPoint."

OPENING A PRESENTATION

You can open an existing presentation in several different ways:

- Select More Presentations in the Open a Presentation section of the New Presentation task pane. If this pane doesn't appear, select File, New.

Tip from
Patrice-Anne Rutledge

You can also open directly one of the previous four PowerPoint files you used by selecting it at the top of the Open a Presentation section of the New Presentation task pane. The File menu also displays these files at the end of the list of menu options.

PART
I

CH
2

- Click the Open button on the Standard toolbar.
- Press Ctrl+O from within PowerPoint.
- Choose File, Open from the menu within PowerPoint.

Note

You can also double-click a PowerPoint presentation from within Windows Explorer to open it directly and bypass the Open dialog box.

The Open dialog box appears, shown in Figure 2.13.

Figure 2.13
The Open dialog box includes many additional features, including file management and search capabilities.

[Open dialog box figure with labels: Search the Web, Up One Level, Create New Folder, Back, Delete, Views, Tools]

From the Open dialog box, follow these steps to open a file:

1. Select the folder in which the file you want to open is located from the Look In drop-down list. From here, you can click the various server and folder icons to navigate to the file you want.

Tip from
Patrice-Anne Rutledge

You can also use the History, My Documents, Desktop, Favorites, and Web Folders buttons on the left side of the dialog box to navigate to the file you want to open.

⚠ **Can't find a presentation you know you saved?** See "Finding a Saved Presentation" in the "Troubleshooting" section near the end of this chapter.

2. If necessary, select the type of file you're looking for from the Files of Type drop-down list. This is useful if you have a large number of files on your computer.

3. When you locate it, click the file you want to open. Its name will appear in the File Name field.

4. Click Open to open the selected presentation.

The down arrow to the right of the Open button provides several other options. You can also

- **Open Read-Only**   Opens the file as read-only. For example, if you've applied a password to the presentation, others may only be able to open it read-only. To make changes and save this file, choose File, Save As from the menu and save with another name.

- **Open as Copy**   Opens the presentation as a copy of the original. You might do this if you want to keep your original and create another presentation based on it.

- **Open in Browser**   Opens a presentation saved in a Web page format (.HTM, .HTML, .HTX, or .ASP) in your default browser.

⚠ *Can't open your Web presentation in a browser? See "Opening a Presentation in a Browser" in the "Troubleshooting" section near the end of this chapter.*

EXPLORING THE OPEN DIALOG BOX

The top portion of the Open dialog box includes several buttons that assist with both opening files and file management. These include

- **Back**   Returns you to previous folders or drives you have viewed. It lists the name of the folder as the button name. Click the down arrow to view previous folders.

- **Up One Level**   Moves up one level in the directory structure.

- **Search the Web**   Opens the Pick a Search Engine page on the Microsoft Web site.

- **Delete**   Deletes the selected file.

- **Create New Folder**   Opens the New Folder dialog box in which you can enter a name for a new folder.

- **Views**   Includes several options for displaying your files and arranging icons by name, type, size, and date.

- **Tools**   Displays a menu that enables you to find, rename, delete, or print files, as well as add them to your Favorites folder, map to a network drive to find a file, or display file properties.

Note

You can perform sophisticated searches by choosing Tools, Search, which opens the Search dialog box. The functionality in this dialog box is nearly identical to what you can do with the Search task pane.

→ To learn more about the Search task pane, **see** "Using the Search Task Pane" in Chapter 1, "Introducing PowerPoint 2002."

SETTING VIEW OPTIONS

You can view files in several different ways in the Open dialog box. Click the down arrow next to the Views button and choose the view option you prefer:

- **Large icons**   Displays files as large icons (six across and four down).
- **Small icons**   Displays files as small icons (five columns of files).
- **List**   Lists all files, without any detail.
- **Details**   Lists file size, type, and date last modified.
- **Properties**   Displays a property sheet for the selected file.
- **Preview**   Displays a preview of the actual presentation for the selected file.
- **Thumbnails**   Previews presentations as thumbnails.
- **WebView**   Previews presentations you've saved in a Web-based format.

DELETING A PRESENTATION

To delete a PowerPoint presentation you no longer want, select it in the Open dialog box and press the Delete key on the keyboard. A warning dialog box appears, verifying that you want to delete the file and send it to the Recycle Bin. Figure 2.14 shows this dialog box. Click Yes to confirm the deletion.

Figure 2.14
PowerPoint confirms that you want to delete a presentation.

Confirm File Delete   ✕

    Are you sure you want to send 'Investments' to the Recycle Bin?

                                           Yes   No

Tip from
Patrice-Anne
Rutledge

You can also delete a PowerPoint presentation in Windows Explorer. To do so, click on the presentation file in Explorer and press the Delete key to remove the file to the Recycle Bin.

RENAMING A PRESENTATION

To rename a PowerPoint presentation, select it in the Open dialog box and choose Tools, Rename. PowerPoint converts the filename to an edit box in which you can overwrite it, as shown in Figure 2.15.

Figure 2.15
Rename a presentation something more meaningful.

Another way to rename a selected file in the Open dialog box is by right-clicking and choosing Rename from the menu that appears. You can also print a file or quick view it from this menu, among other things.

TROUBLESHOOTING

CREATING YOUR OWN TEMPLATE

I don't like any of the existing design templates. What can I do?

You can create your own design template and then save it for future use. Start by modifying an existing template and then save it as a design template in the Save As dialog box. Chapter 6 covers this in more detail.

CHOOSING A SAVE LOCATION

My presentation didn't save in the folder where I thought it would.

By default, your presentation is saved in the My Documents folder unless you manually specify another location in the Save As dialog box. To change this default, choose Tools, Options from the main PowerPoint menu and choose a different Default File Location in the Save tab.

FINDING A SAVED PRESENTATION

I can't find a PowerPoint presentation I saved.

In the Open dialog box, verify that you made the appropriate selection from the Files of Type drop-down list. For example, if you're looking for a PowerPoint presentation or a Web page, be sure you've selected that option. Also, verify that you're searching in the right folder. If you still can't find your presentation, do a search using the Find dialog box (Tools, Search from within the Open dialog box). You can also perform similar searches using the Search task pane.

OPENING A PRESENTATION IN A BROWSER

I want to open my presentation in a browser, but the Open in Browser option isn't available from the menu next to the Open button in the Open dialog box.

You must have saved the presentation in a Web format (such as .HTM, .HTML, .HTX, or .ASP) in order to open it in a browser. To save as a Web page, choose File, Save as Web Page.

DESIGN CORNER: CREATING A PRESENTATION FROM SCRATCH

Although PowerPoint offers many timesaving ways to create presentations, you still might want to start with a blank presentation and build from there. For example, you might be an experienced graphic designer with your own ideas of what you want to create. Or you might just want to create a basic presentation with your company logo and company colors, and none of the existing design templates really match. Even if you're not a designer, throughout this book you'll learn techniques that will enable you to design your own presentations from scratch if you want to.

BEFORE

Figure 2.16

AFTER

Figure 2.17

Logo

Custom color scheme

Additional design element

EDITING AND FORMATTING PRESENTATIONS

CHAPTER 3

WORKING WITH TEXT

In this chapter

UNDERSTANDING POWERPOINT'S TEXT CAPABILITIES

Adding and formatting text is a fairly straightforward task in PowerPoint. What's often more difficult is choosing the appropriate fonts, colors, and effects for your presentation. PowerPoint offers sophisticated text formatting and customization options, and it also provides a great deal of automation if you're in a hurry or have limited design skills. When you're done adding text to your presentation, you can verify that its spelling and style are error free with PowerPoint's spelling checker.

ADDING TEXT

In PowerPoint, you need to add text in a text placeholder, title placeholder, or text box. Figure 3.1 illustrates an example of a text placeholder.

Figure 3.1
A text placeholder is a tool PowerPoint uses for entering text.

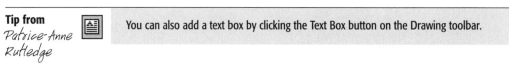

Title placeholder

Click to add title

o Click to add text

Text placeholder

If you use the AutoContent Wizard or add a slide that includes a text or title placeholder, you can immediately start creating text.

If you want to add your own text box to a blank slide, choose Insert, Text Box. You can then draw a text box on the slide using the mouse. As you add text, the box expands. Figure 3.2 shows a text box.

Tip from
Patrice-Anne Rutledge   You can also add a text box by clicking the Text Box button on the Drawing toolbar.

⚠ **Your text doesn't fit in the text box?** See "Making the Text Fit" in the "Troubleshooting" section near the end of this chapter.

Figure 3.2
A text box is another tool that PowerPoint uses to enter text.

FORMATTING TEXT

PowerPoint's design templates include preselected colors, fonts, font sizes, and other formatting parameters that are designed to work well together—a real timesaver and also very useful for people who are new to presentation design.

→ To learn more about how typefaces and fonts affect your presentation, **see** "Choosing Typefaces and Fonts" in Chapter 23, "The Media—Designing Visual Support."

You'll need to apply extensive text formatting only if you create a text box on a blank slide in a presentation without an attached design template. In most cases, you'll either use the formatting that the design template suggests or make only minor modifications to it.

→ To learn more about how to modify text and formatting on slide masters rather than on individual slides, **see** "Modifying the Slide Master" in Chapter 21, "Customizing PowerPoint."

The following are some changes you may consider to enhance the presentation of your slides:

- **Enlarge or reduce font size to fit the page** For example, if your title is too long to fit across one line, you might want to reduce the font size slightly. If you have only a few bullet points on a slide, you might want to increase their size to fill the page. Be sure, however, that the font size is still appropriate for the presentation. For example, be careful that all text is still readable on the slide and, if you're going to do an onscreen presentation, that it isn't too small to be seen by viewers in the back of a room.

- **Replace one font with another** You might have a particular font you prefer to use in presentations. Be careful, however, not to be too creative with unusual fonts. You want to be sure everyone can clearly read your presentation.

- **Add boldface, italics, or color** Use these to emphasize a point with a certain word or words.

Caution

Unless you have experience in graphic design, you're better off using the preselected fonts, colors, and font sizes included in one of PowerPoint's design templates or making only very minor modifications.

You can format text in two ways:

- Use the Font dialog box to make a number of changes in one place and to set font defaults.
- Apply text formatting individually using the buttons on the Formatting toolbar.

USING THE FONT DIALOG BOX

To use the Font dialog box to format text, follow these steps:

1. Select the text you want to format and choose Format, Font. The Font dialog box appears, shown in Figure 3.3.

Figure 3.3
Make numerous font changes quickly using the Font dialog box.

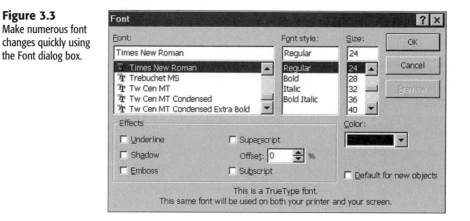

2. Select the font you want to use from the Font list. Scroll down the list to see additional font selections.

3. Select a Font Style: Regular, Bold, Italic, or Bold Italic.

4. Choose a Size: Choose a preset size from 8 to 96 points, or enter an exact size in the edit box.

5. Apply additional desired effects by checking the check box next to any of the following:

    - **Underline** Underlines the selected text.
    - **Shadow** Applies a slight shadow to the lower right of the text.
    - **Emboss** Creates an embossed effect on the selected text.
    - **Superscript** Raises the text above the baseline and reduces the font size. Sets the Offset to 30%, which you can adjust.
    - **Subscript** Lowers the text below the baseline and reduces the font size. Sets the Offset to –25%, which you can adjust.

Offset refers to the percentage the text displays above or below the baseline, or standard, text. For example, because subscript text is below the baseline, its offset will be a negative number.

→ To learn how to create innovative text objects with PowerPoint WordArt, **see** "Inserting WordArt" in Chapter 14, "Creating and Formatting Objects."

    6. Choose a color from the palette that is displayed by the Color drop-down list. For additional color choices, click More Colors from the palette to open the Colors dialog box.

→ To learn more about color theory and how it relates to emotions, **see** "Understanding Background Colors and Emotions" in Chapter 23.

→ To learn more about the Colors dialog box, **see** "Using the Colors Dialog Box" in Chapter 14.

    7. Click Preview to view the selected font changes on your slide.

    8. If you want the selected font formatting to be the default for future text, select the Default for New Objects check box.

    9. If you want to accept these changes, click OK to close and apply the font formatting.

PART

II

CH

3

USING THE FORMATTING TOOLBAR

You can use the Formatting toolbar (see Figure 3.4) to apply individual formatting elements such as bold, italics, and shadows to selected text.

Figure 3.4
The Formatting toolbar includes buttons for commonly used text effects.

Table 3.1 lists the formatting options on this toolbar.

TABLE 3.1   FORMATTING TOOLBAR BUTTONS

Button	Name	Description
Times New Roman	Font	Applies a font to the selected text.
24	Font Size	Sets the size of the font from 8 to 96 points or any size you enter in the edit box.
B	Bold	Bolds the selected text.
I	Italic	Italicizes the selected text.
<u>U</u>	Underline	Underlines the selected text.
S	Shadow	Applies a shadow to the selected text.

TABLE 3.1   CONTINUED

Button	Name	Description
	Align Left	Aligns text to the left margin of the object.
	Center	Centers text across the slide.
	Align Right	Aligns text to the right margin.
	Numbering	Applies numbering to the selected text.
	Bullets	Applies bullets to the selected text.
	Increase Font Size	Increases the font size of selected text by one increment.
	Decrease Font Size	Decreases the font size of selected text by one increment.
	Decrease Indent	Outdents the selected text.
	Increase Indent	Indents the selected text.
	Font Color	Applies the color you choose from the drop-down list to selected text.
Design	Design	Opens the Slide Design task pane.
New Slide	New Slide	Creates a new slide and opens the Slide Layout task pane.

To apply specific formatting, select the text you want to format and click the toolbar button. Clicking the Bold, Italic, Underline, Text Shadow, Numbering, or Bullets button a second time acts as a toggle and removes the formatting.

With the Font drop-down list, you can preview what each font actually looks like.

REPLACING FONTS

If you want to replace all occurrences of one type of font in your presentation with another font, you can easily do so by following these steps:

1. Choose Format, Replace Fonts to open the Replace Font dialog box (see Figure 3.5).

2. Select the font that you want to replace from the Replace drop-down list. Only those fonts that currently exist in your presentation are listed.

3. Select the replacement font from the With drop-down list. All available fonts in PowerPoint are listed.

4. Click Replace to replace all matching fonts in your presentation.

5. Click Close to return to the presentation.

Figure 3.5
Replace fonts throughout your presentation with this dialog box.

> → If you find you are making several text changes to all slides in a presentation, consider using the slide master. To learn how, **see** "Working with Slide Masters" in Chapter 21.

CHANGING TEXT CASE

PART
II
CH
3

You can also automate a change of text case in your presentation, such as changing from lowercase to all capitals. Do so by following these steps:

1. Select the text that you want to change.

2. Select Format, Change Case to open the Change Case dialog box, shown in Figure 3.6.

Figure 3.6
You can quickly change case if something doesn't look right.

3. Choose the case to which you want to change. Options include

- **Sentence case**   Only the first word in a sentence is capitalized.
- **lowercase**   All letters appear in lowercase.
- **UPPERCASE**   All letters appear in uppercase.
- **Title Case**   The first letter of every title word is capitalized. Exceptions include words such as *the, and, to,* and so on, which remain lowercase in titles.
- **tOGGLE cASE**   Toggles all existing cases. Lowercase becomes uppercase, and uppercase becomes lowercase.

4. Click OK to apply the case changes to the selected text.

Caution

Remember that an unusual use of case may be difficult to read, particularly uppercase and toggle case. With text, you need to strive for readability and clarity.

 Only part of your text changes? *See "Making Your Case Work" in the "Troubleshooting" section near the end of this chapter.*

Tip from
Patrice-Anne
Rutledge Another way to change case is to select some text and press Shift+F3 to cycle through PowerPoint's case options.

SETTING LINE SPACING

To specify the amount of vertical space between text (such as single or double spacing), follow these steps:

1. Select the text you want to format and choose Format, Line Spacing. Figure 3.7 shows the Line Spacing dialog box that appears.

Figure 3.7
Appropriate line spacing can make a presentation easier to read.

In this dialog box you can set either lines or points for line spacing, space before paragraphs, and space after paragraphs.

2. Select the numeric amount from the first field and then choose either Lines or Points from the second drop-down list.

3. Click the Preview button to view the changes in your presentation before accepting them.

4. Click OK to apply the changes.

SETTING ALIGNMENT

To align paragraphs, choose Format, Alignment and then one of the following options:

- **Align Left** Aligns text to the left margin of the object.
- **Center** Centers text across the slide.
- **Align Right** Aligns text to the right margin of the object.
- **Justify** Justifies selected text.

USING BULLETS

Creating a bulleted list of text is a very common PowerPoint task. If you use the AutoContent Wizard, your presentation probably already contains a slide with text formatted as a bulleted list. You can add a bulleted list to any slide that contains text, as well as within a table.

 To change a numbered list or other text to a bulleted list, select the text and click the Bullets button on the Formatting toolbar. The default style for bullets comes from the design template applied to the presentation. You can change this if you want, however. To do so, select the bulleted list that you want to change and choose Format, Bullets and Numbering. Figure 3.8 shows the Bullets and Numbering dialog box that appears.

Figure 3.8
You can choose from many different bullet types.

On the Bulleted tab of this dialog box, you can choose from the seven bullet styles displayed, or you can choose None to remove bullets. In the Size field, you can scroll to enlarge or reduce the bullet size from the default 100%.

To change the color of a bullet, select a new color from the Color drop-down list. For additional color choices, click More Colors to open the Colors dialog box.

→ To learn more about the Colors dialog box, **see** "Using the Colors Dialog Box" in Chapter 14.

→ To change the bullets in your entire presentation, do so on the master slide; **see** "Modifying the Slide Master" in Chapter 21.

You can also create picture or character bullets, if none of the seven default bullet styles suits your needs.

CREATING PICTURE BULLETS

To apply a picture bullet, click the Picture button to open the Picture Bullet dialog box, which enables you to choose from a wide variety of more creative bullet styles.

Select your desired bullet from those that appear or enter a keyword in the text box and click Search to locate matching bullets. Click OK to apply. Figure 3.9 shows a presentation that uses picture bullets.

Figure 3.9
A picture bullet can enhance a creative presentation.

Tip from
Patrice-Anne Rutledge

To import your own picture bullets (maybe a logo or something you already use on a Web site or other company literature), click the Import button to open the Add Clips to Organizer dialog box.

CREATING CHARACTER BULLETS

You can choose a character bullet for your bulleted list if you want something a little different. In the Symbol dialog box you can choose from a variety of fonts. Each font displays its character set, from which you can choose a new character bullet.

To apply a character bullet, click the Customize button in the Bullets and Numbering dialog box to open the Symbol dialog box, shown in Figure 3.10.

Select a font from the Font drop-down list, choose the bullet you want from the display area, and click OK. To speed up your insert process, you can view and choose from character bullets you've recently applied to a bullet list from the Recently Used Symbols section.

Figure 3.10
Use a font like
Wingdings for charac-
ter bullets.

PART

II

CH

3

Note You can select a color and size for your character bullet in the Bullets and Numbering dialog box.

USING NUMBERED LISTS

For a sequence of items, creating a numbered list is a good alternative to a bulleted list. For example, a series of procedural steps or a list of dollar amounts from highest to lowest would work well in a numbered list. You can create numbered lists with actual numbers, Roman numerals, or letters of the alphabet.

To change a bulleted list or other text to a numbered list, select the text and click the Numbering button on the Formatting toolbar.

Tip from
Patrice-Anne
Rutledge

You can also create a numbered list by pressing the Backspace key at the beginning of a bulleted list, typing the number 1 (or the letter a if you're using letters instead of numbers), pressing the Tab key, and entering your first list item. PowerPoint then continues the numbering series when you press Enter to move to the second line.

To change the numbering style of selected text, follow these steps:

1. Choose Format, Bullets and Numbering and go to the Numbered tab, shown in Figure 3.11.

2. Select one of the seven number styles that appear. Choosing None removes the numbered list.

3. Set Size as a percentage of the text; 100% (or the same size as text) is the default. Lower the number to reduce the size, increase the number to enlarge the size.

Figure 3.11
A numbered list can
put a series of items
in order.

4. Choose a color from the Color drop-down list. For additional color choices, click More
   Colors to open the Colors dialog box.

→ To learn more about the Colors dialog box, **see** "Using the Colors Dialog Box" in Chapter 14.

5. If you want the numbering to start at a number other than 1, enter that number in the
   Start At field.

6. Click OK to apply the numbering.

CHECKING SPELLING AND STYLE

Creating a quality presentation that is error free and easy to read is a natural objective when
you use PowerPoint, and PowerPoint's spelling and style checkers can offer some assistance
in this area. Keep in mind that, although these automated tools can help you catch errors,
they aren't foolproof and don't take the place of thorough proofreading by a real person. To
set options for spelling and style checks, select Tools, Options and go to the Spelling and
Style tab. Figure 3.12 illustrates this tab.

You can choose any of the following spelling options:

- **Check Spelling as You Type**   Underlines each suspected spelling error as you type it.
- **Hide All Spelling Errors**   Doesn't display red underlining for suspected spelling
  errors.
- **Always Suggest Corrections**   Suggests possible correct spelling options.
- **Ignore Words in UPPERCASE**   Skips any word that is all uppercase in the spell-
  check process.

■ **Ignore Words with Numbers** Skips any word that includes a number in the spell-check process.

Figure 3.12
You can designate several spell-checking options in PowerPoint.

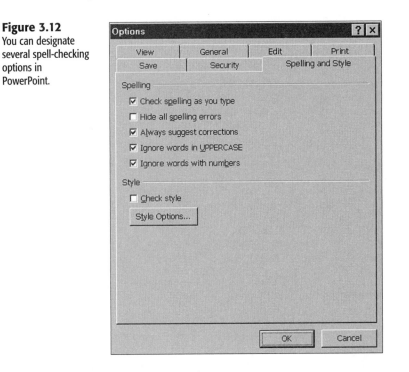

SETTING STYLE OPTIONS

If you also want to check style, select the Check Style check box and click the Style Options button. This opens the Style Options dialog box, shown in Figure 3.13.

Figure 3.13
Setting default case and punctuation helps give a more consistent look to your presentation.

Note

The style checker uses the Office Assistant to check style. If the Office Assistant isn't enabled, PowerPoint prompts you to do so.

Caution

Although having PowerPoint search for potential style errors can help you find mistakes you wouldn't otherwise notice, be careful to look closely at the changes it suggests rather than just automatically accepting all style changes. Sometimes automation can yield unusual and unwanted results.

On the Case and End Punctuation tab, you can select the default case and end punctuation styles for your presentation slide titles and body text. Options include the capability to

- Set Slide Title Style to Sentence case, lowercase, UPPERCASE, or Title Case (the default).
- Set Body Text Style to Sentence case (the default), lowercase, UPPERCASE, Title Case, or Consistent case. Sentence case is your best choice for regular body text because it's the most readable.
- Set Slide Title Punctuation to either Paragraphs Have Punctuation (the default) or Paragraphs Do Not Have Punctuation.
- Set Body Punctuation to Paragraphs Have Punctuation, Paragraphs Do Not Have Punctuation, or Paragraphs Have Consistent Punctuation (the default, which ensures that your punctuation choices match). For example, a bulleted list in a well-designed presentation shouldn't have a mixture of periods and no periods at the end of the bulleted text; it should be consistent.

Select the check boxes next to all options for which you want PowerPoint to search and choose the option from the drop-down list.

Tip from
Patrice-Anne Rutledge

If you want to place a character other than a period at the end of the slide title or body text, enter the appropriate character in the Slide Title or Body Text edit box. For example, you might want to use a colon instead of a period in some cases. In that case, PowerPoint would look for the colon instead of the period.

Note

If you've enabled another language, such as Japanese, additional grammar options may appear for that language.

→ To learn more about foreign language options, **see** Appendix B, "Using PowerPoint's Foreign Language Capabilities."

On the Visual Clarity tab, you can view and revise the existing defaults for font clarity and presentation legibility.

On this tab you can set the

- Maximum number of fonts
- Minimum point size for title text
- Minimum point size for body text
- Maximum number of bullets
- Maximum number of lines per title and per bullet

The Visual Clarity tab already includes default selections for these options that are based on basic design principles, but you can change any settings in the adjacent drop-down lists. When you run PowerPoint's spelling checker, it looks for violations of these constraints.

PART

II

CH

3

> **Caution**
>
> Even though you can change these defaults to suit your needs, consider carefully before doing so. Exceeding the recommended number of fonts and bullets and changing to overly small or overly large fonts can make your presentation difficult to read.

If you make changes to the settings on the Style Options dialog box and want to go back to PowerPoint's defaults, click the Defaults button.

RUNNING A SPELLING AND STYLE CHECK

After you've set the spelling and style options you want, you can check your presentation.

If you set the option to have PowerPoint check spelling as you type, you know immediately when you've possibly misspelled a word. PowerPoint underlines all suspected misspellings, as shown in Figure 3.14.

You can either fix the error yourself or right-click to see some suggested alternatives from which to choose. Figure 3.14 illustrates some suggestions.

⚡ *PowerPoint missing some of your spelling or style errors? See "Checking Spelling and Style" in the "Troubleshooting" section near the end of this chapter.*

You can also spell-check your entire presentation all at once. To do so, follow these steps:

1. Click the Spelling button on the Standard toolbar, or choose Tools, Spelling and Grammar.
2. When PowerPoint encounters an error, it displays the Spelling dialog box, shown in Figure 3.15.
3. The Not in Dictionary field highlights the misspelled word, and the Change To field suggests the most likely alternative. The Suggestions box also provides additional alternatives.

Figure 3.14
When you right-click an underscored spelling error, PowerPoint offers suggested spellings.

Misspelled word ———

Figure 3.15
The Spelling dialog box offers several options for handling potential misspellings.

4. Select the correct spelling or enter it manually in the Change To field.

5. The Spelling dialog box also includes several buttons that provide other options:

   • **Ignore**   Ignores the misspelling and continues checking spelling.

   • **Ignore All**   Ignores all instances of the misspelling in the presentation and continues checking spelling.

   • **Change**   Changes the individual misspelled word to the spelling offered in the Change To field.

   • **Change All**   Changes all instances of the misspelled word to the spelling offered in the Change To field.

   • **Add**   Adds the suspect word to the custom dictionary as a correctly spelled word.

   • **Suggest**   Provides additional spelling suggestions.

- **AutoCorrect**   Adds the misspelled word and its corrected version to the AutoCorrect list.
- **Close**   Closes the dialog box.

→ To learn more about AutoCorrect, **see** "Setting AutoCorrect Options" in Chapter 21.

Tip from
Patrice-Anne Rutledge

To make further modification to your custom dictionaries, go to Microsoft Word and choose Tools, Options from the menu bar. On the Spelling and Grammar tab of the Options dialog box, click the Custom Dictionaries button. The Custom Dictionaries dialog box opens, from which you can make additional modifications to your custom dictionaries.

You'll find custom dictionaries stored as text files in one of three locations, depending on your operating system and configuration: `C:\Windows_folder\Application Data\Microsoft\Proof`, `C:\Windows_folder\Profiles\User_name\Application Data\Microsoft\Proof`, or `C:\Windows_folder\Profiles\User_name`.

Note

PowerPoint also targets unknown words as spelling errors, such as a person's name, a company name, or a product. Be sure to check carefully for these and add the names and words you commonly use in presentations to the dictionary.

When PowerPoint finishes checking spelling, it informs you with another dialog box.

TROUBLESHOOTING

MAKING THE TEXT FIT

My text doesn't fit in my text placeholder.

Select the placeholder and then choose Format, Placeholder to open the Format AutoShape dialog box. Go to the Text Box tab and be sure that you've checked the Resize AutoShape to Fit Text check box.

MAKING YOUR CASE WORK

I tried to change the case of my text, but only part of it changed.

If you select only part of a sentence and change the case, the change applies only to the selected text, not to the entire sentence/paragraph. It isn't enough just to place the cursor in the specified line or paragraph. Select the entire text you want to change and then choose Format, Change Case again.

CHECKING SPELLING AND STYLE

I ran the spelling checker, and it didn't find my spelling or style errors.

PowerPoint checks the spelling only in the basic presentation; it doesn't check text in charts, WordArt objects, or embedded objects.

PowerPoint's style checker looks for only the style flaws you specified on the Spelling and Style tab on the Options dialog box (Tools, Options). It doesn't check for any other style errors.

DESIGN CORNER: DRESSING UP YOUR LIST

To make a bulleted list that's unique to your organization, consider using a logo or other internal image as a picture bullet. To import a logo for use as a picture bullet, click the Import button in the Picture Bullet dialog box. In the Add Clips to Gallery dialog box, select your logo and click Add. Now you can add your logo to a bulleted list just as you would any other picture bullet, adding some additional style and personalization to your presentation.

BEFORE

Figure 3.16

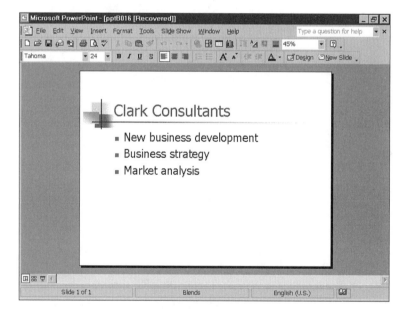

AFTER

Figure 3.17
The company logo with the matching picture bullets.

CHAPTER 4

WORKING WITH TABLES

In this chapter

UNDERSTANDING TABLES IN POWERPOINT

You've probably created tables in other applications such as Word, or maybe even in a previous version of PowerPoint, and discovered what a valuable way to communicate information they offer. A *table* is essentially an object that conveys related information in columns and rows. In addition to making information easier to understand, tables do so using a minimum amount of space. For example, rather than creating three separate bullet list slides, each listing the five most important features of your three main products, you could summarize all of this information in a table on a single slide. You could still present information on individual slides and then summarize everything at the end of the presentation in a table. In PowerPoint, tables offer both convenience and flexibility.

You can include a table in a PowerPoint presentation in one of two ways:

- **Insert a table in PowerPoint**   PowerPoint's basic table insertion feature places a table into a PowerPoint slide based on the number of rows and columns you specify. You can then format, customize, and add data into this table.

- **Draw a table in PowerPoint**   This option is most useful if PowerPoint's regular table insertion feature doesn't meet your needs. It takes longer to draw your own table, so use this option only if what you want to create is too complex for the automated table feature.

Note

You can also integrate existing tables you create in Microsoft Word, Excel, and Access with PowerPoint. To do this, choose Insert, Object to open the Insert Object dialog box. Select the Create from File option and browse to the file that contains the table you want to import.

→ To learn more about using Word, Excel, and Access within PowerPoint, **see** Chapter 19, "Integrating with Office XP."

ADDING A TABLE

New Slide   To add a new slide that contains a table, select Insert, New Slide or click the New button on the Standard toolbar. From the Slide Layout task pane, choose the Title and Table slide layout. Alternatively, you can also choose any slide layout that includes content and click the Insert Table button from the content palette.

→ To learn more about the Slide Layout task pane, **see** "Understanding Slide Layouts" in Chapter 2, "Creating a Basic Presentation."

Note

If you use the AutoContent Wizard to create your presentation, it might already have a slide that contains a table.

→ For more information about creating ready-made presentations with the AutoContent Wizard, **see** "Using the AutoContent Wizard" in Chapter 2.

Figure 4.1 illustrates the start of a sample table slide.

Figure 4.1
You can start adding a table by double-clicking the table object.

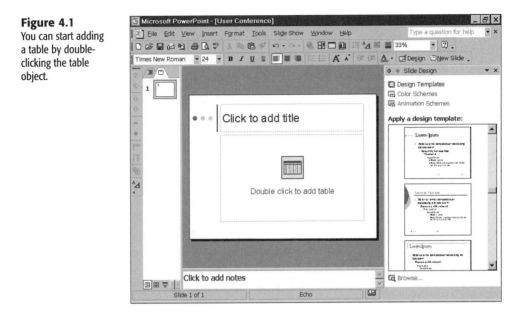

Double-click the Table object to open the Insert Table dialog box, illustrated in Figure 4.2.

Figure 4.2
Choose the number of rows and columns you want to include.

> **Insert Table**
>
> Number of columns:
> 3
>
> Number of rows:
> 4
>
> OK
>
> Cancel

Note

You can also insert a table into an existing slide by clicking the Insert Table button on the Standard toolbar or by selecting Insert, Table.

Choose the number of columns and number of rows to display and click OK.

A blank table appears in your slide, shown in Figure 4.3.

Figure 4.3
Enter the title and table text to complete your table.

Click the title placeholder to remove the directional text and enter an appropriate title for the slide. Next, add the desired text in each cell of the table, clicking inside the table and then tabbing to the cell or clicking in the cell.

→ To learn more about adding text to your presentations, **see** Chapter 3, "Working with Text."

Note

Table text doesn't appear on the Outline tab, just the slide title.

You can format this text as you would any other text. For example, you might want to bold the first row or column or add other special formatting.

FORMATTING A TABLE

PowerPoint enables you to apply a variety of formats and borders to your tables, including the capability to do the following:

- Apply different styles, widths, and colors
- Insert and delete rows and columns
- Merge and split cells
- Align cell text to the top, bottom, or center

You'll want to use the Tables and Borders toolbar to access PowerPoint's table formatting options. If this toolbar doesn't currently appear, you can open it by clicking the Tables and Borders button on the Standard toolbar or by selecting View, Toolbars, Tables and Borders. Table 4.1 lists the buttons on this toolbar.

TABLE 4.1   TABLES AND BORDERS TOOLBAR BUTTONS

Button	Name	Description
	Draw Table	Draws a custom table
	Eraser	Erases column and row lines in a custom table
	Border Style	Applies one of several table border
1 pt	Border Width	Applies a selected table border width
	Border Color	Applies a selected table border color
	Outside Borders	Sets outside and inside border lines
	Fill Color	Applies a fill color to the interior of selected table cells
Table ▾	Table	Lists a variety of menu options for table formatting
	Merge Cells	Merges selected cells into one cell
	Split Cell	Splits the selected cell into two cells
	Align Top	Aligns cell text to the top of the cell
	Center Vertically	Aligns cell text in the center of the cell
	Align Bottom	Aligns cell text to the bottom of the cell
	Distribute Rows Evenly	Resizes rows to make them equal in size
	Distribute Columns Evenly	Resizes columns to make them equal in size

PART

II

CH

4

 You applied multiple formatting changes and want to undo something you did a few steps back? See the "Troubleshooting" section near the end of the chapter.

MERGING AND SPLITTING CELLS

In PowerPoint, you can merge and split cells if you don't want to have the same number of rows or columns throughout your table. For example, you might want to merge all the cells across the top row of your table to serve as a title. You might want to split one cell into two if the content of that cell includes two separate sets of information.

To merge cells, select the cells you want to merge and click the Merge Cells button on the Tables and Borders toolbar. Figure 4.4 illustrates two cells that were merged into one.

Caution

If you already have text in each of the cells you merge, each cell text becomes a line of text in the new single cell.

To split a cell, select the cell you want to split and click the Split Cell button on the Tables and Borders toolbar. Figure 4.4 illustrates a cell that was split into two.

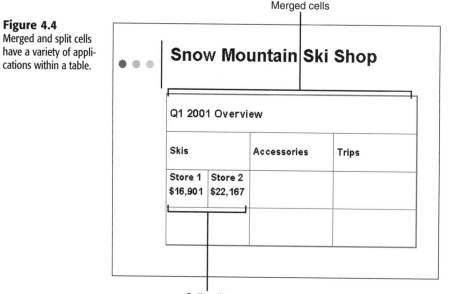

Figure 4.4
Merged and split cells have a variety of applications within a table.

CREATING A BORDER

Borders can add to the visibility of your table and can also add to its dramatic flair. PowerPoint tables include a black, solid line border by default, but you can change this. To apply border formatting options, select the table and then click the appropriate Tables and Borders toolbar button.

SETTING BORDER STYLE

To set the border style, click the Border Style drop-down list on the Tables and Borders toolbar and choose the style of border you prefer. The list includes the option to apply no border, a solid line, or a variety of dashed line styles, shown in Figure 4.5.

SETTING BORDER WIDTH

To set the border width, click the Border Width drop-down list on the Tables and Borders toolbar and choose the width you prefer. Options include point sizes from 1/4 point (a very thin line) to 6 points (a thick line), shown in Figure 4.6.

Figure 4.5
Choose the border style that suits your table.

Figure 4.6
Use a thick border to create more emphasis, a thin border to create less.

SETTING BORDER COLORS

To set the color for the table border, click the Border Color button. The box that appears offers several possible colors from which to choose, based on the presentation's color scheme. For additional color choices, click More Colors to open the Colors dialog box.

→ To learn more about the Colors dialog box, **see** "Using the Colors Dialog Box" in Chapter 6, "Formatting Slides and Presentations."

CREATING OUTSIDE BORDERS

You can specify which parts of your table contain borders—all of it or only specific outside or inside areas.

To set options for outside borders, click the down arrow to the right of the Outside Borders button on the Tables and Borders toolbar. A palette appears with several preselected outside border options, as shown in Figure 4.7.

Figure 4.7
You can have both inside and outside borders on your table.

SETTING TABLE FILL COLOR

You can change the fill color of an individual cell or cells in your table if you want.

Caution

> Be sure that your table text is still readable if you change a cell's fill color.

To change fill color, select the cell or cells that you want to change and click the down arrow next to the Fill Color button on the Tables and Borders toolbar.

You can

- Choose from the colors that appear on the palette. If you applied a design template to your presentation, the colors that appear here complement the design template and will give you the best results.
- Click More Fill Colors to display the Colors dialog box. You can choose from a large number of colors in this dialog box or create a custom color.
- Click Fill Effects to choose from a number of gradients, textures, patterns, and pictures.

→ To learn more about the Colors and Fill Effects dialog boxes, **see** Chapter 6.

To remove a fill you no longer want, click the down arrow next to the Fill Color button and choose No Fill from the palette.

WORKING WITH COLUMNS AND ROWS

After you create a table, you may decide that you need to add additional information or that you want to remove some of the data it currently contains.

INSERTING ROWS AND COLUMNS

To insert a new row into your table, select an existing table row by clicking the mouse in that row and then choosing Table, Insert Rows Above or Insert Rows Below from the Tables and Borders toolbar. PowerPoint inserts a row either above or below the selected row, depending on your menu choice. Figure 4.8 illustrates a table with an added row.

Tip from
Patrice-Anne Rutledge

> You can resize the height or width of any row or column by selecting the row or column separator with the mouse and dragging it to the new location.

Caution

> When you add or delete rows and columns, your table may no longer fit well on the slide. You then need to resize the table by dragging a corner with the mouse. Be careful, however, that you don't hide existing text by making the cells too small during resizing.

Figure 4.8
Add rows if you
didn't create enough
during the initial table
creation.

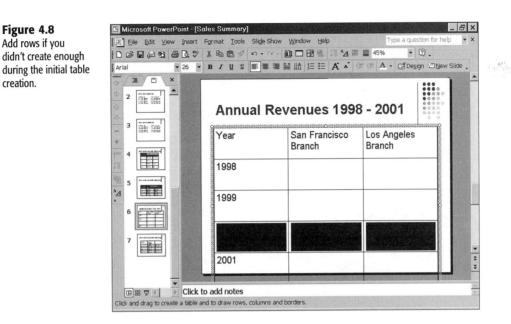

⚠️ *Your table no longer fits after inserting rows or columns?* See the "Troubleshooting" section near the end of the chapter.

If you want to insert multiple rows, select that number of rows before selecting the Insert command. For example, if you select two table rows and then choose Table, Insert Rows Above in the Tables and Borders toolbar, two rows are inserted above the selected rows.

To add a new column to your table, select an existing table column by clicking the mouse in that column and choosing Table, Insert Columns to the Left or Insert Columns to the Right from the Tables and Borders toolbar. PowerPoint inserts a column either to the right or the left of the selected column, depending on your menu choice. Figure 4.9 illustrates a table with added columns.

DELETING ROWS AND COLUMNS

To delete rows or columns, select the areas you want to delete and then choose Table, Delete Rows or Delete Columns from the Tables and Borders toolbar. PowerPoint deletes the entire column or row of the cell(s) you select.

DELETING TABLES AND TABLE CONTENTS

To delete specific text in a table cell, select the text (not just the cell), and press the Delete key.

Caution

You must select the actual text or cell—not just place the cursor in the cell—to delete the text.

Figure 4.9
You can add columns
if your table design
changes.

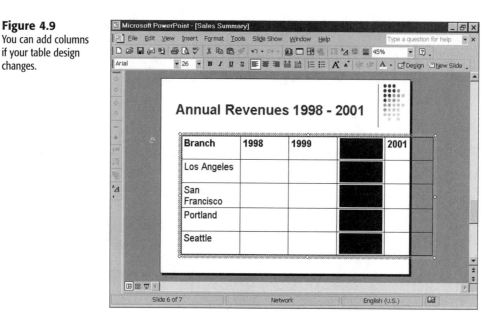

To delete an entire table, choose Table, Select Table from the Tables and Borders toolbar and then press the Delete key. The table disappears and is replaced by the initial Double Click to Add Table directive that appears when you first create a table slide.

Tip from
Patrice-Anne
Rutledge

To delete a table, click the outside border of the table to select the entire table, and then press the Delete key.

FORMATTING WITH THE FORMAT TABLE DIALOG BOX

The Format Table dialog box (seen in Figure 4.10) duplicates much of what you can do from the Tables and Borders toolbar. However, it is a much more powerful tool if you want to do all your formatting from one location or if the Tables and Borders toolbar is closed and you don't want to open it again. You can access this dialog box in one of two ways:

- Click the Table button on the Tables and Borders toolbar and choose Borders and Fill from the menu.
- Select Format, Table from the main PowerPoint menu.

USING THE BORDERS TAB

The Borders tab enables you to set the following attributes:

- **Style** Choose a border style from the available options.
- **Color** Select a color from the drop-down list. For additional color choices, click More Colors to open the Colors dialog box.

Figure 4.10
Apply a multitude of
formatting options
from the Format Table
dialog box.

→ To learn more about the Colors dialog box, **see** "Using the Colors Dialog Box" in Chapter 6.

- **Width**   Choose a border width from the drop-down list.

- **Borders**   Click on the diagram to apply borders where you want them.

USING THE FILL TAB

Use the Fill tab, shown in Figure 4.11, to specify fill color for your table cells.

Figure 4.11
You can apply fill
colors to your tables,
but be sure the text is
still readable.

Click the Fill Color check box if you want to apply a fill color to your selected table cells.
Select a color from the drop-down list. From here, you can also access the Colors and Fill
Effects dialog boxes to apply additional color and fill options.

→ To learn more about the Colors and Fill Effects dialog boxes, **see** "Specifying Colors" in Chapter 14,
"Creating and Formatting Objects."

If you want to make the color display as Semitransparent, click the check box.
Semitransparent colors can make it easier to view the slide's background and text.

PART

II

CH

4

USING THE TEXT BOX TAB

Use the Text Box tab, shown in Figure 4.12, to set alignment and margins in your table.

Figure 4.12
The Text Box tab enables you to set a variety of alignments.

```
┌─────────────────────────────────────────────────┐
│ Format Table                            [?] [X]   │
│ ┌────────┬──────┬──────────┐                      │
│ │ Borders │ Fill │ Text Box │                     │
│                                                   │
│   Text alignment: [Top            ▼]              │
│   ┌─ Internal margin ──────────────────────┐      │
│   │ Left:  [0.1"   ▲▼]   Top:    [0.05"  ▲▼]│      │
│   │                                         │      │
│   │ Right: [0.1"   ▲▼]   Bottom: [0.05"  ▲▼]│      │
│   └─────────────────────────────────────────┘     │
│   ☐ Rotate text within cell by 90 degrees         │
│                                                   │
│         [  OK  ]   [ Cancel ]   [ Preview ]       │
└─────────────────────────────────────────────────┘
```

To set text alignment, click the drop-down list and choose from one of these alignment options: Top, Middle, Bottom, Top Centered, Middle Centered, or Bottom Centered.

You can also set internal margins for the left, right, top, and bottom margins within the table cells.

Select the Rotate Text Within Cell by 90 Degrees check box to rotate selected text vertically.

ADDING BULLETED AND NUMBERED LISTS WITHIN TABLES

 To create a bulleted list within a table cell, select the cell you want to format and click the Bullets button on the Formatting toolbar.

To create a numbered list within a selected table cell, click the Numbering toolbar button.

Tip from
Patrice-Anne Rutledge

For additional bullet and numbering options, select the text you want to format and then choose Format, Bullets and Numbering to open the Bullets and Numbering dialog box. This dialog box offers many additional options, including the capability to create alphabetical lists as well as picture bullets.

DRAWING A TABLE

If the default table options don't provide what you need in a table, you can create a custom table. Drawing your own table enables you to make columns and rows of varying widths, for example. For some people, drawing a table is faster than using the table placeholder method.

To draw a table, select the Draw Table button on the Tables and Borders toolbar. The mouse pointer becomes a pencil. Drag the mouse diagonally across the slide to create the basic table. Then use the mouse to draw lines representing columns and rows.

If you make a mistake or want to imitate the Merge Cell feature, click the Eraser button on the Tables and Borders toolbar. Use this eraser to remove the lines between rows and cells as necessary.

Tip from *Patrice-Anne Rutledge*	To make it easier to create your rows and columns, you can display rulers and guides on your slide. Select View, Ruler to display a ruler. You can also create invisible grids and guides to help you draw and create objects (View, Grid and Guides).

→ To learn more about grids and guides, **see** "Snapping to a Grid or Shape" in Chapter 14.

TROUBLESHOOTING

MAKING ROOM FOR ADDITIONAL ROWS AND COLUMNS

I added some rows and columns to my table, and now they don't fit in the slide.

You can resize your table to fit, but you might hide table text from view by doing this. If you haven't already invested a lot of time in creating and formatting your table, you might be better off deleting the table and starting again.

UNDOING MULTIPLE FORMATTING CHANGES

I applied several formatting options to my table, and I don't like the results.

Click the down arrow next to the Undo button on the Standard toolbar to see a list of formatting tasks you can undo.

DESIGN CORNER: IMPROVING INFORMATION DESIGN THROUGH THE USE OF TABLES

By now, you've learned of the value of using tables to present information in PowerPoint as well as the many ways you can customize tables to blend with the overall design of your presentation. Obviously, including a table in every slide can be monotonous, but the judicious use of tables can definitely enhance your presentation. For example, the bullet lists in the "Before" example convey the information adequately but duplicate it in certain places. Using the column and row format of a table, you can convey the same information without duplication and in a way that's easier for your audience to see the relationship between the table data. The "After" example eliminates these redundancies, and through the use of merged cells and fill colors, provides a more aesthetically appealing look as well.

BEFORE

Figure 4.13

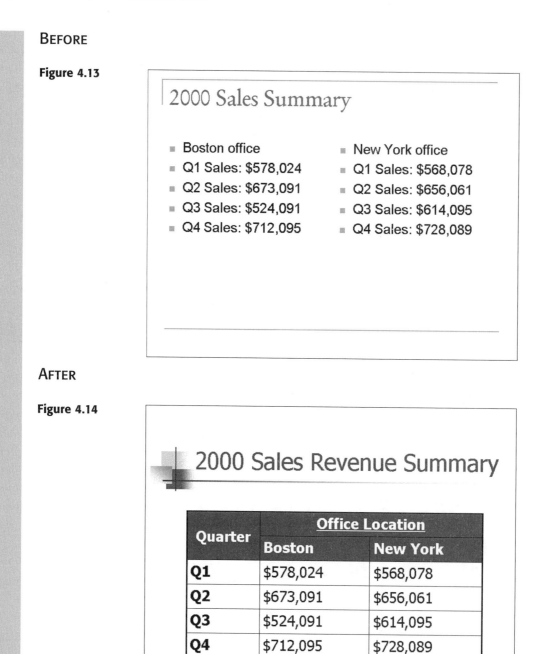

AFTER

Figure 4.14

CHAPTER 5

ORGANIZING PRESENTATIONS IN POWERPOINT

In this chapter

EXPLORING POWERPOINT'S OUTLINING FEATURES

PowerPoint's outlining features make it easy to create a well-organized presentation. There are several ways that you can organize a presentation in PowerPoint, depending on how you work best and whether you've already created an outline in another program. You can use the Outline tab in Normal view to organize and rearrange your presentation easily. For added options, try the Outlining toolbar. This toolbar enables you to promote and demote outline points, as well as move, collapse, and expand them. You can also create a summary slide or display font formatting. If you create outlines in Word or another program, you can import them into PowerPoint. PowerPoint also imports other common file formats, such as RTF and TXT.

ORGANIZING PRESENTATIONS

Before you actually create a PowerPoint presentation, you should determine the presentation's purpose, organize your ideas, and establish the flow of what you're going to say. Essentially, you need to create an outline.

→ To learn some useful outlining techniques, **see** "Creating an Outline and Storyboard" in Chapter 22, "The Message—Scripting the Concept."

PowerPoint offers four ways to create an outline. One of the easiest ways is to create your presentation using the Outline tab in Normal view. If you're more comfortable adding content directly to slides, your information will automatically be displayed on the Outline tab. Creating a presentation using the AutoContent Wizard is a good idea if you want to receive detailed content suggestions for a particular type of presentation; the wizard also creates a basic outline for you. And finally, if you already have an outline in another application, such as Word 2002, or just prefer working in this environment, you can easily import the outline into PowerPoint.

→ To learn what the AutoContent Wizard does, **see** "Using the AutoContent Wizard" in Chapter 2, "Creating a Basic Presentation."

→ To learn how to import existing outlines, **see** "Working with Outlines Created in Other Programs" in this chapter.

As you create your basic outline, keep several things in mind:

- Start nearly every presentation with a title slide that introduces your topic and its presenter.

- Think of several main points to cover and design your presentation around those points.

- Try not to cover more than one main topic or concept in an individual slide.

- Remember that a PowerPoint outline is usually designed to accompany a verbal presentation. Keep in mind what you want your audience to see versus what you want them to listen to during your presentation.

- Keep bulleted lists balanced and consistent. For example, a single bullet on a slide doesn't really make sense; a list should contain at least two bullets. Too many bullets on one slide and very few on another also might not work well.

- Consider using a summary slide to summarize the points you made during your presentation and conclude it.

USING THE OUTLINE TAB

No matter which method you use to create your outline, you'll probably want to use PowerPoint's Outline tab to organize this information at some point. In Normal view, the outline appears on the left side of the window and shares the desktop with the slide itself and related notes.

Note

You can change the size of any pane in PowerPoint by dragging its border to a new location. This can be done when the cursor changes to a double-headed arrow.

To view the Outline tab, click the Normal View button in the lower-left corner of the PowerPoint window. The Outline tab is selected by default, and your presentation's outline will appear on the left side of the window. Figure 5.1 shows the Outline tab.

Figure 5.1
The Outline tab offers a flexible approach to creating an outline.

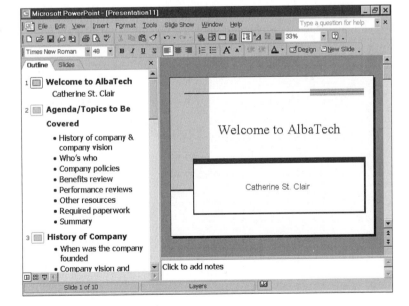

PART

II

CH

5

Each slide in your presentation is numbered and followed by a slide icon and the title text. The body text is listed under each slide, up to five levels. This body text includes bulleted and indented lists, as well as other text information. The title text is also referred to as the *outline heading* and each individual point in the body text as a *subheading*. Clip art, tables, charts, and other objects don't appear in the outline.

Note

Any text that you enter other than in the Click to Add Title or the Click to Add Text placeholder doesn't display in the outline.

Adding new outline information is simple. Enter the content and press the Enter key to move to the next point. To delete a point you no longer need, select it and press the Delete key.

USING THE OUTLINING TOOLBAR

You can use the Outlining toolbar to help organize and rearrange your slides on the Outline tab. To display the toolbar, choose View, Toolbars, Outlining. It appears vertically on the left side of the Outline tab. Table 5.1 lists the buttons on this toolbar.

TABLE 5.1   OUTLINING TOOLBAR BUTTONS

Button	Name	Description
⬅	Promote	Applies the style and formatting of the level that is one step above the level of the selected text.
➡	Demote	Applies the style and formatting of the level that is one step below the level of the selected text. Demoting a slide title moves the text of the selected slide to the previous slide.
⬆	Move Up	Moves the selected text ahead of the previous item in the outline.
⬇	Move Down	Moves the selected text beneath the next item in the outline.
➖	Collapse	Hides all body text for the selected slides.
➕	Expand	Displays all body text for the selected slides.
⬆☰	Collapse All	Hides all body text in the outline.
⬇☰	Expand All	Displays all body text in the outline.

TABLE 5.1   CONTINUED

Button	Name	Description
	Summary Slide	Creates a slide that summarizes the presentation by listing slide titles.
	Show Formatting	Shows the actual presentation font formatting on the Outline tab.

Note

You can move the Outlining toolbar to another location on the screen by dragging the move handle (above the Promote button) to another location.

PROMOTING AND DEMOTING OUTLINE POINTS

You can demote outline headings and promote and demote subheadings to reorganize and rearrange your presentation. Promoting a first-level subheading makes it a heading (slide title) in a new slide. Promoting a secondary-level subheading (such as indented text or lower-level bullet) moves it up to the next level. Conversely, promoting indented text outdents it.

For example, if you select the text of a second-level bullet in the outline and click the Promote button, the bullet becomes a first-level bullet (see Figures 5.2 and 5.3).

Figure 5.2
The bulleted list item you want to change is currently indented.

Organization chart

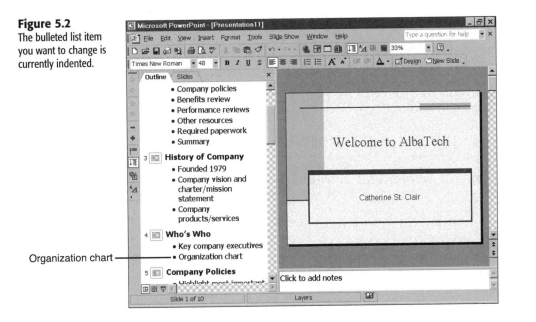

PART

II

CH

5

Figure 5.3
Promoting the
bulleted list item
moves it up one
level but doesn't
change its location.

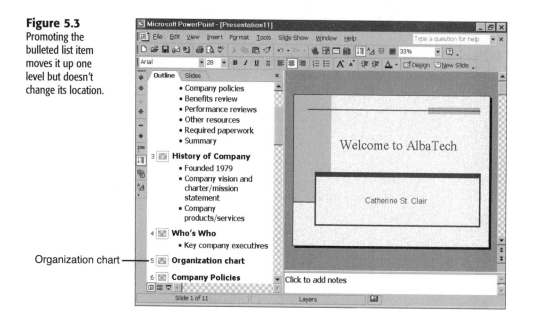

Organization chart ─────

If you promote a first-level bullet, it becomes a slide title, and PowerPoint inserts a new slide into the presentation.

The Demote button works in much the same way as the Promote button. Demoting a sub-heading such as a first-level bullet moves the bullet point to a second-level bullet. Demoting other text indents the text.

Tip from
Patrice-Anne
Rutledge

You can also easily demote a specific heading by selecting it and pressing the Tab key.

Demoting an outline heading (slide title) deletes the slide and moves its text content to the bottom of the previous slide. PowerPoint verifies this action before doing it if your slide contains notes or graphics.

⚠ ***Do you lose notes and graphics when demoting?*** *See the "Troubleshooting" section near the end of the chapter.*

MOVING OUTLINE POINTS UP AND DOWN

In addition to promoting and demoting outline points, you can also move the location of each point. For example, to move a numbered list item from the second to the first position in the list, select that second item and click the Move Up button.

Let's say you want to move the first of three bulleted list items from one slide to the top of the list in the following slide. To do this, click the Move Down button three times (see Figures 5.4 and 5.5).

Figure 5.4
The original bullet position.

Retirement plan

Figure 5.5
Its position after clicking the Move Down button three times.

Retirement plan

→ To learn more about the different ways you can organize slides in PowerPoint, **see** "Rearranging Slides" in Chapter 6, "Formatting Slides and Presentations."

Tip from
Patrice-Anne Rutledge

Use Slide Sorter view to view your actual slides as you rearrange them.

→ For details about viewing slides in Slide Sorter view, **see** "Using the Slide Sorter View" in Chapter 6.

COLLAPSING AND EXPANDING OUTLINE POINTS

To make it easier to read a long outline, you can collapse and expand slides and their body text.

 To collapse the body text of an individual slide, select it and click the Collapse button. The slide number and title remain, but the related body text is hidden from view. Figure 5.6 shows a collapsed slide.

Figure 5.6
Collapsing a slide hides its body text.

Select the slide again and click Expand to display the hidden text.

To collapse the entire outline, click the Collapse All button. Figure 5.7 illustrates an outline that is entirely collapsed.

To display the outline details again, click the Expand All button.

Tip from
Patrice-Anne Rutledge

If you want to collapse and expand more than one slide, but not all slides, press Shift, choose the consecutive slides, and then click the Collapse or Expand button. Note that the slides you select must be consecutive.

Collapsing and expanding your outline make it easier to print as well. You can print an entire outline in detail, only certain sections in detail, or only a collapsed summary outline.

→ To learn how to print outlines, **see** "Printing an Outline" in Chapter 10, "Creating and Printing Presentation Materials."

Figure 5.7
Collapsing an entire presentation creates a presentation outline summary.

CREATING A SUMMARY SLIDE

You can create a slide that summarizes the outline headings (the slide titles) for all or selected slides in your presentation. You can then use that slide to introduce your presentation, to highlight the areas you're going to discuss, or to close your presentation by summarizing it. To create a summary slide, select all the slides you want to include in the summary.

Note

You need to choose either all slides or a series of consecutive slides when you create a summary slide from the Outline tab in Normal view. Create a summary slide from Slide Sorter view if you want to choose multiple, non-consecutive slides.

Usually it's easier to do this if you collapse all the headings by clicking the Collapse All button on the Outlining toolbar.

Tip from
Patrice-Anne Rutledge

You can easily select all slides in the presentation by selecting the first slide and dragging the mouse down to the last slide or by pressing Ctrl+A.

Next, click the Summary Slide button. PowerPoint automatically creates a summary slide that contains a bulleted list of all the selected slide titles in your presentation. The summary slide is inserted before the first selected slide, but you can move it to another location if you want. Figure 5.8 shows a sample summary slide.

Figure 5.8
Create a summary slide
to introduce or close
your presentation.

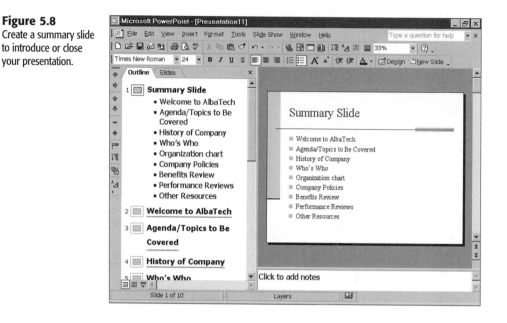

SHOWING SLIDE FORMATTING

By default, the Outline tab displays each heading and subheading in the same font, bolding the headings for emphasis. If you want the outline to appear using the actual fonts and formatting of the presentation itself, click the Show Formatting button on the Outlining toolbar. Figure 5.9 shows a sample outline with formatting.

Figure 5.9
This outline displays
text formatting.

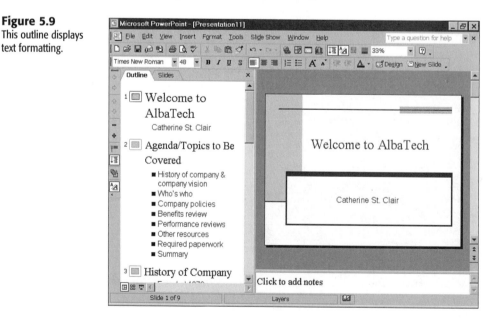

The specific font and attributes—such as size, bolding, italics, underlining, and shadow—now appear in the Outline tab. The font color, however, does not display.

WORKING WITH OUTLINES CREATED IN OTHER PROGRAMS

If you create outlines in other Office XP programs, such as Microsoft Word, you can either export them from their original application or import them directly into PowerPoint. PowerPoint can work with outlines in many different formats, such as the following:

- Word documents (.doc)
- Rich Text Format (.rtf)
- Text files (.txt)
- Excel worksheets (.xls)
- HTML (.htm)

For example, if you create an outline in Word, you use heading 1, heading 2, and heading 3 styles to format your document. When PowerPoint imports your outline, each heading 1 becomes a slide title, each heading 2 becomes first-level text, and each heading 3 becomes second-level text. Figure 5.10 shows a Word outline and its components.

Figure 5.10
Outline in Word and then export your outline to PowerPoint.

If the file you export doesn't contain these heading styles, PowerPoint uses paragraph indentations and tabs to determine the structure of the outline. Use the Outlining toolbar buttons to reorganize the outline if the initial format isn't correct.

To export an outline to PowerPoint from within Word, choose File, Send To, Microsoft PowerPoint. PowerPoint automatically creates a presentation from this information. Apply a design template, graphics, and other pizzazz, and your presentation is complete. Figure 5.11 illustrates an example of an exported outline.

Figure 5.11
The outline now appears in a PowerPoint presentation.

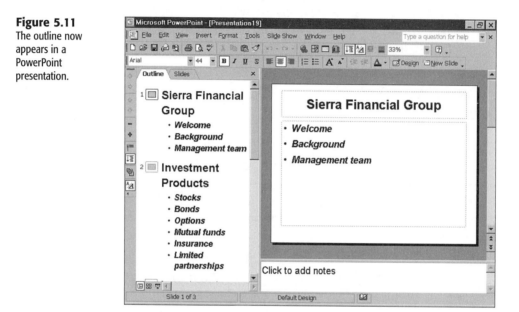

Although this is the easiest way to create a PowerPoint presentation from a Word outline, there are other ways to import different types of outlines into PowerPoint. You can

- **Import an outline from within PowerPoint**   To do this, click the Open button to display the Open dialog box, select All Outlines from the Files of Type drop-down list, choose the outline you want to import, and click Open. With this method, PowerPoint creates a new presentation. Note that you may be prompted to install a converter if one isn't already installed.

- **Import an outline into an existing presentation**   To do this, select the slide on the Outline tab after which you want to insert the new outline. Choose Insert, Slides from Outline to open the Insert Outline dialog box. Choose the outline you want to import and click Insert.

Does your imported outline look strange? See the "Troubleshooting" section near the end of the chapter.

- **Copy the outline text from the source application**   Then just paste into PowerPoint and reformat to create a basic presentation quickly.

TROUBLESHOOTING

PREPARING FILES TO IMPORT

I imported an outline, and it doesn't look right.

Remember that PowerPoint imports an outline from another application "as is." Before importing, be sure that the existing document makes a suitable outline. For example, a lengthy text file or detailed spreadsheet might not make sense as an outline.

DEALING WITH DEMOTIONS

I demoted a slide, and the text moved to the previous slide, but the notes and graphics disappeared.

When you demote a slide using the Demote button on the Outlining toolbar, the text content remains and carries over to the previous slide, but any graphics or notes are deleted.

DESIGN CORNER: REORGANIZING A SLIDE'S CONTENTS IN THE OUTLINE TAB

Use an outline to ensure a logical flow of thought through your presentation. Creating an initial outline often can call attention to such problems. PowerPoint's outlining features make it easy to correct and perfect your outline.

For example, let's say that you need to present the process for selecting a new accounting software program to your team. You entered the basic points on your introductory slide, but after reviewing this slide you realize that the subtopics aren't indented correctly under the main topics you want to cover. You can correct this easily with the Outlining toolbar:

1. Click on the Outline tab in Normal view. If the slide's contents aren't clearly visible, drag the pane's border to resize it.

2. Select the Goals and Objectives bullet points on the Outline tab and click the Demote button on the Outlining toolbar.

3. Select the Final deadline: May 1, 2001 bullet point and click the Promote button on the Outlining toolbar.

BEFORE

Figure 5.12
Demote these two
bullet points, which
are part of the project
introduction.

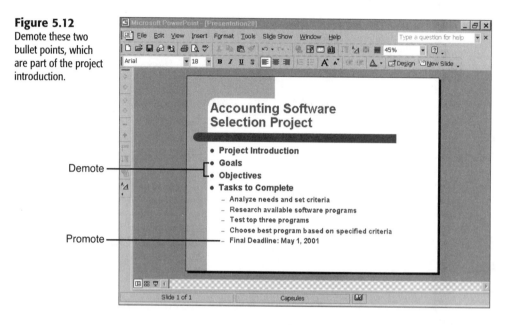

Demote

Promote

AFTER

Figure 5.13
Promote this bullet
point, which is its own
topic.

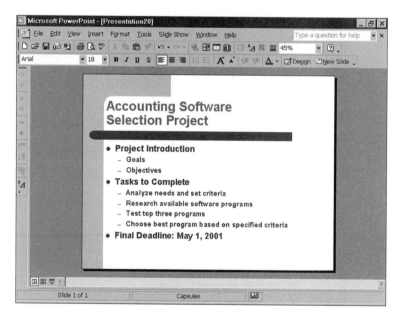

CHAPTER **6**

FORMATTING SLIDES AND PRESENTATIONS

In this chapter

EXPLORING POWERPOINT FORMATTING OPTIONS

After you create a presentation, you may want to make some changes to it. Adding, deleting, rearranging, copying, and moving slides are simple tasks in PowerPoint. You can also make more detailed changes to the original format of your presentation. For example, you can apply a new design template, change colors and color schemes, and apply a special effects background.

ADDING SLIDES

After you create a presentation, you may want to add new slides. To add a new slide to an open presentation, click the New Slide button on the Formatting toolbar or press Ctrl+M. PowerPoint adds a new slide immediately following the current slide and opens the Slide Layout task pane. Select the slide layout you want to use; PowerPoint applies that layout to the slide (see Figure 6.1).

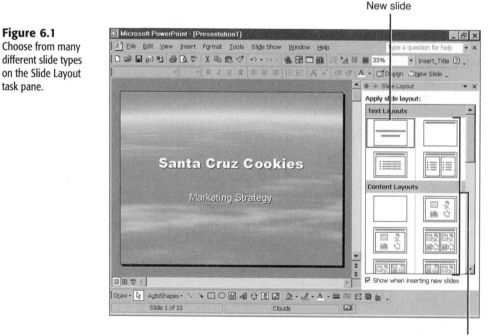

Figure 6.1
Choose from many different slide types on the Slide Layout task pane.

New slide

Slide Layout task pane

→ To learn more about each layout type, **see** "Understanding Slide Layouts" in Chapter 2, "Creating a Basic Presentation."

DELETING SLIDES

If you no longer need a slide or make a mistake and want to start again, you can delete it. In Normal view, select the slide on either the Outline tab or the Slides tab, and press the Delete key. If these tabs don't appear, click the Normal View button in the lower-left corner of the PowerPoint window to restore them.

To delete multiple consecutive slides, press the Shift key and select the slides you want to delete before pressing the Delete key. You can delete multiple nonconsecutive slides in Slide Sorter view by holding the Ctrl key, selecting the slides you want to delete, and pressing the Delete key.

REARRANGING SLIDES

You can rearrange slides in three different locations in PowerPoint. These include the

- Outline tab in Normal view
- Slides tab in Normal view
- Slide Sorter view

Select the icon of the slide you want to move and drag it to a new location. Which method is best? The Outline tab is useful if you want to read the content of your slides as you reorganize. The Slides tab is a good choice if you know exactly what you want to move and want to do it quickly. If you have major reorganization to do on your presentation, you may want to use Slide Sorter view because it provides more flexibility as well as the capability to view the contents of your slides as you rearrange them.

Tip from
Patrice-Anne Rutledge

If you want to do a major reorganization of a presentation that contains numerous slides, consider printing handouts with either six or nine slides per page first so you can more easily analyze your entire presentation before making changes.

→ To learn more about using Slide Sorter view to organize your slides, **see** "Using the Slide Sorter View" later in this chapter.

→ To discover more outlining techniques, **see** "Moving Outline Points Up and Down" in Chapter 5, "Organizing Presentations in PowerPoint."

USING THE SLIDE SORTER VIEW

You can use the Slide Sorter view to organize and rearrange your slides. To open this view, click the Slide Sorter View button on the lower-left corner of the PowerPoint window or select View, Slide Sorter. Figure 6.2 displays this view.

Figure 6.2
Analyze and organize slides in Slide Sorter view.

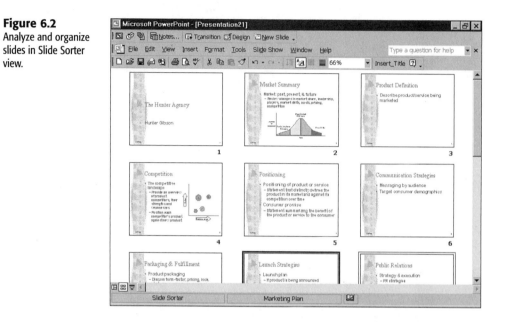

In this view, you see smaller versions of your slides in several rows and columns. By viewing the basic content of each slide, you can more easily rearrange their order.

To move a slide in the Slide Sorter, select it and drag it to a new location.

To view a particular slide in more detail, click on the desired slide and select the Normal View button at the lower-left corner of the PowerPoint window (see Figure 6.3).

Figure 6.3
Choose how you want to view your presentation.

Normal View button

Select any slide.

To delete a slide in Slide Sorter view, select it and press the Delete key. To select multiple slides to delete, press Ctrl, select the slides, and then press the Delete key.

Tip from	Occasionally, you may also want to hide slides from view during an onscreen presentation but not delete them from the presentation itself. To do that, select the slide or slides you want to hide and click the Hide Slide button on the Slide Sorter toolbar. The slides remain in the presentation, but they aren't displayed when you run your slideshow. This is often easier than creating a custom show, particularly if you don't plan to repeat this version of your presentation.
Patrice-Anne Rutledge	

The Slide Sorter toolbar also includes buttons for applying optional effects, such as transitions, animation effects, and speaker's notes, which we discuss later in this book.

→ To learn why you might want to use speaker's notes, **see** "Creating Notes and Handouts" in Chapter 10, "Creating and Printing Presentation Materials."

→ To learn how to create transitional effects, **see** "Setting Slide Transitions" in Chapter 15.

COPYING AND MOVING SLIDES FROM ONE PRESENTATION TO ANOTHER

Using the Slide Sorter view, you can either copy or move slides from one PowerPoint presentation to another. To do this, open both the source and destination presentations in Slide Sorter view. Choose Window, Arrange All. PowerPoint displays both presentations in different window panes in Slide Sorter view, shown in Figure 6.4.

To copy a slide, select it and then drag it with the mouse to the desired location in the other presentation. PowerPoint places the slide in the destination presentation, but it also remains in the source as shown in Figure 6.5.

To move a slide, select it, click the Cut button on the Standard toolbar, position the mouse in the new destination location, and click the Paste button. The slide is removed from the source presentation and inserted in the destination presentation. To move or copy more than one slide at a time, press Ctrl as you drag slides from the source presentation.

If each presentation uses a different design template, the slide changes to the template of the new presentation and the Paste Options button appears. If you want to retain the design template of the source presentation, click the down arrow to the right of the Paste Options button and choose Keep Source Formatting. To go back to the design template of the target presentation, choose Use Design Template Formatting.

PART

II

CH

6

Figure 6.4
By splitting panes between two presentations, you can copy or move slides between them.

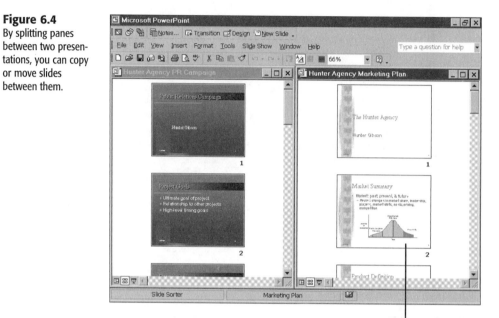

Slide you want to move or copy

Figure 6.5
Copying a slide is easier than creating it again.

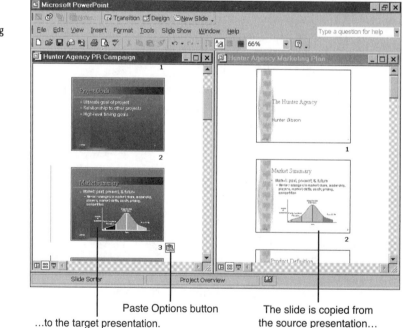

...to the target presentation.

Paste Options button

The slide is copied from the source presentation...

Caution

Although you can combine multiple design templates in a single presentation, think carefully before doing so. Combining design templates can make your presentation confusing unless done properly.

Problems with multiple design templates? See the "Troubleshooting" section near the end of this chapter.

To remove the dual window view, click the Close button in the upper-right corner of the presentation you no longer want to view and then the Maximize button in the upper-right corner of the presentation you want to keep active.

If arranging both presentations in one window is too distracting, you can put them in separate windows:

1. Open the presentation from which you want to copy or move slides.
2. Click the Slide Sorter View button at the lower-left side of the screen to display the presentation in this view.
3. Select the slides you want to copy or move. To select multiple noncontiguous slides, press the Ctrl key and then choose slides.
4. Press Ctrl+C to copy the slides; press Ctrl+X to cut the slides if you would rather move them.
5. Open the presentation in which you want to place the selected slides.
6. Click where you want to insert the slides and press Ctrl+V to paste them.

Note

If more than one presentation is open at a time and each is in a maximized window, you can press Ctrl+F6 to cycle through each one. This helps when you want the full-screen view and want to copy/move from one presentation to the next without having to use the Window menu.

Lost slides when you copied from one presentation to another? See the "Troubleshooting" section near the end of this chapter.

PART

II

CH

6

APPLYING A NEW DESIGN TEMPLATE

You can easily change the design template originally applied to your presentation. To do so, click the Design button on the Formatting toolbar. The Slide Design task pane appears, displaying all available design templates in preview format (see Figure 6.6).

The existing design template used in the current presentation appears at the top (if there is one), followed by the most recently used templates, and then all other available templates.

Select the template you want to use. PowerPoint applies this new design to your presentation.

Figure 6.6
Choose a design template that matches the mood and goals of your presentation.

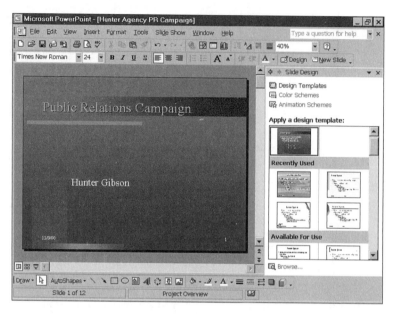

Caution

Not all design templates are already installed. If PowerPoint displays a warning that you need to install a template, be sure to have the program CD in your CD-ROM drive, and then follow the installation instructions in the warning.

→ To learn more about design templates and how to use them best, **see** "Understanding Design Templates" in Chapter 2.

→ To learn how to apply a design template to a presentation when you create it, **see** "Creating a Presentation Using a Design Template" in Chapter 2.

Note

To download additional design templates from the Web, choose Help, Office on the Web or go directly to http://officeupdate.microsoft.com.

PREVIEWING DESIGN TEMPLATES

If you want to view larger previews of the design templates, click the down arrow to the right of any template preview and choose Show Large Previews from the shortcut menu that appears. The preview templates will increase in size. To go back to the normal-size previews, simply select this option again to remove the check mark. Figure 6.7 illustrates design template in large previews.

Figure 6.7
Preview lets you see what a presentation looks like before you apply it.

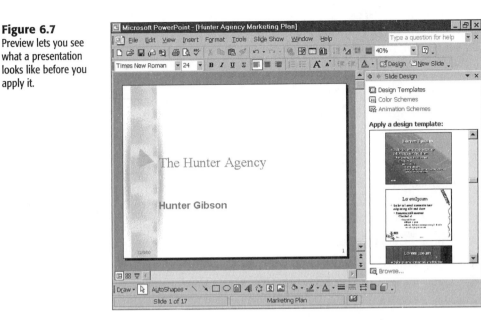

APPLYING MULTIPLE DESIGN TEMPLATES TO A SINGLE PRESENTATION

PowerPoint 2002 offers the flexibility of using multiple design templates in a single presentation. Although it's very easy to do this, you should carefully consider whether it's a good idea or not. Too many contrasting styles and designs can make your presentation confusing and difficult to follow. Even if you decide to apply multiple design templates, your best bet is to keep them reasonably similar. Here are some suggestions for when multiple design templates would be appropriate:

- You want to use one design template for your title slide and another for the rest of your presentation. For example, the title slide could include a logo that the rest of the presentation doesn't have.

- Your presentation is broken into several distinct sections and you want to use a separate design template for each. For example, let's say that you're giving a summary presentation about three divisions of a large corporation and each division uses a different default design template for its PowerPoint presentations. You might want to use the standard template for each division for that part of the presentation.

- You want to make minor design template modifications based on the content of the slide. For example, you could create two similar design templates, one with a graphic image in the lower right corner and one without. On slides with extensive content, you might prefer to use the design template without the graphic image.

To apply a different design template to a selected slide, follow these steps:

1. Select the slide or slides to which you want to apply a separate design template.
2. Select the preview of that template on the Slide Design task pane.

PART

II

CH

6

3. Click the down arrow to the right of the selected template.

4. Choose Apply to Selected Slides. PowerPoint applies the design template only to the selected slides. The unselected slides still retain the original design template.

To return to a single design template, select that template and choose Apply to All Slides from the menu that appears when you click the down arrow.

CREATING YOUR OWN DESIGN TEMPLATE

Sometimes none of the existing design templates offers exactly what you're looking for. In that case, you can either modify an existing template or create one of your own. The following are some ideas of things you might want to do to customize or add to a blank slide:

- Change the master title or text style to a different font (View, Master, Slide Master).
- Change the background color (Format, Background).
- Change the slide color scheme (choose Color Schemes from the Slide Design task pane).
- Change the bullet styles (Format, Bullets and Numbering).
- Add objects such as a logo, picture, or WordArt image.

To save a customized design template for future use, follow these steps:

1. Choose File, Save As to open the Save As dialog box.

2. In the Save As Type drop-down list, choose Design Template. The Save In drop-down list selects the folder in which you store design templates by default.

3. Enter a name for your design template in the File Name field.

4. Click the Save button.

The saved design template is available the next time you open the Slide Design task pane.

Note

To delete a design template you no longer want or created by mistake, select the template in the Open dialog box and press the Delete key.

CHOOSING A NEW SLIDE COLOR SCHEME

Each design template includes several color schemes from which you can choose. A color scheme is a set of eight coordinated colors that applies to the following parts of your slides:

- Background
- Text and lines
- Shadows
- Title text

- Fills
- Accent
- Accent and hyperlink
- Accent and followed hyperlink

For example, you may like a basic design template but prefer to use different colors. You may want to use the same presentation for both onscreen and overhead delivery, but they require different color schemes.

APPLYING A NEW COLOR SCHEME

To apply a new color scheme to your presentation, follow these steps:

1. Click the Design button on the Formatting toolbar. The Slide Design task pane opens.
2. Click the Color Schemes link on the Slide Design task pane. The available color schemes for the design template of the current presentation appear (see Figure 6.8).

Figure 6.8
You can modify your presentation's color scheme.

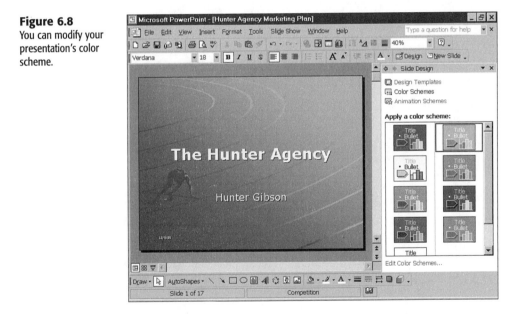

3. Select a new color scheme; PowerPoint applies it to your presentation.

→ For more information about color theory, **see** "Using Color" in Chapter 23, "The Media—Designing Visual Support."

PREVIEWING COLOR SCHEMES

If you want to view larger previews of the available color schemes, click the down arrow to the right of any scheme and choose Show Large Previews from the shortcut menu that appears. The preview schemes will increase in size. To go back to the normal-size previews, select this option again to remove the check mark.

PART
II
CH
6

APPLYING MULTIPLE COLOR SCHEMES TO A SINGLE PRESENTATION

To apply a different color scheme to selected slides, follow these steps:

1. Select the slide or slides to which you want to apply a separate color scheme.
2. Select the preview of that scheme on the Slide Design task pane.
3. Click the down arrow to the right of the selected scheme.
4. Choose Apply to Selected Slides. PowerPoint applies the color scheme only to the selected slides. The unselected slides retain the original design template.

To return to a single color scheme, select that scheme and choose Apply to All Slides from the menu that appears when you click the down arrow.

Caution

Although the capability to apply multiple color schemes to your presentation adds flexibility and creativity, be sure not to overdo it. Consider carefully before applying more than one color scheme to verify that your presentation is still consistent and readable.

APPLYING A COLOR SCHEME TO NOTES AND HANDOUTS

In addition to applying a new color scheme to your actual presentation, you can also apply color schemes to notes or handouts that you create.

To apply a color scheme to notes, select View, Notes Page and then apply a color scheme from the Slide Design task pane.

To apply a color scheme to handouts, select View, Master, Handout Master and then apply a color scheme from the Slide Design task pane.

CREATING A CUSTOM COLOR SCHEME

Occasionally you may want to customize the individual colors in a color scheme. For example, you may like a particular scheme but want to modify only the background color. To do this, follow these steps from the Slide Design task pane:

1. Click Edit Color Schemes to open the Edit Color Schemes dialog box with the Custom tab selected, displayed in Figure 6.9.
2. Choose the object whose color you want to change, such as the background or title text.
3. Click the Change Color button, which displays the Background Color dialog box. Figure 6.10 shows this dialog box.
4. Choose a color from the Standard tab or formulate a custom color on the Custom tab. The New preview box compares this new color with the Current color.

→ For more details on color selection dialog boxes, **see** "Specifying Colors" in Chapter 14, "Creating and Formatting Objects."

Figure 6.9
Change the color of
certain areas of your
presentation to cus-
tomize it.

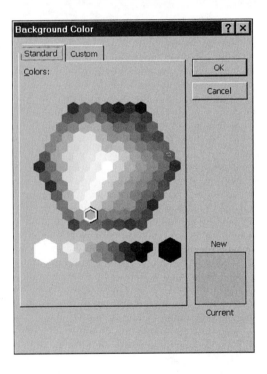

Figure 6.10
Choose a standard
color or specify a cus-
tom color.

5. Click OK to return to the Edit Color Scheme dialog box.

6. Click the Preview button to preview this new color in your presentation.

7. Click Apply to apply the color scheme.

8. Click the Add As Standard Scheme button if you want to add this scheme to your selections on the Slide Design task pane (see Figure 6.11).

Figure 6.11
The color scheme you created is now a standard selection.

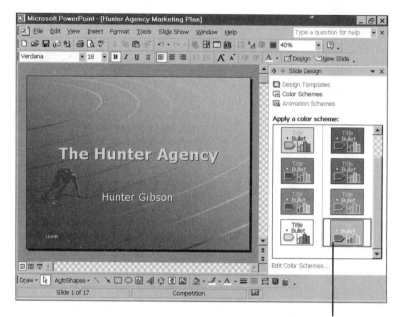

New color scheme

You can now apply this new color scheme as you would any other color scheme.

You can delete a color scheme just as easily as you created a new one. To delete a color scheme, go to the Standard tab on the Edit Color Scheme dialog box, select the scheme you no longer want, and click the Delete Scheme button.

APPLYING A BACKGROUND

In addition to specific color backgrounds, you can also add special background effects such as shading, patterns, textures, and pictures to your presentation. To apply a special background, choose Format, Background to open the Background dialog box, illustrated in Figure 6.12.

Figure 6.12
You can apply a special effects background to your presentation.

From the drop-down list in the Background Fill group box, you can choose

- One of the compatible colors under the Automatic color box.
- More Colors to open the Colors dialog box, in which you can select from many other colors or even specify your own custom color.

→ For more information about the Colors dialog box, **see** "Specifying Colors" in Chapter 14.

- Fill Effects to open the Fill Effects dialog box, where you can apply special effects such as gradients, textures, patterns, and pictures.

→ For more information about the Fill Effects dialog box, **see** "Specifying Fill Color" in Chapter 14.

After you select the background you want, you can click the Preview button to see the effects before applying them, Apply to the current slide only, or Apply to All the slides in your presentation.

TROUBLESHOOTING

COPYING VERSUS CUTTING PRESENTATIONS

I thought I copied slides from one presentation to another, but now they've disappeared from my original presentation.

Be sure to use Ctrl+C (copy) rather than Ctrl+X (cut) if you want to keep the original slides in place. Moving slides removes them from their original location; copying just creates duplicates.

CONSOLIDATING DESIGN TEMPLATES

I copied slides from several other presentations to my current presentation and ended up with multiple conflicting design templates.

To use a single design template, select the template you want from the Slide Design task pane and choose Apply to All Slides from the menu that appears when you click the down arrow.

DESIGN CORNER: MODIFYING AN EXISTING DESIGN TEMPLATE

Often you'll find a design template whose basic design and concept you like, but the colors are wrong or you'd like to change other design elements. In PowerPoint, it's easy to modify an existing design template to create a new one.

For example, let's say that you like the Eclipse design template, but would prefer a dark background and some other color changes and would also like to change the bullet styles. To do so, follow these steps:

1. Apply the Eclipse design template to your presentation from the Slide Design – Design Template task pane and then click the Color Schemes Hyperlink.

2. Choose a new color scheme from those that appear; PowerPoint applies it to your presentation.

3. Click the Edit Color Schemes hyperlink to open the Edit Color Schemes dialog box.

4. Choose the item whose color you want to change, such as Title Text, and click the Change Color button to open the Title Text Color dialog box.

5. Choose your new color and click OK.

6. Continue applying color changes in this manner until you're done; click Apply to close the Edit Color Scheme dialog box.

7. Select the bulleted text and choose Format, Bullets and Numbering to open the Bullets and Numbering dialog box.

8. Choose a new bullet style and click OK.

You can apply these changes only to the current presentation or save them as a new design template (choose Design Template as the file type in the Save As dialog box).

BEFORE

Figure 6.13

AFTER

Figure 6.14

New bullet style   Modified Font colors

Modified color scheme

CHAPTER 7

COLLABORATING ON PRESENTATIONS

In this chapter

DEFINING WAYS TO COLLABORATE IN POWERPOINT

Being able to get feedback easily on a presentation you've created or work collaboratively with a group of people on a presentation is important for many organizations. PowerPoint 2002 offers new collaborative features that make tracking, reviewing, and merging changes among multiple reviewers an easier task.

There are two ways to handle the physical process of sending and receiving reviews: with Microsoft Outlook and without Microsoft Outlook (for example, using another e-mail program, a network server, or disks). If you use Outlook, you can take advantage of special features that make collaborative reviewing easier, particularly if you want to monitor the feedback of multiple reviewers. But you can also review without using Outlook, especially if you don't really need its added functionality.

No matter which method you use, there are four main steps to a review cycle:

1. The original author sends the presentation out for review.
2. The reviewer (or reviewers) reviews the presentation, either by making changes directly to it or by adding comments.
3. The reviewer returns the presentation to the original author.
4. The original authors merges, compares, and finalizes the presentation.

How you use PowerPoint's reviewing features depends on both the method you choose to handle the physical review and your goals for the review process. You may simply want to send your presentation to one person for review. In that case, you need to decide if you want to use PowerPoint's advanced reviewing tools (such as the Revisions pane) or if you'd rather just have your reviewer adds comments where necessary and send the presentation back to you.

If, on the other hand, you want to track all reviews formally or incorporate the comments and revisions of multiple reviewers, using tracking tools and the Revisions pane would be useful. In any case, PowerPoint's review and collaboration features are both powerful and flexible enough to suit most requirements.

SENDING A PRESENTATION FOR REVIEW

The first step in collaborating on a PowerPoint presentation is to send the presentation out for review. Depending on the method you use to handle reviews, how you do this can vary slightly.

To send a presentation for review using Outlook, follow these steps:

1. Open the presentation you want to send for review.
2. Choose File, Send To, Mail Recipient (for Review). Microsoft Outlook opens with an e-mail ready to send (see Figure 7.1).

Figure 7.1
Your presentation is set up automatically to draw the attention of a reviewer.

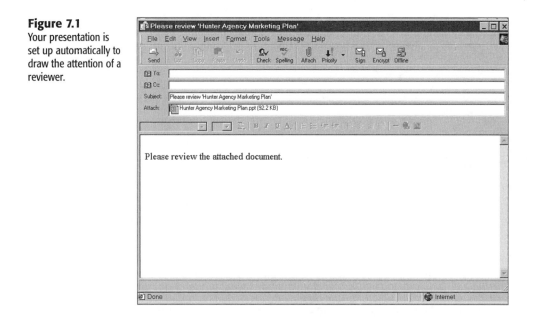

3. Enter the e-mail address of the person to whom you want to send the presentation.

4. Click the Send button to send your presentation.

To create a review copy of your presentation that you can send using another e-mail program, place on a network server, or copy to a disk, follow these steps:

1. Open the presentation you want to send out for review.

2. Choose File, Save As. The Save As dialog box opens, shown in Figure 7.2.

Figure 7.2
Save your file as a presentation for review.

3. Enter a name for the review copy in the File Name field.

4. Choose Presentation for Review in the Save as Type drop-down list.

5. Click Save.

From here, you can send your presentation to reviewers using your preferred method—e-mail, network server, or disk.

PERFORMING THE REVIEW

What happens during the actual review depends on a number of things: the methodology the original author communicated to the reviewers, the amount of change required, the type of review (quick glance versus detailed content analysis), and the preferences of the individual reviewer.

In PowerPoint, reviewers can either make changes to the presentation itself or add comments about individual slides in the presentation. If a reviewer revises the actual presentation, the original author will be able to use the Revisions pane to determine what changes were made. If the reviewer uses comments, these will be readily visible in yellow boxes on the screen. When a reviewer changes the actual content of a presentation, PowerPoint tracks these changes. Table 7.1 lists the types of changes PowerPoint tracks, in addition to the actual text itself.

TABLE 7.1 REVIEW CHANGES POWERPOINT TRACKS

Change	Description
Presentation-level changes	Slide size Content and list of named shows Headers and footers for slides, title slides, and notes
Slide-level changes	Color scheme Animation settings List of shapes Slide master IDs and locked templates Slide master list of color schemes, default text styles, background, and objects Slide transition and layout Headers and footers
Shape-level changes	Action settings Recolor information External objects
Paragraph-level changes	Bullet typeface, color, size, animation schemes, margins, and tabs Paragraph indent, alignment, direction, margin, and tabs East Asian word wrap and alignment settings
Text-level changes	Font typeface, color, and size Languages Hyperlinks

USING THE REVIEWING TOOLBAR

The Reviewing toolbar offers features that are useful both to reviewers and to authors reconciling reviews. Depending on the stage of the review cycle and the review activity you're performing, some of the Reviewing toolbar buttons may be unavailable or hidden.

The Reviewing toolbar displays automatically during certain reviewing activities, such as adding comments or reconciling reviews. You can also open it manually by choosing View, Toolbars, Reviewing.

Table 7.2 lists the buttons on the Reviewing toolbar and explains how they're used.

TABLE 7.2	REVIEWING TOOLBAR BUTTONS	
Button	**Name**	**Description**
	Markup	Toggles the display of comments and changes on and off
Reviewers...	Reviewers	Enables you to select the reviews/comments of specific reviewers
	Previous Item	Cycles back to the previous comment in a presentation
	Next Item	Cycles forward to the next comment in a presentation
	Apply	Enables you to apply all changes to the current slide or the current presentation
	Unapply	Enables you to unapply all changes to the current slide or the current presentation
	Insert Comment	Inserts a comment box on a slide
	Edit Comment	Enables you to edit a selected comment
	Delete Comment	Deletes a selected comment or all markers on the current slide
End Review...	End Review	Enables you to end the review, losing any unapplied changes
	Revisions Pane	Toggles the Revisions pane on and off

⚡ **Can't find buttons on the Reviewing toolbar?** See the "Troubleshooting" section at the end of the chapter.

ADDING COMMENTS TO SLIDES

The capability to add comments to slides is a useful reviewing utility that is shared with other Office XP applications, such as Word and Excel. You can use comments as part of PowerPoint's collaborative reviewing process or use the comments feature on its own.

Note

Comments aren't the same as notes. You add comments within a presentation to provide input on specific slides. Comments are usually deleted after you read them and update your presentation. Notes are information you keep with your presentation to provide additional information as you speak.

→ For details on creating notes, **see** "Creating Notes and Handouts" in Chapter 10, "Creating and Printing Presentation Materials."

To add a comment to a slide, click the Insert Comment button on the Reviewing toolbar or choose Insert, Comment. If it isn't already open, the Reviewing toolbar appears when you insert a comment.

→ To learn more about the buttons on the Reviewing toolbar, **see** "Using the Reviewing Toolbar" in this chapter.

A yellow box appears at the top-left corner of your slide; your name appears as the reviewer. Figure 7.3 illustrates a sample comment box.

Figure 7.3
Comments provide a way to get feedback on your presentation.

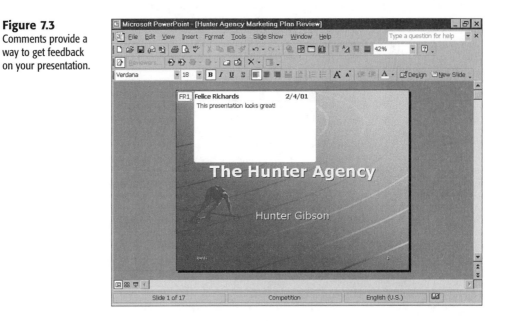

Note

You can't add a comment in Slide Sorter view; this option is dimmed on the menu.

PowerPoint places all general comments in the upper-left corner of the slide by default. If you add more than one comment to the slide, it is placed on top of the existing comment, covering most of it. You can move the comment from its default location by selecting it and dragging it with the mouse.

You can also attach a comment to a selected element on the slide. For example, you could create a comment about the overall content that appears in the top-left corner and then attach individual comments to selected text or a selected graphic object as well.

Enter your comments in the yellow box, which expands to fit the length of your comment.

To change the reviewer name, choose Tools, Options, and enter a new name in the User Information group box on the General tab.

REVIEWING COMMENTS

If you don't plan to use the Revisions pane to review comments in a presentation, you can use the Reviewing toolbar to move from comment to comment, evaluating each comment as you progress. To review comments, click the Markup button on the Reviewing toolbar if comments don't appear.

Don't want comments to appear in your presentation? See the "Troubleshooting" section at the end of the chapter.

In general, comments should be apparent because of their bright yellow color. In a long presentation, it can be easier simply to jump to the next comment rather than look at each slide. To do this, click the Next Item button on the Reviewing toolbar.

Note

To jump back to a previous comment and look at it again, click the Previous Item button.

Note

When you reach the end of a presentation, clicking the Next Item button brings you back to the first comment of the presentation.

After you read a comment, you might want to delete it. To do so, select it and click the Delete Comment button on the Reviewing toolbar.

PART

II

CH

7

SENDING BACK THE REVIEW

After entering all comments and changes, the reviewer needs to send the presentation back to the author for final reconciliation. A reviewer who received a presentation through Outlook can send it back by choosing File, Send To, Original Sender from within PowerPoint.

If the reviewer uses a previous version of PowerPoint to perform the review, such as PowerPoint 2000 or 97, choose File, Send To, Mail Recipient (as Attachment) to return the presentation to the author.

Unless instructed otherwise, reviewers receiving a presentation as an e-mail attachment, on a network, or on a disk should save the presentation and return it to the author in the same way it was received.

RECONCILING REVIEWS

If you're the author of a presentation, the final step includes merging the reviews, checking the comments and changes of all reviewers, accepting or rejecting their suggestions using the Revisions pane or Reviewing toolbar, and saving your final presentation.

Tip from
Patrice-Anne
Rutledge

There is no one right way to handle the review and reconciliation process. You can use a combination of features on the Revisions pane List and Gallery tabs and on the Reviewing toolbar to complete your presentation.

COMPARING AND MERGING PRESENTATIONS

If you're using Outlook to do revisions, open the e-mail that contains the reviewed presentation, double-click it, and click Yes in the prompt dialog box that asks if you want to merge this presentation. PowerPoint automatically merges this presentation with the original.

If you're using another e-mail program, a network server, or a disk to handle reviews, follow these steps:

1. Open the original presentation in PowerPoint.
2. Choose Tools, Compare and Merge Presentations. The Choose Files to Merge with Current Presentation dialog box opens (see Figure 7.4).
3. Select a file (or files) to merge and click the Merge button. The presentations are merged and the Revisions pane opens. Other buttons may be added to the Reviewing toolbar.

USING THE REVISIONS PANE TO RECONCILE REVIEWS

The Revisions pane enables you to view and reconcile the comments and changes of multiple reviewers. It should appear automatically when you compare and merge presentations, but you can also open it manually by choosing View, Toolbars, Revisions Pane. Figure 7.5 illustrates the Revisions pane.

Figure 7.4
Comparing and merging your presentation enables you to see all reviewers' comments in the same place.

Comment   Change marker

Figure 7.5
Use the Revisions pane to look at reviewers' changes and accept or reject them.

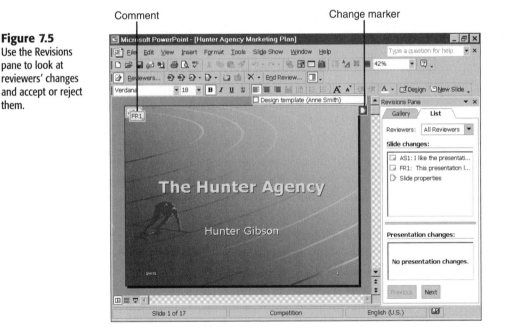

The List tab displays color-coded comments and changes for each reviewer. To see those for specific reviewers, select them from the Reviewers drop-down list. The default is to display the comments of all reviewers.

On the List tab, you can click an individual comment to view it and then click the Delete Comment button on the Reviewing toolbar to remove it from your presentation. Depending on the contents of the comment, you might want to make additional changes to your presentation. If the comment is informational only ("Great presentation!"), you can continue to the next review item.

On the List tab, you can also click a change marker to display its contents and click in the check boxes if you want to accept the changes. You can also hover the mouse over a change marker on your slide to view the proposed change. Then click on that change marker to display the menu with check boxes for accepting changes (or in some cases, an individual change).

To move to the next slide, click the Next button on the pane. To go back to a previous slide, click Previous.

On the Gallery tab, you view thumbnails of the changed slides by reviewer.

On this tab, you can click the check box next to the name of a reviewer to apply all changes suggested by that reviewer. You can click the down arrow next to the thumbnail to view a list of other options, including the capability to apply changes, unapply changes, view only a specific reviewer's changes, preview animation, or tell PowerPoint that you're done with that reviewer.

TROUBLESHOOTING

HIDING COMMENTS

I don't want to see comments on my slides, but I don't want to delete them, either.

If you don't want to delete your comments, you can hide them so they don't appear on a slide. To do so, click the Markup button on the Reviewing toolbar to toggle off the comments. Comments will never appear in an actual slideshow.

LOCATING MISSING BUTTONS

The button I need doesn't appear on the Reviewing toolbar.

Many of the buttons on the Reviewing toolbar appear as a result of an action in the review process. For example, you might need to open a presentation for review to activate some buttons or merge presentations to view others. If you can't find the button you want, be sure you've completed the prerequisite steps to get where you want to be in the review process.

USING SPEECH AND HANDWRITING RECOGNITION

In this chapter

UNDERSTANDING SPEECH AND HANDWRITING RECOGNITION

Speech and handwriting recognition is a new feature of Office XP, shared among all Office applications as well as Internet Explorer and Outlook Express. Using speech recognition, you can dictate the content of PowerPoint slides or use voice commands to perform basic tasks such as formatting text. Speech recognition requires the use of a speech recognition engine; Microsoft currently offers three engines—in U.S. English, Japanese, and Simplified Chinese.

Note

If you're a native speaker of English from a country other than the United States (such as the U.K. or Australia), the speech recognition engine may not work as well for you because it's trained to recognize American accents.

Using handwriting recognition, you can "write" using a handwriting input device, such as pen stylus and tablet (or even your mouse), and have your written text transcribed into typed text in PowerPoint. Handwriting recognition requires the use of a handwriting recognition engine. Microsoft currently offers five engines—in U.S. English, Japanese, Simplified Chinese, Traditional Chinese, and Korean.

The uses and advantages of both speech and handwriting recognition are numerous, with the most important being the ability to cut down on keyboard and mouse time while still remaining productive. These tools are an acquired taste, however, and may take some time to get used to. If you're interested in seeing how they could assist in your own productivity, it's worthwhile—and fun—to at least give them a try. Remember though, that speech and handwriting recognition can't be a complete substitute for working with a keyboard and mouse. They're most effective when working in conjunction with these traditional tools if you want to achieve the best results.

LOOKING AT HARDWARE AND SOFTWARE REQUIREMENTS

Office XP's speech and handwriting recognition tools have specific hardware and software requirements. They also have specific minimum requirements in terms of computer speed and memory.

Caution

Although you may be able to activate speech and handwriting recognition tools with less than the minimum specified requirements, their performance will be problematic or unreliable.

To use speech recognition, you'll need

- A close-talk headset microphone with gain adjustment support to modify microphone amplification for appropriate sound recognition. Microsoft recommends a USB (universal serial bus) microphone.
- A 400MHz or faster computer.
- 128MB of memory or more.
- Internet Explorer 5.0 or later.
- Windows 98 (or later) or Windows NT 4.0 (or later).

Note

If you're using Microsoft Windows 98, but not the second edition, you'll need to download the Microsoft Active Accessibility Redistribution Kit (RDK) from the Microsoft Web site (www.microsoft.com) to use voice commands in dialog boxes.

To use handwriting recognition, you'll need

- A 75MHz or faster computer
- 24MB of memory or more with Windows 98 or ME; 40MB of memory or more with Windows NT 4.0 or later
- As a writing tool, a mouse (minimum) or a handwriting input device such as a pen stylus and tablet connected through a serial or USB port (recommended)
- Windows 98 (or later) or Windows NT 4.0 (or later)

INSTALLING SPEECH AND HANDWRITING RECOGNITION

To install speech recognition automatically, choose Tools, Speech from the menu bar and then proceed with the step-by-step setup guidance. To install handwriting recognition, you'll need to return to the Office setup CD. You can also install speech recognition from this setup CD.

→ For a more in-depth explanation to set up the speech recognition feature, **see** "Setting Up Speech Recognition" later in this chapter.

To install these features from the Office XP CD, follow these steps:

1. Insert the Office XP Setup CD in your CD-ROM drive to reopen the Microsoft Office Setup dialog box (see Figure 8.1).
2. Select the Add or Remove Features option button, and click Next to continue.
3. Click the plus sign next to Office Shared Features and then the plus sign next to Alternative User Input.
4. Click the down arrow next to Speech and/or Handwriting and choose Run from My Computer from the menu that appears. Figure 8.2 illustrates both speech and handwriting recognition installed.

5. Click the Update button to update your system with the selected changes.

Figure 8.1
You can add or remove speech and handwriting recognition features.

Figure 8.2
Running these features from your computer means that they're installed.

Note

If you want to uninstall either of these features, choose Not Available from the menu.

Once you install speech and handwriting recognition for one Office application, it's available in the other Office applications as well.

SETTING UP SPEECH RECOGNITION

Before you can set up speech recognition, you need to verify that both your microphone and speakers are connected and work properly. Because the specific hardware you're using will vary, consult the manual that came with your microphone and speakers if you have any issues regarding setting them up. Once your hardware is connected, you're ready to begin. Position the microphone to the side about an inch from your mouth; close enough to hear your words, but not so close as to hear your breath.

Setting up speech recognition is essentially a two-step process: Configure your microphone, and complete a voice training session so that PowerPoint recognizes your speech when you dictate or issue voice commands. Although you can perform these steps separately or go back to make adjustments to each, PowerPoint walks you through the entire process step-by-step the first time you use speech recognition.

To set up speech recognition for the first time, follow these steps:

1. Choose Tools, Speech to open the Welcome dialog box (see Figure 8.3) and click Next to continue.

Figure 8.3
The initial dialog box welcomes you to speech recognition.

2. From the Microsoft Wizard Welcome dialog box, click Next to continue to the first step of the Microphone Wizard, shown in Figure 8.4.

Figure 8.4
The Microphone Wizard walks you through microphone setup step by step.

3. Follow the instructions in the wizard, shown in Figure 8.5, reading the sentence indicated to test the microphone volume. Click Next to continue.

Figure 8.5
Adjust your microphone using the Microphone Wizard.

Note

To readjust the microphone at a later time, return to the Speech Recognition tab of the Speech Properties dialog box and click the Configure Microphone button.

4. Follow the instructions in the wizard, reading the sentence indicated to test the positioning of the microphone. If you don't have a headset microphone, you can skip this step. Click Finish to continue to the Voice Training series of steps. Figure 8.6 illustrates the first step.

Figure 8.6
Voice training helps the speech recognition engine get used to your voice.

5. Continue through the voice training steps, carefully following the detailed instructions and tips on the screen as you read sample text that the speech recognition engine will record and analyze. Be sure you're in a quiet room and the microphone is positioned correctly.

Note

If you want to do additional voice training, click the More Training button before you finish.

6. When you reach the final step, click Finish to close the dialog box.

Now that you've set up speech recognition, you can use it in PowerPoint or any other Office XP application. You can start using the speech tools right away or make further customizations based on how you plan to use this feature. But first, you should get acquainted with the Language bar, which contains all the buttons and menus you'll need to access both speech and handwriting recognition tools.

USING THE LANGUAGE BAR

After you install speech or handwriting recognition, the Language bar automatically appears. With this toolbar, shown in Figure 8.7, you can use and customize Office XP's speech and handwriting recognition tools.

Figure 8.7
The Language bar provides all the buttons and menus you'll need.

> 🖉 Microphone | 🖳 Dictation | 🔎 Voice Command | Dictation | 🖳 Tools | ✍ Handwriting |

The Language bar is also available if you activate an *IME* (*input method editor*, used to enter Asian characters). Microsoft refers to speech and handwriting recognition, IMEs, and alternative keyboard layouts as *text services*.

The exact buttons that display may vary, according to the text services you've installed and the Office applications you have running. For example, if you have both Word and PowerPoint open and are currently using Word, the Correction button appears on the Language bar. Switch to PowerPoint, and this button disappears from the Language bar.

Tip from
Patrice-Anne Rutledge

Text services are very memory intensive and can affect your computer's performance, particularly if you don't have a state-of-the-art system. If you aren't planning to use a specific text service, you should remove it.

→ To learn more about removing a text service, **see** "Adding and Removing Text Services" later in this chapter.

To move the floating Language bar, pause the mouse over the vertical bar on the left side of the Language bar and drag it.

SPECIFYING LANGUAGE BAR OPTIONS

You can set a variety of Language bar options from the menu that appears when you right-click the Language bar. These include

■ **Minimize** Minimizes the Language bar, so that it remains open but is out the way and appears as an icon in the taskbar. You can also click the Language bar's Minimize button (upper-right corner of the bar) to minimize in one step.

Note

To restore the Language bar, click the Language bar icon in the taskbar and then choose Show the Language Bar from the menu that appears.

■ **Text Labels** Serves as a toggle to add or remove text labels on the Language bar. Text labels (the default) are an advantage if you're unfamiliar with the Language bar, but they do take up additional space. Figure 8.8 illustrates the Language bar with traditional toolbar buttons rather than text labels.

Figure 8.8
If you're familiar with the Language bar, you may not need text labels.

■ **Additional Icons in the Taskbar** Places icons for specific text services directly on the taskbar, for easy access without displaying the Language bar on the desktop. Simply click the taskbar icon to perform the specific service, such as speech and handwriting recognition.

■ **Close the Language Bar** Closes the Language bar and removes it from the desktop. If you installed an IME, you can't close the Language bar. However, you can still minimize it to get it out of the way.

To reopen the Language bar after closing it, choose Start, Settings, Control Panel and then double-click the Text Services icon. In the Text Services dialog box, click the Language Bar button and select the Show the Language Bar on the Desktop check box.

Caution

Closing the Language bar isn't the same thing as removing specific text services; these services will remain installed and continue to take up computer memory unless you remove them.

SPECIFYING TEXT SERVICES SETTINGS

Click the Settings option from the Language bar menu to open the Text Services dialog box, shown in Figure 8.9.

Figure 8.9
You can add and
remove text services in
this dialog box.

Here, you can select your default input language and access other text services options.

→ For more information on speech recognition engines in other languages, **see** "Changing to Another Speech Recognition Engine" later in this chapter.

ADDING AND REMOVING TEXT SERVICES

In the Installed Services group box, you can add and remove installed text services for the language you selected in the Default Input Language drop-down list. If you don't plan to use a specific text service, you should remove it here because each installed service takes up valuable computer memory. To add a text service, click the Add button to open the Add Input Language dialog box, shown in Figure 8.10.

Figure 8.10
Select the specific
text service you
want to add.

Select the Input Language from the drop-down list and then click the check box for the text service you want to add (Keyboard Layout/IME, Handwriting Recognition, or Speech). Choose the specific option or component you want from the drop-down list and then click

OK to close the dialog box. If certain options are grayed out, they're either already installed or aren't available.

To remove a text service, select it from the Installed Services list on the Text Services dialog box and then click the Remove button.

> **Caution**
>
> You can't remove all text services; at least one must remain.

SPECIFYING LANGUAGE BAR SETTINGS

Click the Language Bar button to open the Language Bar Settings dialog box, shown in Figure 8.11.

Figure 8.11
You can further customize the Language bar.

In this dialog box, you can select

- **Show the Language Bar on the Desktop**   Displays the Language bar on the desktop. Selected by default.
- **Show the Language Bar as Transparent when Inactive**   Enables you to view what's behind the Language bar when it appears on the desktop.

> **Caution**
>
> Language bar transparency is available only with Windows 2000; it won't work with Windows 98, Me, or NT 4.0.

- **Show Additional Language Bar Icons in the Notification Area**   Places icons for available text services on the taskbar.
- **Show Text Labels on the Language Bar**   Displays text labels on all Language bar buttons, making it easier to view the Language bar, but also increasing its size. Selected by default.

If you choose not to display text labels on the Language bar, pause the mouse pointer over the button to view a ScreenTip with the button's label.

VIEWING ADDITIONAL LANGUAGE BAR SETTINGS

You can view additional options from the Language bar Options menu. To view this menu, click the Options down arrow on the Language bar (it's the small down arrow on the lower right of the bar). From this menu, you can add or remove Language bar buttons (a check mark indicates that a button appears on the bar), click Settings to open the Text Services dialog box (refer to Figure 8.9), or click Restore Defaults to restore the Language bar to its default settings.

Restoring defaults only restores Language bar buttons, not any changes you made to text labels or Language bar transparency. You must change these manually.

DISPLAYING LANGUAGE BAR MESSAGES

You can display informational messages on the Language bar that provide help as your work with speech recognition tools. The messages vary, depending on the tool and mode you're using. For example, the message balloon could tell you that you're speaking too softly for Dictation mode to understand your words or let you know that you're currently dictating (see Figure 8.12).

Figure 8.12
Let Language bar messages provide helpful tips.

Language bar message

To activate these messages if they don't already appear, click the Tools button on the Language bar and choose Show Speech Messages on the menu that opens. Clicking on this option again will hide the speech messages.

USING SPEECH RECOGNITION

Before you begin using speech recognition, be sure to place your mouse pointer in a location that can accept text, such as a bullet list or other text area on a slide. To improve accuracy, talk in a consistent, even tone. Speaking too slowly or quickly can decrease the level of recognition. Also, don't stop and start. Pauses and gaps make it harder to recognize your speech.

USING DICTATION MODE

To dictate text using the speech recognition engine, follow these steps:

1. Click the Microphone button on the Language bar to turn on the microphone. Alternatively, you can say the word "microphone" to toggle the microphone on and off.

2. Click the Dictation button on the Language bar (or say "dictation") to activate speech recognition.

3. Dictate your text into the microphone.

Of course, getting dictation to work exactly as you want it to is more complicated than 1-2-3, but the basic premise is really quite simple. When you're finished dictating, be sure to turn off the microphone; the speech recognition engine will continue to record your words until you do so.

> **Note**
>
> You can use Dictation mode with the Ask a Question box. Simply place the insertion point in the box and dictate your question.

Problems getting your microphone to recognize your speech? See the "Troubleshooting" section near the end of the chapter.

DICTATING PUNCTUATION

During dictation, you'll probably need to add some form of punctuation or a special character to your text. You can do this easily using one of the many dictation commands the speech recognition engine recognizes. For example, if you want to place a period at the end of a bullet point, just say "period." If you want to include a Web address, the engines will know what you mean when you say "dot." Table 8.1 lists the most common dictation commands.

TABLE 8.1 SAMPLE DICTATION COMMANDS

Say	Result
Ampersand	&
Asterisk	*
At	@
Colon	:
Comma	,
Dot	.
Exclamation point	!
Period	.

TABLE 8.1 CONTINUED

Say	Result
Question mark	?
Semicolon	;
Backslash	\
Slash	/
Vertical bar	|
Hyphen	-
Double dash	--
Equals	=
Plus	+
Pound sign	#
Percent	%
Dollar sign	$
Underscore	_
Tilde	~
Ellipsis	...
Greater than	>
Less than	<
Caret	^
New line	Enter
New paragraph	Enter twice
Left bracket	[
Right bracket	]
Left brace	{
Right brace	}
Left parenthesis	(
Right parenthesis	)
Open quote	"
Close quote	"
Open single quote	'
Close single quote	'

DICTATING NUMBERS

If you're going to dictate numbers using Dictation mode, here are a few things to keep in mind. The speech recognition engine

- Spells out numbers less than 20

- Inserts numbers greater than 20 as digits

- Inserts fractions as digits (one-fourth becomes ¼)

- Recognizes a series of seven numbers as a telephone number and formats it as such (555-1234)

- Enables you to insert all numbers as digits if you say "forcenum" before saying the numbers

SPELLING OUT UNCOMMON WORDS

There are going to be times when the speech recognition engine simply won't be able to recognize what you say. This is particularly common when you say the name of a company, product, or person or use specific industry jargon. In these circumstances, you can quickly spell out the word or words you want to dictate. To do so, say "spelling mode" and then begin spelling letter by letter. Another option is to add these common words to the speech recognition dictionary.

→ To learn how to add words to the dictionary, **see** "Adding Words to the Speech Recognition Dictionary" later in this chapter.

CORRECTING SPEECH RECOGNITION ERRORS

As you know, Office's speech recognition tools may accurately recognize only 80% to 95% of your speech. To fix errors, you have two choices:

- Select the error (either a single word or section of text) and repeat your dictation.

- Manually fix the error using the keyboard.

USING VOICE COMMAND MODE

Voice command functionality has a variety of uses. You can use voice commands to say the name of

- An active toolbar button to perform its command. For example, you could say "save" to save the presentation you're currently working on or "bold" to apply a bold format to selected text. If you're not sure of the name of a toolbar button, pause the mouse over it to display its ScreenTip.

- A menu to open it. For example, say "insert" to open the Insert menu. From there, you can say the name of the menu item you want to choose or say "expand" instead of clicking on the double down arrows to view additional menu options.

- A dialog box tab to move to that tab.

- A dialog box option to select it. For check boxes, saying its name again acts as a toggle to remove the check mark.

- A hyperlink in a task pane to activate it.

- A punctuation command, such as comma, period, or colon, to enter the symbol for that command.

- The individual letters of words that the speech recognition engine would have trouble recognizing (say "spelling mode" before doing this).

Note

To create a new blank presentation from the New Presentation task pane, say "new file."

→ For more information on spelling mode, **see** "Spelling Out Uncommon Words" earlier in this chapter.

ISSUING VOICE COMMANDS

To activate voice commands, first verify that your microphone is on and then click the Voice Command button on the Language bar (or say "voice command"). If you were in Dictation mode, PowerPoint no longer transcribes your words as dictation, but instead understands them as commands. Try out all the suggested ways to use voice commands to determine which ones will help in your own personal productivity. You can control a great deal of PowerPoint's functionality with voice commands, but you'll probably need to experiment for a while to learn how to use this new way of working more effectively.

EXPLORING VOICE COMMANDS

You can also use voice commands to navigate within PowerPoint in addition to control menus, toolbars, and fields in dialog boxes and task panes. Table 8.2 lists some additional voice commands to try.

TABLE 8.2 SAMPLE VOICE COMMANDS

Say	Result
New line	Moves to the next line
New paragraph	Starts a new paragraph
Mic off	Turns off the microphone
Tab	Tabs once
Enter	Presses the Enter key
Spelling mode	Enters spelling mode, enabling you to spell out difficult words letter by letter
Forcenum	Enters a numeral rather than spelling the actual word (for example, "three" becomes "3")

TABLE 8.2   CONTINUED

Say	Result
Right-click	Right-clicks the current object (to display a menu, for example)
Backspace	Deletes the previous character
Last word	Moves to the last word
Space	Inserts a space
Escape	Presses ESC
Up	Moves up one line
Down	Moves down one line
Left	Moves left one character
Right	Moves right one character
Previous Page	Moves to the previous page
Next Page	Moves to the next page
Page Down	Moves down one page
Page Up	Moves up one page

CUSTOMIZING SPEECH RECOGNITION

After you've tried using speech recognition to dictate and issue voice commands, you may decide you want to customize it a bit. For example, you could create an additional profile for another location in which you work, customize audio settings, add words to the speech recognition dictionary, or perform additional voice training.

Tip from
*Patrice-Anne
Rutledge*

> If you're the only person using your computer, you might not think multiple profiles would be useful. But if you're mobile and work in a variety of locations—home, office, in the field, and so forth—creating a profile for each location can help increase accuracy. Even if you're working in a very temporary location such as a hotel room, it's worthwhile to create a new profile if you're planning to use speech recognition.

WORKING WITH SPEECH RECOGNITION PROFILES

A recognition profile stores the speech data PowerPoint records and analyzes when you do voice training. When you set up speech recognition for the first time, PowerPoint automatically records your speech in the default user profile. If you're the only person using speech recognition on your computer and you use your computer in only one location, this may be the only recognition profile you need.

You can, however, create multiple profiles in PowerPoint. This is useful if more than one person uses your computer, but it can also be useful if you want to use speech recognition with different microphones or in different environments (for example, if you have a note-book computer and work in a variety of locations). Creating a separate profile of your speech under each of these conditions helps to ensure that the speech recognition tools take these environmental changes into consideration as well.

CREATING A NEW SPEECH RECOGNITION PROFILE

If you want to create a recognition profile other than the default profile, follow these steps:

1. Click the Tools button on the Language bar, and choose Options from the submenu that appears. The Speech Properties dialog box will open, shown in Figure 8.13.

Figure 8.13
Adding a new speech recognition profile is just one of the tasks you can perform in the Speech Properties dialog box.

2. On the Speech Recognition tab, click the New button. Figure 8.14 illustrates the Profile Wizard dialog box that opens.

Figure 8.14
Give your new profile a name.

3. Enter your name in the Profile text box. If you're creating multiple profiles of your speech in different environments, you could enter something like "Pat Smith—Office."

4. Click Next to continue to the first step of the Microphone Wizard.

5. Continue on from step 3 in the earlier section "Setting Up Speech Recognition" to complete setup, which is nearly identical to setting up your first speech recognition profile (the default user).

MODIFYING RECOGNITION PROFILE SETTINGS

To modify recognition profile settings, click the Settings button on the Speech Recognition tab of the Speech Properties dialog box. The Recognition Profile Settings dialog box will open, shown in Figure 8.15.

Figure 8.15
Customizing settings
is another option.

In this dialog box, you can set specifications on pronunciation sensitivity and accuracy versus recognition response time, as well as choose to have the system automatically adapt to your voice to increase accuracy.

To restore your default settings, click the Restore Defaults button.

DELETING A SPEECH RECOGNITION PROFILE

To delete an existing recognition profile, return to the Speech Recognition tab of the Speech Properties dialog box. Select the profile you want to delete from the Recognition Profiles group box and click the Delete button.

Performing Additional Voice Training

You can perform additional voice training when you set up speech recognition by clicking the More Training button before you complete the setup process. You also can return at a later time to do additional training. The more samples Office has of your voice, the better it will be able to recognize your speech. You don't need to do all the training at once, however. It's often a good idea to do the initial training, see how accurate your results are when you use the speech recognition tools, and then go back and do more training.

To continue with additional voice training at a later time, click the Tools button on the Language bar and choose Training from the submenu. The Voice Training dialog box shown in Figure 8.16 opens for the current user. Here you can choose from additional training sessions.

Figure 8.16
Additional voice training helps increase your accuracy.

Note

To change the current user, click the Tools button on the Language bar and then choose a user from the Current User menu.

At first, your accuracy may only be around 85%–90%, but after additional training it should increase to around 95%.

Adding Words to the Speech Recognition Dictionary

If you want to add unusual words that might not easily be recognized to Office's speech recognition dictionary, you can do so manually. This is particularly useful if you want to add proper names, company names, or industry terms that might not be included in the standard dictionary or easily recognized. To add and delete words to this dictionary, follow these steps:

1. Click the Tools button on the Language bar.
2. Click Add/Delete Word(s) to open the Add/Delete Word(s) dialog box, shown in Figure 8.17.

Figure 8.17
Add uncommon or
unfamiliar words to
the dictionary.

3. Enter the word you want to add to the dictionary in the Word text box.

4. Click the Record Pronunciation button and speak the word into the microphone. When the speech recognition engine recognizes the word, it adds it to the dictionary list.

5. To delete a word from the dictionary, select it in the list and click the Delete button.

Note

To spell out an unfamiliar word, say "spelling mode" when you're in Dictation or Voice Command mode and then spell the word letter by letter.

CHANGING TO ANOTHER SPEECH RECOGNITION ENGINE

If you plan to use speech recognition in more than one language, you need to switch speech recognition engines. To do so, follow these steps:

1. Click the Tools button on the Language bar and choose Options from the submenu that appears. The Speech Properties dialog box opens (refer to Figure 8.13).

2. On the Speech Recognition tab, choose the alternative engine from the Language drop-down list. If you're speaking U.S. English, the default engine will be Microsoft English ASR Version 5 Engine.

3. Click OK to close the dialog box.

You'll need to restart PowerPoint for this change to take effect.

CHANGING TO ANOTHER SPEECH RECOGNITION PROFILE

If you've created multiple speech recognition profiles, you need to switch to the appropriate profile before using PowerPoint's speech recognition tools. To change profiles, click the

Tools button on the Language bar, choose Current User, and then select the profile you want to use. The submenu displays all profiles you've recorded (default, those for other users, those for other environments such as office or home, and so forth).

ADJUSTING AUDIO INPUT SETTINGS

On the Speech Recognition tab of the Speech Properties dialog box, you can adjust the audio input settings of your microphone by clicking the Audio Input button. Figure 8.18 illustrates the Audio Input Settings dialog box.

Figure 8.18
Adjust audio input settings if you like.

On this dialog box you can choose the preferred (default) audio input device or select an alternative device from the drop-down list.

Note

To specify the audio input line you want to use, click the Properties button. To adjust volume, click the Volume button. Note that unless you have advanced knowledge of audio systems or settings, you'll probably want to use the defaults rather than make any changes.

USING HANDWRITING RECOGNITION

Using handwriting recognition, you can enter text on your PowerPoint slides, as well as in other Office applications, without the constraints of having to use a keyboard. Although writing with a mouse isn't practical for more than a few words here or there, with a pen stylus and tablet you can essentially write your content manually and convert it to text onscreen. This is useful for people who need to limit their use of the keyboard for some reason as well as those who just don't like to type.

Office XP's handwriting recognition engine doesn't require any training. You can start using it as soon as you install the feature. Handwriting recognition tools include several components:

- A Writing Pad, which enables you to "write" text in a window with a lined note pad.

Note

In Japanese and Chinese, you'll use the Boxed Input window rather than the Writing Pad.

- The Write Anywhere window, which enables you to write anywhere on your screen.
- A Drawing Pad that's available only with Microsoft Word or Outlook. You'll still see the Drawing Pad option available in menus and on toolbars within PowerPoint, but you won't be able to activate the window until you switch to a program that supports it.
- Onscreen keyboards for entering text and symbols (such as foreign language characters). These keyboards are designed for use with a touch-screen computer. You can still use them with a mouse if you don't have touch-screen capabilities, but they won't be very practical.

You can access these components by clicking the Handwriting button on the Language bar and then choosing the appropriate component from the drop-down menu.

USING WRITING PAD

To open the Writing Pad window, Click the Writing Pad button on the Language bar, or say "writing pad." If you don't see the Writing Pad button, click the Handwriting button and choose Writing Pad from the menu that appears. Figure 8.19 illustrates the Writing Pad.

Figure 8.19
The Writing Pad enables you to write text on an onscreen note pad.

Position the insertion point where you want to insert the text on your PowerPoint slide. Using either your handwriting input device or your mouse, "write" the text you want to enter on the solid line in the Writing Pad. The handwriting recognition engine recognizes your writing and converts it to text at the insertion point.

Note

The handwriting recognition engine works with any AutoCorrect options you've set. For example, if you set an AutoCorrect entry that automatically corrects your entry of "js" to "John Smith," entering "js" on the Writing Pad will automatically correct to "John Smith" as well.

On the right side of the Writing Pad is a palette of buttons (also available on the Write Anywhere window) that you can use for editing and navigation. Table 8.3 describes these buttons.

TABLE 8.3 WRITING PAD AND WRITE ANYWHERE BUTTONS

Button	Description	Result
	Ink	Enters the actual words you write as handwriting rather than converting them to text. This button is active only in Microsoft Word and Outlook.
	Text	Converts what you write to text.
	Backspace	Deletes the previous character.
	Space	Enters a space.
	Enter	Moves to a new paragraph line.
	Tab	Tabs once.
	Recognize Now	Enters what you've written on your slide if you haven't set Automatic Recognition on the Handwriting Options dialog box.
	Write Anywhere	Switches to the Write Anywhere window.
	Drawing Pad	Switches to the Drawing Pad in Microsoft Word and Outlook. In PowerPoint, clicking this button has no effect.
	On-Screen Standard Keyboard	Switches to the On-Screen Standard Keyboard.
	Up Cursor	Moves the cursor up.
	Left Cursor	Moves the cursor to the left.
	Right Cursor	Moves the cursor to the right.
	Down Cursor	Moves the cursor down.
	Correction	Displays correction options (not available in PowerPoint).
	Clear	Deletes what you've entered on the Writing Pad.
	Reduce	Reduces the number of buttons that appear on the Writing Pad.
	Expand	Expands the buttons that appear on the Writing Pad.

Button in the Writing Pad or Write Anywhere window not working? *See the "Troubleshooting" section near the end of the chapter.*

USING WRITE ANYWHERE

The Write Anywhere window enables you to write anywhere on your screen rather than on the lined Writing Pad. To open the Write Anywhere window, click the Write Anywhere button on the Language bar, or say "write anywhere." If you don't see this button, click the Handwriting button and choose Write Anywhere from the menu that appears. Figure 8.20 illustrates the Write Anywhere window, which consists of a series of buttons similar to those on the Writing Pad window. Refer to Table 8.3 for a description of these buttons.

Figure 8.20
You can write any-where on your screen.

Using either a handwriting input device or your mouse, "write" your text in the location you prefer on your screen. By default, the handwriting recognition engine immediately transcribes your text.

CORRECTING HANDWRITING RECOGNITION ERRORS

If the handwriting recognition engine doesn't interpret your handwriting correctly, you can select the incorrect text and either use your handwriting input device to rewrite the text or make the correction manually using the keyboard.

SETTING HANDWRITING OPTIONS

To set handwriting options, click the down arrow in the upper-left corner of the Writing Pad or Write Anywhere window and choose Options from the submenu that appears. Figure 8.21 illustrates the Handwriting Options dialog box that opens.

On the Common tab, you can customize the pen color and pen width from the choices available from the drop-down lists.

Select the Add Space After Insertion check box to add a space after every word you insert. Select the Automatic Recognition check box to recognize what you write automatically rather than wait for you to click the Recognize Now button on the Writing Pad or Write Anywhere window.

If you want to speed up or slow down the rate at which the handwriting recognition engine recognizes your writing, adjust the Recognition Delay scrollbar accordingly.

Finally, you can customize the appearance of the toolbar buttons on the Writing Pad in the Toolbar Layout group box. Choices include moving the buttons to the left or right and making the buttons smaller or larger to suit your needs.

Figure 8.21
Specify exactly how you want your handwriting tools to appear.

If you make customizations and want to return to the default settings, click the Restore Default button.

On the Writing Pad tab, you can customize the background color of the Writing Pad (choices include the default yellow as well as white, parchment, and system colors) and the number of lines that appear.

TROUBLESHOOTING

RESOLVING MICROPHONE PROBLEMS

I spoke into the microphone, but nothing happened.

First, verify that you've installed and set up speech recognition, you've clicked the Microphone button on the Language bar, and clicked the appropriate speech button (either Dictation or Voice Command) on the Language bar. Also, verify that your insertion point is in a location that can accept text. If the software doesn't seem to be the problem, take a look at your actual microphone. Be sure that you've turned it on, connected it properly, and haven't pressed a mute button. If you still have no luck, try the microphone with another program to see if it works. If it doesn't, refer to your microphone manual for additional troubleshooting advice.

UNDERSTANDING POWERPOINT'S SPEECH AND HANDWRITING RECOGNITION LIMITATIONS

The buttons in the Writing Pad and the Write Anywhere window don't work.

Not all handwriting recognition functionality works in all Office applications. For example, when you click the Drawing Pad, Ink, or Correction button from within PowerPoint, it won't work because PowerPoint doesn't support those functions. Switch to Word 2002, and they will become active.

Design Corner: Using Office XP's New Speech and Handwriting Recognition Tools

Using Office XP's new speech and handwriting recognition tools in PowerPoint can increase your productivity, but these new features are most effective when combined with the more traditional keyboard and mouse. As an example, you could open PowerPoint, click Voice Command on the Language bar, and then say the verbal commands "file, new" to open the New Presentation task pane. From there, say "new file" to create a new presentation. Say "design" to open the Slide Design task pane and apply a design template. Switch to Dictation mode and then dictate a title and subtitle. You can add a new slide by saying "new slide" and, if you choose a bulleted list, you can dictate each bullet followed by "new line." Finally, say "save" to open the Save As dialog box and then say "save" again to save your presentation in progress.

MAKING PRESENTATIONS

9

PRESENTING A SLIDESHOW

In this chapter

SETTING UP A SHOW

After you create all the slides you want to include in your presentation, you'll want to plan how you're going to present them in a slideshow. Fortunately, PowerPoint makes it easy to set up and rehearse your presentation, as well as configure it to work with a projector.

You can deliver a PowerPoint presentation in three different ways:

- **Present it live with a speaker**   This is the most common method of delivering a PowerPoint presentation, full screen in front of an audience.

- **Browse it individually through the PowerPoint browser**   This option enables someone to view your presentation at any convenient time in a browser window with navigation elements such as a scrollbar.

- **Browse it at a kiosk**   This method enables you to create a self-running presentation. Its appearance is full screen, similar to a presentation presented by a speaker. This show type automatically loops continuously. A tradeshow demonstration is one example of when you might want to set up your show to be browsed at a kiosk. Using automatic timings and continuous looping, you can continually display the same show over and over for new viewers. You can add voice narration, if you want, but be sure that your show plays in a location where the narration will be audible.

Before you deliver a PowerPoint presentation, you should think through its entire visual flow. This is the time to rehearse in your mind what you want to present and how you want to present it, as well as plan for the technical aspects of your presentation.

→ To learn more about how to prepare yourself to deliver a presentation, **see** Chapter 25, "The Mechanics of Function—Developing Internal Presentation Skills."

→ To learn about staging, projectors, overheads, and using laptops, **see** Chapter 26, "Exploring Technicalities and Techniques."

After you've visualized your presentation, you can start to set it up within PowerPoint. To do this, follow these steps:

1. Choose Slide Show, Set Up Show to open the Set Up Show dialog box (shown in Figure 9.1).

2. Select a Show Type. Options include Presented by a Speaker (Full Screen), Browsed by an Individual (Window), or Browsed at a Kiosk (Full Screen). Figure 9.2 illustrates a full screen presentation; Figure 9.3 shows you the navigation elements of the PowerPoint browser window.

Note

If you choose Browsed by an Individual, you can select the Show Scrollbar check box to display a scrollbar on the right side of the browser when viewing. An individual can then use the scrollbar to navigate your presentation.

Figure 9.1
Specify the type of presentation you want to make in this dialog box.

Figure 9.2
Having a speaker present a slideshow is the most common way to deliver a presentation.

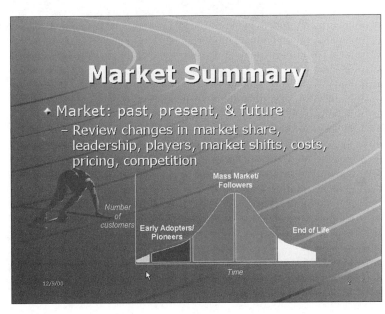

→ If you want to learn how to use the Slide Transition dialog box, **see** "Setting Slide Transitions" in Chapter 15, "Working with Animation."

 Can't browse your presentation at a kiosk? *See the "Troubleshooting" section near the end of this chapter.*

→ To learn about the advantages of rehearsing timings, **see** "Rehearsing Timings" later in this chapter.

    3. Specify the Show Options you want to set:

        • Select the Loop Continuously Until 'Esc' check box if you want your presentation to play over and over until you press the Esc key. This check box is available only if you select the Presented by a Speaker or Browsed by an Individual option. A presentation loops continuously by default if browsed at a kiosk.

Figure 9.3
Choosing the Browsed by an Individual option enables users to view your presentation on demand.

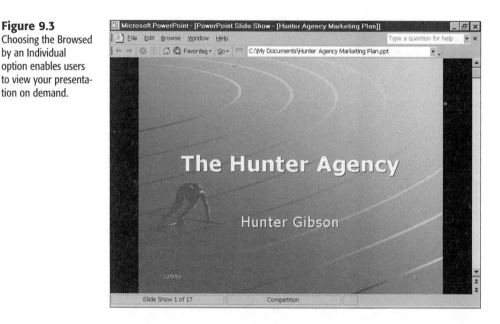

- Select the Show Without Narration check box to deactivate any accompanying narrations temporarily. For example, if you are presenting at a show, narrations might be either inaudible or distracting.

→ For more details about creating narrations, **see** "Recording a Voice Narration" later in this chapter.

- Select the Show Without Animation check box to deactivate any accompanying slide animations temporarily. For example, you may want to include animations to use in some situations but not all.

→ If you want to add animation to your presentation, **see** Chapter 15.

- Specify a Pen Color if you're going to use the pen function when presenting. This option is available only if you chose Presented by a Speaker as your show type. You can either choose one of the default colors that appear when you click the down arrow to the right of this field, or click More Colors to open the Colors dialog box. In this dialog box, you can choose from a wider variety of colors or create a custom color.

→ To learn more about using the pen function during your presentation, **see** "Setting Pointer Options" later in this chapter.

4. Specify the slides you want to include in your presentation. Options include All, a certain range of slide indicated by the From and To boxes, and a Custom Show that can be selected from the drop-down list. The Custom Show option is active only if you've created a custom show.

→ To learn how to create a custom show, **see** "Working with Custom Shows" later in this chapter.

5. To advance slides, you can choose either Manually or Using Timings, If Present. To advance the slide manually, you need to press a key or click the mouse.

Note

Choosing Manually in this field overrides any timings you previously set.

→ For more information about slide transitions, **see** "Setting Slide Transitions" in Chapter 15.
→ To learn more about timings, **see** "Rehearsing Timings" later in this chapter.

6. If you're using multiple monitors, select the monitor on which to present your slideshow.

7. If you're concerned about performance, select the appropriate options in the Performance group box. For example, 800 × 600 resolution will give you higher quality but slower performance. 640 × 480 will be faster, but the quality won't be as good.

8. Click OK to close the Set Up Show dialog box.

PART

III

CH

9

REHEARSING TIMINGS

PowerPoint enables you to set fixed slide transition timing and rehearse the time it takes to deliver your presentation. After you rehearse a presentation, you can save those timings to deliver automatically.

You may not always want to move automatically from slide to slide, however. For example, it can sometimes take you more or less time to discuss a slide in person, or an audience member may interrupt your presentation with a question. Even if you don't want to automate your slide transitions, rehearsing timings can be useful because it helps you adjust your presentation to fit into an allotted amount of time.

To rehearse and set timings, choose Slide Show, Rehearse Timings. The presentation appears in Slide Show view, opening the Rehearsal toolbar in the upper-left corner, shown in Figure 9.4.

Begin talking through your presentation, clicking the Next button in the toolbar to advance to the next slide. If you need to stop temporarily, click the Pause button. If you make a mistake and want to start over, click the Repeat button.

The elapsed time of the current slide appears in the Slide Time box in the center of the toolbar. You can also enter a time in this box manually. The time field on the right side of the toolbar shows you the elapsed time of the entire presentation.

Note

You can enter timings manually in the Slide Transition dialog box as well.

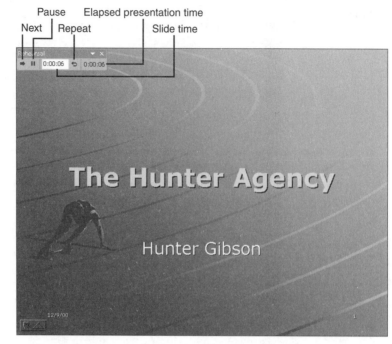

Figure 9.4
The Rehearsal toolbar helps you rehearse and record slide timings.

→ To learn more about slide transitions, **see** "Setting Slide Transitions" in Chapter 15.

After you rehearse the last slide, PowerPoint displays a message box that asks if you want to save the timings. If you click Yes, the presentation opens in Slide Sorter view with the timings displayed under each slide.

If you record and save timings but don't want to use them to automatically advance your presentation, you can select the Advance Slides, Manually option in the Set Up Show dialog box.

RECORDING A VOICE NARRATION

A voice narration is useful for many reasons. You can record your own voice-over to accompany

- A Web-based presentation.
- An on-demand presentation that people can listen to at any time.
- An automated presentation, such as one you run continuously at a tradeshow booth.
- A presentation delivered by a speaker that includes special recorded commentary by a particular individual. An example of this would be a human resources representative delivering an employee orientation that includes voice narration from the CEO.

Before recording your narration, you should create a script and rehearse it several times until it flows smoothly and matches your presentation.

Caution

You need to have a microphone and a sound card to record a narration. And remember—the better quality equipment you use, the more professional your narration will sound.

⚠ *Can't hear your other sound files after recording a voice narration?* See the "Troubleshooting" section near the end of this chapter.

To record a voice narration, follow these steps:

1. Choose Slide Show, Record Narration to open the Record Narration dialog box, shown in Figure 9.5.

Figure 9.5
Add voice narrations to your slideshows.

2. Before you record your narration, you can verify that your microphone is set up properly. To do this, click the Set Microphone Level button. The Microphone Check dialog box appears (see Figure 9.6).

Figure 9.6
Set your microphone level to record properly.

3. Read the sentence that appears into the microphone, and the Microphone Wizard automatically adjusts your microphone level. Click OK to return to the main dialog box.

4. To change the sound quality to CD, radio, or telephone quality, click the Change Quality button to open the Sound Selection dialog box. The better the sound quality, however, the larger the file size.

5. To store the narration as a separate file, click the Link Narrations In check box. Your narration will be stored in a separate .WAV file in the same folder as your presentation. To store your narration in another folder, click the Browse button and choose the appropriate folder in the dialog box that appears. If you want to embed the narration in the presentation, be sure the Link Narrations In check box is cleared.

Tip from
Patrice-Anne Rutledge

Linking a narration is a good idea if you want to easily transport your presentation without the accompanying narration, such as on a disk or via e-mail. Otherwise, it's easier to just embed the narration in the presentation without creating a separate .WAV file.

If you want to embed the narration in the presentation, be sure the Link Narrations In check box is cleared.

6. Click OK to start recording. PowerPoint displays your presentation in Slide Show view.

7. Continue narrating as the slide show is displayed.

8. When you reach the end of the presentation, a message box prompts if you want to save the timings with each slide. If you do, click Yes.

The presentation is displayed in Slide Sorter view with the slide timings appearing below each slide if you chose to save them with the presentation.

Tip from
Patrice-Anne Rutledge

To delete the narration from a slide while in Normal view or Slide view, select the sound icon that displays in the lower-right corner and press the Delete key. You need to repeat this for each slide that has a corresponding narration.

WORKING WITH CUSTOM SHOWS

Custom shows enable you to create customized PowerPoint presentations designed for different audiences or purposes without having to create multiple, nearly identical presentations.

For example, you might want to create a sales presentation that you can use with three different types of prospective clients. Let's say the first seven slides of your show cover information about your company and its history, which remains the same for all three types of prospects. But you've also created individual slides for each of your three prospect groups that detail your successes in those industries. You can then design three custom shows, each of which includes the seven main slides, plus the specific slides that pertain only to a certain prospect type. This helps save you time and effort when you need to update information in the seven main slides; this way, you need to do it only once.

To create a custom show, follow these steps:

1. Choose Slide Show, Custom Shows to open the Custom Shows dialog box, shown in Figure 9.7.
2. Click the New button to open the Define Custom Show dialog box, shown in Figure 9.8.

Figure 9.7
Customizing your slideshows saves time and reduces duplication.

PART

III

CH

9

Figure 9.8
Add a new custom show in this dialog box.

3. Replace the default name in the Slide Show Name text box with a title for your show.
4. From the Slides in Presentation list, choose the first slide you want to include in your custom show.
5. Click the Add button to copy this slide to the Slides in Custom Show list.
6. Repeat steps 4 and 5 until you've copied all the required slides to this list. If you need to remove a slide from the Slides in Custom Show list, select it and click the Remove button.

Tip from
Patrice-Anne Rutledge

Use the up and down buttons on the right side of the dialog box to rearrange slides you highlighted.

7. Click OK to save the custom show and return to the Custom Shows dialog box. From this dialog box you can now edit, remove, or copy any selected custom show.

Tip from

Patrice-Anne Rutledge

Copying a custom slideshow is useful if you want to create several similar versions of a custom show and don't want to repeat the same steps over and over.

8. To preview what the show will look like, click the Show button. The show previews in Slide Show view.

9. Click the Close button to close the Custom Shows dialog box.

To play a custom show, select it from the Custom Show drop-down list in the Set Up Show dialog box. Then either press the F5 key or select the Slide Show, View Show menu command.

INSERTING SLIDES FROM OTHER PRESENTATIONS

As an alternative to creating a custom show, you can insert slides from another presentation into your current presentation. This helps save time and redundancy as well.

Note

A major difference between custom shows and inserting slides is that inserting makes a copy of the slide and, if you change the original, the copy isn't affected. Custom shows "link" to the slides, so they are stored only once.

To insert slides, follow these steps:

1. Select the slide after which you want to start inserting other slides and choose Insert, Slides from Files to open the Slide Finder dialog box, shown in Figure 9.9.

Figure 9.9
The Slide Finder helps you add slides from other presentations.

2. From the Find Presentation tab, click the Browse button to open the Browse dialog box (see Figure 9.10). You can also enter the filename and path directly in the File field in the Slide Finder.

Figure 9.10
Browse to find your
source presentation.

3. Locate your desired file and click Open. The Browse dialog box closes, and the slides appear in the Select Slides section of the Slide Finder, as shown in Figure 9.11.

Slide Sorter button

Figure 9.11
Display the presenta-
tion in the lower por-
tion of the dialog box.

Outline button

4. The Slide Sorter button is selected by default, and displays visual images of three slides across the Select Slides area. If you prefer, you can display a text-based outline of your slides with one visual at a time. To do so, click the Outline button to the far right of the Select Slides area. Figure 9.12 illustrates this view.

Figure 9.12
Use an outline to find the slide you want to insert.

5. Select the slide you want to add and click Insert, or click the Insert All button to insert all slides in the current presentation.

6. Select the Match Destination Formatting check box if you want the design template of the slide you insert to match the design template of the destination presentation. Leave this check box blank if you want to retain the existing design template of the inserted slide.

7. Continue selecting and inserting slides until you finish. The slides are inserted in the order you select them, following the active slide in the current presentation.

8. Click the Close button to exit the dialog box.

If you frequently insert slides from the same presentation, you can add them to a favorites list. Click the Add to Favorites button to do so. The next time you want to insert slides from this presentation, you can go to the List of Favorites tab in the Slide Finder dialog box (see Figure 9.13) to locate them.

Note

In addition to inserting slides, you can also hide them. To hide a selected slide or slides, choose Slide Show, Hide Slide. This doesn't delete the slide; it simply prevents it from appearing in the show.

Figure 9.13
Using the List of
Favorites tab makes it
easier to find com-
monly used slides.

PART

III

CH

9

VIEWING YOUR SHOW

After you plan and set up your PowerPoint presentation, it's time to present it. To do this,
select Slide Show, View Show or press F5.

> **Note**
>
> Before presenting your show live, you should preview it to test content, flow, and nar-
> ration. After you determine that your show itself is flawless, you should work on per-
> fecting your delivery, particularly if you don't deliver live presentations on a regular
> basis. By simulating live conditions as much as possible in your practice sessions, you'll
> increase your odds of delivering a perfect presentation.

PowerPoint presents a show using the settings you enter in the Set Up Show dialog box.
For example, you can view in a browser or full screen, depending on what you entered in
this dialog box. Whether you need to advance each slide manually depends on your choices
in this dialog box. How you navigate the presentation also depends on how you view it:

- **Full screen**   You'll display full screen if you choose the Presented by a Speaker or the
  Browsed at a Kiosk option in the Set Up Show dialog box. The major difference between
  the two is that when you present by a speaker, you have numerous navigation options
  available because a person is in control of the presentation. When you browse at a kiosk,
  these navigation options aren't available because this type of show is self-running.

- **PowerPoint Browser**   You'll view in the PowerPoint browser if you choose Browsed
  by an Individual in the Set Up Show dialog box. This is similar to other browsers, such
  as Internet Explorer or Netscape Navigator. You can use the scrollbar to scroll through

the presentation if it's available, or you can use the Page Up and Page Down keys to navigate manually. To switch to the full screen view, choose Browse, Full Screen from within the PowerPoint browser.

Tip from
Patrice-Anne Rutledge

Displaying a scrollbar can make it easier for viewers to navigate your show. Specify whether to display a scrollbar in the Set Up Show dialog box.

→ For more information about the Set Up Show dialog box, **see** "Setting Up a Show" earlier in this chapter.

Note

To present the show starting with the current slide, click the Slide Show button in the lower-left corner of the window.

NAVIGATING A SHOW FULL SCREEN

If you choose to present your PowerPoint slideshow by a speaker, you'll display your presentation full screen. In this type slideshow, you have several ways to advance each slide manually if you choose this method of advancing slides, rather than by automatic timing. Table 9.1 lists a variety of ways to navigate a slideshow.

TABLE 9.1   SLIDESHOW ACTIONS

Slideshow Action	Method
Advance to next slide	Left-click the mouse Press the spacebar Press the letter N Press the right-arrow key Press the down-arrow key Press the Enter key Press the Page Down key
Return to previous slide	Press the Backspace key Press the letter P Press the left-arrow key Press the up-arrow key Press the Page Up key
Go to a specific slide	Enter the number of the slide and press the Enter key
Black/unblack the screen (toggle)	Press the letter B Press the period key
White/unwhite the screen (toggle)	Press the letter W Press the comma (,)
Display/hide the arrow (toggle)	Press the letter A Press the equal sign (=)

Table 9.1 Continued

Slideshow Action	Method
Stop/restart a timed show (toggle)	Press the letter S Press the plus sign (+)
End the show	Press the Esc key Press Ctrl+Break Press the minus (–) key
Erase screen drawing made with pen	Press the letter E
Advance to hidden slide	Press the letter H
Rehearse using new timing	Press the letter T
Rehearse using original timing	Press the letter O
Return to the show's beginning	Press both mouse keys
Activate the pen	Press Ctrl+P
Activate the arrow pointer	Press Ctrl+A
Hide pointer/button	Press Ctrl+H
Automatically show/hide pointer	Press Ctrl+U

PART III
CH 9

Tip from
Patrice-Anne Rutledge

Right-click anywhere on the screen and choose Help from the shortcut menu to display this list of shortcuts within your slideshow.

Note

The capability to toggle a black or white screen is a useful tool. For example, if you want to explain a detailed concept and want your audience to focus on what you're saying and not on the slide, you can temporarily make the screen either black or white. This is also useful during breaks for long presentations.

You have other ways to navigate a PowerPoint show. Right-click the mouse anywhere on the screen and choose Go from the shortcut menu. You can choose any of the following navigational options:

- **Slide Navigator** This displays the Slide Navigator dialog box (see Figure 9.14), in which you can choose the show and slide titles you want to view. Simply select the slide you want and click the Go To button. The Show field is available only in presentations that include custom shows and enables you to choose the custom show that contains the slides you want to view.

- **By Title** Displays a menu listing all slides in your presentation. Click the one you want to view.

Figure 9.14
The Slide Navigator
dialog box helps you
find slides.

■ **Custom Show**   Displays a menu listing available custom shows. Click the one you want to view.

■ **Previously Viewed**   Displays the previously viewed slide again.

Tip from
Patrice-Anne
Rutledge

Although the options that appear on the Go menu are useful for finding a specific slide you want to display, you'll probably want to avoid using these features during an actual presentation because a break in your flow can be distracting. One case in which you might want to do so during a presentation would be when you have to go back to previous slides to answer questions or clarify a point and don't want to page through numerous slides to do so.

SETTING POINTER OPTIONS

You can use an arrow pointer during a PowerPoint presentation, write with a pen, or hide all pointers. To choose these options, right-click the mouse anywhere on the screen, choose Pointer Options from the shortcut menu, and select Arrow, Pen, or Hidden from the menu that appears.

The Arrow option displays a standard mouse pointer arrow on your screen, which you can use to point to specific areas. If you want to actually draw on the screen, choose the Pen option. Using a pen enables you to draw circles around important words to highlight them, draw shapes and objects to emphasize a point, or even write text on the screen. Writing text is a bit hard to read, however, so you'll probably want to do this sparingly. To erase your pen markings, right-click the mouse and choose Screen, Erase Pen or press the letter E. Annotations are also erased when you advance to the next slide. If you don't want any pointer to appear, choose the Hidden option.

Figure 9.15 shows the standard arrow pointer with which most people are familiar.

Figure 9.15
Use a pointer during your slide presentation.

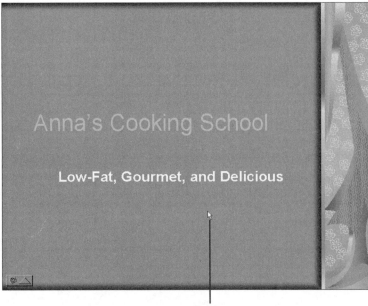

Pointer

Figure 9.16 illustrates a sample use of the pen feature.

Figure 9.16
Use the pen to add comments or illustrations to the presentation.

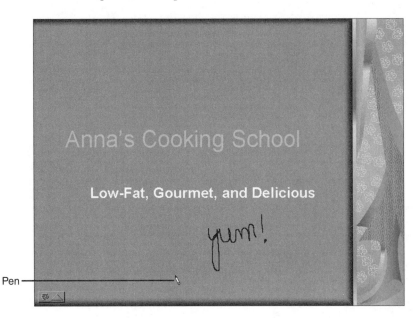

Pen

You can choose your pen color in the Set Up Show dialog box, or you can set it by right-clicking the mouse, choosing Pointer Options, Pen Color, and selecting a color from the list that appears.

→ To set up the pen color in the Set Up Show dialog box, **see** "Setting Up a Show" earlier in this chapter.

USING THE MEETING MINDER

The Meeting Minder enables you to take meeting minutes and assign action items. You can also export your minutes to Outlook if you want to e-mail them to others or to Word if you want to edit, format, and print them. To use the Meeting Minder, right-click the mouse anywhere on the screen and choose Meeting Minder. Figure 9.17 shows the Meeting Minutes tab of the Meeting Minder dialog box where you can enter detailed minutes from your presentation.

Figure 9.17
The Meeting Minutes tab of the Meeting Minder enables you to keep track of what happens during a meeting.

In the Action Items tab (see Figure 9.18), you can enter multiple action items (like a "to do" list) for specific people that come up during the course of a meeting.

Figure 9.18
Record action items in the Action Items tab.

To add an action item, enter its description, the name of the person to whom it's assigned, and a due date. Then click the Add button to add this item to the action item list below. You can also edit and delete selected action items by clicking the Edit and Delete buttons.

To export the meeting minutes and action items to Outlook or Word, click the Export button. Figure 9.19 shows the Meeting Minder Export dialog box.

Figure 9.19
Export meeting min-
utes to Word or
Outlook.

⚠ ***Can't see the Post Action Items to Microsoft Outlook option?*** *See the "Troubleshooting" section near the end of this chapter.*

The Export Options offered are

■ Post Action Items to Microsoft Outlook

■ Send Meeting Minutes and Action Items to Microsoft Word

Choose one or both options and click the Export Now button. Figure 9.20 shows a sample export to Microsoft Word.

Figure 9.20
In Word, you can for-
mat meeting minutes.

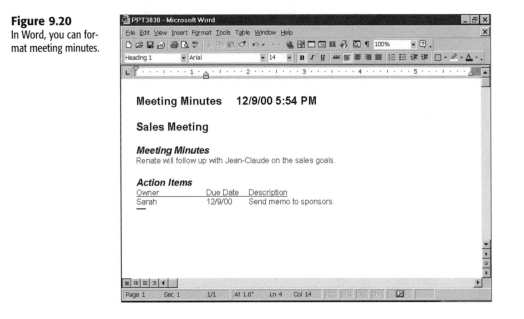

Click the Schedule button in the Meeting Minder dialog box to open Outlook and display an appointment.

Note

If you haven't installed Microsoft Outlook, the option won't activate.

Click OK to exit Meeting Minder. You'll notice that PowerPoint adds a slide that contains your recorded action items to the end of this presentation (see Figure 9.21).

Figure 9.21
PowerPoint adds a
slide summarizing
your action items.

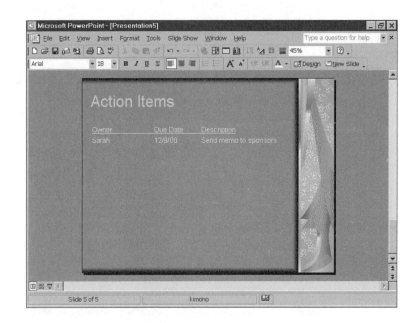

Note

In addition to taking your own meeting minutes, you can also refer to your speaker's notes during your presentation (the notes you enter on the Notes pane in Normal view). To do this, right-click the mouse and choose Speaker Notes from the menu. The notes from the current slide are displayed.

USING THE PACK AND GO WIZARD

The Pack and Go Wizard enables you to package your presentation for delivery on another computer. You can also simply copy your presentation to a disk or move it to a network location, and then present it on another computer, if you're sure that the other computer has the same version of PowerPoint and the same fonts as your original computer. If you're not sure, the Pack and Go Wizard can verify that you have everything you need:

1. Choose File, Pack and Go to open the Pack and Go Wizard, shown in Figure 9.22.
2. Click the Next button to continue and choose which presentation you want to package (see Figure 9.23).
3. Specify whether you want to package the active presentation or another presentation.
4. If you select Other Presentation(s), you can enter its name in the edit box or click the Browse button to locate it in the Select a Presentation to Package dialog box (see Figure 9.24).

Figure 9.22
With the Pack and Go Wizard, you can deliver your presentation on another computer.

Figure 9.23
You can package the active presentation or choose another.

Figure 9.24
Choose the presentation you want to package in this dialog box.

5. If you use the Select a Presentation to Package dialog box to locate your presentation, choose the presentation you want and click the Select button to return to the wizard. The pathname you selected appears in the Other Presentation(s) field in the Pack and Go Wizard.

6. Click Next to determine where you want to save the packaged presentation, shown in Figure 9.25.

Figure 9.25
Save the file to any drive you specify.

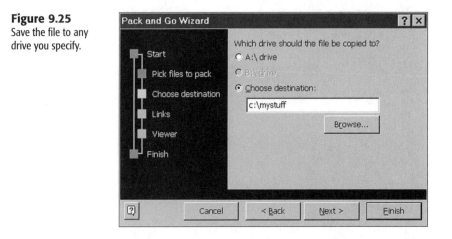

7. Specify where to save the packaged presentation. Options include drive A:, drive B:, or another drive.

Caution

The Pack and Go Wizard can compress additional files with your presentation, such as linked files, embedded fonts, and a viewer. If the final presentation package is too large for a single disk, you'll receive a message prompting you to insert additional disks.

Tip from
Patrice-Anne Rutledge

If you want to save on another drive—one on a network, for example—you can click the Browse button and choose this drive from the Specify Directory dialog box.

8. Click Next again to specify what linked files and fonts you want to include (see Figure 9.26).

9. Indicate whether you want to choose the Include Linked Files and Embed TrueType Fonts options. Choosing both ensures that all external clip art images, media clips, sounds, and special fonts are included in the package.

Figure 9.26
Include linked files and fonts to form a complete package.

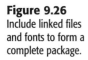

> **Note**
>
> You can embed TrueType fonts that come with Windows. You can embed other TrueType fonts that you install only if they aren't restricted by license or copyright. You'll receive an error message if you try to embed a restricted font. To embed fonts directly in a presentation before using the Pack and Go Wizard, choose File, Save As and then choose Tools, Embed TrueType Fonts from the Save As dialog box. Embedding fonts makes the file you're saving larger.

10. Click Next to continue and specify if you want to include the PowerPoint Viewer, as shown in Figure 9.27.

Figure 9.27
You can also include the PowerPoint Viewer.

11. If you're going to present on a computer that doesn't have PowerPoint installed, you can include the PowerPoint Viewer within the package. Choose either Don't Include the Viewer or Viewer for Microsoft Windows, as appropriate.

Note

If you haven't already downloaded the PowerPoint Viewer, click the Download the Viewer button (which only appears only if you don't have the Viewer). You are then prompted to download it from Microsoft's Web site and install it on your computer.

→ To learn what this viewer is and how it works, **see** "Using the PowerPoint Viewer," the next section in this chapter.

12. Click Next to advance to the summary step (see Figure 9.28).

Figure 9.28
The final step summarizes your actions.

13. This step summarizes what the wizard will do, such as compress the files to a specific drive, include the PowerPoint Viewer, and more. Click Finish.

PowerPoint compresses your file to its target destination in a file named PRES0.PPZ. It also includes an application file named PNGSETUP.EXE. When you're ready to deliver your presentation on the new computer, run PNGSETUP.EXE, which extracts the presentation and runs it.

USING THE POWERPOINT VIEWER

The PowerPoint Viewer (PPVIEW32.EXE) is an application that enables people who don't have PowerPoint installed on their computers to view a PowerPoint presentation. You can freely distribute the Viewer without any license fee. Using the Pack and Go Wizard, you have the option of including the Viewer in your presentation package.

→ To learn more about how to use this wizard and how it works with the PowerPoint Viewer, **see** "Using the Pack and Go Wizard," the previous section in this chapter.

Note

PPVIEW32.EXE is also compressed when you use the Pack and Go Wizard and is extracted to the folder you indicate when you run PNGSETUP.EXE to decompress your presentation.

To run the Viewer, follow these steps:

1. Double-click PPVIEW32.EXE from within Windows Explorer. Figure 9.29 illustrates the Microsoft PowerPoint Viewer dialog box.

Figure 9.29
The PowerPoint Viewer enables you to deliver slideshows on computers without PowerPoint.

2. Navigate to the presentation you want to view or enter its name in the File Name field.

3. Specify whether you want to advance slides Manually or Using Timings, If Present.

4. Click the Print button if you want to print this presentation. The standard Print dialog box appears, in which you can set print options.

5. Click the Options button to set presentation and viewer settings, shown in Figure 9.30.

6. In the Options dialog box, you can select Use Settings Saved with File or Override Saved Settings. These are the settings you specified in the Set Up Show dialog box.

→ For more information on the Set Up Show dialog box, **see** "Setting Up a Show" earlier in this chapter.

Figure 9.30
Specify settings in this
dialog box.

7. If you want to override saved settings, you have the following options:

   - **Loop Continuously Until 'Esc'**   Plays the presentation over and over again until you press the Esc key.
   - **Show Without Narrations**   Temporarily deactivates any accompanying narrations.
   - **Show Without Animation**   Temporarily deactivates any accompanying animations.

8. You can also set the following Viewer Settings:

   - **Popup Menu on Right Mouse Click**   Displays a subset of the menu options that are available within PowerPoint during a slideshow.

→ To learn how to use these options, **see** "Viewing Your Show" earlier in this chapter.

   - **Show Popup Menu Button**   Displays the pop-up menu button in the lower-left corner.
   - **End with Black Slide**   Finishes the show with a black slide.

9. After making your selections, click OK to return to the main dialog box.

10. Click the Show button to run the show with the parameters you set.

11. Click Exit to close the PowerPoint Viewer dialog box.

You can also play multiple shows with the Viewer by creating a playlist file with Notepad. To do this, follow these steps:

1. Open Notepad by choosing Programs, Accessories, Notepad from the Start button.

2. Enter each presentation and its path on a single line in Notepad, avoiding any spaces between lines. Figure 9.31 provides an example.

3. Choose File, Save to open the Save As dialog box, shown in Figure 9.32.

Figure 9.31
Enter multiple
presentation files in
Notepad.

Figure 9.32
Save your playlist.

4. Enter a name for the file in the File Name text box and click Save. You can't use long filenames or folder names in a playlist—stick to eight characters.

5. Choose File, Exit to close Notepad.

Next, you have to rename the playlist with the extension .LST. The playlist must have this extension or it won't run. You can then return to the PowerPoint Viewer and run the playlist. Be sure to select Playlist in the Files of Type field.

Tip from
*Patrice-Anne
Rutledge*

For more information about the parameters you can use in setting up a playlist, click the About button in the Microsoft PowerPoint Viewer dialog box.

TROUBLESHOOTING

DISPLAYING HIDDEN SLIDES

My presentation doesn't display all the slides I created.

Be sure you don't have any hidden slides. To verify this, open your presentation in Slide Sorter view and verify that none of the slide numbers has a strikethrough, which indicates it's hidden. To unhide a slide, select it and choose Slide Show, Hide Slide.

ADVANCING SLIDES AT A KIOSK

I want to browse my presentation at a kiosk, but the slides don't advance.

Be sure you set automatic timings if you want to browse at a kiosk because you can't do this manually. Also verify that you chose the Using Timings, If Present option in the Set Up Show dialog box.

LISTENING TO A VOICE NARRATION

I added a voice narration, and now I can't hear other sound files I've included.

If you insert media clips such as sounds, and then add a voice narration, the narration takes precedence over the media clips. As a result, you'll hear only the narration. To resolve this, delete the narration if the media clips are of more importance, or find a way to include the other sounds in the narration you record.

EXPORTING ACTION ITEMS

I want to export an action item from the Meeting Minder to Microsoft Outlook, but that option isn't available in the Meeting Minder Export dialog box.

You must click the Add button to add at least one action item to the Action Items tab before you can export that item. If you just enter one action item without clicking the Add button, the Post Action Items to Microsoft Outlook option won't be available.

DESIGN CORNER: CREATING MINUTES AND ACTION ITEMS IN WORD

PowerPoint makes it easy to edit and format your meeting minutes and action items in Microsoft Word before printing or sending to meeting participants and other team members. To do so, follow these steps:

1. Present your show by pressing F5; right-click anywhere on the screen, and choose Meeting Minder from the shortcut menu.

2. In the Meeting Minder dialog box, enter your meeting minutes and action items as your presentation progresses.

3. Click the Export button to open the Meeting Minter Export dialog box.

4. Select the Send Meeting Minutes and Action Items to Microsoft Word check box and click Export Now. PowerPoint exports the minutes and action items to Word, opening the new Word document.

5. In Word, edit and format your minutes as desired.

BEFORE

Figure 9.33
Meeting Minutes and Action Items come directly from the Meeting Minder dialog box in PowerPoint.

AFTER

Figure 9.34

CHAPTER 10

CREATING AND PRINTING PRESENTATION MATERIALS

In this chapter

EXPLORING PRESENTATION OUTPUT OPTIONS

You can create a variety of printed output from PowerPoint: slides, notes, handouts, and outlines. You can use these materials to proof your slide content, remind yourself of what you want to say while presenting, or give to audience members who attend your presentation. If you don't have a color printer, you can print your presentation in either grayscale or pure black and white. PowerPoint also includes numerous customization options for printing auxiliary materials. You can export these to Microsoft Word for even more flexibility.

CREATING NOTES AND HANDOUTS

In addition to slides and outlines, notes and handouts are two of the most common forms of printed output. You create notes in the Notes pane, which is visible in Normal view. Figure 10.1 illustrates a Notes pane in which you can create detailed speaker's notes about your presentation.

Figure 10.1
Add notes for yourself or your audience in the Notes pane.

Notes pane

Note

Notes are not the same as comments. A comment appears in a yellow box on top of your presentation and provides commentary about its content. You use comments most often during the review process to get feedback from others, and you usually delete them later. Notes are designed to be kept with a presentation as a reference for the speaker or audience members.

→ For details about the use of comments, **see** "Adding Comments to Slides" in Chapter 7, "Collaborating on Presentations."

You can use notes to remind yourself of what you're going to present, to create an entire script for your presentation, or to provide information you print out for audience members.

Printing handouts is similar to printing slides, except that with handouts you can print up to nine slides on a page. This can greatly reduce the number of pages and amount of printer toner required to print your presentation. When you print handouts, you see only the slides, not the accompanying notes.

→ To learn more about how and when to use handouts, **see** "Creating Handout Materials" in Chapter 23, "The Media—Designing Visual Support."

PREPARING TO PRINT YOUR PRESENTATION

To avoid wasting paper, you'll want to ensure that your PowerPoint presentation is truly ready to print before sending it to the printer. This includes setting page and print options, customizing headers and footers, and previewing your presentation in the color scheme in which it will print. If you're going to provide hard copy handouts of your presentation to your audience, you'll definitely need to print your presentation. But even if you plan to deliver your presentation onscreen only, it's still a good idea to view your presentation on paper. When proofing a hard copy version of your presentation, you'll often notice problems that you didn't catch onscreen.

Tip from
Patrice-Anne Rutledge

> If you're going to provide your audience with handouts, it's usually a good idea to hand them out *after* you're finished presenting. Why? You want to be sure your audience is focusing on what you're saying and not on reading handouts during your actual presentation.

→ For more details on proofreading and spell-checking your presentation, **see** "Checking Spelling and Style" in Chapter 3, "Working with Text."

SETTING PAGE SETUP OPTIONS

Before you print, you'll want to set up page options such as a default output and orientation. To do this, follow these steps:

1. Choose File, Page Setup to open the Page Setup dialog box, shown in Figure 10.2.

2. Select your output from the Slides Sized For drop-down list. Options include On-screen Show, Letter Paper, Ledger Paper, A3 Paper, A4 Paper (international standard), B4 (ISO) Paper, B5 (ISO) Paper, 35mm Slides, Overhead, Banner, and Custom.

Figure 10.2
Set up page orientation and other defaults in the Page Setup dialog box.

Tip from
Patrice-Anne Rutledge

If you want to create 35mm slides from your PowerPoint presentation, you can send it to a service bureau (often electronically) to have this done. Genigraphics (www.genigraphics.com) is one example of a bureau that specializes in PowerPoint presentations.

3. The Width and Height settings appear in inches automatically, based on your selection in step 2. You can customize these settings, if necessary.

4. In the Number Slides From field, select the number to use on the first slide.

5. Choose either a Portrait or Landscape orientation for your slides. Landscape is the default.

6. Choose either a Portrait or Landscape orientation for your notes, handouts, and outline. Portrait is the default for these, but you can switch to landscape if your presentation doesn't fit on the page with portrait orientation.

7. Click OK to close this dialog box.

CUSTOMIZING HEADERS AND FOOTERS

You can also add headers and footers to your outline, notes, and handouts when you print them. To do this, choose View, Header and Footer and go to the Notes and Handouts tab on the Header and Footer dialog box, seen in Figure 10.3.

You can add any or all of the following when you print notes, handouts, or outlines:

■ **Date and Time**   Select this check box and then either choose to update the date automatically or enter a fixed date. If you choose to update automatically, you can pick a format from the drop-down list. Options include displaying the date only, the time only, or the date and time in up to 13 different ways. You can also choose your base language and calendar type (depending on the language selection). If only English is enabled, the Calendar Type and Language buttons aren't active. The date and time appear on the upper-right corner of the page.

→ For details on multilingual presentations, **see** Appendix B, "Using PowerPoint's Foreign Language Capabilities."

Figure 10.3
Indicate the headers
and footers you want
to print.

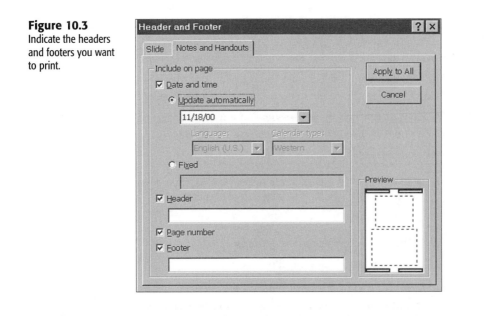

Note

The date options you can choose from the Update Automatically drop-down list are based on your choice of language/country. For example, choosing English (UK) results in date options that display a dd/mm/yy format rather than the mm/dd/yy format that is used in the United States.

- **Header** Prints the header text you enter in the text box on the upper-left corner of the page.
- **Page Number** Prints the page number on each page on the lower-right corner of the page.
- **Footer** Prints the footer text you enter in the text box on the lower-left corner of the page.

Click Apply to All to close the dialog box.

PREVIEWING A POWERPOINT PRESENTATION

Before you print your presentation, you can preview it using PowerPoint's Print Preview feature.

 To preview, click the Print Preview button on the Standard toolbar, or choose File, Print Preview.

You have several formatting and output options from this view:

- **Previous Page** Goes back to the previous page.

- **Next Page** Moves forward to the next page.

- ■ **Print** Opens the Print dialog box, from which you can print your presentation.

→ For more information on the Print dialog box, **see** "Printing PowerPoint Presentations" later in this chapter.

- ■ **Print What** Enables you to select what you want to print from a drop-down list. Options include Slides, Handouts (from one to nine per page), Notes Pages, and Outline View.
- ■ **Zoom** Reduces or enlarges the size of the content on your screen. Sizes range from 25% to 400%. You can also choose to fit the slide to the screen.

Tip from
Patrice-Anne Rutledge

Clicking the slide is another way to zoom in and out. Clicking serves as a toggle between a 100% view and fitting the slide to the page.

- ■ **Landscape** Displays the presentation in Landscape mode.
- ■ **Portrait** Displays the presentation in Portrait mode.
- ■ **Options** Opens a submenu with additional options including the following:
  - • **Header and Footer** Opens the Header and Footer dialog box, where you can modify headers and footers for printing.

→ For more information on the Header and Footer dialog box, **see** "Customizing Headers and Footers" earlier in this chapter.

  - • **Color/Grayscale** Displays a submenu from which you can preview your presentation in Color, Grayscale, or Pure Black and White.

→ For more information on color previewing, **see** "Previewing in Grayscale and Black and White" later in this chapter.

  - • **Scale to Fit Paper** Changes the size of slides to fit the paper, making them either larger or smaller as appropriate.
  - • **Frame Slides** Includes a border around the slides.
  - • **Print Hidden Slides** This option is available only if your presentation includes hidden slides.
  - • **Include Animations** Displays animated graphics in your presentation as icons on the printed page.
  - • **Include Comment Pages** Prints comment pages with your presentation.
  - • **Printing Order** Displays a submenu from which you can choose to print slides horizontally or vertically. This isn't the same as printing in portrait or landscape orientation, but rather refers to how multiple slides appear on a single page. Look at the preview to the right of the option buttons to see how the printing order changes depending on whether you select Horizontal or Vertical.
- ■ **Close** Closes the preview and returns to the presentation.

PREVIEWING IN GRAYSCALE AND BLACK AND WHITE

If you don't have a color printer, you can print a color presentation in two different ways: grayscale or black and white. Table 10.1 illustrates how each PowerPoint object appears when printed in grayscale or black and white.

TABLE 10.1   GRAYSCALE AND BLACK-AND-WHITE OBJECTS

Object	Grayscale	Black and White
Bitmaps	Grayscale	Grayscale
Charts	Grayscale	Grayscale
Embossing	None	None
Fill	Grayscale	White
Frames	Black	Black
Lines	Black	Black
Patterns	Grayscale	White
Shadows (object)	Grayscale	Black
Shadows (text)	None	None
Slide backgrounds	White	White
Text	Black	Black

To preview what your color presentation will look like in grayscale, click the Color/Grayscale button on the Standard toolbar and choose Grayscale from the submenu.

To preview the same presentation in black and white, choose Pure Black and White from the submenu. To return to viewing your presentation in color, choose Color from the Color/Grayscale submenu.

The Grayscale View floating toolbar appears when you preview in grayscale or pure black and white (it doesn't appear when you're viewing in color). You can manually change how an object prints in either grayscale or black and white with this toolbar. To do so, click Setting from the Grayscale View toolbar and choose the color option you prefer.

To close the Grayscale View toolbar, either return to viewing your presentation in color, or click the Close Grayscale View or Close Black and White View button on the Grayscale View toolbar.

PART
III

CH
10

PRINTING POWERPOINT PRESENTATIONS

To print an open PowerPoint presentation, follow these steps:

1. Choose File, Print to open the Print dialog box, shown in Figure 10.4. You can also click the Print button on the Standard toolbar if you want to print with the defaults, rather than setting options in the Print dialog box. Be sure that your default settings match your desired output, such as grayscale or black and white. You can set these defaults in the Print dialog box.

2. Select the printer you want to use from the Name drop-down list.

Figure 10.4
You can specify numerous print parameters in the Print dialog box.

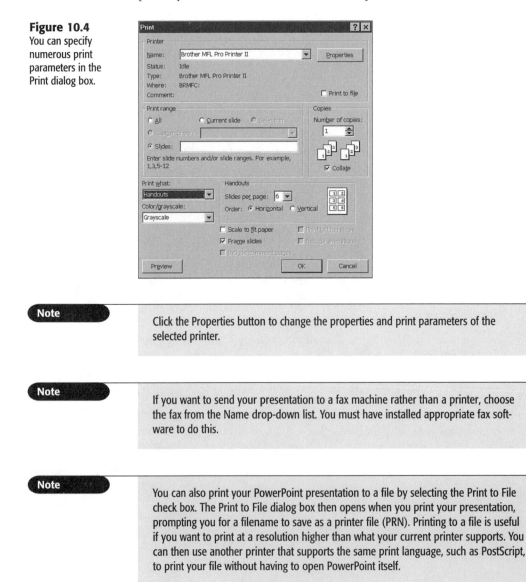

> **Note**
>
> Click the Properties button to change the properties and print parameters of the selected printer.

> **Note**
>
> If you want to send your presentation to a fax machine rather than a printer, choose the fax from the Name drop-down list. You must have installed appropriate fax software to do this.

> **Note**
>
> You can also print your PowerPoint presentation to a file by selecting the Print to File check box. The Print to File dialog box then opens when you print your presentation, prompting you for a filename to save as a printer file (PRN). Printing to a file is useful if you want to print at a resolution higher than what your current printer supports. You can then use another printer that supports the same print language, such as PostScript, to print your file without having to open PowerPoint itself.

3. In the Print Range group box, select the slides you want to print. Choices include

- **All** Prints all slides in the presentation.
- **Current Slide** Prints only the currently selected slide.
- **Selection** Prints the selected slides. For example, if you select specific slides on the Outline tab, only these slides are printed.
- **Custom Show** Enables you to select a custom show to print. This option isn't available if you haven't created at least one custom show.

→ For more information on custom shows, **see** "Working with Custom Shows" in Chapter 9, "Presenting a Slideshow."

- **Slides** Enables you to pick and choose multiple slides. Enter the numbers of the slides you want to print. For example, you could enter 1-4, 10 to print slides 1, 2, 3, 4, and 10. Page numbers must be selected in ascending order.

4. Enter the Number of Copies you want to print. If you choose to print more than one copy, specify whether or not to collate. Collating keeps multiple copies in sequence. If you print five copies of a presentation without collating, for example, you will print five copies of page one first, then five copies of page two, and so on.

5. Specify what you want to print in the Print What drop-down list. Options include Slides, Handouts, Notes Pages, and Outline View.

6. If you choose to print handouts, the Handouts group box becomes active. Indicate how many slides you want to print per page—up to nine—in the Slides per Page field and choose either Horizontal or Vertical Order for the flow of slides on the page.

PART
III
CH
10

Tip from
Patrice-Anne Rutledge

If you choose to print three slides per handout, PowerPoint provides lined spaces to the right of each slide on which you can write notes. If you choose another number of pages, you won't have this note space.

7. From the Color/Grayscale drop-down list, choose the color options you want. Options include

- **Color** Prints the presentation in color, optimized for a color printer. If you select this option and print to a black-and-white printer, the presentation will print in black and white.
- **Grayscale** Prints the presentation as grayscale (using shades of black, white, and gray) which optimizes a color presentation for a black-and-white printer.
- **Pure Black and White** Prints the presentation in black and white only, without any gray.

8. Next, choose any of the following print options that apply:

- **Scale to Fit Paper** Changes the size of slides to fit the paper, making them either larger or smaller as appropriate.
- **Frame Slides** Includes a border around the slides. Not available when you print Outline view.

- **Include Comment Pages**   Prints comment pages with your presentation.
- **Print Hidden Slides**   This option is available only if your presentation includes hidden slides.
- **Include Animations**   Displays animated graphics in your presentation as icons on the printed page.

9. Click the Preview button to see what your printed presentation will look like, based on your selected options. When you're satisfied with your print choices, click OK to print to your printer.

 Having trouble printing? *See "Resolving Print Problems" in the "Troubleshooting" section near the end of the chapter.*

Tip from	You can customize printing defaults for the existing presentation in the Options dialog box. To access it, choose Tools, Options and go to the Print tab.
Patrice-Anne Rutledge	

→ For more information about printing, **see** "Setting Print Options" in Chapter 21, "Customizing PowerPoint."

PRINTING AN OUTLINE

In the Print dialog box, you can choose to print a presentation's outline by selecting the Outline View option in the Print What drop-down list.

→ For more detailed information about printing, **see** "Printing PowerPoint Presentations" in this chapter.

Before you do this, however, you might want to set up your outline for printing.

 To display the entire contents of each slide, click the Expand All button on either the Standard or Outlining toolbar. If the Outlining toolbar doesn't appear, choose View, Toolbars, Outlining.

 To print only the title of each slide, click the Collapse All button on the Outlining toolbar.

 To print an outline with the same formatting as the presentation itself (font styles and sizing, line spacing, and the like), click the Show Formatting button on the Standard or Outlining toolbar.

→ To better understand outlines, **see** "Collapsing and Expanding Outline Points" in Chapter 5, "Organizing Presentations in PowerPoint."

PRINTING A POWERPOINT PRESENTATION WITH MICROSOFT WORD

If you want to make more customizations than PowerPoint provides, you can also send your presentation to Word, customize it, and print from that application. Choose File, Send To, Microsoft Word to open the Send To Microsoft Word dialog box, shown in Figure 10.5.

This dialog box includes several choices on how to display the PowerPoint presentation in Word.

You can either paste or paste link the slides into Word. Pasting is the equivalent of embedding. If you embed a PowerPoint presentation into Word and later change that presentation in PowerPoint, those changes won't appear in the Word document. If you paste link the PowerPoint presentation into Word and later make changes in PowerPoint, these changes appear the next time you open the document in Word.

Figure 10.5
The Send To Microsoft Word dialog box includes several options for exporting to Word.

→ To learn more about linking objects, **see** "Linking Office Objects" in Chapter 19, "Integrating with Office XP."

→ For more information on embedding, **see** "Working with Embedded Office Objects" in Chapter 19.

Click OK to send your presentation to Word and open it in that application. After your presentation is opened in Word, you can use all of Word's features to customize your notes and handouts.

ENSURING A SMOOTH PRINT PROCESS

The following are some tips to help ensure a smooth process in printing your PowerPoint presentation:

■ If you want to continue working with PowerPoint while printing a large presentation, choose Tools, Options, and select Background Printing on the Print tab. With some printers, background printing can also be a setting of the printer itself. For example, if your printer enables you to set up print spooling, this has the same effect as background printing.

■ If your print job is moving too slowly, turn off background printing.

 Not printing fast enough? See "Speeding Up the Print Process" in the "Troubleshooting" section near the end of the chapter.

- Proof your presentation carefully before printing it to save time and money. Run the spelling and grammar checker, verify the content, look at the placement of all graphics, and ensure that the color scheme and design templates are appropriate. When you're confident about your presentation, then print.

- If the fonts in your presentation don't print out properly, try substituting other fonts. For example, if you don't use TrueType fonts and your printer can't recognize a font you selected, it prints a different font, one that may not be what you want. Embedding fonts as graphics is another way to avoid this problem.

What should you do if your graphics don't print in their entirety? *See "Resolving Incomplete Graphics Printing" in the "Troubleshooting" section near the end of the chapter.*

- If you're going to distribute notes or handouts to audience members, carefully consider the quality and color of paper you use. Although heavier paper might make attractive handouts, not all printers are equipped to handle the heavier weight. Specialty paper is also more expensive. In terms of color, light colors other than white can work well, but be wary of paper that's too dark or bright. It can make your presentation hard to read.

TROUBLESHOOTING

RESOLVING PRINT PROBLEMS

I can't print. What should I do?

If you're having problems printing, first verify that your printer is turned on, that you selected the right printer in the Print dialog box, and that you checked for error messages in the Printers folder. To further isolate a printing problem, check to see if you can print another PowerPoint presentation or a document from another application. If not, the problem is probably with the printer and not PowerPoint or your presentation.

SPEEDING UP THE PRINT PROCESS

My print job is printing too slowly. How can I speed up the print process?

Turn off background printing to speed up the print process. To do so, choose Tools, Options and remove the check mark by Background Printing on the Print tab of the Options dialog box.

RESOLVING INCOMPLETE GRAPHICS PRINTING

My graphics don't print completely. How do I fix this?

First, verify that a document without graphics prints properly. If so, your printer may not have enough memory to complete a print job with complex graphics. Refer to your printer manual for information about memory and memory upgrades.

DESIGN CORNER: CREATING CUSTOM POWERPOINT HANDOUTS

If you're just going to provide handouts for internal reference, PowerPoint's handout creation feature may easily handle all your needs. But if you need to create polished, professional handouts (for an important client presentation, for example), you might need a bit more flexibility and sophistication. This is where the integrated power of Office XP comes in handy—create your presentation in PowerPoint and then polish up the handouts in Word. With Word's advanced formatting features, you can create a custom PowerPoint handout that meets your exact specifications. Just choose the page layout options you want in the Send To Microsoft Word dialog box (File, Send To, Microsoft Word) and then customize the output in Word.

BEFORE

Figure 10.6

AFTER

Figure 10.7

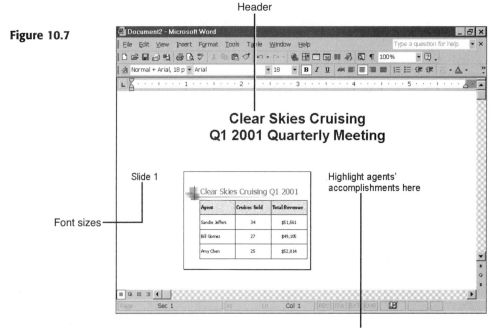

Header

Slide 1

Font sizes

Highlight agents' accomplishments here

Custom fonts

PART **IV**

WORKING WITH GRAPHICS, CHARTS, AND MULTIMEDIA

CHAPTER **11**

WORKING WITH CHARTS

In this chapter

EXPLORING POWERPOINT CHART POSSIBILITIES

PowerPoint charts can be as simple or as complex as you like. You can create a basic chart using the Microsoft Graph application from within PowerPoint or insert a chart you create using Microsoft Excel. You can choose from common chart types such as column, bar, line, or pie charts; try something out of the ordinary, such as a doughnut or radar chart; or create a chart type of your own. PowerPoint charts are preformatted based on the attached design template, but you can also make extensive modifications to nearly every aspect of a chart if you like—its color, text, labels, and more.

A chart, also referred to as a graph, can be a useful tool for communicating numeric information in a concise format. You could create a chart illustrating sales revenue per region or the percentage of sales allocated to each of your products, for example. As you begin to work with charts, you'll discover a multitude of uses for them.

UNDERSTANDING CHARTS IN POWERPOINT

In PowerPoint, you can use the Microsoft Graph application to create powerful charts in your presentation or you can insert charts created in another application, such as Excel. Using Microsoft Graph from within PowerPoint is the easiest alternative if you need to create a chart from scratch and don't need to apply Excel's calculation and formula capabilities to your chart data. If you've already created a chart in Excel or you need to analyze complex data, inserting an Excel chart is the best solution.

Note

For the sake of consistency, we use the term *chart* throughout this chapter to match PowerPoint's interface. You'll note, however, that the application you use to create charts is called Microsoft Graph. Essentially, *chart* and *graph* are synonyms for any kind of graphical representation of numeric information.

In addition to the common chart types such as column, bar, line, and pie, you can also create doughnut, radar, cone, bubble, stock, and other chart types.

Before you start creating a chart using Microsoft Graph from within PowerPoint, you should become familiar with the terms associated with charts. Table 11.1 lists these terms and their definitions.

TABLE 11.1 CHART OBJECT TERMINOLOGY

Term	Definition
Axis	A line that frames one side of the plot area. The two most common axes are the value axis and the category axis.
Datasheet	A sheet with rows and columns that resembles a spreadsheet, in which you can enter data for your chart.

TABLE 11.1   CONTINUED

Term	Definition
Data label	A label that describes a specific data marker or series of data markers. This label can be a numeric value, text, percent, or combination of these items.
Data marker	A value that represents a single cell or data point in a datasheet.
Data series	Data series are the main categories of information in a chart and are usually reflected in a chart's legend and in the first cell of each datasheet row or column.
Data table	A table that displays in the chart listing the exact data in the datasheet.
Gridlines	Lines that display across the category or value axes, which enhance a chart's readability. By default, major gridlines are in increments of 10 and minor gridlines in increments of 2.
Legend	A box that lists and color-codes all data series.
Trendline	A line that forecasts future values based on current data.

Figure 11.1 shows some of these chart objects.

Figure 11.1
Learn the basic objects of a chart before you create one.

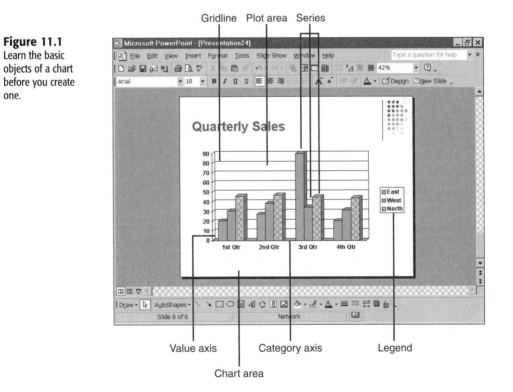

ADDING A CHART

The fastest way to add a chart to your PowerPoint presentation is to apply a slide layout that contains a chart. To do so, click the New Slide button on the Formatting toolbar and then choose an appropriate layout from the Slide Layout task pane. The next step varies depending on the slide layout you choose.

If you choose any of the layouts in the Content Layouts or Text and Content Layouts sections, you need to click the Insert Chart button on the content palette that displays (see Figure 11.2) to activate the chart and Microsoft Graph.

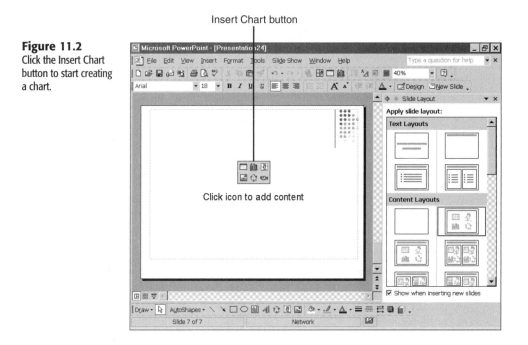

Figure 11.2
Click the Insert Chart button to start creating a chart.

If you choose one the layouts containing a chart in the Other Layouts section, you need to double-click the chart placeholder to activate the chart and Microsoft Graph. Figure 11.3 shows a sample chart slide with a chart placeholder.

Tip from
Patrice-Anne Rutledge

If you want to create a slide with a single chart and no other content, choose the Title and Chart slide layout.

→   To learn more about how slide layouts affect your presentation, **see** "Understanding Slide Layouts" in Chapter 2, "Creating a Basic Presentation."

Note

If you use the AutoContent Wizard to create your presentation, it might already have a slide that contains a chart.

Placeholder

Figure 11.3
You can start adding a chart by double-clicking the placeholder.

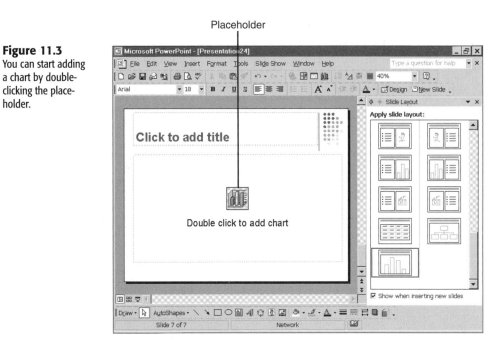

Figure 11.4 illustrates a preliminary chart in Microsoft Graph, which you'll see after either clicking the Insert Chart button on the content palette or double-clicking the chart placeholder. You can also insert a chart into an existing slide by clicking the Insert Chart button on the Standard toolbar or by selecting Insert, Chart.

Figure 11.4
PowerPoint displays a chart with sample data.

A sample 3D clustered column chart displays by default and the related datasheet opens. The menu bar and toolbars are also customized for Microsoft Graph. The menu bar now includes Data and Chart menu items, and the Standard toolbar includes several new options, explained in Table 11.2.

TABLE 11.2   STANDARD TOOLBAR CHART OPTIONS

Button	Name	Description
Plot Area ▼	Chart Objects	Enables you to select the chart object you want to format or work with, such as plot area, chart area, legend, axis, or series.
	Format	Opens a Format dialog box tailored to the selected chart object.
	Import File	Opens the Import File dialog box from which you can import chart data from another file, such as an Excel worksheet, into your chart.
	View Datasheet	Displays the datasheet for this chart.
	By Row	Displays the datasheet row data as the data series (the default).
	By Column	Displays the datasheet column data as the data series.
	Data Table	Displays a table with all the datasheet data in your chart.
	Chart Type	Enables you to apply a new chart type from the palette that displays.
	Category Axis Gridlines	Displays category axis gridlines.
	Value Axis Gridlines	Displays value axis gridlines.
	Legend	Displays a legend for your chart.
	Drawing	Displays the Drawing toolbar.
	Fill Color	Enables you to apply fill color and fill effects to selected objects.

→ To learn more about object-formatting options in PowerPoint, **see** "Using the Format Dialog Box" in Chapter 14, "Creating and Formatting Objects."

If you don't see these menu and toolbar options, Microsoft Graph isn't active. To activate it, double-click the chart in PowerPoint and you'll then be able to view the Data and Chart menus and chart toolbar options.

Note

Many of these toolbar buttons act as a toggle. For example, clicking the View Datasheet button displays the datasheet if it's closed, but closes it if the datasheet already displays.

To determine what each object is in a chart you've created, place the mouse on that object or part of the chart and a chart tip displays its name. Figure 11.5 shows an example of a chart tip with the name and numeric value for a data series.

Figure 11.5
This chart tip lets you know the name of the chart object as well as its value.

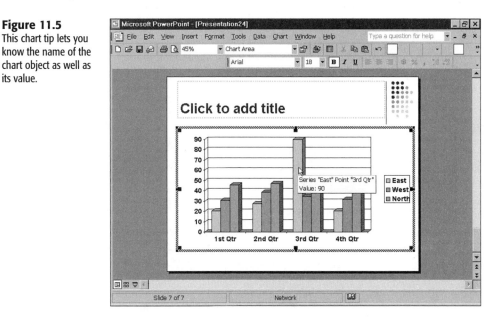

If the chart tip doesn't display, activate Microsoft Graph by double-clicking the chart, choose Tools, Options, and then verify that the Show Names and Show Values check boxes are selected on the Chart tab of the Graph Options dialog box (see Figure 11.6).

Figure 11.6
PowerPoint displays names and values in chart tips by default.

MODIFYING YOUR CHART

You can create a basic chart quickly in PowerPoint or you can make numerous enhancements and formatting changes. After you activate Microsoft Graph to create a chart, it's easiest to proceed in the following order:

1. Change the chart type if you don't want to use the default (a 3D column chart).
2. Edit the datasheet data (the text and numbers for your chart).
3. Enter a title for the chart slide.
4. Modify and format chart objects as needed.

Tip from
Patrice-Anne Rutledge

Before creating an actual chart, design a paper sketch of the chart you want to create. This can help you understand which chart type is right for your specific chart.

Note

For help in using Microsoft Graph, choose Help, Microsoft Graph Help. This opens the help file specific to this application.

SELECTING A CHART TYPE

PowerPoint offers numerous chart types and chart sub-types for almost every kind of graphic representation you could want to create. Sub-types offer variations on the basic chart type, such as 3D options. PowerPoint includes the following basic chart types:

- **Column** Creates vertical columns to compare the values of categories of data. Column, bar, and line charts work well if you want to compare values over a time period such as months or quarters. Figure 11.7 illustrates a sample column chart.
- **Bar** Creates horizontal bars to compare the values of categories of data.
- **Line** Creates a line with markers for each data value.
- **Pie** Creates a pie that analyzes percentages of a total number. Use a pie chart if you want to see the contribution of each item to a total. For example, you might want to see how much each line of items you sell contributed to total revenues for the year. Figure 11.8 displays an example of a pie chart.
- **XY (Scatter)** Creates a chart that compares sets of values.
- **Area** Creates a chart that displays the trend of values in a single solid area.
- **Doughnut** Creates a pie chart that can contain more than one series.
- **Radar** Creates a radar image with markers for each data point.
- **Surface** Creates a single 3D surface that analyzes trends in value.
- **Bubble** Creates a comparison of three sets of values displayed as bubbles.
- **Stock** Creates a chart that displays a stock's high, low, and close figures.

- **Cylinder**   Creates columns shaped like cylinders.
- **Cone**   Creates columns shaped like cones.
- **Pyramid**   Creates columns shaped like pyramids.

Figure 11.7
A column chart makes it easy to compare series of data.

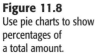

Figure 11.8
Use pie charts to show percentages of a total amount.

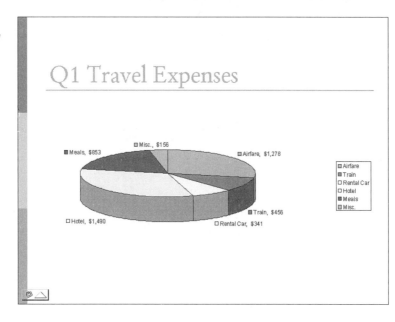

If you already know that you want to create a 3D clustered column chart, which is the PowerPoint default, you don't need to do anything to select a chart type. However, if you want to use a different chart type, you should select it before you enter any data or make any other modifications. There are two ways to change the chart type in PowerPoint. You can click the down arrow next to the Chart Type button on the Standard toolbar and select the chart type you want to apply from the palette that appears. Place the mouse over a specific chart type button to view a chart tip that tells you the name of the chart type. PowerPoint applies the chart type to your chart, which automatically reformats itself in the new type. Not all chart types are available through the Chart Type button, however. If you can't find what you need on the palette that appears, try the Chart Type dialog box (Chart, Chart Type).

In either case, if you don't like the new chart type you applied, click the Undo button on the Standard toolbar to return to your original selection.

To apply a new chart type using the Chart Type dialog box, follow these steps:

1. In Microsoft Graph, choose Chart, Chart Type from the menu. The Chart Type dialog box appears, as shown in Figure 11.9.
2. On the Standard Types tab, select the type of chart you want from the Chart Type list. A variety of sub-types appears in the Chart Sub-Type box.
3. Click the image of the sub-type you want. The text box below provides detailed information about this sub-type.
4. To preview what an actual chart of this type looks like, click the Press and Hold to View Sample button. A sample chart temporarily replaces the Chart Sub-Type box, as shown in Figure 11.10.
5. If you want to change this to your default, select the Set as Default Chart button.
6. If none of the chart types in the Standard Types tab suits your needs, click the Custom Types tab to view more options. Figure 11.11 illustrates this tab.
7. Click the Built-In option button to display PowerPoint's ready-made custom charts.

Figure 11.9
PowerPoint offers many different chart types.

Figure 11.10

You can preview changes before making them.

Figure 11.11

Custom charts provide variety and options.

Note

Custom charts include detailed formatting and some are customized specifically for a certain kind of output, such as onscreen presentations. The text box beneath the sample indicates these details.

Note

You can also add an active chart in your current presentation to the list of chart types. Simply select the User-Defined option button on the Custom Types tab, click the Add button, and enter details about this active chart to the Add Custom Chart Type dialog box that displays. Microsoft Graph adds this chart to its list of custom chart types.

8. Select the chart type you want to use from the Chart Type list. A sample displays in the Sample box.

9. Click OK to apply the chart type and return to your presentation.

ENTERING DATA IN THE DATASHEET

The default datasheet that opens when you first create a chart includes four columns and three rows. This is a common chart format—comparing specific categories over periods of time—but only one of the hundreds of possible formats. Figure 11.12 illustrates this datasheet.

Figure 11.12
Enter chart data in a datasheet, similar to an Excel worksheet.

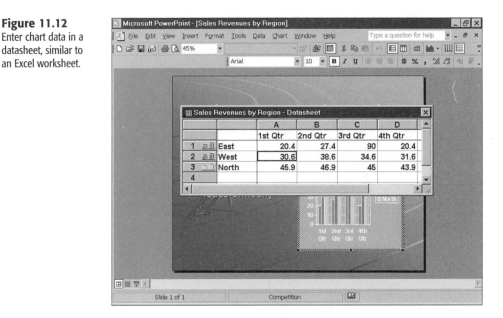

The first row and column of a datasheet serve as headers for the information in the datasheet. Therefore, the second row begins with the number 1 and the second column with the letter A. In this example, the columns display as the category axis, the rows display as the data series listed in the legend, and the cell data (A1:D3) represents the value axis.

Tip from
Patrice-Anne Rutledge

To reverse the chart and use the column data as the data series instead of the row data, click the By Columns button on the Standard toolbar. Microsoft Graph redesigns the chart based on this change. For example, if you changed the default chart to display as in columns, the quarters would appear in the legend and the locations in the category axis.

To modify the default data, you can simply overwrite the existing information in each cell.

⚠ **_Does your chart have extra spaces?_** _See the "Troubleshooting" section near the end of this chapter._

 If the data you need is already in an Excel spreadsheet, you can import directly from Excel without re-entering this information in the datasheet. To do so, click the Import File button on the Standard toolbar to open the Import File dialog box. Choose the Excel file you want to import and click Open. The Import Data Options dialog box guides you through this process. Note that you can import from Lotus 1-2-3 and text file formats as well.

INSERTING AND DELETING DATASHEET ROWS AND COLUMNS

To delete a row or column, place the cursor within the appropriate row or column and choose Edit, Delete from the menu. To remove the contents of a cell rather than the cell itself, choose Edit, Clear, Contents. Clearing the contents is best when you want to remove existing data and replace it with new data. If you no longer need the row or column, you should delete it. You can delete a row or column by selecting its heading and pressing the Delete key.

Note

You can also cut (Ctrl+X), copy (Ctrl+C), and paste (Ctrl+V) data in the datasheet by using keyboard commands or by choosing the appropriate buttons on the Standard toolbar.

To insert a new row, select the row below where you want to place the new row and choose Insert, Cells from the menu. Microsoft Graph inserts a new row directly above the selected row.

To insert a new column, select the column heading to the right of where you want to place the new column and choose Insert, Cells. Microsoft Graph inserts a new column directly to the left of the selected column.

If you want to insert a new cell, rather than a complete row or column, select the cell adjacent to where you want to insert; choose Insert, Cells; and choose either Shift Cells Right or Shift Cells Down in the Insert dialog box (see Figure 11.13).

Figure 11.13
Determine the direction to move the existing cells in the Insert dialog box.

PowerPoint inserts a new cell and shifts the row to the right or shifts the column down, depending on your selection. You can undo insertions and deletions by clicking the Undo button or pressing Ctrl+Z.

FORMATTING DATASHEET COLUMN WIDTH

To format the datasheet's column width, follow these steps:

1. Select the column heading of the column whose width you want to adjust.

2. Choose Format, Column Width. The Column Width dialog box appears, as shown in Figure 11.14.

3. Enter the number of spaces you want to include in the Column Width field. To adjust to the standard width, select the Use Standard Width check box.

4. Click the Best Fit button to have the columns adjust automatically based on the existing data.

5. Click OK to return to the datasheet.

Figure 11.14
You can customize the width of a datasheet column.

FORMATTING DATASHEET NUMBERS

You can format the text and numbers in your datasheet if you want. To format numerical data, select the cell or cells you want to format and choose Format, Number. The Format Number dialog box appears, as shown in Figure 11.15.

Figure 11.15
Customize the way numbers appear in this dialog box.

Select the type of number format you want from the Category list, such as date, time, or currency format. Based on your category selection, the right side of the dialog box offers additional formatting options related to the category.

For example, if you choose Currency, the right side of the dialog box lets you choose the currency symbol such as the dollar, pound, or yen. Several of the numeric categories also let you choose the number of decimal places you want to include.

Click OK to accept the formatting changes and to update your chart.

 Do your datasheet numbers display in an exponential format? *See the "Troubleshooting" section near the end of the chapter.*

INCLUDING AND EXCLUDING ROWS AND COLUMNS

You can include rows and columns in your datasheet, but temporarily hide them in your presentation. To do that, select the column or row that you want to hide, and choose Data, Exclude Row/Col. The row or column appears shaded in your datasheet and temporarily disappears from your presentation. Figure 11.16 shows an example of a hidden column in a datasheet.

To include this information again, choose Data, Include Row/Col.

Figure 11.16
This hidden column will temporarily be removed from the chart.

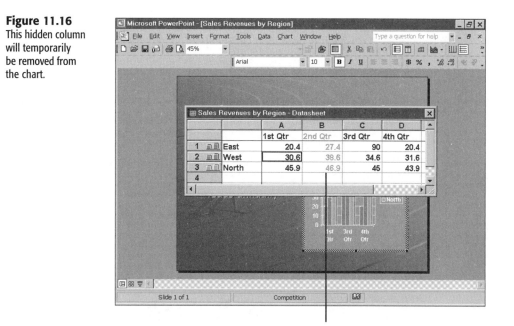

Hidden column

Tip from
Patrice-Anne Rutledge

You can also double-click the row or column head to include or exclude the rows. In this case, the action serves as a toggle.

RETURNING TO THE PRESENTATION FROM THE DATASHEET

When you finish formatting and modifying the datasheet, you can close it and return to the presentation itself by clicking the View Datasheet button on the Standard toolbar. Or you can return to working on the presentation while the datasheet remains open by clicking on any section of the presentation.

To open the datasheet after closing, click the View Datasheet button again.

FORMATTING A CHART

You can set overall chart options or format specific objects in a chart. Microsoft Graph offers detailed precision in chart creation and the opportunity to make numerous formatting changes. Before making major changes to the chart default, be sure to carefully consider your reason for customizing. Different isn't always better, unless it adds value or clarity to your chart.

Note

If the chart isn't active, you won't see the chart menu and toolbar options. Double-click the chart to select it and display the appropriate options.

SETTING OVERALL CHART OPTIONS

You can set overall chart options for the chart type you selected in the Chart Options dialog box. In Microsoft Graph, choose Chart, Chart Options to display this dialog box, shown in Figure 11.17.

We'll use the clustered 3D columnar chart type as an example as we explore the tabs of this dialog box. Remember, however, that if you select a different chart type (such as a pie), the options and tabs may differ slightly.

Make any necessary changes within the tabs of this dialog box, and then click OK to apply them to your presentation.

Figure 11.17
Set a variety of chart-formatting options in this dialog box.

ENTERING CHART TITLES

On the Titles tab, you can enter titles for the overall chart and the available axes such as category, value, or series. The sample to the right previews these changes in your chart.

Caution

The chart title isn't the same as a slide title. If you create a chart title, your chart will have two separate titles—one for the slide and one for the chart.

FORMATTING AXES

On the Axes tab, shown in Figure 11.18, you can choose whether or not to display category, series, and value axes. If a particular axis isn't available, you won't be able to choose it. In this example, the category axis displays the data you entered in the first row of cells in your datasheet. The value axis displays a numerical series based on the values you entered in the datasheet.

Figure 11.18
Specify whether or not to display a particular axis.

FORMATTING GRIDLINES

In the Gridlines tab (see Figure 11.19), you can choose whether or not to display major and minor gridlines for all available axes.

Figure 11.19
Major gridlines, selected by default, can make values easier to read.

Note

Pie and doughnut charts don't have gridlines.

DISPLAYING A LEGEND

On the Legend tab, shown in Figure 11.20, you can choose to display a legend by selecting the Show Legend check box.

Placement options include placing your legend at the bottom, corner, top, right, or left of your chart.

Figure 11.20
A legend makes a chart easier to understand.

Note

After you place a legend on your chart, you can select it and drag it with the mouse to a new location.

DISPLAYING DATA LABELS

A data label makes data in your chart easier to identify. You can display a value, percent, text label, text label and percent, a bubble size, or no label at all. Figure 11.21 shows the Data Labels tab.

Figure 11.21
Data labels are optional means of identifying chart information.

Note

Depending on the chart type you select, not all data label options are available.

If you do choose to display a data label, the Legend Key check box appears. Check this box if you want to display a color-coded box next to the data label to associate it with the legend.

DISPLAYING A DATA TABLE

If you want to include a table with all your datasheet data in your chart, you can choose the Show Data Table check box in the Data Table tab (see Figure 11.22).

Figure 11.22
If your chart contains complex numerical data, a data table can make this information more meaningful.

If you do select this option, you also have the choice to Show Legend Keys if you want to display a color-coded box in the table columns to associate them with the legend.

FORMATTING CHART OBJECTS

You can format individual chart objects, such as the chart area, axes, series, legend, and gridlines. To format a specific chart object, select it from the Chart Objects drop-down list on the Standard toolbar, and then click the Format button to the right of the drop-down list. A Format dialog box customized for the type of object you select appears. For example, you might see the Format Axis dialog box or the Format Data Series dialog box, depending on the selected chart object. If the Format button isn't available, no formatting options exist for the selected chart object.

You can modify a multitude of formatting options from the Format dialog box, including pattern, font, placement, scale, alignment, and shape. Remember, though, that numerous changes don't always enhance a chart and you might want to make only a small number of formatting enhancements on a regular basis.

→ To learn more about the available options in this dialog box, **see** "Using the Format Dialog Box" in Chapter 14.

Some things you may want to consider changing include the following:

- Apply a different color to the data series fill areas. To do this, select the data series you want to modify from the Chart Objects drop-down list and click the Format button. Figure 11.23 illustrates the Format Data Series dialog box.

PART
IV

CH

11

Figure 11.23
Change fill color in
this dialog box.

Choose a new color from the Area group box and click OK. PowerPoint updates the color in the presentation.

■ Increase or decrease font size to make text more readable or to make it fit a specific area. For example, to change the font size of the legend, select the legend in the Chart Objects drop-down list and click the Format Legend button to display the dialog box of the same name (see Figure 11.24).

Figure 11.24
Adjusting font size is a
common formatting
change.

From the Font tab, you can increase or decrease the font size as needed.

■ Adjust the value axis scale. To do this, select the value axis from the Chart Objects drop-down list and click the Format Axis button. Figure 11.25 shows the Scale tab in the Format Axis dialog box.

Figure 11.25
You can adjust the axes and gridlines in the Format Axis dialog box.

You can change the minimum and maximum values or the major and minor gridline units on the Scale tab. For example, you could change the minimum value from 0 to 100 if all the values in your chart are more than 100 and you want to see the variations in the existing values more clearly. PowerPoint updates the presentation, making the differences between the three data series much more apparent.

FORMATTING 3D VIEW

If you choose a 3D chart type, you can format 3D viewing options such as elevation, rotation, height, and perspective. Table 11.3 explains each of these options.

TABLE 11.3   3D VIEW OPTIONS

3D View Option	Description
Elevation	Enables you to control the elevation level from which you view the chart. The range is from –90° to 90° with a default of 15°.
Rotation	Enables you to control the plot area rotation around a vertical axis. The default rotation is 20° with a possible range of 0° to 360°. On bar charts, the range is up to only 44°. Be careful not to overdo rotation, however. A 90° rotation on a typical column chart will yield some rather unreadable results, for example.
Height	Enables you to control the height of the value axis as a percentage of the length of the category axis. A height of 150% would make the chart height one and a half times the length of the category axis.
Perspective	Enables you to control the chart depth view in degrees. With a default of 30°, the range is from 0° to 100° and measures the ratio of the chart front to back. This option is unavailable when the Right Angle Axes check box is selected or when the chart type is a bar.

To format these options, follow these steps:

1. In Microsoft Graph, choose Chart, 3-D View to open the 3-D View dialog box, as shown in Figure 11.26.

Figure 11.26
Modify the way your chart displays 3D objects in this dialog box.

> **Caution**
>
> Again, the default settings for 3D options are designed to work with this chart. Carefully consider any changes you make. Major modifications to a chart's elevation, rotation, height, or perspective can make it unreadable.

→ To learn more about 3D, **see** "Adding Shadow and 3D Effects" in Chapter 14.

2. Enter a new elevation in the Elevation field or click the up and down arrow buttons above this field to adjust elevation. The box to the right displays an example of what the selected change looks like.

3. Enter a new rotation or click the left and right arrow buttons to the right of the field to change the rotation. The sample box previews this change.

4. Click the Auto Scaling check box to automatically scale the chart to fit the slide.

5. If you remove the check mark from the Auto Scaling check box, the Height field appears. In it, you can set height as a specific percentage of the base.

6. If you remove the check mark from the Right Angle Axes check box, the Perspective field appears. Set the perspective manually or use the buttons to modify perspective.

7. Click the Apply button to view the effects of potential changes to chart.

8. Click the Default button to set the changes you've made as your new default.

9. Click OK to apply the changes and return to your presentation.

Tip from
Patrice-Anne Rutledge

If you make a mistake, click Close to exit the dialog box without saving changes.

ADDING A TRENDLINE

You can display a trendline in unstacked area, bar, column, line, stock, XY (scatter), and bubble charts that don't have a 3D effect. A *trendline* creates a forecast of future trends based on existing data. For example, you can use a trendline to predict future revenues based on existing revenue data in a chart. This is also referred to as *regression analysis*.

You can use trendlines to make basic forecasts, but a solid understanding of regression analysis and statistics is necessary to make the best use of this feature. To create a trendline, follow these steps:

1. Choose Chart, Add Trendline to open the Add Trendline dialog box, shown in Figure 11.27.

Figure 11.27
Predict future values by creating a trendline.

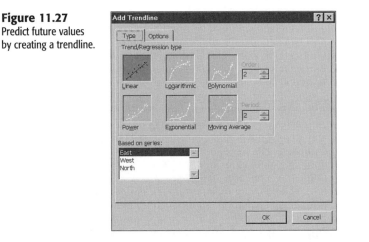

⚡ **Can't access the Add Trendline menu option?** See the "Troubleshooting" section near the end of this chapter.

2. Choose the Trend/Regression Type, such as Linear or Moving Average, from the group box.

3. Select the data series on which you want to base the trend from the Based on Series list.

4. Click the Options tab for more options, shown in Figure 11.28.

5. You can enter your own custom name for the trendline or accept the default. The default uses the type of trendline you selected in the Type tab, followed by the series name in parentheses.

6. Indicate how many periods you want to forecast either forward or backward. For example, if your chart displays data for four quarters and you choose to forecast four periods forward, PowerPoint displays trends for the next full year in quarterly increments.

7. Click OK to apply the trendline.

PART
IV

CH
11

Figure 11.28
Specify the period
of time you want
to forecast.

Figure 11.29 shows a sample trendline forecasting sales for the next year for a specific region based on its actual data for the current year.

Figure 11.29
This chart illustrates
both current values
and future predictions.

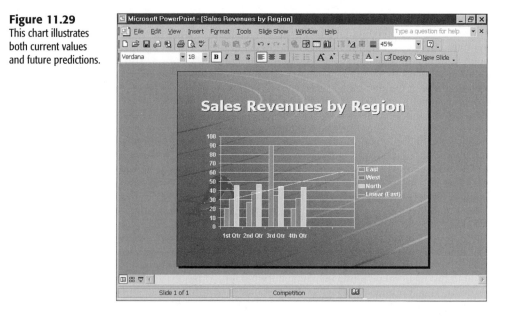

TROUBLESHOOTING

LOCATING MISSING MENUS AND TOOLBARS

I can't find the menus or toolbar buttons you mention.

Be sure that Microsoft Graph is active if the text mentions that this menu or toolbar button is part of that application. If you're in PowerPoint, the Graph options won't display. To activate Microsoft Graph, double-click your chart and it appears within PowerPoint.

RESOLVING DATASHEET FORMAT PROBLEMS

My datasheet numbers display in exponential formatting.

You need to apply a formatting category other than the default General formatting if your numbers exceed 11 characters. To do so, choose Format, Number from within Microsoft Graph and change to a Category such as Number or Currency.

FINDING THE ADD TRENDLINE MENU OPTION

I can't see the Add Trendline option from the Chart menu.

You can only create a trendline with unstacked area, bar, column, line, stock, XY (scatter), and bubble charts that don't have a 3D effect. Otherwise, this menu option won't be available.

REMOVING EMPTY SPACES

My chart has empty spaces where there should be a data series.

If you don't need one of the existing datasheet rows or columns, you need to remove it entirely from the datasheet, not just the contents. Otherwise, it can display as an empty space on your chart and disrupt formatting. If a series you entered is missing, verify that none of your columns or rows is hidden. To include a hidden row/column, choose Data, Include Row/Col from within Microsoft Graph.

DESIGN CORNER: USING CHART FORMATTING OPTIONS

PowerPoint, in combination with Microsoft Graph, offers numerous chart-formatting options to help you create visually appealing and memorable charts. This example shows how even minor changes can enhance your chart.

For example, you could create a basic column chart by choosing the Title and Chart layout from the Slide Layout task pane (see the "Before" figure). To liven up the chart (see the "After" figure), follow these steps using the techniques you learned in this chapter:

1. With your chart active, choose Chart, Chart Options to open the Chart Options dialog box.
2. On the Titles tab, enter a title for your chart.
3. On the Legend tab, place your legend on the bottom.
4. Click on the down arrow to the right of the Chart Type button on the Standard toolbar to display a palette of options.
5. Click on the Bar Chart button to change to a bar chart format (pause the mouse pointer over the buttons to identify the right button).

In only a couple minutes, you enlivened your chart and made its format better suit your needs.

BEFORE

Figure 11.30

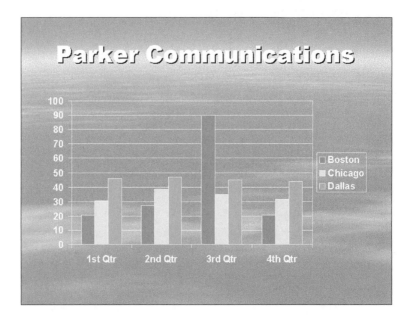

AFTER

Added chart title

Figure 11.31

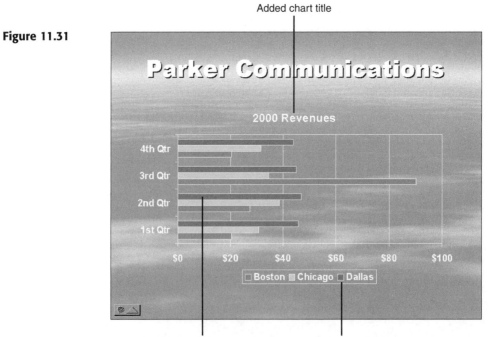

Changed chart type   Moved legend to bottom

CHAPTER 12

WORKING WITH DIAGRAMS AND ORGANIZATION CHARTS

In this chapter

UNDERSTANDING DIAGRAMS AND ORGANIZATION CHARTS

In PowerPoint you can insert detailed diagrams and organization (org) charts directly in your presentations. PowerPoint's new diagram functionality is just one of several ways to insert dynamic, conceptual illustrations in a slide. Using diagram options such as Cycle, Radial, Pyramid, Venn, and Target, you can visually represent a variety of concepts and ideas—and then make the diagrams match the color scheme and look of your overall presentation. And the revised org chart functionality enables you to display a hierarchical structure of your organization—and more. Although org chart terminology—subordinate, co-worker, and so forth—is directed to a corporate environment, you can use an org chart anywhere you need to set up a hierarchy of people. For example, an org chart could describe a volunteer committee, school organization, club, or not-for-profit group. You can even use org charts to organize ideas and projects, not just people.

GETTING STARTED WITH DIAGRAMS AND ORGANIZATION CHARTS

The fastest way to add a diagram or organization chart to your PowerPoint presentation is to apply a slide layout that contains one. To do so, click the New Slide button on the Formatting toolbar and then choose an appropriate layout from the Slide Layout task pane. The next step varies, depending on the slide layout you choose.

If you choose any of the layouts in the Content Layouts or Text and Content Layouts sections, click the Insert Diagram or Organization Chart button on the content palette that displays to open the Diagram Gallery (see Figure 12.1).

If you choose the Title and Diagram or Organization Chart layout in the Other Layouts section, double-click the placeholder to open the Diagram Gallery. Figure 12.2 shows a sample slide with this placeholder. If you want to create a slide with a diagram or org chart and no other content, choose this slide layout.

→ To learn more about how slide layouts affect your presentation, **see** "Understanding Slide Layouts" in Chapter 2, "Creating a Basic Presentation."

Alternatively, you can also insert a diagram or org chart by clicking the Insert Diagram or Organization Chart button on the Drawing toolbar.

Figure 12.3 illustrates the Diagram Gallery, which offers not only an org chart option, but Cycle, Radial, Pyramid, Venn, and Target diagram options as well. If you're unsure of the best use of any of these diagram options, single-click its image on the Diagram Gallery and explanatory text will appear below.

Figure 12.1
Click the Insert Diagram or Organization Chart button to get started.

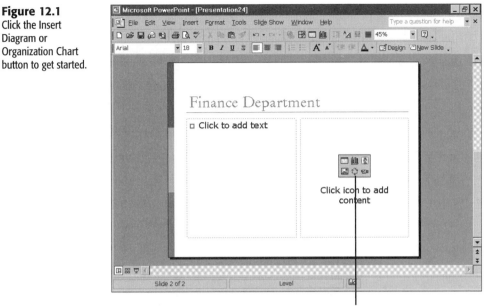

Insert Diagram or Organization Chart button

Figure 12.2
You can also start by double-clicking a placeholder.

Double-click the placeholder to open the Diagram Gallery.

Organization Chart

Figure 12.3
The Diagram Gallery enables you to add a variety of diagrams and an org chart to your presentation.

Cycle Diagram

Radial Diagram

Target Diagram

Venn Diagram

Pyramid Diagram

Figures 12.4 and 12.5 illustrate examples of each of these diagrams or charts.

Cycle diagram

Figure 12.4
There are a variety of ways to illustrate information in PowerPoint.

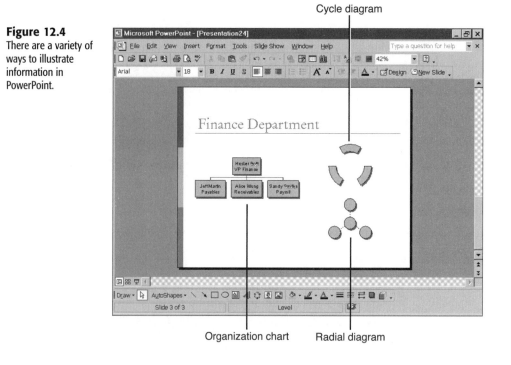

Organization chart   Radial diagram

Venn diagram

Figure 12.5
Additional diagram
options are also
available.

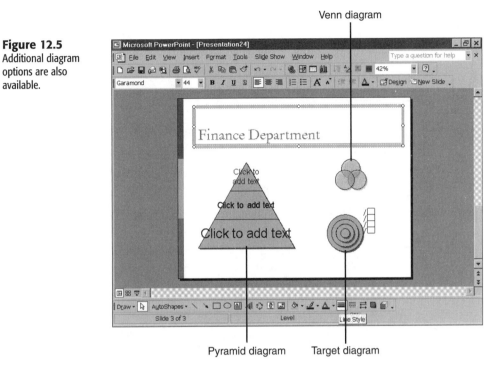

Pyramid diagram   Target diagram

ADDING A DIAGRAM TO YOUR PRESENTATION

To add a diagram, choose one of the five diagram styles in the Diagram Gallery and click
OK. If you find that the diagram type doesn't suit your needs, you can always change it
later.

 Can't find the right diagram? See the "Troubleshooting" section near the end of this chapter.

PART
IV
CH
12

Note

Remember that diagrams are only one way to visually present information in
PowerPoint. You can also create flowcharts and other illustrations, for example, to convey similar information using PowerPoint's AutoShape functionality.

→ To learn how to use AutoShapes to create flowcharts or other diagrams, **see** "Adding AutoShapes" in
Chapter 14, "Creating and Formatting Objects."

PowerPoint inserts the diagram in your presentation and opens the Diagram and Drawing
toolbars. The Diagram toolbar includes the following options:

- ⚬ Insert Shape **Insert Shape** Inserts an additional shape in your diagram. For example, if you have a pyramid diagram with four levels, clicking Insert Shape would add a
  fifth level.

→ For more information on using the Drawing toolbar, **see** "Using the Drawing Toolbar to Create Objects" in Chapter 14.

- **Move Shape Backward**   Moves the selected shape backward.

- **Move Shape Forward**   Moves the selected shape forward.

- **Reverse Diagram**   Reverses the positioning of the selected diagram.

- **Layout**   Displays a menu with the following options:
  - **Fit Diagram to Contents**   Resizes the diagram to fit the allotted space.
  - **Expand Diagram**   Expands a smaller diagram to fit the allotted space.
  - **Scale Diagram**   Rescales the diagram proportionally to the allotted space.
  - **AutoLayout**   Applies an AutoLayout.

- **AutoFormat**   Opens the Diagram Style Gallery where you can choose from many different styles for your selected diagram type. The box to the right previews the style you select. Click Apply when you find the style that suits your presentation. Figure 12.6 illustrates this style gallery.

Figure 12.6
Choose from a variety of style options for your diagram.

The Diagram Style Gallery is a useful tool that provides a lot of flexibility and creativity in terms of style options. Be sure, however, that your choice still makes your diagram readable and matches your overall presentation tone before choosing something too unique.

- **Change To**   Displays a menu of other diagram styles so you can quickly modify your diagram if your original choice (which is dimmed on the menu) wasn't quite right. Options include Cycle, Radial, Pyramid, Venn, and Target.

ADDING TEXT TO YOUR DIAGRAM

You can add text to radial, pyramid, and venn diagrams by clicking the Click to Add Text placeholder or by right-clicking and choosing Edit Text from the context-sensitive menu. Clicking this placeholder removes the temporary text and inserts the cursor in a text box where you can type your text. You can format the text in this box like any other text, applying bolding, a new font, and so forth.

Even if you chose a diagram that doesn't support adding text in this manner, you can add text in the form of a text box. To add text in the form of a text box, click the Text Box button on the Drawing toolbar to place a text box.

→ For more information on using the Drawing toolbar and creating a text box, **see** "Using the Drawing Toolbar to Create Objects" in Chapter 14.

FORMATTING YOUR DIAGRAM

You can format a diagram just as you format any other PowerPoint object. For example, you can reposition your diagram, change its colors, modify fonts, and so on. Formatting your diagram can not only make it more visually appealing, but also make it better match the design scheme of your overall presentation. You'll primarily handle formatting tasks in the Format dialog box or by using the Drawing toolbar.

→ For more information about the Format dialog box and the Drawing toolbar, **see** Chapter 14.

You can also animate a diagram to add additional emphasis during a presentation. For example, you could animate a pyramid diagram by having each level of the pyramid display one at time on your slide. Using the Custom Animation task pane, you can easily apply sophisticated animations like this to the parts of your diagrams.

→ To learn more about animating diagrams, **see** Chapter 15, "Working with Animation."

PART

IV

CH

12

DELETING A DIAGRAM

To delete a diagram, select it and press the Delete key. Either the content palette or placeholder appears, depending on which slide layout you chose. If you want to create another diagram, you can start over from here, accessing the Diagram Gallery by clicking the palette or placeholder. If you want to delete the diagram entirely, select the frame around the palette or placeholder and press the Delete key again.

ADDING AN ORGANIZATION CHART TO YOUR PRESENTATION

To add an organization chart, choose the Organization Chart option in the Diagram Gallery and click OK.

Tip from
Patrice-Anne
Rutledge

> You should design your org chart on paper first, particularly if you're not familiar with this application. This enables you to focus on creating the chart rather than on content.

PowerPoint inserts the org chart in your presentation and opens the Organization Chart and Drawing toolbars. The button image for each option on these toolbars shows you what its layout style looks like. The Organization Chart toolbar includes the following options:

- **Insert Shape** Displays a menu of types of boxes to insert when you click the down arrow to the right of this button. Choices include Subordinate, Co-worker, and Assistant. If you're familiar with Microsoft Organization Chart 2.0, which worked with PowerPoint 2000, this functions a little differently. Choosing a shape from this menu directly inserts a new shape related to the currently selected shape.

Caution

> If you've selected the top-level position in the organization, you won't be able to add a co-worker and this option will appear dimmed.

- **Layout** Displays a menu of layout options, including the following:
  - Standard
  - Both Hanging
  - Left Hanging
  - Right Hanging
  - Fit Organization Chart to Contents
  - Expand Organization Chart
  - Scale Organization Chart
  - AutoLayout
- **Select** Enables you to select a specific part of your org chart so that you can format that selection. Options include Level, Branch, All Assistants, and All Connecting Lines.
- **AutoFormat** Opens the Organization Chart Style Gallery where you can choose from a variety of different styles for your selected org chart type. The box to the right previews the style you select. Click Apply when you find the style that suits your presentation. Figure 12.7 illustrates the Organization Chart Style Gallery.

Caution

> The Organization Chart Style Gallery is a useful tool that provides a lot of flexibility and creativity in terms of style options. Be sure, however, that your choice still makes your chart readable and matches your overall presentation tone before choosing something too different.

Figure 12.7
Choose from a variety
of style options for
your org chart.

ADDING TEXT TO YOUR ORGANIZATION CHART

You can add text to your org chart by clicking the Click to Add Text placeholder that
appears in the shapes that comprise your chart. Depending on the size of the shape, this
placeholder may not be visible; if not, just click in the shape itself. Enter the desired text in
the shape; it automatically resizes if what you enter is larger than the existing shape. You
can format org chart text just as you would any other text, by changing fonts, applying bold
and italics, resizing it, and so on.

➔ For a refresher of text formatting techniques, **see** Chapter 3, "Working with Text."

FORMATTING YOUR ORGANIZATION CHART

You can format an org chart just as you format any other PowerPoint object. For example,
you can reposition it, change its colors, modify line width, and so on. You'll primarily do
this in the Format dialog box (right-click and choose Format AutoShape from the menu) or
using the Drawing toolbar.

➔ For more information about the Format dialog box and the Drawing toolbar, **see** Chapter 14.

You can also animate your org chart to provide additional emphasis during a presentation.

➔ To learn more about animating org charts, **see** Chapter 15.

> **Caution**
>
> Remember to consider readability and visual clarity when you modify an organization
> chart's defaults. Some formatting can enhance a chart's appearance, but too much for-
> matting can make it confusing or worse—unreadable.

DELETING AN ORGANIZATION CHART

To delete an org chart, select it and press the Delete key. Either the content palette or
placeholder appears, depending on which slide layout you chose. If you want to create
another chart, you can start over again from here, accessing the Diagram Gallery by

PART
IV
CH
12

clicking the palette or placeholder. If you want to delete the chart entirely, select the frame around the palette or placeholder and press the Delete key again.

TROUBLESHOOTING

FIXING A PROBLEM ORG CHART

I tried creating an org chart for the first time and it's a real mess. Do I have to delete the entire slide?

No, just delete the org chart itself and PowerPoint will redisplay either the placeholder or content palette (depending on which layout you chose). From there, you can begin again.

EXPANDING DIAGRAM CHOICES

I can't create the diagram I want with the Diagram Gallery choices.

Remember that you can apply additional style options using the Diagram Style Gallery. If even those options aren't enough, you can create a diagram yourself from the Drawing toolbar by adding an AutoShape or manually designing an illustration using PowerPoint's drawing tools. As a last resort, create your diagram in another program (such as Visio or Illustrator) and then insert it.

DESIGN CORNER: ENLIVENING YOUR ORGANIZATION CHARTS

You can use PowerPoint's organization chart functionality to create a variety of hierarchical charts and then use the style gallery and other formatting features to enliven your chart and make it coordinate with the rest of your presentation. For example, let's say you created a basic org chart for your department using the default options, showing you as the department manager with an assistant and three staffers reporting to you. It conveys the basic information you want, but lacks pizzazz (see Figure 12.8). You decide that you want to apply a different style, bold the names and titles to make them easier to read, and increase the font size in the shape that contains your name and title (you are the boss, after all). To quickly do this, follow these steps:

1. Click the AutoFormat button on the Organization Chart toolbar to open the Organization Chart Style Gallery.

2. Select the style you prefer (such as Brackets) and click Apply.

3. Click and drag the mouse to form a dotted rectangle surrounding your entire org chart to select it.

4. Click the Bold button on the Formatting toolbar to bold all org chart text.

5. Select the top-level shape; click the Increase Font Size button on the Formatting toolbar to increase the font size of this org chart shape. Figure 12.9 illustrates the improved org chart. If you want, you can make other changes as well—revising font colors, italicizing job titles, modifying the options in the Format Organization Chart dialog box (right-click and choose Format Organization Chart to open), and so forth. There are a multitude of options—just don't go overboard and make your org chart harder to read rather than easier to read.

BEFORE

Figure 12.8

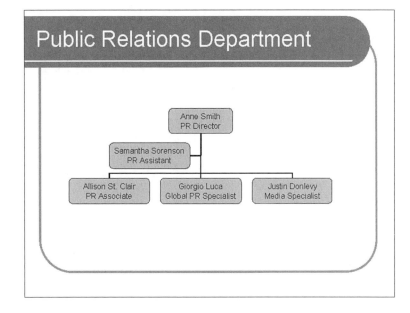

AFTER

Figure 12.9

Increased font size   Bolded text

New diagram style

CHAPTER 13

WORKING WITH MEDIA CLIPS AND THE CLIP ORGANIZER

In this chapter

EXPLORING CLIP ART, PICTURES, MOVIES, AND SOUND

Clip art, pictures, movies, and sounds can add pizzazz and polish to your PowerPoint presentations, creating a full multimedia effect. You can insert picture, sound, or video clips from a variety of sources—clips from the Microsoft Clip Organizer, clips you download from the Microsoft Web site, or your own pictures, sounds, and videos.

UNDERSTANDING CLIP ART

Office XP offers thousands of clip art images that you can use to enliven your presentations. Microsoft's Web site includes even more images. After you insert clip art into your presentation, you can reformat, recolor, and redesign it to suit your needs.

Office XP includes clip art images in the following formats:

- Windows Metafile (WMF)
- Computer Graphics Metafile (CGM)
- Graphics Interchange Format (GIF)
- Joint Photographic Experts Groups (JPEG)

You can also add images in the Portable Network Graphics (PNG) and Bitmap (BMP) formats.

UNDERSTANDING PICTURES

Pictures are similar to clip art. In PowerPoint, pictures refer to images you insert from your own files, or scan in through a scanner or digital camera. They can be drawn images or actual photographs.

UNDERSTANDING SOUND AND VIDEO FILES

PowerPoint includes the capability to insert media clips (sound and video files) into your presentations. To use these features, you need to have a sound card, microphone, and speakers installed on your computer.

Media clips work in much the same way as clip art illustrations and photographs, and are also available through the Microsoft Clip Organizer. Common media clip file formats include the following:

- **MIDI**   Musical Instrument Digital Interface.
- **WAV**   Microsoft Windows audio format.
- **MPEG**   A standard video format.
- **AVI**   Microsoft Windows video format.
- **GIF**   Graphical Interchange Format. Animated GIFs (a series of GIF images that appear animated) are stored with other video files.

Media clips can greatly enhance the multimedia effect of your presentation, but remember that, as with clip art and other images, overuse of media clips can clutter a presentation.

→ To learn more about ways to include multimedia content in your presentations, **see** "Incorporating Multimedia" in Chapter 26, "Exploring Technicalities and Techniques."

A PowerPoint presentation can play a clip automatically during a slideshow, or you can customize the clip to play only by a mouse action. Other multimedia options include recording your own sounds, or playing a CD track as a slideshow background.

INSERTING CLIPS

There are several ways to add clips such as clip art, pictures, photographs, movies, and sound to your PowerPoint presentations. The method you choose depends on where the clip is located (in the Clip Organizer or only on your computer, for example), how you prefer to use PowerPoint, and whether or not you know exactly what you want to insert.

INSERTING CLIP ART

To insert clip art, you can do any of the following:

■ From the Slide Layout task pane, choose any of the content layouts and click the Insert Clip Art button from the content palette. The Select Picture dialog box opens (see Figure 13.1), displaying clips from the Clip Organizer.

Figure 13.1
Inserting a clip from a slide layout is just one option.

PART
IV

CH

13

→ For details on choosing and using layouts, **see** "Understanding Slide Layouts" in Chapter 2, "Creating a Basic Presentation."

Select the picture you want to insert and click OK to insert it on your slide. If you want to search for a specific image, enter its keyword in the Search Text field and then click Search.

> **Note**
>
> If you want to import a clip, click the Import button. This opens the Add Clips to Organizer dialog box where you can choose the clip you want to import.

- From the Slide Layout task pane, choose either the Title, Clip Art, and Text or Title, Text, and Clip Art layout, and double-click the clip art placeholder to open the Select Picture dialog box.
- Choose Insert, Picture, Clip Art to open the Insert Clip Art task pane, shown in Figure 13.2.

Figure 13.2
Search for clip art by keyword.

Search by keyword for the type of clip art you need, and select it. Click the down arrow to the right of the thumbnail and then choose Insert. The clip will be inserted on your slide.

> **Note**
>
> You can also drag your selected picture from the task pane to the slide.

The first time you open the Insert Clip Art task pane, the Add Clips to Organizer dialog box appears. Use this dialog box to have PowerPoint automatically organize your clips for you.

→ To learn more about using the Add Clips to Organizer dialog box, **see** "Opening the Clip Organizer" in this chapter.

■ Choose Insert, Picture, Clip Art to open the Insert Clip Art task pane. Click the Clip Organizer link to open the Microsoft Clip Organizer from which you can view clip art collections. Figure 13.3 illustrates the Clip Organizer.

Figure 13.3
Browsing the collections in the Clip Organizer is another way to locate clip art.

Within the Clip Organizer, you can either copy and paste a clip into your PowerPoint presentation, or drag and drop it if your windows are arranged to accommodate this.

■ Click the Insert Clip Art button on the Drawing toolbar to open the Insert Clip Art task pane. From here, you can either use the task pane's search functionality to search for clip art, or click the Clip Organizer link to go directly to the gallery.

INSERTING PICTURES

To insert a picture on a slide, do any of the following:

■ From the Slide Layout task pane, choose any of the content layouts and click the Insert Picture button from the content palette. The Insert Picture dialog box opens (see Figure 13.4), which is similar to the Open dialog box.

→ To learn more about the advanced features of the Open dialog box that are shared with the Insert Picture dialog box, **see** "Exploring the Open Dialog Box" in Chapter 2.

Select the picture you want to insert and click Insert to insert it on your slide.

■ Choose Insert, Picture, From File to open the Insert Picture dialog box.

■ Choose Insert, Picture, From Scanner or Camera to open the Insert Picture from Scanner or Camera dialog box.

Figure 13.4
Locate and insert a
picture from this
dialog box.

→ To learn more about inserting pictures from scanners or cameras, **see** "Adding Clips from a Scanner or Camera" in this chapter.

■ Click the Insert Picture button on the Drawing toolbar to open the Insert Picture dialog box.

INSERTING SOUNDS OR MOVIES

To insert a media clip (sound or movie file) to your presentation, do any one of the following:

■ From the Slide Layout task pane, choose any of the content layouts and click the Insert Media Clip button from the content palette. The Select Media Clip dialog box opens, displaying available clips from the Clip Organizer. This dialog box is nearly identical to the Select Picture dialog box; simply choose the clip you want to insert and click OK.

A message box asks if you want to play the file automatically in the slideshow. Click Yes if you do. Otherwise, you need to click the file to play it.

Note

To change how the clip is played, you can choose Slide Show, Action Settings to specify mouse click and mouse over effects. You can set additional play options on the Custom Animation task pane. Access this task pane by choosing Slide Show, Custom Animation.

→ For details on using action settings to animate your presentation, **see** "Using Action Settings" in Chapter 15, "Working with Animation."

→ To learn about the advanced options in the Custom Animation dialog box, **see** "Creating Custom Animations" in Chapter 15.

■ From the Slide Layout task pane, choose either the Title, Media Clip, and Text or Title, Text, and Media Clip layout, and double-click the media clip placeholder to open the Select Media Clip dialog box.

- Choose Insert, Movies and Sounds, Movie from Clip Organizer or Sound from Clip Organizer. The Insert Clip Art task pane opens; select one of the options in the task pane or click the Clip Organizer link to open the Clip Organizer.

- Choose Insert, Movies and Sounds, Movie from File or Sound from File. Depending on your selection, either the Insert Movie or Insert Sound dialog box opens, as shown in Figure 13.5.

Figure 13.5
You can insert your own movie or sound file and have it play automatically.

Select the sound or movie you want to insert and click OK. A dialog box asks if you want the clip to play automatically when you display the slide. Click Yes if you want to do this. Otherwise, you need to click the clip to play it.

The clip appears as an icon on your slide. You can move this icon to another part of the slide if you want to.

- Choose Insert, Movies and Sound, Record Sound to open the Record Sound dialog box, from which you can record your own sound.

→ To learn how to record your own sound file, **see** "Recording Sound Files" in this chapter.

- Choose Insert, Movies and Sound, Play CD Audio Track to open the Movie and Sound Options dialog box, where you can specify a CD audio track to play during your presentation.

→ For details on inserting CD audio tracks, **see** "Playing a CD Audio Track" in this chapter.

PART

IV

CH

13

Note

You can also insert a sound or video file by choosing Insert, Object and choosing the appropriate object from the Insert Object dialog box. This uses the Windows Media Player to play the clip rather than the PowerPoint Player. In general, use this method of inserting a media clip only when PowerPoint doesn't support the clip format you want.

RECORDING SOUND FILES

You can record your own sound clips to insert in your PowerPoint presentation. You need to have a microphone and sound card to do this.

Tip from
Patrice-Anne Rutledge

In addition to adding a sound clip to a single slide, you can record a narration for your entire presentation by choosing Slide Show, Record Narration. Narrating your presentation is particularly effective if you're planning to publish to the Web or create a self-running slideshow (such as for a trade show).

→ To learn how to narrate your presentations, **see** "Recording a Voice Narration" in Chapter 9, "Presenting a Slideshow."

To record a sound, follow these steps:

1. Choose Insert, Movies and Sound, Record Sound to open the Record Sound dialog box, which appears in Figure 13.6.

Figure 13.6
Record a sound to play with a particular slide.

Stop button   Record button
Play button

2. Enter a description for this sound in the Name field.
3. Click the Record button to begin recording your sound.
4. Click the Stop button when you finish recording. To play back the sound, click the Play button.
5. Click OK to save the sound with the presentation; click Cancel to exit and start over.

The sound now appears as an icon in your presentation, and you can use it anywhere in that slideshow. For example, you can play the sound when you click a specific object using PowerPoint's action settings.

→ To learn how to play sounds with action settings, **see** "Using Action Settings" in Chapter 15.

PLAYING A CD AUDIO TRACK

You can also play a specific audio track from a CD during a PowerPoint presentation. For example, you might want to include music from a CD as a background or to introduce your presentation. To do this, follow these steps:

1. Choose Insert, Movies and Sound, Play CD Audio Track to open the Movie and Sound Options dialog box, shown in Figure 13.7.

Figure 13.7
Music from a CD can serve as a background sound.

2. Select the Loop Until Stopped check box if you want the track to play continuously during your presentation.

3. In the Play CD Audio Track group box, choose the start and end tracks to play.

4. If you want to play only part of a track, indicate the timespans in the Start At and End At fields. For example, you might want to play only the first two minutes of a track.

5. Click OK to close.

PowerPoint displays a CD icon on the open slide. These steps insert the CD clip into the slide, but you must use the Custom Animation dialog box to set up your presentation to play this file during the slideshow.

→ For details on setting up custom animation options, **see** "Creating Custom Animations" in Chapter 15.

UNDERSTANDING THE MICROSOFT CLIP ORGANIZER

The Microsoft Clip Organizer, available from within Office XP applications, includes thousands of ready-made illustrations, photographs, sound files, and video clips to use in your presentations. You can search the Organizer by keyword or category to find the right clip, import your own clips to the Organizer, categorize clips, or download clips from the Microsoft Design Gallery Live Web site.

OPENING THE CLIP ORGANIZER

You can access the Clip Organizer in several ways:

■ From the Windows desktop, select Start, Programs, Microsoft Office Tools, Microsoft Clip Organizer.

- Select Insert, Picture, Clip Art to open the Insert Clip Art task pane. Click the Clip Organizer link on the task pane.

- Select Insert, Movies and Sound, Sound from Clip Organizer or Movie from Clip Organizer to open the Insert Clip Art task pane. Click the Clip Organizer link on the task pane.

The first time you open the Clip Organizer, the Add Clips to Organizer dialog box opens. Figure 13.8 shows this dialog box.

Figure 13.8
Automatically adding clips to the Clip Organizer can save time and make it easier to find your own clips when you need them.

From here, you can

- Click Now if you want the Clip Organizer to automatically categorize pictures, photos, sounds, and videos it finds on your computer.

- Click Later to close the dialog box and have it remind you to do this later.

- Click Don't Show This Message Again if you don't want to be reminded again about adding clips to the Organizer.

- Click Options to open the Auto Import Settings dialog box, shown in Figure 13.9, which enables you to place a check in all the folders you want categorized and remove the check from any folders you don't want categorized.

Having the Clip Organizer automatically categorize your clips doesn't move them, but rather just creates catalog entries that help you find them within the Clip Organizer.

Note

You might not have time to organize your clips the first time you access this feature, or you may add so many new clips that you want to automatically organize them again. If you want to open the Add Clips to Organizer dialog box at a later time, choose File, Add Clips to Gallery, Automatically from within the Clip Organizer.

Figure 13.9
Specify the folders you want to import automatically.

EXPLORING THE CLIP ORGANIZER

If you're familiar with other Office programs, the Clip Organizer (shown in Figure 13.10) will be easy to navigate and use. You can access the most common features from the toolbar, illustrated in Table 13.1.

TABLE 13.1   CLIP ORGANIZER TOOLBAR BUTTONS

Button	Name	Description
![Search...]	Search	Displays the Search task pane, from which you can search for an image
![Collection List...]	Collection List	Displays the Collection List task pane, which offers a hierarchical view of your clip collection
![Copy icon]	Copy	Copies the selected clip
![Paste icon]	Paste	Pastes the clip from the Clipboard
![Delete icon]	Delete from Clip Organizer	Removes the selected clips from the Clip Organizer

PART

IV

CH

13

TABLE 13.1 CONTINUED

Button	Name	Description
	Thumbnails	Displays the clips in the selected collection as thumbnails
	List	Displays the clips in the selected collection as a list of filenames
	Details	Displays details about the clips in the selected collection, such as filename, type, size, caption, keywords, and date created
Clips Online	Clips Online	Opens the Microsoft Design Gallery Live in a browser window (button active only if connected to the Internet)

Figure 13.10
The Clip Organizer enables you to store, categorize, and view all types of media clips.

NAVIGATING THE COLLECTION LIST

By default, the Clip Organizer displays the Collection List task pane on the left side of the window, and thumbnails of the clips in the selected collection on the right. The Clip Organizer offers four different types of collection folders: My Collections, which stores your own clips that you've added to the Organizer; Office Collections, which stores clips that come with Office; Shared Collections, which stores clips on a file server set up by a network administrator; and Web Collections, which stores online clips, including clips provided by Microsoft partners.

To expand collections, click the plus (+) sign; to collapse them, click the minus (-) sign. When you find the folder you want, click it to display its contents.

In thumbnail view, you can click the down arrow to the right of the thumbnail image to view a list of options for that particular clip, most of which duplicate functions available on the toolbar. One particularly useful item on this shortcut menu is Preview/Properties. This option opens the Preview/Properties dialog box for the selected clip. Figure 13.11 shows this dialog box, which provides details such as file type, resolution, date created, and keywords.

Figure 13.11
Learn more about an individual clip in the Preview/Properties dialog box.

Preview/Properties

Name: j0090386.wmf
Type: WMF File
Resolution: 213 (w) x 182 (h) pixels
Size: 33 KB
Duration:
Created: 8/14/98 9:09:18 AM
Orientation: Landscape
Open with:
Keywords:
buildings
homes
houses

Caption:

< Refresh > Edit Keywords...

Paths
File: c:\Program Files\Microsoft Office\media\cagcat10\j0090386.wmf
Catalog: c:\Program Files\Microsoft Office\media\cagcat10\CAGCAT10.MMW

Close

ADDING CLIPS TO THE CLIP ORGANIZER

The Clip Organizer contains clips from the Office XP product. Adding your own clips (clip art, photos, sound files, and videos) located on your hard drive or network can make this feature even more useful. You can add clips to the Clip Organizer in three ways: automatically, independently, or through a scanner or digital camera.

⚠ *Clips don't appear in the Clip Organizer?* See the "Troubleshooting" section near the end of the chapter.

ADDING CLIPS AUTOMATICALLY

To have the Clip Organizer automatically add and categorize your clips, choose File, Add Clips to Organizer, Automatically. The Add Clips to Organizer dialog box opens, from which you can specify how you want the Clip Organizer to perform this task.

→ For details on how to use the Add Clips to Organizer dialog box, **see** "Opening the Clip Organizer" in this chapter.

ADDING CLIPS ON YOUR OWN

To add clips to the Clip Organizer on your own, follow these steps:

1. From within the Clip Organizer, choose File, Add Clips to Organizer, On My Own. The Add Clips to Organizer dialog box opens (see Figure 13.12). You'll notice that this version of the dialog box looks very different from the dialog box of the same name that you use to import clips automatically.

PART
IV

CH
13

Figure 13.12
Adding clips on your own gives you total control as to how and where they're added.

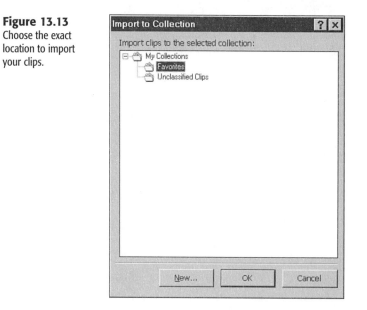

2. Select the clip you want to add to the organizer and click the Add To button. The Import to Collection dialog box will open, shown in Figure 13.13.

Figure 13.13
Choose the exact location to import your clips.

3. Select the collection to which you want to add the clip. If you don't select a collection, the Clip Organizer places the clip in the Unclassified Clips folder.

To create a new collection, click the New button and enter the new collection's name in the New Collection dialog box.

4. Click OK to return to the Add Clips to Organizer dialog box.

5. Click Add to add the clip to Clip Organizer.

ADDING CLIPS FROM A SCANNER OR CAMERA

It's also easy to use a scanner or digital camera to add clips to the Clip Organizer. To do so, follow these steps:

1. From within the Clip Organizer, choose File, Add Clips to Organizer, From Scanner or Camera. The Insert Picture from Scanner or Camera dialog box opens (see Figure 13.14).

Figure 13.14
If you use a digital camera or scanner, you can easily import your photos into the Clip Organizer.

2. Select the device from which you want to transmit the clips, such as a specific scanner or digital camera connected to your computer, from the Device drop-down list.

3. Select the resolution to use—either Web Quality or Print Quality.

4. Click Insert to begin the import process. Depending on the hardware device you're connected to, any remaining steps could vary.

Note

Click Custom Insert to specify custom details such as resolution, color, scanning area, and size before importing.

ADDING OBJECTS TO THE CLIP ORGANIZER

You can also add objects you create in PowerPoint or other Office applications to the Clip Organizer. Examples include pictures, WordArt, or AutoShapes you create and want to reuse. To add these objects to the Clip Organizer, follow these steps:

1. In PowerPoint, select the object you want to add, such as a picture, WordArt image, or AutoShape.

2. Click the Copy button on the Standard toolbar.

3. Choose Insert, Picture, Clip Art to open the Insert Clip Art task pane.

4. Click the Clip Organizer link on the task pane.

5. In the Clip Organizer, select the collection to which you want to add the object.

6. Click the Paste button. The Clip Organizer will add the object to the specified collection.

ADDING CAPTIONS AND KEYWORDS

After you add new clips to the Clip Organizer, you'll probably want to add captions and keywords that make them easy to find in the future. To do so, follow these steps:

1. Select the clip to which you want to add or edit keywords.

2. Choose Edit, Keywords. The Keywords dialog box opens, with the Clip by Clip tab selected (see Figure 13.15).

Figure 13.15
Specifying keywords for your clips makes them easier to find, particularly with large collections.

3. Add or edit the caption, which is a name for the clip.

4. Enter the keyword you want to add in the Keyword field and click the Add button. The keyword will be added to the Keywords for Current Clip list.

5. To delete a keyword, select it and click Delete.

6. Click OK to save your changes and exit the Keywords dialog box. The next time you search on the keywords you added, the selected clip will appear with the matching results.

To save time, you can apply the same keyword to multiple clips, such as a group of photos of Carmel, California, to which you want to add the keyword Carmel. To do so, open the collection that contains the clips, press Ctrl+A to select them all, and go to the All Clips at Once tab in the Keywords dialog box to add your keywords.

SEARCHING FOR A CLIP

To search for a clip based on its location or keyword, follow these steps:

1. Click the Search button on the Clip Organizer toolbar. The Search task pane appears, shown in Figure 13.16.

Figure 13.16
You can search for clips by collection or keyword.

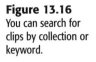

This task pane is also available from within PowerPoint itself.

2. Enter the keyword you want to search for in the Search Text field. If you know the name of the clip (its caption), you also can enter that here.

There are several things to keep in mind when you enter search text:

- Use wildcards to expand your search. A question mark (?) matches a single character, and an asterisk (*) matches multiple characters. For example, pr* would match both presentation and present. Pr? would match pro, but not presentation or present, because it looks only for single characters.

- Use parentheses to search for specific phrases such as "Phil's Photos." Entering Phil's Photos without the parentheses would search for anything that included both these words, not just that specific phrase.

- Use a comma to set OR criteria. Entering carmel, photos would search for clips that match either carmel or photos, whereas entering carmel photos would search for both words.

3. In the Search In field, select the collection you want to search from the drop-down list. To expand a collection, click the plus (+) sign; to collapse it, click the minus (-) sign. When you find the collection you want, place a check mark in the box that precedes it.

> **Note**
>
> If you have no idea where the clip is located, choose Everywhere to search in all locations. Be aware, however, that it takes longer to search all collections than to focus on specific collections.

4. Select the type of files to look for in the Results Should Be drop-down list. Options include All Media File Types, Clip Art, Photographs, Movies, or Sounds.

5. Click the Search button to begin the search process. The Clip Organizer finds matching clips and displays them in the task pane.

⚡ ***Can't find a clip by keyword?*** *See the "Troubleshooting" section near the end of the chapter.*

WORKING WITH THE CLIP ORGANIZER

One of the best things about the Clip Organizer is that it makes your clips easy to find. After you've added clips to the gallery, you might want to move, copy, or delete them:

- **Create a new collection**   Choose File, New Collection; in the New Collection dialog box, enter the name of the new collection, choose a location, and click OK.

- **Move a clip to another collection**   Select the clip you want to move; choose Edit, Move to Collection; choose the new collection in the Move to Collection dialog box; and click OK.

- **Copy a clip to another collection**   Select the clip you want to move; choose Edit, Copy to Collection; choose the new collection in the Copy to Collection dialog box; and click OK.

- **Rename a collection**   Select the collection you want to rename; choose Edit, Rename Collection. You can rename only a collection you've created, not one that comes with the Clip Organizer.

- **Delete a clip**   Select the clip you want to delete; choose Edit, Delete from "Collection" or Delete from Clip Organizer. A prompt confirms the deletion before proceeding. The clip is deleted from the location you specified in the Clip Organizer, but it still remains on your computer's hard disk.

- **Delete a clip collection**   Select a collection you added from the Collection List task pane, right-click, and choose Delete "collection" from the shortcut menu. The Clip Organizer will delete the collection and its associated clips.

COMPACTING THE CLIP ORGANIZER CATALOG

Compacting the Clip Organizer helps repair data corruption and can assist in avoiding or resolving problems such as missing clips or data corruptions. To perform the compacting process quickly, choose Tools, Compact. The Clip Organizer displays a message telling you that it's compacting the Organizer. The compacting process doesn't remove any files from the Organizer.

USING THE CLIP ORGANIZER'S ONLINE FEATURES

Click the Clips Online hyperlink or button in either the Clip Organizer or PowerPoint's Insert Clip Art task pane to open the Microsoft Design Gallery Live Web site. Click the Accept button to accept the end user license agreement and access the site, shown in Figure 13.17. From the Design Gallery Live, you can search for clip art, photos, and sound and motion files and download selected clips to your own computer.

Figure 13.17
Search for the right image from a vast collection of design options.

MODIFYING CLIP ART IMAGES

After you insert a clip art image or picture into a PowerPoint presentation, you can modify it to suit your needs. Using the Picture toolbar, you can make both minor and major adjustments to an inserted clip, such as changing its color or adjusting its contrast. Table 13.2 describes each button on the Picture toolbar.

PART
IV

CH
13

TABLE 13.2   PICTURE TOOLBAR BUTTONS

Button	Name	Description
	Insert Picture	Opens the Insert Picture dialog box from which you can choose another image
	Color	Enables you to convert the image to a grayscale, black-and-white, or washout image
	More Contrast	Enhances the contrast of the selected image
	Less Contrast	Reduces the contrast of the selected image

Button	Name	Description
	More Brightness	Increases the image's brightness
	Less Brightness	Decreases the image's brightness
	Crop	Enables you to crop the image to another size
	Rotate Left	Rotates the image to the left
	Line Style	Displays a list of varying line widths and styles from which to choose
	Compress Picture	Enables you to compress the picture, reducing its file size
	Recolor Picture	Enables you to change the color of a clip art image
	Format Picture	Offers numerous options for formatting an image's lines, color, size, and position
	Set Transparent Color	Converts a single color to a transparent image
	Reset Picture	Returns the image to its original state

TABLE 13.2 CONTINUED

To open the Picture toolbar, choose View, Toolbars, Picture.

→ To get more ideas on how to format images in PowerPoint, **see** Chapter 14, "Creating and Formatting Objects."

RECOLORING A CLIP ART IMAGE

You can recolor a Windows metafile image (WMF), such as a clip art image, after you place it in a PowerPoint presentation. This can be useful, particularly if you want the image to match the colors of a selected design template.

Tip from
Patrice-Anne Rutledge

The capability to recolor a generic clip art image can be a useful feature, particularly if you want to ensure the consistency of your PowerPoint presentation. For example, you could recolor a picture to match the colors in your corporate logo or to match the colors in the design template you've chosen.

 Can't recolor your image? See the "Troubleshooting" section near the end of the chapter.

To recolor a WMF image, follow these steps:

1. Select the image you want to recolor and click the Recolor Picture button on the Picture toolbar. The Recolor Picture dialog box opens, as shown in Figure 13.18.

Figure 13.18
Change the color of a
WMF image to match
your presentation.

2. Select the Colors option button to change the actual image colors or the Fills option button to change background colors.

Note

Selecting Fills doesn't affect line colors.

3. Under Original, place a check mark next to the color you want to change.
4. Select a color from the New drop-down list.

Note

Click More Colors from the drop-down list of colors to open the Colors dialog box, which offers a wide array of custom colors from which to choose.

→ To learn more about applying colors to objects, **see** "Specifying Colors" in Chapter 14.
→ For details on color theory, **see** "Using Color" in Chapter 23, "The Media—Designing Visual Support."

5. Click the Preview button to view the suggested color changes before you make them.
6. Click OK to apply the changes to the presentation.

PART
IV

CH
13

FORMATTING CLIP ART IMAGES

When you place a clip art image in your presentation, you can make changes to its lines, size, and position in the Format dialog box. You can also combine clip art with WordArt pictures to create a complete graphic image such as a logo.

→ For details on using the Format dialog box and working with WordArt, **see** Chapter 14.

To create this image, place both a WordArt picture and clip art on the slide and adjust their positions to create the image you want. You should also group these two images together to make them one.

→ For instructions on how to group PowerPoint objects, **see** "Grouping Objects" in Chapter 14.

TROUBLESHOOTING

FINDING YOUR OWN CLIPS IN THE CLIP ORGANIZER

The Clip Organizer doesn't contain my own pictures and photos.

You need to add your clips to the Clip Organizer before the Search function of the Insert Clip Art task pane can find them.

SEARCHING BY KEYWORD

The Search task pane can't find my clips by their keywords.

First be sure that your clips are actually in the Clip Organizer. Then verify that the keyword you used is actually associated with the clip (click the down arrow next to the clip and choose Preview/Properties to verify the list of keywords). Click Edit Keywords to make keyword modifications if necessary.

RESOLVING RECOLORING PROBLEMS

I can't recolor my clip art image.

You can't recolor BMP, JPG, GIF, or PNG images. Instead, you have to use an external program, such as Microsoft Photo Editor, to convert the color of these images.

DESIGN CORNER: ENLIVENING YOUR PRESENTATION WITH MULTIMEDIA

You can enliven any presentation by adding multimedia options such as clip art, pictures, sound, and movies. For example, you could take a simple bulleted list and make it both more interesting and more meaningful to your audience with a few simple additions.

Create this slide by choosing the Title, Text, and Clip Art layout from the Slide Layout task pane (click the New Slide button to open the task pane). Add your bullet items on the left side and then double-click the clip art placeholder. Select a picture from the Select Picture dialog box which appears (enter some search text to narrow down your choices).

From here, you can add a music clip to play in the background as an introduction; again, something that relates to your topic works best. How about music from your company's radio or TV ads, or something motivating if you want to inspire your employees? To do this, choose Insert, Movies and Sounds, Sound from Clip Organizer to view the sound files in the Insert Clip Art task pane. When you choose the appropriate sound file, you can specify that PowerPoint play it automatically in your slideshow. Adding a movie clip would be another option (Insert, Movies and Sounds, Movie from Clip Organizer). With a quick click, you could demo your company's latest TV ad. Sound and movie files can display visually on your slides or you can hide them (as illustrated in this example).

BEFORE

There's nothing wrong with this slide, but it isn't very exciting either.

Figure 13.19

Creative Brainstorming

- Determine the problem
- Start with traditional solutions
- Expand out of the box
- Think "big sky"
- Look to the future
- Do a reality check

AFTER

Add clip art and other multimedia effects to enliven your presentation.

Figure 13.20

CHAPTER **14**

CREATING AND FORMATTING OBJECTS

In this chapter

EXPLORING OBJECT CREATION AND FORMATTING

PowerPoint includes more drawing and object formatting options than you'll probably ever use. These features are simple enough to meet the needs of the casual user, yet powerful enough to handle the customization requirements of a sophisticated PowerPoint designer. The Drawing toolbar is the centerpiece of PowerPoint's suite of drawing tools and includes buttons that enable you to insert images, shapes, WordArt, and clip art. This toolbar also provides access to detailed and varied options for coloring, positioning, formatting, and manipulating objects you create or insert. In addition, PowerPoint 2002 offers new technology named GDI+ for displaying objects and pictures, which enhances quality by enabling better blending, transparency, and antialiasing.

USING THE DRAWING TOOLBAR TO CREATE OBJECTS

You can use the toolbar to add a variety of visual objects to your PowerPoint presentation, such as rectangles, ovals, AutoShapes, WordArt, and clip art. You can also modify existing objects using the toolbar buttons to apply shading, 3D, color, and other effects.

To open this toolbar, choose View, Toolbars, Drawing. Table 12.1 lists all the buttons on this toolbar.

TABLE 14.1   DRAWING TOOLBAR BUTTONS

Button	Name	Description
Draw ▾	Draw	Displays a menu with a variety of drawing options such as placement and formatting
▨	Select Objects	Activates a pointer that enables you to select drawing objects
AutoShapes ▾	AutoShapes	Displays a menu of AutoShape types from which to choose
╲	Line	Enables you to draw a line
↘	Arrow	Enables you to draw an arrow
▢	Rectangle	Enables you to place a rectangular shape on your slide
◯	Oval	Enables you to place an oval shape on your slide
▣	Text Box	Enables you to place a text box on your slide
◢	Insert WordArt	Opens the WordArt Gallery
▦	Insert Diagram or Organization Chart	Opens the Diagram Gallery from which you can insert a diagram or org chart

Table 14.1   Continued

Button	Name	Description
	Insert Clip Art	Opens the Insert Clip Art task pane
	Insert Picture	Opens the Insert Picture dialog box from which you can insert a picture, such as a GIF or JPEG, on your slide
	Fill Color	Displays the Fill Color palette from which you can choose a fill color or pattern
	Line Color	Displays the Line Color palette from which you can choose a line color or pattern
	Font Color	Displays the Font Color palette from which you can choose a font color
	Line Style	Displays a series of line styles you can apply to a selected line
	Dash Style	Displays a series of dash styles you can apply to a selected line
	Arrow Style	Displays a series of arrow styles you can apply to a selected arrow
	Shadow Style	Displays a Shadow palette from which you can choose a shadow to apply to a selected object
	3D Style	Displays a 3D palette from which you can choose a 3D effect to apply to a selected object

This chapter covers the functionality of all these toolbar buttons with the exception of Insert WordArt, Insert Diagram or Organization Chart, Insert Clip Art, and Insert Picture. Separate chapters exist to cover each of these PowerPoint features.

→ For more information on inserting diagrams and organization charts, **see** Chapter 12, "Working with Diagrams and Organization Charts."

→ To learn how to use clip art and pictures in PowerPoint, **see** Chapter 13, "Working with Media Clips and the Clip Organizer."

→ For details on using WordArt, **see** "Understanding WordArt" later in this chapter.

Adding Lines and Arrows

You can add lines and arrows to your presentation for emphasis. For example, you might want to add a line beneath a word or phrase to draw attention to it. You might also use an arrow to point to text or an object of special importance.

> **Note**
>
> To underline selected text, you can also click the Underline button on the Formatting toolbar. The line drawing feature, however, provides more flexibility in terms of the color, position, and width of line you use.

CREATING A LINE

To draw a line on your presentation, click the Line button on the Drawing toolbar. Use the mouse, whose pointer becomes a plus sign, to draw a line in the exact location you want to place it. If the line looks crooked or is the wrong length, select it and adjust the ends.

Tip from
Patrice-Anne Rutledge

Press the Shift key as you drag the mouse to create straight horizontal or vertical lines. This enables you to draw lines at angles evenly divisible by 15 (0, 15, 30, 45, and so forth), which makes it much easier to create a straight line. Press the Ctrl key as you drag the mouse to draw a line from a center point, lengthening the line in both directions as you drag.

To specify line style, select the line and click the Line Style button on the toolbar. The Line Style palette displays, shown in Figure 14.1.

Figure 14.1
Create thick or thin, single, double, or triple lines in your presentation.

| ¼ pt |
| ½ pt |
| ¾ pt |
| 1 pt |
| 1½ pt |
| 2¼ pt |
| 3 pt |
| 4½ pt |
| 6 pt |
| 3 pt |
| 4½ pt |
| 4½ pt |
| 6 pt |
| More Lines… |

You can choose from a variety of single and double lines as well as one triple line from 1/4 point to 6 points in width. You can also change your line to a dashed line by clicking the Dash Style button. For additional options, select More Lines, which opens the Format AutoShape dialog box where you can set additional line options. You can also open this dialog box by right-clicking on the line and choosing Format AutoShape.

→ To learn more about this dialog box, **see** "Using the Format Dialog Box" in this chapter.

→ For more details about coloring lines, **see** "Specifying Line Color" in this chapter.

You can use the Line Style palette for more than just formatting lines. You can use this palette to format lines associated with arrows, rectangles, ovals, AutoShapes, and other objects as well.

CREATING AN ARROW

To draw an arrow on your presentation, click the Arrow button on the Drawing toolbar. Use the mouse (the pointer becomes a plus sign) to draw an arrow in the location you want to place it.

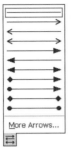 To specify an arrow style, select the arrow and click the Arrow Style button on the toolbar. The Arrow Style palette displays, shown in Figure 14.2.

Figure 14.2
Arrows can point to areas you want to emphasize.

You can choose from a variety of arrow types—both single and double arrows. For additional options, select More Arrows, which opens the Format AutoShape dialog box.

→ For details on the available options in this dialog box, **see** "Using the Format Dialog Box" in this chapter.

Figure 14.3 shows a slide that utilizes both lines and arrows.

Figure 14.3
Use lines and arrows to add clarity and visual effect.

ADDING RECTANGLES AND OVALS

You can draw rectangular and oval shapes directly on your PowerPoint presentation. Using shapes enables you to emphasize important information (contained in your shape) or to illustrate other ideas or concepts.

PART

IV

CH

14

To draw a rectangle, click the Rectangle button on the Drawing toolbar and use the mouse (the pointer becomes a plus sign) to draw a rectangular or square shape.

Tip from
Patrice-Anne Rutledge

To draw a square, press the Shift key while drawing your shape.

 To draw an oval or circular shape, click the Oval button on the Drawing toolbar and use the mouse (the pointer becomes a plus sign) to draw the desired shape.

Tip from
Patrice-Anne Rutledge

Pressing the Shift key while creating an oval shape forms a perfectly shaped circle.

Figure 14.4 shows the use of rectangular and oval shapes in a slide.

Figure 14.4
You can add images such as squares and circles to your presentation.

You can then reshape and resize these images or apply other formatting to them.

You can add text to a rectangular or oval shape. If you only want to add a word or two, select the object and type in the text you want to enter. Or click the Text Box button on the Drawing toolbar and create a text box inside the original object. Be sure, however, that the text box fits into the object without overlapping its borders.

ADDING TEXT BOXES

You can create a text box to add text to your slide other than in your original text place-holders or to frame special text. Note that you can't add text to a slide other than in a text placeholder or text box. Click the Text Box button on the Drawing toolbar, click where you want to place the text box on the slide, and start entering text to create the box. Figure 14.5 illustrates the use of a text box.

Figure 14.5
A text box calls attention to something you want to say in your presentation as well as enables you to place text exactly where you want it.

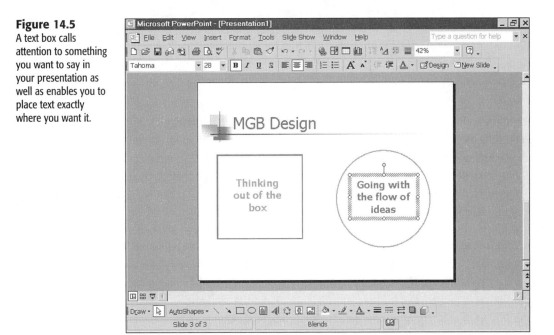

You can format the text in a text box as you would any other text, including formatting the font, font size, color, and style.

→ For more details on ways to format text in PowerPoint, **see** "Formatting Text" in Chapter 3, "Working with Text."

→ To learn how to make changes to a text box you add, **see** "Formatting a Text Box" in this chapter.

ADDING AUTOSHAPES

An *AutoShape* is a drawing object such as a hexagon, triangle, or star. Rectangles and ovals are also referred to as AutoShapes. AutoShapes make creating callouts, flowcharts, block arrows, and other special objects much easier and provide additional flexibility and creativity within PowerPoint.

To insert an AutoShape, click the AutoShapes button on the Drawing toolbar and choose the type of AutoShape you want from the menu. Options include the following:

■ **Lines**   Includes special line forms such as curves, scribbles, and freeform.

- **Connectors**   Offers three different kinds of connectors to connect objects—straight, elbow, or curved. Even if you move one of the connected objects, its connector stays attached and moves with it.

Tip from
Patrice-Anne Rutledge

To ensure that the connection between two objects is the shortest possible distance, you can reroute connectors. To do this, click the Draw button from the Drawing toolbar and choose Reroute Connectors.

- **Basic Shapes**   Includes shapes such as a hexagon, moon, triangle, box, arc, and plaque.
- **Block Arrows**   Offers large block arrows similar to regular line arrows, but much thicker.
- **Flowchart**   Offers flowchart images such as process, document, input, and terminator.
- **Stars and Banners**   Offers waves, scrolls, explosions, and pointed stars.
- **Callouts**   Includes several types of callout images that you can use to call attention to a particular part of the slide.
- **Action Buttons**   Includes several action button options, such as beginning, forward, and next.

Choose the specific AutoShape you want from the palette that displays when you select a menu option and place it on the slide by dragging the mouse. You can then format the AutoShape as you would any other object. Figure 14.6 shows some sample AutoShapes.

Figure 14.6
Callouts are just one example of an AutoShape.

Choose More AutoShapes from the AutoShapes menu to display the Insert Clip Art task pane, which offers even more options.

→ To learn how to insert clip art images, **see** Chapter 13.

SPECIFYING COLORS

You can apply color to objects, text, and lines using three different Drawing toolbar buttons. The Fill Color, Font Color, and Line Color buttons all operate in basically the same way, with slight differences based on the object they are coloring. To select the default color, click the button directly. To select another color, click the arrow to the right of the button to display a palette with additional options. You can also specify color in the Format dialog box.

→ To learn more about formatting options, **see** "Using the Format Dialog Box" in this chapter.

SPECIFYING FILL COLOR

 To set an object's fill color, select it, and click the arrow next to the Fill Color button. The Fill Color palette displays, shown in Figure 14.7.

Figure 14.7
You can add colors or patterns to fill an object.

You can do one of the following in this palette:

- Click No Fill to remove the existing fill color. The object becomes transparent and displays the color of the existing slide background.
- Choose one of the compatible colors under the Automatic color box option.
- Click More Fill Colors to open the Colors dialog box in which you can select from many other colors or even create your own custom color.
- Click Fill Effects to open the Fill Effects dialog box in which you can apply gradient, texture, pattern, and picture effects.

USING THE COLORS DIALOG BOX

Click More Fill Colors on the palette to open the Colors dialog box, illustrated in Figure 14.8.

PART

IV

CH

14

Figure 14.8
The Colors dialog box provides numerous options for color selection.

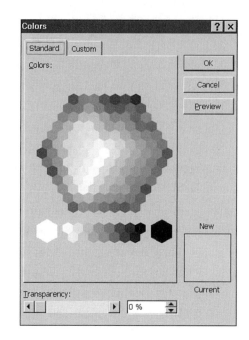

Select a new color from the palette on the Standard tab. It displays in the New section of the preview box to contrast with the Current color.

Note

You can set transparency (making the color appear transparent) by dragging the Transparency scrollbar or by entering a specific transparency percentage.

Click the Preview button to preview what the color will look like in your presentation. Click OK to return to the presentation or Cancel if you do not want to apply the color changes.

USING A CUSTOM COLOR

To create and add a custom color, click the Custom tab on the Colors dialog box, shown in Figure 14.9.

On the Custom tab, you can create a custom color by adjusting its hue, saturation, and luminance, or by specifying the level of red, green, and blue. Click the Preview button to preview your suggested changes and then click OK to save.

Note

If you're not familiar with color theory, *hue* refers to the actual color, *saturation* refers to the intensity of the color, and *luminance* refers to the brightness of the color. In general, the lower the number, the lighter or less intense it is.

Figure 14.9
Create a custom color
to suit your exact
needs.

→ For more information about color theory, **see** "Using Color" in Chapter 23, "The Media–Designing
Visual Support."

SPECIFYING FILL EFFECTS

To specify fill effects, select the object you want to format and click the arrow next to the
Fill Color button. From the palette that displays, choose Fill Effects to open the Fill Effects
dialog box. Figure 14.10 illustrates this dialog box, in which you can choose from a variety
of special fill effects.

This dialog box includes four different tabs—Gradient, Texture, Pattern, and Picture—that
guide you in selecting special effects fills.

APPLYING A GRADIENT FILL To apply a gradient (shading) effect, select the Gradient tab on
the Fill Effects dialog box. In the Colors group box, choose one of the following:

- **One Color** Applies a gradient effect with just one color. You choose the base color
  from the Color 1 drop-down list and specify how dark or light to make the contrast.

- **Two Colors** Choose the two colors you want to use from the Color 1 and Color 2
  drop-down lists.

- **Preset** Displays a drop-down list of preset color combination options such as
  Daybreak, Peacock, and Rainbow.

PART

IV

CH

14

Figure 14.10
Choose from gradient, texture, pattern, and picture effects.

Next, you can set the transparency by dragging the Transparency scrollbar or by entering a specific transparency percentage.

Finally, you can choose how to apply the gradient in the Shading Styles group box. Options include Horizontal, Vertical, Diagonal Up, Diagonal Down, From Corner, and From Center. Pick the option you prefer in the Variants group box; it displays in the Sample box. Click Preview to view the selection in your actual presentation and then click OK to apply.

APPLYING A TEXTURED FILL To apply a texture, select the Texture tab on the Fill Effects dialog box and scroll down the available textures until you find one you like. Select it and click OK. Figure 14.11 illustrates the Texture tab.

To choose an external texture graphic file that you have on your computer, click the Other Texture button to open the Select Texture dialog box. In this dialog box, you can choose the texture you would like to use and click the Insert button to display it in your selected object. You can choose to search among all pictures or specify a particular graphic format, such as a Windows metafile or bitmap image.

APPLYING A PATTERNED FILL To apply a pattern, select the Pattern tab on the Fill Effects dialog box (see Figure 14.12).

Figure 14.11
Textures can provide variety and visual depth to a presentation.

Figure 14.12
PowerPoint provides many different pattern effects.

Choose Foreground and Background colors and then select from the many available patterns.

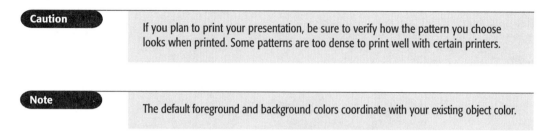

Caution

If you plan to print your presentation, be sure to verify how the pattern you choose looks when printed. Some patterns are too dense to print well with certain printers.

Note

The default foreground and background colors coordinate with your existing object color.

Click Preview to preview the fill effect, and then click OK to apply the fill.

APPLYING A PICTURE FILL To insert a picture fill inside the selected object, select the Picture tab on the Fill Effects dialog box. Figure 14.13 illustrates this tab.

Figure 14.13
Use your own image, such as a logo, as a fill.

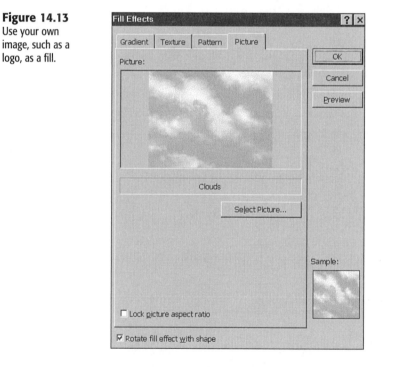

Click the Select Picture button to open the Select Picture dialog box, shown in Figure 14.14.

Locate and select the graphic image you want to use and click Insert to return to the Fill Effects dialog box. Click OK to close.

Figure 14.14
Choose a picture
of your own to apply
as a fill.

Caution

Although selecting a picture or graphic file of your own can definitely personalize and customize your presentation, be sure that it works as an effective fill.

SPECIFYING LINE COLOR

To add color to a selected line, choose the arrow to the right of the Line Color button on the Drawing toolbar. The Line Color palette displays, shown in Figure 14.15.

Figure 14.15
Format or remove
lines in the Line
Color palette.

Choose from the following options:

- Click No Line to hide the existing line.
- Choose one of the compatible colors under the Automatic color box.
- Click More Line Colors to open the Colors dialog box in which you can select from a variety of other colors or even create your own custom color.

→ To learn more about color options, **see** "Using the Colors Dialog Box" in this chapter.

PART
IV
CH
14

→ For details on expanding your color options, **see** "Using a Custom Color" in this chapter.

- Click Patterned Lines to open the Patterned Lines dialog box. This dialog box is almost identical to the Pattern tab on the Fill Effects dialog box.

Note

Unless you create a very thick line, patterns in a line probably won't be visible.

→ To learn how patterns work as fill colors, **see** "Applying a Patterned Fill" in this chapter.

SPECIFYING FONT COLOR

To add color to selected text, choose the arrow to the right of the Font Color button on the Drawing toolbar. The Font Color palette displays, shown in Figure 14.16.

Figure 14.16
Specify the color of
your text here.

You can either choose one of the compatible colors under the Automatic color box or click More Colors to open the Colors dialog box in which you can select from a variety of other colors. If you don't want to use one of the compatible colors coordinated to work with the current design template, be sure that the color you do select is clear and readable on your slide.

→ To learn more about what's available in the Colors dialog box, **see** "Using the Colors Dialog Box" in this chapter.

→ To learn how to insert a custom color, **see** "Using a Custom Color" in this chapter.

USING THE FORMAT DIALOG BOX

You can use the Format dialog box to apply numerous object formatting changes all in one place. The Format dialog box duplicates some of the functions of the Drawing toolbar, but also has some special features of its own. Depending on the object you're formatting, the full name of the Format dialog box may vary (Format AutoShape, Format Text Box, and so forth).

To open the Format dialog box for a selected object, double-click that object or right-click and choose Format from the menu that displays. Figure 14.17 shows a sample Format dialog box—Format AutoShape.

Depending on the type of object you're formatting, only the tabs and fields that pertain are available.

Figure 14.17
The Format AutoShape dialog box enables you to make many changes in one place.

FORMATTING COLORS AND LINES

On the Colors and Lines tab, you can set colors and styles for fills, lines, and arrows. Most of these options duplicate what the Line Color, Line Style, Dash Style, and Arrow Style Drawing toolbar buttons also achieve. The drop-down lists provide palettes that are very similar to the ones you access from these buttons. The effect is the same whichever method you use to apply a specific color or line format. The only difference is the way you choose to apply the formatting.

→ To learn the best way to use these objects in your presentation, **see** "Adding Lines and Arrows" in this chapter.

→ To learn how to use the Line Color button, **see** "Specifying Line Color" in this chapter.

Click the Preview button to preview the changes in your presentation. Click the Default for New Objects check box to make these customizations your default for future objects you create in this presentation.

FORMATTING SIZE

On the Size tab (see Figure 14.18), you can manually set size, rotation, and scaling options.

You can specify the exact height and width of an object, rather than resizing it with the mouse, if you want. This is useful if you want to create several objects of the same size and need greater precision than you can achieve by resizing with the mouse. You can also specify an exact rotation percentage, rather than rotate using menu options.

PART

IV

CH

14

Figure 14.18
Specify the exact size of the selected object on this tab.

→ For details on rotation and flipping, **see** "Rotating and Flipping Objects" in this chapter.

To resize the selected object by scale, you can adjust the percentages in the Scale Height and Width fields. For example, you might want to reduce an object to 50% of its original size.

⚠ **Is your rescaled object distorted?** See the "Troubleshooting" section near the end of this chapter.

You can also set the object's size as Relative to Original Picture Size or as Best Scale for Slide Show to automatically set the proper proportions.

FORMATTING POSITION

On the Position tab, shown in Figure 14.19, you can specify the exact position of the object on the slide.

Enter the exact Horizontal and Vertical positions for the object. For example, to move an object currently 2.75 inches from the margin one inch to the left, you would enter 1.75 in the Horizontal field. You can also set the position at either Top Left Corner or Center.

FORMATTING A PICTURE

If the selected object is a picture, the Picture tab (see Figure 14.20) offers several formatting options.

Tip from
Patrice-Anne Rutledge

Another quick way to create multiple objects of the same size is to copy and paste from the same master object.

Figure 14.19
With this dialog box, you can easily set an exact position.

You can crop a picture if you don't want to include the entire image in your presentation. Select the inches to crop in the Left, Right, Top, and Bottom fields. The inches you select are removed from the picture.

Figure 14.20
Set options for a picture, such as a clip art image, on the Picture tab.

Note

You can also crop a picture using the Crop button on the Picture toolbar if you prefer cropping by using the mouse.

Select a coloring format from the Color drop-down list. Options include Automatic, Grayscale, Black & White, and Washout. Figure 14.21 illustrates examples of each for the same picture.

Figure 14.21
The appropriate color format is an important factor in a successful presentation.

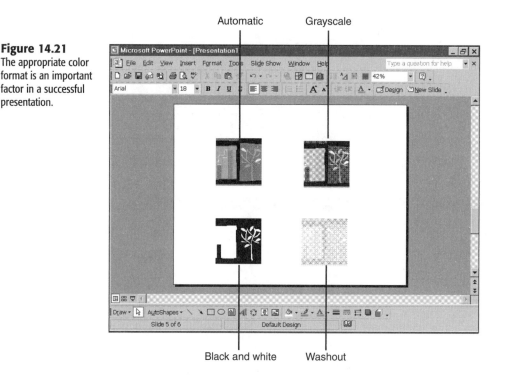

→ For interesting information about color theory, **see** "Using Color" in Chapter 24.

You can also specify brightness and contrast for this selected picture.

Click Recolor to open the Recolor Picture dialog box in which you can change the color of a PowerPoint object or a WMF clip art image.

Click Preview to see what the changes would look like in your presentation before you save them. Click Reset to restore everything to its original setting.

Tip from
Patrice-Anne Rutledge

Click the Compress button to open the Compress Picture dialog box where you can reduce the size of the pictures in your presentation, thereby reducing the size of the presentation itself.

→ To learn more about all these picture formatting options, **see** Chapter 13.

FORMATTING A TEXT BOX

If the selected object is a text box or any other shape that contains text, you can specify additional formatting options in the Text Box tab. Figure 14.22 illustrates this tab.

Figure 14.22
You can make several text box customizations.

You can set a Text Anchor Point to align your text in the text box. Options include Top, Middle, Bottom, Top Centered, Middle Centered, and Bottom Centered.

The Internal Margin section enables you to determine how much open space—or internal margin—to display within the text box. You can select fractions of inches in the Left, Right, Top, and Bottom fields.

Other options include the following:

■ **Word Wrap Text in AutoShape**   You should choose this option if you want to place text within an AutoShape object; otherwise, the **text** displays straight across the shape, rather than neatly inside it.

■ **Resize AutoShape to Fit Text**   Resizes the AutoShape object to fit the text exactly. For example, if you have one word inside an AutoShape, it reduces the shape to a size that precisely surrounds that word.

■ **Rotate Text Within AutoShape by 90°**   Rotates horizontal text to a vertical format.

PART

IV

CH

14

FORMATTING WEB INFORMATION

On the Web tab (see Figure 14.23), you can enter the text you want to display while this image is loading on the Web (through the HTML IMG tag's ALT attribute), which also displays as a ScreenTip when you pause the mouse over the image. This information is useful only if you're going to give a Web presentation.

Figure 14.23
In this dialog box, indicate what you want people to see while your Web graphic is loading.

Format Text Box	? ×

Colors and Lines | Size | Position | Picture | Text Box | Web

Alternative text:

Loading object.

Web browsers display alternative text while pictures are loading or if they are missing. Web search engines use alternative text to help find Web pages. Alternative Text is also used to assist users with disabilities.

OK | Cancel | Preview

MANIPULATING OBJECTS

You can easily cut, copy, paste, move, and resize PowerPoint objects.

To cut a selected object, click the Cut button on the Standard toolbar or press Ctrl+X. To cut more than one object, hold down the Shift key while selecting objects or drag a rectangular shape around all the objects with the mouse.

Note Click the Undo button to undo cutting an object.

To copy a selected object, click the Copy button or press Ctrl+C.

Tip from
Patrice-Anne Rutledge

To copy the attributes of a particular object and apply them to another object, use the Format Painter button on the Standard toolbar. For example, selecting an object with 3D effects, clicking the Format Painter button, and then selecting another object would apply 3D effects to the new object as well.

To paste a cut or copied object to another location, such as another slide, click the Paste button or press Ctrl+V.

Note

PowerPoint's Clipboard includes the capability to store 24 different copies. To see what the Clipboard currently contains, choose Edit, Office Clipboard to open the Clipboard task pane.

To move a selected object, use the mouse to drag the object to a new location.

Resizing an existing object is also an easy procedure. When you select an object, resizing handles display around its edges. Figure 14.24 illustrates these handles.

Figure 14.24
Resizing handles make it easier to adjust the size and shape of your object.

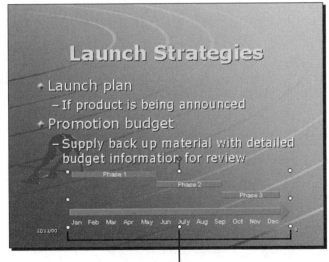

Resizing handles

Drag the handles with the mouse to make the object smaller, larger, or a different shape. Notice that depending on which sizing handle you select—a corner or interior handle—you can either enlarge the entire object or totally change its shape. To resize the selected object proportionately from a corner, press the Shift key and drag a corner handle to the appropriate size.

PART
IV

CH
14

ADDING SHADOW AND 3D EFFECTS

You can add shadow and 3D effects to objects, including AutoShapes, WordArt, and clip art.

→ To learn more about adding an AutoShape object to a slide, **see** "Adding AutoShapes" in this chapter.

→ For details on how to effectively use WordArt to enhance your presentation, **see** "Understanding WordArt" in this chapter.

→ To learn what clip art images are available and how to use them, **see** "Inserting Clip Art" in Chapter 13.

 Select an object and click the Shadow Style button on the Drawing toolbar to display the Shadow palette, shown in Figure 14.25.

Figure 14.25
Shadows can add a dramatic effect to a presentation.

Choose the shadow style you want to apply from the available palette options.

Tip from
Patrice-Anne Rutledge

To remove a shadow immediately, click the Undo button. To remove a shadow later, select the shadowed object, click the Shadow button on the Drawing toolbar, and choose No Shadow.

You can also customize the shadow by specifying its exact position and color. To do this, select Shadow Settings from the Shadow palette. The Shadow Settings toolbar displays, as described in Table 14.2. Figure 14.26 shows an object with a shadow.

→ To learn how to nudge an object to move it slightly, **see** "Nudging Objects" in this chapter.

→ For details on the effects of this dialog box, **see** "Using the Colors Dialog Box" in this chapter.

TABLE 14.2   SHADOW SETTINGS TOOLBAR BUTTONS

Button	Name	Description
	Shadow On/Off	Acts as a toggle to remove and replace the shadow
	Nudge Shadow Up	Moves the shadow up slightly
	Nudge Shadow Down	Moves the shadow down slightly
	Nudge Shadow Left	Moves the shadow slightly to the left

TABLE 14.2   CONTINUED

Button	Name	Description
	Nudge Shadow Right	Moves the shadow slightly to the right
	Shadow Color	Enables you to select a standard color, apply a semi-transparent image, or go to the Colors dialog box for additional color choices

To add 3D effects, select the object you want to modify and click the 3-D button on the Drawing toolbar. The 3-D palette displays, illustrated in Figure 14.27.

Figure 14.26
Get dramatic with shadows.

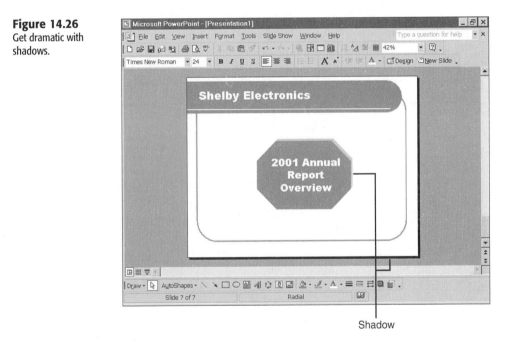

Shadow

Figure 14.27
Get creative with 3D, but be sure your object doesn't become too distorted.

Choose the 3D style you want to apply from the available palette options.

Can't apply 3D effects? See the "Troubleshooting" section near the end of the chapter.

Tip from
Patrice-Anne Rutledge

To immediately remove a 3D effect, click the Undo button. To remove 3D later, select the object, click the 3-D button on the Drawing toolbar, and choose No 3-D.

You can also customize the 3D effect by specifying its tilt, depth, direction, lighting, surface, and color. To do this, select 3-D Settings from the 3-D palette. The 3-D Settings toolbar displays, described in Table 12.3.

TABLE 14.3   3-D SETTINGS TOOLBAR BUTTONS

Button	Name	Description
	3-D On/Off	Acts as a toggle to turn the 3D off and on
	Tilt Down	Turns the object slightly downward
	Tilt Up	Turns the object slightly upward
	Tilt Left	Turns the object slightly to the left
	Tilt Right	Turns the object slightly to the right
	Depth	Enables you to adjust the depth from 0 points to infinity
	Direction	Enables you to set the direction, using either perspective or parallel options
	Lighting	Enables you to set the direction and intensity of the lighting
	Surface	Enables you to choose from a wire, matte, plastic, or metal surface
	3-D Color	Enables you to select a standard color, apply a transparent image, or go to the Colors dialog box for additional color choices

→ To learn more about the options available in this dialog box, **see** "Using the Colors Dialog Box" in this chapter.

Figure 14.28 shows an object with 3D effects.

Figure 14.28
Properly used, 3D effects can enhance a presentation.

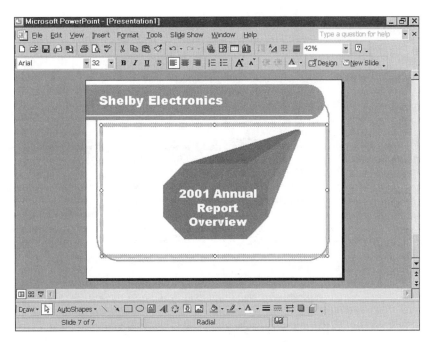

SETTING OBJECT ORDER

Sometimes you might want to layer objects in a presentation to create a special visual effect. By layering two or more objects, you place one on top of another, hiding the part of the bottom layer that is overlapped by the layer on top of it. You can do this for pure visual effect or to indicate that the overlapping objects have a relationship to each other. To rearrange the order that an object appears in this layer, choose it, select the Draw button on the Drawing toolbar, and choose Order from the menu. You can also right-click the mouse and choose Order from the shortcut menu.

Tip from
Patrice-Anne Rutledge

If the object you want to select is hidden from view, press the Tab key to cycle through all objects to find the one you want.

This shortcut menu includes four options:

- **Bring to Front**   Brings the selected object to the front layer of the stack, placing all other objects behind it.
- **Send to Back**   Sends the selected object to the back layer of the stack, bringing all other objects closer to the front.

PART

IV

CH

14

- **Bring Forward**   Brings the selected object one layer closer to the front. This is most useful with more than two objects.
- **Send Backward**   Sends the selected object one layer to the back. Also most useful when you have more than two objects.

Figure 14.29 includes an example of layering three objects.

Figure 14.29
You can layer objects for a special effect.

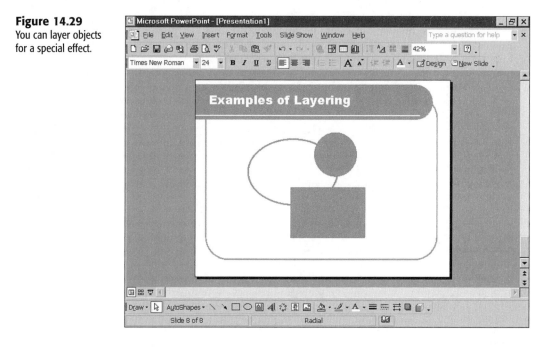

ALIGNING OBJECTS

You can align objects in much the same way that you align text. Select the objects you want to align, click the Draw button on the Drawing toolbar, choose Align or Distribute from the menu, and then select one of the following menu options:

- **Align Left**   Aligns selected objects by their left edge.
- **Align Center**   Aligns selected objects horizontally by their center.
- **Align Right**   Aligns selected objects by their right edge.
- **Align Top**   Aligns selected objects by their top edge.
- **Align Middle**   Aligns selected objects vertically based on their middle point.
- **Align Bottom**   Aligns selected objects by their bottom edge.
- **Distribute Horizontally**   Aligns three or more selected objects horizontally across the slide.

- **Distribute Vertically** Aligns three or more selected objects vertically across the slide.
- **Relative to Slide** Aligns selected objects relative to the slide, rather than the other objects. For example, if you choose Relative to Slide and Align Left, all objects align to the left of the slide itself, rather than to the object that is farthest to the left.

NUDGING OBJECTS

If you want to move an object only incrementally, you can nudge it. To do this, select the object you want to nudge, click the Draw button on the Drawing toolbar, choose Nudge, and then select one of the following directions: Up, Down, Left, or Right. You might need to nudge an object several times to achieve the desired results. The advantage to nudging is that you can control very small movements, which is difficult to do if you move an object with the mouse.

Tip from
Patrice-Anne Rutledge

Alternatively, you can also select an object and use the arrow keys to nudge the object in the direction of the arrow.

SNAPPING TO A GRID OR SHAPE

When you align or move objects, the objects snap to an invisible grid, which guides their positioning. This helps you more precisely align and position objects in your presentation, creating a more polished and professional look. If you want to use other objects as a positioning guide, you can snap to shapes. To choose these options, click the Draw button on the Drawing toolbar and choose Grid and Guides to open the Grid and Guides dialog box (see Figure 14.30).

Figure 14.30
Snap objects to a grid or another object.

In this dialog box, you can choose to snap objects to either a grid or other objects. You can also indicate the spacing of your grid in inches (from 1/24th of an inch to two inches).

Select the Display Grid on Screen check box to activate the grid. You'll see checkerboard-style squares on your screen in the spacing width you specified, which will help you position

PART
IV

CH
14

your objects. Although the grid appears onscreen, it doesn't appear in print or during an actual presentation.

Another option is to use adjustable drawing guides by selecting the Display Drawing Guides on Screen check box. This will place one adjustable vertical line and one adjustable horizontal line on your screen, which you can drag to position where you want them. These, too, are invisible in print or during a presentation.

To set these options as your default, click the Set as Default button. Click OK to close the Grid and Guides dialog box.

GROUPING OBJECTS

You can group two or more PowerPoint objects in order to treat them as one object. For example, if you combine WordArt with a clip art image to create a logo, you might want to group these objects so that they stay together when you move them. A grouped set of objects moves in unison, always remaining in the same position in relation to each other as when you grouped them. When you format grouped objects, the formatting applies to all the objects. For example, let's say you have two grouped objects that were originally different colors. If you now recolor them, the new color applies to both objects, not just one. To make individual changes, you have to ungroup the objects.

To group selected objects, click the Draw button on the Drawing toolbar and choose Group. The object handles now treat the objects as one, shown in Figure 14.31.

Figure 14.31
Group objects to treat them as one.

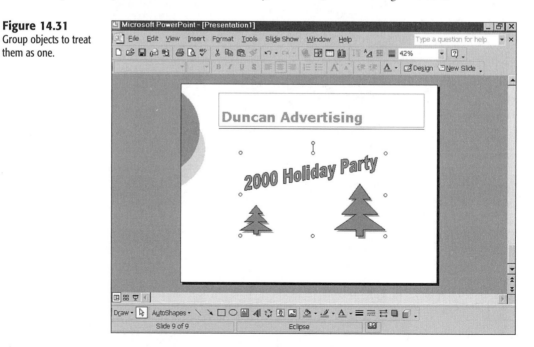

You can ungroup selected objects by clicking the Draw button again and choosing Ungroup.

Choose Regroup from the Draw menu to regroup items you just ungrouped.

ROTATING AND FLIPPING OBJECTS

Many times when you add an AutoShape or clip art image, it ends up facing the wrong direction. For example, you might add a callout to draw attention to specific text, but the callout is pointing the wrong way.

To rotate or flip a single object in a group, you need to ungroup it first and then regroup after changing its direction.

To quickly rotate an object, select it, and place the mouse pointer over the green rotate handle that appears at the top of the object (attached by a line to the top-most resizing handle). Drag this handle to rotate the object as desired.

You can also use rotation options from the Drawing toolbar. To rotate or flip a selected object, click the Draw button on the Drawing toolbar, choose Rotate or Flip, and then select one of the following menu options:

- **Free Rotate**   Enables you to openly rotate the object.
- **Rotate Left**   Moves the object counterclockwise.
- **Rotate Right**   Moves the object clockwise.
- **Flip Horizontal**   Turns the object horizontally.
- **Flip Vertical**   Turns the object vertically.

UNDERSTANDING WORDART

WordArt is an application you can use within PowerPoint to create special text effects such as shadowed, rotated, stretched, or multicolored text. PowerPoint treats WordArt pictures as drawing objects, not text, so the properties that apply to other drawing objects—such as formatting, the use of 3D, and the like—also apply to WordArt.

→ To learn how to apply 3D effects to WordArt, **see** "Adding Shadow and 3D Effects" in this chapter.

Spell check doesn't work with WordArt because it's a drawing object, not text. You must check spelling manually in WordArt pictures.

Figure 14.32 provides some samples of the type of text formatting you can do with WordArt.

Figure 14.32
WordArt provides numerous options for creating words with special graphic effects.

Be careful not to overuse WordArt in your presentation or it can become cluttered and confusing. WordArt should be used for emphasis only.

INSERTING WORDART

To insert a WordArt image in your slide, follow these steps:

1. Select Insert, Picture, WordArt to open the WordArt Gallery dialog box, shown in Figure 14.33.

 You can also open the WordArt Gallery dialog box by clicking the WordArt button from the Drawing toolbar.

2. Select the WordArt style you want and click OK. The Edit WordArt Text dialog box appears, as shown in Figure 14.34.

3. Enter the text that you want to format using WordArt.

4. Format this text by choosing an appropriate Font and Size and by clicking the Bold and Italic buttons if you want to add these effects.

5. Click OK to place the WordArt drawing on your slide.

Figure 14.33
Preview WordArt
styles before you
choose one.

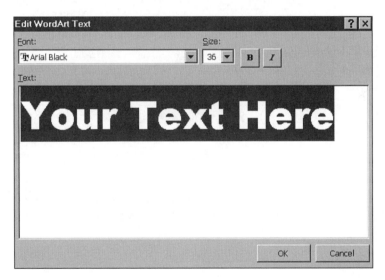

Figure 14.34
Enter the word or
words you want to for-
mat in this dialog box.

FORMATTING WORDART

After you insert a WordArt image, the WordArt toolbar appears. You can use this toolbar to apply additional formatting options. Table 14.4 describes the WordArt toolbar buttons.

PART

IV

CH

14

TABLE 14.4 WORDART TOOLBAR BUTTONS

Button	Name	Description
	Insert WordArt	Opens the WordArt Gallery so that you can add an additional WordArt image
Edit Text...	Edit Text	Opens the Edit WordArt Text dialog box so that you can revise the text of the existing WordArt image
	WordArt Gallery	Opens the WordArt Gallery so that you can apply a new style to the existing WordArt image
	Format WordArt	Opens the Format WordArt dialog box in which you can format color, lines, size, and position
	WordArt Shape	Displays a palette of additional shapes that you can apply to your WordArt picture
	WordArt Same Letter Heights	Makes all letters in a WordArt picture the same height
	WordArt Vertical Text	Rotates a WordArt picture to make it vertical
	WordArt Alignment	Enables you to set WordArt alignment, including left, right, center, and justified alignments
	WordArt Character Spacing	Enables you to make character spacing looser or tighter than normal or to set a specific spacing percentage

Tip from
Patrice-Anne
Rutledge

Use the buttons on the Drawing toolbar for other formatting options, such as changing the fill color of a WordArt picture, adding a shadow, or applying a 3D perspective.

→ For more details on the powerful design capabilities of this toolbar, **see** "Using the Drawing Toolbar to Create Objects" in this chapter.

FORMATTING WORDART CHARACTERS

You can customize several aspects of character spacing and orientation using WordArt.

Click the WordArt Character Spacing button on the WordArt toolbar to choose spacing options from a menu that displays.

You can also set a Custom percentage for character spacing. The default is 100%—a higher percentage loosens the text; a lower percentage tightens the text. Select the Kern Character Pairs option if you want to adjust sets of characters together.

Click the WordArt Same Letter Heights button to make all the letters in your WordArt picture the same height as the highest character.

Click the WordArt Vertical Text button to change the WordArt picture from a horizontal to a vertical orientation. You might have to resize the picture to make it fit properly by dragging the bottom side with the mouse.

Figure 14.35 illustrates examples of text spacing modifications.

Figure 14.35
Spacing and orientation make WordArt adjust to your presentation needs.

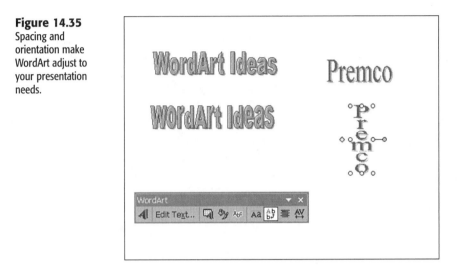

Note   Click the Undo button to undo any WordArt formatting option that you apply.

MODIFYING WORDART

To modify an existing WordArt picture, select it to redisplay the WordArt toolbar again. Use the toolbar buttons to change or further customize the WordArt picture.

TROUBLESHOOTING

UNDERSTANDING 3D LIMITS

I want to add 3D effects to a selected object, but the effects on the 3-D palette are dimmed and unavailable.

If you can't apply 3D effects to the selected object, the 3-D palette won't be active. For example, you can't apply 3D effects to pictures or text boxes, because it wouldn't make sense to do so.

RESCALING OBJECTS

I tried to rescale an object in the Format dialog box, but it became distorted.

To preserve the ratio of height to width in an object that you're rescaling, be sure to check the Lock Aspect Ratio check box. Otherwise, the object may become distorted.

DESIGN CORNER: ENHANCING PRESENTATIONS WITH FORMATTING EFFECTS

By adding special formatting effects such as AutoShapes, shadows, and line styles, you can greatly enhance your presentation. For example, you can take an existing presentation and within a few minutes add some pizzazz to enliven it. Or you can design a presentation from scratch with a goal of using special formatting to create something truly unique and customized. To understand what works and what doesn't, you need to experiment a little. Take a sample presentation and try out some of the various formatting techniques to find your favorites. One word of caution, though. It's easy to get carried away with special formats and effects. If you're creating a basic business presentation, you'll want to use these effects to *enhance* your presentation, not overwhelm it. Even if you're creating something other than a business presentation, remember to add formatting effects sparingly. In the example shown here, a somewhat bland presentation was made more visually appealing by adding lines and shadows, as discussed in this chapter.

BEFORE

Figure 14.36

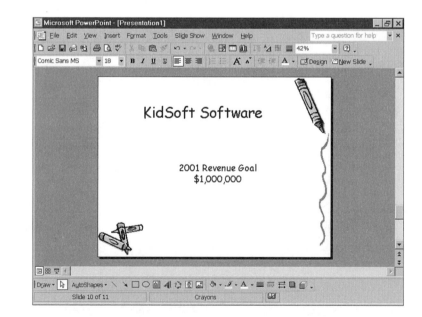

AFTER

Figure 14.37

Block arrow AutoShape

Arrow with
3-point line style

Oval shape with
shadow effects

CHAPTER 15

WORKING WITH ANIMATION

In this chapter

UNDERSTANDING ANIMATION

PowerPoint includes a multitude of animation options. You can use animation to change from one slide to another in your presentation or to introduce objects and text on a slide. You can also customize these basic animations in a variety of ways. Additional animation options include the capability to have action buttons or other objects perform a specific action in your presentation, such as opening a Web page on the Internet.

Like most of PowerPoint's capabilities, animation can be either very simple or detailed and complex. It all depends on how creative and sophisticated you want to make your presentation. Animation can definitely enliven any presentation, but as with any special effect, be careful not to overdo. Too much animation can actually detract from your presentation; it also increases its file size.

→ To learn more about animation and visual design, **see** Chapter 23, "The Media—Designing Visual Support."

PowerPoint includes a variety of animation options, which can be overwhelming if you're not sure about what each one does. Depending on what you want to animate (slide, text, drawing object, chart, media clip, and so forth) and what type of animation you want to use (a direction or an action), you have several ways to create the desired animation effect in PowerPoint. Your basic choices include the following:

- **Slide transitions**   Enable you to determine how to change from one slide to the next in your presentation.

- **Animation schemes**   Enable you to animate PowerPoint objects, such as text or drawing objects, using directional effects similar to slide transitions. For example, you can use an animation scheme to dissolve or wipe title text into your presentation.

- **Custom animation**   Enables you to set more sophisticated animation options, such as the order and timing of multiple animation objects in one slide. You can also use custom animation on charts and media clips such as sound and movie files.

- **Action settings**   Enable you to attach a mouse action to a PowerPoint object. For example, you can open a Web page, go to another slide, or start an external program by clicking the mouse or even just passing the mouse pointer over the selected object. An action setting differs from the previous types of animation in that it performs an action rather than defines how to introduce directionally an object or slide.

- **Action buttons**   Enable you to attach an action to a specific button. An action button is a predefined object that includes an action setting. You can attach an action setting to an object you create, or you can use one of the existing action buttons instead.

SETTING SLIDE TRANSITIONS

Setting slide transitions is one of the most common PowerPoint animation effects. You can set slide transitions that apply to the entire presentation or just to the current slide. PowerPoint offers a variety of transition options, including the capability to fade, dissolve, wipe, or even display items as a newsflash.

Within each of these main categories, you have other directional choices. For example, you can wipe up, down, left, or right. It's best to use a limited number of slide transition effects for your slideshow unless you have a good reason for applying several. Too many transitions can make your presentation confusing and inconsistent, detracting from your original purpose and message.

You can set slide transitions in either Normal view or Slide Sorter view. Follow these steps:

1. Choose Slide Show, Slide Transition. The Slide Transition task pane appears, shown in Figure 15.1.

Figure 15.1
You can specify how you want to move from one slide to another slide during a presentation.

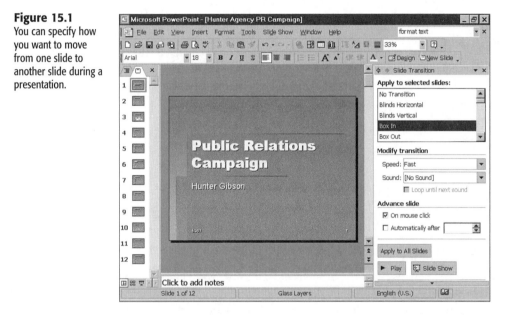

Tip from
Patrice-Anne Rutledge

If you already have a task pane open, you can click the down arrow at the top of the pane and select the Slide Transitions task pane from the menu that appears.

2. Select the slide or slides to which you want to apply the transition in either Normal view or Slide Sorter view.
3. From the Apply to Selected Slides list, select the transition you want to apply.

Tip from
Patrice-Anne Rutledge

Verify that the AutoPreview check box is selected so that you can preview your transitions as you apply them. Depending on your screen resolution and whether your PowerPoint window is maximized, this check box may be hidden from view. If it is, pause your mouse over the small arrow at the bottom of the task pane, and the pane will scroll up so that you can see the hidden fields.

4. Choose a transition speed of Slow, Medium, or Fast, depending on how quickly you want the transition to occur in a slideshow.

5. To add sound effects to your transition, select from the Sound drop-down list. To add a sound other than one of the default WAV files, select Other Sound from the drop-down list to open the Add Sound dialog box. You can choose another sound. If you want the sound to continue playing until the presentation encounters another sound file, click the Loop Until Next Sound check box.

⚠️ **Can't hear your sound files?** See the "Troubleshooting" section near the end of this chapter.

6. Select the On Mouse Click check box to advance to the next slide when you click the mouse or press a key such as the spacebar, Enter, Page Up, or Page Down. This is selected by default.

7. If you would rather have PowerPoint automatically change to the next slide after a specified amount of time, select the Automatically After check box and enter a specific time in the field beside it. Any timings you've already added to your slideshow appear in this box automatically.

8. Click the Apply to All Slides button to apply the transitions to all slides in your presentation.

9. Click the Play button to preview the selected transitions within your current view (or preview it again if you selected the AutoPreview check box); click the Slide Show button to start a slideshow.

→ To learn more about running slideshows, **see** Chapter 9, "Presenting a Slideshow."

USING ANIMATION SCHEMES

In addition to animating the transitions of your slides, you can also apply preset animation to the text on selected slides. You do this using animation schemes. Animation schemes provide numerous options, ranging from subtle to highly creative animations. Pinwheel, Neutron, and Boomerang and Exit are just a few examples of PowerPoint animation schemes. To preview their effects, try out a few to find the one that's right for your presentation.

To apply an animation scheme to a selected slide or slides, follow these steps:

1. Choose Slide Show, Animation Schemes. The Slide Design task pane, shown in Figure 15.2, opens with the Animation Schemes option selected.

Tip from
Patrice-Anne Rutledge

If you already have a task pane open, you can click the down arrow at the top of the pane and select Slide Design–Animation Schemes from the menu that appears.

---

2. Choose the animation you want from the Apply to Selected Slides list. The list displays the Recently Used animation schemes first and then divides the remaining schemes by category, such as Subtle, Moderate, and Exciting.

Figure 15.2
Animation Schemes offers a fast and simple way to animate your slides.

Animation Schemes option

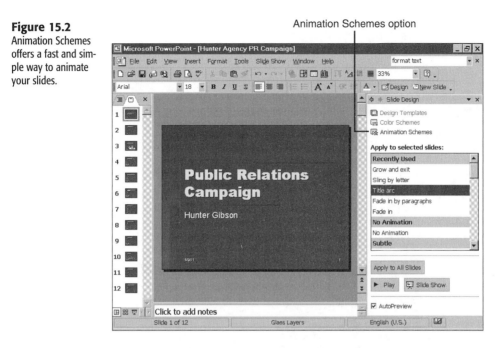

Tip from
*Patrice-Anne
Rutledge*

Verify that the AutoPreview check box is selected so that you can preview your animations as you apply them.

3. To preview what this animation effect looks like within the current view (or preview it again if you selected the AutoPreview check box), click the Play button. To start a slideshow, click the Slide Show button.

→ To learn more about running slideshows, **see** Chapter 9.

4. To apply the animation scheme to the entire presentation, click the Apply to All Slides button.

If you later decide you don't want a particular animation scheme, choose the No Animation option in the Apply to Selected Slides list in the Slide Design—Animation Schemes task pane.

CREATING CUSTOM ANIMATIONS

The Custom Animation task pane offers more advanced animation options, such as the capability to set order and timings or to animate certain parts of a slide. You also use this task pane to set animation effects for charts, diagrams, organization charts, and media clips. If animation schemes don't provide the flexibility you need, try custom animation.

Note that if you've already applied an animation scheme to a slide, these animation events will appear in the Custom Animation list on the Custom Animation task pane. For example, the Grow and Exit animation scheme appears as five separate animation events on this task pane.

You can either delete these animations and start over with custom animation by clicking the Remove button on the task pane or add more enhancements to your animation schemes.

→ To learn more about animation schemes, **see** "Setting Special Animation Effects" later in this chapter.

Note

Applying a custom animation is far more complicated than applying an animation scheme. Be sure that you really need the power offered by custom animations before you spend the time to set them up.

To apply a custom animation to a selected text or object, follow these steps:

1. Choose Slide Show, Custom Animation to open the Custom Animation task pane, shown in Figure 15.3.

Figure 15.3
Custom Animation offers more complex options.

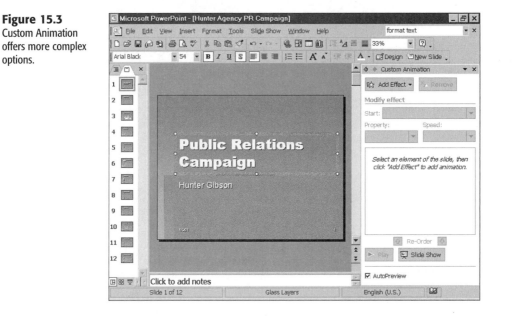

Tip from
Patrice-Anne Rutledge

If you already have a task pane open, you can click the down arrow at the top of the pane and select the Custom Animation task pane from the menu that appears.

2. Click the Add Effect button to display a menu of additional options:

   • **Entrance**   Determines how the selected text or object enters the slide. Options include Blinds, Box, Checkerboard, Diamonds, and Fly In.

   • **Emphasis**   Adds emphasis to the selected text or object. Options include Change Font, Change Font Size, Change Font Style, Grow/Shrink, and Spin.

- **Exit** Determines how the selected text or object exits the slide. Options include Blinds, Box, Checkerboard, Diamonds, Fly Out, and Whip.
- **Motion Paths** Sets a directional path that the selected text or object follows. Options include Diagonal Down Right, Diagonal Up Right, Down, Left, Right, and Up. You can also draw a custom path based on a line, curve, freeform, or scribble shape.

Note

Not all options are always available, depending on what you select to animate. For example, the text-based animation options such as Change Font or Change Font Size are only available if you select text.

---

3. Click the type of effect you want and choose from the submenu of additional options. It will appear in the Custom Animation list.

Tip from
Patrice-Anne Rutledge

Verify that the AutoPreview check box is selected so that you can preview your transitions as you apply them.

---

4. To see a complete list of effects, choose the More Effects menu option, which opens a dialog box of related effects, such as the Add Entrance Effect or Add Emphasis Effect dialog box (see Figure 15.4).

Figure 15.4
Additional custom effects are available, ranging from subtle to extravagant.

The effects in these dialog boxes are grouped by style—basic, subtle, moderate, or exciting, for example. If the Preview Effect check box is selected, you can preview an example of the effect on your slide when you click it in the dialog box. If you want to use one of these effects, select it and click OK to close the dialog box.

5. From the Start drop-down list in the Custom Animation task pane, choose when you want the animation to start. All choices might not appear in the drop-down list, depending on the sequence of the animation.

6. Depending on which custom animation you choose, additional drop-down lists might appear, such as Direction, Speed, Font, Duration, and so forth. Select the options you prefer.

7. Click the Play button to demonstrate the selected transitions within your current view; click the Slide Show button to display the animations in a slideshow.

→ To learn more about running slideshows, **see** Chapter 9.

Each animation event you add appears in the Custom Animation list in the order you enter it. The icon that precedes it tells you the type of animation it is and corresponds to the icons that precede the choices on the Add Effect menu (Entrance, Emphasis, and so forth). Pause the mouse over the animation in the list to display more information, such as the start option and effect type. If you have multiple animations in this list, the list is numbered and the numbers also appear on your slide to show where the animations are located. These numbers don't appear in print or during a slideshow, however. Figure 15.5 illustrates a list of animation options.

Figure 15.5
PowerPoint lists your custom animations in sequence.

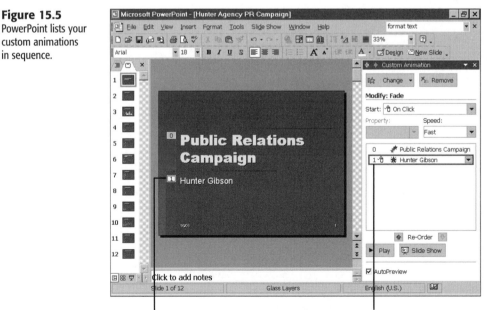

Sequence number—Slide   Sequence number—Custom Animation list

SETTING SPECIAL ANIMATION EFFECTS

The Custom Animation task pane also offers the option to add more animation effects, set timings, reorder animation events, and animate parts of diagrams, organization charts, media clips, or other charts you've added to your slides.

SETTING ADDITIONAL EFFECTS

To add effects to an animation event in the Custom Animation list—such as directional, sound, text, and color enhancements—click the down arrow to the right of an animation in the list and choose Effect Options from the menu that appears. A dialog box opens with the Effect tab selected (see Figure 15.6).

Figure 15.6
Continue to customize your custom animation with the options in this dialog box.

The name and content of the dialog box depend on the type of animation event you're customizing. For example, if you choose the Box entrance effect, the Box dialog box appears. We'll look at the Box dialog box to explore the range of customizations you can make, but remember that depending on the effect you choose, this dialog box could have different fields or tabs.

The Effect tab on the Box dialog box has the following options:

- **Direction** Specify a direction for the selected animation, such as In, Out, Horizontal, or Vertical.

Note

Only those directions that apply to the selected animation event will appear in this drop-down list.

■ **Sound** Select a sound effect from the drop-down list. If you don't want to include a sound, choose No Sound, which is the default option. For additional options, choose Other Sound to open the Add Sound dialog box.

■ **Volume** Click the Volume button to raise or lower the volume level of the sound effect. You can also choose to mute the effect here.

■ **After Animation** Specify how to end your animation in this drop-down list, such as displaying the object in a new color or hiding it after animation. Options include

• **Standard colors buttons** Enables you to apply a color from the default palette, which changes the object's color after animation.

• **More Colors** Displays the Colors dialog box in which you can choose from a variety of other color options.

→ To learn more about the Colors dialog box, **see** "Specifying Colors" in Chapter 14, "Creating and Formatting Objects."

• **Don't Dim** Continues to display a static image of the object after animation.

• **Hide After Animation** Hides the object after animation.

• **Hide on Next Mouse Click** Hides the object when you click the mouse.

■ **Animate Text** From the drop-down list, choose a method for introducing text: All at Once (the default), By Word, or By Letter.

■ **% Delay Between Words** If you choose the By Word or By Letter option, you can indicate the percentage of delay between introducing those characters.

SETTING TIMINGS

To set exact timing effects for your custom animations, click the down arrow next to an animation in the Custom Animation list and choose Timing from the menu that appears. A dialog box opens with the Timing tab selected, as shown in Figure 15.7.

Figure 15.7
Make additional timing modifications on the Timing tab.

Remember that the name of this dialog box reflects the type of animation effect whose timing you want to customize. On the Timing tab, you can set the following options:

- **Start** Specify whether you want to start the animation On Click, With Previous (simultaneous with the previous animation in the list), or After Previous (after the previous animation in the list).

- **Delay** Enter the delay in seconds.

- **Speed** Select a speed level, from very slow to very fast.

- **Repeat** Indicate how many times you want the animation to repeat. Options include none; two, three, four, five, or ten times; until the next click; or until the next slide.

- **Rewind when Done Playing** Select this check box if you want to rewind (return to its original position) the animation when you're done playing it.

- **Triggers** Click the Triggers button to display two additional fields on this tab: Animate as Part of Click Sequence and Start Effect on Click Of. You can choose one of these triggers, but not both. In PowerPoint, you'll use a trigger to start an animation.

  - **Animate as Part of Click Sequence** Select this radio button to animate as part of the click sequence in the Custom Animation list.

  - **Start Effect on Click Of** Select the specific animation to target this trigger from the drop-down list, such as a title or text.

You can also display the Advanced Timeline, which enables you to further customize timings by dragging the timeline's scrollbar. To open this timeline, right-click the Custom Animation list and choose Show Advanced Timeline. Figure 15.8 illustrates this timeline.

PART

IV

CH

15

Figure 15.8
Define specific timings to give your presentation a professional polish.

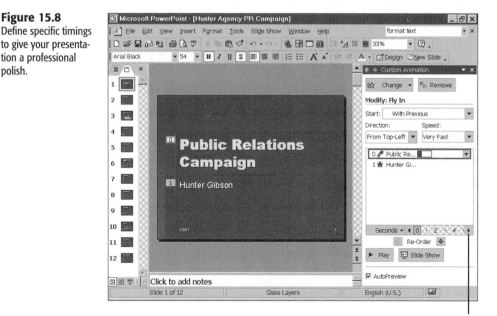

Advanced timeline

To close the timeline, right-click again and choose Hide Advanced Timeline.

ANIMATING CHARTS

You can add more effects to a chart to which you've applied a custom animation. To do so, click the down arrow next to the chart in the Custom Animation list and choose Effect Options from the menu. Figure 15.9 illustrates the dialog box that appears (remember that the dialog box name will reflect the type of effect you've applied, such as Box or Spin, and not the fact that you're animating a chart).

Figure 15.9
Animating a chart is another possibility.

Click the Chart Animation tab and, from the Group Chart drop-down list, indicate how you want to introduce the chart elements. Options include As One Object, By Series, By Category, By Element in Series, and By Element in Category.

Tip from	If you choose any option other than As One Object, the Animate Grid and Legend check box activates, enabling you to include the chart grid and legend in the animation effect.
Patrice-Anne Rutledge	

→ To learn how to create a chart, **see** Chapter 11, "Working with Charts."

ANIMATING DIAGRAMS

Animating parts of diagrams or organization charts is another animation customization you can apply. To do so, click the down arrow next to the diagram in the Custom Animation list and choose Effect Options from the menu. Figure 15.10 illustrates the dialog box that appears with the Diagram Animation tab selected.

From the Group Diagram drop-down list, choose the way you want to introduce the diagram onto the slide: As One Object; All At Once; Each Branch, Shape by Shape; Each Level, Shape by Shape; or Level by Level.

Figure 15.10
Animating parts of a diagram is another custom animation option.

ANIMATING MEDIA CLIPS

You can also customize animations to media clips such as a sound or video file. For example, to customize a sound clip animation, click the down arrow next to the clip in the Custom Animation list and choose Effect Options from the menu. Figure 15.11 illustrates the Play Sound dialog box that appears with the Effect tab selected. The Effect tab includes choices for starting and stopping the playing of the media clip.

Figure 15.11
The Effect tab adds fields for animating media clips.

REORDERING ANIMATIONS

The animations in the Custom Animation list appears in the order you enter them, but you can change this order if you like. To specify the order in which to animate multiple objects on a single slide, select the object you want to reorder and click either the up or down Re-Order button. Dragging an animation to another location in the list is another way to reorder the animation events in the Custom Animation list.

MODIFYING ANIMATIONS

After you apply custom animations to a slide, you may decide that you want to modify them. For example, you might want to change the type of effect you applied from Box to Diamond or from Grow/Shrink to Spin. To do so, select the animation in the Custom Animation list on the Custom Animation task pane and click the Change button. From here, you can select a new custom animation to apply.

Note

The Change button is the same as the Add Effect button. Its name changes when you modify an existing animation rather than add a new one.

DELETING ANIMATIONS

To delete a custom animation, select it in the Custom Animation list on the Custom Animation task pane and click the Remove button. To delete all animations, select the first animation in the list, press the Shift key, select the last animation in the list, and then click the Remove button.

 If you make a mistake and want to restore your deletions, click the Undo Custom Animation button on the Standard toolbar.

USING ACTION SETTINGS

Use the Action Settings dialog box to start an action by clicking an object with the mouse or simply by passing the mouse pointer over it.

For example, you can place an object, such as a rectangle, in your presentation and have it connect to the Web, play a sound, run a macro, or ⬝en another program when you click it or pass the mouse over it. This can be useful when you want to demonstrate other applications during your presentation, but don't want to take the time to try to locate and open them in the middle of a slideshow.

To add an action to a PowerPoint object, follow these steps:

1. Select the object to which you want to add an action.
2. Choose Slide Show, Action Settings to open the Action Settings dialog box, shown in Figure 15.12.

Figure 15.12
Use a mouse click or mouse over to perform actions in your presentation.

PART

IV

CH

15

3. Choose the Mouse Click tab if you want to start the action with a mouse click; choose the Mouse Over tab to start the action by passing the mouse over the object. The Mouse Click and Mouse Over tabs are nearly identical. The only real difference is the method by which you start the action.

> **Caution**
>
> Passing the mouse over an object to start an action is the easier method, but be careful not to get too close to the object too soon or you might start the action before you intend to.

4. PowerPoint provides five main action choices in this dialog box, as well as the capability to activate a sound. Choose one of the following:

   - **None**   No action occurs. Choose this option to remove a previously placed action.
   - **Hyperlink To**   Creates a hyperlink to a selected slide within your presentation, another PowerPoint presentation, another file on your computer, or a Web page.

→ For further explanation about using hyperlinks in PowerPoint, **see** "Adding Hyperlinks" in Chapter 16, "Using PowerPoint's Web Features."

   - **Run Program**   Runs the program whose path you specify in the text box. You can click the Browse button to open the Select Program to Run dialog box, where you can search for the appropriate program.

Tip from
*Patrice-Anne
Rutledge*
You can also use Run Program to open a file in another program. For example, enter-ing c:\budget.xls would open Excel and the Budget worksheet.

- **Run Macro**   Lets you choose from a list of PowerPoint macros you've created.

→ To learn how to create macros, **see** "Running a Macro from the Toolbar" in Chapter 20, "Working with PowerPoint Macros."

- **Object Action**   Enables you to open, edit, or play an embedded object. This option is available only for objects that you can open, edit, or play, such as a media clip or an organization chart.
- **Play Sound**   Enables you to play a sound you select from the drop-down list. You can select other sounds by choosing Other Sound from the drop-down list.
- **Highlight Click/Highlight when Mouse Over**   Highlights the selected object when you perform the mouse action.

5. Click OK to close the Action Settings dialog box.

⚠ *Are your animation effects not working when using PowerPoint 2000? See the "Troubleshooting" section near the end of the chapter.*

USING ACTION BUTTONS

Action buttons are another alternative for using PowerPoint objects to perform certain actions. PowerPoint includes 12 different action buttons.

These buttons function in much the same way as applying an action setting to an existing object. In fact, when you place an action button on a slide, the Action Settings dialog box appears. You can then specify mouse actions for the action button. Many action buttons per-form common tasks such as moving to a previous slide; this action is already defined by default in the Action Settings dialog box.

To place an action button on a PowerPoint slide, choose Slide Show, Action Buttons. The Action Buttons palette appears, as shown in Figure 15.13.

Tip from
*Patrice-Anne
Rutledge*
You can also create an action button from the Drawing toolbar by choosing AutoShapes, Action Buttons.

Click on a button on the palette to open the Action Settings dialog box, in which you can accept the default action setting or specify the action to attach to this button. Enter the required information and click OK. The action button now appears on your PowerPoint slide, as illustrated in Figure 15.14.

Figure 15.13
This palette includes
several ready-made
action buttons.

Figure 15.14
Use action buttons in
your presentation for
added flexibility and
convenience in chang-
ing to other slides or
applications.

You will probably want to resize and move the button on the slide.

→ To learn how to move, resize, copy, delete, and format an object, such as an action button, **see** Chapter 14.

TROUBLESHOOTING

RESOLVING SOUND FILE PROBLEMS

I can't hear sound files I embedded in my presentation.

You must have a sound card and speakers to hear sounds that you add to your presentation. Also, verify that your volume is turned up sufficiently to hear the sounds.

WORKING WITH PREVIOUS VERSIONS

I opened my presentation in PowerPoint 2000, and the animations don't work.

The features and functionality of PowerPoint 2002 aren't always available in previous versions of the software. With animations, PowerPoint either converts animations to effects supported by the software version you used to open the presentation or eliminates the animation effect entirely, depending on the type of PowerPoint 2002 animation effect you applied.

DESIGN CORNER: SPICING UP YOUR PRESENTATION

With PowerPoint's animation features, you can enliven presentations using transitions, action buttons, or preset animation. Before you apply animation to your presentation, you should have a plan. First, be sure you understand PowerPoint's animation options and how best to use them. If you're not sure, experiment a little. Trial and error can often be the best teacher in learning what works and what doesn't. Second, create a cohesive plan for integrating animation into your presentation (where, how much, what kind, and so forth). Remember that a little can go a long way and that over-animating can have detrimental effects, such as cluttering your presentation and making its file size too large. Finally, implement your plan by adding the actual animations (this is the easy part). When you're done, be sure to preview the entire presentations to verify that what you've planned is truly effective.

In the example shown here, an informative slide is made more eye- and ear-catching by adding animation and sound effects.

BEFORE

Figure 15.15

AFTER

Apply multimedia effects such as looping to a sound object.

Figure 15.16

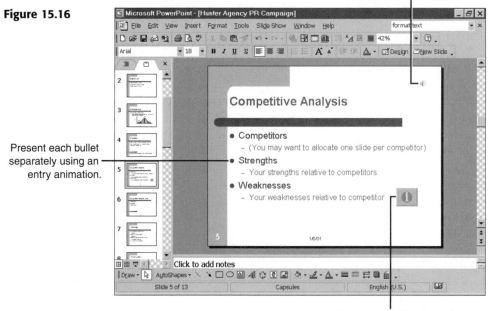

Present each bullet separately using an entry animation.

Include an action button to perform an action such as linking to a Web page from your presentation.

PART V

Working with PowerPoint on the Web

CHAPTER 16

Using PowerPoint's Web Features

In this chapter

WORKING WITH HYPERLINKS

If you've ever surfed the World Wide Web, you're already familiar with *hyperlinks*. Simply put, by clicking your mouse on a linked object, you can jump to another location in your PowerPoint presentation, to another program, or even to a location on the Web.

Unlike a book or a typical slideshow where you must proceed sequentially through the material, a hyperlinked PowerPoint presentation enables you to go where you need to go and to present what you need to present when you want to present it. Suppose, for example, you are making a presentation to the board of directors of your entertainment company. You suspect some board members will want to know more about current promotions by a rival company. You can create a hyperlink in your slideshow that opens up your Web browser, connects to the Internet, and displays your competitor's Web site. Of course, if no one asks or if time is running short, you don't even need to use the link. But you know it's there, just in case.

ADDING INTERNET HYPERLINKS

The first step in creating an Internet hyperlink is to identify the object to link. You can link any object, including text, clip art, WordArt, charts, AutoShapes, and more. To create a link, follow these steps:

1. While in Normal view, select the text or object you want to link (see Figure 16.1).

Selected text

Figure 16.1
Select text or any other object to which you want to add a hyperlink.

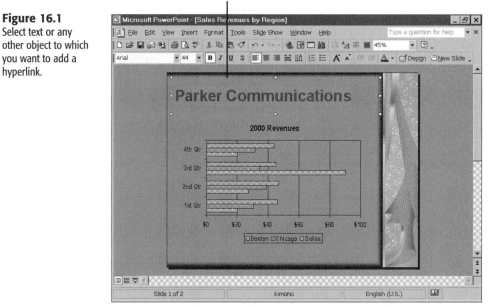

2. Click the Insert Hyperlink button. Alternatively, you can choose Insert, Hyperlink or press Ctrl+K. PowerPoint displays the Insert Hyperlink dialog box (see Figure 16.2).

Figure 16.2
Use the Insert Hyperlink dialog box to specify the location you want to link to the selected text or object.

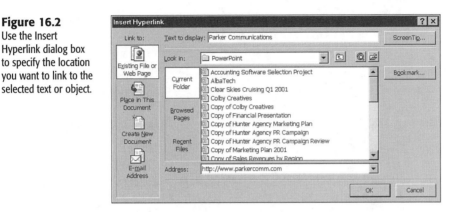

Note

When you create a hyperlink for the first time, you use the Insert Hyperlink dialog box. If you change the hyperlink, the name of the dialog box changes to Edit Hyperlink. However, both are identical except for the Remove Link button found in the Edit Hyperlink dialog box.

3. Type the Internet URL in the Address field.

Caution

Be sure to type the URL carefully, including all special characters (such as the tilde ~). Generally, you should use lowercase characters. Some Web servers distinguish between uppercase and lowercase characters, and using an uppercase character in the URL might not work.

4. Click OK.

If you added a link to text, that text now appears underlined and in a different color (see Figure 16.3). The actual color you see depends on the PowerPoint design template you are using. If you added the link to any other object, you do not see any difference in the appearance of the object, but the object is linked, nonetheless.

When you access the Insert Hyperlink dialog box, PowerPoint displays the Link to Existing File or Web Page view by default. This view enables you to find the URL you want in several ways:

■ If you know the URL, simply type it in the Address field.

■ If the link is to a location that you have visited recently, you can select it from the list of displayed URLs.

Linked text

Figure 16.3
Linked text appears underlined and in a highlighted color.

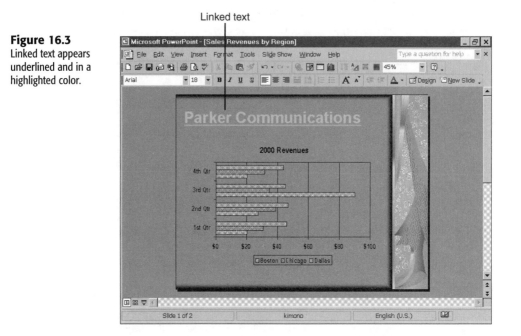

- If you don't remember the location by its URL, you can click the Browsed Pages button and choose the location from a list of places you've recently visited on the Web.

- You can click the Browse the Web button to go to your browser, enabling you to browse for the Internet location you want. When you find the location, you switch back to PowerPoint (use the Windows taskbar or press Alt+Tab), and the URL from your browser appears automatically in the dialog box.

Note

Don't forget that you must be connected to the Internet if you want to browse for a URL. Generally, those connected directly to a network need not be concerned; those using dial-up connections must first make sure they are connected.

- If you want to jump to a specific location within a Web page after inserting the URL, click the Bookmark button. PowerPoint displays a list of all bookmarks found in the Web page (see Figure 16.4). Select a bookmark and choose OK. PowerPoint adds the pound sign (#) and the bookmark name to your URL.

CREATING INVISIBLE HYPERLINKS FOR TEXT

Linked text appears markedly different from the nonlinked text around it (it's underlined). You might not like the look this creates, but you still want to be able to click that text and jump to the linked page or document. The solution is really quite simple: Draw an AutoShape—such as a rectangle—that covers the text you want to link, link the AutoShape, and then make it invisible.

Figure 16.4
If you need to link to a
bookmark, PowerPoint
can connect to the
Web site and return a
list of bookmarks in
the target Web page.

➜ For more information about creating AutoShapes, **see** "Adding AutoShapes" in Chapter 14, "Creating
and Formatting Objects."

To create an invisible hyperlinked object, follow these steps:

1. Use the Drawing toolbar to draw a rectangular box that covers the text you want to link
   (see Figure 16.5).

2. With the AutoShape selected, click the Insert Hyperlink button (or choose Insert,
   Hyperlink or press Ctrl+K).

Figure 16.5
To create the effect
of linked text without
making it look linked,
use an AutoShape
graphic image to
create the link, and
then make the
image invisible.

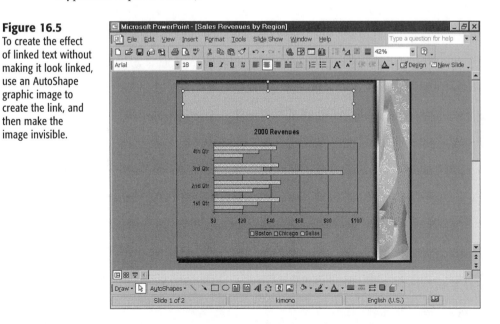

PART

V

CH

16

3. Type the Internet URL in the Address field.

4. Click OK. This creates the link to the AutoShape image.

5. Right-click the AutoShape, and choose Format AutoShape; or choose Format, AutoShape from the menu bar. PowerPoint displays the Format AutoShape dialog box (see Figure 16.6).

Figure 16.6
Use the Format AutoShape dialog box to remove fill color and line color, thus making the AutoShape invisible.

6. Click the Fill Color drop-down list and choose No Fill.

7. Click the Line Color drop-down list and choose No Line.

8. Click OK.

An invisible linked object now appears over the text you want linked (see Figure 16.7). When you play your slideshow, you simply move the mouse pointer to that text area and click when the mouse pointer changes to a hand. To the audience, it appears that you are clicking on text, although you are really clicking a linked invisible graphic shape.

An additional benefit to using an invisible link is that no one except you has to know the link is there. If you don't use it, no one will ever know. Text linked in the normal manner, on the other hand, begs to be clicked because the text around it is so obviously different.

JUMPING TO OTHER SLIDES

In addition to Web sites—and perhaps of more practical use—you can also create links that enable you to jump to other slides within your presentation, or even to a slide within another PowerPoint presentation.

Linked AutoShape

Figure 16.7
An invisible
AutoShape can be
linked, making it
appear that the text
beneath it is linked.

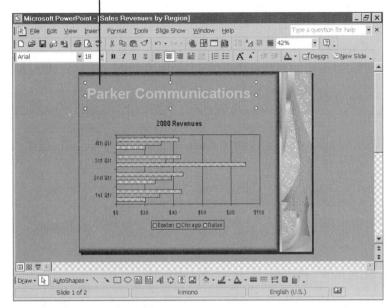

Creating links to other slides helps you customize your slideshow so that you can go quickly
to those slides you need. For example, after your opening title slide, you might want to
include a table of contents slide, with hyperlinks from each topic to a specific location in
the slideshow. On the last slide for each topic, you could include a link back to the table of
contents slide. To create this type of internal link, follow these steps:

1. Select the object to be linked and access the Insert Hyperlink dialog box.
2. Click the Place in This Document button. PowerPoint displays a list of slides in the
    current slideshow (see Figure 16.8).

Figure 16.8
To link to a slide in
your current presenta-
tion, click Place in This
Document and select
the slide you want.

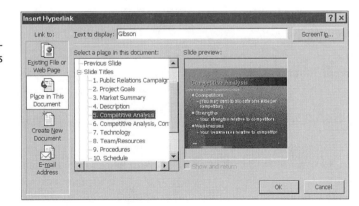

3. Select the slide to which you want to jump.

4. Click OK.

To create a link to another presentation, do the following:

1. Select the object to be linked and access the Insert Hyperlink dialog box.

2. Click the Existing File or Web Page button.

3. Choose the PowerPoint presentation to which you want to jump. Use the Browse for File button if necessary (the third small button to the right of the Look In drop-down list).

4. Click the Bookmark button. PowerPoint displays the Select Place in Document dialog box (refer to Figure 16.4).

5. Select the slide to which you want to jump.

6. Click OK twice to return to the PowerPoint editing screen.

JUMPING TO ANOTHER FILE

PowerPoint also enables you to create a hyperlink to another document, either on your own computer or on the network, if you are connected to one. When you jump from your PowerPoint presentation to another file, the application that displays that file starts automatically. Other PowerPoint files appear in PowerPoint, of course. Word documents appear in Word, HTML files are displayed in your browser, and so on.

To link to a file from the Insert Hyperlink dialog box, you can do the following:

- Type the name of the file, including its full pathname (for example, c:\my documents\sales.xls).

- Click the Recent Files button to display a list of recently accessed files.

- Click the Browse for File button and browse your computer or your network files for the file you want.

CREATING OTHER TYPES OF LINKS

Finally, you can insert links to files you haven't even created, as well as links to send electronic mail. Creating a link to a new file (by clicking the Create New Document button) is a handy way to create a hyperlink and create a new PowerPoint presentation at the same time. And adding a link to an e-mail address can be useful if you publish to the Web and want your audience to be able to contact you after viewing your presentation (see Figure 16.9).

To create a link to an e-mail address, click the E-mail Address button in the Insert Hyperlink dialog box. Type the address in the E-mail Address field and enter a subject. You can even select the e-mail address from a list of recently used e-mail addresses (see Figure 16.10).

Figure 16.9
You can even link to a yet-to-be-created document.

Figure 16.10
Create a link to an e-mail address, enabling a viewer to send a message.

Tip from
Patrice-Anne Rutledge

As a shortcut, just enter your e-mail address directly in PowerPoint (jsmith@work.com). PowerPoint recognizes common e-mail formats and creates a link for you automatically.

Note

Traditionally, PowerPoint presentations were designed to be presented to an audience by a speaker. PowerPoint is now designed so that viewers can also be allowed to run the presentation by themselves. PowerPoint presentations placed on a company network or on a Web site can be designed so that viewers can navigate and even interact with the presentation at their own pace.

CUSTOMIZING THE SCREENTIP

When you point your mouse at a linked object during a presentation, a ScreenTip appears, detailing the location of the link. You can customize the ScreenTip to make it easier for you (or the audience) to know just where you will go if you click the linked object.

To change the ScreenTip, follow these steps:

1. Select the object to be linked and access the Edit Hyperlink dialog box.

2. Click the ScreenTip button. PowerPoint displays the Set Hyperlink ScreenTip dialog box (see Figure 16.11).

Figure 16.11
Customize the ScreenTip that appears when you move the mouse pointer to a linked object.

3. Type the text you want to appear in the ScreenTip in the ScreenTip Text field. The note about ScreenTips in Internet Explorer refers to slideshows viewed in the browser, not to slideshows presented normally.

4. Click OK twice to return to the PowerPoint editing screen.

MODIFYING HYPERLINKS

The Edit Hyperlink dialog box is a powerful tool for quickly and efficiently modifying your hyperlinks. To change the URL for a hyperlink you created, follow these simple steps:

1. Click or select the linked object.

2. Right-click the object and choose Edit Hyperlink; or choose Insert, Hyperlink; or press Ctrl+K. PowerPoint displays the Edit Hyperlink dialog box (see Figure 16.12).

Figure 16.12
The Edit Hyperlink dialog box enables you to update or change an existing hyperlink.

3. Type the new URL or use one of the dialog box tools to select what you want to link to.

4. Choose OK to update the hyperlink.

REMOVING HYPERLINKS

After inserting a hyperlink, you may decide you don't want that link or that you need to link it to another object on the screen. To remove a hyperlink, simply select the object, access the Edit Hyperlink dialog box, and click the Remove Link button.

CHANGING A HYPERLINKED OBJECT'S ACTION SETTINGS

The most important action for a linked object is to jump to a desired location. However, using PowerPoint's action settings feature, you can control how you activate the hyperlink and also add some pizzazz to the linked object.

→ To learn more about action settings, **see** "Using Action Settings" in Chapter 15, "Working with Animation."

PART
V
CH
16

To access the Action Settings dialog box:

1. Select the linked object.

2. Right-click and choose Action Settings, or choose Slide Show, Action Settings. PowerPoint displays the Action Settings dialog box.

If you've created a hyperlink, Hyperlink To is already selected, and the location of the link is listed. Note that the action appears on the Mouse Click tab, which means that you have to click the linked object to activate the hyperlink. The Mouse Over tab offers the same options, but actions are activated merely by passing the mouse pointer over the linked object, without clicking.

Note

You might be able to save some time by selecting an object and using the Action Settings dialog box both to create the hyperlink and to set any actions you want.

Caution

You don't want surprises during your slide presentation. Unfortunately, the Mouse Over option for activating hyperlinks can take you places before you're really ready to go there. Generally, you should activate hyperlinks only by clicking the mouse.

You can add some pizzazz to your presentation by creating actions that produce sound effects or that highlight linked objects. For example, you can require a mouse click to activate a hyperlink, but you can highlight the object (graphic objects only) or add a sound effect when the mouse pointer is passed over the object.

To add Mouse Over sound and highlighting effects:

1. Select the object to which you want to add the effects.

2. Right-click and choose Action Settings, or choose Slide Show, Action Settings. PowerPoint displays the Action Settings dialog box.

3. Click the Mouse Over tab (see Figure 16.13).

Figure 16.13
Add action settings to a link that are activated when you pass the mouse pointer over the linked object.

4. Click the Highlight When Mouse Over check box (you cannot select this option if the object you have selected is text).

5. Click the Play Sound check box.

6. Click the Play Sound drop-down list, and select the sound effect you want to use.

> **Note**
>
> You can associate any WAV-formatted sound file with the object. Simply choose Other Sound from the drop-down list and browse until you find the sound you want.

> **Note**
>
> If you add action settings to an object, the Action Settings dialog box opens when you click the Insert Hyperlink button (rather than the Insert Hyperlink or Edit Hyperlink dialog box). You can still edit the URL, but you have to remove any action settings if you want to access the Edit Hyperlink dialog box.

TESTING HYPERLINKS

More likely than not, you will test your hyperlinks as you go. Nevertheless, before you present to an audience, you'll want to test all your hyperlinks to verify that you set them up correctly.

Note

Don't forget that you must be connected to the Internet, either via a network or through a dial-up connection, if you want to test links to the Web.

To test a hyperlink, follow these steps:

1. Go to the slide you want to test.

2. Click the Slide Show view. Choosing Slide Show, View Show (or pressing F5) starts you at the beginning of your presentation, not at the currently selected slide.

3. Move the mouse pointer to the linked object.

4. Check that the ScreenTip appears properly.

5. Note whether action settings work properly (such as the sound effect on mouse over).

6. Click the linked object and verify that you are taken to the appropriate Web location, slide, or file.

7. Return to your slideshow by closing the linked location. Usually, this involves closing the application, although you can also just minimize the application if you want it to start more quickly the next time you use it.

When you complete your slideshow, you should test all the links in the entire presentation. This means starting the slideshow at the beginning and trying out each hyperlink. (We'll talk about how to do that in the next section.) Stop and fix any hyperlink that doesn't work the way you expect it to.

Tip from
Patrice-Anne Rutledge

If you're presenting at a remote location and want to use hyperlinks to the Internet, be sure to arrive early to test your Internet connection and hyperlinks again. Even if you tested your hyperlinks at home and they worked fine, you need to verify your network connectivity at an unfamiliar location and have enough time to resolve problems before you present.

Navigating a Hyperlinked Presentation

You would probably never get lost in a sequential slide presentation, but in a hyperlinked presentation, you can become disoriented—and even get lost—very easily.

You can minimize the likelihood of getting lost by rehearsing your presentation many times, trying out various links, and learning what will happen and how to get back on track.

Some typical techniques for returning to the right place in your presentation include the following:

■ If you go to a browser, you can use the browser's Back button to return to PowerPoint. Generally, this doesn't close the browser, but keeps it open in case you need to use it again during the presentation.

- If you jump to another PowerPoint presentation, you can right-click the slide in the new presentation and choose Go, Previously Viewed to return to the original presentation. If your browser was open prior to opening a second slideshow, the browser might be closed.

- If you link to another document that opens up another program, such as Word, you can switch back to PowerPoint without closing the application you jumped to by pressing Alt+Tab.

- If you are linking primarily to other slides within your own presentation, you can also add navigational links, such as linked action buttons, that help you stay on course.

LINKING TO THE WEB DURING A PRESENTATION

The more elements you add to your presentation, the more complex it becomes, thus increasing the chances that something will go wrong. This can be particularly true when you link to the Internet during a presentation. Try to determine what parts of your presentation are most critical, and have a backup plan in case things don't work the way you hope they will. Make allowances that minimize your risk, and consider the following:

- Test links thoroughly. Remove broken links and update incorrect ones.

- Test your links for speed relative to other sites. If the linked URL contains a lot of graphics, uses Java, or is served by a slower Web server, you might not want to wait during your presentation for the site to appear.

- Always evaluate and reevaluate just how important the link is. If you don't need it, don't use it. What takes a few seconds to load in your office will seem like an eternity when you're standing in front of your audience.

- Have a backup plan in case your hyperlinks don't work. One method is to copy the files from the URL to your local computer (or network) and display them from there. However, the complexity of some sites, as well as copyright considerations, might make this impractical.

- Consider creating other slides that convey the same information as the Web site you wanted to connect to. They might not measure up to the actual Web site, but then again, you won't have to stand there waiting for the URL to come up, only to find that network congestion prevents it from doing so.

- If you're using a slower dial-up connection to the Internet during your presentation, be sure to consider page download times. Even a short delay while a page loads can distract an audience.

PUBLISHING TO THE INTERNET

The World Wide Web has taken the world by storm. Everyone wants either to receive or to disseminate information via the Web. PowerPoint makes it easier than ever to convert your presentation into a format that can be viewed by Web browsers, such as Internet Explorer or Netscape Navigator.

Before doing so, however, you should consider the following:

- A Web version of your presentation can be viewed by anyone who has access to your Web server. Unless your server is limited to your company (such as a corporate intranet), anyone from anywhere in the world can look in.

- A Web version enables your viewers to see the presentation at their convenience. This can be particularly important for global audiences in vastly different time zones.

- You have less control over a Web version of your presentation. No longer can you dictate the sequence of the slides, nor can you add clarifying comments if they are needed.

- In the case of classroom presentations, will a Web version encourage students to skip class, knowing they can get the presentation off the Web at another time?

- Will your potential Web audience have the necessary computer hardware and software to view your presentation the way you intend it to appear?

PART

V

CH

16

After you determine that you really want to publish your presentation to the Web, you next need to be sure that the slideshow is well designed for Web use. Consider the following:

- Use good presentation design principles. If the slideshow works for an audience that sits before you, it will probably work well on the Web.

- Because the presentation will be viewed unattended, be sure you have abundant navigational aids so that viewers don't get lost. Include a table of contents or Home, Back, and Forward buttons to assist the viewer.

- Be more judicious in your use of graphics, animations, and other multimedia effects. What works well from a hard disk or over a local area network might be deadly slow over a modem connection. Keep such elements small or eliminate them altogether, if they don't really add to the presentation.

- Be aware of issues related to accessibility for disabled users. For example, consider whether you need an alternative text-based page for the visually impaired who use special voice readers.

Do you have the right folders in the right place on your Web server, but some of your files are not appearing in the Web slideshow? See "Restoring Missing Files" in the "Troubleshooting" section near the end of this chapter.

Caution

Be careful to understand and follow copyright laws and guidelines when publishing your slideshow to the Web. If any of your material is copyrighted by someone else, you may be required to limit access to the material or not even use it at all if you don't first obtain permission.

SAVING A PRESENTATION AS A WEB PAGE

PowerPoint not only enables you to save your work directly in HTML format, but also lets you open your HTML slideshows directly into PowerPoint, edit them, and save them again in HTML. As you will see, this is not only easy, but it saves lots of time and space because you don't have to keep an original PowerPoint show and convert it each time.

Publishing your show to the Internet involves two steps: saving the presentation in HTML format and transferring the resulting files to a Web server. If you're lucky enough to be connected directly to your Web server over a company intranet, you don't even have to worry about transferring files because you can save the show directly at the Web site.

To save a slideshow as a Web page, follow these steps:

1. Choose File, Save as Web Page, and PowerPoint displays a somewhat modified Save As dialog box (see Figure 16.14).

Figure 16.14
Saving a PowerPoint presentation as a Web page can be quite simple, or you can customize the Web page.

2. Browse to the location where you want to save your presentation, displayed in the Save In field.

> **Note**
>
> Saving your show as a Web page generates several separate files. To make it easier to locate these files, to delete them, or to transfer them to a Web server, it's a good idea to create a separate folder for the Web version of your slideshow. Click the Create New Folder button and supply the name of the folder for your Web files.

3. Edit the filename if you want. Note that the filename ends in .htm, a standard extension for HTML files.

4. Click the Change Title button to change the page title in the Set Page Title dialog box. This title appears in the browser's title bar.

5. Click Save to save your presentation as a Web page.

Note

> If you know that PowerPoint's Web options are set the way you want them, you can save time by choosing Save. By default, this gives you a frame-based Web page that includes an outline, navigation buttons, and other tools, along with the slide. The HTML file is also optimized for use with Internet Explorer 4.0 or later.

If you want to customize the way you present your slideshow as a Web page, follow these steps:

1. Choose File, Save as Web Page.

2. In the Save As dialog box (refer to Figure 16.14), click Publish to customize the Web page display. PowerPoint displays the Publish as Web Page dialog box (see Figure 16.15).

Figure 16.15
Publishing a presentation as a Web page enables you to customize how the page will appear on the Web.

3. Choose the options you want (see the next section, "Customizing a Web Presentation").

4. Click Publish to save your presentation as a series of HTML files that work together to display your slides on the Web.

CUSTOMIZING A WEB PRESENTATION

The many options for saving your presentation as a Web page enable you to tailor your Web page to match the needs of your viewers. For example, some browsers won't be able to view animations, while others can.

To customize a Web presentation, you must first decide exactly what you want to publish to the Web: the entire presentation, selected slides, a custom show, and/or speaker's notes (refer to Figure 16.15).

You can also optimize the Web presentation for browsers that audience members are likely to use by selecting the following options under Browser Support:

■ To attain the highest fidelity to your original presentation, publish the presentation for use by selecting Microsoft Internet Explorer 4.0 or Later (High Fidelity). This option enables viewers with the latest browsers to see animations and to experience other multimedia features.

Tip from
Patrice-Anne
Rutledge

You must decide whether to ignore users with older browsers or force them to upgrade to view your Web page. If you're pretty sure that most browsers are up to date, optimize for the highest quality. Otherwise, you might want to choose an option that allows all browsers to view the Web page.

■ To enable users of older Web browsers to view your Web page content, choose Microsoft Internet Explorer 3.0, Netscape Navigator 3.0, or Later. Some of the pizzazz of your PowerPoint presentation may be lost with this conversion.

■ All Browsers Listed Above is a special dual-HTML feature that enables viewers to see the best presentation they can, based on the browser they use. This option creates larger files, which means slower downloads, but it helps you avoid having to guess which browsers your audience members are going to use.

The Web Options button takes you to the Web Options dialog box (shown in Figure 16.16), where you have many other options.

Figure 16.16
General Web options determine how the Web page is to be laid out and whether animations will be active.

On the General tab, you can set several appearance options, including the capability to add slide navigation controls, show slide animation while browsing, or resize graphics to fit the browser window.

Note

> The options on the General tab affect only those slideshows prepared for and viewed by Internet Explorer 4.0 or later. However, navigation control color options, even when turned off, do affect the navigational outline in Web pages targeted for Internet Explorer 3.0 and Netscape Navigator 3.0 or later.

PART

V

CH

16

On the Browsers tab (see Figure 16.17), you can choose the browser your viewers will use.

Figure 16.17
Set the optimal browser viewing options on this tab.

The earlier the browser version you choose, the smaller your Web pages will be. However, an earlier browser version might not support all the functionality of PowerPoint 2002, such as animations. You can also set a browser preference in the Publish as Web Page dialog box.

Based on your browser selection, the Options check boxes have the following default options selected:

- **Allow PNG as a Graphics Format** PNG (Portable Network Graphics) is a Web graphics format that is smaller in size and can have better color and transparency control. However, older browsers (pre–Internet Explorer 4.0) don't support this type of graphic format.

- **Rely on VML for Displaying Graphics in Browsers** VML (Vector Markup Language) is a method for describing 2D graphics in a text format. VML works only with the latest browsers, such as Internet Explorer 5.0. If your audience might be using older browsers, do not use this option.

■ **Save an Additional Version of the Presentation for Older Browsers**   This option ensures that the maximum number of viewers can view your presentation clearly, but it increases the space required for your presentation.

■ **Save New Web Pages as Web Archives**   Saves in a Web archive format, which enables you to store all parts of your Web site into a single file (text, graphics, other content, and so on). This option uses the MHTML (MIME encapsulated aggregate HTML) file format, which is supported by Internet Explorer 4.0 and later.

Click the Files tab in the Web Options dialog box to access file naming and location options. Here you can specify to organize supporting files in a folder, use long filenames, and update links on save (see Figure 16.18).

Figure 16.18
File options enable you to specify how files will be named, how they'll be organized, and whether you can edit the resulting HTML files in PowerPoint.

The Pictures tab provides the option to target monitor screen size. If you have chosen the Internet Explorer 4.0 Browser Support and the Resize Graphics to Fit Browser Window options, changing this setting has no effect. However, if you publish your presentation for use on older browsers, this option enables you to specify how large the slides should be.

Tip from
Patrice-Anne Rutledge

Using a screen size that matches the target browser screen setting usually results in a slide that is too small for the available screen. If you want to fill up the browser window with a larger slide, select the next-highest resolution (for example, select 1024 × 768 if the target screen is 800 × 600).

Finally, the Encoding and Fonts tabs enable you to modify the output for use in browsers that support other languages.

→ For more information on the use of other languages in your presentations, **see** Appendix B, "Using PowerPoint's Foreign Language Capabilities."

TRANSFERRING YOUR WEB PAGE TO A WEB SERVER

Typically, you create your presentation and save it as a Web page on your local hard disk. Working offline saves time and, in some cases, dial-up connection charges. When you're finally ready to make your presentation available to the rest of the world, you must transfer your files from your own computer to the Web server that will host your Web page.

If you are connected to a company intranet, you may be able to publish your Web page directly to the Web server. Check with your network specialist to find out if this is possible and how to do it.

If you aren't connected directly to your Web server, you will have to transfer files to it following the instructions provided by your Internet service provider (ISP), just as you would any other Web site or pages.

PART
V

CH

16

TESTING YOUR WEB PAGE

More likely than not, you will test your Web page as you go. At the bottom of the Publish as Web Page dialog box, you can check the Open Published Web Page in Browser option so that each time you publish your presentation, your default browser starts and displays the page using files saved on your local computer (see Figure 16.19). If you find something wrong or want to try other options, simply return to PowerPoint and publish the presentation again.

Figure 16.19
A Web page published for Internet Explorer 4.0 or later includes an outline, the slide, and several navigation buttons.

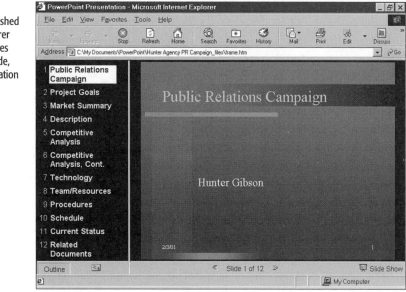

After you transfer your files to your Web server, you should again test your presentation in your browser over the Internet. Some things you should check for are the following:

- All files should be in their proper place. If you find missing pages or graphics, be sure you have transferred files to folders and locations that correspond *exactly* to the folders on your hard disk.

■ Links should be tested individually to be sure they work as you expect.

> The World Wide Web is a dynamic, constantly changing medium. Links that work today might not work tomorrow. If your Web page contains links, you should check periodically to be sure they're still active.

■ If some of your intended audience use dial-up connections, test how long it takes to download your presentation using a modem. You might discover that certain slides simply take too long to download because of large graphics, sound, or even video elements. You have to determine just how important those elements are and consider eliminating them to speed up the presentation.

■ Not all browsers are created equal! You should test your Web page using both Internet Explorer and Netscape Navigator, including new and older versions of those programs. If you want, you can download older versions of browsers from the Microsoft and Netscape Web sites.

■ Not all computers and screen settings are the same, either. Test your pages on standard VGA screens (640 × 480), on Super VGA (800 × 600), and on XGA screens (1024 × 768).

■ Test your Web page on Macintosh screens (or any other operating system you anticipate your audience might use). Screen resolution and colors sometimes are very different on the Macintosh.

Note

> If your intended audience uses the same browser and has the same type of computers (for example, in a corporate intranet setting), you might not need to perform such extensive testing. If you have a wider audience and you want to look good on a wide variety of computer screens (for example, in a university setting), you can't assume everyone uses the same computer and browser that you do.

MODIFYING OR UPDATING YOUR WEB PAGE

If you find during testing that you need to change your Web page, or if at a later date you want to update the information in your presentation, you can still use PowerPoint to edit the presentation.

The easiest way to edit a PowerPoint Web page is to open the main HTML page directly into PowerPoint. Because it uses XML and other advanced HTML processes, the HTML page retains all of PowerPoint's special features, including the use of animations and other multimedia objects.

Tip from
*Patrice-Anne
Rutledge*

> You don't need to keep both a PowerPoint (PPT) and an HTML version of your presentation on your local computer. Keep only the HTML copy, which you can open, edit, and play just as you do any regular PowerPoint presentation.

After you make the changes you want, simply save the presentation again as a Web page and transfer the resulting files to your Web server, if necessary.

TROUBLESHOOTING

RESTORING MISSING IMAGES

Why are some of the image files from my presentation not appearing in the HTML slideshow?

If you place your supporting files (such as images) in a subfolder, you must create the same folder structure on your Web server and transfer your files to their correct locations. If you transfer all your files to the same location, without subfolders, your slideshow will not work properly.

RESTORING MISSING FILES

I have the right folders in the right place on my Web server, but some of my files are still not appearing in the Web slideshow. What else can I do?

You must create filenames and folder names *exactly* as you created them when you published your Web page locally, including uppercase and lowercase characters. Using the wrong case in even one character of a filename or folder name can prevent your Web page from working properly.

DESIGN CORNER: CREATING INVISIBLE LINKS

Linked text in your slideshow can make it easy to jump from one place to another, but because the links themselves look markedly different from the text around them, they can also distract from the overall design of your slide (see Figure 16.20). To remedy this, follow these steps:

1. Enter the text to which you want to add a hyperlink.
2. Select the Rectangle button on the Drawing toolbar and create an AutoShape that covers your text.
3. Select the AutoShape and click the Insert Hyperlink button on the Standard toolbar.
4. Enter your hyperlink in the Insert Hyperlink dialog box and click OK.
5. Right-click the AutoShape; set the fill color to No Fill and the line color to No Line in the Format AutoShape dialog box and click OK.

An invisible linked object now appears over the text you want linked, while the text itself has not changed in appearance from the text around it. When you present your slideshow, you simply move the mouse pointer to that text area and click when the mouse pointer changes to a hand (see Figure 16.21). To the audience, it appears you are clicking on text, although you are really clicking a linked invisible graphic shape.

BEFORE

Figure 16.20

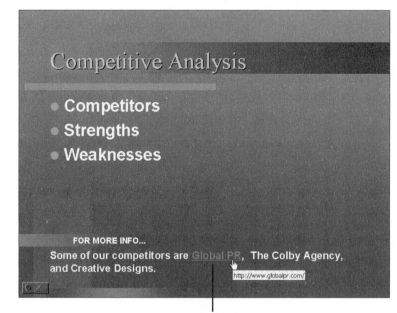

Linked text

AFTER

Figure 16.21

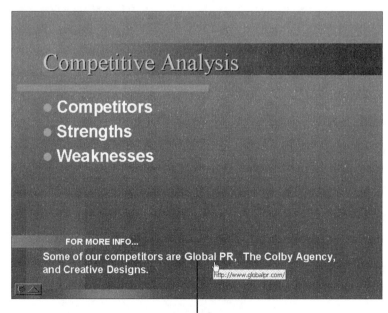

Hidden link

CHAPTER 17

WORKING WITH WEB SCRIPTS

In this chapter

UNDERSTANDING WEB SCRIPTS

With PowerPoint 2002's Web functionality, you have the ability to save presentations as HTML documents and edit them in the Microsoft Script Editor. If you know HTML, you can edit HTML tags in this editor. If you know a scripting language, such as VBScript or JScript, you can create powerful scripts to augment and automate your Web-based presentations.

Today's two most popular Web browsers, Microsoft Internet Explorer and Netscape Navigator, have embedded inside them the general-purpose core of the lightweight, object-oriented programming language referred to as both JavaScript (in the case of Navigator) and JScript (in Internet Explorer). Possessing this embedded code enables browsers to read segments of the scripting language that have been written directly into HTML documents. This is referred to as *client-side* scripting.

Understanding the client-side/server-side distinction can be tricky, and it has slightly different connotations depending upon its application. For the purpose of this discussion, the *server* is the Web server, where Web pages actually reside. The home PC of a user connecting via the Internet is considered the *client*. This raises a question, however: If the Web page with embedded script is sitting on the Web server, why isn't this a *server-side* script? The answer is that the client home PC and its browser are reading the embedded code and executing it, and it is there that the execution takes place. This is the significant point in terms of the client/server relationship.

Scripting can also be applied on the server side, when code inside an HTML document points to a script file sitting on the Web server. The script is then executed, and the result is sent back to the client. This is especially useful for generating HTML content on-the-fly.

CREATING AND EDITING WEB SCRIPTS

The Microsoft Script Editor is a powerful tool for HTML and Web script editing that provides a high level of functionality and ease of use for the experienced developer as well as the novice. Please note that this chapter is not intended to teach you the VBScript or JScript languages, and assumes that you already possess some prior knowledge of both scripting and HTML.

➔ To learn more about VBScript or JScript, **see** "Expanding Your Knowledge of Web Scripts" later in this chapter.

The Microsoft Script Editor gives you the ability to view and edit the HTML files you generate when saving your presentation as a Web page. From here you can add scripts, whether they are VBScript or JScript.

Thanks to the comprehensive Document Object Model (DOM) supported by Microsoft products, with Microsoft Script Editor you can create event handlers for virtually any element in a PowerPoint presentation. *Event handlers* are scripts that run in response to actions by the user, such as mouse clicks or the browser's loading of the document.

Editing features aren't limited to event handlers. You can also use the Microsoft Script Editor to create independent blocks of script to contain any script you choose.

Caution

Use the Microsoft Script Editor to edit only .htm and .asp files. If you edit other files (such as .doc files), ID parameters, <SPAN> and <DIV> tags, and some VALUE parameters might be changed when you save or refresh the file.

From within PowerPoint, you can open a presentation in the Microsoft Script Editor by following these steps:

1. Save your presentation as a Web page (.htm format) by choosing File, Save as Web Page.

2. Name your file and select a folder in which to save it.

3. Click Save.

4. With your presentation onscreen, choose Tools, Macro, Microsoft Script Editor. This opens the Microsoft Script Editor, as shown in Figure 17.1.

Document Outline window   Project Explorer

Figure 17.1
You can also open the
Microsoft Script Editor
by pressing
Alt+Shift+F11.

HTML window   Properties window

The Web page you view in the Microsoft Script Editor is actually a separate copy of your actual presentation. If you make changes to this copy of the Web page while in the Microsoft Script Editor, the changes are out of sync with the copy of your Web page in

PowerPoint. Any changes made to the presentation in PowerPoint while the Microsoft Script Editor is open are out of sync, as well. To update the unchanged copy of your Web page with the changes you made, be sure to click Refresh on the Refresh toolbar when you return to the unchanged copy in PowerPoint. The Refresh toolbar is a floating toolbar that appears in PowerPoint after you make changes in the Microsoft Script Editor.

SCRIPTING IN THE MICROSOFT SCRIPT EDITOR

The Microsoft Script Editor consists of four primary windows for working with Web scripts: the Document Outline, HTML, Project Explorer, and Properties windows.

The Document Outline window uses a hierarchy tree similar to that seen in Windows Explorer to represent the scripts within a document. The HTML window is the repository of the hard code for the presentation you're working with. As in the Document Outline window, the Project Explorer window uses the tree metaphor to display the associated files in a presentation. The Properties window is where certain HTML and scripting attributes are set.

LOOKING AT THE DOCUMENT OUTLINE WINDOW

The Document Outline window provides a graphical display of the object model for your presentation (see Figure 17.2).

Figure 17.2
The Document Outline window is divided into folders, or nodes, representing the object model of the open file.

From here, you can

- Display a tree view of all elements in your presentation that have already had their ID or NAME attributes set
- Display the events for each element

- Quickly navigate to any script in the page
- Generate new event handlers for any element in the presentation

Table 17.1 describes the use of each node in the Document Outline window. Depending on what you're doing in the Microsoft Script Editor, not all these nodes might appear.

TABLE 17.1 THE DOCUMENT OUTLINE WINDOW'S NODES

Document Outline Window's Nodes	Function/Use
Client Objects & Events	A hierarchy of the elements that support client scripts or have client scripts attached. Under the node for each element is a list of the events for which you can write handlers.
Client Scripts	A set of nodes for each client script on the page. There is a node for each script block on the page and a separate node for each function or subroutine defined within a script block. There is also a node for inline scripts defined as part of a control definition, as in this example: `<INPUT TYPE="button" NAME="button1" ONCLICK="alert('Clicked!')">`.
Server Objects & Events	A list of nodes for each element that supports server scripts or that has server scripts attached. Under each node is a list of the events for which you can write handlers. The Server Objects & Events node also displays the Microsoft Internet Information Server object model, including the Session object, Application object, and so on. In the Document Outline window, these objects do not display events.
Server Scripts	A set of nodes for each server script on the page. Functions and subroutines are identified by name. Inline server scripts appear in a tree, but are not identified by name.

Note

The Document Outline window doesn't include elements that are added to a page using an INCLUDE file.

LOOKING AT THE HTML WINDOW

The HTML window (see Figure 17.3) enables you to view and edit scripts.

This window was designed for working with the raw code of a Web document, providing for more precise control over the attributes in a given page. It enables you to switch between visual and text representation of all controls on the page using the Design and HTML tabs.

Figure 17.3
Edit and view code in
the HTML window.

Design view is not available for pages created in Microsoft PowerPoint or any other Office application. You can use Source view to modify the script, but design changes must be made in the Microsoft Office program. Design view is available only for pages that are opened from within the Microsoft Script Editor.

If you accessed Microsoft Script Editor through PowerPoint and want to take advantage of Design view's capabilities, close the HTML window and select File, Open, File. From here you can navigate to the folder containing the associated files for your presentation in the Open File dialog box. By enabling Design view in this manner, you are able to extend the WYSIWYG attributes of the editing environment.

To preview your presentation in a browser, choose File, View in Browser.

LOOKING AT THE PROJECT EXPLORER WINDOW

The Project Explorer window displays the associated file in the folder created when you saved your PowerPoint presentation. From here, double-click a file's icon to open its source code in the HTML window. You can add the individual .htm files of the presentation you generated by saving each file as a Web page and simply repeating the steps outlined above to enable Design view for your presentation.

LOOKING AT THE PROPERTIES WINDOW

The Properties window (see Figure 17.4) displays the various HTML and scripting properties within the Web page.

Figure 17.4
Use the sort buttons to view your attributes.

Alphabetic sort
Categorized sort
Click here to open the Property Pages dialog box.

PART

V

CH

17

From this window, you can change default settings such as client and server script types. This window provides three tool buttons with which to view and edit page attributes: Sort Properties Alphabetically, Sort Properties by Category, and Property Pages.

The Property Pages button opens the Property Pages dialog box shown in Figure 17.5, in which you can define specific document properties.

Figure 17.5
Select HTML and scripting attributes in the Property Pages dialog box.

You can also click in the far-right column of the Properties window, which displays individual properties, and make your selection there.

NAVIGATING TO SCRIPTS

You can use the Document Outline window to move between scripts by first clicking the appropriate node to expand the Document Outline tree until you see the script you want to view, and then clicking the script's name. The insertion point in the HTML window moves to the script's location in the file. If you are working on a script in the HTML window, you can match up your location in the Document Outline window to see where you are in the context of the overall page.

To synchronize your position with the Document Outline window, right-click and choose View, Synchronize Document Outline.

ADDING WEB SCRIPT COMMANDS TO YOUR TOOLS MENU

To facilitate scripting in PowerPoint, Microsoft has provided you with three specialized commands you can add to your Tools menu:

- Insert Script
- Remove All Scripts
- Show All Scripts

To insert these items, follow these steps:

1. In PowerPoint, choose Tools, Customize. This opens the Customize dialog box, as shown in Figure 17.6.

Figure 17.6
From the Customize dialog box, you can drag new tools to your menus.

2. In the Categories box, click Tools.

3. Scroll down in the Commands box until the scripting commands become visible.

4. Drag Insert Script from the Commands box to the Tools menu on the main PowerPoint menu bar. From here, drag down to the Macro submenu. When the Macro submenu opens, drag to where you want the Insert Script command to appear and then release the mouse button.

5. Repeat steps 3 and 4 for the Show All Scripts and Remove All Scripts commands.

6. Click Close.

The Insert Script command invokes the Microsoft Script Editor, placing the cursor at the insertion point you've selected. The Show All Scripts command provides a toggle that displays what Microsoft refers to as a *glyph* to mark the location of a script while still in PowerPoint. As the name suggests, Remove All Scripts removes the scripts from a presentation.

If at any time you want to remove a command from the Tools menu, simply select Customize and reverse the process by dragging the undesired command off the Macro submenu.

PART

V

CH

17

CREATING EVENT HANDLERS

The Document Outline window shows you all scriptable elements in your page, and for each element, the events for which you can write handlers. This window divides the elements and scripts into those that will run on the client and those that will run on the server.

When you expand an object node in the Document Outline window (as shown in Figure 17.7), a list of potential event handlers for that object displays. If the event name is bold, a handler already exists for that event.

Figure 17.7
Click the plus sign next to the node to see the available event handlers.

To create a new event handler, expand the appropriate object node until you see the event name for which you want to create a script; then double-click the name of the event. When you double-click the event name, the editor performs the following actions:

- Creates or moves to one of the following script blocks at the top of the document, depending on where the script will run and what language it will be in:
  - `clientEventHandlersJS`
  - `clientEventHandlersVBS`
  - `serverEventHandlersJS`
  - `serverEventHandlersVBS`
- If the script will be in JScript, adds an event attribute (for example, `onclick=`) to the element.

Finally, the editor inserts a new script block for the event you selected with a bare handler function that you then must flesh out to suit your needs.

The handler is created in the default language for the current context. For example, if you are creating a server script, the handler is in the default language for the server, as set in the Property Pages dialog box for the current document.

For VBScript functions, the format is

```
Sub elementID_event
{insert code here}
End Sub
```

For JScript functions, the format is

```
function elementID_event(){
{insert code here}
}
```

When creating JScript event handlers, the editor also adds the following attributes to the HTML element itself:

```
event="return elementID_event()"
```

SETTING THE DEFAULT SCRIPT LANGUAGE

In the Properties window, scroll down until the `defaultClientScript` or `defaultServerScript` category is visible in the bottom-left column, as shown in Figure 17.8. To change the default settings, select the category in the left column and then click on the facing cells of the far-right column to display a drop arrow. Clicking this arrow displays the options JavaScript (or JScript) and VBScript.

Figure 17.8
VBScript has been chosen instead of the default language, JavaScript.

CREATING STANDALONE SCRIPTS

In addition to creating event handlers, you can create standalone script blocks. This is useful if you want to create procedures (subroutines or functions) called by other scripts, or if you want to create a global script that runs as soon as the browser loads the page.

To create a new standalone script block, follow these steps:

1. Select the HTML window.

2. Position the cursor where you want the new script to appear.

3. Right-click and choose Insert Script Block, Client, or Server.

The Script Editor then generates a new <SCRIPT> block. If you choose Server, the script tag contains the attribute RUNAT=SERVER. The script block's LANGUAGE attribute is set to the default language for the client or server.

 Can't get your scripts to work? Not sure where to place them? See the "Troubleshooting" section at the end of this chapter.

EXPANDING YOUR KNOWLEDGE OF WEB SCRIPTS

If you don't have a background in creating scripts with JScript or VBScript, but this initial exploration of the Microsoft Script Editor has piqued your interest, take a look at the Microsoft Script Editor Help window. From within the Microsoft Script Editor, choose Help, Microsoft Script Editor Help. Here you'll find reference guides and tutorials for both JScript and VBScript as well as an HTML reference.

You don't need to become a programming expert to learn enough of one of these scripting languages to make some worthwhile enhancements to your Web-based PowerPoint presentations, but if you'd like to delve further into these topics, consider *Special Edition Using JScript* and *Special Edition Using VBScript*, also by Que.

TROUBLESHOOTING

GETTING SCRIPTS TO WORK

Why won't my simplest scripts work?

Proper syntax is always a concern in programming. Consequently, it is important to pay strict attention to detail when writing scripts. If you mean for a particular parameter to be a string, for example, you will run into trouble if you forget to enclose it in quotation marks when you type it.

PROPERLY PLACING YOUR SCRIPTS

Is there a difference in where I put my scripts on the HTML page?

The scripts you write are interpreted as part of your Web browser's HTML parsing process. This means that if the script you create is located inside the <HEAD> tag in a document, it will be interpreted before any of the <BODY> tag is looked at. If you have objects that are created in the <BODY> tag, they don't exist at the instant the <HEAD> is being parsed and, therefore, can't be manipulated by the script.

CHAPTER 18

USING ONLINE BROADCASTS AND MEETINGS

In this chapter

UNDERSTANDING ONLINE BROADCASTS AND MEETINGS

By this time, you should have polished your presentation thoroughly. It's clear, organized, and to-the-point. Your visuals are coordinated, your script is down pat, and maybe you've even added background sound to make the presentation really move. Now it's time to deliver. This chapter shows you how to use PowerPoint 2002's presentation broadcast and online meeting tools to do exactly that.

PowerPoint can run a live, simultaneous broadcast of your presentation from your PC to tens, hundreds, or even thousands of other PCs tuned in to hear what you have to say. You can also add live audio or video content to the presentation as you make it. Using PowerPoint to do a presentation broadcast is much more convenient than gathering your audience physically into one room and getting the necessary facilities, large-screen computer projectors, and sound equipment organized.

By itself, PowerPoint can transmit a presentation broadcast to as many as 10 other people. Your audience will need Internet Explorer 5.1 or later to view this broadcast. For broadcasts to 11 or more people, you need to have access to a Microsoft Windows Media Server. This is a digital media platform that supports streaming media in your presentation (such as audio and video). If you don't have access to a Windows Media Server, you can sign up for an account with a third-party service provider to handle these technicalities. If your company or organization has an IS department, you should contact its staff for advice on using Windows Media Server within your network environment.

Note

Broadcasting to a large audience and using Windows Media Server can be complex. To learn more about broadcasting PowerPoint presentations to large audiences, refer to the Microsoft Office Resource Kit (http://www.microsoft.com/office/ork/).

In addition to showing you how to conduct a PowerPoint presentation broadcast, I'll also cover PowerPoint's other broadcast feature, online meetings. Online meetings are a nice complement to presentation broadcasts. A *broadcast* is a one-way connection between you and your audience, whereas an *online meeting* is a two-way channel. In an online meeting, everyone can communicate with everyone else to brainstorm, hash out a tough decision, or even create a presentation together.

CHOOSING A BROADCAST OR MEETING

Online meetings also require some additional software to work. To use the feature, you'll need to have Microsoft's NetMeeting group collaboration software installed on your computer, and so will everyone else who takes part in the meeting. NetMeeting is included on your Office CD, and, if it isn't already on your system, it will be installed automatically the first time you try to use it.

Here are some guidelines to help you decide which online presentation approach is right for you.

Choose a presentation broadcast when

- You want to reach a large number of people at once.
- You want to save your presentation broadcast so people can watch it later.
- You want your presentation to be one-way.
- Your audience doesn't have very powerful computers or fast network connections (all they need is Internet Explorer 5.1 or later to see your broadcast).

Presentation broadcasts can be used in corporate training sessions, general company announcements, and online presentations to business partners or clients.

Choose an online meeting when

- You want to interact with the people to whom you are presenting.
- You don't need to reach many people (say 10 or fewer).
- Your audience has powerful enough computers with fast enough network connections to handle Microsoft NetMeeting (and the computers have the NetMeeting software installed). As a rough guide, meeting participants need at least Pentium-class computers with 32MB of RAM and a 56Kbps modem network connection.

Online meetings can be used for group brainstorming sessions (especially those now done with videoconferencing equipment), online staff meetings, and one-on-one planning meetings with a colleague.

Later, we'll cover a third online collaboration tool—Web discussions.

PART
V

CH

18

RECORDING AND SAVING A BROADCAST

Because running a live presentation broadcast can be complicated, it's usually better to practice recording and saving a broadcast before presenting it live. Even if your ultimate goal is to conduct a live broadcast, doing several "practice runs" in which you record, save, and replay your broadcast can help you perfect your presentation and delivery—and make you more confident when it's time to go live.

To get started, choose Slide Show, Online Broadcast, Record and Save a Broadcast. If this is the first time you've tried to create a presentation broadcast, a message appears telling you that PowerPoint needs to install some extra software to enable this feature (see Figure 18.1). Choose Yes to install the software.

Figure 18.1
The first time you try to set up a presentation broadcast, PowerPoint needs to install its presentation broadcast feature.

A message box appears, showing you the installation progress. You can click the Cancel button if you want to stop the install for any reason. After the online broadcasting feature is installed, the Record Presentation Broadcast dialog box opens (see Figure 18.2).

Figure 18.2
Enter a title and description for your recorded presentation broadcast.

The Record Presentation Broadcast dialog box sets up the basic information your audience will see in the presentation lobby page and enables you to configure more advanced broadcast options. Enter a title and description for your broadcast, as well as the speaker's name and, if you want, the e-mail address of the person organizing the broadcast. You can also add copyright and keyword information. You should provide sufficient detail here so that potential audience members will know what the presentation will be about and for whom it was designed. Specifying the length of the presentation is also a good idea. Click the Tips for Broadcast button to display related content in the PowerPoint Help window.

CONFIGURING BROADCAST SETTINGS

After you've entered information on the Record Presentation Broadcast dialog box, you'll need to specify a few more technical broadcast settings. Click the Settings button on the Record Presentation Broadcast dialog box to open the Broadcast Settings dialog box (see Figure 18.3).

Figure 18.3
The Broadcast Settings dialog box enables you to set various presentation options.

The first group of options on the Presenter tab (Audio/Video) enables you to specify whether or not you want to have live audio or video (or both) broadcast with your presentation. Regardless of what you choose here, audio in the presentation itself (such as a saved narration or slide transition sounds) doesn't get broadcast.

If you want to broadcast audio, you'll need to have a sound card and a microphone set up at your computer. If you want to provide video (usually a picture of you talking along with the presentation, although you could also use a VCR as a video source), you'll need to have a video camera and video capture card installed at the broadcast station. Remember that the people tuning into your broadcast need to have audio-capable computer hardware to hear any sound.

You can also choose whether to let audience members see your speaker notes by selecting the Display Speaker Notes with the Presentation check box.

In the Save Broadcast Files In edit box, enter the file location where you want to save your broadcast. Because you're recording and saving this broadcast, rather than presenting it live, you can save either on your own C:\ drive or in a shared network location. For your audience to view your final broadcast, however, you'll need to move the main broadcast Web page and its associated folder to a shared network location at some point. Network locations are typed in using the format \\servername\sharename.

From the Slide Show Mode drop-down list, specify whether to display a full screen or a resizable screen. If you plan to access other programs during your broadcast (for example, to demonstrate other software), you should use a resizable screen.

The Advanced tab of the Broadcast Settings dialog box (see Figure 18.10) includes options you'll primarily use for live broadcasts.

→ To learn more about the options available on the Advanced tab of the Broadcast Settings dialog box, **see** "Scheduling a Live Broadcast" later in this chapter.

PART

V

CH

18

Note
You can also access the Broadcast Settings dialog box directly by choosing Slide Show, Online Broadcast, Settings from the menu bar.

RECORDING YOUR BROADCAST

Click the Record button on the Record Presentation Broadcast dialog box to open the Broadcast Presentation dialog box, shown in Figure 18.4.

Note
If you're rerecording your broadcast, PowerPoint will display a dialog box verifying that you want to overwrite the existing broadcast.

Figure 18.4
In the Broadcast Presentation dialog box, you'll prepare to record your broadcast.

PowerPoint verifies that the network locations you typed in earlier are valid; then it checks that your audio and video inputs are working correctly (if you enabled those options in the Broadcast Settings dialog box when you set up the presentation broadcast).

If you selected real-time audio, PowerPoint displays a Microphone Check dialog box (see Figure 18.5) to verify that your audio levels are set correctly.

Figure 18.5
Read this window's text into your microphone to check your audio levels.

After you've read the text out loud (and you've seen the horizontal volume bar move), choose OK to continue. If you want to check the microphone level again, click the Recheck Microphone button.

If you selected real-time video, PowerPoint displays a Camera Check dialog box in which you can preview the video you'll transmit to your audience. Click the Recheck Camera button to check the video again.

When the Broadcast Presentation dialog box flashes "Press Start When Ready," click the Start button to begin. Your presentation appears in Slide Show view (see Figure 18.6); record your broadcast, speaking into your microphone (and looking into the camera, if you're including video).

In many ways, this process is similar to presenting a live, in-person slideshow. When you finish recording, a message box appears telling you where PowerPoint has saved your broadcast (in an HTML format).

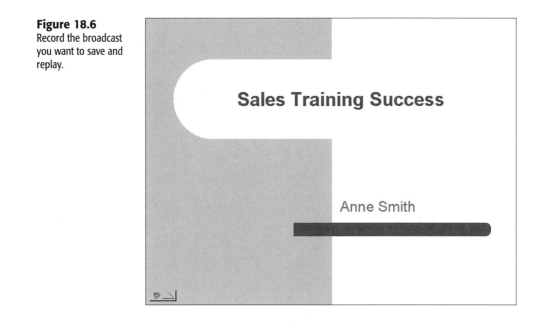

Figure 18.6
Record the broadcast you want to save and replay.

→ To learn more about presenting a live, in-person slideshow, **see** "Setting Up a Show" in Chapter 9, "Presenting a Slideshow."

Click Replay Broadcast to immediately replay the broadcast and preview what your audience will see. Click Continue to return to PowerPoint.

REPLAYING YOUR BROADCAST

If you clicked the Replay Broadcast button when you finished recording, your broadcast will display in Internet Explorer (see Figure 18.7).

In the upper-left corner of the browser, live video displays within the Windows Media Player window if you've included video in your broadcast. If your broadcast is audio only, the Windows Media Player logo will appear in this window.

Immediately below it, you'll see basic information about the broadcast (title and presenter's name) that remains throughout the broadcast.

The upper-right corner of the browser window offers links to View Previous Slides, Email Feedback, and Help.

The lobby page displays in the slide area, providing additional presentation information and the Replay Broadcast button. Click this button to start the actual broadcast, which appears in the slide area. Figure 18.8 illustrates an example of a broadcast.

Video displays here.   Click these links for other options.

Figure 18.7
The lobby page of
your recorded broad-
cast appears.

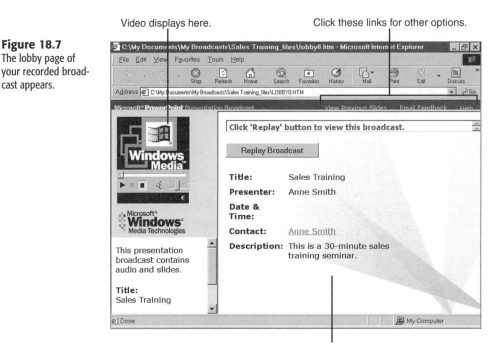

Your PowerPoint presentation appears in the slide area.

Presentation appears in the slide area.

Figure 18.8
View your PowerPoint
presentation in the
slide area of the
browser.

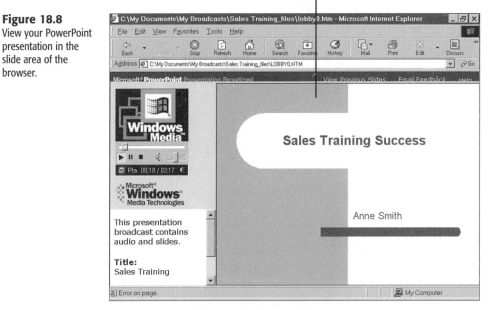

If you saved your broadcast to your C:\ drive, you must move it (the HTML file in the My
Broadcasts folder as well as the associated folder of the same name) to a shared network

location before others can view it. Send an e-mail with a link to the HTML lobby page to people you want to view the broadcast. When viewers load this Web page, instruct them to click the Replay Broadcast button to start.

 Get an error message about VML when you try to replay? *See the "Troubleshooting" section near the end of the chapter.*

SCHEDULING A LIVE BROADCAST

The first step in presenting a live online broadcast is to schedule it. This step prepares PowerPoint to broadcast your presentation and sets up a special Web page (called a *lobby page*) that your audience will use as an online gathering place before the presentation starts.

Tip from
Patrice-Anne Rutledge

You can schedule your broadcast on a machine different from the one you actually use to make the broadcast. As long as you have your PowerPoint file with you (which contains your broadcast settings inside it), you can use any computer you want to do the broadcast. Remember, the broadcast computer needs sound and video capabilities if you want to include those features, and it must have PowerPoint 2002 installed and a fast network connection.

As part of setting up a schedule, you can also send electronic mail to people whom you'd like to view the presentation, inviting them to the show and telling them how to view it.

To start the scheduling process, open the presentation you want to broadcast and choose Slide Show, Online Broadcast, Schedule a Live Broadcast. The Schedule Presentation Broadcast dialog box opens (see Figure 18.9), which is similar to the Record Presentation Broadcast dialog box (refer to Figure 18.2).

PART

V

CH

18

Figure 18.9
Enter a title and description for your upcoming presentation broadcast.

Schedule Presentation Broadcast	? X
Please enter presentation information here. This information will appear on the lobby page.	

Title: Sales Training
Description: This is a 30-minute sales training seminar.

Windows Media Technologies
You can use PowerPoint to broadcast a live presentation to other users on your network. You can send slides, audio and video. A Web browser is used to view the broadcast.

Speaker: Anne Smith
Copyright:
Keywords: Sales Training;Anne Smith
Email: Anne Smith

Settings...   Tips for Broadcast...   Schedule...   Cancel

Refer to the earlier section "Recording and Saving a Broadcast" for instructions on how to specify broadcast options and settings in this dialog box. In the Broadcast Settings dialog box (open it by clicking the Settings button), you'll note several options on the Advanced tab for live broadcasts (see Figure 18.10).

Figure 18.10
Using a Windows
Media Server enables
you to broadcast to a
large audience.

To use a remote Windows media encoder, enter the name of its computer in the edit box.

To enable participants to have real-time chat during your broadcast, enter a valid URL in the URL for the Audience Chat Room field. You must already have a chat room (not part of PowerPoint) set up to use this feature. Check with your network administrator to find out what's available at your company, if you're not sure.

Finally, you can specify Windows Media Server settings. Remember that you'll need to use Windows Media Server if you're broadcasting to more than 10 participants. Your choices include

- **Do Not Use a Windows Media Server**   Select this option if you have 10 or fewer participants, and don't need a Windows Media Server to broadcast.

- **Use This Local Windows Media Server on This LAN**   Enter the name of the server or computer that has the Windows Media Server you'll use for your presentation.

- **Use a Third Party Windows Media Service Provider**   Enables you to search for a third-party service provider for a live presentation only.

Note

You can still change your presentation after you've scheduled a broadcast; nothing's set in stone. You can even switch to presenting a completely different file if you want to, without redoing your broadcast schedule setup.

→ To learn more about how to reschedule a broadcast, **see** "Rescheduling a Broadcast" later in this chapter.

After you've finished entering your broadcast description, broadcast settings, and server options, you're ready to actually schedule the broadcast. Click the Schedule button on the Schedule Presentation Broadcast dialog box to continue.

PowerPoint starts your e-mail client to send an announcement to the people you'd like to invite to your presentation. If you're using Microsoft Outlook as your e-mail client, you'll be able to schedule the presentation using Outlook's group meeting facilities.

You've finished scheduling your presentation. PowerPoint displays a confirmation message to let you know your presentation broadcast settings have been saved. Press OK to close the message.

RESCHEDULING A BROADCAST

If you decide you want to change the broadcast time or other settings before the show actually starts, you can modify your settings easily. To do so, open the presentation you want to reschedule and choose Slide Show, Online Broadcast, Reschedule a Live Presentation to open the Reschedule Presentation Broadcast dialog box (see Figure 18.11).

Figure 18.11
Even though you've already scheduled your broadcast, you can change your mind later.

This dialog box is nearly identical to both the Record Presentation Broadcast and Schedule Presentation Broadcast dialog boxes. Note that you must have a previously scheduled presentation open to see the Reschedule a Live Presentation option from the Slide Show menu. Otherwise, you'll see the Schedule a Live Presentation option.

→ To learn more about modifying the settings of the Record Presentation Broadcast and Schedule Presentation Broadcast dialog boxes, **see** "Recording and Saving a Broadcast" earlier in this chapter.

To notify audience members that you're rescheduling your broadcast, click the Reschedule button. Your e-mail client will open, and you can send an e-mail to your participants. You can also cancel a scheduled broadcast this way as well.

STARTING THE BROADCAST

You can broadcast a presentation that you've already scheduled, or broadcast a new, unscheduled presentation. If you want to start a broadcast you haven't previously scheduled, you still need to specify which options and settings you want to use. You should start a broadcast about 30 minutes before you actually want to present to allow time for your presentation to be uploaded to the server. This also gives you time to send messages to waiting viewers before the presentation starts.

→ To learn more about how to schedule a broadcast presentation, **see** "Scheduling a Live Broadcast" in this chapter.

PART

V

CH

18

> **Note**
>
> You can tweak your presentation until the moment you click the Start button. After that, your presentation files are copied to the server for broadcast. If you still want to change the presentation, you can close the Broadcast Presentation window by clicking Close; making your changes; and then choosing Slide Show, Online Broadcast, Start Live Broadcast Now.

To start an actual broadcast, follow these steps:

1. Open the PowerPoint presentation you're going to broadcast and then choose Slide Show, Online Broadcast, and Start Live Broadcast Now. The Live Presentation Broadcast dialog box appears (see Figure 18.12).

Figure 18.12
Choose the event, either scheduled or unscheduled, to broadcast.

2. Select the broadcast you want to present from this list, which includes both scheduled and unscheduled broadcasts for the open presentation.

3. Select the Record This Live Presentation check box if you want to record your live broadcast and save it for later viewing.

> **Note**
>
> If you want to make additional changes to the settings of a previously scheduled broadcast, click the Modify Info button to open another version of the Live Presentation Broadcast dialog box (see Figure 18.14). This is nearly identical to the other presentation broadcast dialog boxes you've seen in this chapter.

4. Click the Broadcast button to continue. If you selected a scheduled broadcast, the Broadcast Presentation dialog box opens (shown in Figure 18.13), and you can skip to step 8. If you selected an unscheduled broadcast, the Live Presentation Broadcast dialog box opens (see Figure 18.14), from which you can establish broadcast settings and invite participants.

5. Click the Settings button to open the Broadcast Settings dialog box (refer to Figure 18.3). In this dialog box, you can specify the exact broadcast settings you need for this presentation.

→ To learn more about the settings in the Broadcast Settings dialog box, **see** "Configuring Broadcast Settings" earlier in this chapter.

Figure 18.13
Do your last-minute checks from this dialog box.

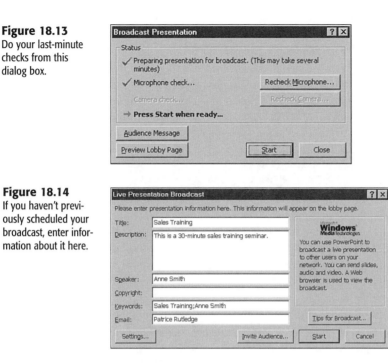

Figure 18.14
If you haven't previously scheduled your broadcast, enter information about it here.

6. Click the Invite Audience button to open your e-mail client (such as Microsoft Outlook) and send an e-mail to your audience.

7. Click the Start button to open the Broadcast Presentation dialog box (refer to Figure 18.13).

8. PowerPoint verifies that the network locations you typed in earlier are valid; then it checks that your audio and video inputs are working correctly (if you enabled those options in the Broadcast Settings dialog box when you set up the presentation broadcast).

9. If you selected real-time audio, PowerPoint displays the Microphone Check dialog box (refer to Figure 18.5) to verify that your audio levels are set correctly. After you've read the text out loud (and you've seen the horizontal volume bar move), choose OK to continue. If you want to check the microphone level again, click the Recheck Microphone button.

10. If you selected real-time video, PowerPoint displays a Camera Check dialog box in which you can preview the video you'll transmit to your audience. Click the Recheck Camera button to check the video again.

11. To send a message to all waiting audience members, click the Audience Message button (handy if you want to announce a brief delay); enter a message in the Audience Message dialog box and click Update.

12. To preview the presentation's lobby page, click the Preview Lobby Page button, and a browser window will open (refer to Figure 18.7). When your audience is ready to view the presentation, they'll use their Web browsers to go to this lobby page, which

PART
V

CH
18

is specific to your presentation broadcast. There they'll find out how long it is before the presentation actually starts, as well as the presentation title and description you typed in.

13. When the Broadcast Presentation dialog box flashes "Press Start When Ready", click the Start button to begin.

CONDUCTING THE BROADCAST

Now that you've accessed your broadcast, audience members need to arrive as well. This is a simple process—they just need to click the URL to the broadcast lobby page that you provided them in your broadcast invitation e-mail.

A broadcast presentation won't look any different to you (the presenter) than if you were running a slideshow on your computer. Just move through your presentation as you normally would, but remember to not go too quickly. It takes 10–15 seconds for your clients to download each new page.

Tip from
Patrice-Anne Rutledge

You might want to set up a nearby computer and log in as a participant so you can see what your audience is actually seeing. Based on tests, the time it takes for each slide to reach client systems varies from slow to really slow. Take your time and double-check to be sure you're not getting ahead of your audience.

→ To learn how to hold your audience's attention when you're not physically in front of them, **see** Chapter 27, "Presenting in a Variety of Settings."

What audiences see in a Web broadcast slide area (refer to Figure 18.7) is close to what they would see if they were actually looking at your screen in person. PowerPoint's pen and pointer features don't work over presentation broadcasts, however; if you want to use them, consider switching to an online meeting, which does support them. It's best to just go with a simple design and format when using presentation broadcasts. You can go back and forth through the slides in your presentation using your Page Up and Page Down (or Space and Backspace) keys as you normally would.

⚠ **Can't connect to the broadcast?** See the "Troubleshooting" section near the end of the chapter.

ENDING THE BROADCAST

When you've finished your broadcast, just press Esc to end it (if any questions have been e-mailed in during your presentation, you might want to answer them verbally before you wrap things up). You'll be asked to confirm your decision to end the broadcast. Your audience will be sent back to the presentation lobby page, which will tell them that the presentation has ended.

USING INTERACTIVE ONLINE MEETINGS

In addition to presentation broadcasts, PowerPoint also provides a much more interactive way of sharing your ideas with others: online meetings. PowerPoint has had interactive meeting features for some time. For example, you can use PowerPoint's Meeting Minder (Tools, Meeting Minder) to jot down minutes and action items while you're presenting to a group of people. Online meetings take the concept of interactive presentations online, where you can bring together a group of people from around the world to present your ideas and then discuss them.

Just as with presentation broadcasts, online meetings enable you to show your live presentation to others, including real-time audio and video commentary. However, online meetings also let your audience in on the action. Instead of passively watching your presentation, participants in a PowerPoint online meeting can jot down ideas on a shared whiteboard; interactively send messages back to you and the group; and even take control of the presentation in midstream, make some changes to the presentation, and then give control back to you. Online meetings are much better suited to roundtable discussions and for immediate decision making than presentation broadcasts are.

STARTING AN ONLINE MEETING

The first step in starting an online meeting is to open the presentation you want to present in the meeting. Then choose Tools, Online Collaboration, Meet Now to start the program PowerPoint uses for online meetings. This group collaboration tool, called Microsoft NetMeeting, is installed as part of Microsoft Office.

PART
V

CH
18

Note

If for some reason you don't have NetMeeting installed on your computer, you can download it from the Microsoft Web site (`http://www.microsoft.com/windows/netmeeting`). This site also includes detailed information and resources about NetMeeting. If you've never used this application before, you should familiarize yourself with its basic functionality before you start an online meeting in PowerPoint.

If you've run NetMeeting before, the Find Someone dialog box opens (see Figure 18.15).

If you haven't used NetMeeting before, the NetMeeting dialog box will ask for your name, e-mail address, and your NetMeeting directory server. You can choose any server you want from the list, or you can type in your company's private NetMeeting directory server (ask your network administrator for its name). All the people that will be joining this meeting have to log in to the same NetMeeting server, however, so you'll have to let your audience know which server to use ahead of time.

Setting up an online meeting in NetMeeting is different from running a broadcast presentation. Instead of letting your audience come to you, you need to bring in people one by one, just as in a telephone conference call.

Figure 18.15
Conference someone into your meeting by typing his or her name and then choosing Call.

The Find Someone dialog box gradually displays a long list of logged-in users as NetMeeting downloads the server user list.

Caution

> The most common problem at this point is that your selected server might become too busy to handle numerous login requests, for both your meeting and other parties' meetings. If this happens, participants should just try to log in again by selecting that server's name from the Directory box.

Type in the name of the person you want to conference in to your online meeting to quickly jump to his or her name in the list. When you've found the person you want to call, select that name and then click the Call button.

NetMeeting tries to make the connection and, if the other person accepts the call, the Find Someone dialog box disappears, and the Online Meeting toolbar appears (see Figure 18.16).

Figure 18.16
The Online Meeting toolbar provides all the tools for conducting your online meeting.

⚠ **Can't get online meetings to work?** See the "Troubleshooting" section near the end of the chapter.

JOINING AN ONLINE MEETING

If you want to have more than two people in the meeting, just call more people by clicking the Call Participant button on the Online Meeting toolbar, and repeat the process. Your guests can also call in on their own using NetMeeting. If they do, they'll be told that you're in a meeting, but they can ask to join the meeting. You, as the meeting host, are then notified of an incoming call and asked whether you'd like to accept it.

PRESENTING YOUR IDEAS

After you have all the right people connected at the same time (which can take some effort, depending on how busy the NetMeeting servers are), you're ready to start presenting.

Each of the people you've called (or who have called you) now see on their screen an exact duplicate of what's on your PowerPoint screen. This is a live view, so whatever you do appears on all the meeting attendees' screens—all your menu choices, mouse movements, typing, everything.

Sound is the one exception, however. Any transition sounds you have in your presentation won't be sent over the broadcast because the NetMeeting software is already using your sound hardware for itself.

Tip from
Patrice-Anne Rutledge

Consider using your phone to do an audio conference call along with the online meeting to get around the sound limitations.

Right now, with the exception of sound, you've got close to the same result as you would have had using a broadcast presentation. What's really different about the NetMeeting approach is that it enables other meeting attendees to interact with each other.

USING ONLINE CHAT AND WHITEBOARDS

The easiest way for online meeting participants to interact is through NetMeeting's chat window. Click the Display Chat Window button of the Online Meeting toolbar to open the chat window (see Figure 18.17). You can send a text message to everyone in the meeting by typing whatever you want into the Message box and then clicking the Send button.

Figure 18.17
A chat window makes it easy to communicate with everyone at the same time in an online meeting.

Untitled - Chat - chatting with 2 other(s)	
File Edit View Options Help	
Fred Wharton	What about slide 4, foks? Do we need to get into double-clicks at all?
Bill Hammond	I think they're going to be around for a while.
Bill Hammond	Let's put in some extra practice sessions on those. It's hard for some people to get the speed right.
Timothy Dyck	I've seen that in my training classrooms too.

Message:

Send to: Everyone In Chat

Welcome to Chat

 You can also open a graphical whiteboard by clicking the Display Whiteboard button; the whiteboard works just like the chat window (except you can draw on it). Figure 18.18 illustrates the whiteboard.

ENABLING ONLINE GROUP EDITING

The ultimate form of interaction in online meetings goes even further than chat and whiteboard windows, however. With your permission, meeting participants can take direct control of your PowerPoint window and type as if they were sitting at your desk. This is a great way of creating a presentation together—if someone is having a hard time getting across what she'd really like to see, she can take control and drive for a while.

Figure 18.18
A whiteboard is another online collaboration tool.

To enable application sharing, you, as meeting host, have to tell PowerPoint it's okay for others to take control. Click the Allow Others to Edit button on the Online Meeting toolbar to do so.

The other people in the meeting can now double-click the image of your screen (displayed in their monitors) and take control. They'll be able to type right into the presentation open on your computer, add new slides, change slide order, and anything else you could do by yourself.

To take back control, just click anywhere in your PowerPoint window. You might want to turn off the Allow Others to Edit button just so people don't accidentally take control. It can be tricky to know who's in control sometimes.

Note

Note that application sharing doesn't require that anyone but the meeting host have PowerPoint installed on his computer. The only software other people need to have is NetMeeting.

Tip from
Patrice-Anne Rutledge

You can tell who's in control when using application sharing by looking for that person's initials in tiny letters at the bottom right of the mouse pointer.

ENDING AN ONLINE MEETING

To end an online conference, click the End Meeting button on the Online Meeting toolbar. Individual attendees (except for you, the meeting host) can individually join and leave as they like during the meeting; the host facilitates these entries and exits. When you end the meeting, everyone gets disconnected.

SCHEDULING AN ONLINE MEETING

Although the method we've covered here enables you to start an online meeting whenever you want, PowerPoint also has hooks into Outlook that make it easy to schedule an online meeting.

Choose Tools, Online Collaboration, Schedule Meeting. PowerPoint starts an Outlook meeting request, which includes a specified online meeting directory server location and your e-mail address (see Figure 18.19). You can even have Outlook automatically start NetMeeting when the meeting begins.

Figure 18.19
Schedule a future online meeting using Outlook.

PARTICIPATING IN WEB DISCUSSIONS

PowerPoint's online collaboration capabilities don't stop with presentation broadcasts and online meetings. You can also access Office XP's Web-based discussion forums from PowerPoint as you can with all the other Office applications.

These forums work like an Internet newsgroup and enable you to carry on a discussion with others without all of you having to be present at the same time. Presentation broadcasts and online meetings, on the other hand, work in real-time. Web forums aren't real-time; they're there whenever you have a chance to check in to see what's new. It's handy to have the choice between the two approaches.

STARTING A WEB DISCUSSION

To start a new Web discussion (or access a previously created one), choose Tools, Online Collaboration, Web Discussions. The first time you run the command, you'll see the Add or Edit Discussion Servers dialog box (see Figure 18.20), which asks you for the name of your discussion server.

Figure 18.20
You need to type in the server name of your Office discussion server to access a Web discussion.

Note

Your network administrator must set up a discussion server ahead of time. A discussion server is a Web server with special software, called the Office Server Extensions, installed on it.

Type the server name that your network administrator has provided into the top box of this window and, if you want, type an easy-to-remember name into the bottom box of the window. This name will be your identity during the discussion. Then choose OK to finish this step.

You'll then see PowerPoint's Discussion Options dialog box (see Figure 18.21). Here you can add, edit, or remove Office discussion servers, as well as decide which fields you'd like to see displayed on the discussion server. The default settings are usually adequate, so you can just click OK.

Figure 18.21
You can add new discussion servers here as well as configure what kind of information appears on them.

When you close the Discussion Options dialog box, the Web Discussions toolbar appears on your screen (see Figure 18.22). Table 18.1 describes the buttons on this toolbar.

Figure 18.22
The Web Discussions toolbar provides all the functionality you'll need to conduct a Web discussion.

TABLE 18.1   WEB DISCUSSIONS TOOLBAR BUTTONS

Button	Name	Description
Discussions ▼	Discussions	Displays a drop-down list of options enabling you to insert a discussion about the presentation; filter, refresh, or print the discussion; or redisplay the Discussion Options dialog box.
	Insert Discussion About the Presentation	Displays the Enter Discussion Text dialog box, which enables you to enter a comment about the presentation. Comments appear at the bottom of the screen.
Subscribe...	Subscribe	Displays the Document Subscription dialog box, where you can tell the Office Discussion Server that you'd like to be notified by e-mail when this document changes or when someone else adds a comment to the discussion database.
	Stop Communication with Discussion Server	Stops communication with the discussion server.
	Show/Hide Discussion Pane	Serves as a toggle to display or hide the discussion pane.
Close	Close	Closes the Web discussion.

TROUBLESHOOTING

RESOLVING A VML ERROR MESSAGE

When I try to view a broadcast, I get an error message telling me to download a VML.

If your presentation contains rotated graphics, you might get an error message when you try to view a broadcast, stating that you need to install vector graphics rendering (VML) components. If the message doesn't take you directly to a location where you can download, click the Windows Start button and choose Windows Update. On the Microsoft Windows Update Web site, click Product Updates and then Select Software. Choose the Vector Graphics Rendering option; downloading will take only a few minutes.

RESOLVING BROADCAST CONNECTION PROBLEMS

People trying to watch the presentation broadcast get a message saying that their computers can't connect to the broadcast.

Be sure that the network location you specified for the location of the presentation broadcast files is accessible by everyone you want to see the broadcast. (People outside your company won't normally be able to access your presentation broadcast location, for example.)

DISPLAYING THE LOBBY PAGE

When audience members open the broadcast lobby page, the Web page is nearly empty.

Be sure that all your viewers are using Microsoft Internet Explorer 5.1 or later as their Web browser. Netscape Navigator won't display the presentation broadcast correctly.

CALLING ONLINE MEETING PARTICIPANTS

When I try to call someone using PowerPoint's Online Meeting tools, I get a message saying, "The person you called is not able to accept Microsoft NetMeeting calls."

The person you are calling either doesn't have Microsoft NetMeeting started or hasn't logged in to the same NetMeeting directory server you have. You have to let meeting participants know ahead of time that they should have NetMeeting open and be logged in to your chosen directory server so they can get your call. (They can also configure their systems to always have NetMeeting run unobtrusively in the Windows taskbar so that their computers are always "listening" for incoming NetMeeting calls.)

CONNECTING TO THE DIRECTORY SERVER

When I try to log in to a NetMeeting directory server, I get a message saying that there was a problem connecting to the directory server.

Any network problem between you and the NetMeeting directory server (or an overloaded server) will cause these kinds of problems. Just reselect the name of the server from the Directory box to connect to the directory server again. If the problem persists, try switching to a different directory server or use the Advanced button to call people using their Internet hostname or IP address.

DESIGN CORNER: REHEARSING FOR A LIVE BROADCAST

Conducting your first live presentation broadcast can be both exciting and unnerving. To ensure that everything goes well, you should first record, save, and replay your broadcast several times, perfecting both your technical understanding of the process and your actual delivery. This also gives you a chance to hear and/or see yourself present as well as let others critique your recorded broadcast. To record and play back your presentation, follow the steps outlined in "Recording and Saving a Broadcast" in this chapter. When you replay it, first verify that everything is working correctly—you can access the broadcast and see it clearly, the sound is audible, and the video quality is crisp. Then take a second look for content, aesthetics, and pacing. Does your presentation still look good as a broadcast? Do your words adequately convey your message? Are you speaking too quickly or too slowly? Do you look professional and at ease in the video window? Undoubtedly, you'll find things you want to change. Go ahead and make improvements, recording and replaying your presentation again...and again if you need to.

ADVANCED POWERPOINT

CHAPTER 19

INTEGRATING WITH OFFICE XP

In this chapter

UNDERSTANDING OFFICE INTEGRATION

One of the primary benefits of working with a suite of programs such as Office XP is the interoperability that the suite's programs offer. Because easy and efficient integration and interoperability exist between the Office applications, you can use all the applications together to build more effective documents. PowerPoint may be the one application within Office that makes the greatest use of the other applications within the suite. By its nature as a presentation tool, PowerPoint can work with all your other applications, tools, and documents to create a single powerful and effective slide presentation.

LINKING OFFICE OBJECTS

By now, you've probably used the Clipboard to cut or copy content between and within Office applications. The Clipboard is one of the most significant tools that Windows offers, and Office makes it even more powerful by giving you the capability to cut, copy, and paste several objects as a group or one at a time.

For all that power and convenience, however, the pasting process is limited. For example, after you've pasted an Excel chart into your PowerPoint slide, any changes made to the Excel chart or to the data that supports it are no longer reflected in the pasted copy of the chart in PowerPoint. Simple pasting establishes no connection between the copied chart and its source. To establish such a connection, you must link the source and the target so that the target can be updated when opened to reflect changes in the source.

USING PASTE SPECIAL TO CREATE A LINK

A link between two applications is established by using the Edit, Paste Special command, as described in the following steps:

1. In the source document, select the content to be copied to your PowerPoint slide (the target). Figure 19.1 shows a section of an Excel worksheet, selected for copying.
2. Choose Edit, Copy or click the Copy button.
3. Switch to or open your PowerPoint presentation, and go to the target slide.
4. Choose Edit, Paste Special. The Paste Special dialog box opens (see Figure 19.2).
5. Click the Paste Link option. If more than one type of object is in the As box, select the one that most closely matches the source of your content.
6. If you want your linked object to appear as an icon, select the Display as Icon check box. The content of the object will be visible only if you (or a person viewing your presentation) want to see it. To view a link icon, double-click it.
7. Click OK to insert the linked content.

After you insert the linked object, test the link—go back to the source application and make a change to the content. Switch back to the target slide, and view the updated content. It now reflects the change made to the source.

Figure 19.1
When selecting content from another application, imagine it in your slide—will it fit? Does its content effectively communicate your information or message?

Figure 19.2
When pasting Excel worksheet content, PowerPoint displays that object type in the As box.

Note

You can resize the linked object by dragging diagonally from the object's corner handles. Drag inward to shrink the object, outward to increase its size.

Caution

Excel doesn't work properly unless you make sure you save the workbook file before creating the link the first time.

Your pasted Excel content lost its formatting? *See the "Troubleshooting" section near the end of this chapter.*

UPDATING LINKS

After a link is established, PowerPoint prompts you to update that link each time you open the target presentation (see Figure 19.3).

Figure 19.3
You can update the target file with any changes that have been made to the source content.

> **Microsoft PowerPoint** ☒
>
> ⓘ The presentation C:\My Documents\Q1 Travel Expenses.ppt contains links that can be updated.
>
> [Update Links]   [Cancel]   [Help]

This prompt enables you to choose whether to allow any changes that have occurred in the source document to update the linked content in your PowerPoint presentation. To update, click the Update Links button.

Tip from
Patrice-Anne Rutledge

Why would you choose not to update your target file? Maybe you need to print the presentation with the older data or save it before changes are made. Or perhaps your presentation pertains to second quarter sales, and the source content has been updated with third quarter data, which you're not ready to use. If for any reason you want to maintain the target data in its current form, click Cancel.

If you choose not to update the links at the time you open the file, you can always update them later by following these steps:

1. Choose Edit, Links. The Links dialog box opens (see Figure 19.4), displaying a list of files that are linked to your open document.

Figure 19.4
Click the Open Source button to view the linked data before updating it.

> **Links** ? ☒
>
> | Links: | Type | Update | |
> |---|---|---|---|
> | Book1!Sheet1!R3C1:R8C2 | Worksheet | Automatic | [Close] |
> | | | | [Update Now] |
> | | | | [Open Source] |
> | | | | [Change Source...] |
> | | | | [Break Link] |
>
> Source: Book1!Sheet1!R3C1:R8C2
> Type: Microsoft Excel Worksheet
> Update: ⦿ Automatic   ○ Manual

2. Choose the link you want to update, and click the Update Now button.

3. Click Close to update the target with any changes to the source.

MAINTAINING LINKS

For the most part, links you establish between files with Paste Special require little or no active maintenance on your part. To be sure your links remain intact, simply follow these basic rules:

- Don't rename the source or the target file.
- Don't move or delete the source file.
- Don't move or delete the target file.

If you must move or rename either the source or target file, you will have to reestablish the link through the Links dialog box while in the target file. Click the Change Source button and navigate to the source file's new location, as shown in Figure 19.5.

Figure 19.5
The Change Source dialog box enables you to find, select, and reestablish a link between a source and target if one of the files has been moved or renamed.

When making changes to your source document, remember that it is linked to a target file. Whether you're editing content or applying formats, make sure that these changes will be useful in the target document. If you need to make changes to the source that won't be appropriate in the target, consider breaking the link. You'll have to update the former target manually (to make content changes), but you won't risk unwanted changes to the target file.

Caution

If you aren't the only person using the source or target file, be sure to alert other users to changes you make to the source that may not be appropriate in the target file. If another user chooses to update a link, he might be unhappy with the resulting changes.

REMOVING THE LINK BETWEEN SOURCE AND TARGET FILES

After a link is established, it remains in force (even if updates between the source and target are rarely or never performed) unless one or both of the files are moved or renamed. Moving or renaming either the source or target file breaks the link between the files because the files can't find each other anymore.

Although this method technically breaks the link, it doesn't do a very clean job. The target document continues to store a record of a link back to a moved or renamed file. To make a clean break, severing all ties and any record between your source and target files, follow these steps:

1. In the target file, choose Edit, Links.
2. In the Links dialog box (refer to Figure 19.4), select the link you want to break.
3. Click the Break Link button.

After the link is broken, the pasted content remains in the target document, but it retains no connection to the source data. Changes made to the source are not reflected in the target, and when opening the target file, you will not be prompted to update your link.

Note	A linked paragraph or table from Word or a worksheet section from Excel is seen as an object. After a link is broken, the pasted content is seen as a picture, a simple graphic component of your slide.

Tip from *Patrice-Anne* *Rutledge*	One benefit of breaking a link by moving or renaming the source or target file is that the link can be reestablished easily by putting the file back where it was or renaming it to the original filename. Many users use this technique to make a temporary break, allowing changes to the source without the risk of updating the target until it becomes appropriate.

WORKING WITH EMBEDDED OFFICE OBJECTS

Whereas linking connects two applications through a pasted file or a portion of a file, embedding places an entire document and makes the tools of its native application available within another application file. Your choice to embed (rather than link) is based on what you want to do with the object and, in some cases, who will be using the application in which the embedded object resides. The following are two situations that support the decision to embed an object:

■ **Limited system resources**   Rather than have two applications open at once, embed one in another by embedding an object. While the object is active, the object's application is also active (and its tools appear in the target application window). The source application can then be closed after any editing of the object is performed, leaving the object in the target file, and freeing system resources for the target application.

■ **Simplicity**   Instead of linking (and having to decide when and if to update links), embed an application object and build the content you need, using the embedded application's tools. There is no need to restrict your moving and renaming of the file because no other files are linked to it.

EMBEDDING NEW AND EXISTING FILES

Embedded objects can be blank, meaning that you have to build the content within the object after it's embedded, or they can be derived from a file with existing content. The latter approach can save you some work because the content is already there. Consider some of these examples of embedded objects in a PowerPoint presentation:

■ **Excel worksheets**   Whether you need a block of cells on your slide or need tools for formatting and performing calculations, embed an existing Excel worksheet (if the content of the worksheet will fit on the slide), or start with a blank worksheet and build it within the object.

■ **Excel charts**   Build a chart in your PowerPoint presentation, using Excel's formidable charting tools. The object will consist of a worksheet with a Chart tab and a Sheet tab, enabling you to enter data and then watch it turn into any sort of chart you need. This is an excellent approach for a user who spends more time in PowerPoint than Excel, but who needs Excel's superior charting and spreadsheet tools to create an effective chart for a PowerPoint presentation.

■ **Word text**   If your content is intended only for use in your PowerPoint presentation, you needn't create it in Word first and then copy it to PowerPoint. Instead, create it in PowerPoint through an embedded Word object. Without switching between applications, you're able to take advantage of Word's extensive text formatting tools. You can use this technique to embed an existing Word document, as well.

Tip from	You can also embed a PowerPoint presentation in a Word document or an Excel worksheet. This can be especially useful when sending a presentation and its supporting data to someone for review.
Patrice-Anne Rutledge	

EMBEDDING A NEW OBJECT

A new object is one that has no content and is not based on an existing file. All content will be built within the embedded object, and the object and its content will exist nowhere beyond the slide in which you embed it.

To embed an object in your PowerPoint presentation, follow these steps:

1. Go to the slide that will contain the object.
2. Choose Insert, Object.
3. In the Insert Object dialog box (see Figure 19.6), choose Create New.

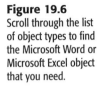

Figure 19.6
Scroll through the list of object types to find the Microsoft Word or Microsoft Excel object that you need.

4. Select the Object Type.

5. If desired, click Display as Icon. This option is useful when you want to save visual space. The object will open up only for entry and editing (or for simply viewing the content) when the icon is double-clicked.

6. Click OK to insert the object.

When inserted, the object can be edited in terms of content or formatting, using the tools of the object's native application. Figure 19.7 shows an embedded Excel chart and the Excel toolbar in a PowerPoint presentation window.

Figure 19.7
An inserted object can be selected for movement or resizing, or activated for editing.

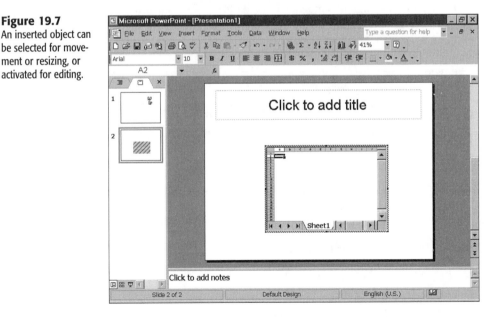

Tip from
Patrice-Anne
Rutledge

When the embedded object's application tools appear, they are formatted in the source application. If you turned off the option to have the Standard and Formatting toolbars share one row, they appear on two rows in the embedded application as well.

EMBEDDING AN OBJECT FROM AN EXISTING FILE

Embedding an existing file gives you much of the same power as a linked object. Your content need only be updated in one place—and offers all the convenience of an object that lives within the target presentation. Because the file and its content already exist, you need only to edit and reformat the embedded version of the file if or when it's required. When such changes are necessary, you have the source application tools at your disposal without having to open a separate application—the object's application tools appear in the target application window as soon as the object is activated by a double-click.

To embed an existing file in your PowerPoint presentation, follow these steps:

1. In your open PowerPoint application, go to the slide in which you want to embed the file.
2. Choose Insert, Object.
3. In the Insert Object dialog box, click the Create from File option (see Figure 19.8).

Figure 19.8
Save yourself the time and effort of entering your object's content by embedding an existing file.

PART
VI

CH
19

4. Type the pathname and filename of the file you want to embed, or click the Browse button to find it.
5. If desired, click the Link check box to establish a link between the source file and the embedded object. This embedded link, however, isn't the same as a pasted link. An embedded link gives you the power to use the tools of the original application (such as Excel or Word) to make changes in PowerPoint as well as in the original application.

Caution

If you choose to establish a link between the source file and the embedded object, be sure to update the link only when you're sure that changes to the source won't conflict with editing that may have been applied to the embedded object. This is especially true when more than one person will be accessing and editing one or both files.

6. When the correct pathname and filename appear in the File box, click OK to insert the object and close the dialog box.

USING WORD TABLES

Just as tables are a powerful feature in Word, they are equally powerful and effective in a PowerPoint presentation. For this reason, PowerPoint's Slide Layout task pane offers several options for inserting tables, and the Insert Table button appears on the Standard toolbar in your PowerPoint application window. However, if you're more comfortable using Word's table tools (and the complete Table menu found in Word) or you already have an existing Word table and don't want to duplicate efforts, you can build your table there and paste it into your PowerPoint presentation.

INSERTING A WORD TABLE

A Word table is simple to insert, and with a little forethought (how many columns and rows do you need?), you can add one to any slide in a matter of seconds. You'll use Word's tools to create it and then bring the table into your PowerPoint presentation with the following steps:

1. Build your table in Word, using your familiar Word tools (found in the Table menu or using the Insert Table button).
2. You can enter your content after building the table, or you can wait until the table is in your PowerPoint slide.
3. Copy the table to the Clipboard using Edit, Copy or by pressing Ctrl+C.
4. Switch to or open your PowerPoint presentation, and go to the slide (in Slide view) into which you want to paste the Word table.
5. Choose Edit, Paste, or press Ctrl+V to insert the copied table.
6. Edit the content and dimensions of the table using the Tables and Borders toolbar, which appears whenever the table is active (see Figure 19.9).

→ For more info on using PowerPoint's own table creation tools, **see** Chapter 4, "Working with Tables."

Tip from
Patrice-Anne Rutledge

If your Word table already exists and you want to use it in a PowerPoint slide, you can link it to your slide so that future updates to the table's content appear in the PowerPoint version as well.

Figure 19.9
Use the Tables and Borders toolbar to perform a variety of table-formatting tasks.

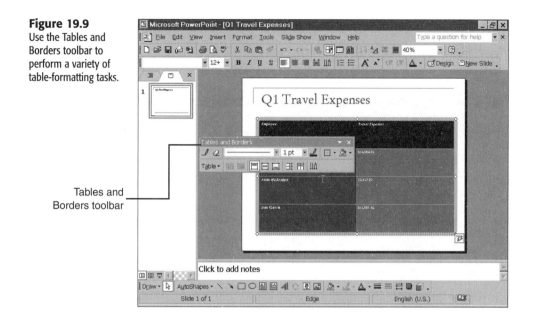

Tables and Borders toolbar

Note

Like any slide component (regardless of its source), a table can be deleted easily. Click the table to select it, and then click its border to disable the cursor in the table's cells. To remove the table from your slide, press the Delete key.

USING POWERPOINT PRESENTATIONS IN OTHER APPLICATIONS

PART
VI

CH
19

Throughout this chapter, we discuss bringing content or tools from Word and Excel into your PowerPoint slides. Although this is the most common type of Office integration when working with PowerPoint, you will find that you can use PowerPoint content and slides in Word and Excel as well.

Any PowerPoint slide content—graphics, organization charts, text boxes—can be added to a Word document or Excel worksheet by using the Clipboard to copy the content from the slide and paste it into the target Word or Excel file. The pasted content can also be linked (as discussed previously in this chapter), so that changes to the PowerPoint content are reflected in the Word or Excel target.

Another way to use PowerPoint content in other applications is to use entire slides. You can save an individual slide in virtually any graphic file format (such as GIF, TIF, JPG, PNG, or BMP), enabling you to insert it as a graphic in any Word or Excel document.

To save a PowerPoint slide as a graphic file, follow these steps:

1. Select the slide you want to save as a graphic.

2. Choose File, Save As to open the Save As dialog box (see Figure 19.10).

Figure 19.10
Before saving the file, it pays to check which formats are acceptable to your target application. Choose the most commonly used formats for greatest usability.

3. In the Save as Type list, scroll through the formats and select a graphic file format such as JPG, TIF, GIF, or BMP (common graphic formats).

Tip from
Patrice-Anne Rutledge

It's a good idea to experiment with the graphic format you choose as the quality and results can vary. For example, high-color presentations don't save well as GIFs because they are reduced to 256 colors. And JPG compression could make your presentation look grainy. Saving as a BMP or TIF creates the best quality output for insertion in another Office document, at the expense of large file size.

Tip from
Patrice-Anne Rutledge

If you'll be using the graphic on a Web site, save it in GIF format. This format is acceptable to most Web design programs and creates small files, which is desirable for creating fast-loading Web pages.

---

4. Type a name for your file in the File Name box.

5. Click Save. A prompt appears, asking if you want to export every slide in the presentation or just the selected slide.

6. Click Current Slide Only, which exports (saves) only the selected slide.

When you save as a graphic, use the Insert, Picture command in Word or Excel to insert the graphic. The graphic can be sized for legibility and formatted using the Picture toolbar.

TROUBLESHOOTING

RETAINING EXCEL FORMATTING

When I paste Excel content into another file, I lose my formatting.

Excel formatting should be retained when worksheet cells or charts are pasted into your PowerPoint slides. If the pasted content looks different than the source content, however, consider these solutions:

- Delete the pasted content and repeat the Copy and Paste procedure.
- If you're using Paste Special to link the content to the PowerPoint slide, be sure that you choose the correct object type.

If neither of these options solves the problem, consider embedding an Excel object in the slide and pasting the content there. You'll be able to edit and format the content in its own application, negating the possibility of lost formatting.

DESIGN CORNER: PRESENTING WITH EMBEDDED OBJECTS

PowerPoint becomes a natural place to combine the best results of your efforts in Word and Excel to create an effective presentation. You can use the Clipboard and OLE tools to reuse existing Word and Excel content as well as to create new slide elements through embedded Word and Excel objects. This saves both time and effort and assures consistency throughout your Office documents.

For example, using the techniques described in "Working with Embedded Office Objects," you can embed an Excel chart in your PowerPoint presentation. To the presentation audience, the tools used to build the chart are invisible, but to the presenter, having an entire Excel worksheet available through a simple double-click is a significant convenience, despite the costs of larger files and increased use of system resources during editing.

BEFORE

The entire three-sheet workbook is available, although only
part of it (the chart) needs to be shown on the actual slide.

Figure 19.11

AFTER

Figure 19.12

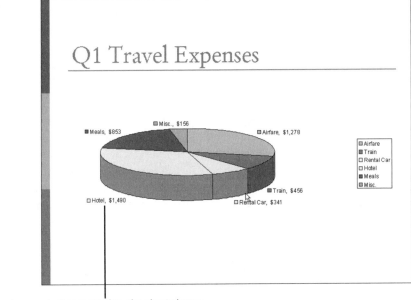

In an actual presentation, the chart shows
no sign of its roots as an Excel object.

CHAPTER 20

WORKING WITH POWERPOINT MACROS

In this chapter

UNDERSTANDING MACROS

Macros are programs that automatically execute a series of functions in PowerPoint to achieve a particular goal. You can easily create a macro without programming by recording a series of tasks that you would otherwise perform yourself. You can record any number of steps in a task, from applying a format to running a slideshow, and choose from a variety of ways to run the macro in the future. Macros are simple to create, easy to run, and can be used throughout an office to standardize the development process, as well as the appearance of presentations. In addition to recording macros, you can create them as Visual Basic for Applications programs.

Note

> Macros use Visual Basic for Applications (VBA) as their programming language. Don't worry, however; recording, editing, and using macros requires little or no knowledge of VBA. You can improve your ability to edit and troubleshoot your macros by becoming acquainted with VBA, but many (if not most) users don't interact directly with VBA to create, change, or run their macros.

The applications found in Microsoft Office XP contain so many tools and menu commands that perform such a wide variety of seemingly automatic tasks, it might seem unnecessary for you to ever build your own macros. How could PowerPoint possibly work faster? What tasks require too many steps to be convenient?

Your first impression may be that the software makes it so simple and quick to develop a great presentation that further automation isn't needed. If you spend a great deal of time with PowerPoint, however, or if the presentations you create have many common elements, you'll no doubt benefit from this chapter as you find ways to make repeated tasks simpler, faster, and, most importantly, more consistent in their outcome.

Perhaps you're stumped—you can't imagine how you could use macros to speed up or simplify your use of PowerPoint. Check the following list for some ideas:

- **Getting started**   Your macros can be run as soon as your toolbars appear and the first slide is onscreen. Create a macro to apply a design template and create a series of standard slides for your presentation. After that, all you have to do is add any extra slides that aren't part of your standard presentation, and enter your content. Much of your content entry also can be done with macros.

- **Building an outline**   If you create the same sales or productivity presentations every quarter, don't reinvent the wheel each time, and don't reuse your old presentations and risk overwriting them or leaving old data behind. Create a macro that builds the basic presentation, from choosing slide layouts to entering slide titles. Then, all you have to do is enter the new data and your presentation is complete.

- **Making changes to the master**   Create a series of macros that insert a logo on your slide master, add a slogan to your title master, or change the font of your text on all masters. Any changes that you find yourself making on all or most of your presentations can be automated with macros.

- **Setting up a slide**   If your slide layout needs are not met by any of the installed layouts, simply create a macro that inserts chart objects, tables, text objects, and graphics. The macro can include your placement and sizing of these objects, so that when the macro is run, all you need to do is fill in the blanks—double-click and insert the chart data, edit the organization chart, or type your text—and the layout is done for you.

- **Inserting hyperlinks**   Do all your presentations have links to your company Web site or an internal database? Create a macro that inserts the hyperlink. This includes choosing the linked site or file and entering the text or graphic that serves as the link.

- **Building an organization chart**   With the exception of the names of new or relocated people, the organization charts of most companies don't vary from presentation to presentation. Rather than having to manually copy and paste a chart from a previous presentation, you can record a macro that inserts your company's completed organization chart. After running the macro, all you have to do is edit the names and titles to reflect changes in the roster since you recorded the macro. If, over time, the changes are significant, you can simply edit the source chart so that when the macro inserts it, the majority of the needed changes have already been made.

- **Running a slideshow**   Rather than make your audience sit through the process of opening the presentation and starting the show, record a macro that can be run as soon as you open PowerPoint. You'll have rehearsed your show and set any automatic slide timings before recording the macro, so that all the macro needs to do is start the show.

CREATING A MACRO

When you record a macro, it's as though you've turned on a video camera that watches your keystrokes, mouse movements, and command selections—the macro recorder notes every move you make and converts your actions to programming code. After you name your macro and perform all the steps you want to automate, you stop the recorder, and by using the name you've given the macro, you can run it at any time. A macro enables you to perform a virtually unlimited series of steps in just seconds.

Note

> In earlier versions of Office, the Word, Excel, and PowerPoint programs didn't have features such as AutoCorrect and AutoText. Before these features existed, users created macros to correct common misspellings and turn abbreviations into words, phrases, and paragraphs. As Office evolves, the number of common tasks you'll need to automate by yourself will continue to decrease.

PART
VI

CH
20

RECORDING A MACRO

Before you begin to record a macro, you need to do some planning. Think about where you are in the process of developing or running a presentation when the macro you're about to create is invoked. What situation must exist for the macro to be successful? If the macro formats existing slide content, the content must be displayed and selected before the macro is run. If the macro runs a slideshow, the presentation must be placed in the same folder where the macro was recorded. In short, set the stage for your macro to begin, and record it only when the scenario is appropriate.

After you set the stage, record your macro by following these steps:

1. Choose Tools, Macro, Record New Macro.

2. In the Record Macro dialog box (see Figure 20.1), enter a macro name to replace the default name. Your macro's name cannot contain any spaces. If your macro name is more than one word, use the underscore to separate the words.

Figure 20.1
Give your macro a short yet descriptive name.

3. As needed, type a description of the macro in the Description box. It's a good idea to leave the name and date text that is already in the box and add your description at the end of that text.

4. Click OK.

5. Perform the steps you want to record, using the mouse or keyboard to issue commands.

6. When your steps are complete and you reach the end of the procedure you want to automate, choose Tools, Macro, Stop Recording.

Caution

Try to test your macros immediately, especially if you've developed them for others to use. This will prevent any unpleasant surprises when you or another user attempts to use the macro, and enables you to edit it as needed while the procedures are fresh in your mind. The process of running a macro is discussed later in this chapter.

Can't get your macro to run the way you want? See the "Troubleshooting" section near the end of this chapter.

CREATING A MACRO IN THE VISUAL BASIC EDITOR

If you're familiar with VBA, you can build a macro without recording your steps as described in the previous section of this chapter. Instead, you can type the macro programming code directly into an editing window provided by Office XP's Visual Basic Editor (see Figure 20.2).

Project window   Module window

Figure 20.2
Even a novice VBA user can learn a lot from building and editing macro code in this window.

Properties window —

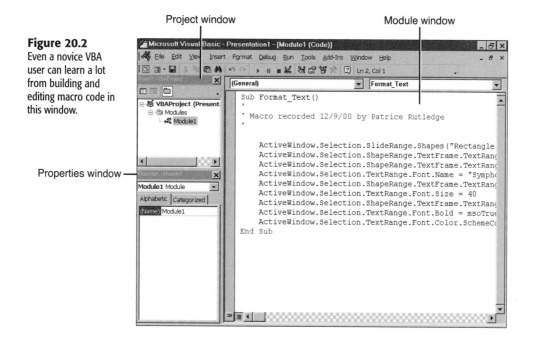

To enter the editor, select Tools, Visual Basic Editor, and then choose the macro you want to edit from the Declarations drop-down list (on the upper-right corner of the large module window). The editor consists of three separate windows, each designed to assist you in the creation and editing of a macro:

- **Project** The Project window shows a hierarchical tree, displaying the various modules of your macro. A simple macro will probably only consist of one module.

- **Properties** This window again lists the modules involved in the project, but in this window, they're listed alphabetically or by category.

- **Module** The macro code appears in this central window. Type new or edit existing VBA code in this window.

Figure 20.3 shows the Module window with the parts of a simple formatting macro identified.

To create a macro in the Visual Basic Editor, follow these steps:

1. Choose Tools, Macro, Visual Basic Editor.
2. Click inside the Module window to make it active.
3. As needed, choose Insert, Module. This creates a blank module for you to begin writing your code.
4. Type Sub followed by the name of your macro and press Enter. Your End Sub statement is added automatically (see Figure 20.4).

PART

VI

CH

20

Description of the macro

Name of the macro

Figure 20.3
A knowledge of VBA is required for building a macro from scratch in the Visual Basic Editor.

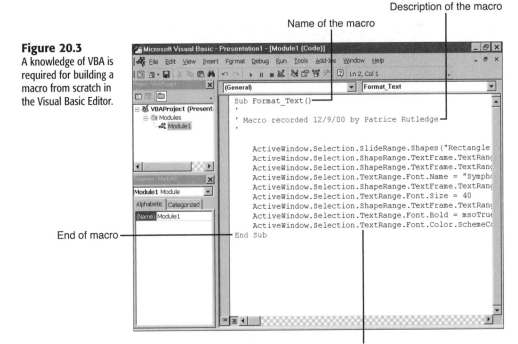

End of macro

Procedures performed by macro

Figure 20.4
If the name of your macro includes spaces, use the underscore character to represent them, as in Format_Title.

5. Type your lines of code for the steps your macro should perform.

6. Choose File, Close and Return to Microsoft PowerPoint.

EDITING A MACRO

You can use the Visual Basic Editor again whenever you want to edit a macro. Unless you're familiar with creating macro code in this editor, however, it's probably a good idea to delete and re-record a macro if it's not working or requires significant changes to work properly. But for simple changes, even a user unfamiliar with VBA can use the editor to make minor modifications. You can change text entries that the macro inserts. Any text appearing in quotes is text that the macro adds to your presentation (see Figure 20.5). Edit or retype this text as needed.

Misspelled word in macro

Figure 20.5
Misspell something while recording your macro? Fix the text in the Visual Basic Editor window.

You can choose different formats and fonts, depending on your needs. Figure 20.6 shows how you can change Times New Roman to Bookman.

You can also select a different element. For example, if your macro currently types text into a title box and you want the macro to type it into a subtitle box, change the code and redirect the entered text.

PART
VI

CH
20

Tip from
Patrice-Anne Rutledge

Interested in learning more about VBA or want to decipher what a snippet code really means? Choose Help, Microsoft Visual Basic Help from within the Microsoft Visual Basic window. Here, you can view detailed reference materials or search on a specific topic.

Font changed to Bookman

Figure 20.6
Change your font by
editing the program-
ming code.

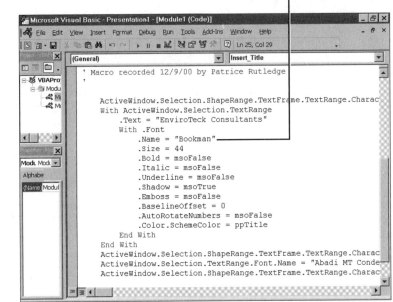

```
' Macro recorded 12/9/00 by Patrice Rutledge
'
        ActiveWindow.Selection.ShapeRange.TextFrame.TextRange.Charac
    With ActiveWindow.Selection.TextRange
        .Text = "EnviroTeck Consultants"
        With .Font
            .Name = "Bookman"
            .Size = 44
            .Bold = msoFalse
            .Italic = msoFalse
            .Underline = msoFalse
            .Shadow = msoTrue
            .Emboss = msoFalse
            .BaselineOffset = 0
            .AutoRotateNumbers = msoFalse
            .Color.SchemeColor = ppTitle
        End With
    End With
    ActiveWindow.Selection.ShapeRange.TextFrame.TextRange.Charac
    ActiveWindow.Selection.TextRange.Font.Name = "Abadi MT Conde
    ActiveWindow.Selection.ShapeRange.TextFrame.TextRange.Charac
```

DELETING A MACRO

Perhaps your macro is obsolete, or has so many problems that you find it easier to delete it
and start over than to edit it. In any case, deleting a macro is simple if you follow these
steps:

1. In the presentation that contains the macro, choose Tools, Macro, Macros. The Macro
    dialog box opens (see Figure 20.7).

Figure 20.7
See a list of your cur-
rent macros, created
for the open presen-
tation.

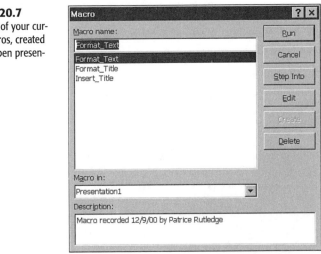

2. Select the macro you want to delete.

3. Click the Delete button. A prompt appears, asking you to confirm your intention to delete the selected macro. Click Yes.

Caution

After a macro is deleted, it cannot be retrieved. Be careful to read the description box for each macro before you delete it, especially if you have several similarly named macros or if your macro names are not terribly illustrative.

Creating a Macro Template

If you want to build a series of macros to use in all your new presentations, create a blank presentation template that includes all your macros. Whenever you want to build a presentation that utilizes your macros, simply start the presentation based on that template by choosing File, New, and selecting the appropriate template.

RUNNING A MACRO FROM THE TOOLBAR

Macros save time and effort by automating repetitive tasks. The process of invoking a macro, however, can be prohibitive because it requires the use of two levels of menus and a dialog box. To speed up the use of your macros, try assigning them to toolbar buttons with the following steps:

1. In the presentation that contains the macro(s) you want to assign to the toolbar, choose Tools, Customize to open the Customize dialog box.

2. Click the Commands tab (see Figure 20.8).

Figure 20.8
Select Macros in the Categories list to view all the macros available in the open presentation.

Customize

Toolbars | Commands | Options

To add a command to a toolbar: select a category and drag the command out of this dialog box to a toolbar.

Categories: Commands:

Table   Format_Text
Window and Help   Format_Title
Drawing   Insert_Title
AutoShapes
Outlining
Web
Control Toolbox
Macros
Built-in Menus
New Menu

Selected command:

Description   Modify Selection

Close

PART
VI

CH
20

3. Scroll through Categories and select Macros.

4. A list of your macro names appears in the Commands box. Click and drag a macro name (one macro at a time) up to the toolbar.

5. When your mouse pointer is on the spot where you want to add the macro button, release the mouse.

6. Right-click the new button (which appears with the macro name on it, as shown in Figure 20.9), and choose Change Button Image from the shortcut menu.

Figure 20.9
If your macro name is long, it might be better to have a picture represent the macro rather than to take up a lot of space on the toolbar.

Text face on button

Palette of button images

7. Click to select one of the graphic images from the palette.

8. Whether your macro name is long (and is wasting toolbar space) or you feel you don't need to see the name to remember which button performs the macro, remove the text portion of the button image. Right-click the button and choose Text Only (in Menus). The text name of the macro disappears, and the graphic image remains.

9. Click the Close button to exit the Customize dialog box.

Tip from
Patrice-Anne Rutledge

While the Customize dialog box is open, you can move and delete any of the existing toolbar buttons, including any new macro buttons you place.

→ For more information on customizing PowerPoint toolbars, **see** Chapter 21, "Customizing PowerPoint."

Troubleshooting

Resolving Macro Problems

The macro I created doesn't work properly, and I'm not sure why.

PowerPoint macros (and macros in any Office XP application, for that matter) might not work as expected when the following situations exist:

- Items required by the macro (slides from another presentation, fonts, graphics, sound files) are not available. Once you create a macro that inserts something into your chart, be sure not to rename or delete that item.

- The stage isn't set for the macro to run. If your macro was designed to move from slide 4 to slide 8, it might not work as expected if you invoke it while on slide 5. If your macro will be run during an important slideshow, be sure to test it ahead of time and note the circumstances that must be in place for the macro to do its job.

- You've run out of system resources. PowerPoint presentations contain so much graphical content that a machine with marginal resources (memory, speed) may crash or begin to work poorly if your macro opens a presentation or inserts or runs a memory-intensive file. In this situation, it's the hardware, and not the macro, that is at fault. Be sure to close all unnecessary programs before running your slideshow, so that PowerPoint and the necessary files are all that are open during your show.

Design Corner: Using a Macro to Insert a Title

As you've seen from this chapter, macro automation can simplify repetitive tasks and help you become more productive and efficient. To find good macro targets for your presentations, think of the tasks you repeat again and again. For example, if you create a variety of presentations that include your company name, you could create a macro that automatically enters this name in the location you specify. Of course, you could use AutoCorrect to do this as well, but with a macro you can add formatting and other steps. In this example, Figure 20.10 shows a blank slide with the Insert Title toolbar macro available, and Figure 20.11 shows the results of running this macro. If you create a number of macros to help you automate your presentation creation, you could create a Macros menu (or toolbar) and place all your macros in one easy-to-access location.

To create the macro that inserts the title "EnviroTech Consultants" and make the macro available from the toolbar, follow these steps:

1. Position the cursor in the title text box of a slide in your presentation.
2. Choose Tools, Macro, Record New Macro to open the Record New Macro dialog box.

3. Enter the name and other details about your macro and click OK to start the recording process.

4. Enter the text EnviroTech Consultants and apply the following formats from the Formatting toolbar: the Abadi MT condensed font, font size of 48 points, and a shadow effect.

5. Choose Tools, Macro, Stop Recording.

6. Choose Tools, Customize to open the Customize dialog box; select the Commands tab.

7. Scroll down the Categories list and choose Macros and then select the macro you want to place on the toolbar from the Commands list.

8. Drag the macro name from the Customize dialog box to the specific location on the toolbar where you want to place its associated toolbar button.

9. Click Close to exit the Customize dialog box.

BEFORE

Figure 20.10

Insert Title toolbar macro

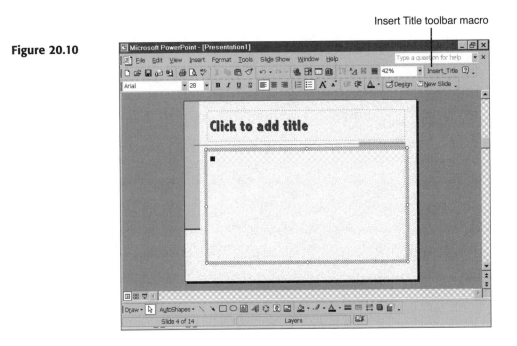

AFTER

Title text is inserted automatically and with the desired formatting.

Figure 20.11

CHAPTER 21

CUSTOMIZING POWERPOINT

In this chapter

CUSTOMIZING TOOLBARS

Toolbars help make PowerPoint and other Windows programs easy to use. A quick click on a button and you avoid having to search through endless menus to get to the command you want. PowerPoint has several predefined toolbars and by default places a few of them at various locations around the screen. For example, the Standard and Formatting toolbars display by default at the top of the screen, whereas the Drawing toolbar appears at the bottom, above the application bar (see Figure 21.1).

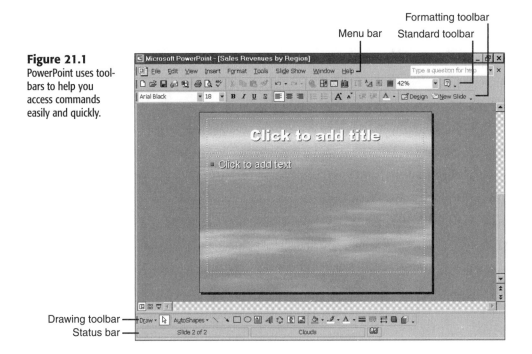

Figure 21.1
PowerPoint uses toolbars to help you access commands easily and quickly.

Formatting toolbar

Menu bar   Standard toolbar

Drawing toolbar
Status bar

DISPLAYING OR HIDING TOOLBARS

The Standard and Formatting toolbars contain buttons for the most commonly used PowerPoint procedures, such as saving, printing, editing, and formatting. If you need to have other features easily at hand, you can choose additional toolbars for specific tasks. To display toolbars, choose View, Toolbars, and scroll through the list that displays to choose the toolbar you need. The choice of toolbars include:

■ **Control Toolbox**   This toolbox is handy for building dialog boxes using Visual Basic. Most PowerPoint users will probably never need it.

■ **Drawing**   This toolbar enables you to draw and enhance objects in your presentation.

■ **Outlining**   If you click the Outline tab in Normal view, the Outlining toolbar automatically appears along the left side, ready to help you create or edit the slideshow outline.

> Some toolbars appear automatically when you select a feature or command related to that toolbar. For example, the Picture toolbar automatically appears if you select a picture.

- **Picture** When you click a picture object, the Picture toolbar appears to help you modify the picture's colors, brightness, contrast, lines, and so on.
- **Reviewing** This toolbar assists in collaborative editing of a slideshow. Reviewers can add comments or review comments by others, create Outlook tasks, or send the show as an attachment via e-mail.
- **Revisions Pane** Displays the Revisions pane, in which you can see what changes reviewers have suggested.
- **Tables and Borders** With this toolbar, you can quickly and easily draw or edit free-hand tables and borders.
- **Task Pane** Opens the New Presentation task pane.
- **Visual Basic** For advanced users, this toolbar assists in the creation of Visual Basic scripts.
- **Web** This toolbar can help you add hyperlinks and search for and link useful information from the Internet.
- **WordArt** Add or modify WordArt objects quickly and easily with this handy toolbar.

You never actually remove a toolbar. Instead, you simply hide it from view. Suppose, for example, that the Web toolbar displays, but you really don't need it and want to reclaim the screen space it takes up. Simply choose View, Toolbars, and click Web to deselect that toolbar.

> You can also right-click any toolbar to display the Toolbar menu. You then select or deselect the toolbar from that menu.

To close a floating toolbar, click the Close button at the right side of the title bar.

> When you close a toolbar that opened automatically, that toolbar no longer automatically opens when needed. You must open the toolbar from the menu to display it and also to make it appear automatically in the future.

REPOSITIONING TOOLBARS

Typically, you expect a toolbar to appear at the top of the screen. However, you've already noted that the Drawing toolbar is located at the bottom. When you select other toolbars, they may appear vertically along the side of the screen. Toolbars that appear on any side of the screen are said to be docked, whereas floating toolbars can be found in the middle of the screen.

You can reposition a toolbar simply by dragging it to the desired location. For example, to move the Standard toolbar to the left side of the screen, follow these steps:

1. Place the mouse pointer on the Move handle on the toolbar. A four-way arrow appears (see Figure 21.2).

Figure 21.2
Drag a toolbar by clicking and dragging the toolbar's Move handle.

2. Click and, while holding the left mouse button down, drag the toolbar away from the edge. PowerPoint displays the toolbar along with a title bar (see Figure 21.3). If you release the mouse button at this stage, the toolbar appears as a floating toolbar.

3. Continue dragging the toolbar to the desired location—for example, along the left edge.

4. When the toolbar's title bar disappears and the Move handle reappears, release the mouse button to dock the toolbar along the edge of the screen (see Figure 21.4).

Note

It's easy to lose toolbars as you drag and drop them. For example, if you accidentally drop a toolbar on top of another one, you might not notice that they've been combined. Use the Move handle to drag one toolbar from on top of another one.

Figure 21.3
A floating toolbar also displays a title bar and can be placed anywhere on the screen.

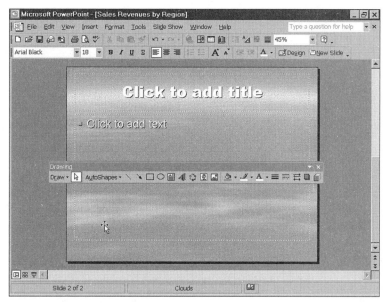

Outlining toolbar   Standard toolbar   Formatting toolbar

Figure 21.4
Docked toolbars can appear at any side of the screen.

Drawing toolbar

Note

If you drag a toolbar to a new location, it remains there until you move it again, even if you close PowerPoint.

ADDING AND REMOVING TOOLBAR BUTTONS

Everyone uses PowerPoint differently. You use some of the buttons on the PowerPoint tool-bars on a regular basis, whereas you rarely or never use others. PowerPoint makes it easy to add or remove buttons.

ADDING AND REMOVING BUTTONS FROM THE TOOLBAR

To add or remove toolbar buttons directly from the toolbar, follow these steps:

1. Click the Toolbar Options down arrow at the right end of the toolbar.

2. Choose Add or Remove Buttons from the menu.

3. Choose the name of the toolbar you want to customize from the menu, such as Standard or Formatting. A complete list of currently selected and commonly used buttons associated with that particular toolbar displays (see Figure 21.5).

Figure 21.5
Select or deselect commands to add or remove buttons from this list.

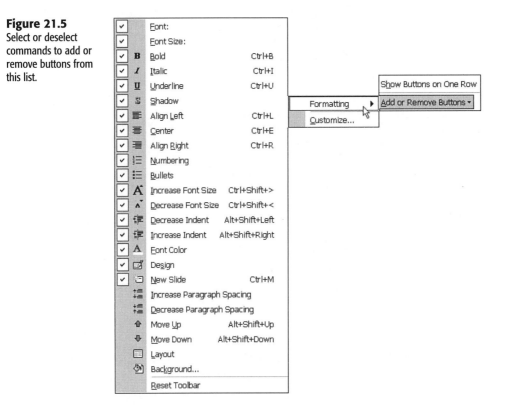

4. Click a button to add or remove it from the toolbar. Buttons that are currently active on the toolbar display a check mark in front of them. PowerPoint automatically adds buttons to the end of the toolbar or removes buttons from wherever they're located on the toolbar.

5. Click anywhere on the screen to close all menus.

If you want to go back to the original toolbar but forget which buttons it contained, simply scroll to the bottom of the Add or Remove Buttons menu and click Reset Toolbar.

ADDING AND REMOVING BUTTONS IN THE CUSTOMIZE DIALOG BOX

You can also add or remove toolbar buttons using the Customize dialog box, which offers additional options. To add buttons using this method, follow these steps:

1. Select View, Toolbars, Customize to open the Customize dialog box, shown in Figure 21.6.

Figure 21.6
The Customize dialog box offers numerous options for customizing your toolbars.

2. On the Toolbars tab, select the toolbar you want to modify, if it doesn't already appear on the screen. Active toolbars have a check mark in the check box that precedes them.

3. Click the Commands tab to display a comprehensive list of standard PowerPoint buttons by category (see Figure 22.7).

4. Locate the command for the button you want to add. For example, if you want to add a button to help you quickly view your color slides in black and white (as they might be printed on a laser printer), first click View in the Categories list, and then scroll through the Commands list until you find Black and White.

> **Note**
>
> If you're not sure what a command is used for, select the command and click the Description button.

5. Click and drag the button to the target toolbar.

Figure 22.7
The Commands tab displays commands you can add to a toolbar.

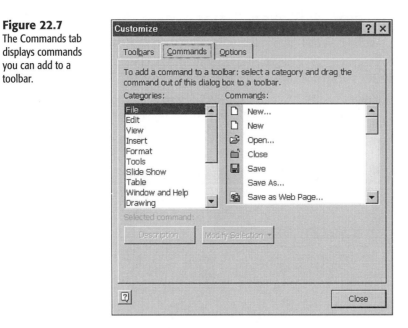

6. Position the button using the I-beam mouse pointer as a guide (see Figure 21.8).

Drag the toolbar button.

Figure 21.8
Drag a command button to the target toolbar and use the I-beam pointer to position it.

7. Release the mouse button to add the button to the toolbar.

8. To save changes to the toolbar, click the Close button to close the Customize dialog box.

To remove a button from the toolbar, open the Customize dialog box, select the button you want to remove, and drag it from the toolbar.

You can also reposition buttons on the toolbar by simply dragging them to their new locations. Note that you can't drag and drop toolbar buttons if the Customize dialog box isn't open.

⚠ **Customized your toolbar too much and want to start over?** See the "Troubleshooting" section near the end of this chapter.

ADDING COMMANDS TO MENU BUTTONS

Some toolbar buttons also function as menus. For example, the Font Color button on the Formatting toolbar displays a menu of color options (also referred to as a palette). Figure 21.9 illustrates this menu.

Figure 21.9
The Font Color toolbar button also displays a menu of options.

You can customize menu buttons by adding and removing commands. To add a new command to an existing menu button, follow these steps:

1. Open the Customize dialog box by choosing View, Toolbars, Customize and click the Commands tab.

2. Locate the first command you want to add to the toolbar button's menu (for example, Insert, Duplicate Slide).

3. Drag the command from the Customize dialog box to the desired toolbar button and wait until the menu drops down.

4. Position the new command where you want on the menu, using the I-beam as an insertion guide (see Figure 21.10).

5. Drop the command where you want to place it on the drop-down menu.

6. Repeat steps 2–5 until you have added all the menu commands you want.

7. Click Close to close the Customize dialog box and to save changes to your toolbar menu.

PART

VI

CH

21

To remove a command from a toolbar button's menu, simply select the command and drag it off the toolbar. You need to have the Customize dialog box open to do this, however.

Figure 21.10
An I-beam shows where to position a command you want to add to a drop-down menu from a toolbar button.

MODIFYING TOOLBAR BUTTONS

The power and ease of use derived from using toolbars instead of menus depend largely on the ease with which you can visually identify a button and its function. If you find that one of PowerPoint's standard toolbar buttons simply doesn't convey to you the visual information you need to quickly identify what the button does, you can modify the button or even create an entirely new one.

To modify a toolbar button, follow these steps:

1. Open the Customize dialog box by choosing View, Toolbars, Customize.
2. Select the button on the toolbar that you want to modify. A black border surrounds it.
3. Right-click the selected button to display the Modify Selection menu (see Figure 21.11).

> **Note**
>
> You can also access this menu by selecting the Commands tab and clicking the Modify Selection button. Note that this button is only available if you've already selected a toolbar button to modify.

4. Select one of the following modifications:
   - **Reset**   Restores the button to its original PowerPoint default. Any changes you have made to the button will be lost.
   - **Delete**   Removes the button from the toolbar.

- **Name**   This is the text version of the button that is used if you choose to display text along with or instead of the button, or if the command appears in a toolbar menu. Also, if you point the mouse at the button, a text prompt appears to remind you what the button does. If you add the ampersand (&) before a letter in the name, that letter appears underlined in menus where you can select the command using the keyboard.

Figure 21.11
The Modify Selection menu enables you to customize a toolbar button.

> **Note**
>
> The name you choose can be important in making it easy to identify the function of a button. Be as descriptive as possible, but also try to keep the name brief because the name may appear in menus as well.

- **Copy Button Image**   Copies the selected button image to the Clipboard.
- **Paste Button Image**   Pastes a copied button image to the current selected toolbar button.

> **Note**
>
> Although you can do so, you should avoid having two identical images on the same toolbar. Furthermore, you should avoid using images that are commonly used for other functions (such as Save, Print, and so on).

- **Edit Button Image**   Opens the Button Editor dialog box, shown in Figure 21.12. In the Button Editor dialog box, you can move the direction of your button's image, change its color, or even design a new image by adding colors pixel by pixel. Click the Preview button to preview your changes before accepting them.

Figure 21.12
Let your creative side take over as you create or edit new button images.

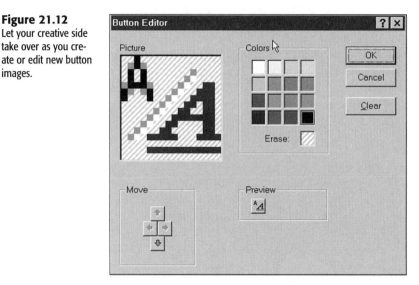

Even if you plan to create your own image, you can get a head start by first changing the image to something that closely resembles what you want to create. You then simply edit that image instead of completely starting from scratch.

- **Reset Button Image**   Resets the button image to its original state.

- **Change Button Image**   Displays a palette of optional button images (see Figure 21.13) you can apply to your toolbar button. If you don't like your selection, you can choose Reset Button Image to restore the original image.

Figure 21.13
If you don't like the current button image, you can choose from a palette of alternative images.

- **Default Style**   Displays the button as an image when it appears as a button, and as image and text when it is located in menus.

- **Text Only (Always)**   Ignores the image and displays only text, including the underlined character when appropriate.

- **Text Only (in Menus)**   Displays an image when the command is a button, but ignores the image when the command is located in menus.

- **Image and Text**   Displays both image and text, even when the command is a button.

- **Begin a Group**   Adds a vertical line to the left of the button, helping to establish the beginning of a group of buttons.

> As you add, move, or delete buttons, you might find that you want to group your buttons so they're more easily distinguished by function. You can do this by adding a vertical line between buttons on the toolbar. You might not notice these vertical lines right away, but if you look to the left of the Bold button and to the right of the Underline button on the Formatting toolbar, you can view existing group lines.

- **Assign Hyperlink**   Enables you to add a link to the button which, when clicked, takes you to the Web or to another document or program.

→ For details on adding links to PowerPoint objects, **see** Chapter 16, "Using PowerPoint's Web Features."

Tip from
Patrice-Anne Rutledge

> Don't be afraid to experiment with changing toolbar buttons. You want to create buttons that work for you, and you can always reset the images if things go awry.

5. Click the Close button to close the Customize dialog box.

CREATING A NEW TOOLBAR

If you're like many of us, it seems that the buttons we use on a regular basis are scattered about on different toolbars. Perhaps you'd like to create your own toolbar with all those buttons you use the most. Creating your own toolbar also means you won't have to modify PowerPoint's original toolbars.

To create your own toolbar, follow these steps:

1. Choose View, Toolbars, Customize to access the Customize dialog box.

2. Click the Toolbars tab.

3. Click the New button. PowerPoint displays the New Toolbar dialog box (see Figure 21.14).

Figure 21.14
Create a new toolbar using the New Toolbar dialog box.

New Toolbar

Toolbar name:

My Tools

OK   Cancel

4. Create the name of the toolbar (for example, "My Tools") in the Toolbar Name text box.

5. Click OK and PowerPoint displays a new floating toolbar (see Figure 21.15).

Add buttons to your
toolbar to make it complete.

Figure 21.15
A new toolbar also
needs command but-
tons to make it com-
plete.

6. Click the Commands tab to add and arrange buttons and groups.

→ To learn more about accessing the Commands tab, **see** "Adding and Removing Buttons in the Customize Dialog Box" earlier in this chapter.

7. Dock the toolbar along one of the sides of the screen, or position the floating toolbar where you want it to appear when you access it.

8. Click the Close button to close the Customize dialog box.

RESETTING THE TOOLBAR

If you make many changes to a toolbar, you'll find it's nearly impossible to remember which buttons are original to the toolbar and which ones you added. If you decide you want to restore your original toolbar, you can do this in one of two ways.

Click the Toolbars tab in the Customize dialog box, select the toolbar you want to restore, and click Reset. PowerPoint asks if you're sure you want to do this, and if you're sure, just click OK.

You can also click the Toolbar Options down arrow at the right end of the toolbar, choose Add or Remove Buttons from the menu, choose the name of the toolbar you want to cus-tomize from the menu, and click Reset Toolbar.

CUSTOMIZING MENU COMMANDS

By default, PowerPoint menus tailor themselves to the way you work. Initially, only the most commonly used commands appear on the menus (see Figure 21.16). If you click the double arrows at the bottom of the menu or wait a few seconds, the menu expands to include other commands you have used rarely or not at all (see Figure 21.17). If you begin to use a command regularly, PowerPoint then adds that command as a regular menu item.

Figure 21.16
By default, PowerPoint displays only the most common menu commands along with recently used commands.

Click here to expand the menu.

Figure 21.17
Clicking the arrows at the bottom of a menu displays the full range of menu commands.

Note

Although customizing menus is activated by default in PowerPoint, this option can be turned off on the Options tab of the Customize dialog box (View, Toolbars, Customize).

You can further customize how menus work by changing menu options, adding or deleting menu commands, and even adding entirely new menu categories.

CHANGING MENU OPTIONS

You customize menu options using the same dialog box you use for customizing toolbars. Access the Customize dialog box by right-clicking the menu bar and choosing Customize. Then click the Options tab. PowerPoint displays the following options (see Figure 21.18):

- **Show Standard and Formatting Toolbars on Two Rows** Select this option to display these two frequently used toolbars on separate rows; to save screen space, deselect this option to display both toolbars on one row. On high-resolution screens, you may be able to see all of the buttons from both toolbars. On other screens, however, the toolbars are collapsed and you must click the More Buttons button to see and use the entire list of buttons.

Figure 21.18
Set menu options on
the Options tab.

- **Always Show Full Menus** Select this check box to always show the full menu.
- **Show Full Menus After a Short Delay** This option allows the full menu to appear after a few seconds. Otherwise, you must click the Expand button (the double arrows) at the bottom of the menu to see the entire menu.
- **Reset My Usage Data** Suppose you use a command quite often for a specific project, but don't otherwise use it very much. You can click this button to reset the history of your use of PowerPoint's commands so that only the default menu commands appear. You then begin establishing once again a history of commands as you use them.

■ **Large Buttons** This option displays the buttons about four times larger than usual. You probably won't use this option unless you are visually impaired or you have a very high-resolution screen and have the room required for large buttons.

Tip from
*Patrice-Anne
Rutledge*

Although the Large Buttons option takes up a lot of space, you can create a custom toolbar with a minimal set of buttons that fit on a single row. (See "Creating a New Toolbar" earlier in this chapter.)

■ **List Font Names in Their Font** By default, PowerPoint displays font names in the toolbar font list using the actual fonts (see Figure 21.19). This might cause the list to appear slowly, especially on older, slower computers. To list them in a standard Windows font, deselect this option.

Figure 21.19
Display font lists using the fonts themselves or a standard Windows font.

■ **Show ScreenTips on Toolbars** When you point at a toolbar button, PowerPoint displays the name of the button in a small yellow box. This helps identify the button if you can't discern its use by the button image alone. If you want to turn off this option, deselect it.

■ **Show Shortcut Keys in ScreenTips** Believe it or not, lots of people still prefer to use the keyboard whenever possible. This option enables them to see whether a toolbar button command has an equivalent keystroke, such as F5 to View a Slide Show or Ctrl+S to save a presentation.

Tip from
*Patrice-Anne
Rutledge*

Although using the mouse may make it easier to find features and commands you don't often use, usually you can access commands more quickly by using keyboard equivalents. For example, if you're already typing, pressing Ctrl+S to save the presentation is faster than moving your hand to the mouse, and then finding and clicking the Save button on the toolbar. Use toolbar button ScreenTips to learn keystrokes that can save you time.

PART
VI

CH
21

■ **Menu Animations** If you want to add some pizzazz to the way your menus display, choose Unfold, Slide, or Random (which alternates the first two methods). Slide simply slides the menu down from the top. Unfold slides the menu both from the top and from the left. The default is None, probably because either method can be rather distracting.

CREATING A NEW MENU ON THE MENU BAR

If you find using menus easier than using toolbars, you can create and add your own menus to the menu bar. Suppose, for example, you want your own Quick Stuff menu, using the letter *Q* as the hotkey. On that menu, you intend to add items from the Formatting toolbar because you plan not to display that toolbar.

Note

The menu bar functions and is modified in exactly the same way as toolbars. That is, not only can you add menu items to toolbars, but you can add commands to the menu bar as well. Information in preceding sections about modifying toolbars also applies to customizing menu bars.

To create a new menu and to add items to that menu, follow these steps:

1. Open the Customize dialog box by right-clicking the menu and choosing Customize.
2. Click the Commands tab in the Customize dialog box.
3. Scroll to the bottom of the Categories list and click New Menu.
4. Drag the New Menu button from the Commands list to the menu bar. You can place the button anywhere on the menu bar, not only at the end (see Figure 21.20).

Figure 21.20
Create new menu items and place them anywhere on a menu or toolbar.

5. Click the Modify Selection button. PowerPoint displays the Modify Selection menu (see Figure 21.21).

Figure 21.21
The Modify Selection menu enables you to customize new menus.

6. Choose Name and edit the text to change the name from "New Menu" to something more descriptive of the menu's purpose (for example, "My Menu"). If you want to make *M* the hotkey, place an ampersand (&) before the letter *M*. Press Enter or click anywhere outside of the menu to close the menu.

7. Next, locate the first button you want to add to the custom menu (for example, Format, Bold).

8. Drag the command button to the new menu (for example, My Menu) and wait until a menu drops down. The first time you do this, the menu consists of nothing more than a blank gray square (see Figure 21.22).

Figure 21.22
Drag and drop commands to the blank square beneath a new menu entry.

9. Drop the command on the drop-down menu (or blank square). As you drag the button up and down the menu, a horizontal line indicates where you will drop the button.

10. Repeat steps 7–9 until you have added the menu commands you want.

To remove a new menu or menu command, drag it off the menu bar when the Customize dialog box is open.

SETTING AUTOCORRECT OPTIONS

PART
VI

CH
21

AutoCorrect is a useful feature that can help save you time and automatically correct mistakes you frequently make. If you need to enter a long term or name frequently, it can save you time and effort if you enter a shorter term and have PowerPoint automatically enter the longer term. For example, let's say the name of your latest product is "All Natural, Fat-Free Chilly Cherry Sorbet." You're tired of typing that phrase over and over, so you set up an AutoCorrect entry named "CCS" and have PowerPoint automatically enter "All Natural, Fat-Free Chilly Cherry Sorbet" any time you type the letters "CCS". Entering your initials instead of typing your full name is another example of how you could use this feature.

In addition, if you know you always misspell a particular word, you can enter the word as you normally misspell it in the Replace field and the correct spelling in the With field.

To view the current AutoCorrect options as well as make modifications, additions, and deletions to these options, select Tools, AutoCorrect Options. The AutoCorrect dialog box for your installed language opens, shown in Figure 21.23.

Figure 21.23
You can view and modify automatic correction options in this dialog box.

Basic AutoCorrect options include:

- **Show AutoCorrect Options Buttons**   Displays the AutoCorrect Options button after an automatic correction occurs. Place the mouse over the small blue box beneath the correction and click the down arrow to view a menu of options. From here, you can revert back to your original entry, stop automatically correcting this type of entry, or open the AutoCorrect dialog box. Figure 21.24 illustrates an example of the AutoCorrect Options button.

- **Correct TWo INitial CApitals**   Corrects instances where you accidentally enter two initial capital letters in a row. You can enter exceptions to this rule if you like (such as ID, and so on).

- **Capitalize First Letter of Sentences**   Capitalizes the first letter of all sentences.

- **Capitalize First Letter of Table Cells**   Capitalizes the first letter of a word in a table cell.

- **Capitalize Names of Days**   Capitalizes days of the week such as Monday, Tuesday, and so forth.

- **Correct Accidental Use of cAPS LOCK Key**   Turns caps lock off if you start typing regular sentences and corrects the words you started entering incorrectly.
- **Replace Text as You Type**   Replaces AutoCorrect entries as you type them.

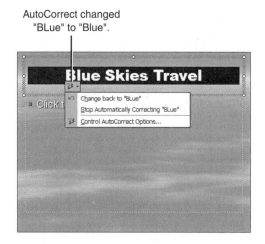

AutoCorrect changed
"BLue" to "Blue".

Figure 21.24
Choose from several options when you automatically correct text entries in PowerPoint.

CUSTOMIZING AUTOCORRECT ENTRIES

You can also customize individual AutoCorrect entries. The lower portion of the dialog box includes a list of existing automatic corrections.

To delete an existing entry, select it and click the Delete button.

To modify an existing entry, select it and enter the new data in the Replace and/or With fields as needed.

To add a new entry, enter the term to replace in the Replace field and the term to replace it with in the With field.

SPECIFYING AUTOCORRECT EXCEPTIONS

To specify exceptions to these rules, click the Exceptions button. Figure 21.25 illustrates the AutoCorrect Exceptions dialog box.

On the First Letter tab, you can specify any abbreviations that end with a period that you don't want to treat as the end of a sentence. PowerPoint ignores standard rules of capitalization here and doesn't capitalize the next letter after the period. Terms such as etc. and abbr. are automatically included here, but you can also add your own or delete any existing entries.

On the INitial CAps tab, shown in Figure 21.26, you can enter any capitalized terms that you don't want PowerPoint to covert to lowercase.

PART
VI

CH
21

Figure 21.25
If you want to make exceptions to AutoCorrect functionality, you can do it here.

Figure 21.26
Automatically resolve capitalization problems on this tab.

For example, to avoid having the word ID converted to Id based on the normal rules of capitalization, you would enter it on this list.

AUTOFORMATTING AS YOU TYPE

The AutoFormat As You Type tab of the AutoCorrect dialog box enables you to replace and apply a number of formatting options as you type. This helps save you time by eliminating the need to manually format. Figure 21.27 illustrates this tab.

Figure 21.27
You can view and modify automatic correction options in this dialog box.

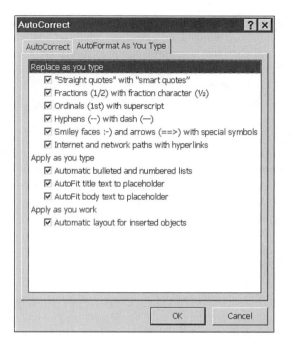

Options include

- **"Straight quotes" with "smart quotes"**   Replaces straight quotes you enter using the keyboard with properly formatted "smart quotes" for printing.

- **Fractions (1/2) with fraction character (½)**   Replaces fractions you enter by typing the slash between two numbers with a fraction character.

- **Ordinals (1st) with superscript**   Replaces manually entered ordinals with superscript ordinals.

- **Hyphens (--) with dash (—)**   Replaces manually entered hyphens with an em dash.

- **Smiley faces :-) and arrows -- > with special symbols**   Replaces the smiley face with ☺ and the arrow with ➔.

- **Internet and network paths with hyperlinks**   Automatically applies a hyperlink to an Internet address so that it will open a browser when you click on it. For example, AutoCorrect would convert www.microsoft.com to www.microsoft.com.

- **Automatic bulleted and numbered lists**   Automatically applies bulleted or numbered lists when PowerPoint detects that you're creating a list (when you use an asterisk for a bullet, for example).

- **AutoFit title text to placeholder**   Automatically resizes text if it won't fit in a title text placeholder. For example, the title text is 44 points by default, but can be reduced if your title is extremely long. When this option is activated, the AutoFit Options button appears. Click the down arrow on the right side of the button to display a menu from which you can accept or reject automatic fitting, as well as open the AutoCorrect dialog box. Figure 21.28 illustrates the AutoFit Options button.

PART

VI

CH

21

Figure 21.28
Use the AutoFit Options button to modify PowerPoint's automatic formatting.

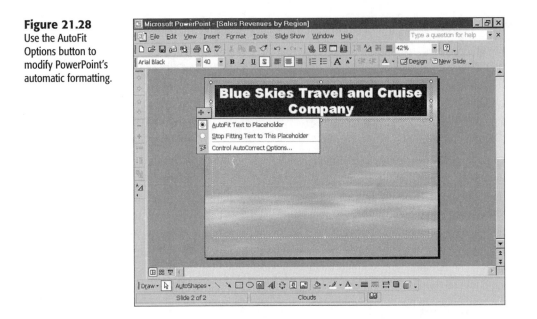

- **AutoFit Body Text to Placeholder**   Automatically resizes text if it won't fit in a body text placeholder. This option works in much the same way as the AutoFit Title Text to Placeholder option.

- **Automatic Layout for Inserted Objects**   Automatically sets the layout for objects you insert.

These options are all selected by default, but you can remove the check mark if you want to deactivate them for any reason.

SETTING POWERPOINT OPTIONS

PowerPoint enables you to change many basic options, such as how you edit, save, or print your presentations, as well as how you view PowerPoint screens.

Note

Changes you make in the Options dialog box become your new default settings until you change them again.

Tip from
Patrice-Anne
Rutledge

Whenever you use a new program or an update to a program, your first inclination is to try to make the program do things the "old way" or the way you're used to doing them. Although it can be tempting to jump right in and make changes to PowerPoint's default settings, you probably should use PowerPoint "as is" for a while, at least, until you decide whether those default settings might actually be better.

To access the Options dialog box, choose Tools, Options (see Figure 21.29).

Figure 21.29
The Options dialog box is used to change many of PowerPoint's default settings.

SETTING VIEW OPTIONS

Click the View tab to display options that affect what you see as you create and edit a slideshow, as well as what you see when you play the slideshow.

Show options include the following:

- **Startup Task Pane** Displays the task pane upon startup.
- **Slide Layout Task Pane When Inserting New Slides** Displays the Slide Layout task pane when you insert a new slide into your presentation.
- **Status Bar** Displays the status bar at the bottom of the screen. Although the status bar does take up a bit of territory, it shows you which slide you're editing as well as the design you're using. Also, the spelling button appears with a red x if anything on the current slide is misspelled.

Note

If you double-click the design name on the status bar, PowerPoint displays the Slide Design task pane, enabling you to quickly change the design template. Double-clicking the spelling button begins the spelling feature.

PART
VI

CH
21

- **Vertical Ruler**   Displays a vertical ruler along with the horizontal ruler if you choose to display rulers (View, Ruler).

- **Windows in Taskbar**   Displays a separate Taskbar icon for each open Office window. If you remove this check box, only a single icon will display. Note that this option isn't available for Windows NT 4.0.

Slide Show options include the following:

- **Popup Menu on Right Mouse Click**   When presenting a slideshow, you need an easy way to access navigation and other options. With this option, you can right-click on the slide to display a menu of options.

- **Show Popup Menu Button**   By default, when you play a PowerPoint slideshow, PowerPoint displays a small button at the lower-left corner of the slide. Clicking this button gives you the same menu as the one you get when you right-click the slide. If you don't want this button on the screen, deselect this option.

- **End with Black Slide**   If you deselect this option, PowerPoint returns to the PowerPoint editing screen when you conclude your slideshow. Leaving this option active makes for a cleaner ending.

You can also specify your default view from the Open All Documents Using This View drop-down list. Options include the following:

- The view saved in the file

- Normal—outline, notes, and slide

- Normal—thumbnails, notes, and slide

- Normal—outline and slide

- Normal—thumbnails and slide

- Normal—notes and slide

- Normal—slide only

- Outline Only

- Slide Sorter

- Notes

SETTING GENERAL OPTIONS

Click the General tab to change information about yourself and other items not easily grouped into a specific category (see Figure 21.30). General options include the following:

- **Provide Feedback with Sound to Screen Elements**   To add sound effects for menus, buttons, and other screen elements, select this option.

Figure 21.30
The General tab of the Options dialog box offers miscellaneous PowerPoint settings.

```
Options                                                    ? X
┌─────────────┬──────────────┬─────────────────────┐
│    Save     │   Security   │  Spelling and Style  │
├─────────────┼──────────────┼──────────┬──────────┤
│    View     │   General    │   Edit   │  Print   │
└─────────────┴──────────────┴──────────┴──────────┘
 ─ General options ─────────────────────────────────
   ☐ Provide feedback with sound to screen elements

   ☑ Recently used file list:  4 ⬍  entries

   Link sounds with file size greater than 100 ⬍ Kb
 ─ User information ─────────────────────────────────
   Name:   Patrice Rutledge

   Initials:  PAR

   Web Options...


                             ┌───── OK ─────┐  ┌─── Cancel ───┐
```

Note

Changing this option in PowerPoint changes it for all Office XP applications. However, you may have to restart Windows for this option to take effect. Also, you may find that other sound schemes take precedence over these sound effects.

- **Recently Used File List:** *n* **Entries** By default, PowerPoint displays the four most recently opened files at the bottom of the File menu. You can increase this number up to nine or reduce it to none.

- **Link Sounds with File Size Greater than** *nn* **Kb** PowerPoint normally saves sound files as part of the PowerPoint presentation itself. However, large sound files can make a presentation unwieldy. Selecting this option means that files larger than the size specified are *not* included with the slideshow, but instead are linked from their current file location.

- **Name** Whenever you use options that require your name, such as in the Properties Summary (File, Properties), PowerPoint automatically uses the name found here.

- **Initials** Whenever user initials are required—for example, during a NetMeeting— PowerPoint automatically uses the initials found here.

- **Web Options** Opens the Web Options dialog box where you can set various Web output options, including formatting, graphic formats, and the like.

→ For more information on Web options, **see** Chapter 16.

PART
VI

CH

21

SETTING EDIT OPTIONS

Click the Edit tab to change options for editing text and charts (see Figure 21.31). These options include the following:

- **Show Paste Options Buttons**   Displays a Paste Options button that enables you to make choices about how you want to paste a copied object or text, such as whether to keep source or target design template formatting.

Figure 21.31
The Edit tab of the Options dialog box offers options for text and chart editing.

- **Use Smart Cut and Paste**   The spacing around added or deleted text adjusts to add a space between words or to remove a space before a period, unless you deselect this option.

- **When Selecting, Automatically Select Entire Word**   If you want to select only portions of words when using a mouse, deselect this option.

- **Drag-and-Drop Text Editing**   Clicking selected text and dragging it to a new location is the same as cutting and pasting. If you find this happens accidentally too often, you may need to deselect this option.

- **New Charts Take on PowerPoint Font**   If you clear this option, charts will use a generic default font (for example, Arial) instead of the font and style being used in the current slide.

Tip from
Patrice-Anne
Rutledge

Although it might seem like a good idea to use the default PowerPoint fonts when creating a new chart, more generic fonts may actually look better. You might want to create test charts using both font methods before actually developing the data or making other modifications.

- **Maximum Number of Undos:** *nn*   By default, you can undo the last 20 actions. You can decrease the number of undos to as few as three or increase it to as many as 150.

Caution

Increasing the number of undos increases the size of your document and also increases the risk of corrupting your document. Unless you really need more, stay with the default number, or fewer.

 Taking too long to save or perform other tasks? See the "Troubleshooting" section near the end of this chapter.

- **New Animation Effects**   Disables the new animation effects in PowerPoint 2002. This is useful if you're going to share presentations with users of previous versions of PowerPoint that employ a different kind of animation effects.

- **Multiple Masters**   Disables the use of multiple slide masters which can cause problems when opened with a previous version of PowerPoint.

- **Password Protection**   Disables the use of password protection, so that users of previous PowerPoint versions not supporting password protection can still open your presentations.

CHANGING PRINT OPTIONS

To change general printing defaults or to change settings for the current document only, click the Print tab (see Figure 21.32).

→ For details on printing PowerPoint presentations, **see** Chapter 10, "Creating and Printing Presentation Materials."

General printing options include the following:

- **Background Printing**   This option enables you to continue editing your slide presentation while PowerPoint prints slides in the background. Depending on the printer you're using, it might already be set up for background printing. If so, your printer will print in the background regardless of your selection here. If your printer isn't already set up to do background printing, the selection in this check box determines whether background printing occurs or not.

- **Print TrueType Fonts as Graphics**   If your printer has trouble printing the fonts used in your presentation, it could be that your printer cannot recognize them or you are using too many fonts for your printer to keep track of. Choosing this option sends text to the printer as graphics, thus bypassing the downloading of fonts to your printer. However, this option generally makes printing much slower.

■ **Print Inserted Objects at Printer Resolution**   This helps match graphic resolutions to the printer that's printing them. For example, your graphic image might have been created at only 72 dots per inch (dpi), but your printer can print at a much crisper 600 dpi. Selecting this option may slow printing.

Figure 21.32
The Print tab of the Options dialog box offers several default printing options.

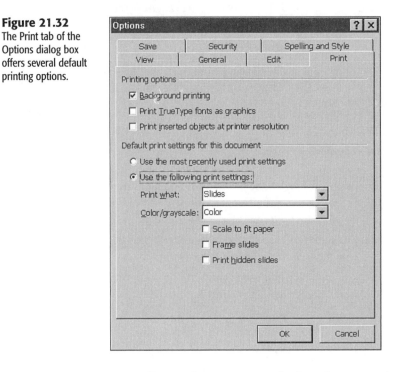

When you print your current document using the Print button on the Standard toolbar, by default you use the most recently used PowerPoint print settings. You can also choose to Use the Following Print Settings:

■ **Print What**   Enables you to choose exactly what you want to print and its format. Options include

  • **Slides**   This is the default printing format.

  • **Handouts**   You can print two, three, or six slides per page.

  • **Notes Pages**   This prints a small version of the slide, along with any speaker notes you might have created.

  • **Outline View**   This printout appears exactly as it does in PowerPoint's Outline view.

■ **Color/Grayscale**   Enables you to choose the color option for print. Choices include Color, Grayscale, or Pure Black and White.

Note

To preview your printout in another color format, click the Color/Grayscale button on the Standard toolbar and choose Color, Grayscale, or Pure Black and White from the menu.

- **Scale to Fit Paper**   If you're using other than standard-sized paper, this option enables PowerPoint to scale the slides to fit that size paper.
- **Frame Slides**   This option places a single, thin-line border around the entire printed slide.
- **Print Hidden Slides**   If you have hidden slides in your PowerPoint presentation, you can choose to include them in the printed version.

Note

Don't forget that print options selected from the Options menu apply only to automatic printing from the Print button on the Standard toolbar. Choosing File, Print still enables you to choose specific print options before printing.

→   For details on printing PowerPoint presentations, **see** Chapter 10.

SETTING SAVE OPTIONS

Click the Save tab to view and change Save options (see Figure 21.33).

Figure 21.33
The Save tab of the Options dialog box helps change default file saving options.

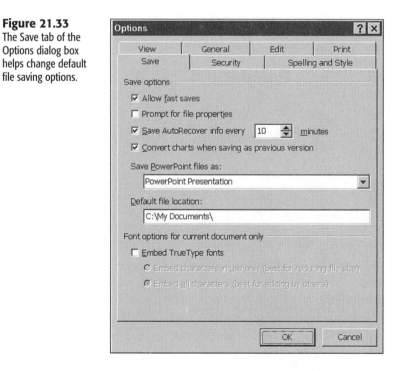

These include

- **Allow Fast Saves** By default, PowerPoint saves only the changes made to a presentation since the last time it was saved, which obviously takes less time than saving the full presentation. However, this also requires more disk space, so if your computer is already fast enough, you might want to consider deselecting this option.

- **Prompt for File Properties** The Summary, found in File, Properties, helps document the authorship and revision history of your slide presentation. If this is important to you, select this option, which automatically brings up the Properties screen the first time the document is saved or whenever it is saved with a different name.

- **Save AutoRecover Info Every *nn* Minutes** This is the automatic backup provision that saves a temporary copy of your presentation (typically in the \Windows\Temp folder) as frequently as you specify with this option. If you exit your document properly, the automatic backup file is erased. If you don't exit properly (for example, due to a power failure), PowerPoint automatically opens this file the next time you use PowerPoint so that you can determine whether it contains data you didn't save.

- **Convert Charts When Saving as Previous Version** When saving the presentation to an earlier version of PowerPoint, use this option to convert charts to a format also understood by earlier versions of PowerPoint.

- **Save PowerPoint Files As** By default, PowerPoint saves its files in the PowerPoint presentation format, which can't be opened in earlier versions of PowerPoint, such as Office 95.

  However, PowerPoint 2002 can open presentations created in earlier versions. If you work in an environment where not everyone is using PowerPoint 2002, you may need to agree upon a common format to be used by everyone. Then, change this option to one of the following formats:

  - PowerPoint presentation, which can be opened and edited in PowerPoint 2002, 2000, or 97
  - PowerPoint 97-2002 & 95 Presentation
  - Web Page
  - Web Archive

Caution

Be aware that saving a PowerPoint 2002 presentation in an earlier format may result in the loss of certain features available only in PowerPoint 2002.

- **Default File Location** PowerPoint saves your presentations in the folder you specify. Initially this is usually C:\My Documents, but that may vary depending on how PowerPoint was installed.

- **Embed TrueType Fonts** Select this option if you want to embed TrueType fonts in the current document. Options include embedding only characters in use to reduce file size or embedding all characters so that others can edit.

SETTING SECURITY OPTIONS

The Security tab (see Figure 21.34) enables you to set a variety of security options for PowerPoint, which can be useful if you share your presentations with other users or place them on a network, intranet, or the Internet.

Figure 21.34
Protect your presentations using the Security tab.

Options include the ability to

■ **Set a password to open a presentation** Protect your file by entering a password in the Password to Open field. You, or anyone else, will need to enter this password to open the file again. To set further encryption options, click the Advanced button.

■ **Set a password to modify a presentation** Another option is to set a password specifically to modify a presentation. Anyone can still view your presentation, but it will take a password to make changes to it. Enter a modification password in the Password to Modify field.

Caution

If you forget your password, you'll no longer be able to open and/or modify your presentation, so be sure to choose a password that's easy for you to remember, or write it down in a secure location.

PART
VI

CH
21

- **View or modify digital signatures** If you plan to use digital signatures with your PowerPoint presentations, click the Digital Signatures button to view these options. PowerPoint 2002 uses Microsoft Authenticode technology to enable digital signatures using a digital certificate. A *digital signature* is an electronic, encrypted signature stamp that's attached in a certificate to vouch for its authenticity. The average PowerPoint user won't normally set up digital certificates; this is the domain of an organization's IT department.

- **Set privacy options** If you're very concerned about privacy, you can specify that PowerPoint remove any personal information (such as your name) that it stores by selecting the Remove Personal Information from This File on Save check box. Note that this option doesn't remove personal information you add to your presentation yourself (for example, entering your name and address on a slide), but information PowerPoint stores by default.

- **Set macro security** If you regularly receive presentations that include macros, you might want to set special security options to protect from macro viruses. Options include the ability to accept only signed macros from sources you specify, to choose whether or not to accept files with macros, or to disable macro protection. Macros aren't as commonly used with PowerPoint as they are with other Office programs, but you should still set at least some form of macro protection if you're going to share files with others. Click the Macro Security button to set these options.

SETTING SPELLING AND STYLE OPTIONS

Click the Spelling and Style tab to change default spelling and style options.

→ For detailed information on checking spelling and style, **see** "Checking Spelling and Style" in Chapter 3, "Working with Text."

SETTING PRESENTATION PROPERTIES

As you create and modify your presentation, you automatically change many of the presentation's properties. You can view these properties and also change or add other properties to the document by choosing File, Properties. PowerPoint displays a dialog box with the name of your presentation. This dialog box includes the following tabs:

- **General** Specifies the type, size, and location of the file; the dates it was created, last modified, and last accessed; as well as any attributes it carries.

- **Summary** Enables you to enter custom information about your presentation (see Figure 21.35).

  This information is useful when you have to find the file because you can use keywords, for example, even if you can't remember the name of the file.

  To customize the presentation's summary, simply fill in the information you think is important. Assuming you created the document and that you supplied your name when you installed PowerPoint, the author's name appears automatically. The title is taken from the first slide of the presentation, but you can change that if desired.

The Save Preview Picture option simply enables you to see a preview of the first slide when you browse the file. If you deselect this option, you cannot preview the file in the Open dialog box.

Figure 21.35
Presentation properties add information to your file that can be used for finding and organizing your presentations.

Note

Using the Save Preview Picture option also increases the size of the saved file. To decrease the size of the file, deselect this option.

■ **Statistics** Displays detailed statistics about the presentation, including the number of words it contains, how many times it has been revised, total editing time, and more. Figure 21.36 illustrates this tab.

■ **Contents** Displays other basic information about your presentation, including which fonts you've used, the design template you applied, and so on.

■ **Custom** Enables you to create a series of customized properties that further categorize your document (see Figure 21.37). Unless you have a great number of presentations that need a high degree of organization, you'll probably never use this option. If you do, refer to PowerPoint's online help for information about creating a custom property.

PART
VI

CH

21

Figure 21.36
Go to the Statistics tab to learn how much time you've spent working on your presentation.

Figure 21.37
Custom properties help you find presentations by searching for unique characteristics you define.

USING ADD-IN PROGRAMS

Add-ins are special supplemental programs, usually provided by third-party sources to extend and enhance the capabilities of PowerPoint. Add-ins range from programs that add multimedia capabilities to those that simply enhance PowerPoint's default menus or toolbars.

Some add-ins are free; others you have to purchase. You can even write your own custom add-in programs by using PowerPoint's Visual Basic Editor. Also, you can find many add-ins on the Web. Look at the Microsoft Web site for those provided by Microsoft or do a Web search for "addins" and "PowerPoint" to find possible PowerPoint enhancements elsewhere on the Web.

Suppose you find an add-in that enhances the shadow control toolbar. Although not an earthshaking add-in, it does add some helpful controls for dealing with object shadows. To add this, or any other add-in, follow these steps:

1. Choose Tools, Add-Ins. PowerPoint displays the Add-Ins dialog box that lists add-ins that have already been installed (see Figure 21.38).

Figure 21.38
Add-ins add powerful functionality to PowerPoint.

2. Choose Add New. PowerPoint opens the Add New PowerPoint Add-In dialog box. By default, PowerPoint looks in the AddIns folder (for example, `C:\Windows\Application Data\Microsoft\AddIns`) to find add-in programs that have a `.PPA` filename extension. If the add-in you're looking for isn't in the default folder, browse to its location.

3. Select the add-in you want to install, and then choose OK.

4. If the add-in contains macros, as virtually all add-ins do, a warning message appears that allows you to disable the macros. However, if you want the full functionality of the add-in, you'll need to enable the macros.

> **Caution**
>
> Macros can contain viruses that in turn can wreak havoc on your computer. You should always exercise caution when enabling macros from unknown sources. Knowing the source of the add-in can help protect you from such viruses. If you've installed an anti-virus program on your computer and have updated it with the latest virus definitions, you should be reasonably safe.

5. After the add-in is installed, its name appears in the Available Add-Ins list with an x to the left of it. This means that the add-in is also loaded and ready to use.

6. Choose Close to return to PowerPoint.

You now can use the add-in as you work with your PowerPoint presentation.

> **Tip from**
> *Patrice-Anne Rutledge*
>
> Add-ins do use some memory and can slow PowerPoint's performance. When you're not using an add-in, unload it by choosing Tools, Add-Ins, and then after selecting the add-in, choosing Unload. The add-in remains installed but inactive, and you simply load it again when you need it.

WORKING WITH SLIDE MASTERS

PowerPoint is designed to help you achieve a consistent look in your slide presentations. You want your audience to focus on the message and not be distracted by poor and inconsistent design from one slide to the next.

You achieve this consistency by using *design templates*, or predesigned slide presentations that coordinate background colors and designs, font styles and placement, and other graphic design elements.

When you apply a design template to your presentation, PowerPoint also applies a related slide master. If you apply a new design template, a new slide master will also be applied. The slide master contains details about the fonts, placeholders, background, and color scheme of the related design template. If you want, you can customize the slide master to suit your needs. For example, you could change the default fonts, placeholders, background design, color scheme, or bullets; reposition placeholders; or add a logo.

→ For information on using design templates or how to change slide backgrounds and color schemes, **see** Chapter 6, "Formatting Slides and Presentations."

MODIFYING THE SLIDE MASTER

To modify your slide master, choose View, Master, Slide Master. PowerPoint displays the Slide Master layout and editing screen (see Figure 21.39).

Figure 21.39
The Slide Master editing screen helps you change the overall look and layout of your custom design templates.

Object area

You can modify either the slide master itself, which affects the design of the entire presentation, or the title master, which affects the design of the title slide only.

> **Note**
>
> All changes to the title or other text while in the slide master editing screen apply to all slides in your slide presentation except those based on the title master, thus helping you achieve consistency from slide to slide.

Place the mouse pointer over the thumbnails to the left side of the screen to display which thumbnail is for the overall slide master and which is for the title master. If the thumbnails don't display, close the slide master, choose View, Normal (Restore Panes) from the main menu, and then choose View, Master, Slide Master. Select the thumbnail to make formatting changes to the desired master.

The master includes several areas you can modify:

- Title Area
- Subtitle Area
- Object Area

- Date Area
- Footer Area
- Number Area

In the Date, Footer, and Number areas, you normally don't add text, but instead format the <date/time>, <footer>, and <#> placeholders. This information is added when you edit the Header and Footer (View, Header and Footer). An exception might be the page numbering where you could add and format "Page" before the <#> placeholder.

To modify an area, click in it and apply the desired formatting changes either from the Slide Master View toolbar, another toolbar, or the menu.

If you modify the slide master first, perhaps little needs to be changed for the title slide. However, you might make the title font larger, position it differently, or add a graphic object to the screen. Furthermore, you can delete the Date, Footer, or Number area boxes and create a different date or footer for the title slide.

You don't need to delete the date, footer, or page number placeholders if you don't want them on the title slide. Instead, when you choose View, Header and Footer to display footers for your slideshow, simply check the Don't Show on Title Slide check box.

Be sure you have modified the Slide Master before changing the Title Master. Initially the Title Master uses the same fonts and other attributes as the Slide Master.

Table 21.1 lists all the buttons on the Slide Master View toolbar.

TABLE 21.1   SLIDE MASTER VIEW TOOLBAR BUTTONS

Button	Name	Description
	Insert New Slide Master	Inserts a new slide master.
	Insert New Title Master	Inserts a new title master.
	Delete Master	Deletes the selected master.
	Preserve Master	Prevents a slide master from being deleted if you apply a new template.
	Rename Master	Opens the Rename Master dialog box in which you can enter a new name for your slide master.

TABLE 21.1   CONTINUED

Button	Name	Description
	Master Layout	Displays the Master Layout dialog box in which you can choose to add a specific placeholder. If all placeholders display on your master, the fields won't be active.
Close Master View	Close Master View	Closes the slide master view and returns to the current presentation.

MODIFYING THE HANDOUT AND NOTES MASTERS

In addition to the presentation itself, PowerPoint enables you to modify the handout and notes masters.

To modify the handout master, choose View, Master, Handout Master. PowerPoint displays the Handout Master editing screen and Handout Master View toolbar (see Figure 21.40).

Figure 21.40
The handout master defines the default layout for your template's printed handouts.

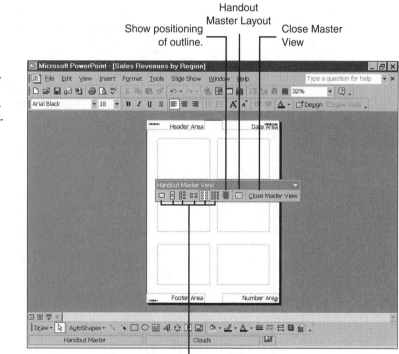

Show positioning of outline.

Handout Master Layout

Close Master View

Show positioning for one to nine handouts per page.

On the handout master you can

- Choose the number of slides you intend to include on each handout page by clicking a slide-positioning button (such as the Show Positioning of 6-per-Page Handouts button) on the Handout Master View toolbar. Choices include one, two, three, four, six, or nine handouts per page.

- Show the positioning of the outline by clicking the Show Positioning of the Outline button on the Handout Master View toolbar.

- Modify, reposition, or delete the Header, Footer, Date, and Page Area text boxes.

Note

You can easily change the number of slides to be included in the handouts in the Print dialog box when you actually print the handouts.

To modify the notes master, choose View, Master, Notes Master. PowerPoint displays the Notes Master editing screen (see Figure 21.41).

Figure 21.41
The notes master defines the default layout for your template's printed notes.

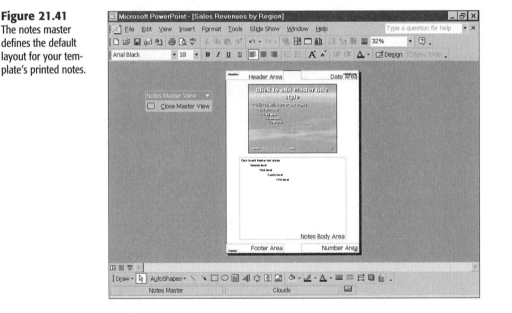

On the notes master you can

- Reposition or resize the slide area, depending on how much area you want for the text (notes).

- Reposition or resize the notes area.

- Modify, reposition, or delete the Header, Footer, Date, and Page Area text boxes.

Note

Although you can change the background colors and color schemes for the handout and notes masters, you probably won't want do so. Handouts and notes are usually printed, and background colors aren't necessary or desired. You can, however, add a graphic element, such as a company logo, which then appears on each printed page.

TROUBLESHOOTING

RESETTING A TOOLBAR

After experimenting with customizing my toolbar, I can't remember which buttons should be on the toolbar and which ones shouldn't. How do I reset a toolbar?

PowerPoint makes it easy to return to the original default toolbar settings. Just access the Customize dialog box (View, Toolbars, Customize), click the Toolbars tab, and click Reset. Be careful, however, because you lose all customizing you might have added to the toolbar.

SPEEDING UP PRESENTATION PERFORMANCE

After working with a presentation for some time, I notice that it takes longer to save or to perform certain tasks that were faster before. How can I make a leaner, faster presentation?

Several things can make your presentation grow unnecessarily, which in turn can slow it down. Try some of the following to reduce your file size or to otherwise speed up your work with PowerPoint:

- Reduce the number of undos (Tools, Options, Edit). By default, PowerPoint saves the last 20 changes, but you probably don't need more than 10.
- Turn off the option to save a preview picture with the file (File, Properties, Summary, Save Preview Picture).
- Unload any add-ins you may have loaded (Tools, Add-Ins, Remove).

DESIGN CORNER: MODIFYING MENUS AND TOOLBARS

Modifying menus and toolbars is often one of the most useful customizations you can make, particularly if you use certain commands frequently. Including a special menu with your most common menu tasks or placing frequently used buttons on your toolbar can be big timesavers.

For example, if you insert many Excel charts into your PowerPoint presentations, having the Insert Microsoft Excel Worksheet button on either the Standard or Formatting toolbar can save you a lot of time. To do this, follow these steps:

1. Choose Tools, Customize to open the Customize dialog box; click the Commands tab.
2. Choose Insert from the Categories list and Microsoft Excel Worksheet from the Commands list.

3. Drag the Microsoft Excel Worksheet command to the location where you want to place it on a toolbar (most likely, either the Standard or Formatting toolbar) and release the mouse button.

4. Click Close to close the Customize dialog box. The Insert Microsoft Excel Worksheet button appears on the toolbar, ready for use.

As another example, let's say you want to add a "My Stuff" menu command on the menu bar so that you'll have easy access to menu items you use frequently. This is a more involved process, but you should be able to create a custom My Stuff menu in about five to ten minutes by following the steps in "Creating a New Menu on the Menu Bar" in this chapter.

When you're done customizing, all of your most commonly used features and functions will be at your fingertips.

BEFORE

Figure 21.42

AFTER

Figure 21.43

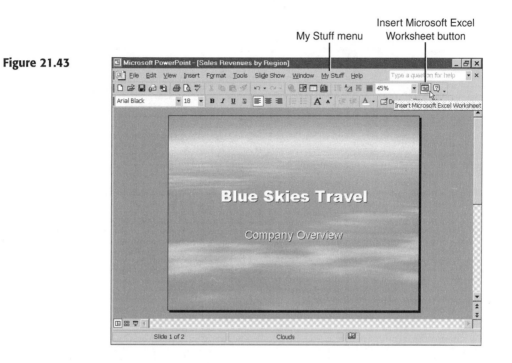

FROM CONCEPT TO DELIVERY

CHAPTER 22

THE MESSAGE—SCRIPTING THE CONCEPT

In this chapter

by Tom Mucciolo

EXPERIENCING IDEAS

You know what I like? I like other books. You know, the other books out there that deal with presenting, public speaking, and communications. I figure that anyone who has a plan that works and puts it in writing is probably giving good advice. Of course, that statement might not apply to every how-to book ever written, but you get the idea. While most advice is mainly subjective, when rooted in something believable, it can be of great value. I encourage you to investigate the topic of business presentations through the eyes of many experts and gather their viewpoints. You can learn a lot from those who have found success.

UNDERSTANDING THE PROCESS

Basically, there are only three things you have to think about when putting a presentation together.

The first is development of the concept; the second involves the design of the visuals; and the third concentrates on the delivery of the message to the audience. You might be involved in one or more of these stages.

To see the big picture, you have to understand where you are in the process of presenting. This is a good time to touch on how this chapter relates to the ones that follow, as the process is unveiled.

The chapters ahead are separated to cover each part of the process. While this chapter examines the message and teaches you how to script the concept into a workable presentation, Chapter 23, "The Media—Designing Visual Support," concentrates on the media and offers you advice on designing the visuals. This helps you make the visual expression of the message the best it can be. Chapter 24, "The Mechanics of Form—Developing External Presentation Skills," and Chapter 25, "The Mechanics of Function—Developing Internal Presentation Skills," both deal with the mechanics of presenting. The presentation skill is separated into two chapters, one covering external form and the other concentrating on internal function. I arranged these chapters in the order of theory to practice to personal skill.

Chapter 26, "Exploring Technicalities and Techniques," is dedicated to the environmental issues concerning a presentation, such as the room, the equipment, the seating arrangements, and other elements that might affect the performance of the message.

Chapter 27, "Presenting in a Variety of Settings," applies elements of the presentation process to many different situations, including conference rooms, small group meetings, and the outdoors, as well as interactive videoconferencing sessions.

PUTTING PEOPLE FIRST

One thing all the experts can agree on is that the success of communication is dependent on the presenter. The visuals are secondary to the concept, which is subject to the delivery skills of the person. All three elements are important, but without the presenter, you really can't call it a presentation.

If you think the content and the visuals are most important, try this at your next presentation. Arrive early and place a chair in the front of the room, right about where you are expected to stand. For added effect, place your jacket over the back of the chair. Now, with a cassette player running a voice recording of your presentation, let the PowerPoint visuals advance automatically for the audience. Then, using an egg timer, see how long the group remains in the room!

Communication is about people. Competition is so strong that products or services in the same category are starting to look the same. From household goods to cars to electronics—everything seems on par with everything else. The offerings of a company don't make the difference; instead, the people skills used to express those offerings are often what causes us to make a decision. The role of the presenter has taken on new meaning for companies that expect to compete in the new century.

BECOMING A VISUAL PRESENTER

Most people, especially those under the age of 40, are visual creatures. They get their information and stimulation from television, movies, computers, and video games. All of these forms are driven by action. Visual creatures demand action. In fact, they crave it. Think about it. Where do you get most of your news information? TV, right? That's because you like all the little pictures. Who doesn't? We're visual creatures. To be successful, presenters need to match the needs of an audience of visual creatures by becoming visual presenters. A visual presenter embodies a message and delivers it with action, creating a lasting impression on the audience.

My development of the concept, the design, and the delivery follows a consistent set of principles based on over 15 years of experience. The MediaNet approach focuses on messages, media, and mechanics in order to blend concepts and visual support with a person's individual delivery style.

A Method to the Madness
The processes and skills discussed in this book are simply the fundamentals. You can easily advance beyond the basics; one approach to gaining more comprehensive skills is MediaNet's "Presentation Skills Mastery Program," which builds a person's presentation style though four levels: Development, Competence, Achievement, and Mastery. The goal of the program is to master the skills and become a complete visual presenter, capable of delivering a variety of topics across a wide range of media.

This method has proven to be a practical, easy-to-understand, and extremely potent technique for changing ordinary business presentations into very memorable events. The techniques and tactics discussed in this book are designed for a visual presenter. This process advances a personal skill, allowing an individual to reach his or her own potential as an expert communicator. The results are immediate and easily applied to new situations.

Although this book discusses one method of presenting unlike any other you are likely to encounter, it is not the only way of developing and delivering better presentations;

it's just one way. But, I really believe if you apply these techniques, you will enhance your proficiency, increase your effectiveness, and develop your own style. Hopefully, your style will incorporate some or all of the skills of a visual presenter, from concept to delivery.

MAKING A LASTING IMPRESSION

People remember people, not data. Very few people will come up to you at the end of your presentation and say, "You know. The third pie chart? The fourth slice? Loved it. The other slices, nahhhh, but the fourth slice, wow!"

But a person might say, "You know. The story you told about the young woman and the two kids? I'll never forget that."

How long after the presentation is your message still memorable? Remember: Quality content stimulates thinking and makes a lasting impression.

When you develop content for a presentation, the messages you place in the script should stay with an audience long after the event takes place. It's not about the messages alone; rather, it's about the way those messages are conveyed. People communicate ideas to people. Quality content is only quality content if presented that way. Obviously, if an actor plays Hamlet poorly, the quality of the content is lost.

Now don't over-analyze when you read this chapter—just let the stuff sink in slowly. The messaging issues are broken down to the smallest components so that you can see how to build lasting impressions. The good news is that you probably instinctively know most of this already without even reading it.

People and ideas need to be brought together for content to flourish and for messages to be remembered. To create a lasting impression, you'll need to pay attention to the way messages are created for both the presenter to deliver and for the audience to grasp. The trick is to get this process to the point where you are constantly saying the right things to the right people at the right times. Having said that, the three areas we need to address when scripting a message are constructing the argument, qualifying the participants, and assuring consistency.

Note

I chose the development of the message as the starting point. Many believe that the first step in creating content is to analyze the needs of the audience. Then, after meeting those needs, the message is developed. Although I agree these two issues are closely related, the process of creativity dictates that the message needs to be developed before the audience is targeted. You really have to have a reason to say something and have something to say before you can ask someone to listen. Religion, politics, and theater are everyday examples of how messages need to exist before audiences can be reached.

CONSTRUCTING THE ARGUMENT

Whenever you take on the task of conceptualizing and creating a presentation, you probably have more information at your fingertips than you really need. Sometimes, the sheer quantity of data forces you to try to use every piece of the puzzle at any opportune moment. The problem with that process is the entire presentation becomes a "data dump" on the audience. The visuals become cluttered and the presenter stands there reading the information on each visual to a gradually dozing crowd. Sound familiar? Who has the time to be bored with more stuff than can be remembered?

The good news is that this clutter problem can easily be avoided. You just need to understand that developing quality content is a process, and the more you are involved in this process, the more you will recognize similar patterns and familiar sequences of ideas, intentions, and information. Don't be concerned with details when you begin, just concentrate and focus on the larger issues. To collect all the details, you need to understand the whole concept.

Zero Out Your Brain

A painter starts with a fresh canvas. You need to clear your mind, relax your brain, and let your inner creative state begin to work. To do this, say the following out loud, "What do I want to talk about?" In fact, sit back in a chair and look up at the ceiling when you say it. You will be amazed at how quickly you'll "zero out" most of the rubble in your head and focus on the development of the message. Of course, there's more to this than a one-sentence exercise, but I want you to understand that the initial creative process is based on very simple actions that take place in a very relaxed atmosphere.

If you just take a step back, look at the bigger picture, relax your mind, and think clearly, you can easily find the simple pattern to a successful presentation.

ESTABLISHING A PURPOSE

From an organizational perspective, you really need to start with a reason for creating the presentation in the first place. If you know why you are creating a presentation, you can learn how to convey it most effectively. The key to all communication is action and this is most important to visual creatures who demand constant action to understand information.

Although the word "purpose" answers the question "why," the word "objective" adds "to what extent." If you think about your purpose in the form of an objective, you'll get the impression of some action or some intention associated with the word objective.

This action in your message stems from your purpose or objective, and the resulting reaction is what you expect from the audience.

Your expectation is also known as your call to action. If you know what you want the audience to do at the end of the presentation (call to action), you can set an objective (course of action) that will get you to the result.

Let's say you want your friends to go with you to a comedy club rather than to the museum, as originally planned. Your call to action (what you want your friends to do) is to get them to choose the comedy club. Your course of action (objective) is to convince them that the comedy club is the only choice. If your argument is convincing, they will see only one choice—comedy club.

ACTION DRIVES CONTENT

In keeping with the approach of developing content for a visual presenter, action-driven concepts are the way to go.

Therefore, your objective must always be stated in terms of action, and you must express your objective actively in the form of "to do something." Whether it is to sell, to motivate, to persuade, or any other action, the entire script must adhere to the chosen objective.

After you state the "to do" objective using an active verb, it becomes easier to shape the story to fit the objective. For example, if the purpose or objective is to persuade, then every item in the presentation must, in some way, directly persuade the audience.

If there are components in the presentation that do not directly match the objective, you should remove them. If not, these extraneous bits of information, although indirectly supporting your topic, will become a waste of time for your live audience. This will transform them into a dead audience. It is better to place such additional information and any extensive details in the handout materials.

Tip from *Tom Mucciolo*	Avoid redundancy. If you have several ways of displaying similar information, such as a pie chart and a bar chart, don't use both. The test for such wordiness is to examine the sequence of support items and see whether you can interchange their order. If, for example, you can switch the order of a pie chart and bar chart, then one of them is probably extra and can be dropped from the story line. Think theater! Can you simply switch scene one with scene two without messing up the chronology of the play?

When your purpose or objective is clear, it's easier to capture ideas and gather only the relevant supporting information needed to advance the objective.

A well thought-out objective reduces information overload because it takes less data to support a single objective than it takes to support a number of different objectives.

FINE-TUNING THE OBJECTIVE

Sometimes the definition of the objective needs to be stronger. To make the objective stronger, you need to let action act on something or someone. An action verb (to do) needs to act on a noun (to do what) for a more specific result to occur. (You didn't realize how important those fourth-grade language classes were, did you?)

For example, the objective to sell might not be as emphatic as to excite and stir emotions. Notice how your approach to the script feels different by adding the noun *emotions*. The noun gives you a target. The type of information you would gather to support the stronger objective would be more extreme or more crucial than otherwise might have been used. Nouns help fine-tune the expression of the objective so you can narrow down the choices of support material.

Consider the expression "to paint detailed pictures." The type of information needed for this objective would contain precise elements that accurately depict the story so that there would be no question in the minds of the audience as to how to interpret the data. Now you know to look for data elements that show detail, such as segmented vertical bar charts showing individual comparisons at specific points in time, rather than line charts that show general comparisons to a trend over time. But that is not all to consider. You might begin to gather stories and examples from real life to continue to support your objective. These might or might not be depicted visually, but they could be described vividly to help paint a picture for the audience.

The strong or powerful expression "to force a single choice" makes it easier for the audience to agree to your point of view. You could have used this objective for the comedy club mentioned earlier, for instance. This fine-tuned objective tends to make you gather information that is mostly one-sided and not subject to much interpretation or argument. Data elements might include comparative tables or listings, pie charts showing percentages of the whole, and horizontal bar charts that are always used to show items at a single point in time. Stories and analogies will be clearly biased to your point of view to enhance this objective. It is not important right now to know the exact information and statistics buried in your support data. You just have to have an idea of the effort you will need to gather the level of support information you think you might use in your visuals.

The whole point of fine-tuning the objective is to stimulate your brain and get your juices flowing. Compare "to convince" with "to burn an indelible mark on the soul." Which one pushes your creative buttons more?

OBJECTIVE CHARACTERISTICS

The characteristics of the objective might further define the kinds of information required for support of the message. You use an active verb (to do) to express the objective and you may add a noun (to do what) to fine-tune the objective. If you also apply an adjective (by when or for what reason) to the objective itself, you give it character and depth.

Think of being stuck in an airport. Your objective is to get to your destination, right? What if you apply a characteristic of time to that objective? Let's say it's the beginning of your business trip rather than the end. Your objective will not only be more urgent, but the means to your destination might suddenly include a car, train, or boat to get there.

The following are examples of characteristics:

- Specific
- Measurable
- Time-based

- Achievable (but not already achieved)
- Relevant

For example, if the objective is to force a single choice, a measurable characteristic such as comparing features and benefits of products will match the objective because forced choice is a result of measuring comparisons. Later, when you select support information for the presentation, you will know to look for more comparative items that measure differences.

Or, if the objective is to motivate the creative team, a time-based characteristic, such as establishing a deadline for a given project, will match well with the objective, because the motivation for the team is to meet the deadline in order to avoid a consequence. When you select support information, you can narrow your choices to those items that relate to motivating the creative team by a certain date.

When the purpose or objective of the presentation is clearly defined and carefully fine-tuned, the number of required supporting elements is less. This is because a well-thought-out objective lets you get to the point quickly without displaying data that doesn't directly support the theme. You are able to focus on gathering the right information to put into the presentation. Less information means less distraction!

> **Note**
>
> Although you must have an objective, you don't have to fine-tune the objective or even find a characteristic to help shape that objective. However, you should consider it as an exercise in reducing data clutter. I've spent the last 15 years showing organizations how the weaknesses in their messages ultimately limit the effectiveness of their presenters. Fine-tuning and identifying characteristics of an objective help to avoid this data overload trap.

When you think about the whole purpose behind the message, you need to come up with a compelling reason to get that message into the minds and hearts of the audience. That's why working with your objective makes sense and why you have to understand the importance of this early phase of the process. After you get your brain thinking in these terms, every script you create will follow a similar pattern, even though the content itself will keep changing.

HOW DO YOU SELECT AN OBJECTIVE?

We covered that an objective must be action-driven and contain an active verb. You've also seen how it helps to fine-tune the objective into a more descriptive expression and even more beneficial to understand certain characteristics of the objective. But how do you make the choice from the start?

Is the objective chosen at random? Is it based on any secret formula? Is it an educated guess? In reality, you can be very accurate in your choice of objective by simply knowing what you plan to say at the very end of the presentation. Your conclusion is critical to your strategy and contains key points that you want to cover.

Think about it. If you tell a joke, you must know the punch line. If you get in a car, you need to know the destination. You prove to yourself all the time that you need to know the end before you know where to start.

DO YOUR CONCLUSION FIRST

The key to selecting your objective is to create your last impression first. This doesn't mean you should present the last visual at the beginning of your presentation; rather, do your conclusion first to set the pattern or direction for all of the supporting elements to be presented.

Your last impression, or conclusion, is the verbal description of your overall objective. Think of your conclusion as a dartboard and each of the concepts as a dart. Each concept and support item must be directed at the dartboard in order to be effective. All components of the script must point to the bull's-eye, or the overall objective.

Remember that call to action we talked about earlier? Well here it is again.

The call to action that you expect from your audience is directly related to the expression of your objective. For example, if you plan on concluding your presentation with the phrase, "Thank you very much and I hope you will each buy one of our products," then you must have been trying to sell. Each component of your script would then support the objective of selling something to the audience, whether it is a product, a concept, or an idea.

If the last thing you plan to say is, "Thank you very much and I hope you learned everything about PowerPoint," then you must have been trying to educate. Every part of your script would have to support the objective of educating the audience, in some direct way, on the features, benefits, processes, or procedures of PowerPoint. Your closing remark summarized your expectation of the group ("I hope you learned") and it was originally expressed as the objective to educate.

Naturally, you can always fine-tune the objective and match a characteristic to the objective to help narrow your choices of support material. But the original selection process comes from knowing what you want to have happen when the presentation is over.

As Stephen R. Covey, author of *The Seven Habits of Highly Effective People*, says, "Start with the end in mind."

CAPTURING IDEAS

Despite what you might have heard, great ideas are not found on supermarket shelves, they are not a dime a dozen, and they certainly aren't driven by genius. Coming up with truly great ideas usually involves brainstorming, a process that allows the mind to spontaneously bring forth ideas. At times, the development of the message is left strictly to one person; other times that brainstorming process is shared.

The good news is that in both cases the methods by which we capture ideas vary and there is no exact science as to what will produce the perfect script for a presentation. However, several techniques will help you to selectively choose related concepts from the available pool of ideas. These tools help narrow your choices so that the next part of the process, the outline and storyboard, can be easier. The four most common techniques are discussed in the next few sections.

FISH-BONE DIAGRAM

The *fish-bone diagram* links supporting visuals to a consistent theme (objective). Supporting visuals are linked by like causes while supporting the root cause. Confused yet? A good analogy might be to imagine a highway and the exit ramps off the highway. Then, think of the roads that connect to the exit ramps. That's the picture I'm painting here. Be careful how far you stray from the main highway with supporting information or else the audience might not be able to follow the map to your final destination.

Look at Figure 22.1. The end result (call to action) is supported by three categories for grouping your ideas. The most important category is placed closest to the end result because it represents ideas nearest the purpose (objective) of the message. Categories father from the end result represent more supportive ideas for the argument.

Figure 22.1
This is the layout you can use for a fish-bone diagram. Notice how supporting ideas (sub-category, elements) branch from main (category) ideas.

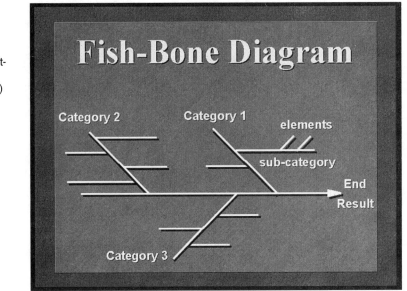

Tip from
Tom Mucciolo

> A good rule is to structure three groups that support the main message and then have no more than three supporting messages beneath each group. If you branch out too far, the audience might not be able to get back on track.

When capturing ideas to a fish-bone diagram, fill in the blank lines where needed with ideas that support the closest or most immediate concept and look for data elements (support information) that match those ideas.

FLOW CHART

A *flow chart* forces you to think in "stages" of action and tends to show that one step leads to another. Similar to the fish-bone diagram, flow charts, however, are mostly used when showing decision-based branching or interactivity. For example, nonlinear electronic presentations might allow a particular subject or issue to be explored further only if the presenter prefers it that way—usually based on some cues or questions from the audience.

If you look at Figure 22.2, you'll see how the flow chart helps you place your ideas in sequence, noting any areas where choices might be made to further the message to its conclusion. Maybe after making your first point you check for agreement in the crowd. If they agree, you move on; if not, you bring in more evidence to support your argument. In an electronic presentation, this might mean selecting an object on the visual that contains an action to display another visual, not necessarily in sequence, which holds more information.

Figure 22.2
Here's how you "flow chart" your ideas. This shows how backup or supplemental data can be used by the presenter only if needed to force a decision at that point.

→ For more information on how to create interactive elements within an electronic presentation, **see** "Using Action Buttons" in Chapter 15, "Working with Animation."

The key to a flow chart is in the logical flow of continuous action. Remove an element and the flow is broken. You can create a flow chart out of a simple day in your life.

If you think about your commute to work, your morning activity, your lunch hour, your afternoon, and your commute home, you have a flow chart. Now, imagine that as a giant flow chart across the wall of your bedroom. But don't lose any sleep over it. The process is a simple one.

The point is to keep it simple, logical, and flowing. If you have a process-driven presentation, consider using the flow chart as a tool to incorporate ideas into the process. You will easily see how some ideas, although seemingly important on their own, actually do not fit the flow chart's process-oriented structure. This reduces the number of ideas you can squeeze into one continuous flow of information.

AFFINITY DIAGRAM

An *affinity diagram* helps you sort out your ideas into categories. Think about dropping your ideas into a bunch of different buckets, all of which relate to the main theme. If you look at Figure 22.3, you'll see how the categories are decided in advance, before brainstorming the ideas needed to support each of the categories.

Figure 22.3
The affinity diagram limits your ideas to predefined categories, or buckets. This helps you focus on the exact message and prevents you from including nonessential information.

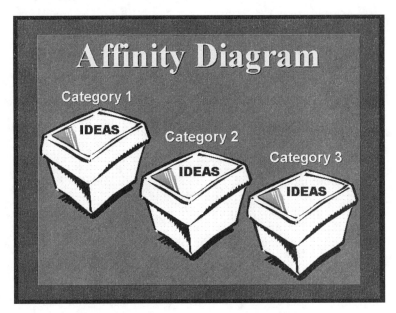

By grouping closely related activities, you outline ideas based on agreed-upon categories—or buckets—of information. By tossing ideas into these specific buckets, you fill each category with the main points that you know you have to make in order to satisfy the category. The key to this method of capturing ideas is to agree on the categories in the first place.

For example, Figure 22.4 shows the agreed-upon information buckets to drop ideas into for this presentation. Perhaps this is how the meeting went that day. Someone said, "We have to talk about pricing," and the idea about pricing was placed in the financial category. Someone else mentioned "memory" and the idea of memory was placed under features. But another person said, "We should discuss the service policies of the company." Even though service is an important part of the company, the idea didn't fit any of the categories originally defined. Unless we stretch the meaning of what can be included in a specific category, there won't be any service-talk in this presentation.

Figure 22.4
A filled-in affinity diagram showing how the tossed-in ideas or discussion points are grouped according to four different predefined categories.

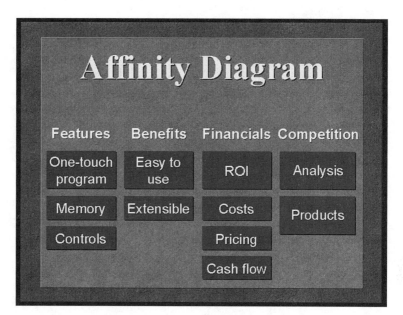

Although the service policies are important, it is not the right information to be brought up during this particular presentation. Think of it this way: Ford makes cars and trucks, but they are not shown in the same commercial.

Tip from
Tom Mucciolo

Limit your categories to three or four, and limit your ideas per category to about the same number. You'll need at least one item of visual support for each idea. If you have too many categories or ideas within categories, the presentation might drag on too long.

MIND MAP

If Felix Unger is the affinity diagram, then Oscar Madison is the *mind map*. But don't assume chaos is a bad thing. In fact, when it comes to brainstorming, it's quite the opposite.

Mind mapping is a technique that starts with a major theme or concept and then looks for immediate supporting issues. After the main issues are defined, additional support can be considered. Each idea you write down might spawn another related idea and so on. The underlying support for each of the main issues ultimately supports the overall theme.

However, as you place ideas farther from the center of the map, you attach a lower importance to the idea, and, as a result, you need less support information for that idea. A mind map template, shown in Figure 22.5, illustrates the placement of ideas in relation to a central theme or core concept.

Figure 22.5
A sample mind map, showing how ideas are placed in relation to the core concept. A second idea is one that supports an original idea, which supports the core concept.

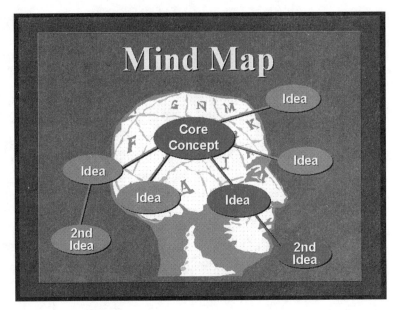

Although this appears similar to the affinity diagram, the mind map adds a different dimension to gathering ideas. It allows many ideas to make it to the table, and then tries to categorize each idea into a particular mainstream concept. The added dimension is distance. Once an idea is placed on the mind map, you are able to see how close to the center of the map it is and, therefore, determine its importance in the presentation.

Because mind maps are usually associated with concepts and concepts are abstract, one supporting idea might be usable in more than one area of the mind map. Where you decide to place the idea will determine the amount of support you'll need for that idea. If, however, you use an idea more than once on the map, then you might need to use different levels of support for the same idea at different points in the script. Is your brain hurting yet?

For example, in Figure 22.6, the idea Recognize appears in two areas of the map. It is part of the Fun Workplace concept under Recruiting, which is one of the issues of Management Control. Recognize also appears as part of Motivate, a subset of Ownership, which stems from Authority, which relates to Accounting (yet another issue of Management Control). The two ideas are at different distances from the center of the map. When you look at each idea called Recognize, you can count the levels each sits from the core. In one area there are two levels to pass through to reach the core; in another area there are four levels to pass through.

In the first instance, the idea of recognition is closer to the core or central theme of management control (count the levels). Knowing this, you should use more support and explanation during the discussion of Recognition at this point in the presentation than during the other reference. So after seeing where in the map the idea appears and how close to ground zero it really is, you can gather your support information accordingly.

Figure 22.6
A mind map shows levels of the thought process.

The other advantage of the mind map is that, at a glance, you can decide if the ideas are straying too far from the core, causing the presentation to become more drawn out. I suggest you keep the levels to no more than three: main theme (core), supporting issues, and supporting data for those issues. This makes for a shorter, more concise presentation.

CREATING AN OUTLINE AND STORYBOARD

After you have gathered the main ideas and concepts that support your overall objective, you can create an outline and storyboard. The *outline* is simply a list of headings with some degree of detail attached to a few items. The *storyboard* is a visual example of the items in the outline.

You don't really have to create both an outline and a storyboard, but it helps to see a list of items categorized in sections as well as a visual sketch of those items.

ELECTRONICALLY CREATING AN OUTLINE AND STORYBOARD

PowerPoint simultaneously updates your outline and your storyboard (visuals) as you add content. The good news is that you can move items around quickly in PowerPoint, which is especially useful after all of your ideas have been entered into the outline.

→ For more information about outlines and storyboards, **see** "Understanding PowerPoint Views" in Chapter 1, "Introducing PowerPoint 2002."

→ To learn more about working with different slide layouts, **see** Chapter 5, "Organizing Presentations in PowerPoint."

When you create an outline or storyboard in PowerPoint, some serious visual design is already happening. The very nature of the software is designed to *multitask* and to do two things at once for you. Let the software do the work and don't worry. Rather than be concerned about the design issues at this point, just try to get your ideas into the outline and then organize those ideas similarly to the way you captured them. Remember, you're not designing the visuals yet, only sketching ideas into a rough visible format.

MANUALLY CREATING AN OUTLINE AND STORYBOARD

If you are creating a storyboard on paper for later input into PowerPoint, simply make a rough sketch of how you see each idea visualized. For example, at my company (MediaNet, Inc.), we have created over 1,000 PowerPoint presentations from handwritten notes and sketches sent to us by clients. This is probably a familiar process in your company as well. Lots of people scribble out some rough-looking visuals just to help them visualize the information. Although it is much easier to use PowerPoint for the task of organizing content, you can also tackle the process manually on paper.

On paper, you can create the outline in a hierarchical (first to last) structure. Just remember a few of the outlining rules from school, such as "every A needs a B" (meaning that you can't have only one supporting point for a major idea—you need at least two).

The outline is easy, but the storyboard is a bit more difficult when created manually. The design of the visuals is usually taken from the original sketches in the storyboard. All the information chosen to support the story needs to be presented in a clearly readable format.

Most people belong to the "8 1/2 × 11 crowd." That is, those who use an entire sheet of paper, squeeze as much information as possible onto it, and then expect to later convert the clutter into a presentation visual. It's true. You take a standard sheet of paper and a magic marker (no one thinks of using a pencil with an eraser!), and you write on both sides of the sheet. You call it—a visual. The days of the full page of typewritten text with the little letter "o" for the bullet are gone.

A storyboard sketch of each visual should not take up a full, 66-line, typewritten sheet of paper. When projected, the final image from that original sketch needs to be clearly seen from a distance. This means the text and any other elements should be large, and the only way to ensure that is to limit the amount of data placed on the visual in the first place.

The best way to limit what can be placed on a single visual is to take a piece of standard paper and fold it in half before you design anything. Of course this doesn't mean you should write twice as small. But it does force you into a smaller workspace and help you avoid cluttering the image with extensive information that might not be readable for the audience when projected.

Another option is to use 5" × 7" index cards to storyboard your ideas. The advantage of index cards is that they can be spread on a flat surface, like a table, and can be moved around as needed to organize your storyboard images into a proper flow. This is the manual version of the slide sorter in PowerPoint. You can probably now see how valuable the software is to the planning process when you consider the alternative of doing this manually.

The goal is to limit the information so the audience can spend more time listening and watching. Studies have shown that people retain only 10% of what they read but 70% of what they see and hear. Use this as a hint to stop the data, spare us the details, and save the presentation. Can I make this any clearer? Fewer words on the screen means more words in your mouth. Remember the KISS principle—Keep It Simple, Stupid!

STRUCTURING IDEAS INTO A FLOWING SCRIPT

An outline and a storyboard help organize captured ideas into a format ready for design. But another issue must be addressed and that is making the presentation presentable. To support the notion of a visual presenter in terms of the script, the strategy is to link ideas so that a person can convey them. The script itself—the story line—must be structured so that the ideas flow easily from paper to people.

Earlier I asked you to think about the big picture when examining the purpose; now you should start thinking about the finer details. When you structure your ideas into some cohesive format, you might think it's easiest to give the audience the big picture and then back that up with the smaller details. That might work in some instances, but you should really consider the opposite strategy, as well.

Our world is complex and we seek simplicity. You will be more effective if you first get right to the immediate issue of the presentation and then offer the larger-than-life view.

One way to look at it is to think of a presentation as a big dinner. The menu is the view of the meal, but the selection is the anticipation of the taste. Then consider how the chosen meal is served: one course at a time. Each course needs to be segmented or cut into bite-size pieces in order to be consumed.

If the courses are the big picture items and the bite-size pieces are the details, from the server's (presenter's) point of view, the order of information should be from bigger to smaller. But, if you look at it from a taster's (audience's) point of view, the food on the fork is more important than the rest of the stuff on the table.

Maybe I've only succeeded in making you hungry, but I want you to begin to see how the details of the argument actually stimulate the anticipation of the audience more than the big picture.

No matter which way you choose to present the information, you still have to develop a pattern or a structure to the script so the information can be absorbed properly.

Think of the structure as the type of script that is used to convey the message. Most presentations follow a linear pattern, which moves from an opening through the body and, finally, into the closing. This open-body-close process is common and usually expected as the metaphor for receiving information. The good news is that you have a choice of about five types of scripts you can use to convey a message in a linear presentation, all discussed in the following sections.

MATCHING IDEALS

This structure is really a setup for the audience. The plan is that you describe the ideal product or service, which, of course, you know will closely resemble your product or service. Because the audience accepts your description as the premise of the argument, it is quite easy to match your argument to the premise you set up in the first place. This structure is usually used more for products than for services because attributes of a product are more tangible (visible) than qualities of a service.

For example, you selectively mention the ideal attributes of a good car. You say, "The ideal car has front-wheel drive, dual air bags, a rear defrost, and a trunk release." You naturally get the audience's agreement that these are the ideal attributes of a good car. Then you describe your car in terms of the ideal, making sure you only compare to about 90% of the ideal. You say, "Our car has front-wheel drive, dual air bags, a rear defrost, and we're still working on the trunk release." You see, you never want to compare to 100% because that would mean you have the perfect product (which no one does), and it would leave you no room for improvement (how do you improve on perfection?).

The matching ideals script is designed to lead the audience to an understanding that the product (or service) is the best one for the job, but it might not do the whole job.

MAIN POINTS

Typically, this structure is used with information-based presentations such as those dealing with financial results and other historical data. The process follows the familiar pattern of

> *Tell 'em what you're gonna to tell 'em.*
>
> *Tell 'em.*
>
> *Tell what you told 'em.*

One way to identify this structure is the appearance of an agenda early in the presentation and a corresponding summary at the end. This lets the audience know what to expect and then expect what to remember.

The summary at the end is critical because main points can be hard to remember, especially when a large number of supporting points is discussed. The audience might get lost unless they are constantly made aware of how the supporting information relates to the main points.

QUESTION AND ANSWER

Question and answer scripting is similar to educational activities of "pre-test" and "post-test." This is useful in training sessions with a lot of unrelated, yet comprehensive, information.

First you pre-test the audience's knowledge of a subject using easy-to-answer questions (true/false, multiple choice). The questions cover all the major points you expect to convey during the session. Then, during the session, you reveal the correct answers using supporting visual elements to explain each answer as you elaborate. Finally, you ask the audience as a group to answer the original questions (post-test).

A question and answer scripting structure can be used in a variety of situations, including surveys, polls, and research studies. The important point to remember is that the objective should address how the information will be used by the audience to achieve a specific result. One way to ensure that the information is more than just a data dump is to repeat key points and summarize conclusions at several stages of the presentation. Repetition will aid in the retention of concepts and ideas. Repetition will aid in the retention of concepts and ideas. Repetition will aid in the retention of concepts and ideas. Any questions?

MEETING NEEDS

Sometimes called the *helping hand script*, this structure starts with the needs of the audience in mind. This is often used in sales presentations where you put the needs of the customer up front and then show how you can address those needs.

For business, at first glance, this meeting needs script might seem an easy task. But more often than not, presentations using this format tend to treat all needs on an equal basis. This becomes a problem because if all needs are truly equal, then priorities cannot be set and decisions take longer to reach. If, however, you attach importance to specific needs, you create a sense of gratification by meeting those needs in the order of their importance. This builds value for you in the eyes of the audience.

Once you know the priority of the customer needs, you can address those important issues first. Then, you can summarize how you can help with other issues that might not have been verbalized as a top priority, but might be important to the scope of the project or activity. The point is that many issues are brought into a presentation, some of which can have a negative impact on your objective. By concentrating on primary needs, you limit the attention placed on less important and perhaps frivolous needs that could have otherwise stalled the process.

PROBLEM-SOLUTION

Also known as the *divide and conquer script*, the *problem-solution structure* is one of the most effective scripts you can use, especially for high-level, decision-based presentations. Whereas the meeting needs structure focuses on the goals ahead, the problem-solution structure concentrates on the mistakes of the past. That's why I love this script. It concentrates on failure, it thrives on fear, it accentuates the negative—and it leaves the door open for a hero to save the day. It's like Superman!

The process follows a simple pattern. First, the overall problem is described and presented in a manner that makes it look bleak or negative. Then, you dissect the problem into smaller sections that can be addressed individually. Finally, the solutions to the smaller areas will solve the big problem, as well, and the result will always look positive.

Politicians use the problem-solution scenario frequently. The political candidate announces, "The country is going downhill, crime and inflation are out of control, your children have no future." Immediately you feel depressed hearing the problems at hand. Seconds later, the candidate continues, "but our party has the solution!" Suddenly you feel better, as if the day has been saved. Okay, it really isn't exactly that way, but you get the idea.

From a business presentation perspective, the problem-solution script can be highly effective because it plays on a very powerful human emotion: Fear. If problems can't be solved, then the consequences might be harmful. This can cause fear and anxiety.

Problem-Solution Scenario

Many times I find that presentations are poorly constructed using the problem-solution approach. I usually suggest this pattern. The opening of the presentation should state the case in this order: problem, consequence of inaction, sense of urgency, and solution.

For example, let's say your company markets a software program that keeps track of Internet access. The following quoted text is an example of the conceptual script that might be used.

First, you quickly tell the audience the problem. You state how "employees spend a growing percentage of the workday accessing the Internet for non-business-related information."

Next, examine the consequence of inaction. In other words, what happens if nobody does anything about the problem? You indicate that without action, the "consequence will be a reduction of productivity in the workplace."

Okay, here's the clincher. Attach a timeframe to action in order to establish a sense of urgency. After all, without urgency there is less need to solve the problem today. In other words, if they do see the problem, how long can they wait to do something about it? You mention that "less productivity from lost time reduces the ability to adapt quickly to constant changes in the industry."

Finally, you must address the problem with your specific solution. Without a link to your special way of solving the problem, you will only end up educating the audience by increasing general awareness of the problem. Therefore, you show that your software "limits Internet access to nonbusiness information using a unique process, thereby allowing a company to maximize productivity into a competitive advantage."

This entire scenario—problem-consequence-urgency-solution—should be shared up front with the audience in less than one minute to set the stage for the rest of the presentation.

The problem-solution script positions the presenter as a solution provider for existing problems. Because most people are cautious and conservative, this kind of script appeals to a sense of urgency.

Of all the structures available, I most prefer the problem-solution type. Any scripts that involve a sense of urgency will always be the most effective because urgency relates to the limits of time, and time, once lost, can never be retrieved.

USING AN OPENING HOOK

We spent a lot of time covering objectives, ideas, and structures, and by now you should have some grasp on how to construct the argument in order to move an audience to some call to action. But now we have to think about jump-starting the presentation with an opening hook.

A hook is used for the purpose of changing something about the way an audience thinks. A hook can be any credible or even doubtful piece of information, which, when presented, causes the audience to immediately react. Whether it be a bit of research, a little known but interesting fact, a revelation, a controversial opinion, a current event, or simply a smile in the face of defeat, the opening hook sets the stage for the rest of the presentation.

I find a statistic can make for a great opening hook. For example, an opening hook I use for my "Electrifying Presentations" seminars is a series of statistics which position the physical presentation skill, the actual art of delivery, as contributing to over 90% of the communication message. It doesn't mean that content is unimportant; rather, that content needs to be clear and concise because we process more of what we see than anything else.

That hook is important because it forces the audience to make a choice—do they agree or disagree? For those who agree, they spend the rest of the presentation nodding their heads as the evidence to support the hook is presented. For those who disagree, they spend the rest of the presentation tilting their heads looking for more evidence as to why they should change sides. Both groups are forced to change the way they think in order to keep sitting through the presentation.

What happens is this: An audience arrives at the presentation in neutral. Their emotions and thoughts have yet to be swayed. Your goal is to get them in gear—forward or reverse—it doesn't matter, but you must create a sense of action. Just as the objective is positioned to do something, the audience needs to be pushed to do something, too. Think of them as sitting on a fence and trying to push them to one side or the other. If I'm still on the fence at the end of your presentation, I haven't accomplished anything and neither have you. We both lose. You have to influence the group in some way.

Rarely is this done visually onscreen, as in a before/after comparison. The hook is more of a fact or statement that challenges the status quo or belief system. Even if you displayed a visual of something powerful, such as natural disaster or a victory celebration, you would still have to verbally interpret the hook for the audience. A visual that supports your hook needs to be placed in context and described. Usually, you don't need the visual at all because the description is likely to stand on its own.

The value of the hook is in the timing. When the presentation starts, how long does it take before the group is being influenced by your objective (to sell, to motivate, to convince, or whatever)? How long do you let them sit on the fence?

The longer it takes you to employ your objective, the harder it gets to arrive at the call to action. However, using an opening hook can instantly affect the audience and get them to make choices about your message.

For example, if you started a presentation by saying, "By the end of the day you will lose all excess weight, look 10 years younger, and add one million dollars to your income!" I'd say that's a pretty good hook. Sign me up!

Note

Don't use a fact for no reason. For example, mentioning that over 83% of all Paul Newman movies have the letter H somewhere in the title might be factual, but is really just trivial, especially because the audience can't control the likelihood that future Paul Newman movies won't have an H somewhere in the title!

The hook can even tap into an audience's sense of urgency for the presentation to be over. One of the best opening hooks I heard a presenter give was to a group of time-starved executives at the beginning of a sales presentation. The presenter said, "This can take five minutes or five hours, but you're going to buy something!" Each person in that room glanced at the clock and was instantly swayed from thinking "Do I want to buy?" to wondering "Do I want buy now or five hours from now?"

ALLOWING FOR TIMELY GRABS

Although an opening hook creates action in the minds of the audience, timely grabs are used to hold the attention of the audience across sections of the script. These grabbers pepper the script at specific points with interesting information, personal experiences, or other stimulating items that relate to or help further the message.

Grabbers include

- Stories
- Examples
- Analogies
- Statistics
- Interaction
- Questions
- Repetition
- Shock
- Suspense
- Special Effects (animation, sound, video)

Tip from	When using analogies, try to make them as real-world as possible. The advantage of drawing a likeness between something in your content and an everyday activity is that the audience transfers the benefits of the very real experience to your information.
Tom Mucciolo	For example, a simple analogy for a maker of digital video cameras might be to specify that a particular model is the Cadillac of the industry. The public impression of Cadillac is one of quality and a transfer is made by the audience to the digital camera as having a high quality.
	Typical real-world analogies include references to transportation, household appliances, food, travel, and entertainment. The more the reference applies to everyday experience, the faster the connection is made by the audience.

Grabbers should directly relate to the topic, but can come from nowhere and be completely unrelated to anything you're discussing. It depends on what you want to do with the audience. Unrelated grabbers are used typically to inject life into the crowd. Let's say it's one hour after lunch. You might notice the audience is losing focus, appearing glassy-eyed, getting a bit drowsy. Although it's possible you are boring them to sleep, the head-bobbing is more from the blood leaving the head to travel to the stomach to digest food.

You might have to do something unrelated. I have a full-day seminar/workshop, which has a topic called "Multimedia vs. Multimania." It's one of the eight topics for the day, but it is strategically placed about one hour after the lunch break. In the middle of the lecture is a 10-minute game show on the order of a "Name That Tune" contest. It has less to do with the guidelines for using multimedia than it does to wake the audience up from a low energy point. Plus, it's fun. And you know something, you can have fun and learn at the same time!

UNDERSTANDING NONLINEAR ISSUES

Nonlinear presentations offer the greatest flexibility for a repetitive presentation with a changing audience. With experience, presenters learn where the questions arise and to what extent backup, or supporting information, is needed.

The technique employed in these presentations relates to features within PowerPoint, specifically Action buttons and hyperlinks. See Chapters 15, "Working with Animation," and 16, "Using PowerPoint's Web Features," for more information on the use of these features.

Using a nonlinear structure, you can

- Answer expected or unexpected questions with backup support information
- Analyze "what if" scenarios by linking to spreadsheets and other data
- Show generic presentations to different audiences and use backup data only where necessary

If you decide to display backup information based on audience responses, be sure the information is general enough to warrant display.

If you decide to do what-if scenarios in front of an audience where a software application needs to be used, be sure you know the software well and don't get caught up in details or small changes.

The following situations are some in which a nonlinear approach might be effective:

- Show only the overview to busy executives and more detailed levels to subordinates
- Adapt to an audience's knowledge level by giving details only where needed
- Respond to different audiences' priorities by showing most important information to that particular audience first

The same way you tell a story based on limited time is the way to think about nonlinear access to information. If you have the time, show it. But show limited amounts of information—enough to make the point.

You might have to preplan a lot of this branching information and you might not be asked to show it all. Usually, a presentation done several times to different audiences tells a presenter where the supporting information belongs.

Be sure you incorporate a go-back button. Don't leave someone in la-la land wondering how to get back to the original story! Nonlinear navigation can be confusing if you don't have a way to get back on track after you've branched off to a supporting item. This is why nonlinear presentations are usually meant for an audience of one (such as at a kiosk); or, they are thought-out so far in advance to cover every interactive possibility that they end up falling into the pattern of a typical linear presentation. The key thing to remember is not to lose control of the event.

QUALIFYING THE PARTICIPANTS

So what do you really know about the speaker and the listeners? The ability to understand attributes of both the presenter and the audience is critical to the message. The objective and the target audience for that objective are so closely intertwined that you should consider them as coexisting.

The message is buried between the speaker and the listener. In fact, all presentations follow a standard communication model (Sender—Message—Receiver). For visual presenters the model can be described more theatrically as Actor—Action—Audience. Regardless of the terms, the human elements of the process—the sender (presenter) and the receiver (audience)—are key to the presentation process and crucial to message development.

LEARNING THE TRAITS OF THE PRESENTER

If you are the presenter of your own message, then you already know your own likes, dislikes, habits, and so forth. But if you have to prepare a message or even the visual support for the message for another person to deliver, then the following section can offer you some helpful information.

To construct a believable message, it helps if you know certain characteristics or traits of the presenter. The more the presenter is involved in the message, the better the delivery.

Some points to consider for knowing the traits of the speaker include personal attributes, delivery style, expertise level, and media preferences, all discussed in the following sections.

In the real world, you might never have the time to really gather this information. In fact, many of those who create content do so for others to present. In a number of situations, the content providers never even see the presenters. Some actually might feel that's a good thing, but, collaboration is the key to effective messaging. You have to find ways of working together with a presenter who might be delivering your content. The goal is to get a dialogue going. When a presenter has input, the script becomes more personal and will be delivered more emphatically.

Tip from
Tom Mucciolo

Send only the outline of the presentation to one or more presenters and ask for suggestions on the order of topics to be covered (not the content, just the order). Wherever a person makes comments, marks, or notes is where the script is more personal and appeals to the presenter.

PERSONAL ATTRIBUTES

One of the things I like to do immediately when working with a presenter is to ask one of three favorites: I want to know his or her favorite type of movie (action, mystery, romance); favorite type of music (rock, jazz, classical); and favorite type of sport to watch or play (football, golf, tennis).

For example, let's say I'm coaching you. You tell me that you prefer action movies. I would look for some obvious characteristics about action movies, such as split-second decision-making, sense of urgency, attention to detail, even a hero who saves the day. Perhaps you have some or all of those traits or at least admire those traits in others.

I then look for parts of the script that relate (or could relate) to decision-making, especially the split-second kind. I would search for other parts that involve sense of urgency or attention to detail. There might even be a part in the script where a problem is solved and the hero saves the day. At those specific points in the presentation, I would ask you, the presenter, to recount personal experiences (stories), cite specific examples, or use some other informative grabbers for the audience. Your energy and enthusiasm will be greater during any moment that is closer to some attribute of your personality. If you have a greater stake in the details, you will deliver the information with more confidence.

Note

The more personal a message is to you, the more you will express it with conviction. It's not about what the topic means—it's about what the topic means to you.

DELIVERY STYLE

Whenever I am working with someone, I look for special elements in the person's delivery style. Style is an interesting word that can mean so many things. If you need to find out more about a presenter, ask some questions.

For example, is she outgoing? Does she like to interact with the audience? Is she comfortable in front of her superiors? The answers to questions such as these will help you frame the message from a presenter point-of-view.

A presenter who likes to interact and get in close with the audience, for example, might be more at ease sharing personal experiences rather than displaying numerous statistics. Someone who loves details and trivia might prefer to point out the hidden meanings by reading between the lines or going inside the numbers.

When you know more about the personality of the presenter, it can make your job easier as a content-provider for a speaker who needs less support data than you might have expected. As you shape the message with a presenter in mind, you might find additional opportunities for unique grabbers, such as humor, simply based on the delivery style of the presenter.

EXPERTISE LEVEL

Knowing how in-depth a presenter understands the topic and the key concepts associated with the message is extremely helpful in your efforts to shape the quantity of content.

For example, if a presenter has a great deal of expertise, the content can be more visual than verbal, more conceptual than concrete. Ah, but keep in mind that we favor the visual presenter. The script should contain broad concepts and limited data so that the audience spends more time listening, watching, and interacting with the presenter and less time reading the screen.

However, there are times when the expertise leads to wordiness, and the audience is bombarded with too many long-winded explanations. What I've noticed is the greater your vocabulary, the harder it is for you to get to the point. It's true. For some reason, when a presenter has more command of language, the longer it takes for him or her to get to the heart of the matter.

That's why a lot of times when I'm coaching someone I'll say, "You probably write well, don't you?" People who write well tend to speak like they write. They keep adding phrases and lengthier descriptions as they deliver the message. They'll say "What's important here, what you really need to understand, what is truly critical to note, in this instance . . ." Just get to the point!

I'm not saying that poor language skills make for better presenters; instead, full command of the language needs to be regulated to entice an audience to want to know more. If you have presenters that drone on and on, make them move through the script more quickly. Teach them three little words to say as quickly as possible: "You may leave."

MEDIA PREFERENCES

One other trait of the presenter has to do with media preference. You might have to develop the message differently based on a particular media type such as 35mm slides, overhead transparencies, or electronic images. If you know the media preference of a presenter, you can develop support for the message accordingly.

For example, for a 20-minute presentation, a person familiar with using PowerPoint to electronically deliver content will need about 35 electronic images. A person preferring overheads needs about 10 transparencies to cover the topic during the same 20 minutes. That's because you can't scale overheads like Frisbees to try to change visuals as rapidly as you might advance an electronic show.

As the creator of the message, you might have to make some adjustments. For the person with the electronic show, you might include several builds as part of the 35 impressions, leaving the presenter some room for stories, analogies, and other grabbers. For the person with the overheads, you might have to fill each transparency with more data—leaving less time for grabbers. Or, you might make the transparencies with limited data, forcing the presenter to have more in-depth knowledge of the topic because fewer visual cues are available during the presentation.

PART
VII
CH
22

> **Note**
>
> MediaNet has a software utility called Show*STARTER*, which uses artificial intelligence to help a person plan a presentation. By answering 10 simple questions, a 10-page report is available that outlines the visual design, text attributes, proper colors, lead-time, and number of visuals, all tied to a selected objective. You can use a free, online miniversion, Show*STARTER Express,* by visiting MediaNet's Web site at www.medianet-ny.com.

KNOWING THE PARTICULARS OF THE AUDIENCE

Knowing the audience is the most difficult task imaginable. This is why marketing professionals lose sleep at night. Just when they think they can predict the market, the market changes. Although we want to avoid turning analysis into paralysis on this issue, understanding your target audience is very important to the development of the message.

Here's my take on audiences. I think people are basically the same. I'm not discounting diversity in any way, but I use the philosophy that whatever is true for me in my own heart is probably true for everyone else on a very basic level. Our similarities allow us to share entertainment, sports, and all types of social activities. Our differences are what business presentations try to isolate and somehow address.

Knowing how to target differences in people is important in building effective messages. We can learn more about an audience in several ways, including direct contact, demographics, and motivators.

DIRECT CONTACT

The difference between learning the traits of the presenter and knowing particulars of the audience is direct contact. You have greater access to the presenters. They work with you. You can call them, e-mail them, fax them, see them. This interaction helps you understand them.

You might have little contact and interaction with your audience until the presentation is starting. This is not uncommon. It happens a lot, especially to those pitching a new business. However, you might have other presentations in which the same group convenes on a regular basis. This might happen with internal presentations or briefings such as those on a monthly, quarterly, or annual basis.

The more direct contact (experience) you have with a particular audience, the easier it is to design a targeted message. Think about your family, friends, or even co-workers. You know how to handle these groups because you see them more often. Of course, in some situations you might prefer not to see them!

DEMOGRAPHICS

Experience through direct contact is getting harder to gain in the real world. Our lives are getting so busy that many of us just don't have the time to get to know a consistent audience. Be honest, aren't you amazed when you actually reach someone on the phone? You might quickly say, "What? No voice message? You're probably not that busy today, are you?" Direct contact is becoming a rare commodity.

When you can't have direct contact with the audience, you still have to try to define them or categorize them to look for differences. This analysis will help you design the right message for the right group. You can use demographics to gather certain information, including age, gender, expertise, and culture. Note how these measurements are general and not job specific.

For example, if your audience is primarily individuals who speak English as a second language, your message might have to be designed in very general and conceptual terms, using fewer details and wordy descriptions.

Nostalgia Theory

Knowing the average age of the audience is a significant piece of information that can be used effectively. The nostalgia theory works like this: Experiences and events that occurred during the mid-teen years (near puberty) are memorable for life. In other words, you can remember more things from when you were about 15 years old than almost any other time in your life. You recall specific songs, political issues, sporting events, and even the first person you fell in love with—remember?

If the average age of the audience is 43 and it's the year 2001, you know they were 15 in the year 1973. References to events from the late '60s and early '70s will be quickly recognized. The end of the Vietnam war, the last songs of The Beatles, Armstrong on the moon, Nixon resigning, and so on. You can reflect on history to develop examples and analogies to support your message.

MOTIVATORS

Motivators are the emotional elements that induce action. Now we're talking about the juicy stuff! Some of the more basic motivators are pride, profit, love, fear, and need.

Note

Although the basic motivators are general, the type of motivator can be more specific. Need might be refined to necessity, obligation, urgency, requirement, or even compulsion. You can fine-tune the motivator, just as you can fine-tune the objective.

Decide which will best motivate your audience and fine-tune your original objective in order to help achieve the emotional response. Stop! You don't change your objective; you only fine-tune it.

How a Motivator Affects the Objective

Let's say your topic is a discussion about sales quotas. The talk is given to different groups such as marketing, senior management, and sales. Initially, you choose the objective "to inform."

You notice your next presentation of this material is at the annual sales conference. You decide that pride is the motivator for this particular audience, the sales force. You fine-tune the original objective—to inform—and it becomes to inspire to great heights.

You inspire by reinforcing the group's accomplishments and encourage them to achieve more. You add individual success stories. You use support information, including comparisons to last year, growth in market share, perhaps even a testimonial from the president of the company.

Do you see how influential a motivator can be in the development of the message? Your original objective didn't change. It only became more specific.

You might find that more than one motivator moves an audience at different points in the presentation. You just have to match supporting elements in your script to the motivator that targets the type of response you seek. For example, if the best motivator is profit, a less obvious motivator might be fear. Thus, a chart showing the consequences of overspending might tap fear, while still supporting the underlying motive for profit.

UNDERSTANDING FILTERS

People react to information in many ways. What you say and what you show might be quite different from what the audience sees and hears. This happens every day. I say one thing; you hear something different. It's not a matter of who's right—it's a matter of agreement. Because you can't change this about people, don't even try. Just figure a way to deal with it.

Demographics and motivators affect the way an audience filters or classifies information. Each audience member puts his or her own spin on information based on how data is filtered to the brain.

A *filter* is the slant you apply to a message to make it your own. When someone says "The way I see it," you can be sure the person is applying a filter to the information in order to understand it.

The goal is to create a clear message that minimizes the distortion the audience tends to place on information. As we distort messages, we develop barriers because we make personal judgments. For example, when you see a stop sign, you know the message is the same for everyone. When you see a sign that says "Authorized Vehicles Only," you instantly become a member of a distinct group. You then form an opinion about the other group. You begin to question their right to even be authorized! Who are these people and why?

Avoid Clichés

Stereotyping is just one expression of how we filter information. This is a problem in itself because it leads to misconceptions, misunderstanding, and prejudice. Clichés also exist in business, especially when considering organizational duties.

Don't fall into the trap of shaping the message to a job function cliché. Accountants do not prefer only numbers. Engineers are not limited to processes. Sales and marketing people can handle details.

If the clichés for business were applied to art or entertainment, then there would have to be separate versions for everyone. Can you imagine *Gone with the Wind* for computer programmers and a different version for financial planners? How about a version of baseball only for doctors, called *Medicine Ball*?

The job doesn't make the person. The person makes the job. If you changed your profession or industry tomorrow, would you really be a different person than you are today?

Avoid the job title cliché. If members of the executive team are expected to be in the audience, the message must still be created for the entire audience. If the entire audience is only the executive team, then the message is still tailored to the needs of that specific group, based on generalities, not specifics. It wouldn't matter if the CEO likes fishing. If you make every reference about fishing, the remainder of the group is likely to miss the boat! Job titles might cause anxiety for the messenger, not the message.

I avoid clichés like the plague. They're old hat. They end up making a mountain out of a molehill.

Because filters exist, a good script finds ways of overcoming those filters. Table 22.1 shows some examples of where filters are used by the audience and the method used to break through the filter.

TABLE 22.1   HANDLING DEMOGRAPHIC FILTERS

Demographic	Method for Breaking Through Filter
Language	Simplify the words
Age	Appeal to generation styles
Gender	Avoid stereotypes
Expertise	Adjust conceptual complexity

For example, in the preceding table, the filters associated with the demographic of age might be addressed by using analogies, references, and other data that earmark a cross section of the audience by generation. You would have less reason to make a comparison of events from the 1950s if the audience is composed of recent college graduates.

Audiences apply their own filters to motivators, too. People put unique slants on emotional responses. After all, who can truly agree on how fear or pride affects any individual? The abstract concepts associated with any motivator lead to very subjective viewpoints for each person experiencing that motivator at any given time. Thus, each person applies a filter to a motivational element based on given circumstances and conditions prevailing at the time. Table 22.2 shows how to handle motivational filters.

TABLE 22.2   HANDLING MOTIVATIONAL FILTERS

Motivator	Method for Breaking Through Filter
Pride	Show comparisons and achievement
Fear	Use reassurance and historical data
Profit	Offer reachable goals
Love	Demonstrate teamwork
Need	Meet with urgency

For example, when a company is faced with a crisis situation and the employees are motivated by fear, the initial effort should be to reassure by pointing to how such situations were dealt with in the past, as opposed to immediately suggesting alternatives for the future. Stop the bleeding before you recommend a new brand of bandages.

ASSURING CONSISTENCY

Until now, we've looked at the micro view of the presentation message. The effort has been to examine all the intricacies and nuances of purpose and people to arrive at a finely tuned message.

Now we have to readjust, take a macro view of the message, and examine it according to a much bigger picture. The ultimate objective and the basic philosophy of an organization play a role in the development of the message used for the presentation. We must move beyond words and begin to apply the notion of a visual presenter to the entire organization and its global expression.

The growth of the World Wide Web is enabling any organization, regardless of size, to have a presence. As technology advances, the visibility and reach of an organization become more global. We won't be typing to one another to converse; instead, we'll be seeing one another though the eyes of a display device. Electronic communication will be more visual, allowing the diversity of our organizations to become the portal to our profits.

To assure consistency, you must create presentations that can be delivered by a number of people in your organization to diverse audiences in a variety of settings.

This portability across presenters is easier when you design presentations that are high on conceptual ideas and low on technical information. When designed, the message will need to be scripted for the presenter, either conceptually or literally.

MAINTAINING THE CORPORATE IMAGE

Companies create and protect their corporate identities by spending millions of dollars on logos, signage, packaging, stationery, and public relations. Likewise, each employee's ability to tell the company story consistently helps establish a verbal corporate image.

Anyone who publicly delivers a message represents his or her company. In fact, the higher you are in the company, the more "you are the company." If you see the president of General Motors presenting poorly, you might instantly have a negative impression about the cars GM produces. These are not related, but in your mind they are. There is no logic to this, but it happens. The leaders are the company. In fact, the higher your level of responsibility, the tougher my coaching sessions. My logic is that if you make the big bucks, then you should present like you deserve the big bucks.

Concepts, visuals, and presenters are each part of the corporate identity. One of the goals of the presentation must be to match the consistency of your company image as demonstrated in other marketing venues. Start taking advantage of those TV ads!

For example, let's take a car company like Volvo. For years the marketing messages for Volvo have consistently stressed safety. Their TV commercials, advertisements, and brochures have always put safety first, as a way to differentiate their product. This doesn't mean Volvo's competitors' cars are not safe; rather, it simply means Volvo has made safety a primary issue. They are spending big advertising dollars to make this point.

Okay, so let's say you are developing the concepts for a new sales presentation for Volvo. One way to assure consistency in theme across other public image venues is to build references to safety into the script. Safety is related to security, protection, and even confidence. If you find stories, analogies, and other grabbers that relate to security or confidence, you will match the existing image portrayed in other marketing endeavors. In other words, you will be supporting the investment the company is already making through its advertising.

The presentation message represents the verbal corporate image, and it should try to support an image that the company is already vested in through other marketing efforts.

USING PORTABLE CONCEPTS

Just as the corporate image is expressed in different venues such as advertising and public relations, the same image is also expressed through multiple presenters. When your message is thought all the way through the corporate philosophy, those in the company who've embraced that philosophy will have an easier time delivering the message.

This "through-line of action" takes the traits of the presenter and matches them as closely as possible to the elements within the script, as well as to the components of the corporate philosophy. When all three areas—personality, message, and philosophy—are in a direct line, the audience receives the highest communication.

If your personality trait is an appreciation for truthful analysis and the message contains elements about accurate reporting and your company philosophy is built around showing specific details, then a through-line of action exists. It is at these points in the presentation that your energy level and your commitment to the argument will be at its peak.

Tip from	See if your presenters understand the company philosophy in the same way. Ask your
Tom Mucciolo	presenters to list the three most important things the company does or provides. Then look at the company mission statement and see how many of those things match. Two out of three is good. Anything less means the presenter doesn't get it. Now if you find that a lot of presenters in your company don't get it, maybe the executives need to communicate better to those embracing the wrong message!

Concepts need to be portable in the sense that more than one person in the company is able to express those concepts in a variety of circumstances. Naturally, a growing company is likely to have multiple presenters. However, the complexities of the supporting elements for your message might be more difficult for some presenters than others.

Your letterhead might look the same across office locations, but your presenters are all different, even if they all work in the same building. Even though you expect each to deliver your message in basically the same way, it is the individual style that shapes your message for that particular audience.

For example, if you are creating a presentation for a remote sales force and the supporting elements to your objective include several detailed charts and graphs, some of your presenters might be more confident with such details than others. Those who have a better grasp of the material will handle the delivery of the concepts with little problem. Those less certain of their knowledge of the details will present the message with difficulty. Because each presenter places his or her personal spin on the information being conveyed, individual style will breed inconsistency.

To assure a consistency among multiple presenters, consider developing support items with limited details. When faced with less information, a presenter defers to actual experience, personal philosophy, and general concepts to express the verbal corporate message. In essence, they express themselves throughout the presentation, and the result is a more believable statement of knowledge for the audience.

So now I'll add another little twist to the plot. You need to script information conceptually and develop yourself as a visual thinker to be able to provide information suitable for a visual presenter. The more conceptual the message, the easier for individual presenters to personalize the message.

Developing Portable Concepts

To enhance your skill as a visual thinker and learn to develop portable concepts, try this exercise. You will need three blank sheets of paper and a candy bar. Place the candy bar away from the paper, but within reach. Now place the sheets of paper in front of you.

On the first sheet, write a one-sentence description of what your company does or what your specific department is responsible for within the company. Imagine this sentence will be part of a press release or be announced on the local news. Be descriptive, but limit your narration to one complete sentence. This is the way you naturally think about the message.

On the second sheet, create three bullet points that cover the one sentence description you wrote on the first sheet. Imagine you are creating a PowerPoint visual using a bulleted list format. This is the way you currently think about designing the visuals.

On the third sheet, reduce the three bullet points to one word for each bullet and, if possible, make each word begin with the same letter of the alphabet. In addition, make sure the structure is the same. If the first one is a verb, they should all be verbs to maintain a parallel structure. This is the way you visually think about developing portable concepts.

If you did this right, your third sheet of paper has three words on it, possibly each beginning with the same letter of the alphabet. Okay, you can have the candy bar now!

Portable concepts offer less experienced presenters an opportunity to appear knowledgeable without sacrificing the consistencies already made public by more experienced personnel. That's a polite, sophisticated way of saying that even the new people can deliver the message when the message is simple.

The disparity between newcomers and seasoned veterans is less obvious when specific details are left to the speaker and not to the speaker support. Save the details for the handouts and spare the clutter on the visuals. Both your presenters and their audiences will be more appreciative!

PROVIDING "DO" AND "SAY" SCRIPTS

One of the last stages of the scripting process is the actual process of providing the script. At times you might simply provide an outline or you might wait until the visuals are created and provide the presenter a copy of the presentation in print form. In either case you haven't assured a consistency in delivering the essence of the message you've created. You need to provide a script.

There are basically two kinds of scripts—those that do and those that say. Both are designed for the presenter, and they normally show the description of each visual (or the actual visuals) and the related message for each visual. The message can be conceptual (driven by actions) or concrete (driven by words).

A do script is conceptual and a say script is concrete. The do script contains suggested actions to convey each element in the presentation. A say script contains the actual words to use during the presentation. A say script is basically a written speech linked to the support material.

For example, you created the message and supporting data for a sales presentation and you expect each of the sales people to deliver the presentation in a local market. You need to provide each person with a script that matches each visual with a related suggestion as to how to deliver the information.

One way to guide the sales force through your message is to provide a do script which suggests actions for each concept or supporting idea. Figure 22.7 is one visual taken from a sample do script. Table 22.3 highlights a segment of the storyboard, including the reference to the visuals. The left column shows the sequence, name, and type of visual, while the right column describes the action a presenter might take to deliver the information.

TABLE 22.3   A SEGMENT OF A DO SCRIPT

Storyboard Visual and Type	Supporting Script
#18—Customer Satisfaction (Survey shown as a table)	Tell a story that describes a personal experience in which you helped solve a customer's problem that resulted in extreme satisfaction and repeat business.
#19—Domestic Locations (U.S. map with dots showing office sites)	Describe your relationship with other sales people around the country and give examples of how you share information and collaborate to achieve sales goals.

Do scripts enhance the authenticity of the delivery and help each presenter develop a unique delivery style. This method requires very little memorization, which reduces the chances for error and inconsistency. Simple visuals that don't lead or confine the presenter are the key to effective conceptual presentations.

Another way to guide the same sales force through your message is to provide a say script that offers the exact wording (speech) for each concept or supporting idea. Figure 22.8 is one visual taken from a sample say script, basically the same example as the do script used earlier. Table 22.4 highlights a segment of the storyboard, including the reference to the visuals. The left column shows the sequence, name, and type of visual, while the right column gives the actual words a presenter should say when delivering the information.

Figure 22.7
A customer survey showing "out of one hundred" satisfaction ratings for a series of products and services. This visual appears as #18 in the storyboard script.

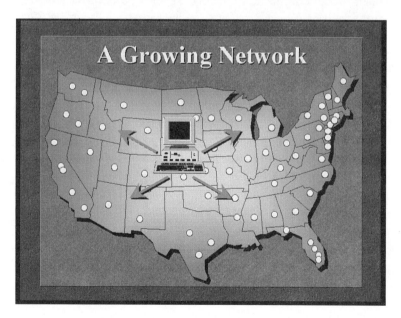

Figure 22.8
A U.S. map showing office locations and demonstrating the concept that the offices are connected by a communications network. This visual appears as #19 in the storyboard script.

TABLE 22.4   A SEGMENT OF A SAY SCRIPT

Storyboard Visual and Type	Supporting Script
#18—Customer Satisfaction (Survey shown as a table)	"As a world class provider of widgets, this survey shows our leadership in building customer satisfaction into every product and process we deliver."
#19—Domestic Locations (U.S. map with dots showing office sites)	"We have sales and service offices in 40 cities in the U.S. alone. Each office is networked through a sophisticated computer system that allows our sales force to expedite orders and share data."

Say scripts seem to offer more consistency than do scripts because all the correct words to support the message have been decided. Sometimes exact wording is necessary, either because someone prefers to work that way and is good at memorization (very rare) or because the person is presenting in a situation where precise timing and complete accuracy are crucial. Examples of these are presentations or speeches prepared for the media, such as TV or videotape.

Say scripts tell a presenter exactly what to say and require that the presenter memorize or read the script word-for-word. Because very few people can memorize a scripted speech, say scripts are usually more effective when using a TelePrompTer. The prompter gives the appearance that eye contact is being maintained as the presenter conveys the message.

Note

Because the average person can't memorize a speech, he or she will usually read it to the audience. When we see someone reading, we have less faith in that person's knowledge of the subject. In fact, we might even doubt the person's sincerity if the message is emotional.

One way to help someone with a written speech is to have them go through the presentation without the words. The more someone understands the basic flow of information and can express the ideas and main points in his or her own words, the easier it is to later substitute the words of another.

In the theatre, the actors hear the first reading of the play, then play each scene in their own words (improvisation) to get familiar with actions and intentions. Later, when they learn the lines they are able to make the playwright's words more personal because those words are tied to actions and intentions already experienced.

Otherwise, say scripts become cards or notes delivered from a lectern by a presenter who spends most of the time looking down to catch the next sentence in the script rather than looking up to catch the next response from the audience.

To support the notion of a visual presenter, you need to provide the kind of script that offers the best opportunity for the message to be received by the audience. Although do scripts offer the greatest expression of individual style, say scripts conform to a higher expression of consistency.

As you construct the argument and qualify the participants, both presenter and audience, you will seek a consistent expression of the intended message. That message, converted into visual support, must be delivered in an effective manner in order to move an audience to action. Such are the qualities of successful presentation.

I know we covered a lot of information in this chapter and I don't want you to feel overwhelmed. You can't apply everything I mentioned to a presentation you expect to give two hours from now. But, you can start to think more clearly about the message itself.

Maybe you'll be involved in twenty PowerPoint presentations this year at some level. If some of those scripts are in your control at the message stage, then revisit this chapter and find the elements that help you most in designing a clear, concise, and captivating message!

TROUBLESHOOTING

SCRIPTING WITH A TIMELINE LAYOUT

Is there any quick, easy, one-two-three method for scripting a presentation?

Actually there is. It's called a timeline layout. There are three segments in the timeline, based on chronology, following the pattern of past, present, and future. Some people use the metaphor of "where we were, where we are, where we're going." You can probably use this process with almost any type of script or situation and it's certainly easier to remember your key points when you use the timeline approach.

For example, let's say you have to give a short talk on the progress of a particular project. First, you determine the outcome of the talk (the call to action). You decide you want the group to continue to support the project. Nothing major, just "continued support." People give continued support to things that have a track record of satisfaction. So the objective is to demonstrate satisfactory results. You have an objective and a call to action. Now you need a script. Of the noted types found in this chapter, you select "problem-solution."

Using the timeline layout, you apply the problem-solution scenario to the past, present, and future using no more than three issues for each segment of the timeline. Thus, for the past you mention three specific problems which led to the need for the project, and you identify at least one solution that came about to address one of those problems. This begins your journey to providing satisfactory results (remember the objective?).

Next, you focus on current issues (present) and how several initiatives are being used to address the remaining problems from the past. In addition, you show how the solution to some of the problems has opened new concerns, which might develop into problems if left unchecked. For example, you might show that the implementation of a new procedure while streamlining communication has created the need for advanced technology and additional expertise. This is your first indication to the group that you will require their continued support for the increasing scope of the project (remember the call to action?).

Then, you discuss the strategy or plan for the future and the results you expect based on the already demonstrated and satisfactory past performance. You show how the investment in already-proven, additional resources will continually improve the specific business function that the project was originally intended to address. You close by showing that, without continued support for the project, the original problems that created the need for the project will return but the effect of those problems will be magnified based on the current economic and competitive conditions.

Your ability to remember and discuss information is based on your understanding as to where that data fits along the timeline of past, present, and future. Just make sure that everything you present matches the objective (satisfactory results) and leads to the call to action (continued support).

BEING CONSISTENT, YET UNIQUE

How can I maintain consistency in all my messages yet keep them unique?

The easiest way to create and deliver messages with consistency and impact is to find yourself in the message. The closer the message is to your heart and your belief system, the easier it is to be consistent.

But don't confuse consistency with conformity. When you try to conform to the message, you make sacrifices and trade-offs in order to fit yourself into the message. This cannot be done with any sincerity because your heart and soul will not allow it. When you are consistent with the message, you make the message conform to you and the message is expressed naturally, through your actions.

If I coached you to higher levels of this presentation skill, I would force you to find where in a given message you have the strongest tie. In other words, what part of the message is closest to your heart? Once you match a core principle (belief) of your life to a particular element in the message, a link is established between you and the message. That is the starting point for developing a consistency. You might have to modify the message by slanting it to your way of thinking. But that's the beauty of shaping a message to your personal and natural style.

For every message thereafter, you will use the same process to find the elements in the message that match at least one of your core principles. Messages will change, but you must remain true to your own beliefs. This is why I am able to work with so many different people from such diverse groups. The consistency in the coaching is to simply create the link between the message and the messenger.

And don't think you can't match the message. A message and a corporate philosophy are created by individuals who are part of the same race—the human race. For all the diversity that exists, we still share basic instincts and characteristics simply by the fact that we are human. So, start from the premise that you are able to find elements of a message or a philosophy that fit you. The consistency in your own heart must be the watermark for all ideas and concepts you expect to support.

COMMUNICATING CHANGE

In my company, the messages are top-down and the training is bottom-up. This causes a big gap between employees and executives. Who should change?

Change is inevitable for everyone. From a presentation perspective, change is more difficult for those at the top. Technology is a factor. As computers and communication systems evolve, the skills required to deliver information become more visual. Companies that recognize the need to provide presentation-skills training usually start from the bottom-up. This approach is incorrect because the newest employees are already visually driven and will adapt naturally to visual communications. The top-level executives need the skills training the most because they are probably not visual presenters. Having coached for more than 15 years, I see these problems affecting the bigger companies more than the smaller companies.

For example, I once dealt with the Director of Communications for a major fast food service company—we're talking major with a capital *M*—the leader in the industry. Although many of the mid-level managers had experienced the initial stages of my company's coaching, the director felt that I was not the right fit to coach the top-level executives. When I asked why, the director told me that my personality and my approach would adversely influence the top executives in a way that might affect the corporate message. He was afraid to expose the leaders to the exact skills that others in the company were experiencing and using. This indicated the director's lack of confidence in the executive team's ability to change. In an effort to protect the top-level executives, the director created a gap between management levels. This gap will eventually widen until the mid-level managers move up or until they move on (usually to a competitor).

As a company develops a visual presentation strategy, those nearest the top need the training first. Why? Because they usually deliver the core messages of the company in the most public forums to extremely diverse groups. If the leaders can't change, then the followers will change the leaders!

CHAPTER 23

THE MEDIA—DESIGNING VISUAL SUPPORT

In this chapter

by Tom Mucciolo

BRINGING YOUR STORY TO LIFE

"Image is everything," "Seeing is believing," "You oughta be in pictures"—you've heard it all before. The look and feel of your visuals will certainly make a difference in your business presentations; you just want to make sure the difference is positive.

For instance, I can look at any presentation and within the first three visuals tell how good or bad the presentation will be, just from a media viewpoint. In most cases, the visuals are pretty bad. Some simple techniques can help even a first-time presenter avoid making the most common mistakes.

A well-conceived script containing a clearly defined objective should be enhanced with good visual support. The features and functions of PowerPoint help bring your outline and storyboard to life, giving you the opportunity to create visuals with impact. This chapter focuses on the effective design of the support elements used to direct your message.

A lot of people take for granted the importance of having well-designed visual support for the presentation. The components of the event, especially those that are most visible, can make or break the moment. If you keep following our notion of a visual presenter, you can begin to see how the support for your message must be highly visual.

CHOOSING A MEDIUM FOR YOUR MESSAGE

When Marshall McLuhan said, "The medium is the message," he was referring to the power of television and its influence on how we interpret information. Television is one type of medium used to express information. Canvas is one type of medium for a painter's artistic expression. The medium of expression is basically the link between the message and the mind.

> **Note**
>
> Media is plural and medium is singular, but sometimes media is used as a collective noun to describe a larger set (the newspaper media, for example). Rather than asking you to consider semantics and form, from here on out, I will refer to everything as simply media, including flip charts, slides, overheads, electronic images, and other related items associated with the visual support used in a presentation.

The media choice represents the physical form of the message. It definitely affects the manner in which the presentation is delivered. For example, using overheads requires a different approach in delivery than an electronic presentation simply because the transparencies need to be handled (touched). Having one more thing to do affects the way in which the presenter delivers the message.

Although your delivery style is affected by the media choice, your objective should remain independent of the media. The very definition of visuals as "speaker support" implies that you should be able to present your message without supporting media. I'm not trying to burst the PowerPoint bubble and suggest not using visuals at all. On the contrary, presentations with no visual support force the presenter to have the most exceptional delivery skills. Think about music. Without the orchestra, a singer is required to have perfect pitch to be a success. Unless you want to be an *a cappella* presenter, I suggest you stick with visual support.

UNDERSTANDING MEDIA TYPES

Presentations involve a number of support options, including transparencies, 35mm slides, and electronic visuals. I place them in order from most to least interactive. Overheads will require changing, slides may involve changing carousels, and electronic presentations are mostly hands free. Multimedia is just an extension of the electronic presentation, although a degree of interactivity does occur when you use elements triggered by the keyboard or mouse.

Flip charts and videotapes are omitted to limit this discussion to the most likely media types you would consider when using PowerPoint to design your presentation.

PART
VII
CH
23

Note

PowerPoint calls the visuals you create "slides." However, in their electronic form (on your PC), they are really "visuals" or "images." If they are produced as 35mm slides, only then do they become slides. If they are printed to transparency film, they become overheads. In fact, I always describe an electronic presentation as a screen show, not a slideshow.

I am not trying to change the software, but throughout this part of the book, I will continue to use the words "visual" and "image" when referencing the media.

Overheads and slides are tangible and require an output device (printer or slide camera) to produce. Electronic visuals, although seemingly intangible, still require an output device to be viewed. In all cases, the support is part of an overall production.

You're probably aware that I think overheads and slides come in second in the media race. Electronic presentations work best. They offer so much more in the way of variety, interactivity, portability, and flexibility—just to name a few reasons. In fact, as you develop presentations for a visual presenter to deliver to an audience of visual creatures, additional components such as sound, animation, and video will become considerations in the design of the visuals. The real power in PowerPoint is in the design of effective electronic events. The electronic presentation is currently the most effective media choice for delivering business presentations.

I'm not saying never to use slides or overheads, but I am saying that an audience of visual creatures has come to expect more. It used to be that presenting electronically had to be justified in some way. Today, you'll have a hard time explaining why you chose not to present with a computer.

You may even have to explain it environmentally. Electronic presentations are "green"—that is, nothing has to be discarded at a later point that would affect the environment. Slides and overheads are not biodegradable. This is just one of many of the arguments for using electronic presentations.

In keeping with the notion of a visual presenter, you cannot ignore the growing acceptance of electronic presentations over slides and overheads. In fact, black-and-white overhead presentations are the most difficult for an audience to observe and still remain attentive to the message.

The Case for Color

When you watch a black-and-white overhead presentation, it doesn't take long before you start shifting in your seat, updating your daily planner, and checking the stack to see how many overheads are left.

Black text on a white background is called "print," and print is meant for an audience of one. That's why you can work at your computer with its paper-white display. You can look away whenever you want and examine information for as long as you prefer.

A presentation is meant for an audience of more than one. An audience of more than one demands color. Color is what real life is made of; black and white is simulated and, therefore, less than real life. When people are faced with less than real visuals, they become distracted. When you present, you want the smallest amount of distraction possible. Present in color.

If you evaluate types of media based on overall impact, color always supersedes black and white. In fact, if you're not using color, you shouldn't even be thinking about 35mm slides or electronic presentations. Instead, you should stick with overheads. With color, however, the impact is greater, depending on the media type. The more flexibility you have with the media, the better the presentation.

Currently, electronic images offer the greatest flexibility when compared with slides and overheads. If you have several media choices available to you, choose the one with the most flexibility, which I find in most cases is electronic.

If you are already convinced of the benefits of presenting electronically, you can skip the rest of this section on media types. If you need to justify a media choice, however, take a look at the following comparisons.

Flexibility in media can be examined based on the CCC Model, or Cost, Convenience, and Continuity. These three major considerations can help you decide which media choice to use for your color presentation. To better understand media types, we can apply the CCC Model to overheads, slides, and electronic images.

COST OF OVERHEADS

Sometimes referred to as transparencies, foils, or acetates, overheads are one of the most commonly used yet least flexible media types in business.

Often a company will try to use existing audiovisual equipment before investing in new technology, and the overhead projector is the most common in business. This makes sense.

Moreover, for black-and-white presentations, the simplicity of inserting transparency material into a printer makes this choice an easy one with minimal cost.

> **Note**
>
> The easier it is for you to prepare the presentation, the harder it is for the audience to stay attentive to your message. If you quickly create a few transparencies with lots of lengthy phrases, you create a presentation meant to be read and not viewed. Easy for you, tough for the audience. If you take the time to design effective visuals, the audience will find it easier to watch the presentation.

When overhead presentations involve color, the cost issues change. After you prepare your presentation in PowerPoint, you can outsource the production of color overheads to a creative services company, or you can use in-house equipment.

The cost of outsourcing the production of the overheads may appear to be higher because the price is reflective of the original investment in equipment, the supplies used, and the time required to monitor the process. In addition, profit is built into the price. However, in-house production has similar costs associated with the output.

In-house production of color overheads involves the cost of acquiring a color printer and the recurring cost of supplies. In addition, the cost of time associated with the output process itself is a factor.

> **Note**
>
> The factor of time is associated with equipment-related issues and not the time it takes to create the visuals in PowerPoint. That effort is generally the same regardless of the final form of the output. Your investment of five minutes to create a bar chart in PowerPoint doesn't change if you use slides, overheads, or electronic images as the final output.

Let's use the same type of example for comparisons to slides and electronic images. Suppose that a company makes only one 20-minute presentation each week. That's our reference point: one 20-minute presentation per week.

For 20 minutes of presenting, you'll create about 10 color overheads. Over one year, that's 500 overheads. The supplies aren't free. You have to buy them. You can be more exact on supply cost if you know the actual cost of the transparency material (film) and color cartridge (toner, ribbon, or ink). On average, each color overhead costs about $1.00. If you also factor in the cost of the equipment, even a $500 color printer adds another $1.00 to the supplies cost, if you spread the cost of the printer over a single year.

We have one other cost factor. In addition to supplies, you need to consider the cost of time to manage the process of producing the color output. Someone has to do this, whether it is you or some other member of the company. The process includes setup of the printer, maintaining supplies, fixing jams, and waiting for each transparency to print.

If you count changes, mistakes, setup, and other interruptions, about 30 minutes each week is required for the 10-overhead presentation. Although the hourly wage of whoever is managing the process makes a difference, even a $10 per hour wage adds another $0.50 per overhead to the cost.

The cost of producing 10 color overheads in-house might be as much as $2.50 each when you factor in supplies and time. That's $25 a week, assuming you have only one presentation per week.

If you outsource the color overheads by sending a PowerPoint presentation to a service bureau, you'll probably pay twice that or higher, depending on turnaround time. This is something to consider when weighing color overheads against slides or electronic presentations.

COST OF 35MM SLIDES

For 35mm slides, the cost of production also includes investment in equipment, plus the actual cost of developing and mounting the slides. Some companies have in-house equipment to complete the entire process, but many own a slide-imaging device (film camera) from which the 35mm film is sent to a local development lab for processing.

Although the time to maintain the equipment and manage the process is far less than for color overheads, the number of slides needed to make the same points is much higher. If you have 10 overheads in your 20-minute presentation, the same 20-minute presentation using 35mm slides would require you to use about 30 slides. The reason is simple. You use media types differently. Slides in a carousel advance more rapidly than overheads changed manually.

Note

> MediaNet designed ShowSTARTER as a planning tool for a presentation. One of the calculations this software utility makes is to estimate the number of visuals you should have, based on the length of the presentation. Another factor it considers is whether you're using overheads or slides. A person normally changes overheads every two minutes or so, using a landscape orientation; portrait overheads require even more time because they usually contain additional text. Slides stay up for less time because the aspect ratio is different (22/35) and less space is available for data. To cover the same information, you usually need more slides, which means you spend less time on each slide (they change faster). So for example, you'd need about 30 slides for a 20-minute presentation, but only 10 overheads.

Even though film cameras cost more than color printers, the cost per slide is similar to color overheads because you will use more slides per presentation. If you produce 30 slides per week for a year, and you invested in a $3,000 slide camera, your cost per slide is about $2.00. Add to that the actual cost of the roll of film and the developing charge, and it's about another $0.50 per slide. For about $2.50 per slide, you could do it yourself.

If you send a PowerPoint file to an imaging bureau, the cost of production will be somewhere between $5 and $10 or higher per slide, depending on turnaround time. Obviously, because you are using their camera equipment, their personnel, and their profit margin to image the slides, you will pay a higher cost.

COST OF ELECTRONIC IMAGES

One important advantage with electronic images is that they require no additional production output, as with slides or overheads. This is important if you're time-starved like me. I know I wait until the last minute to do stuff because there's always too much stuff to do. If I can work on my presentation and fine-tune the images on the plane, that's a better use of my time than sitting around waiting for film to develop.

The good news is that after you complete your PowerPoint presentation, you can use your PC to launch the screen show (slideshow) using a display device. Nothing is free, however, and you need to consider the cost factor of the device used to project or display the image. Typically, LCD projectors are used with notebook computers to present electronic PowerPoint presentations.

For cost analysis, you should use only the cost of the projection device. Don't add the cost of the PC because the computer has many more business uses beyond presentations. Also, you can't really assign a cost to each image because there is no extra charge to make 10 more electronic visuals in a presentation.

Using ShowSTARTER to calculate the number of visuals, our 20-minute presentation will require 35 images, compared to 10 overheads and 30 slides. This is because the change from one electronic image to another is a little faster than with slides. Hence, more visual impressions are possible when the duration stays the same (20 minutes).

Looking at cost per presentation, the equipment needed to project the image can be in-house (owned) or outsourced (rented). An LCD projector varies in price, depending on feature/function issues, but if we assume owning one requires an investment of about $4,000, your weekly electronic presentation will cost about $80 ($4,000 divided by 50 weeks). Compared to 10 color overheads ($25) or 30 slides ($75), this appears to be the least cost-effective choice. In fact, if you go out and rent the LCD projector, your costs for that one presentation will be even higher ($200 or more). However, outsourced costs are always higher.

Tip from
Tom Mucciolo

One way to know if you should buy or rent the display device is to estimate the minimum number of electronic presentations you expect to give in one year. Divide that number into the cost of a projector. If the answer is lower than a typical rental charge for that type of projector, then you might want to consider a purchase.

For example, suppose you plan on giving 50 presentations this year. You set your sights on a shiny new projector that costs $8,000 to buy. $8,000 divided by 50 is $160. If it costs you more than $160 to rent the same kind of projector, it makes sense to buy the unit.

Use a one-year scenario even though your equipment will naturally last longer. To remain current with technology, you would have to upgrade every year, so the rent-or-buy comparison is done in a one-year time frame to take the most conservative view. A five-year comparison would surely make you choose to buy every time. In fact, most rental prices are based on the equipment paying for itself within one year.

One big issue is that electronic images have no incremental costs per additional visual. Thus, your hard disk can store hundreds of visuals, any of which can be accessed as backup or support information. Electronic presentations offer the flexibility to make changes and updates, create builds and overlays, and even allow for more advanced activity using multimedia and hyperlinks.

From a cost standpoint, that kind of flexibility makes electronic visuals the best choice.

CONVENIENCE OF OVERHEADS

Convenience is about portability and relevancy. I mention portability because overheads are tangible. You have to carry them around and handle them. The handling factor makes overheads a less attractive media choice.

A three-ring binder of 50 color overheads in vinyl protective sleeves weighs about five pounds. Some presenters carry two or three times this much for certain presentations, which can amount to about 15 pounds of plastic. In addition, overheads can accidentally fall from the stack, and many presenters have experienced the "transparency crawl" in an attempt to get everything back into the original sequence quickly.

Another issue of convenience is relevancy, or keeping things current. Many presentations, especially financial ones, rely on the most up-to-date facts to drive home the message. Color overheads limit this timeliness of information to the availability of the nearest color printer. In fact, the more specialized the printer you use, the less likely it is that you will find a similar type when you are offsite at a presentation and you want to make changes or updates to several of your color overheads. This media is device dependent and usually reproduces consistently only when using the same device that made it.

One other issue involves the lack of convenience in printing color overheads. After your visuals are created in PowerPoint, you typically have to leave your desk and go to the location of the color printer. In larger settings, this is not the office printer located a few steps from your desk. Instead, it usually resides in a more central location and may end up being shared by a larger number of users. More people waiting to use the same device will result in longer lines.

CONVENIENCE OF 35MM SLIDES

There are eight different ways to load 35mm slides into a carousel and only one way is correct. This can pose a problem if you are running out of time.

Tip from	The fast way to load 35mm slides into a carousel is to face the carousel so the first slot
Tom Mucciolo	(number one) is to your left. This would be the same as if you were standing in front of the lens looking down at the tray. Take a slide and hold it up to the light so it is correctly oriented as you look at it. Now simply flip it backward (which will turn it upside-down) and drop it into the slot. This look, flip, and drop process can be done fairly quickly.

Remember that convenience is about portability and relevancy. For slides, the portability issue is not so much that they are heavy (like carrying 100 overheads). Instead, you have some limitations concerning how many you can use.

For instance, the number of slots in a carousel limits slides. Glass-mounted slides are limited to 80 per carousel tray. With cardboard or plastic mounts, you can use a carousel that holds 140 slides, but the risk of the slides getting jammed increases with the thinner and lighter mounts. You can bring several carousels, but the convenience of portability is affected.

You actually have less flexibility for making changes when using 35mm slides. It's not that you'll have trouble finding a development lab to process 35mm film; rather, how will you get the slides shot in the first place? The good news is that you can electronically send your PowerPoint file to a 24-hour service for processing. The bad news is that turnaround time is at least a day if you are out of driving range. It is not likely you'll be able to make changes to the slides conveniently.

It's not all negative with slides. (No pun intended.) For certain presentations, the slide's emulsion, a maximum of 5,200 horizontal lines (resolution), offers the best contrast for color and image definition. If you are giving a medical presentation and the audience needs to see the changes in skin tissue to determine a medical condition, the subtle shades and color variations will be most accurate with 35mm slides. Electronic LCD projectors and color printers do not have the resolution (yet) to match slides, so you need to consider the importance of color definition in your support visuals.

High-color definition requirements, such as images rendered in computer-aided design and manufacturing (CAD-CAM) applications, are another instance in which I would recommend 35mm slides over electronic images.

CONVENIENCE OF ELECTRONIC IMAGES

When your images are stored on your notebook computer, you are ready to present. Now that is convenience. When you look at portability and relevancy, electronic images pass those two tests with flying colors.

Portability regarding storage issues for visuals is virtually nonexistent. Your notebook computer doesn't weigh more each time you add more images. You can store as many visuals as your hard disk can hold. There is no slide carousel to limit you.

Electronic images address portability in a different way. It has to do with transfer. The capability to transfer or disseminate information through other electronic methods makes the electronic presentation more useful. Check out Part V, "Working with PowerPoint on the Web," if you want to stimulate your thinking about information sharing.

Welcome to the Machine

Electronic presentations made today can be delivered in similar form, before and after the actual event. You can reinforce your message to create lasting impact.

For example, you can send a self-running overview of your presentation to people in advance. Nothing prevents you from e-mailing your PowerPoint show to expected attendees that contains information that helps support your message. This may even prompt better attendance.

After the event, you might have a more detailed version of the presentation available on your Web site, for example, for people to download and reference. The idea of electronic color hard copy takes on a whole new meaning in terms of cost and convenience.

Clearly you don't have the same flexibility with slides and overheads as you do with the electronic form.

I think relevance is the best quality of this media type. Instant updates, timely changes, and custom versions enable a presenter to tailor current content to more specific audiences. You might have a product presentation for both users of your product and your resellers (distribution channel). Many of the visuals are the same, but the users aren't going to see the visuals about wholesale pricing and the channel-promotion program. You can either have multiple versions of this presentation on your computer or simply go to PowerPoint's Slide Sorter view and hide the images you don't want displayed to certain groups.

The electronic presentation format also offers the convenience of instant access. Action buttons and hyperlinks enable easy navigation to back up and support information, including links to other applications on the computer. The capability to do "what-if" scenarios lends a dimension in presenting that you cannot even consider with more traditional media such as slides and overheads.

From a convenience perspective, electronic images have too many advantages to ignore.

CONTINUITY OF OVERHEADS

The real clincher when deciding on a media type for the presentation is continuity, which is really about keeping the attention of the audience. If there is any break in the action—any interruption of the flow, any distraction at all—the continuity of the presentation will erode. This reduces the impact of the message.

From a continuity viewpoint, color overheads carry a limitation during the presentation process. For one thing, the audience is subjected to the blast of white light each time there is a change to the next color overhead.

To overcome the white light issue, some presenters choose to shut off the projector between changes, but that still doesn't eliminate the problem of guessing if the next visual placed on the projector will be straight when the light pops on. If the image is slanted or skewed in any way, the audience is distracted. You have to touch these things and manually place them on the projector, and you don't always get it right.

Even if the transparency is perfectly straight, the presenter, trying to make fast changes, eventually drifts closer to the projector. Soon, the presenter ends up blocking the view of the screen of some of the audience.

Finally, continuity is broken if a presenter has to search for support information. I've seen many instances in which an audience member brings up a specific issue, and the presenter spends a few minutes searching the stack of overheads for the visual proof of the point. During all that time, the rest of the crowd is generally distracted and begins thinking more about dinner than discussion.

CONTINUITY OF 35MM SLIDES

You have fewer continuity problems with 35mm slides simply because there are no handling issues. Slides can get jammed occasionally in a projector, but for the most part, this media type addresses the continuity issue nearly as well as electronic images.

One difference is quantity of images. The carousel is limited (80 to 140), and changing carousels during the presentation breaks the continuity. Of course, you don't want to keep an audience without a break for more than an hour, so 80 slides in a carousel should be more than enough to make it to each break.

The only minor continuity problem that 35mm slides pose is the on/off transition to the next slide. Audiences get used to the pattern after a while, and it's not really a big deal. In fact, many slide presentations incorporate more than one projector and cross-fade between projected images, which simulates an electronic presentation.

However, if you go to that extent, why not use the computer?

PART

VII

CH

23

CONTINUITY OF ELECTRONIC IMAGES

Certain continuity issues demand the use of electronic images. They include builds and overlays, action buttons and hyperlinks, live applications, and multimedia options.

Builds and overlays, which reveal segments of information (text or graphics), help an audience understand more complex information. These techniques are most effective when done electronically. You can use slides for these effects, but you are limited in the number per carousel. You can attempt a text build with overheads. You know, the magic piece of paper that reveals yet another bullet.

Naturally, action buttons and hyperlinks enable nonlinear navigation using the computer. This requires electronic presentations. However, the instant access is what maintains the continuity of support information to the central theme.

Live software demonstrations, real-time computer applications, and multimedia presentations can only be done electronically; otherwise, the continuity of the event is completely missing. Imagine showing up to a lecture on using PowerPoint, and the presenter is displaying only screen shots of the software on overheads! The media must match the message.

The issues of cost, convenience, and continuity seem to point in the direction of electronic images as being the most effective media choice for business presentations. Selecting the proper medium should be your first consideration, before you start designing any visuals.

Let's Back Up!

So, you think we should put an end to slides and overheads? Not so fast! Let me tell you a little story about the need for back-up.

There was this sales event, sort of like a tradeshow, where makers of new products were presenting to potential distributors. It cost $1,000 per minute to present to about 15 potential buyers. Landing just one deal could be worth millions.

I was brought in to coach the presenters before each would make the big pitch. I worked with one guy named Jerry. His product was quite visual. Jerry made some changes to the presentation here and there and left feeling much more confident.

Thirty minutes before his presentation, he arrived at the conference center, set up his laptop and LCD projector, launched his PowerPoint presentation, and made sure everything was working. As he waited for the audience to arrive, he stepped into the restroom next door for a few minutes. When he returned, his PC and projector had disappeared! Not as in "Look, magic!"; they disappeared as in "Look, stolen!"

Luckily, he still had his briefcase in which he had seven 35mm slides from an older presentation on the same topic. Those few visuals along with several of his handwritten sketches using a flip chart helped him secure an order. They might have felt sorry for him for losing his equipment, but he couldn't know that in advance, even if it were true. The back-up medium saved him.

Computers can be stolen, but no one wants your slides or overheads. You won't find some guy on the corner opening his jacket when you pass by, saying "Pssst! Check it out—corporate slides!" It just doesn't happen.

Having a set of back-up materials, whether it be slides or overheads, makes those media types a very viable and important part of the presentation process. They might come in handy someday.

CREATING HANDOUT MATERIALS

Almost every presentation has some form of handouts. The nature and the timing of these materials are two very important issues. When you decide to give people information to walk away with, you have to think about exactly what they will be given and when they will receive it.

NATURE OF HANDOUTS

Handouts should always be different from the presentation. Let's think about the relationship between the handouts and the presentation. Typically, you might fall into the trap of printing out a hard copy of your visuals for the audience to take away with them. You can look at this in two ways—conceptually or specifically.

If your presentation is designed for a visual presenter, it is conceptual in nature. The images are clear, readable, easy to understand, and very supportive of the stories and analogies used by the presenter. A copy of these visuals will be useless after a short time. When the event is over, people will not have the presenter available to explain the concepts. Someone will find a copy of the handout about three weeks later under a pile of desk rubble. He will see a visual with an arrow, a circle, and a big number 11 and have absolutely no clue as to what it means. That is a useless handout.

Same scenario, except the handout reads like a book. Lots of text on each image, very wordy phrases, full sentences, extremely detailed charts, and complex tables of numbers. The handout is designed specifically. Nice handout and useful for a long time, but I pity the person who attended that presentation! It was probably a data dump on the audience with a presenter who simply read from the visuals most of the time. I have seen so many of these that one look at the handouts and I pretty much know how the presentation went.

A handout must be different from the presentation in the same way a book is different from the movie. How would you feel if you went to a movie and the book was on the screen, its huge pages turning slowly?

Tip from
Tom Mucciolo

Use the Notes feature (see Chapter 10, "Creating and Printing Presentation Materials") to enter the concept or actual script for each visual. If you print a set of these for the audience, they can review the comments long after the presentation is over. This makes the handout more useful.

If you plan on having the audience take notes, you can consider a note-taking handout, which you can make in PowerPoint (see Chapter 10). It should include a combination of your visuals and an area for notes so that the audience can create personal references for later review.

To leave people with supporting documents is better than to bombard them with tons of data on every visual. Specification sheets, detailed charts, advertisements, articles, and even free samples are just some of the support items that you can provide to tout your message long after you're gone.

A Pattern to Remember

Hand out more than you say–say more than you show–show it simply!

To hand out more than you say is to provide more material for later review than you cover verbally during the presentation.

To say more than you show means that more words are always coming out of your mouth than people are reading on the screen. Remember that the visuals are speaker support, not the speaker. Do not read the visuals to the audience unless you plan to use a white bouncing ball over the text to help them follow along.

To show it simply is self explanatory. No one ever complains about a business presentation that is clear and easy to understand. Simple visuals force the audience to listen to the presenter's explanation of the intended message.

TIMING OF HANDOUTS

When is the best time to distribute handouts—before or after the presentation? There is no definite answer one way or the other. It depends on your objective and your ability to keep the attention of the group.

I start with a very simple question. Do you think the handouts will distract the audience from your presentation? If the answer is yes, distribute handouts at the end. If the answer is no, you can give them out at the beginning or the end.

For example, one of my seminars, "Presenting Made Easy," is a full-day workshop covering eight different topics. The audience receives a kit containing a book, a CD-ROM, additional handouts, and other information about technology discussed during the seminar.

Although the handouts are not necessary to follow along through the topics, the information is provided at the beginning so that the audience can have a reference available during the day. In addition, the scope of the material helps the audience decide how much note-taking is necessary. The more depth to the handouts, the fewer notes to take. There is a risk of distraction, but that makes the presenter (in this case, me) work that much harder to keep attention focused on the issue at hand.

Consider the opposite scenario: If I give a two-hour lecture as a keynote speaker, I provide handouts only after the session. I prefer to limit the distraction of people reading ahead and maintain the highest attention for the event. Because my handouts are not copies of each visual, the audience would not be able to follow along anyway, so why give them out ahead of time?

You have to examine the handout materials and judge how critical a role they play in the presentation. Can the audience respond to your message without the handouts in front of them?

Regardless of when you distribute handouts, always announce them at the beginning of the presentation. Let people know what you have, what it covers, and when they can expect to receive it.

CONTROLLING EYE MOVEMENT

We know that eight seconds is the average attention span on any visual. You can leave the visual up as long as you want, but the first eight seconds sets the tone for how long someone reads and how quickly that person can begin to listen. You can't read and listen at the same time. To test this, hand a newspaper article to another person. Begin speaking right away. You'll hear, in an angry tone, "How can I read this if you keep talking?"

Given the need to direct the eye quickly, ask yourself some questions. When a visual is displayed, where does a person look first? At what point on the image is the concentration of attention? Where does a person look next? If you can control a physical element of the audience, you will command more attention per visual. You can do this by controlling eye movement. The part of the body most used by an audience member is the eyes. A presentation is mostly watched. You need to find effective ways to direct the eye to the most important element in the visual.

> **Note**
>
> For this discussion, I'll use the word "eye" to mean both eyes. Another way to think about the word "eye" is as a focal point.

ESTABLISHING ANCHORS

An *anchor* in a visual is really just the solid footing for the brain. It's where we dock our attention to a focal point to begin processing the information. Usually, the starting point is the upper-left corner of the visual because our reading pattern in the English language is left to right. But all visuals are not the same. Text size changes, charts are used, artwork appears, lines are drawn, and shapes are placed in varying spots. It can get very confusing.

Figure 23.1 is a simple text chart. The typical way your eye moves on the visual is to first read the word "agenda" in the title. Then you begin reading the numbers on the left side of the visual. Because they look the same, you scan them downward. At about the third line (12:00), you say, "Wait, I should be reading this left to right." In the few moments it takes to adjust and start again, you have not been listening to the presenter.

Figure 23.1
Without an anchor, the eye initially scans the text as if it were two separate columns.

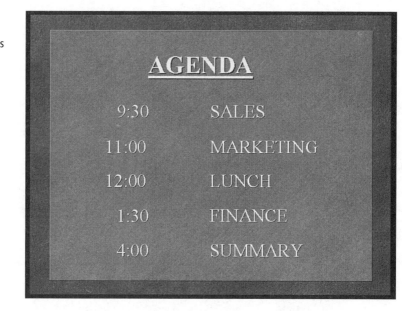

In Figure 23.2, the geometric shape in the background helps guide the eye across instead of down. Text alone cannot guide the eye. Geometric shapes guide the eye.

Geometric shapes are universal. They are not subject to cultural limitations in the way languages are. A square is the same shape in Toronto as it is in Tokyo. We process universal shapes first and the language next.

In Figure 23.3, the list of items covers the basic steps necessary for launching a hot air balloon. It is a text chart with no geometric shapes.

In Figure 23.4, your eye stops after the question mark in the heading and jumps to the tip of the arrowhead. But once you start checking out a geometric shape, you have to finish it to form the image in your mind. Your eye travels to the end of the arrow at the bottom-left corner of the visual to complete the shape. You then process the next shape (the bottom balloon) and after that, the text element near it ("Assemble Balloon"). Without thinking, you'll read the steps from bottom to top (backward, technically).

Figure 23.2
The geometric shape provides an anchor to guide the eye horizontally, allowing a faster scan of the information.

Figure 23.3
While looking at this visual, your eye will move from top to bottom, as in reading a list.

Figure 23.4
The arrow is an anchor in the background. It forces you to find its origin (lower-left corner), and you end up reading the text upwardly.

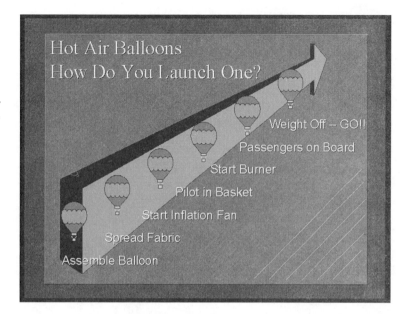

The whole image is designed to redirect your eye. Even the thin diagonal lines on the right side of the visual continue to help your eye move upward. In fact, as the visual forces your eye upward from the bottom, it matches the concept of launching a balloon from the ground.

Parallel Anchors

Another method for anchoring the eye is to keep text parallel, especially in bulleted lists. If you examine only the first word in a list of bulleted items, see if they follow the same pattern. For example, if one word is a gerund (ends with "ing") and another word is a plural noun and another word is a verb, it is not parallel.

If the first word is "Teaches," then each bullet should answer a "What else does this do?" question. Other bullets might begin with "Helps," "Gives," "Makes," "Offers," and the like.

If the first word is "Teaching," then each bullet should answer a "What else is this doing?" question. Other bullets might begin with "Helping," "Giving," "Making," "Offering," and so forth.

Keeping things parallel lets the audience anchor to the pattern and enables them to scan the visual more quickly. A faster visual scan gives the audience more time to listen to the message.

CHOOSING TYPEFACES AND FONTS

The eye moves from the simplest shapes to the more complex. Geometric shapes are easiest, and text gets more difficult. The letters of the alphabet are shapes, but because you need to interpret text (language), you can understand why the eye scans text last. That means the design of the letters (the typefaces and fonts) affects the eye movement of the audience.

Basically there are only two kinds of typefaces: *serif* and *sans serif.* You can be sure that all the fonts you have on your computer fall into one of those two categories. Serif typefaces (such as Times Roman) have little curls (called serifs) at the ends of the letters; sans serif typefaces (such as Arial) don't. To clearly see the difference, just compare the same word displayed in each of these two typefaces. The eye slows down on the serif fonts and speeds up on the sans serif ones. Think of the font as a road. The more hooks and turns, the longer it takes to travel that road. Serif fonts have more contours (hooks and turns), so we read them more slowly.

Tip from *Tom Mucciolo*	If you use two different fonts (please—no more than two!), use a serif typeface for the heading (title) and a sans serif typeface for the body of the chart. When you make a presentation, you want the eye to slow down while reading the heading (which has the key words) and speed up when reading the body of the chart (where there tends to be more text). Once the audience locks in on the title, they are more likely to get the rest of the text that follows. The heading is where the emphasis belongs because it's usually the first place the person looks.

The use of fonts and typefaces is the opposite of that in a newspaper. When you see a newspaper, the headlines are usually bold, Helvetica (sans serif), so that you can quickly scan them as you walk past the newsstand. But the body of the paper, in Times Roman serif), takes longer to read and therefore increases comprehension. That's why I keep my e-mail messages in a plain font (Arial).

If you look at Figure 23.5, you can see that the contours of the letters themselves cause distraction because the patterns keep changing. The eye travels along the contours of each letter and gets distracted as the different text shapes keep appearing.

Capitalization also affects eye movement. Take a look at Figure 23.6. Did you read it again? It's true. A series of all capital letters makes the text look the same. Our language thrives on ascends and descends, as seen in letters such as *b* and *g.* These extenders give letters character. ALL CAPS leave no room for emphasis or inflection. This causes the eye to read the information again. If the words in all caps were read out loud, the sound would be monotone.

By structuring text phrases similarly to the way we read (uppercase and lowercase), you can use capitalization to place emphasis at a particular point on the visual. Figure 23.7 shows the verbal inflection. If you read the text out loud in this example, the capitalized words would sound louder than the rest.

Figure 23.5
The heading, "NEW PRODUCTS," is a Times Roman font. In contrast, the word "Radios" in the first bullet is Helvetica, which is a sans serif font.

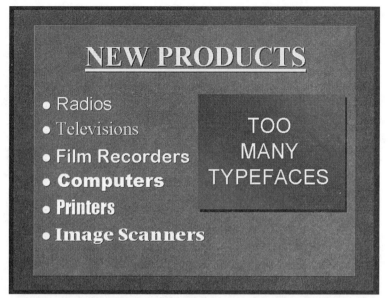

Figure 23.6
When all the words have equal weight, it makes it harder to know what's important.

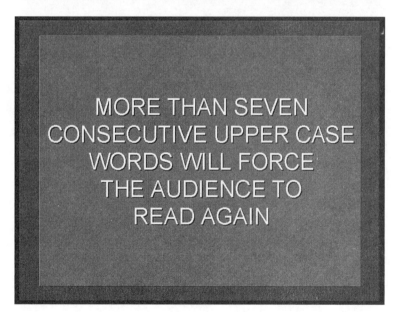

Figure 23.7
The proper use of upper- and lowercase enables the visual to speak for itself by indicating the intended inflection.

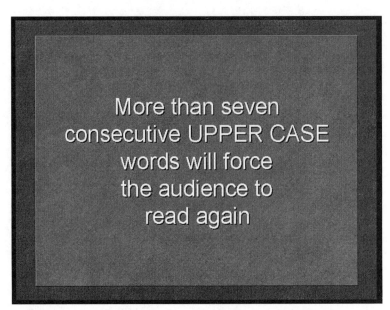

One other capitalization issue involves the use of initial caps, or first caps as some refer to it. This is the choice to capitalize the first letter of every major word in a given text line to create emphasis. The problem is that there is a lack of consistency on which words to initial cap. After all, what is a major word? Is it one with more than four letters? Is it one that is not a preposition? How do you decide? If you are not consistent, the audience begins to get distracted because reading initial caps is not the norm, especially if the pattern is not consistent.

Stick to the natural way we read by initial capping only the first word of a text line, rather than using inconsistent or distracting capitalization methods.

USING BUILDS AND OVERLAYS

Eye movement can be affected by the sheer amount of information the audience is allowed to see on a given visual. Sometimes I look at a visual and think the heading should start with "It was the best of times, it was the worst of times," as though this visual were the start of a great novel.

Obviously, it's easy for me to tell you to reduce the clutter. But the real world doesn't always work that way. The visuals get wordy for one reason or another, and maybe you can't be the one to say *stop*. What can you do?

One way to soften the blow for the audience is to use the build sequence. This simple technique is used to reveal elements of a visual in stages to maintain a steady focus for the audience.

Examine Figures 23.8, 23.9, and 23.10. They are shown as three visual impressions, even though only one visual would appear if you look in the Slide Sorter. That's because the build is a transition effect in PowerPoint.

Figure 23.8
The first in a series using builds. One line appears and limits the distraction from additional items to maintain focus.

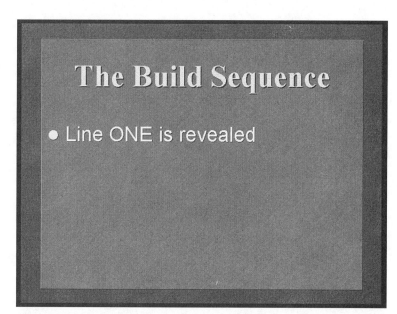

Figure 23.9
The next item in the build sequence is revealed while using the dim-down approach to darken or dim the color of the previous item.

Figure 23.10
The last bulleted point in the build sequence is revealed, and you can still see the dimmed text as a reference to what has been covered.

Figure 23.10
The last bulleted point in the build sequence is revealed, and you can still see the dimmed text as a reference to what has been covered.

→ For more information about slide effects, **see** "Setting Slide Transitions" in Chapter 15, "Working with Animation."

Figure 23.8 shows the beginning of a build sequence with the first line revealed and the remaining information hidden. The presenter is able to concentrate on this element of the visual until the next item is needed.

When he is ready, the presenter reveals the next bulleted item, as shown in Figure 23.9. I prefer using the *dim-down*—or *gray-down*—approach for a more effective text build sequence. Dimming the color of the prior item—usually to a shade of gray—then revealing the next item enables the eye to focus on the brighter and most current element and still maintains some visibility for what has already been covered.

Figure 23.10 shows the next bulleted item, which is revealed at whatever pace the presenter chooses, enabling direct manipulation of eye movement in a downward pattern throughout the entire visual.

Another sequencing method that helps with data clutter is when you reveal information one section at a time. Text, data, and graphic elements—each of which contains a complete thought—are revealed in segments called overlays.

If you show the audience the completed image, too many elements will distract the eye and reduce the effectiveness of the visual. When the eye is bombarded with multiple activities or thoughts, it doesn't know where to look first. If it takes time to design the visual, you have to give the audience time to digest it.

However, if the audience clearly sees the creative thought process that went into the complete visual, they will not be confused. Imagine a busy puzzle. If you watch the pieces of the puzzle fall into place, you can appreciate the whole picture. Have you ever put together a model or a toy with a lot of pieces? There's always that diagram in the instruction pamphlet that shows the "exploded" view of how all the pieces come together to form the object. The exploded view diagram lets you see the pieces spread apart and helps you understand how they fit together.

Figures 23.11, 23.12, 23.13, and 23.14 show the base image and the three subsequent overlays used to show a communications network linking certain office locations in the United States and connected to a central hub. The image can be separated into several little stories or thoughts that, when combined, create the final impression. Consider the amount of information on each of your visuals. Ask yourself if it would be more effective to reveal some of the elements in stages by using overlays.

Figure 23.11
The base image for an overlay sequence. The map of the U.S. appears with only a title above it.

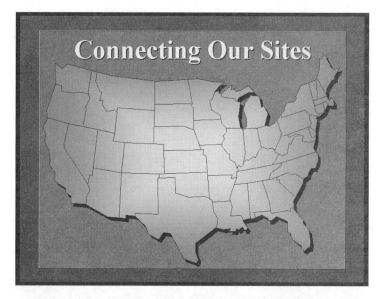

Figure 23.12
The first overlay or "layer" appears, showing the office locations (dots) that the communications network will link together.

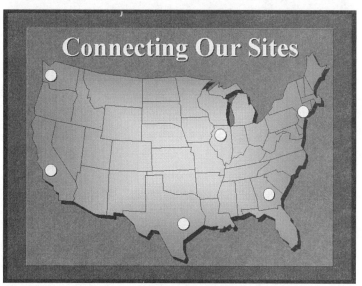

Figure 23.13
The next piece of the overlay puzzle shows the communications network connecting the locations.

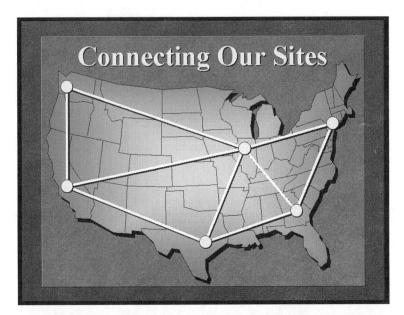

Figure 23.14
The last overlay in the sequence shows the hub or central communication area noted by the star in the center of the map (Chicago).

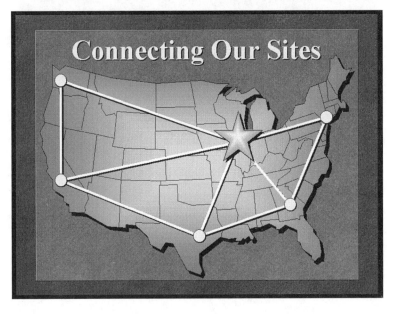

CREATING EMPHASIS

You can control eye movement by designing ways for the audience to know immediately where to look when the visual is displayed. If people are searching around, looking for something on the screen that remotely matches your words, you have a problem. When people don't get it, the attention span drops, and boredom sets in very quickly. You can guide the eye using words or pictures. Headlines and arrows are effective when designing guidance into visual content.

HEADLINES

How would you feel if every time you picked up the morning paper the headline read "News"? Every day the same thing, News. You wouldn't be as interested. Headlines sell newspapers.

The best way to direct the eye to the important area of a visual using words is to start with emphatic headlines. Too many visuals have flat titles.

In Figure 23.15, the two charts contain the same data. In the one to the left, I have a 25% chance that the audience will be looking at the exact part of the line chart I will refer to, even before I begin speaking. The heading is flat. However, in the same figure, the chart to the right includes the emphatic headline "Fourth Quarter Sales Post Record Highs!" This directs the eye quickly to the part of the line chart I want attention brought to—the fourth quarter, as opposed to the other quarters. In fact, the headline even tells the audience how I feel about the information. Don't waste the valuable real estate in the heading. If something is important, try to emphasize it in the title of the visual. You can't do this on every visual, but you can at least review all your headings and see where emphasis can be placed. Used wisely, emphasis in the right areas of a visual can affect both the physical and emotional reactions of the audience.

PART

VII

CH

23

Figure 23.15
The headline tells a story. On the left, a flat heading doesn't help guide the eye. On the right, the headline quickly gets you to the exact part of the visual to be discussed.

LASER POINTERS

You're watching a movie. The killer is lurking in the bushes. Suddenly, a big hand floats over the screen with a finger pointing to a spot near a tree. You'd shout, "Get that thing off the screen!" That's because the visual (camera) has to do the work to guide the eye of the audience.

You should never have to use a laser pointer or any pointing device during a presentation. To use one means you couldn't figure out how to guide the eye with the visual. You needed a prop.

You instantly have problems when using a laser pointer. First, no one can hold it steady. If you forget to shut it off, you must apologize for searing the eyes out of the people in row three. But mostly you have to spend time directing the pointer to a spot on the screen, which causes you to look away from the audience and interact with the screen. Visual creatures (the audience) demand eye contact. If you're looking at the screen and we're looking at the screen, then who's presenting? You can't interact with things that don't breathe, such as the visual.

The only time a pointer makes sense is when the visual is moving, like a video clip. Because the image is in motion, the pointer helps steady the eye to a specific area within the motion. But for still images in presentations, the eye can be directed by creating emphasis.

Sometimes pointing to the screen is required in a presentation. You should always do this from a distance and never touch the screen. Touching the screen causes the visual to move or vibrate, and it forces you to step in front of the image. Never block the light source, because the visual is designed for a flat surface.

You can use your voice to target specific areas. You can say, "If you look at the center of the visual" or "The object in the upper-right corner represents." You can verbally help guide the eye quickly through very complex information.

ARROWS

The simplest graphic element for controlling eye movement is the arrow. In many instances, using arrows as part of the visual can create the emphasis you need. Arrows not only show direction, but they can also indicate conflict, options, choices, and trends.

Be careful with arrows. Eye movement can easily be distracted when arrows point in too many directions on the same visual. Take a look at Figure 23.16. The eye scans the visual elements and eventually wanders or gets lost. The colors, text sizes, inconsistent capitalization methods, and variety of geometric shapes add to the confusion. Try to limit the number of arrows used for emphasis on a single visual.

Figure 23.16
This chart uses too many arrows. Your eye movement is actually disrupted rather than enhanced. When this happens, it takes longer to scan the image, which reduces attention to the message being delivered.

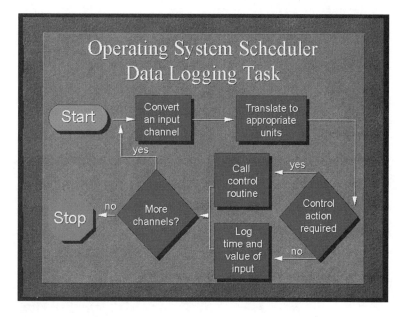

USING COLOR

I have always been fascinated with color. Over the years I've learned that correct color choices can have a tremendous impact on the success of the presentation. At the beginning of this chapter, I pointed out that presentations delivered in black and white are less effective than those in color. We live in a world of color and that, in itself, is an anchor to our understanding of information.

INCORPORATING SYMBOLS

Although geometric shapes are more universal, often you'll find that you need to use actual objects to describe something or make a point. The use of imagery in a visual can be very helpful.

Symbols represent ideas. Clip art is a collection of symbols depicted as artistic renderings and available in PowerPoint or from other sources. You've already learned about symbols and graphics in Chapter 13, "Working with Media Clips and the Clip Organizer." Let's concentrate on how these elements can be used effectively or, for that matter, ineffectively.

I look for flexibility with symbols. Can I use one in the background of the visual? Can I make it into a silhouette for more utility? Can I avoid the distraction of details?

DEPTH

There is an area in the background of each visual just waiting to be used. Sometimes a template is used to fill the background. If the template already contains a lot of elements, you have less chance to use symbols as part of the background. That's why I like simple templates.

Figure 23.17 is a text chart showing how employees spend their time. It's clear, readable, and to the point. The background template is pretty simple. This gives you the option of adding a symbol to support the message.

Figure 23.17
This is a simple text chart containing a series of percentages, arranged from highest to lowest.

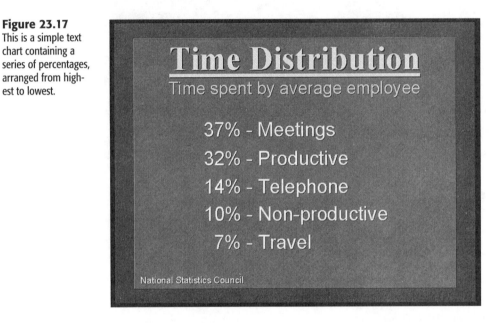

You see the word "time" in the heading, and in the clip art library for a descriptive symbol, you find the stopwatch. As shown in Figure 23.18, if you use just a two-dimensional approach, you'll shift the text to one side and put the clip art on the other side. This is fine, but the clip art is still pretty small and less obvious from a distance.

If you think deep into the visual, there is another interpretation possible. The percentages could be displayed as a pie chart. A pie chart is round; the stopwatch is round. Instead of making the graphic part of the chart, you can make a chart part of the graphic. Figure 23.19 shows a three-dimensional view of the information. This approach creates depth while allowing the data to take a more graphical form, a pie chart. The symbol is in the background but still retains its meaning. You know it's a hand, even though text covers some of the fingers. You know it's a stopwatch, even though there's a pie on its face. The symbol and the text occupy similar space on the visual, only in layers, and create the illusion of depth.

Figure 23.18
The stopwatch clip art is added and the text is moved to one side to make room for the artwork.

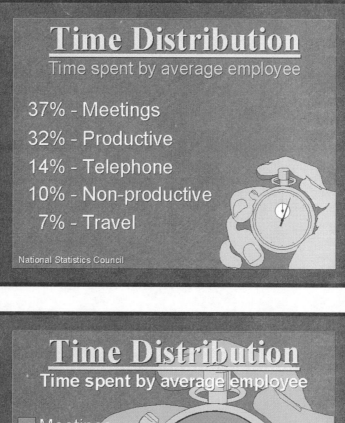

Figure 23.19
The clip art is sized to fill the background.

One of the best uses of the background is to incorporate photographs or natural images. A photo is the real-life symbol of an idea. Figure 23.20 is one example of how a photograph of people in a situation adds to the message in a way that clip art can't. In keeping with our recurring theme of a visual presenter, it makes a lot of sense to use real people in real situations, not only in the message but in the media as well.

Figure 23.20
The photograph in the background is blurred, but it still representative of the "team" concept in the title.

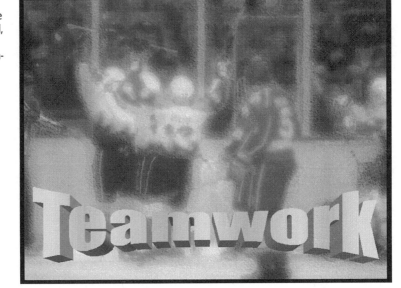

Keep in mind that photos usually contain hundreds of thousands of colors in various degrees of brightness. If you add text or other elements on top of a photo, be aware of light and dark spots. Sometimes the foreground information will blend right into the photo and not be as visible. This usually happens with text. You may have to adjust the brightness and contrast of the entire photo for lighter text to be readable.

All the Lonely People

Ever notice how many solutions are discussed in presentations but no people are shown using them? Photographs are really helpful when you are trying to get an audience excited about a product or a process. If you have a "solution" message, odds are the solution is going to help people. By using photographs of people in the background, you can add the human touch that might be missing among all the charts and tables in your presentations.

I'm not saying you need photos everywhere, but look at your visuals and see where pictures might enhance the story. For example, if you are describing a new project to add facilities for a growing company, photographs or even renderings may be used. But think about using photos of people working in offices, gathered around a water cooler, sharing a cup of coffee, walking through a parking lot, taking the sun with a sandwich, or just burning the midnight oil.

Scenes like these help the message appear closer to reality. Visual presenters and visual creatures are first and always people. The foundation of all communication is people.

SILHOUETTES

I like symbols that translate well across media. Sometimes you have to think about the utility of symbols in a variety of venues. One of the things I look for is the capability to make the symbol into a silhouette. If you fill the symbol completely with black, does it still translate its meaning? Since a silhouette is only two-dimensional, the loss of depth may cause the original object to lose its meaning. For example, a stack of quarters when silhouetted would look like a cylinder. The link to money is gone. A coffee cup would lose depth, but it would still maintain its shape as a cup.

I find this important when printing in pure black and white. Sometimes, objects in the background end up printing like big blobs and no one knows what they are. Printers today are sophisticated enough to print grayscale images, but what if you have to fax a copy of the printouts to someone?

Not every element can or needs to be a silhouette. If the symbol translates well to a purely solid shape, you can use the shape in a lot of situations.

DISTRACTIONS AND DISTORTIONS

Clip art images, if filled with many details, can actually become a distraction when the visual stays in view too long. The audience can get caught up in the artwork and begin to forget about the message. This can happen from the use of hokey-looking graphics that have a cartoonish or silly appearance. It can also happen from very sophisticated renderings that resemble a Rembrandt. The look of something is really up to you. If you don't like it, don't use it if you don't have to.

A more obvious distraction is a distortion. This happens when you do something to the symbol to alter its natural appearance. The alteration forces the audience to concentrate on what the symbol looked like before the distortion.

In Figure 23.21, the original bars in the chart are replaced with clip art in the form of pencils, to match the subheading of office supplies. You should always try to match a symbol closely to a concept to help clarify the message.

Figure 23.21
The pencil symbols are sized to match the height of the original bars.

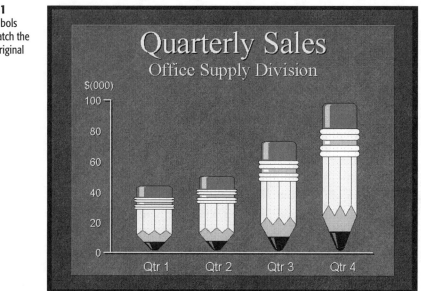

In this case, the pencils are the proper shape to substitute for the vertical bars.

It doesn't always work out so conveniently. Figure 23.22 shows what happens if the height of the first pencil is less. Would you give someone a pencil this little? That deformed, stubby little pencil looks ridiculous. Just because you have access to a clip art library doesn't mean you have to incorporate colorful symbols on every chart.

Figure 23.22
To match the value for the actual data, the first pencil image is distorted to the point of being a distraction.

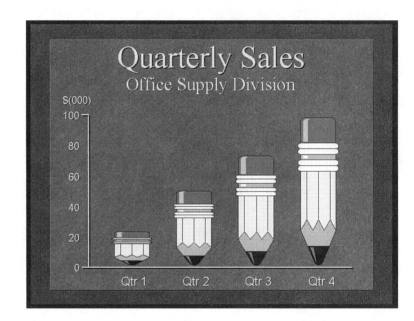

Also, be aware of the geometric shape you replace with a symbol. The bars in the previous examples were all vertical. The choice of pencils made sense. What if you decided to use a stapler as the symbol? Although a stapler is an office supply item, it is meant to be viewed horizontally, not vertically. This means you would have to rotate the stapler and stand it on end to fit the vertical form of the chart.

If you have to rotate a piece of clip art, you probably picked the wrong clip art. The audience is going to have to reorient the clip art in their minds just to place it in context. It's even worse when you rotate text. The only people who can read text quickly at any angle are librarians. The rest of us have to tilt our heads.

Avoid distractions and distortions when incorporating symbols into your visuals.

INVESTIGATING PERCEPTION AND CONTRAST

Although numerous studies have shown the beneficial results of using color in presentations, the most important reaction to color is more of a reflex. Perception is a reflex you cannot change. It happens so quickly that you barely notice it.

Try this audio perception test. As fast as you can, spell the following three words out loud and then answer the question. The key is to spell the words out loud.

Spell the word **MOST**.

Now spell **POST**.

Now spell **HOST**.

What do you put in a toaster?

If you said toast—wrong! You put bread in a toaster. It comes out as toast, but goes in as bread. If you said toast, it's because you followed the natural reflex of perception to spell the three **O-S-T** words and then respond with "toast" instead of "bread."

Figure 23.23 is a test in content perception. Read each of the phrases in the triangles out loud. Did you read the words in both triangles? Now read the phrase in each triangle, backward, one word at a time. Notice anything different on the way back? In both phrases you'll see a duplicate word.

Figure 23.23
Are you reading too much into these phrases, or not enough?

Tip from
Tom Mucciolo

Always proofread your visuals backward, one word at a time. Reading phrases backward lets you spot not only typos but other mistakes as well.

If you scanned the visual and didn't notice the duplicate words, it's because you've probably heard the phrases so many times that you perceived your version to be correct. The anticipation happens because the mind moves faster than the mouth.

Color perception works much in the same way. Depending on contrast, some elements may appear closer to the eye, which may or may not enhance the message.

Figure 23.24 shows how color can change perception, but it also explains why black-and-white presentations are a problem. The two red squares (the dark inside squares) are compared against contrasting backgrounds. The shapes appear to be different sizes but are really the same size.

Figure 23.24
The inside squares are set against contrasting outer squares of white and black. Can you see a difference?

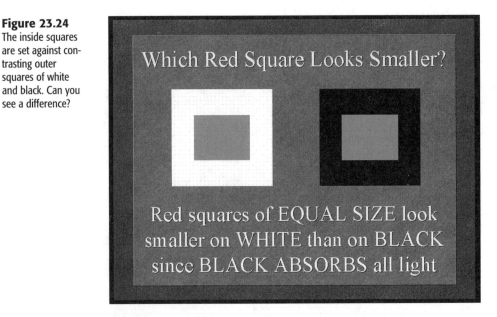

A MATTER OF CONTRAST

Remember that black absorbs all light. The darker the color, the more light it absorbs; therefore, it seems to push the object away from the eye. White reflects all light. The lighter the color, the closer the object appears to the eye. In presentations, contrast between background and foreground is critical. The objects in the background should be darker, and those in the front should be lighter.

This is the major reason why black-and-white overhead presentations are less effective. The contrast is opposite from the norm. The data on a black-and-white overhead is black. It pulls the eye into the visual because the information seems more distant. The clear (white) background is reflecting white light into the audience. The problem is that the body cannot handle white light reflected into the eye for very long. It's too distracting. When you use your computer, you can look away whenever you want. But when you watch a presentation, you are being asked to keep your attention fixed for a longer period. Proper contrast is needed to keep attention.

Because too much white light is a distraction, after a while the eye tries to avoid the conflict and, with it, the content of the presentation. Try staring at a fluorescent light for a while or glancing at the sun for a few moments. Your body simply rejects massive quantities of white light.

The rule of contrast for presentations is to use darker-color backgrounds and lighter-color foregrounds.

This is why I can never understand why anyone using an electronic presentation would choose a bright background and a dark foreground. The only time I recommend this option is if you will be in a room with so much ambient light that your visuals are washed out. In that case, the backgrounds would be less visible and wouldn't matter anyway. That's the only time I would recommend dark foregrounds.

Of course, the software is partly to blame. For many years I have been critical of all software programs, not just PowerPoint, for having only about half the templates following the dark background/bright foreground model. Perhaps this is one of the reasons why so often someone presenting electronically ignores effective contrast—he picked the wrong template!

No Room for Black and White?

The white light problem does not mean that black-and-white overhead presentations are totally useless. You may find times when you have to present without color. You need to be aware of the distraction caused by the amount of white light and consider ways to reduce the effect of the problem.

This might mean designing the visuals more conceptually rather than more technically. Fewer words on each visual let the audience scan the image faster and concentrate more on the presenter than on the screen.

Reducing the number of black-and-white visuals to be presented might be more effective, as well. To compensate for using fewer visuals, more detailed handouts could be given for later reference. You have ways you can limit the impact of white light distraction. Awareness of the problem is the first step toward solving it.

Nonetheless, it is my personal belief that presentations should be in color to be most effective.

Red/Green Deficiency

Certain color combinations may pose a problem for some people, particularly men. Some studies show that nearly 15% of men have a red/green deficiency; MediaNet's research has shown that close to 22% of men have some form of this deficiency. Women do not suffer from this problem (in significant numbers), but they should be aware of this fact when selecting colors for visuals.

If you have this deficiency, you might see purple more as blue, or you may mix up brown and green. The effect is not as noticeable with large areas of color as it is with small areas.

For example, if a line chart has three lines with one beige line, one tan line, and one orange line, it's possible that someone with a red/green deficiency will not be able to tell the difference between the three lines. The result will be confusion and a loss of attention. Try to avoid red-green color combinations, especially in small areas.

EARTH-TO-SKY COLOR THEORY

When you have related elements in the foreground, arrange them in a darker-to-lighter pattern from the bottom of the chart, upward. This "Earth-to-Sky" pattern is the way we view color naturally, from the earth to the sky. The earth is darker than the trees, which are darker than the sky, which is darker than the clouds. It's the same way a room generally appears as you look from floor to ceiling. It's even a pattern in the way we dress, with darker colors usually toward the bottom.

When you have related foreground items of different colors, you can choose an order of those colors from darker to lighter.

For example, in Figure 23.25, the segmented vertical bar chart shows the darker-to-lighter Earth-to-Sky pattern used effectively. If the top segment had been the darkest color, the chart would appear top heavy. The arrangement of colors, done naturally, allows the eye to scan the visual more quickly. A faster scan gives the audience more time to listen to the message. Since the order of the colors can make a difference, why not use it to your advantage?

Figure 23.25
The Earth-to-Sky color theory applied to a segmented vertical bar chart. Note the arrangement of colors in a dark-to-light pattern from the bottom upward.

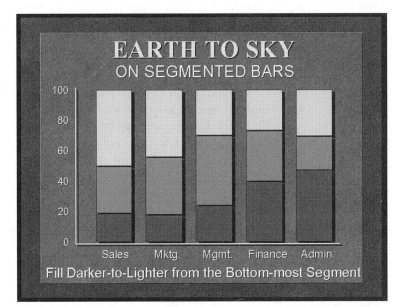

When displaying clusters of bars, as in Figure 23.26, choose a darker-to-lighter pattern, starting from the leftmost bar in each cluster. Don't use the "piano-key" approach by putting the lightest color between surrounding darker colors. When looking from left to right, the eye scans colors more easily when the arrangement is a dark-to-light pattern, similar to the Earth-to-Sky pattern.

Figure 23.26
For related elements such as clusters of bars, keep the darker-to-lighter pattern, beginning with the leftmost bar in each cluster.

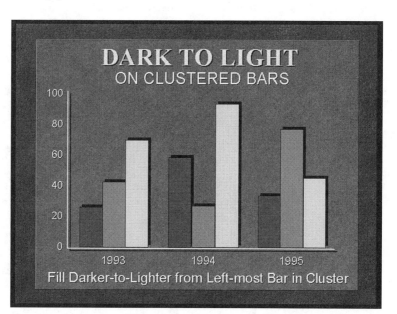

Remember that the Earth-to-Sky theory is for the foreground elements in the visual, not the background color. If you choose gradient shading in the background of the visual, it doesn't matter if it's darker at the top, bottom, left, or right or fans out in both directions from the center. Specifically, the theory is most useful in a data-driven chart, which usually shows a series of related items distinguished by color.

UNDERSTANDING BACKGROUND COLORS AND EMOTIONS

Color affects the nervous system, and the longer you see a particular color, the more it stimulates your emotions. During a presentation, it's best to stay consistent with your backgrounds, so the audience ends up seeing the background more often than each different foreground. The colors in the foreground keep changing and do not really affect the general feeling that the audience gets from the entire event. It's the background color choice that determines the emotional response from the audience.

Note

I suggest you maintain a consistent background color and template for the entire presentation. If you have several different topics to cover, you can switch background colors and even design templates. I have a number of different seminar topics I deliver, and the backgrounds are different in all of them, although throughout any one of the topics, the visual template is the same.

Keep in mind that a society makes psychological associations with colors based on appearances or cultural habits. Figure 23.27 shows some of these associations shared in the United States. Green is associated with money, for example. True, it is the color of money in the United States, but does green actually mean money? That would have to be true for all people everywhere. Is green the color of money all over the world? Then it can't mean money. Otherwise, the color gold would have meant money in the United States 100 years ago.

Figure 23.27
Even though the cultural associations made with certain colors are not universal, it's interesting to see what some colors mean in American society.

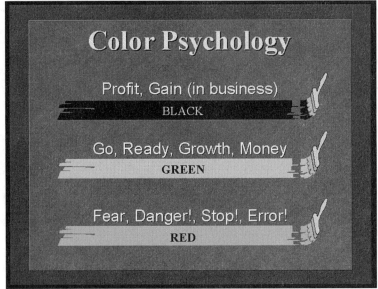

We all live under the same light of the sun. Blue looks the same in Borneo as it does in Bolivia. The effect of color on our emotions is from nature, not heritage. All people, regardless of culture, share a universal range of emotions, such as happiness, sadness, excitement, anxiety, desire, passion, and so forth. Tapping into these emotions using correct color choices can increase the effectiveness of the presentation.

Note

Be careful with colors. Don't make the presentation look like a circus. The use of too many foreground colors with a poorly selected background will become a distraction for the eye and result in an ineffective presentation.

Studies have shown that the background color of a visual produces an emotional response from the audience. Although there may be a number of different cultural interpretations of colors, the physical effect of the color is always the same. For example, red is the warmest color in the spectrum and is seen that way, regardless of any negative cultural associations we make, such as "the company is in the red."

Lots of books and articles are available about color, but the following may help you in choosing a background color for your presentation. These recommendations are based on MediaNet's experience in developing over 2,500 presentations.

GRAY

- Neutrality
- Border between directions
- Uncommitted and uninvolved
- Concealment from other emotions
- Escape from anxiety and discontent

Gray represents neutrality and lack of commitment. Depending on how persuasive you need to be, use of gray backgrounds may be a help or a hindrance. I would avoid using gray backgrounds when displaying any critical business information where you need to sway the audience. However, when the information is left for the audience to make a decision, gray frees the presenter from influencing the audience to respond to the issue.

For best readability, we recommend charcoal or dark gray. Anything brighter than medium gray will cause glare from the visual, and any brightly colored items in the foreground will be harder to see.

BLUE

- Complete calm
- Increased sensitivity
- Loyalty, security, contentment
- Tied to tradition and lasting values
- Reduces blood pressure and pulse rate

Blue represents a conservative, secure, yet more vulnerable approach to information. Deep, dark blue is the color of the night sky. When you sleep, you're at peace with the world and most trustful in that vulnerable state.

Blue has a calming effect on the emotions and is useful for when you want to create a conservative or traditional impression. You can definitely put critical information on blue backgrounds. The blue helps to develop credibility with the audience, especially when you introduce data based on tested facts and figures rather than speculation.

A blue background also tends to make the statement "This is the worst-case scenario." It takes the "hype" out of the information and seeks to elicit an emotion of trust for the argument being presented.

Tip from *Tom Mucciolo*	When in doubt about colors, choose dark blue backgrounds with yellow and white shadowed text. This combination is the easiest to read from any distance.

GREEN

- Operation of the will
- Resistance to change
- Analytical, precise, accurate
- Opinionated and self-assertive
- Need to impress and exercise control

Green stimulates interaction because it represents the operation of the will. If you want to involve your audience in a discussion of the topic, you should use green backgrounds. Green brings out the opinions in people.

In fact, presentations requiring feedback such as management issues or policy decisions may be more effective when green is used in the background.

I would choose deep forest green or olive green or even a teal (blue-green) background in those situations. Avoid very bright green because foreground colors such as yellow or white will not contrast enough to be seen.

RED

- Impact of the will
- Impulse, desire, passion
- Vitality and intensity of experience
- Urge to achieve results and succeed
- Increases blood pressure and pulse rate

A red background is stimulating. Red is a warm color, and warmer colors are linked to arousal of emotion. In presentations that seek to heighten the emotions of the audience, such as sales or marketing events, or for any situations that strive to motivate the audience to action, choose a red background.

Since red is the warmest color of the spectrum, the tendency is for the eye to move toward red more quickly than other colors. This eye movement is most evident with foreground elements, such as a red slice in a pie chart.

From a background perspective, when you look at the color red, your pulse rate increases. You can keep looking at red and keep liking it. You see this in advertising all the time. What color is the fast car, the woman's dress, the uniform of the guy shooting the basket?

Typically, it's red. Red backgrounds tend to be stimulating for the audience and can lead to a heightened sense of realism about the topic, even to the point of increasing enthusiasm. Want to pump up that sales meeting? Go red!

The intensity of the red you choose is important. I suggest you stick to the darker shades such as maroon or crimson as opposed to fire engine red or bright cherry red. It's better to tone down the intensity of the red and use a dark contrast for readability.

BLACK

- Negation of emotions
- Extinction and nothingness
- Surrender and relinquishment
- Powerful, strong, uncontrollable
- Stubborn protest against current state

Black is the absence of all light. This contrast is what makes black such a powerful color (or should I say non-color?). Because black absorbs all light, anything on a black background will appear closer to the eye than the background itself. An object reflecting more light appears closer to the eye than an object reflecting less light.

Because black reflects no light, it offers no emotional stimulus. When the emotional response to a color is removed, the reaction is one of surrender or relinquishment, as in having no other choice. This can be a very effective tool.

Information on a black background leaves the audience feeling it has no choice on how to react to the data. It exists as it is, and the audience can do nothing about it. Thus, black is usually associated with things that have already occurred and will not change. Financial presentations, especially those filled with a lot of accounting data, are usually best represented on a black background since the data cannot be changed; it has already happened.

VIOLET

- Mystical union
- Magical and enchanting
- Unimportant and unrealistic
- Irresponsible and immature
- Attempts to charm or delight others

Also called purple or magenta, violet is a color that represents something magical or mystical. Violet is the mixture of red and blue, and the result is fantasy. Red and blue are opposites in emotional appeal and for those two colors to get along—that has to be fantasy!

Because purple is more charming, it is also adolescent and somewhat childlike. This is a tough background color to use for critical business information. For one thing, the data might be viewed as unimportant or unrealistic, and second, those who suffer from a red/green deficiency would see the violet background color as a washed-out shade of blue—a color that cannot be easily recognized, named, or judged.

If the viewer can't understand the color, the information carries less importance.

If your objective is to entertain or to amuse, a violet background is great for less critical information such as humor, special effects, or even for the awards dinner presentation at the annual company meeting.

BROWN

- Reduced sense of vitality
- Passive, receptive, sensory
- Establishment of a foundation
- Increased need for physical ease
- Desire for family, a home, solid roots

Pure brown is the search for something permanent to plant your feet on. Brown suggests a need to build a solid foundation that currently doesn't exist. Brown is the mix of red and green, and it creates an uneasy physical condition by toning down the sense of energy that red usually gives.

This reduced intensity makes brown seem more passive. For that reason, I would avoid using pure brown as a business background, especially for critical business information. The data on a brown background may be interpreted as "not standing on solid ground," hence, less credible and somewhat unstable, not the best choice for gaining the support of your audience.

Now the people at UPS hate me.

KEEPING IT IN PERSPECTIVE

The support of your message with well-designed media provides the springboard to the delivery skills you'll use to inspire an audience.

A visual presenter constantly strives to stimulate the audience in as many different ways as possible. Whether it is background colors, eye movement, or a well-placed graphic, the presenter works with the message through the media to get the audience to react.

Although the information in this chapter may appear to be comprehensive, the good news is that if you simply maintain a consistency in layout and design, you'll end up with clear, concise visuals that do what they are supposed to do—support the speaker.

TROUBLESHOOTING

USING A COMPANY LOGO...OR NOT

How important is it to have the company logo on each visual?

In the past, when presentation visuals were prepared mostly by outside services, some slides and transparencies would get mixed up among clients. Sometimes this happened during the mounting of slides or during the printing and collating of the transparencies. Putting the company logo on each individual slide or transparency decreased the likelihood of this. However, for electronic images there is no need to identify each image with the company to keep them intact. A filename and a storage location are all you need to know to identify the owner of the visuals. One approach to this is to decide whether your visual content is *hard* (slides, overheads, print materials, flip charts) or *soft* (electronic images, videotapes, Web sites, software applications). If it's hard, put the logo on each component that can be separated from another component, such as each page of a multipage handout. If the content is soft, the logo makes sense on the first visual or at the very beginning of the electronic event.

Some argue that the company logo on every visual acts as a reminder to the audience. If your audience doesn't know what company you're with by the fourth visual, the logo isn't going to save you. Anything on a visual that doesn't add to its value is a distraction. Some say that after a while the audience doesn't notice the logo, which proves it's not necessary. When you are watching TV, how do you feel when the little transparent logo of the TV station in the right corner stays on the screen?

CHAPTER 24

THE MECHANICS OF FORM— DEVELOPING EXTERNAL PRESENTATION SKILLS

In this chapter   *by Tom Mucciolo*

UNDERSTANDING EXTERNAL PRESENTATION SKILLS

"It's not what you say, it's how you say it!" We've all heard that before. And it's especially true when making a presentation.

A study of relationships found that 55% of everything you say is what you look like when you say it. Another 38% is how you actually deliver the information. And only 7% is what you say. Only 7%! You might say this is a measurement derived from personal relationships and not business ones. I say our personal and business lives are so interrelated that it's hard to separate them. To me, this says that the biggest part of communication is nonverbal.

> **Note**
>
> The referenced study is from work done by Albert Mehrabian, Ph.D., and Professor Emeritus of Psychology, UCLA. Dr. Mehrabian is known for his work in the field of non-verbal communication, particularly body language. His findings on communication are described in his book, *Silent Messages*, which deals with all facets of nonverbal communication and with combinations of verbal and nonverbal messages. The book contains reviews of Dr. Mehrabian's own and others' research findings on important elements of subtle or implicit communication. Communicators, leadership trainers, and political campaign managers often make use of these findings.
>
> Dr. Mehrabian specifically notes, "The equations regarding differential importance of verbal and nonverbal messages were derived from experiments dealing with communications about feelings. Unless a communicator is talking about (his) feelings or attitudes, these equations are not applicable."
>
> In our discussions, feeling is definitely an issue. From a visual presenter's perspective, the emotional link to an audience is critical for an effective delivery of nearly every message and makes this study especially relevant to what is covered in this section of the book. Thank you, Dr. Mehrabian!

Here's more proof: You can speak up to 150 words per minute, but you can listen to over 700 words per minute. Do the math and you'll find that more than 75% of the time you are processing nonverbal cues. These cues are important.

Regardless of the exact percentages, the bottom line is that delivery skills make or break the moment. This is not to say that content needs to be ignored, of course. We just spent two chapters on content! That would be like saying that a playwright's words are meaningless. Not at all. But it is true that the success of the spoken lines depends on the actors.

A Delicate Balance?

I work on a theatre principle called "off-balance" perspective. I apply this view to the message, the media, and most often to the mechanics of a presentation. The off-balance approach is a one-sided push for consistency. If I can shift your position to one side (off-balance), then I've made some change in you.

Your "position" might be your stance on a message. It might be your way of looking at visual content on the screen. It might be your view of the presenter in the room.

It actually matches the rule of thirds in photography. If you look at a framed image in three vertical sections, you should use the outer sections for the subject. In other words, when you take pictures, try not to center your subject. The image is more interesting because a bigger picture emerges for the viewer's eye to complete. This is not always done, but if you glance through magazine photos, you'll notice that most shots of people have them positioned more to one side than the other.

This off-balance approach is very effective. I use it often in developing, designing, and delivering presentations.

The actions of the presenter, from a physical and vocal standpoint, can add value to the visuals and make the entire event more effective. During a presentation, the brain must process a large amount of content. Therefore, the presentation needs to be as streamlined and effective as possible—that is, clear, concise, and to the point.

Now you know that the greatest percentage of your communication effort is physical. It is a combination of your visual and vocal delivery. You need to develop the related skills to become a more visual presenter. But visual and vocal skills are directly linked to the way you think and feel. Your mind and heart play a significant role in your delivery style, just as your body and your voice do.

Through all of this, don't forget to smile. If you're not having a good time presenting, how can anyone have a good time watching? This doesn't mean that you have to tell jokes all the time, but the presenter has more impact with an inside smile. It's called energy. Without this energy, your speaking will be flat, uninteresting, and definitely less effective. It only takes two muscles to smile. Try it.

The mechanics of delivery are partly external (form) and partly internal (function). That's why two chapters are dedicated to these mechanical skills.

Let's start with the external skills, the mechanics of form, because your form is the first impression processed by the audience. The skills covering external form involve conquering the fear, using your body, and using your voice.

CONQUERING FEAR

According to the *Book of Lists*, the number one fear is the fear of public speaking. This eclipses even the fear of death! Wait a minute—if the number one fear is public speaking and not death, it means you'd rather be in the coffin than give the eulogy!

Call it nervousness, call it stage fright, call it whatever you want. If you can't speak in front of a group, you won't get very far in the business world. I'm probably not the first to tell you that. If you have no problem speaking in front of people, then skip this section. But if you have some anxiety when it comes to presenting to groups, pay close attention. Some powerful techniques can help you deal with being scared speechless.

So what gives? Does your fear increase as the next person enters the room? Why does the anxiety level rise in proportion to the number of people in the audience? What really causes this fear? You might think it's a simple lack of confidence. That, however, is just a symptom of a disease for which we need a cure! The fear is actually rooted in your physical presence in the situation. Think about it: If you didn't have to be there, you wouldn't have any fear!

Suppose you split communication into three types: written, spoken, and face-to-face. Match those with the way you work. You create documents such as letters, faxes, and e-mails for the written word. You use telephones and voice mail for conversational correspondence. You have meetings and presentations for the face-to-face method of communicating. Only one of these (face-to-face) requires your complete presence. The other two physically hide you from the receiver of the information.

When you write, you have time to edit and restate your words until you are ready to send them out for response. When you speak on the phone, you have less time to edit, but you are free to sit comfortably, and it doesn't matter how you may be dressed or how you look. In fact, the telephone demands very little effort, especially now that you can screen calls, invent interruptions, and use the ever-handy hold button. Even voice mail gives you a chance to plan your response in advance. These two methods of communicating are less stressful simply because we can't be seen for who we really are at the moment, and we get more time to collect our thoughts. When we are less visible, we have less fear. It's that simple. This protection from people helps get through the communication effort with ease.

So let's take a look at the major problems associated with your physical presence in a situation. You can conquer the fear of presenting in two ways—attacking the causes and learning to relax.

ATTACKING THE CAUSES

Over the years I have found four main reasons why people fear public speaking: looking foolish, being judged, appearing boring, and wasting the listener's time. Possibly hundreds of other reasons exist, but these four usually cover most people's fears.

When you examine these reasons, do you see what they have in common? Each is a result of being self-conscious. It becomes a question of "What will they think of me?" The focus of the problem is internal. It is self-directed.

So here is a good rule to remember: When the problem is internal, the solution is external. You need to concentrate on things outside of yourself in order to remove the doubt. This concentration always involves some type of action. Let's examine the four problems I mentioned earlier and see what solutions—or actions—can be used to combat the dreaded fear of presenting in public.

FOOLS RUSH IN

"I'm afraid that people will think I'm stupid!" I hear this one a lot when people discuss their anxiety concerning public speaking. First I ask, "Are you stupid?" And only the really stupid people take a moment to think about that one. Hey, everyone is stupid at times. Look at me. I'm one of the stupidest people I know. There are hundreds of people who will testify to that. But, then again, I hang around with a lot of stupid people who can't tell the difference. Then, when I'm with the really smart people, all 10 of them, I use the skills in this section of the book to mask my ignorance!

Forrest Gump said that "Stupid is as stupid does"—a brilliant statement about actions speaking louder than words. If you do something crazy, others might think you really are crazy!

For many people, the typical uneasiness of speaking in public comes from this fear of looking foolish. What would cause that? Are you poorly dressed? Have you prepared your information? Are you speaking from a script you honestly believe has merit? Looking foolish is a feeling you get when you don't have as much control of the content as you want to have.

It's no different from the feeling you had in school when the teacher called on you and you didn't give the correct response. You were embarrassed. You didn't have the answer, and you looked stupid! But if you knew the content—and hence the answer—you felt exactly the opposite. Your first action is to get control of content. If you do this, your fear will begin to disappear.

Although you might think that content is controlled though memorization, that is not the case at all. The best way to get control of content is first to conceptualize your information, and then visualize the manner in which that information will be delivered.

→ To learn about conceptualizing and visualizing information, **see** "Providing 'Do' and 'Say' Scripts" in Chapter 22, "The Message—Scripting the Concept."

PART

VII

CH

24

You need to script your message using concepts that link together to form the discussion or the argument. Normally, written scripts, or Say scripts, force you simply to read back the content without really knowing it. Conceptual scripts, or Do scripts, are those that segment the topic into main ideas, each of which has some associated action. The action helps you remember the concept and allows you to present without any notes.

When you link action to your words, you visualize the concept for the audience. Once you have obvious control of content, you won't be singing the "I'm feeling foolish" theme anymore.

JUDGMENT DAY

Another reason you might dread public speaking is the belief that the audience is judging you. What could possibly motivate a group of people to dislike you the moment you step in front of them? Why would such a group suddenly unite in the hopes of squashing you like a bug? What would they gain? Always remember that the audience is made up of people like you. The key to that statement can be found by changing the emphasis. People like you. They do.

When you meet someone for the first time, don't you hope the meeting is positive? You're basically the same as everyone else in the world, and everyone wants to make a positive impression with each new person he meets. Before you open your mouth, the audience starts off by liking you.

Of course, some preexisting situations can cause the audience to not like you. If the circumstances are hostile, negative, or life threatening, then the audience is preconditioned to feel a certain way before seeing you. Otherwise, the audience is on your side. They want you to be effective.

Tip from
Tom Mucciolo

Here's a test you can use to see if the way you judge others has merit: Every time you make a subjective statement using the word "they" or "people," simply substitute the word "I" and see if the statement is still true. Try it.

Say the phrase, "People just don't understand this business." Now substitute "I" for "People" and say it again. Notice a difference? Try the phrase, "They don't care about anything," and then change "They" to "I." Using "I" changes your perception and, hence, the acceptance of the statement as being true. You can't separate yourself from the world. You are an integral part of it.

Think of yourself as a mirror and you will get back what you project to others. In the-ater, acting is reacting. The same is true in life. If you offer a positive, nonjudgmental attitude, it truly does come back to you.

To reduce the fear that people are judging you, just believe in people as you do yourself. Approach an audience with the belief that they are just like you and that they just like you. This will begin to reduce the anxiety of feeling that you are being judged in a bad way.

Okay, time for a reality check. Unfortunately, it is very difficult to remove completely the fear of being judged by simply believing the audience likes you. This may work during the 15 minutes prior to stepping onto the platform, but what happens when you look out into the room and see all those expectant faces?

To overcome the inner feeling of being judged, you'll have to concentrate on something outside of yourself, some action or activity to get your mind off the anxiety. To avoid being judged, you need to become a judge. You can do this by focusing on the anchors in the audience.

Simply select a few people in the room to focus your attention on while speaking. These friendly faces, or anchors, are points of concentration that you must continually seek. This removes the feeling of being judged as you present and puts the judgmental responsibility on you. You are forced to judge whether those anchors are staying attentive, still interested, and still maintaining eye contact with you. In other words, your action is to judge others as to their attentiveness to the message. This will push you to make the effort to keep them awake! If you're doing the judging, then the fear of being judged is transferred to the audience.

THE BORED ROOM

"The stuff I have to talk about is so boring." I hear this a lot, especially from accountants. I used be a public accountant, and I found it to be the best training for a life of crime. That's a lie. Political science is the best training for a life of crime. Accounting is the best training for a life of full employment! But that's another story.

The fear is that your presentation will be boring because the topic is boring. That might be true, depending on your topic. After all, not every topic needs to be delivered as a live pre-sentation. However, the topic is usually not the problem when a speaker fails to capture the attention of the audience. When you finish, if the audience responds with a nice round of indifference, chances are *you* were the problem, not the content.

To combat a boring topic, you need to find significance. The action is to convey the importance of the topic. Look for a sense of urgency. The more you identify the critical components of your script, the more determined you become to discuss those components and get reactions from your audience. Reactions reduce boredom and give the audience something to do.

I'll use the accounting example. A monthly budget report might seem a bit mundane. But suppose you link budget information to ways that money will be allocated to make some specific task easier for everyone. Maybe the budget for computer networking can be increased. No big deal, unless you make it a big deal. If you point out that faster file transfers will reduce waiting time, in one sentence you go from lowly accountant to giver of free time! You can't do this all the time, but if you can connect parts of your message to the needs or desires of the audience, boredom will not be your problem.

TIME FLIES

"I think I'm just wasting everyone's time when I'm up there." This is another anxiety producer.

The feeling of wasting time may come over you during the presentation more often than before it. Suddenly you have an instant loss of confidence, and you can't find a compelling enough reason to ask a group of people to continue to watch and listen to you.

Do you see the problem here? Wasting time can happen only if there is time to waste. It's the opposite problem of being boring. People are bored by monotony and too much of the same thing. Wasting time is when you don't have enough relevant stuff to say.

Believe it or not, the structure of your script might cause you to try to fill up the time. Just because you have an extra 15 minutes doesn't mean you must fill it with poor content. You have to make the best use of time in order to reduce the fear of having wasted it. In some cases, that might even mean letting people leave early. Perish the thought!

The easiest way to make the best use of time is with a form of action known as *interaction*. You can manage your time better by involving the audience throughout the presentation. This requires you to plan ahead, think quickly on your feet, ask questions, stir discussion, and even create controversy. Naturally, this shifts the concentration from yourself to your audience because you have to monitor their involvement. Activities that help audiences experience new things are seen as positive and not perceived as wasted time.

Instead of just planning time for the audience to ask you questions, plan time for you to ask them questions. Be proactive—come up with thought-provoking ideas to stimulate discussion. Not only do you involve people in the topic, you learn from the experience, too. This type of involvement helps reduce the fear that you are wasting the listener's time.

If you can't fill the time with enough information of your own, maybe the audience can help you. Again, you need to redirect the fear inside of you by placing the problem outside of yourself. Hand over to the audience the task of not wasting time. Believe me, they'll perk up.

LEARNING TO RELAX

Some say the nervousness before a performance is both natural and necessary. I say it might be natural, but it is certainly not necessary. If you can reduce a case of the jitters before a presentation, you will be able to deliver your message more effectively. One way to do this is to learn to relax physically. Of course, a limber body is always more relaxed under any pressure. Stretching exercises and aerobic activities, among many other benefits, definitely will help you relax when giving a presentation.

As I mentioned, one way you can help yourself prepare for those opening moments is with some kind of physical exercise beforehand, such as stretching or even something more strenuous. Another way to reduce the adrenaline rush and rapid heartbeat is to create other activity for yourself. For example, you can take a few slow, deep breaths before you begin. This increases the amount of oxygen in the system, but it reduces the heart rate before the adrenaline kicks in. More importantly, taking a few deep breaths gives you something to do, which takes the focus away from thinking about your presentation.

Once you start speaking, you may still experience some jitters. You can still create an external action—something to do to reduce the nerves—without the audience being aware of it. You might try wiggling your toes in your shoes. No one sees this, and your concentration again becomes focused on some physical action. Maybe your mouth becomes dry. No, you can't take a drink of water, but you can bite down slightly on the outer edges of your tongue or on the insides of your cheeks to create saliva and keep your mouth moist.

Again, you simply need to do something physical to reduce the internal nervousness, anxiety, and fear through external means. When the problem is inside, the solution is outside. The goal is to redirect your attention away from the internal workings of the mind onto things that are external to you.

The more you concentrate on actions, the less chance you have of being self-conscious, which ultimately creates nervousness. So take a few deep breaths, wiggle your toes, and start talking!

USING YOUR BODY

Keep in mind that eliminating the fear doesn't mean you automatically will present well. That's the same as being unafraid to sing, but not knowing how to hit the right notes.

You can't present well because you haven't learned the rules. You don't know how to play the game because no one taught you. This is completely understandable. I was the same way. Then I learned to play the game.

The only way to develop a method or systematic approach to any skill is to agree on the parameters that make that skill achievable. In this section, you learn to build a concrete foundation from which to work. With a core set of guidelines, you remain consistent from one presentation to the next, regardless of the content.

POSITIONING AND MOVING

The first thing you have to learn is your relationship to the room. The physical space you occupy must be subject to your control. Like the home-field advantage in sports, if you know the space and feel comfortable within it, you can achieve your goal and deliver a more effective message.

For presentations, understanding the layout of the room, especially the size, the distance from the group, and the placement of the screen (visuals) is very important. All these things will change from place to place, and you might have to make adjustments to get the room situated comfortably for you and your audience.

You want to develop a consistent behavior, regardless of the physical attributes of the room. These universal concepts will help you in every presentation situation because you can control all of them, at any time.

ESTABLISHING AN ANCHOR

When presenting with visual support, you need to set an anchor for the audience to watch and read. Anchor your body to the same side as the starting point to read the language (that is, left-to-right or right-to-left).

For presentations in English (and many other languages), you must stand on the left side of the room (from the audience's point of view). In the English language, we read words from left to right. The eye is less distracted if it sees the presenter speaking from the left, glancing slightly to the right to read the visual, then naturally returning left to view the speaker again, as in the act of reading.

If you stand on the opposite side (the audience's right), the audience has to look at you, then navigate left across the visual to find the beginning of the text, and then read just to get back to you. This extra step is a distraction and a waste of time. Listening is delayed, and effectiveness is reduced.

If you were in Israel (where you read words from right to left), you could be on the other side; in the United States, we read words from left to right, so stand on the audience's left when presenting. This is the way to establish an anchor for the audience, because it matches the reading pattern they're used to.

Note

If you have no visuals, it doesn't matter which side of the room you present from, as long as people can see and hear you. However, it is always better to choose a side and remain in that area.

Off-center is always a good choice because a centered presenter ends up having to work twice as hard by shifting and moving to both sides of the room. The one-sided approach sets a positioning anchor for the audience, which is less distracting, if it is constant and unchanging.

PART

VII

CH

24

You want to present from the side of the room that matches the reading pattern of the language, but don't worry if you get stuck on the opposite side of the room. You should try to avoid it, but you never know what you might be faced with when you haven't set things up yourself. If you have to present from the wrong side, just make fewer references to your visuals during the presentation to limit the distraction for the audience. Naturally you won't be as effective as you could be, but you won't necessarily walk away a failure, either.

BUILDING A TRIANGLE

The biggest problem for most presenters is moving. They have no idea where they are going, and they never really think about it.

Can you imagine if actors had no idea where to go? The actor playing Hamlet would say, "To be or not to be—whoops, oh sorry, Dave didn't see your foot!" as he pulled himself from the floor.

The only way to know how or when to move is first to know where to move. An easy way to learn this is to design an area in front of the audience in which you can move. It's called the *Presenter's Triangle*. It's imaginary because you must create it.

Figure 24.1 shows the triangle. While standing at a fixed distance from your display equipment, construct an imaginary line from the eyes of the person sitting on your far right to the left edge of the screen. This line becomes the long end of the triangle, an angled wall. From each end of this angled wall, draw two lines meeting at a 90-degree angle to complete the shape behind you. Now you are standing inside an imaginary triangle.

The most important point to remember is that the angled wall is a boundary you cannot penetrate. If you step through the wall, people on your right will not be able to see the screen.

Figure 24.1
A top-down view of the Presenter's Triangle.

Note

Naturally, the illustration suggests you position yourself at a fixed distance from any display equipment. If you are using transparencies or are seated at a keyboard, the triangle option is limited to those times when you take a position that does not block the view of anyone. This is another reason why presenting with overheads is so difficult. The line of sight from the audience to the visual is broken for some people.

Okay, here's the good news. There are only three positions of the triangle that your body ever has to occupy—the front, the middle, and the back.

Figure 24.2 shows a close-up view of the triangle with the three positions noted. The front is closer to the audience, the middle is where you should be most of the time, and the back is much closer to the screen. You will never use the full area of the triangle, unless you feel like hiding in the far corner (the shaded area) for some reason. Actually, you are really presenting from inside a corridor within the triangle. You simply move along this little hallway, which follows the path of the angled wall.

PART

VII

CH

24

Figure 24.2
A close-up view of the triangle.

Why are there three positions? Because you have to move. You need to change the position of your body every so often or people won't watch you. If your body is not adding value for the audience, then they have less reason to watch you present the information. If you don't move, then it's talk radio. The audience will spend less time looking at you and more time updating their daily planners.

Does Size Matter?

The dimension of your space is based on the distance from the screen to the first row of chairs. At times you might have a 25-foot area to move around in. Other times, you might have only a few feet between the first seat and the screen.

For example, in a conference room you might have only a few steps between both ends of your triangle. But there is always a triangle, even if the only way to change between positions is to shift your weight. Your body must make visible changes based on the available space in order for the audience to pay attention.

Size doesn't matter for the triangle to exist. However, the more area available to you, the longer it will take to get to different spots. This will have some effect on your delivery. You'll want to make your key points when standing still for more impact. Thus, a larger triangle will force you to create additional words or phrases between those key points to fill naturally the moments needed to move to a new position.

All you have to do is treat the three positions of the triangle like stopping points. You move to these points periodically, but with authority, remembering to stop and remain in a particular position for a while as you speak. You don't want to appear to be running back and forth, meandering aimlessly, drifting from place to place for no apparent reason. Just as you don't add punctuation after every sentence or a pause after each word, you don't want to overdo and have constant movement while you present.

You might be wondering when to use the front, middle, and back of the triangle. Here's a guide. Choose the back of the triangle when the visual is complex. A busy visual forces the audience to keep looking at it. If your body is closer to the screen (the back of the triangle), then there is less distance for the audience to look between your visual and your voice. You don't want people moving their heads back and forth like they're at a tennis match.

Choose the middle of the triangle for the majority of the talk. Think of the middle as the launching pad to move in either direction. It's the midpoint between two extremes.

Use the front of the triangle when your visuals are less busy and you want to be closer to the audience. A simple visual enables the audience to reference it fewer times. This means you can be farther from the screen.

Here's one more point to consider about position. If you want to convince an audience with a key point, which do you think would be most effective: to be in the front, middle, or back of the triangle? Obviously it's the front, where you're closer to the people. That is one of the most valuable lessons of all—choreography drives content, not the other way around. Decide where you want to be at certain points in the presentation and then look at the visual. Does its format enable you to be in that spot? If not, then change the visual.

If you want to emphasize an important point when you move to the front of the triangle, your visual content needs to be simple. If the image is cluttered, half the audience will still be reading while you're addressing the major issue. Change the visual to suit your movement.

Don't let content be your guide. Simply decide where you want to be on a given visual and adjust the complexity of the image according to your position in the triangle.

The triangle is important because it represents part of your physical plan of action. Without some definite planned movement, you end up wandering aimlessly, giving the audience no reason or logic for the direction. Don't forget that the audience is processing your body language more than your visuals or your voice.

PLAY THE ANGLES

While there are only three places to move in the triangle, there are only two body positions you have to worry about. All the power in your presentation rests in your shoulders. The angles of your body enhance communication. Figure 24.3 shows the two body positions or angles used in presenting: rest and power. For most of your talk, you should be at a 45° angle to the room. To create the angle, point your shoulders to the opposite corner of the room. This is a rest position. It's a non-threatening stance that opens your body to both the audience and the screen when you need to gesture or move.

Figure 24.3
You should be concerned about only two body positions: rest and power.

After you establish the rest position, you can use the power of your left shoulder. The shoulder farthest from the audience is always your power shoulder. Because you are on the left side of the room, the power comes from what you do with your left shoulder.

To get power, simply square your shoulders to the back wall of the room. Each time you turn your left shoulder toward the audience, you move into a power position. This signals that the information being communicated is of greater importance. But don't stay in that stance too long or the effectiveness of your words and actions will diminish. Constantly staying in the power position is the body's way of yelling. That's why the rest position is so important.

So, if you plan it right, you can choose the exact moments to add impact to the presentation by switching to the power position from any of the three places in the triangle.

For example, let's say you have 20 minutes to present. You start off in the middle of the triangle in a rest position. On a particularly busy visual, you navigate to the back of the triangle, closer to the screen, but still in a rest position. From that same spot, you square off to a power position just long enough to make a key point, and then you revert to the rest position as you continue. Later in your presentation you might navigate to the front of the triangle to get closer to the audience. You're discussing an experience related to the topic and, at a high point in the story, you square off for impact.

Wait, relax, calm down—you don't have to plan a move for every spoken word. But, if you practice, just like an athlete, the "moves" of your body will develop automatically. If you can get used to being a visual presenter, using the positions of the triangle and angles of the body will add enormous value to your presentation.

MAKING EYE CONTACT

How do you please the crowd? You look at them. It is easy to do. Effective presenters look at people and make eye contact. This is critical to the communication process, especially to a group of visual creatures—the audience. The less time you spend looking at people, the less effective you are going to be.

The Eyes Have It!

When you watch TV, you are constantly exposed to eye contact. Think about it. The newscasters are looking right at you, with the help of a TelePrompTer, of course. I don't understand why they have to use a teleprompter. Why can't they just memorize the news the day before?

Anyway, they make constant eye contact. Characters on TV shows don't look at you, but they look at each other.

Let's face it. We all watch a lot of movies and TV and are used to the idea of continual eye contact. As a visual presenter, you must not fight the expectation that a group is made up mostly of eye-contact hounds.

DIRECT EYE CONTACT

Direct eye contact is easier in a smaller group, simply because you have fewer faces to find. In a conference room with 10 people, for example, it will be easy to look at every person in the room at one time or another during your presentation. In a large audience, say 50 or more people, you can make direct eye contact with several people, but probably not everyone.

If you're afraid to make direct eye contact, here's a trick: You don't have to look directly into a person's eyes. Instead, you can look between the eyes and, from a distance, it looks like you're making eye contact. Just look at the spot where the bridge of the nose meets the eyebrows, and it will seem as if you are looking directly into that person's eyes.

ANCHORED EYE CONTACT

What's the highest number of people you feel comfortable presenting to? Usually there's a number. Suppose your number is 25. Then let's say that one more person walks in the room.

Do you suddenly stop, throw your hands in the air, and shout, "Hey you—out. Twenty-five is my limit."

That the limit is in your imagination doesn't change the fact that a larger group may intimidate you. Your "crowd alarm" goes off because you haven't established anchors in the audience with whom to make eye contact.

During a presentation, your eyes occasionally leave the audience, perhaps for a quick glance to your visual. When your eyes look away and then return to the audience, you suddenly see thousands of eyes staring back at you and—zap!—you lose your train of thought. You forget the next phrase because the group temporarily distracted you.

If you have identified specific people in the crowd, a few friendly faces in separate areas of the audience, then you have a better chance of staying focused. If you look away for a moment, when you look back you will be able to seek out those individuals and make anchored eye contact with any one of those friendly faces.

The anchors you select in the audience should be far enough apart that it looks as if you are speaking to whole sections, even though your eyes are fixed on one person within that section. Split the audience up into a few big areas, maybe two on one side, two on the other, one down the middle, and pick out a single face in each area as your anchor. Then, when you turn away, the next look back will find an anchor instead of having the entire group overwhelm you. Think of it as presenting to just a few people who happen to have lots of other people sitting around them. This way, you maintain your concentration and you don't feel intimidated.

After you have found your anchors, any direct eye contact with other individuals is even more effective. If you've been looking into sections of the audience and then suddenly lock your eyes onto one particular person (not one of your anchors), it will be extremely powerful, especially for that person. It's as if you made personal contact with that individual, as if you singled out someone in the audience, making that person feel special.

You may have experienced this yourself. If you've ever gone to a play or a concert, and the performer suddenly makes direct eye contact with you, it's something you never forget. The more eye contact you make with people, the more involved in the presentation they become.

Using Gestures

What do dance, ballet, mime, and most every sport have in common? They all require the use of the hands. Presenting is no different because your hands control the eyes of the audience. What you do or don't do with your hands when you present makes a huge difference. Unfortunately, most presenters simply don't know what to do with those things at the ends of their wrists.

At times during your presentation, you'll have to guide the eyes of your audience toward your visual. Letting the audience look where they want is one thing, but it's more effective if they look where you want.

Never hide your hands behind your back or inside your pockets. Avoid putting your hands together in front of you for more than three seconds. When your hands stay together for even those few moments of time, the audience tends to look at them and not at your face. Always remember, the eyes travel wherever the hands go. Keep your hands apart but always visible.

> **Note**
>
> When you're nervous, your hands tend to join together, folded in front of you, doing nothing. Because you're a mammal, you have no skeleton in the center of your body, so you tend to protect that area by letting your hands rest together in front of you. You never see anyone with his hands on top of his shoulders saying, "Boy, am I nervous!" Hands clasped in front or locked behind your back indicate nervousness and reduce your effectiveness.

If you aren't making any gestures, return to a simple position with your hands at your sides. If your hands are up, waist high, then avoid bringing them together.

If you are not elevated on a stage or standing on a platform when you speak, gestures are harder to see for everyone except the people in the front seats. For those viewing you from the waist up, keep your wrists higher than your elbows so that gestures are visible. Always be aware of those sitting behind others and the view they might have of you while you speak. Gestures with your wrists lower than your elbows will generally go unnoticed and create little impact or meaning.

If used properly, the hands can orchestrate the eyes of the audience. Casual or emphatic gestures made to the screen or to the audience can create visual inflection. This helps the group recognize what is important. You can use a number of gestures with your hands and with your body that can help make your message more meaningful.

REACHING OUT

The best gesture you can make as a presenter is reaching out. The palm of your hand facing up as your arm extends out to the audience is a very friendly move and can be done with one or both hands. When you reach out to the audience, you appear as if you want them involved in the event. The palm-up and arm-out gesture is generally pleasing to the eye and indicates a warmth of expression for the presenter.

Think about your everyday actions in business. When you greet a person in business, you shake hands by extending your arm with your hand open (an exposed palm). You are reaching out to that person. You might shake hands as a greeting, a parting, or as a result of an agreement.

You can shake hands with the audience by reaching out to them. You reach out to the group as a way of greeting them, parting with them, or bringing them into agreement with you. Just because there's more than one person in the room doesn't mean your personal interactive skills suddenly disappear. When you reach out to the audience, you become more approachable and ultimately more effective.

The reaching-out gesture also works best when you interact with the audience, especially in a question-answer situation. If someone asks a question, reach out to acknowledge that person, but don't stop there. Keep your arm outstretched with your palm up until the person begins to speak, and then casually pull back your arm, almost as if catching the first syllable in your hand.

If you don't leave your arm extended until you get the beginning of a response, you end up with the opposite effect, a gesture that suggests insincerity or indifference. It's called the "Like I Care" gesture. You've seen it. The presenter flings a hand at a person while asking a question, as if to say, "Yeah, right, like I care about your answer." Don't start tossing your limbs at people and then expect interaction.

Tip from
Tom Mucciolo

> The reaching-out technique works best for the first question asked. After you set the stage for a nice way of interacting, the audience will be more inclined to ask additional questions.

USING THE LEFT HAND

Your left hand provides most of the guidance for the audience. If you recall, the screen is always to the presenter's left for languages that read left to right. If you want to guide the eye to the screen, simply lift your left arm and use your left hand to motion slowly in the general direction of the visual. This indicates that the group should glance at the image, but they should remain more focused on you. However, if you raise your left arm and dart your left hand quickly toward the screen, the more emphatic movement tells the audience that the content has more importance.

Tip from
Tom Mucciolo

> If you gesture to the screen and keep looking at the audience, the group has a choice to focus on the screen or on you. This is because you are facing them and, technically, so is your visual. If you turn your head to look at the screen as you gesture toward it, you force the audience to focus more on the visual than on you.

The left hand can also help you move through the triangle. You can walk toward the audience with no gesture, but you can't walk backward without an excuse. The audience needs a reason for any movement away from them. If the body retreats, it is a sign of distrust; it indicates that you are not telling the truth or that you are unsure of your accuracy. You appear to be backing away from the issue.

How do you get from the front of the triangle to the middle or back without retreating? You retreat—with a reason—by using your left hand. If you gesture to the visual while navigating backward through the triangle, the audience accepts the movement because you are gesturing. They allow your retreat because you had to back up to gesture to the screen.

Justifying Movement

The audience needs a reason for your moving away from them. Your gesture to the screen is that reason. But only you need a reason to move toward the audience. Typically, this requires no gestures, just movement. Your reason is to get closer to them. In both cases you have justification for the movement in either direction.

What if you have to move sideways? What if you have to break the triangle and cross to the other side of the room? The only reason to do this must be to get to a visible reference. Most likely that reference is a prop. You cross the room to get something to incorporate into the presentation at that moment.

Of course, if you don't need the item, you can gesture to it without crossing the room. However, if you know you are going to need a prop, you should place it closer to you before you begin your presentation so you don't have to cross the room to get it.

Tip from

Tom Mucciolo

Leaving your left hand in the air can help with the pacing of the presentation. How? When you gesture toward the visual and leave your arm extended, the next time you glance back at the image, you can turn your wrist slightly until the face of your watch is visible as you look over the top of your hand. Now you'll know what time it is, and you can adjust your pacing if necessary. Of course, your watch must be on your left arm for this to work. It's also best to wear an analog watch with a contrasting face and visible hands. A digital watch might not be as easy to read, especially if the lighting in the room is dim.

SHIFTING YOUR WEIGHT

When you are not gesturing, your hands should be at your sides and always visible. The eyes travel wherever the hands go, so never hide your hands from the audience. When you are not gesturing, your feet should be shoulder-width apart, your elbows and knees unlocked, and your weight evenly distributed.

When your elbows and knees are unlocked, you have your best opportunity for movement. When you stand still, the tendency is to lock your knees and even your elbows. If your limbs are locked, you lose energy. If your limbs are unlocked, you unleash energy.

Center of Gravity

Men and women are different. I mean, in terms of the way they stand. Men have a higher center of gravity than women, located in the middle of the chest. A man tends to stand with his feet wider than his shoulders, for balance. For some reason, during the presentation his feet invariably will get farther apart, little by little. When his feet are spread too far apart, he is less likely to move and ends up in the same spot for the entire presentation. So a man should stand with his feet at the same width as his shoulders in order to make movement more likely.

Women have a lower center of gravity, closer to the hips. A woman tends to stand with her feet closer together, sometimes with the heels touching, for balance and posture. However, during a presentation a woman will often establish this position and lock into that one spot for the duration of the talk. If a woman keeps her feet shoulder-width apart, she is more likely to move at some point.

Movement is necessary, and gestures are important. You know this by now. However, if you want to use your hands and make all your gestures look natural, you need to shift your weight.

If both your heels are touching the floor, you can't gesture naturally. Instead, your gestures appear stiff. Stand up and try it. Rest your weight evenly on each foot with both heels on the floor. Now lift your left arm to gesture. Take a look in the mirror. You look stiff because your heels are touching the floor at the same time, and your weight is evenly distributed on each foot.

You have to learn to shift your weight, but first you must know the limits of your body to do the weight-shift thing properly. Stand up and place your feet at the width of your shoulders. Both heels should be on the floor and your weight distributed evenly between both feet. Now take a half-step to your left, just far enough for the opposite heel to lift off the floor. Feel that weight shift to your left foot? Okay, now shift your weight back onto the right foot until your left heel lifts off the floor. Now you know the limits of your body to make gestures look natural. The weight must be on one foot or the other for the gesture to look smooth.

Tip from *Tom Mucciolo*	The easiest way to know if you are shifting your weight properly is to keep the base of your neck lined up with the same foot you're placing your weight on (you could also line your chin up with your knee). Now you can gesture and it will look natural.
	If your neck is not lined up with one of your feet, then your weight is probably evenly distributed and you are most likely resting on both heels. If you gesture from this position, it will look unnatural.

Leaning Can Have Meaning!

Weight shifting combined with gestures can help make your message stand out. Depending on the direction you shift your weight, the effect can be quite dramatic.

For example, if you shift your weight to your left foot, toward the visual, while gesturing with your left hand, you are silently saying to the crowd, "Come with me and let's inspect this information." If you shift your weight to your right foot, away from the visual, while gesturing with your left hand, you are saying, "This information proves the point." It's like the magician who leans into the trick and then leans back to reveal the magic!

If you have a problem-solution script, you might want to lean toward a visual when identifying a specific problem and lean away from the visual when the solution is shown.

MASTERING THE LECTERN

A lectern is what you stand behind, and a podium is what you stand on. However, people use both terms to mean the same thing—a big box between you and the audience.

Actors don't have lecterns. If they did, you would think they didn't learn their lines. A politician giving a speech uses a lectern. Isn't he an actor using the words of a writer? Where do you draw the line?

The problem is that visual creatures expect eye contact. They get a lot of information from body language, gestures, and movement.

That's why the most difficult prop to overcome is the lectern. It covers 80% or more of your body and allows for little mobility. Although the lectern is a convenience to the speaker for reading a speech or for referring to notes, it allows much less direct eye contact with an audience.

As far as I'm concerned, lecterns have no place in the life of a visual presenter. Having said that, lecterns are still used quite a lot. How can you master the lectern if you get trapped behind one? You have a few options to help minimize your losses.

First, place the lectern at a 45-degree angle to the room if you can, matching the non-threatening rest position discussed earlier in this chapter. From that angle, both your hands can rest on or touch the lectern and you'll still be in a rest position. You can easily switch to a power position with just a turn of your upper body, leaving only your left hand resting on or touching the lectern.

If the lectern can't be angled but remains fixed and facing directly to the back wall, you can still use the rest and power positions. Assume the rest position (45-degree angle) while behind the lectern. Only your right hand touches or rests on the lectern until you switch to the power position (by squaring off to the back wall), at which point both hands can rest on or touch the lectern.

Make sure the audience sees your hands as much as possible. If you hide your hands, the interpretation is that you're hiding something. Don't let your hands disappear for too long, even if it is just to turn a page.

Even though you are stuck behind the lectern, the three positions of the triangle still exist for you to use. The middle of the triangle is when your weight is on both feet. Movement to the front or to the back happens by shifting your weight to one foot or the other. These slight changes in body position may help to keep the audience looking at you from time to time. Naturally, the lack of mobility and the fact that you are probably reading your speech or your notes limit effective communication.

Typically, the reason you use a lectern is to give a speech. The lectern supports the pages of the script while you deliver the speech. When you read, you make less eye contact.

Every 20 seconds (or about 50 words) you are allowed to look away from people, but only for about one second. That means that for every minute of speaking (or about 150 words), you're allowed just three seconds to look down and read the next group of words. In effect, you should be spending 95% of the time looking at people and only 5% of the time checking the script.

Unless you are using a see-through teleprompter, as is done on TV, the more you read from the script, the less eye contact you have with the audience. Concepts are the solution. Build a conceptual script around key phrases, and you'll spend more time delivering a personal version of the topic directly because you won't have a lot of words to read, just concepts. Doesn't this sound like a Do script? (See Chapter 22 for more information.)

Don't get caught behind a lectern just reading a bunch of statistics to the audience. Think eye contact and avoid facing the facts.

AVOIDING PROBLEMS

When the audience can't interpret your physical actions, they become preoccupied trying to figure out how the words link to the movements. The audience can't ignore these body distractions, and therefore they need to be eliminated. If you remove these distractions, your message is easier to convey.

UPSTAGING

Sometimes the audience is prevented from hearing your words simply because they can't see your face or your expressions. When a part of the body passes between the speaker's face and the audience, the result is called *upstaging*.

Turning your back to the audience is the most obvious example of upstaging and is depicted in Figure 24.4. If you're facing the screen and the audience is facing the screen, then who's presenting? When you turn your back to the group, you can't see them and they can't see you. You lose valuable eye contact and the chance to use facial expressions. In addition, your voice is projected away from the audience and is therefore less audible, unless you have a microphone.

PART
VII
CH
24

Figure 24.4
Don't turn your back
to the audience.

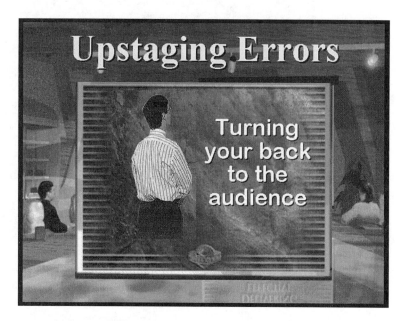

If you have to turn your back to the audience, do it for as short a time as possible. At the same time, increase your volume so the group can still hear what you're saying. Avoid walking into the audience. This happens a lot when you have a U-shaped seating arrangement. You might think that it's more personal to penetrate the "U" to get closer to the person you are interacting with. Not true. Your effort to get closer to one person puts your back toward everyone else as you penetrate the group. Don't alienate one person for the sake of another. You can still make eye contact and reach out to anyone in any part of the room while maintaining your position. The bottom line is that when your back is to the audience, you're least effective.

Tip from
Tom Mucciolo

One easy way to keep from turning your back is to be sure the person seated to your far right can always see the front of your right shoulder. This technique keeps your body facing out to everyone in the crowd as you speak.

Crossing the upper body with your right hand is another example of upstaging, as shown in Figure 24.5. Whenever you gesture to the screen, use your left hand rather than your right. If your right hand goes across the front of your body, it causes a visual distraction that limits your effectiveness.

Figure 24.5
Don't cross your body with one of your arms.

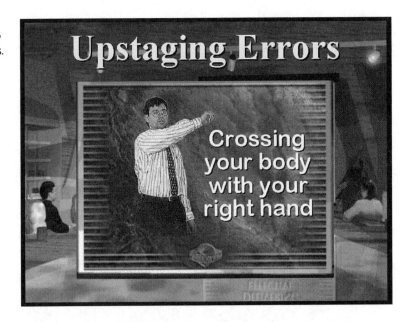

Tip from
Tom Mucciolo

Use your left foot as a guide. To gesture to anything left of your left foot, use your left hand. Use your right hand to gesture to anything to the right of your left foot. This forces you into a more open stance when presenting and allows you to add impact to your delivery style with correct gestures and movements.

THE GUNFIGHTER

One stance to avoid is what I call the gunfighter position, in which your arms are locked at your sides as if your elbows were sewn to your rib cage. This limits the gestures you can make with your hands. To avoid the gunfighter position when presenting, pretend that you must be able to touch your hands to the top of your head without bending your neck. This would be impossible with your elbows still attached to your sides.

THE HEAD WAITER

Be careful about folding your arms in front of you. This head waiter position not only upstages you by putting your arms across your upper body, but it also indicates that you are hiding something from the group. With your hands locked under your arms, your gestures are completely limited.

THE THIRD BASE COACH

Do not clasp your hands together behind your back. This position, the third base coach, forces you to use your shoulders and your chin to create gestures. You'll end up throwing your chin or shoulder forward to acknowledge a question, and the reaction from the audience will be far from positive.

THE HAND TALKER

Avoid conversationalizing your gestures. This happens when you move your hands in the rhythm of your speech. It ends up looking like you have a gesture for every syllable. The trick with gestures is to keep them still and not bounce them around on each word. The audience takes more time to process gestures than it does to process words. Gestures should freeze to add impact to a phrase.

Try this exercise. Say the phrase, "This is very, very, very important," and move both your hands up and down on as many words as you can. Then, say the phrase again, but this time just let your hands come down once and lock them in mid-air as you finish the rest of the phrase. Did you feel a difference? When a gesture stops moving, it is more powerful.

BLOCKING THE LIGHT

The image is meant for the screen. Sometimes you make the mistake of trying to point to something on your visual and you walk in front of the. Never block the light source with your hands or body unless you intend to make shadow puppets for the audience. When you block the light source, the audience finds it difficult to view the distorted image depicted on your clothes.

PINKIE COUNTING

Who started this habit anyway? Pinkie counting is simply counting on your fingers in front of the audience. The action occurs when you hold out your left hand, palm up, and use your right index finger to count on the left pinkie, then ring finger, and so on. The obsession plagues almost everyone from time to time. The audience has no idea when you plan to stop, although five seems to be the limit.

The reason you pinkie count is to keep track of the order of things by giving yourself tactile feedback as you count through the items you relay to the audience. This distraction can be avoided by dropping one hand to your side and simply touching your index finger to the thumb of same hand to maintain the tactile feedback. By inconspicuously using just one hand to count, you don't distract the audience.

If counting is really important to your point, then raise your hand above your shoulder and count so that everyone can see. This will force you to limit those times that you count, and it will add impact to those times that you need to count emphatically.

USING YOUR VOICE

Although I am the first to say that actions speak louder than words, your vocal delivery plays the role of interpreter for the message. If the visual medium is truly the content and the body is definitely the delivery, then the voice is a combination of both. Words carry information and action. To develop the action in your voice, a few issues should be considered, including proper breathing and how to phrase and pause effectively.

BREATHING PROPERLY

Sometimes your choice of where to take the next breath can disrupt the flow of your words. By breathing between phrases rather than during a phrase, you vocalize better. The key to this is having enough air in your lungs to sustain a longer phrase. For example, I have been known to deliver very long phrases with volume and emphasis. I believe that's from knowing how to breathe properly.

When you don't have enough air, you rush through your words, and then they run together from speaking so quickly. Chances are that your emphasis and inflection will be lost. In any case, by having enough air, you can say longer phrases more slowly, which helps to make the message clear.

First, let's find out if you are breathing properly. Stand up and take a deep breath. Did your shoulders go up? Did your chest expand?

If your shoulders went up, you filled your chest with air. Unfortunately, that's not the way you naturally breathe. The air normally goes into the lower abdomen. Try this test. Lie down on the floor, face up, with a book on your stomach. Breathe normally and watch the book. Notice it moving up and down? That's your diaphragm at work. The muscles in your stomach, not your chest, control breathing. Now take a deep breath and force the book upward; it should be easy once you concentrate on the correct muscles for the job.

Next, remove the book, stand up, and take the same deep breath, but don't expand your chest or raise your shoulders. Your stomach should expand. This is the proper way to breathe between your phrases when speaking.

Tip from
Tom Mucciolo

Breathing through your nose makes it easier to expand your stomach (diaphragm). Of course, when speaking, the tendency is to take in air through your mouth also because it is already open. It's not where the air enters but where the air reaches that makes for better vocal control.

Again, the key is having enough breath to complete long phrases or sentences without running out of air. This is important for languages such as English, in which the major points are made at the end of phrases, not at the beginning. Without enough air, your voice might trail off and the audience will not hear the key part (the end) of the sentence. The beginning of the next phrase will be less connected to the important part of the prior one. The result is confusion for the audience.

The following is an exercise for breath control. You should be able to say this entire passage in one breath.

> What a to-do, to die today, at a minute or two to two
>
> A thing distinctly hard to say, yet harder still to do
>
> For they'll beat a tattoo at twenty to two
>
> A rah-tah-tah-tah-tah-tah-tah-tah-tah-too
>
> And the dragon will come at the sound of a drum
>
> At a minute or two to two, today,
>
> At a minute or two to two.

When you develop truly excellent breath control, you will be able to say the above passage two times with one breath.

If you can't remember the above phrase, here's another breathing exercise you can try. In one breath say, "One by one, they went away." Pretty easy, right? Okay, add another to the count, like this, "One by one and two by two, they went away." Try adding another to the count and in one breath say, "One by one and two by two and three by three, they went away." Don't forget that each of these segments has to be done in one breath. You should shoot for as high as "twelve by twelve." With practice, 15 or higher is possible as you get more control of your breathing.

PHRASING AND PAUSING

Take natural pauses between your sentences. Say a phrase, pause, then say a phrase and pause, and so on. By using this technique, you can control the pacing of the presentation. Natural pauses give you a chance to make eye contact, to breathe, or even to think. You end up with smooth transitions and a more consistent delivery.

FILLERS ARE KILLERS

The funny thing about getting up in front of people is that you have an altered sense of time. You think you're going too slow and you begin to pick up the pace, not so much with your speech but more with your thoughts. You begin to think more quickly and between one phrase and another the audience hears "uhhhhhh," "ummmmm," "errrrrr," "ahhhhh," and other fillers, the sounds you make between the words you say. Fillers are not language. They are grunts and groans. The audience can't process fillers. In fact, if you have a lot of them in your presentation, the audience becomes preoccupied with the distraction and ends up concentrating on your fillers, not on your phrases.

Fillers can even be whole words, such as "okay," "right," "you know," "again," and "see," to name a few. Fillers are evidence that you are thinking out loud. You're letting the audience hear you think. To counter this problem, use silence as a filler. It appears that you are taking natural pauses when you speak.

THE OPENING PAUSE

When I'm coaching a person, I always suggest the two-second opening pause. Right after the first phrase, such as "Good morning," you should take a two-second pause. Complete silence for two seconds. It can seem like an eternity, but it gives you the chance to establish two important things: pacing and anchors.

From a pacing perspective, the opening pause sets up the audience. They get to know right away who is in charge of the momentum. People have to know that you are in control. That's the role of the presenter—to control the flow. The role of the audience is to be controlled. If you don't appear rushed, the audience settles into the presentation at the pace you have set.

Those two seconds of silence help you in another way. In our earlier discussion of anchors, we talked about identifying the friendly faces to focus on. Unfortunately, you can't establish anchors in the audience until you first take the stage, because that's when almost everyone is seated. You can't look out in the audience 40 minutes before the presentation and find them. You have to find your anchors during the opening pause. Don't worry, though, it will take you only about two seconds to scan the crowd for those friendly faces. Typically, those sitting in the most light are the easiest to spot.

WHEN IN DOUBT, PAUSE FIRST

Have you ever been asked a question during your presentation and not known the answer? Don't blurt out your ignorance right away. Instead, pause for a moment.

The pause maintains whatever level of credibility you had before the question was asked. By pausing for a moment, you make the audience believe that you could answer the question, given enough time. The group watches you search your mind for an answer, even though you never come up with one.

So, when in doubt, pause first. It buys you time and credibility. Of course, don't stop there. The words "I'll get back to you on that" indicate your intention to follow up at a later point with an answer. Be sure you do.

TARGETING PHRASES

Once you have control over your voice, you can direct your phrases for more impact. You can target your words to entire sections of the audience or simply to one person.

It's a given that everyone in the room has to be able to hear you. Sometimes a microphone will be needed for the entire audience to hear every word you say. Because you can't count on having a microphone in every situation, you'll have to learn to project your voice.

Although proper breathing is important to voice projection, you should also target your phrases toward the back of the room to be sure everyone hears what you say. One way to do this is to play to the back third of the audience. In the theater it's called "playing to the cheap seats." The farthest one-third of the audience is where most of your phrases should be targeted because if they can hear you, everyone can hear you.

You never have to worry about the people in the front. But the people in the back—pretend that they are never sold, never convinced, never in agreement with your message. This forces you to target them. The good news is that this causes you to lift your chin slightly higher in the air, opens your throat, and makes your voice clearer. In addition, you'll find yourself facing forward more often in order to project to the back of the room. The intensity of your phrases, no matter how calm or soft-spoken, become more audible, and your facial expressions more visible.

Voice projection helps when fielding responses from the audience. Sometimes an audience member speaks so softly that only you and a few other people hear him. Be sure you repeat the question or comment so that the entire group can hear it. If you fail to do this, then your response will make sense only to those who heard the question or comment. Also, by repeating a question, you get more time to formulate your answer.

You can also target your phrases directly to a specific person. You can do it with just a look, but you get more impact if you know the person's name. Using names adds a personal touch to your presentation.

When you refer to a person by name, only the first name is needed. This makes it a little easier for you because last names can sometimes be difficult to remember or even pronounce. Of course, if you are speaking to an audience that you have never met before, it will be difficult to identify people by name. During interaction, you could ask that people identify themselves to the audience before they speak. Then, you'll know a person's name and be able to use it in your response.

Targeting your phrases to an entire section or to a specific person makes the audience more conscious of each other and more respectful of your caring to take the time to treat people as individuals when possible.

TRANSITIONING

Transitioning is having something to say during changes in your presentation. Those changes can be a result of movement or from the visuals themselves.

Movement in the triangle can be very obvious when your space is bigger. It might take several steps to get from the middle to the front, for example. You should not be moving on a key phrase. The words have more impact when you are still. Suppose you want to say the words "It saves money" in the front of the triangle. If you are in the middle of the triangle and a few steps away from the front, you have to add a transition or some extra words to allow you time to get to the front. Once there, and not moving, you can say the key phrase, "It saves money." Perhaps your entire phrase (said from the middle while walking to the front) turns into "One of the most important advantages of this new product is that (now you stop at the front) it saves money." The transitional text enables you to move to the next space and deliver the key words while standing still.

Transitions are also useful whenever the visual changes, although this is less of a requirement when using slides or electronic images because they change more rapidly. A more traditional medium, such as overheads, requires verbal transitions.

It takes several seconds to remove one transparency from the overhead projector and replace it with the next. Don't let that time be filled with silence. Have a transition—something to say as you approach the equipment, as you change the visual, as you set the next visual, and as you move away from the equipment. Even in the world of state-of-the-art electronics, a pause to press a remote control is just as obvious as changing an overhead if you leave too big a gap with nothing to say.

Don't confuse silence with timed pauses. A timed pause lasts about one to three seconds and is useful for getting the audience to ponder a question. Dead silence lasts longer and tells the audience you can't really think of anything to say at the moment.

RULE OF THREES

People remember things in sets of threes. Our system of government is based on the number three, many religions are based on three, even the family—mother-father-child—is based on the number three. You can find this rhythm in many political or religious speeches. Key concepts or arguments are constructed around three references. For example, a politician might make the statement: "We'll be more prosperous, we'll pay less in taxes, and our children will have a future." Notice the use of three references in the phrasing to make a point. Many references include a triad of some sort, such as Julius Caesar's "Veni, vidi, vici" ("I came, I saw, I conquered") and the courtroom oath of "the truth, the whole truth, and nothing but the truth." Even the Olympic Games grant three medals: Gold, Silver, and Bronze.

Try to incorporate the rule of threes when presenting your next topic. It's easy, it's simple, and it works like a charm.

AVOIDING VOCAL PROBLEMS

Just as with the body, distractions can occur when using the voice. Most of the time, vocal problems can be corrected, but sometimes our natural speech will sound different to different audiences. An accent is natural to some, but unique to others.

If you have an accent, as most of us do, it means that you might sound different from what the audience is used to hearing. My grandmother, who came from Italy, once said to me in broken English, "Don't laugh at people with accents. They speak one more language than you do." Of course, an accent from speaking a foreign language is no less noticeable than a regional accent. When I spoke at a seminar in Mississippi, the person who introduced me ended his opening remark with "at least you'll like his New York accent." Just as I began to speak, I looked at him and said, "Wait a minute. I thought you had the accent."

The point is that, if you have a well-rehearsed presentation and you can be understood when you speak, your accent should not reduce your effectiveness.

Some believe in eliminating a regional or foreign accent, but I think it helps make the individual stand out for an audience. If you can be understood, then don't worry about an accent. However, some other vocal issues can become major problems if not corrected.

THE MUMBLER

The mumbler is the person who does not enunciate clearly. The lips stay so close together that the audience can't even see the words forming. When the mouth stays very closed, volume decreases and the words are barely audible. Remember to loosen those lips and articulate.

Tip from
Tom Mucciolo

Place a pencil across your mouth between your teeth. Push it as far back as you can, which stretches your lips. Bite down a little on the pencil and begin to talk. Say a couple of phrases for about 30 seconds up to a minute. Take the pencil away and notice how flexible your lips are and how much better you enunciate every syllable.

THE GARBLER

Another person with an enunciation problem, the garbler is the person who speaks so quickly that the audience can't hear the end of one word before the next word arrives. To correct this problem, try saying a short phrase very slowly by stretching out each and every syllable in every word. This helps to reduce the speed of speech.

Tip from
Tom Mucciolo

Find a newspaper article and read the first two sentences out loud. Read them again out loud and you'll probably go even faster. Okay, now read the words in the sentences backward, one word at a time. Hear how slowly you must read and try to match that speed when you speak. Although in practice that pace is definitely too slow, your habit of speaking too quickly will offset the slow speech, and the result will be a closer-to-normal speed.

THE DRONER

The droner has a constant, monotone, expressionless voice and is the best-known cure for insomnia! The problem is from little or no inflection. This is often prevalent among presenters who have limited interest in the topic or those who have been presenting the same information in the same way for too long. They are simply bored with the stuff they deliver. The voice reflects the boredom, gets lazy, and eventually becomes monotonous.

One solution to this problem is to practice placing stress on different words in a sentence. For example, the following list uses ALL CAPS to show the changing emphasis in the same phrase:

> And WE offer the best service.
>
> And we OFFER the best service.
>
> And we offer the BEST service.
>
> And we offer the best SERVICE.

Try saying these phrases out loud and note the difference in the stress of the capitalized words. Placing emphasis in this way forces the voice into higher and lower pitches within a phrase, adding vocal variety to an otherwise droning tone.

THE DROPPER

The dropper is the person who starts out with a lot of volume and then gradually drops off to the point where the audience is straining to hear the disappearing words. This problem is definitely related to improper breathing. The exercises mentioned earlier can help with sustaining longer phrases.

Sometimes the words drop off because you are not completing one thought for yourself before introducing the next. You become anxious to get to the next part of the argument. The key to avoiding this problem is to maintain volume through the end of every phrase.

Tip from
Tom Mucciolo

In addition to breathing exercises, you can also try adding a question at the end of every sentence. Keep in mind that this is only for practice. Don't do this while presenting. For example, add the question, "Is that statement clear?" to every sentence. The question forces a slight raise in pitch and volume. Plus, the extra words make the sentence even longer, forcing you to plan for more air to get to the end. When presenting, you can still silently say the question to yourself if you feel you are dropping off in volume as you present.

When a vocal problem becomes a distraction, you need to take steps to eliminate it. When your voice becomes trained to the point where you can control it effectively, you gain another advantage in conveying the message you intend for the audience.

TROUBLESHOOTING

ENSURING YOUR PRESENTATION WORKS FOR A SMALL GROUP

How do these external skills apply to small group meetings with just a few people sitting around a conference table?

Actually, the skills are the same. The room is just smaller. Good presentation skills work everywhere. This is the same as writing or speaking. Would you tolerate poor grammar or poor enunciation if the crowd were only eight people in a conference room? The key difference is in how you express yourself to fit the size of the group. You are not going to make wide, sweeping gestures, but you would certainly reach out to any size group. You would still use the three positions of the triangle, even though the space is smaller. You would still use the rest and power positions to add emphasis. The point is that your body language is expressed all the time, regardless of the number of people observing you.

If possible, stand up when presenting. This doesn't mean you can't control a meeting while sitting; rather, you get more power when your head is higher than people. That's why kings sit high on thrones, judges sit up high, even pharmacists—they're up on those platforms. It's a power thing.

If you are sitting, you can still create rest and power positions with your body simply by turning in your chair and angling your shoulders to the group. Gestures should be done with your elbows above the edge of the table, and your fingertips can still be used to reach out to include one or more people in the conversation. The actions of your body are always available. Small group meetings require a physical plan in your delivery style just as large groups do.

RESOLVING EYE CONTACT ISSUES

Is there such a thing as too much eye contact?

Obviously, in large groups the chances for direct eye contact are not as great as with smaller groups. Fewer faces for you to look at means more time to look at each face. When there are fewer people in the room, the eye contact with each one should be greater. However, too much eye contact tends to backfire.

Let's use the smallest group scenario: one other person in the room with you. Let's call the other person Debbie. If you are talking with Debbie and you make constant eye contact with her as you speak, after a short time she will have to look away. She won't be able to stare into your eyes continually, so eye contact between you will be broken. That means another object is likely to catch her attention when she looks away. At that point she is no longer listening to you because her attention is diverted to something else.

However, if you break eye contact from time to time while you are speaking, Debbie will have no choice but to remain fixed on your eyes, even as you glance away. You will have greater control of her attention if she is busy fighting for your eyes instead of you fighting for her eyes when you speak. And you really don't look at anything specific when you break eye contact because you are still talking and your eyes are only wandering on occasion in order to keep her more attentive.

When you are listening, you should always maintain eye contact. But when you are speaking, especially to fewer people, you should break eye contact from time to time to keep the attention of your listeners. In presentations, you allow the audience to look away by giving them a chance to glance at the visual on your display screen. The object of their attention, the visual, is still part of your message. In smaller groups, the visuals can be just as useful, but if the interaction is mostly one-to-one without much visual support, allow for occasional breaks in eye contact with your listeners when you are speaking.

CHAPTER 25

THE MECHANICS OF FUNCTION— DEVELOPING INTERNAL PRESENTATION SKILLS

In this chapter

by Tom Mucciolo

GETTING TO THE HEART AND SOUL OF A PRESENTATION

Now that you've learned a bit about external presentation skills, it's time to get internal—into the heart and soul of a presentation. This chapter takes you to another level of presenting, a level that gets the audience to react to how you think and feel about your message.

Teaching about the body and the voice is somewhat easier than talking about feelings because the body and voice are tangible and very measurable parts of the delivery skill. If you're not moving or no one can hear you, it doesn't take a rocket scientist to figure out the problem. If you're not focused or you don't have enthusiasm—people notice that something is not right, but they're not sure what it is. The audience sees external distractions, but they only sense internal ones. External problems make them not want to look at you at the moment. Internal distractions make them not want to watch you again. The mechanics of function are what keep them coming back for more!

Perhaps you've gone to a movie or a play and you left with an empty feeling, unsure as to why you felt that way. This happens because you might not have the expertise to analyze the problems in the performance, but you have the experience to know what a good performance should be. Everyone in the audience has been to a presentation before, and they have the experience of both good and bad events. This is what leads people to arrive at the presentation with a certain expectation.

The good news is that the average audience member at a business presentation expects boredom and talking heads. You can exceed that expectation with well-planned *mechanics of form*, the external presentation skills using the body and the voice. People are always appreciative of your having given them more than anticipated. If you can take the time to prepare on the outside—you know, dress the part, plan the movements, and work the voice—then you need to make the effort to prepare the inside. The inner plan is your character, shaped by thoughts and feelings.

If you truly want your message remembered and linked directly to your personal delivery of that message, you'll have to use the *mechanics of function*, the internal presentation skills. The components of these skills include your mind...and your heart.

USING YOUR MIND

In acting, it takes someone with a lot of intelligence to play the part of ignorance. Carroll O'Connor and Jean Stapleton are brilliant people who played Archie and Edith Bunker on TV's *All in the Family*, a '70s sitcom. Each played ignorance in a special way. But to know all the intricacies of ignorance, a high level of knowledge is required. How would one know what is stupid unless one were smart enough to understand the difference?

Your mind is one of your most powerful assets. As a presenter, you can think on your feet, sway the audience with reason, and persuade people with your logic.

LINKING INTENTION TO CONTENT

This sounds more difficult than it is. The fun in this process is using your imagination to create connections between your actions and the supporting elements in your message. In other words, for every major section of information you are sharing with the audience, you need to identify the intention or subtext that goes along with that information. The intention follows the same pattern as the objective. Based on action and described in the form of "to do" something, it isn't a feeling, although a feeling will always arise out of action. It's like a little objective.

For example, let's say your next presentation's overall objective is to persuade the group to take action on a new budget item. At the beginning of the talk, you plan to bring up a comparison to a similar budget decision that was made in the prior year. Stop. What is your inner intention as you go through the comparison? You know you have to persuade, but use your imagination for a moment. How many ways are there to persuade? Probably a million. Pick one.

Let me pick one for you: Show the absurdity in bringing up what happened a year ago. Stress that this is like comparing apples to oranges, and the data from last year is meaningless to this issue.

Let me give you another one: Proclaim the validity of the comparison to last year. Stress that the decision was made by the same management team evaluating the current project, and their track record on these issues is impeccable.

Your intention is different in each case, yet the visual support looks the same. The angle of your approach is going to change, depending on your inner intention.

In other words, you've got a whole bunch of little things to do inside the big thing you have to do. Just like a wedding, there are a million little details, each with an intensity, an action, and an outcome. Then you have to consider the scope of the entire event. Details exist in so many things you do. Why would your presentation be any different? It's attention to detail that will make it successful.

To do this, dissect your presentation into smaller segments and see what is going on in your mind as you cover each segment. If a few charts are displayed in one part of your talk, what is your subtext; what are you really thinking? Is your intention to distract the audience with the details? Is it to drive home the point? Is it to set the stage for the next section of the presentation?

Don't chop the presentation into such tiny segments that you try to find an intention for every moment. This will result in the analysis-into-paralysis problem. Your intentions typically cover a group of visuals. Maybe you'll have six to eight different intentions for a 20-minute talk. You might use an intention more than once for repetitive items such as humor or storytelling. For example, the intention in each of three different stories might be to teach a lesson.

If you just concentrate on the major sections and the related intentions, the tiny moments take care of themselves. They happen as a result of your natural thinking pattern to accomplish tasks. Trust yourself and give yourself more credit. You wouldn't even be reading this book if you didn't have the ability to express yourself and your intentions. You've been doing this all your life. You just have to apply the process to presenting. If you understand the big segments, then the little things under every single moment will become so natural, you won't have to think about them.

Your inner intentions are buried in your brain, and you have to identify them so that you can be sure that the way you offer the information is the way you expect the audience to understand it. This is what I mean by linking intention to content.

Playing the Stakes

In theater, the actor must "play the stakes" in each scene. The actor searches for the most important moments to make clear in each scene.

The same is true in presenting. Look at any piece of information in your script and decide on its priority to the whole story. The closer it is to being essential, the higher the stakes get if you don't present it well.

You might not convince your audience if you fail to deliver the key information. If you fear your talk will be boring, find the importance in the information and enable the audience to discover the importance with you.

You can play the stakes in a section of the presentation or even on a single visual. If you have a visual that displays several bullet points, you need to decide which of those points is most important to the story at that moment.

Although you may cover all the points anyway, you might find yourself discussing one point in much more detail. This is probably the critical element in the visual, and you should focus more of your attention on delivering that point as clearly and directly as possible. This doesn't mean the rest of the material is unimportant; instead, it helps you use the surrounding information as support for the more important item.

By playing the stakes in each visual, you will add the sense of urgency to the topic that otherwise might appear to you to be too boring for others to experience. In addition, the physical actions you use to play the stakes will heighten the importance of the information.

WORKING WITH DETAILED DATA

Sometimes your visuals contain detailed information. Typically this happens with data-driven charts (bar, pie, line, area, and so on). Most presenters display these charts for the audience and discuss the obvious items, usually the biggest slice, the tallest bar, the upward moving line—the easy stuff. Although nothing is wrong with this, it adds little value to the audience if they could have figured it out for themselves.

A visual presenter reads between the lines and makes the detailed information come to life. It's a process of identifying the means inside the extremes.

Think of the means as internal causes for the extremes. The extremes are the external data elements that are different enough to force a comparison or a discussion.

For example, Figure 25.1 is a vertical bar chart. It contains four selected months of data showing the time (in seconds) it takes to connect to the Internet from home and from business. Wait—don't start calling your Internet service provider and complaining. I made these numbers up just for the example.

Figure 25.1
A simple bar chart showing selected months of activity.

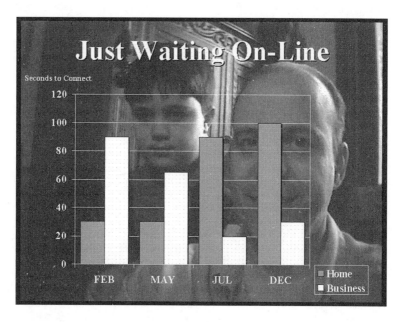

Let's say you select one particular set of extremes related to the home group. You might point out that the connect time in February is much faster than in December. You picked two data elements different enough to stimulate a discussion.

Now you have to stress the means of those extremes. You identify the causes of the difference. An obvious one would be a seasonal issue. The reason it takes longer to connect in December is because of the holiday season and the online calls to friends and family. Maybe you dig deeper into the means. You might bring up a recent article you read that mentioned how the home sales of digital cameras seem to peak in mid-November because people want to have holiday pictures in advance of the holiday season. The effect of more digital photos is their transmission in December over the Internet. These photos are much larger files, resulting in more traffic over the Net and, hence, slower connect times. None of this extra stuff appears on the chart—it's all in your head.

Want to try another? Let's use the same example, but pick two other extremes. Compare home to business in the month of July. What are the means inside those extremes? You could point out that more employees take vacations during the month of July than any other time during the year. Not being at the desk in the office results in fewer connections to the Internet, hence less traffic from the business group. However, vacation doesn't always mean travel away from home, and you might mention that with kids home from school, an increase in Internet activity from home results in more traffic on the Net. Maybe you dig deeper into the means. You cite a statistic from the National Education Extension Outreach Foundation that shows a sharp increase in the number of online college-level courses being taken during the summer months when classroom sessions are fewer. The students in these electronic programs are participating from home, which is another reason for the rise of Internet activity in July and the longer connect times from the home group. Once again, the audience gets none of this from the chart on the screen.

By identifying the means inside the extremes whenever possible, you create a lasting impression with the audience. You become the critical bond for the audience between data and description. Without you as that link, anyone could have presented the topic. A visual presenter would never allow that!

SELECTING FOCAL POINTS

We talked about anchors in the past few chapters. The audience needs anchors and so do you. Anchors don't really move during the presentation—that's why they're called anchors. The anchors are usually big—standing on the left side of the room, five friendly faces in the audience, geometric shapes to help guide the eye—these are all anchors.

But another type of anchor is called a *focal point*. It's more of a temporary anchor, but it is something you can use at various times during the presentation. Many of the focal points you'll use are less apparent, if at all, to the audience. Focal points are visible fixed objects that help you target your attention as you speak.

Have you ever just stared off into space while you were thinking about something? You probably weren't always looking at the night sky when you zoned out. You might have been at your desk or at home and you were looking at something, but you were not focused on the attributes of the object. You were busy thinking. The best example of this is talking on the telephone. Next time you see someone talking on the phone, watch how many places he looks when talking, almost none of which are required for continuing the conversation. You do this a lot yourself. Your focal points change and vary, depending on what your brain is doing.

As a presenter, you need to be aware of these temporary anchors and use them to your advantage.

You can use two kinds of focal points: primary and secondary. Primary focal points include the screen, the display equipment, and the audience. Secondary focal points include the floor, the ceiling, the walls, the furniture, the fixtures, the exit sign, and any other decorative or noticeable objects you might glance at during the presentation.

Primary focal points are referenced a lot in the presentation, and you'll find yourself gesturing to them and interacting with them constantly. Primary focal points help you concentrate your attention, and they are very apparent to the audience.

Secondary focal points are less obvious to the audience. However, they also help connect your thoughts to physical objects in order for your delivery of information to appear more natural.

You can't stare off into oblivion or space out during the presentation, even though you do it in real life. But the very act of staring can be so effective for the audience because they can see you thinking, pondering, and struggling to make information important. Without an object to focus attention on, you can't show the audience that you're thinking. Focal points make thinking a reality.

For example, suppose you're presenting in front of a group of 40 people. You're getting ready to start, and you take note of several objects in the room that catch your attention. On the back wall is a painting of a snow-covered mountain. On the ceiling is a row of track lighting with spotlights facing the sidewall. On the other sidewall is a thermostat and, next to it, a wall telephone. All of these are usable secondary focal points.

Let's say that during the presentation you are telling of a work-related experience in which you had to lead a team of people to accomplish a task. During the story you are reflecting about the experience, and your eyes glance to the painting on the back wall. It only takes a few seconds of your attention on that painting to give the impression to the audience that you are reflecting on the experience. They see you staring into space and believe you are explaining to them what you see in your mind's eye. Without an object to focus on, you might recount the story too quickly and lose some of the impact. The painting gives you a visible focal point that helps demonstrate your thoughts and makes the telling of the story look more natural.

You can't just look off into space; you need something to look at, such as the painting. Because you looked at it prior to the presentation, you are not distracted by the details in the painting. That's why you glance around the room before you begin the presentation. You have to know your focal points in advance. You don't want to be surprised by anything you glance at while speaking.

Sometimes the attributes of a focal point can help in your description. Let's use the same example. It's later in the presentation. You're displaying a line chart and commenting on the rising costs of a current project. You glance at the thermostat briefly and you describe the skyrocketing costs as reaching the boiling point, ready to burst. The thermostat as a focal point created a heat-related image in your mind, helping you build a better description for the problem.

Creating Distance

Focal points have a near or far nature, similar to a camera lens. If the focal point is closer to you, the background blurs; if the focal point is more distant, the foreground blurs.

You can try this by holding your index finger in the air at arm's length, about the height of your eyes. Look at your finger, and everything behind your finger is blurry. Look past your finger at some distant point and your finger (even your hand) is blurry. In fact, you can almost see through your finger by focusing on the background. Don't close one eye or you'll lose all depth perception and your finger will become a solid mass, blocking your view of the background.

The near or far focus is helpful when describing people or things that are not visible to the audience but need to be more real for you. You might stretch your arm out and focus directly on your palm as you describe items from an invisible contract that you're holding. You could be relaying two parts of a conversation, and the face of the invisible other person is the picture frame on the far wall, making it appear that you are conversing with that person.

In both cases, creating distance requires a focal point or something to look at to help you make it appear real.

Focal points are extremely useful, and the more you can selectively use these temporary anchors, the easier it is to show the audience what you're thinking.

USING VIRTUAL SPACE

Just as focal points help you connect your thoughts to visible objects, virtual space helps you connect the audience to invisible objects. You use virtual space to show the audience how your mind is visualizing the concepts you're explaining.

At times during a presentation, you will mention several related concepts to the audience and not really know if the group is following along. You already see the concepts in your mind, but the audience has no idea how to distinguish them.

For example, you mention to the group that three separate departments will be involved in a decision: marketing, sales, and finance. The instant you name the three groups, you have a visual image in your head of each of those departments. You can see where in the building the departments are, you see the faces of people who work in each area, and you are visualizing three distinctly unique departments.

Now you have to get the audience to see three different departments. You do this with virtual space. You physically place the departments in the air for the audience to reference. As you say "marketing," your right hand places the word in the air to your right. As you say "sales," your left hand places the word in the air to your left; as you say "finance," you place the word in the air in front of you, using both hands. In all three moves, your palms would open out to the audience without blocking your face.

The point is that the three departments are floating in virtual space, and you can immediately reference any of the three by physically retrieving it from its floating position. If you say, "The marketing department is going to…," you can gesture to the space occupied by the word marketing, to your right, where you placed it. If instead you use the space to your left, the audience would say, "No, no—that's the sales department over there!" The audience remembers where you placed the references because they have been given focal points. The concepts are floating in virtual space for the audience to see.

Use virtual space to identify concepts as separate and distinct from one another. Don't just use virtual space and then do nothing with the floating anchors you handed the audience. When you place the items in the air for the audience, immediately reference one of them to begin noting the distinction.

Other ways of using virtual space include showing timelines and distance. For example, if you are describing several events from 1990 through the present, you might use your right hand to place 1990 in the air as the beginning of the timeline. Then use your left hand to stretch an invisible thread from your right hand to a place in the air to your left to show the length of the timeline. For showing distance, you might gesture with your left arm fully extended to a point at the far corner of the room while you mention an office location in another state. The group would realize you are referencing a place in the distance and not somewhere nearby.

Keep in mind that the moment you change physical space, virtual space falls to the floor and disappears. For example, suppose you're in the front of the triangle and you use virtual space to distinguish three items. You reference one item, but then you navigate to the middle of the triangle. Because you moved to another physical space on the floor, the virtual references disappear. Those little anchors or focal points for the audience can't float in space if your body is not around to support them. This means that whenever you move in the triangle, you get another opportunity to use virtual space.

HANDLING DISTRACTIONS

When I talked about the mechanics of form in the previous chapter, I mentioned some body and voice problems that the audience might find distracting. Sometimes it's the other way around, and you can get distracted while presenting. With almost every distraction, the result is a loss of concentration. Your mind loses focus on the objective in the presentation. You usually get sidetracked because you were not prepared for the diversion. The following sections discuss some of the external forces at work that might challenge your attention to the message.

THE SLACKER

Activity in the audience is a very common distraction for a presenter, and this usually happens at the beginning of a presentation. It's called tardiness. A latecomer can cause a break in the flow for you while you speak. This is more apparent as the tardy person takes a seat closer to the front because more people have to watch the person get settled.

The best way to handle the distractions caused by someone who arrives late is by finding a way to repeat or recap as much of the story necessary for the person to catch up. The one who is late might be critical to your plan. The tardy person might be the one making the final decision. You never know what role the latecomer plays. Don't chance alienation. Bring that lost sheep back into the fold.

In addition, the distraction of a latecomer usually messes up your current point. Because you'll have to repeat what you just covered for everyone else's benefit, you can sneak in a quick sentence to recap for the slacker.

THE ATTACKER

Sometimes a hostile audience member can distract you. Hostility in the audience usually relates to the content in some way. It's simple: You counter hostility with friendliness.

Sometimes political or market forces are at work, causing frustration for some people, and reactions are negative. I've seen this hostility at employee meetings right after a downsizing took place. It happens at shareholder meetings if profits have taken a hit.

If you are faced with hostility, agree with your adversary as quickly as you can. Then, look at the source of the conflict and ask yourself, "Can I fix this?" Be honest. If you can address the issue, do it. If you can't, then try turning it around. Ask the person, "Do you have a suggestion?" The key to this is that your attempt to solve or ask for help in solving a problem is viewed as a friendly way of working with your adversary.

You usually can't win if you fight back in a public forum. The reason is that the audience believes you know more than you reveal, and fighting back suggests you don't have an answer or will not admit to being wrong. That's why agreement helps soften the blow. I realize this approach can't cover every hostile situation, but it works in most cases.

THE KNOW-IT-ALL

Another distraction is caused by the ego of the know-it-all. Counter the conceit with fellowship. The know-it-all appears more often in small group presentations because the chance to speak out is more readily available. Regardless of the venue, the know-it-all can cause you to lose your concentration.

Like the attacker, you need to side with the know-it-all right away (if possible). For example, suppose you are discussing the tax benefits of a new copy machine for a client. In the meeting is a person from the client's accounting department. We'll call him "Zeno." Now Zeno pipes up very early in your talk and says, "Are you considering this a Section 1231 asset for depreciation purposes?" The rest of the group rolls their eyes, having seen Zeno openly destroy others in the past. No one escapes his wrath. If you are discussing tax benefits, you already understand enough about accounting to handle Zeno easily. You address his concerns and respond with enough information to satisfy his hunger. Still, you also know this is only the beginning. Zeno lives for these moments.

This is when you form the Fellowship of Accountants, in which you and Zeno are the charter members. Soon after responding to Zeno, at the very next accounting issue, you look right over to Zeno and say, "and as Zeno can tell each of you, the equipment." In other words, you make an ally. Zeno becomes your constant resident expert to support nearly every financial point that sounds even remotely confusing.

By making that person your support for complex issues, you always have a very effective way to neutralize the smart-aleck. If you fight the know-it-all, you may gain some sympathy from the rest of the group, but you'll be diverted from your topic and end up being less effective with your message.

THE TALKER

This is the person who distracts by talking during your talk. Usually, talkers travel in pairs, unless they're crazy. So how do you handle people talking when you're talking?

You do nothing. That's right, nothing. Believe it or not, the audience handles them for you. Try this. Go to a movie with a friend. Start talking with your friend. It won't take long before someone whirls around and shushes you. In a play, a ballet, or an opera—anywhere people pay money—fear not, they will quiet the talkers.

People pay to attend a meeting. It's their time, and time is money. Trust the crowd to help you out on this one because the talkers not only disrupt the speaker, they distract the listener, too.

THE BOSS

Of all the distractions in the world, the boss's presence can stop a presenter cold. How do you deal with a superior in the crowd? You usually freak out. The reason is that your effort to impress becomes greater, and you simply try too hard. In the theater it's called overacting, and it usually happens when the actor knows a critic is in the audience.

You may find yourself making more eye contact and directing more of the information to your boss at the expense of the rest of the audience. This is a big mistake because you lose on two counts. First, the audience is slighted from your true attention, and second, your boss may feel singled out during every moment. This is frustrating. When a presenter pays a lot of attention to one person, that person feels obligated to listen even more attentively, almost out of courtesy.

The solution to presenting to a superior is to treat that person the same as all the others in the room. Don't pay any more or any less attention than to anyone else. If you deliver the talk with sincerity and you follow the objective through to the call to action, the presence of your boss will have gone unnoticed. The key here is to neutralize the superiority with equality.

The distractions you might face can break your concentration if you are not prepared to handle the diversion. Typically, you don't fight fire with fire in these cases. You usually play to counter or neutralize the offender. If you stay focused, you remain in control of the presentation, and you hold the attention of your audience as you deliver the message.

USING YOUR HEART

You go to a play and the actor comes to the edge of the stage and he's crying. If you say, "Wow, look at that! Real tears!" you saw technique. If he's crying and you're crying—you are in the moment. You are sharing the emotion, not watching it happen.

You can't limit your skill set to the physical or even the physical and mental. You have to use your heart. You're a whole person—body, voice, mind, and heart. You present with your whole being.

I once had a colleague who had the potential to completely master this skill. She had so much going for her. She perfected physical movement and developed excellent voice control; she used her head, linking intentions with content to convey messages effectively. But she failed to take the last step and use her emotions. This limited her use of humor as well, and it restricted her growth as a consummate communicator. By not committing herself to her own feelings, she let a gap of emptiness exist between herself and her audiences.

The use of emotion is what separates presenting from performing. As a visual presenter you will have to create the emotional link between you and your audience.

UNDERSTANDING MOTIVATION

Think of all the means at your disposal to express your feelings to an audience. Your eyes, facial expressions, voice, and gestures—your whole body emits feeling in order to make words have meaning. But without your personal commitment, your belief, and your motivation, the audience doesn't react as well as expected. Motivation requires inner energy to deliver the information with conviction.

That energy starts with you. You're the catalyst. You have to give an emotion to get an emotion. You have to be motivated before you can expect the group to be motivated. This is one of the most obvious problems I find in working with presenters. They fail to "get into it," but they expect the audience to "get it." If you can't psyche yourself up for the moment, why should the audience be expected to do so? You have to work on yourself to get your heart into it. But before you build the desire (the motivation) to tell the story, you have to believe in your message.

SENSE OF TRUTH

The chance to stir the feelings of a group to truly believe what you believe is the essence of your skill. Your ultimate challenge is to make them believe in your belief in the message. People can't have faith in the message without believing in the person representing the message. People believe in other people. The audience wants above all to believe what you are telling them. It is that simple. That belief starts in your own heart because if you don't buy it, they don't buy it. You must have a sense of truth about your message. This becomes your motivation to deliver that sense of truth with clarity and enthusiasm.

So, ask yourself, "What in the message do I really believe is true?" Everything, something, nothing? Remember that in life, truth is what you know. In presenting, truth doesn't exist until you demonstrate it. Using action, you must show your version of the truth to an audience. But if you can't justify your actions, then the truth is less obvious. Truth and belief are inseparable. You must believe something to show its truth. It reminds me of the saying "Practice what you preach." In almost every coaching session I say, "Do you believe it?"

The best way to develop a sense of truth in your message is to play the devil's advocate with the argument you constructed for the audience. Can you convincingly play both sides of the issue? Can you be the prosecution and the defense? Naturally, the side that wins has more of your sense of truth because it has more of your heart. Truth is in the heart, not the mind. The more the message appeals to you, the more evidence you look for to support it.

Your sense of truth in your topic is directly related to your belief in that topic. Whatever appeals to you most in that truth will be delivered with the most conviction.

THINKING, FEELING, WANTING

Your sense of truth in the message justifies your presenting it. Motivation makes it happen. The motivation to speak is measured by your will, your desire, and your determination. Your feelings and your intellect are both supported by your will. They all work for one another and can hardly be separated. If you use your intellect (mind) to decide on some action, you must call upon your feelings (heart) and your desire (motivation) to make the action happen. You can't separate them. They all work together synergistically. Although action drives emotion, you have to want to create the action in the first place.

For example, let's say you must make a presentation to a group of people about a new product. You know how you will present the message because you've planned it. The planning involved a thinking process, but it doesn't stop there. How do you feel about the plan to present the product? How do you feel about the product itself? How about the people you'll be speaking to, and even the place you'll be presenting in? Considering those feelings, what motivates you to deliver the information at all?

You might say, "My paycheck." Believe it or not, money can motivate only as much as what it gives you—security, luxury, power, and so on. If the motivation is from only a need to present (to get paid), then it is not being driven by desire. It becomes one of those presentations you have to do, but would skip if you could. This, unfortunately, is the case with over 95% of all presentations.

You've heard the excuses. "I just don't have it today," "I'm not into it right now," or "This doesn't interest me." You've probably used these expressions yourself.

When the motivation, the desire, the will is missing, the feelings disappear and the mind is left alone to direct the body and the voice. When this happens, the presenter appears to be going through the motions, and the effect of the message is usually lost.

People Make a Difference

Motivation is a key element to making presentations more effective. I have been giving the same basic skills seminar for a number of years. Often people come up to me who've seen my show more than once and say, "I keep getting more and more out of this seminar; what have you added?" I say, "I've changed nothing." The response is typically, "But something is different."

There is one difference. I'll tell you what it is in a minute.

I've had others ask, "How can you give the same seminar, over and over again, and not be totally bored with the topic?" I respond, "The same way an actor in the theater can play the same role six nights a week for two years and deliver the same part with enthusiasm—because every night is different." It's the same reason my seminar seems different each time.

The answer is different people. When the people change, the event changes because the event is by people, for people. It's a completely new presentation for each new audience. That's the secret behind the motivation. It's the desire and the will to share anew. Whether it's the same information for different people or even new information for the same people, the motivation is a result of change.

Never look to your content to stimulate your will. Look to the people who will be stimulated. It's not the joke that's funny; rather, it's the reaction. Your anticipation of the laughter motivates you to tell the joke. The inspiration you need to present the topic with conviction comes from the simple fact that people are willing to give you their time. If that's not enough to get you excited about your delivery, then consider yourself one of the average communicators—one of the talking heads that people expect to see each time a presentation takes place.

Always visualize the effect of your words on the group and you will understand your motivation. Think of infecting rather than affecting the audience, and your desire to deliver the message will increase.

ADDING STORIES AND PERSONAL OPINIONS

In a world where every product looks the same, the one difference is you. That's what being a visual presenter is all about. Companies differentiate not with products, but with people. If people make the difference, then you can bet that individual experience and personal opinion count for something. Experience means you've been there and have probably formed some philosophy over the years. You've learned some lessons over the course of time. Talk about the lessons, what you learned, and the way you see it. Talk about the way it was, and you'll convince people about the way it should be.

The best presenters tell stories. I can't stress that enough. The advantage of good stories is that they are unique. No one can copy, duplicate, reiterate, reproduce, retransmit, or recount your stories. They are personal references that enable a group of people to know something about what you have been through. Stories and personal experience are ways to share your character with an audience.

TIME, PLACE, AND CIRCUMSTANCE

The rules of storytelling are simple. The audience has to know when it happened, where it happened, and what conditions existed while it happened. If you don't establish time, place, and circumstance, you have less chance of keeping the audience attentive to your story.

Several years ago I was at a big conference and everything was hectic. That's the beginning of my story. How involved are you at this point? What do you really know so far? More important, what do you visualize about the event compared to what I remember about it? Let's break it apart.

"Several years ago"—whatever year you might be thinking of may not be the one I am, so we are not together on that issue. I mentioned "a big conference"—but you are probably visualizing a completely different event in a much different place. Finally, I said, "everything was hectic"—to you, maybe hectic means chaotic, confused, frenzied, or simply wild. Adjectives are tough for everyone to agree on.

Clearly my story doesn't put us on the same page so far. Our references are different. A story works best when we all share a common set of parameters. I need to establish time, place, and circumstance very quickly, to pull you into my story.

It was August 12, 1996. I was inside the San Diego Convention Center at the Republican National Convention, escaping the 100-degree heat. I was with a few thousand people crammed into this closet-of-a-room and suddenly—no air conditioning. Everything was hectic.

Do you see what a big difference those details make? It takes about 20 seconds more to add the description, but you are definitely with me in the story. You know the time (August 1996); you know the place (San Diego, Republican Convention); you know the circumstance (no air conditioning). We both can agree on what hectic means now.

When you specify time, place, and circumstance, you help the listener see what you are recalling in your mind. When you detail with adjectives (crammed, closet-of-a-room, and hectic), you let the listener feel what you are re-creating in your heart.

Storytelling is about attributes and attitudes. Keep that in mind every time you tell a story, and you will be more descriptive of both the facts and the feelings associated with the experience.

PERSONAL OPINIONS MATTER

It's one thing to tell good stories, whether they happened to you or to someone else. It's also important to editorialize. You have to voice your opinion every so often so that people know you're involved in the message. The editorial is the slant on the topic that the audience expects to hear from you. It's the emotional hook that keeps them coming back for more. Just don't be afraid to say the word "I" when you speak.

For example, let's say you're giving a presentation, and you bring up a bullet chart with a list of services your company provides. You may find yourself reciting the list and adding more explanation here and there. How do you feel about these services? The audience would love to know. Maybe you say, "What I really find helpful about" or "One of my favorite ways to use this"—these are personal opinions. Your views tell the audience so much more than your reviews. Don't be afraid to show them your take on life.

That's why we watch talk shows and read those letters to the editor. We are addicted to the unsupported assertions of people we will never meet. If a schoolteacher in West Podunk, Ohio, calls in to *Larry King Live* and criticizes a comment by a state senator from Texas, I'll sit there mesmerized while I dig deeper into my half-gallon of Vanilla-Fudge Swirl. I have no idea why, other than that I have to hear an opinion on anything by anybody, anywhere. Maybe you're not that bad. The point is that we are fascinated by other people's opinions and stories. It's part of the intrigue of being human.

You can be much more effective when you break the pattern of the presentation with stories and personal opinions. It gives the audience an image of a real person who knows how to share information in an interesting way.

USING HUMOR

A traveling salesman walks into a local bar and orders a beer. The bar is crowded, but it's pretty quiet.

Suddenly a voice shouts out, "72!" and everyone just bursts into laughter. The salesman looks puzzled.

The crowd settles, again another voice yells, "114!" and people are just doubling over in hysterics.

The salesman leans to the bartender and says, "What's the deal with the numbers and the laughs?"

The bartender replies, "Oh, this bar has been here for years. Same crowd all the time. Well, they know all the jokes, got tired of telling them, so they numbered them all. When you want to tell a joke, you just yell the number. It's pretty simple!"

The salesman whispers, "Do you mind if I try?"

The bartender says, "Give it a shot."

The salesman clears his throat, waits for a lull, and yells, "84!" Nothing! No response, not even a chuckle. He tries again, even louder, "84!" Dead silence. One more time he shouts, "84!" Blank stares.

Frustrated, he turns to the bartender and says, "What's up? Why don't they laugh? Is something wrong with number 84?"

The bartender shakes his head and says, "Hey, pal, face it. Some people just can't tell a joke!"

I think you get the point. If you aren't funny now, you probably won't be funny when you present. This doesn't mean you can't learn things about timing and rhythm, but humor is exactness, precision, and accuracy. You can miss with tragedy and have some people in tears while others sniffle, but comedy is different. They either laugh or they don't. Smirks and chuckles don't count.

I don't want you to shy away from using humor; rather, I want you to realize how effective humor can be in a presentation. In a world of visual creatures, entertainment ranks high on the list of "what they want." Humor is the best entertainment you can add to an event, because it relaxes people and makes them realize that the world isn't coming to an end after all. The use of humor at the right time with the right inflection can be extremely effective.

OPENING LINES

"I just flew in from New York. Boy, are my arms tired!" That's fine if you are a standup comic. A comedian is expected to be funny. But are you expected to be funny? When someone says, "I want to start off with a joke," I ask why? What makes you think the audience expects an opening joke? For that matter, why not sing? If they expect a joke, surely they expect a song, maybe even a dance! If they've seen you present before and they know you for your humor, then yes, tell the joke. But if they don't know your style, the joke better be really funny. No, I mean really funny. If it's not, it will probably bomb.

Don't just tell an opening joke for the sake of the joke. Whatever opener you choose, make it relate to the topic, the industry, the specific business, or even to a general characteristic about the group, like the fact that they are all in sales or marketing.

I was the keynote speaker at an annual meeting for a global travel agency. My opener was a Henny Youngman joke: "So, I got to the airport, walked up to the ticket counter and said, 'I have three bags here. I want one bag to go to Rome, one to Detroit, and the third one to Dallas.' The attendant said, 'We can't do that!' I said, 'Why not? You did it last week!'" For this group, the joke fit the industry.

STRETCHING THE RUBBER BAND

When I prepare my own presentations, I structure the key issues around the jokes. This is very important because it uses a theater principle called "stretching the rubber band." Think of the emotions of the audience as a simple rubber band. One side is serious; the other side is humorous. When the rubber band is stretched, the distance between the two sides is greater. If you let go of one side, the impact from the other side is bigger. An unstretched rubber band creates less impact.

Applying this principle to presentations, the humor offsets the serious tone of the talk. The timing is the trick. When the humor is at its peak, when you are delivering the funniest line—that's when the rubber band is stretched the most. Immediately following that moment is when you can get the greatest effect from being serious. The seriousness of the message is greater when the audience least expects it. If they are relaxed from a lighthearted comment, then they are vulnerable to the importance of an issue. The timing of your humor can effectively heighten the importance of your message.

INDICATING AND APOLOGIZING

Don't indicate your humor. If you begin to laugh before the audience does, then the effect of the joke diminishes. This is because you indicated or telegraphed the result (laughter) before it could happen for the audience. If you laugh for the crowd, then they won't have to. One other way of indicating humor is by stating, "That reminds me of a joke," or "Here's a really funny story." When you say things like that, you raise the expectation of the group. In that case, it better be funny.

The best way to develop your delivery of humor is to practice telling jokes or funny stories to those closest to you. Family and friends will be the first to tell you if your jokes are funny. But make sure you find the jokes funny as well, or you will not tell them with commitment.

Finally, if a joke falls flat, keep going. Never apologize and never comment on the failure of humor. It's done. Move on. Only a comedian has to worry about being funny all the time. If you bomb out, it only makes the audience relieved that you don't tell jokes for a living.

That reminds me of the two construction workers who...

DEVELOPING YOUR OWN STYLE

Probably the most important issue in the whole skill of delivery is the development of your own style. Think of style not as fashion, but as character.

The audience evaluates your character in relation to the message, the media, and the mechanics. All of these elements are part of the event. If you have developed your own natural way to deliver consistent messages, your style will emerge. People will remember your kind of presentation. Your style will show each time you deliver, regardless of the content.

LEVELS IN YOUR STYLE

One way of assuring your own style is to match three levels of objectives in this order: the objectives for your life, for your role within the organization, and for your current presentation.

Start with your life. Let's say one of the objectives or goals you have in life is to be rich. Then look at your role in your current company. Is there an objective in your job description that possibly can match your life goal of attaining great wealth? Maybe not great wealth, but possibly a raise or a promotion—the steps to greater wealth. Finally, is there anything in the presentation that has to do with attaining great wealth, even if not directly for you but for the company? Look for it.

For example, perhaps part of the presentation discusses company growth. More revenue for the corporation might increase the budget for payroll. That could mean a nice fat raise for you. The extra cash might be what you need for the down payment on that piece of property you've been looking at recently. You know that property appreciates in value, and it would be so nice to have the land as an investment for the future.

During the presentation, the discussion of company growth is in direct line with your goal of attaining great wealth. Chances are that you will cover this topic with more enthusiasm because it matches something that appeals to you—in your heart. That's important in the development of your own style.

Many things in your life appeal to you. If any of them exist in your work and through the presentations you give because of your work, all the better to identify them and use them. Link the little objectives of your talk to the larger objectives of your work and into the even bigger objectives of your life.

THROUGH LINE OF ACTION

Paying attention to everything that comes before, during, and following your presentation develops your character or style. It is one continuous process called a *through line of action*. This is important because it lets you link all of the elements in the presentation with the reality of the way things are.

For example, suppose you are giving a presentation on a Monday morning to a group of people. You begin at 9:00 a.m. and plan to finish at about 11:00 a.m. There will be one 15-minute break at 10:00 a.m. Let's make your through line of action for this example run from the time you woke up until after lunch.

Run through the details of those moments and you'll see a range of events from the very consistent to the very unique. The wake-up routine is probably the same. Depending on where the presentation takes place, locally or out of town, the commute to the event may be more or less familiar. The arrival at the event might be unique, depending on how many times you've done this same presentation for the same people in the same space. The event itself will have some information you've mentioned many times and some new information you are presenting for the first time. You can see how an examination of the continuous action will show you a combination of daily habits and one-of-a-kind activities.

The habits are already a part of your personal style. Don't worry about them at all. The one-of-a-kind moments are part of this through line of action, which eventually may add to your personal style, depending on how often they are repeated. The more you can pinpoint and control the unique moments, the more likely it is that they will recur the next time you present.

DON'T EVEN THINK ABOUT IT!

The examination of your through line of action—that is, the connecting points along the way—is how you develop good habits. Although habits are hard to break, the good ones last forever. You don't even need to think about them after a while because they are part of your natural way of doing things.

Tip from
Tom Mucciolo

Look back at all the segments in Chapter 22, "The Message—Scripting the Concept," through this chapter and put a check mark next to those sections you believe are already part of your style. Put a question mark next to the parts that you think you can achieve for yourself with some effort. Cross out any section that you feel is totally impossible for you to ever accomplish, regardless of how hard you try.

The check-marked items are already yours, and you need not think about them. The question marks represent the work you have to do to make them into check marks.

My guess is that you won't cross out anything because there is nothing you can't accomplish if you try hard enough!

There was a time in your life when, for a few weeks, all you did was spend every single waking moment of your day trying to accomplish a task that today you take for granted. It's called walking. At one time it was a rare privilege; now it's just part of the way you move.

When your presentation skills evolve from a rarity to routine, your own style becomes second nature. This is the result of putting so much of yourself into the mechanics of function—the inner life of your delivery—so that no one else can copy, reproduce, or mimic your personal skill set in any way.

Your body, voice, mind, and heart combine to form the foundation of your skill as a visual presenter. Once developed, your own style will be evident in the message, the media, and the mechanics as you perform your presentation for an appreciative audience. Every move you make, every word you utter, every thought you express, and every feeling you have will be part of your natural style. You'll finally be able to trust your own skills whenever you are truly being yourself in the presentation.

TROUBLESHOOTING

DEMONSTRATING BEFORE A GROUP

What's the best way to do a product demonstration for a group?

Whenever you have to focus the attention of the audience on a prop (a tangible object), you should be concerned about physical perspective. If your physical perspective of the object— your viewing angle—is different from that of the audience, communication is lost. Many product demonstrations fail because the presenter and the audience do not share the same perspective during the demonstration.

For example, let's say the product you need to demonstrate is small enough to rest on top of a table and light enough that you can hold it up to show people. If you are standing and the audience is sitting, the object will be viewed from different angles as it rests on the table. Your angle is from above, and each person in the audience, by virtue of his seat, has a differ- ent viewing angle to the object. That should be your first indication that you need to change the perspective. You might decide to hold the object in the air so people farther back can see, but you still end up with a variety of viewing angles. What can be done to equalize the perspective?

One solution is to reproduce the demonstration for view on a screen. The display screen is the great equalizer of perspective. You can use a still photograph of the object or you can play a videotape of the object in use. You can even use a camera connected to your projector to show the live demonstration on the big screen. There are many ways you can create a visual impression of the object so everyone has the same perspective. This is why movies are so entertaining. The camera is doing all the work for you.

HANDLING TEAM PRESENTATIONS

I give presentations as part of a team. Sometimes two or three of us present different parts of the big picture. Do you have any advice for team presentations?

Teams are very common in high-level sales presentations, initial public offerings (IPOs), and other events where several experts are required to deliver a single message. Whatever the venue, the point is that more than one person is presenting, and that alone changes the dynamics of the event.

The mechanics of function, as discussed in this chapter, play a very important role in the relationships established by the team for the audience. The better the team members know each other, the more cohesive the team appears. I would first suggest you get to know the players on your team. Find out likes, dislikes, hobbies, interests, opinions, concerns, fears, aspirations, and anything else that will help you understand the characteristics of your team members.

Let's put this into perspective using a husband/wife analogy. Even if you aren't married, this can apply to any two partners who know each other very well. You and your partner are at a dinner with several friends. A suggestion is made to commit to doing something the follow- ing Saturday night. You look at your partner and you can sense, within seconds, his interest in the plan. This is because you understand how each of you thinks, feels, and behaves in similar situations. You share a personal history.

When I coach teams, I use exercises to build a personal history to be shared by all team members. I suggest you look for that history in your team members. Have they been through this type of presentation before? Have they experienced a similar turn of events?

Another important element in team presenting is what I call "the exchange." This is the transition between presenters—the awkward moment when one person finishes a section and introduces the next person to continue with the presentation. It is during that moment that an audience looks for a relationship between the two individuals. Do they like each other? Are they friends? Do they get along? Most presenters will simply leave this moment blank. There are no words spoken, no dialogue planned, no exchange.

You should develop a small bit of banter so that the audience gets an immediate impression that the two presenters have a good, healthy relationship. Maybe you plan a humorous story where one person comments on the driving habits of the other "on the way to the presenta-tion." Perhaps you mention a personal hobby or sport that the other person likes. The point is to let the audience see that a relationship exists. If they think you work well together, they will feel more confident in the organization that supports you as well.

Team presenting is about demonstrating relationships, and relationships can be built only from sharing personal information that can be used to help the team function as a unit.

CHAPTER 26

EXPLORING TECHNICALITIES AND TECHNIQUES

In this chapter

by Tom Mucciolo

DEALING WITH THE CONDITIONS

Beyond the message, the media, and the mechanics, the event itself adds another dimension to the planning process. The environment plays a significant role in how the presentation is received by the audience.

For example, when you go to a movie, the lobby, the concession stand, the seats, the size of the screen, and the general conditions of the place will affect how much you enjoy the movie. These environmental elements won't really change from day to day, so they become issues you can learn about in advance of going to that particular theater.

The audience will also make a difference in how much you enjoy the event, but you can't predict the crowd, unless you already have experience with the general group that frequents that theater. You have less control (if any) over the audience than you have over the environment.

You want to be ready for anything when you present and, believe me, anything can happen at even the most well-planned event. This chapter looks at the external factors that can affect your performance.

DRESSING THE PART

The first external element to deal with is what to wear when presenting. When you're not presenting, anything goes, depending on corporate or social standards. You know what you can or can't wear. In front of a group, I suggest you stick to something BASIC: a Believable Appearance is Simple and the Image is Conservative.

Try for that classically conservative look with a dash of personal style. When you dress more conservatively, the audience accepts you more quickly, and you will reduce those first impression biases. A business presentation is contemporary, and your clothing must not overtake the message. A few points to keep in mind to make your clothing go unnoticed are discussed in the following sections.

FOCUSING ON THE FACE

Your face is looked at the most because it carries the message through your voice and your expressions. Nothing should distract the audience from seeing your face. Usually, your clothes can cause a distraction, but in some cases the items around and even on your face can lessen the impact of your expressions, such as a distracting hairstyle, jewelry, makeup, glasses, and so forth. Let's take a look at what it takes to keep the focus on the face.

THE SKIN

My first bit of advice is to the guys—shave! A clean look is an advantage because it lets all your facial expressions show, especially your smile. Women have the advantage of using makeup to accent their features and make expression more visible from a distance. With makeup, be aware of lighting and how the brightness may wash out your features; if possible, apply makeup in the same type of lighting you'll be in while presenting. Cosmetics, like clothing, change style with the seasons, so avoid the makeup time warp. If you have or know of a beauty consultant, it never hurts to get advice. Both men and women presenting under bright lights should use pressed powder to reduce the shine, caused mostly by the heat. This is important as the lighting gets closer.

The Hair

Your hair must be well-trimmed so that it enhances, not hides, your facial expressions. If you wear your hair long, try to keep it pulled back. Otherwise, when you turn your head, your hair might block much of your face. The audience needs to see at least one eye. With your head turned toward the visual, most people get to see only one of your eyes. If it's covered by your hair, it's like having your back to the audience.

Long hair on men is still not generally accepted in all ranks of presenting and, depending on the audience, may generate an undesirable reaction. If you are balding, you have a presentation advantage. You have the added expression of the brow and of making all your facial features appear more dominant. In any case, the hair should not make a statement or the focus will not be on the face.

Eyewear

If eyewear is required, you should first opt for contact lenses because they don't hide eye expressions. If you must wear glasses, try to find ones with a non-glare finish. This will reflect less light, and the audience will be able to see your eyes better. Glass-glare usually is most noticeable in conference rooms and most rooms with average-height ceilings. When you stand and people sit in this type of room, the angle of reflection from the overhead light breaks right at your eyes, regardless of your height. No one knows why this is so, but it is. You could try to raise the earpieces to tilt your glasses forward, but make sure they don't fall off.

Working with Accessories

Collars and necklines should be conservative. You can add a little more expression with ties and scarves. These accessories are great because they naturally draw attention to your face. Bow ties typically are associated with a character trait, and unless the audience already knows you and your bow-tie look, they may not take you seriously. For ties, learn to make a square knot (Windsor knot) so the tie looks symmetrical at the neck. Don't wear those big cartoon ties or the ones with pictures of dead presidents, and avoid the scarves with artistic images of who-knows-what-it-is-or-cares. All these styles distract the audience.

Pins, tie clips, pocket squares, beads, cuff links, and earrings can add polish and style, but wear them sparingly and make sure they don't distract by being reflective or noisy. A watch is your most important presentation accessory because you probably need to keep track of the time. Choose a watch face that is big enough and has enough contrast for you to sneak a look at the time easily as you gesture.

Tip from

Tom Mucciolo

Wear your watch on your left arm when you present, even if you normally wear it on your right. The left hand is the one that gestures to the screen and can be lifted higher than your shoulder. A glance at the face of the watch is easiest from that angle, and because your face is turned away, the audience can't see you look slightly downward to see the time. If you have your watch on your right arm, trying to look at it will be more obvious to an audience member who is looking directly at your face.

Wearing Business Outfits

If the suit fits, wear it. The look, comfort, and style all depend on how well a suit fits and drapes your body. Suits that fit well make you feel better. A suit that is too baggy will look sloppy as you move, and one that's too tight will restrict your movement. Choose a suit that is well constructed and use that suit often. In fact, if you present a lot, I suggest investing in a presentation suit that you reserve for events.

Once again, think conservative. Solid colors or subtle patterns are best. Plaids and large houndstooth patterns tend to "vibrate" and can be quite distracting. As for color, it's best to be traditional and subtle. Dark blue and dark-to-medium gray are the most conservative and traditional choices. Women have more opportunities with color choices than men, but that doesn't mean trendy selections will always work. Choosing the right clothing colors for your complexion can make you seem vibrant and energetic, whereas the wrong colors can make you look tired and gloomy. Color can also complement your figure. In fact, dark colors minimize the figure, and light colors emphasize the figure. Based on your body type, choose accordingly.

On the Top

Shirts and blouses should be fitted for movement and comfort. You don't want very tight outfits, and you should avoid short sleeves while presenting. The reason is that a short sleeve makes the arms look choppy right around the elbow because of the change from cloth to skin. Your gestures are harder to follow because they don't look smooth.

For men, the shirt should be lighter than the suit, and the tie should be darker than the shirt. When in doubt, white is never wrong. For women, the color contrast can vary a bit more, but if you plan to wear a lavaliere microphone, make sure you wear a blouse that buttons up the front or a v-neck top so that the microphone can be clipped in the center and not to one side. Centering equalizes sound pick-up.

Jackets and blazers, like suits, should be fitted for movement and comfort. Watch out for pairing separates of contrasting colors. Think of making a solid line of color from the floor to the neck to draw attention up to your face. A lot of people wonder whether the jacket should be buttoned or unbuttoned. A man must wear his jacket unbuttoned if he plans to move and gesture. This eliminates double-breasted styles because they are meant to be buttoned all the time. If a man buttons a single-breasted jacket and gestures to the screen, for example, the jacket will gape and pucker because men's jackets are cut in a boxy manner.

A woman has the choice to leave her jacket buttoned or unbuttoned because women's jackets are cut to fit the curves of the female frame and tend to move naturally with the figure. However, a jacket usually looks better when buttoned.

TOWARD THE BOTTOM

Men will wear trousers, but a woman has the choice of a skirt or trousers when presenting. Trousers allow easy movement and are generally accepted in the corporate setting when part of a suit. Avoid separates, because they tend to be less formal and more contrasting. With both skirts and trousers, pay attention to hems, making sure the length is tailored and conservative. For both women and men, socks must coordinate with trousers and be long enough to cover the calf. There may be times when you are part of a panel on a platform stage. When you sit, your pants ride up and you don't want the skin on your leg showing. Longer socks prevent this. Women should choose stockings that minimize attention to legs and create a solid look, drawing the eye from the floor to the face.

IT'S GOTTA BE THE SHOES

Footwear is a sound investment because good shoes tend to look and feel good. People judge one another by the shoes. They look at your feet and decide on your grooming habits and even how much money you make, so polish your shoes.

Specifically for women, heels are a symbol of authority and are highly recommended for boosting your credibility (no pun intended). However, heels that are too high affect balance and breathing, so stick to one-inch or two-inch heels.

Platforms are a big trend in footwear right now, mostly among teens and the 20-something crowd. When you're shopping for shoes and hear the word "platforms," think youth before you think presentation. Obviously, lower heels allow easier movement when you navigate backward in your triangle. Although the heels that are usually worn with business suits today are thicker than in the past and fairly comfortable, I have talked with women who've worn heels for most of their careers, and they say that totally flat shoes are actually uncomfortable because their calf muscles are stretching more than with heels.

CHOOSING A FORMALITY

Dress-down Fridays have caused a 20% drop in business for pantyhose makers. Lots of companies have a business casual day at least once a week, and many offices have adapted a relaxed dress code throughout the week. In fact, with the growing number of telecommuters and people working in other nonoffice-like settings, casual attire is becoming more and more accepted. This definitely puts a strain on presenters who aren't sure what to wear and when. Should you always wear the power suit when presenting, or should you match the corporate culture?

When in doubt, wear your suit. Otherwise, try to dress one level above your audience. For example, if they are wearing jeans and chambray shirts, wear khaki trousers and a sweater vest. If they're wearing khakis, wear dark wool trousers and a blazer. If they're wearing blazers, wear the suit. Your goal is to maintain a sense of authority over your audience. Staying one level above in formality will help you look the part.

This whole what-to-wear question is more about sincerity than anything else. Take a look in the mirror or ask a friend to be blatantly honest. It's easy to find the flaws. Focus on what looks right and make it better. If you ever get unsolicited compliments, build on them.

Don't be afraid to consult with professionals. Lots of books cover this topic in depth, and I encourage you to read some of them. From the view of a visual presenter, the focus must be on the face; from that point outward, gestures and movement will create the action in the presentation. Clothing should not get the attention of the audience, because the outfit cannot deliver the message.

SETTING THE STAGE

You might spend a lot of time preparing for a presentation, but when you arrive to deliver, all your difficulties may just be starting. It seems the only things that go according to plan are the problems.

Many things can happen to make the audience uncomfortable, distracted, and even disinterested. Many of these things can be dealt with in advance. Of course, experience is the best teacher. Hundreds of presentations have taught me that well-thought-out logistics of an event (planning and coordinating) make a world of difference for everyone involved, especially me.

The bottom line is that *you* are ultimately responsible for your presentation and the conditions of the event for the audience. If the group expects coffee and there is no coffee, it is your fault. It's certainly not the audience's fault. They did their job; they showed up. The rest of the event is in your hands. Even if you delegate tasks to others, the ultimate responsibility is still yours.

If you plan ahead, you can set the stage for a great event by paying attention to the logistics covered in the following sections.

USING RISERS

If you've already dressed the part, then it makes sense that everyone be able to see as much of your outfit as possible. If you use the Hollywood principle of "more face, more body, and more screen" when planning the room layout, you'll realize a good starting point is to consider risers or stage platforms. I'll use the terms interchangeably, even though a riser is typically lower than a platform.

Remember that ballrooms are designed for dinner and for dancing, not for discussion. The plan to make such a space "presentable" must be well thought out. Line-of-sight is critical: If the audience can't see you or your support information, they can't grasp the entire message.

When you stand on the same level as the chairs, most people see only the top third of your body. In larger settings, always look for the opportunity to use platforms to raise yourself one or two feet from the floor. Platforms give those sitting in the back a chance to see more of you. It is more difficult to communicate when less of your body is visible. When you are on the same level as the audience, I suggest that you at least keep your wrists higher than your elbows when gesturing, so that everyone has a better chance to see those gestures.

If given the chance to place yourself at a higher level than the floor, take it. The audience will get to see more of you and your physical expression of the message. Stage platforms or risers can give you that little lift you need to be seen.

Risers can range from as little as 6 inches high to large platforms that adjust from 18 to 24 inches. You can even use a fixed stage, if available, which is usually 36 inches from the floor. In some corporate auditoriums, the seating is fixed as well, and the rows are sometimes built up on an incline, similar to a playhouse or movie theater.

You won't be able to make changes to fixed structures or stationary seating, but in most hotel situations you can request platforms. Platforms are usually six feet by eight feet and can be rolled into the space and locked together for stability. In some cases, the platforms are four feet by eight feet. In addition, most platforms have extension supports that can change the height from 18 inches to 24 inches.

For audiences of about 50 to 100 people, 18 inches should be the minimum. For more than 100 people, use the 24-inch height setting for maximum visibility. Of course, if the best you can get are 12-inch risers, take them. Any opportunity for the audience to see you better is worth it.

Most platforms are covered with material such as carpeting to dull the hollow sound from your footsteps when you move. If the staging is not carpeted, you'll have to place less of your weight on your heels as you move or simply take smaller steps to minimize any distractions.

Tip from
Tom Mucciolo

Check for the creaks. If possible, walk around the entire stage before the presentation and take note of any creaks or squeaking sounds you hear. If you know that part of the staging makes noise when you walk over it, you should avoid that area as much as possible. The last thing you want is a loud squeak just as you say a key phrase. Many creaks in staging happen where the platforms meet. Some heavy-duty tape can usually eliminate the problem.

Of course, when you are up on risers, avoid leaning forward when you are in the front of the triangle. For people in the front row of the audience, this can appear intimidating. It's best to keep your weight shifted back or stand straight. Depending on platform height and proximity to the first row, the angle of your face gets distorted when you get too close to the edge of the stage.

WORKING WITH LIGHTING AND SOUND

If you can choose only one thing during a presentation, it should be good lighting, followed closely by good sound. The whole notion of a visual presenter revolves around being seen and heard. When an audience watches your presentation, they are getting a lot from your physical delivery, and a tremendous amount of emphasis is given to your facial expressions, including your voice. Bad lighting masks your expressions, and poor acoustics makes the message difficult to hear.

LIGHTING

Good lighting is the key to a good presentation. The audience should see as much of the presenter's face as possible. The goal is to create an unequal distribution of light, with most of the light on the presenter, some light over the audience for note-taking, and no light on the screen (other than from the projected image, of course).

You need only two stage lights to cross-light the presenter effectively. Add a dimmer pack, and you can adjust the light level so that the presenter can still see the audience while speaking.

I recommend using two Leiko lights on trees. A Leiko light is a stage light of 500 to 750 watts (or more) and has four adjustable shutters for directing (cropping) the light into a specific area without spilling onto another area, specifically the screen.

The light is hung from a big metal pole that sits in a round heavy base, with a smaller metal pole across the top that holds one to four lights. When you use stage lights, it's best when the ceiling height is 15 feet or higher and free from obstructions such as low-hanging chandeliers. The lower the ceiling, the lower the lights hang from the tree. Low-hanging lights usually spill into the first few rows of the audience, and you end up with shadows of people in your triangle. You don't want silhouettes all over your body as you move around, which happens when the angle of the light is too low. Higher ceilings allow the light to cast down on you and not spill onto the audience. Use the shutters to crop the light from the bottom if the angles are too low.

Tip from
Tom Mucciolo

In the case of low ceilings, position the light trees closer to the riser on opposite sides of the room and direct the light just a little higher (using a little bounce light from the ceiling). Be sure to keep all light from spilling onto the screen. Depending on the angle, this will be more difficult for the light positioned on the side of the room where the presenter stands. In addition, you may need to arrange a few seats differently so no one's view is blocked by light poles.

A dimmer pack can be a small switch with a round knob, or it can be a complete lighting board with moving levers to reduce the intensity of the lights.

If you are not used to lighting and you stand on a stage with even one light at full intensity, you'll be seeing orange spots for about a week! If you are working with stage lights, make sure you can handle the bright light without excessive blinking or squinting. That's why a dimmer pack is important. Typically, you'll drop the level to about 60% or lower, depending on how much of the audience you need to see. The brighter the lights, the less chance of your seeing a hand raised for questions.

Tip from
Tom Mucciolo

One way to test how bright the lights should be is to bring them up until you see a glare off your cheeks in the lower peripheral of your eyes. The point at which your skin reflects the light into the bottoms of your eyes is the maximum brightness setting.

Two lights are needed to provide cross-lighting. Just a single light from one side creates shadows on your face on the opposite side. Cross-lighting allows light to reach you from each direction and eliminates any shadows, regardless of whether you stand in the rest or power position.

You might think it costs a lot of money to have lighting set up this way, but we're talking about only $250 for everything. Obviously, that's an average price and may be higher, but it's worth checking into when planning the event.

Creative Lighting

If lighting isn't available, you have some inexpensive options, especially if you're at a hotel or conference center. One approach is to rent two 35mm slide projectors and position them on high stands at opposite sides of the room. You can adjust the size of the projected light to fill the presenting area.

You may need a blank, clear slide to let the light pass through the lens, although some slide projectors will project light without a slide in the carousel. To make a blank, simply take any 35mm slide and punch out the film to make a clear opening.

Another lighting option is to rent two overhead projectors. Place them on opposite sides on high stands, keeping in mind that you'll have to place them much closer than slide projectors. You can tape sheets of paper to the overhead projector to shape the light to your exact space, similar to the way shutters work for stage lights.

PART
VII

CH
26

In smaller venues such as a conference room, incandescent lighting works best. These are recessed lights that usually have a dimmer control. Avoid fluorescent lights whenever possible because they are the least flattering and least controlled, and they cast an equal amount of light around the room. When the light is equal, the audience could be distracted by wall hangings, furniture pieces, and worst of all, a clock. By creating an unequal distribution of light, you keep the audience's eyes focused on you and minimize other distractions in the room.

SOUND

Sound is especially important for groups of 50 or more. A wireless *lavaliere* microphone (one that clips to the tie or blouse) is always preferred to allow you the most mobility. The microphone, or *mic* as it is commonly called (pronounced "mike"), should always be clipped in the center—not on the lapel—because most lavaliere microphones pick up sound from only one direction to eliminate background noise. If the microphone is on your lapel, you'll be less audible when you turn your head away.

There are a couple ways to select a microphone. The environment makes a difference. A directional mic is best when you don't want anything but the voice from one direction to be heard. Typically, this is what you will use for presenting. The microphones found on lecterns tend to be omnidirectional, which means they pick up nearby sounds, including your voice, in all directions. That's why you may hear pages turning or thumping when your hand hits the lectern as you speak into the mic.

Tip from

Tom Mucciolo

If you are picking up sound from vibration while at a lectern, try taping another microphone to the existing microphone on the lectern. Shut the lectern mic off and use the other microphone instead. Any vibration caused by your hands bumping the sides of the lectern will be muffled or completely eliminated.

Mics also fall into one of two basic types: *dynamic* and *condenser*. A dynamic mic is durable and usually of the handheld or lectern type. It is very versatile and handles almost any type sound. It doesn't require batteries because it is directly connected to some audio power source.

A condenser mic is smaller and more sophisticated, and is usually found on a wireless lavaliere. This type is best for picking up the richer tones in the voice but are more breakable, especially where the cable meets the mic. It needs a power supply, usually batteries.

Tip from

Tom Mucciolo

If you plan to use a wireless mic for a full-day event, change the battery at lunchtime to ensure quality sound for the rest of the day.

The key to any microphone setup is to make sure the mic is far enough away from your mouth so there is no distortion. For the lavaliere microphone, keep it clipped one hand's width below your neck. Put your thumb at the base of your neck and lay your hand flat so that it rests on the top of your chest. Right past your hand, below your bottom knuckle, is where to clip the mic.

Finally, because the transmitter clips to your belt, place it on your left side, more toward your back, away from your hip bone. It will have less of a tendency to fall off. If you place it on your right side, a gesture you make with your left hand toward the screen is higher and usually tilts your body down to your right. This can lift the transmitter off your right side and possibly make it fall off.

A belt helps, but for some women's form-fitting suits, clipping the transmitter on the side might create a slight bulge through the jacket. You can just as easily clip the transmitter behind you, near your backbone. If your suit jacket is less restrictive, you can even place the transmitter in the inside or outside left pocket, depending on where it is least distracting. If you know you are going to be wearing a mic and transmitter, wear an outfit that will accommodate this equipment with the least problem.

CHOOSING A DISPLAY SCREEN

You have two considerations regarding the display screen, and both involve visibility issues. One is the physical characteristics of the screen, and the other is the placement of the display.

SCREEN TYPES

The most versatile displays are those that allow the best viewing from all angles. For projection screens, I recommend a flat, non-glare, matte-white screen. The image will be just as bright from the sides as from the center. Conversely, glass-beaded screens tend to be very bright when viewed from the center but gradually become dimmer when viewed from wider angles.

Rear-screen projection will be less bright than front-screen, but it is viewable from the same angles. This is good for situations in which people may be crossing in front of the screen, as in an awards ceremony. As the presenter, you should never cross in front of the screen, whether the image is projected from behind or the front.

In addition, the screen should be *keystone-correcting*. An image "keystones" when the projector is positioned lower than the screen. The greater the angle, the more the visual appears like the letter "V," wider at the top and narrower at the bottom. Usually, a tripod screen has an extension bar at the top. When the bar is extended, the screen is able to hook onto the bar at any of several tabs or notches, depending on how far forward you want the screen to lean. The more you tilt the screen toward the projector, the more the image becomes square (less like a V).

Some presentations use a monitor or TV. A monitor takes computer input directly, and a TV needs to change the computer signal using a device known as a *scan converter*. Usually, the more you pay for these converters, the closer the image looks to the original.

Part

VII

Ch

26

Tip from
Tom Mucciolo

> Typically, converters increase the size of the computer's image, and the edges of your visual will be cut off. If you plan to present on a TV using a converter, check your images in PowerPoint's Slide Show view. Then, place your thumb up to the first knuckle on each side of any visual where you think information is close to the edge. The headings and the right side are the most likely problem areas. Anything under your thumb may be missing when the image is sent through the scan converter. If you pretend you have this border or safety zone when creating the visual, you can be sure it will be seen through nearly any scan converter.

A monitor or TV has a light source from within, and therefore the lighting in the room can be quite bright, and the image will still be visible. But the size of these displays is usually limited to about a 35-inch diagonal or less, which limits the number of people able to view the presentation. In addition, monitors are usually set in a wall or mounted in some other fixed position, which makes connecting another piece of equipment pretty difficult. Go for the projection screen whenever possible.

SCREEN PLACEMENT

Look at where the bottom of your visual is in relation to the floor. The bottom of your visual should be higher than your shoulder as you stand on the floor; that way, people seated behind other people will probably be able to see the entire visual. To be sure, try to get the bottom of the visual at least six feet from the floor.

Check this out at the next presentation you attend. If you sit behind someone, you probably can see only the top two-thirds of the image, unless your view is clear. Usually, only the people in the front row have a full view of the screen. In a conference room, the views are usually fairly good for most people, but larger events are the ones with the most problems.

If only the top two-thirds of your image is viewable and you have any data-driven charts showing progress over time, chances are the comparison points are at the bottom. If the content is financial data and the audience can't see the changing dates along the bottom of the visual, how can they understand the chart? For example, Figures 26.1 and 26.2 compare the way a visual can appear, depending on your seat. Figure 26.1 shows a vertical bar chart viewed when sitting in the front row. It is completely visible.

Figure 26.1
A simple bar chart showing activity for selected months in the year. If you sit in the front row, you can see the entire image.

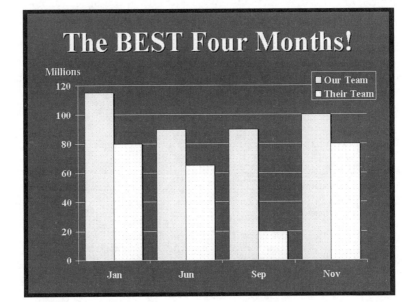

Figure 26.2
The same bar chart seen from a few rows back. When the bottom of the image is not high enough, you have to look around people to see the screen.

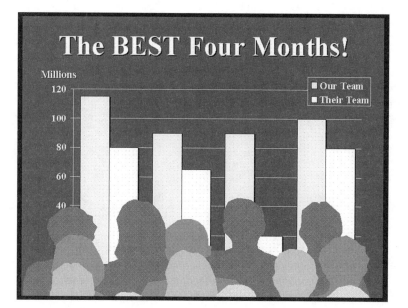

Figure 26.2 is the same visual, but note the way it appears from about row six. From this view, you can't see the lower third of the image, and the heading makes little sense because you don't know which are the best four months. Comparisons are more difficult when people have to make an effort to see the entire image. The harder your audience works to see the full screen, the less effective you will be.

What happens when you can't raise the screen so that the bottom is at shoulder height because the ceiling is too low? As I mentioned before, look for a ceiling 15 feet or higher. In hotels, a ballroom is typical of such height. For example, if you can get a room with a ceiling height of 16 feet, you can use a 9-foot screen and place the bottom of the screen 6 feet from the floor, leaving a foot to spare.

If your ceiling height is too low, then you can try shrinking the overall size of your image so that the bottom of it is higher. If you can get the bottom to a height where anyone can see the entire image from any seat, then the only other thing you have to check is text readability from the back row. Don't shrink the image so that it is totally unreadable from a distance. I'd rather lose some of the visual at the bottom in order for the rest of it to be readable.

DECIDING ON SEATING ARRANGEMENTS

You can use several different styles of seating, but they generally fall into one of two categories—theater or classroom. The difference is tables.

No matter how you arrange the chairs, theater style does not include tables. This style is typical for large groups, and when the seating is not fixed, flexibility improves. You will probably use theater-style seating for groups of 50 or more and for events of short duration (no more than a half-day). Figure 26.3 is MediaNet's suggested room layout for theater-style

PART
VII
CH
26

seating. This diagram, along with more complete setup advice, appears on MediaNet's Web site at www.medianet-ny.com/layout.htm. You can print out these layout considerations and use them to help set up your own event.

Figure 26.3
A suggested room layout with theater-style seating.

If the event is more than a half-day, you should provide tables for a classroom-style approach. Although this reduces the number of people the space can hold by about 60%, the comfort of your audience will be greatly enhanced.

Classroom-style seating can have all the tables facing straight to the front, as the theater setup would be. Classroom style can also have variations. Angling the tables toward the center of the room, called *chevron* seating, can help increase the interaction among audience members because people can see more of one another with the tables on an angle. Interaction is increased even more when you use a U-shape arrangement because almost everyone can see everyone else in the room. The U shape is like a big conference table without the table.

Tip from
Tom Mucciolo

Don't make a perfect U shape. Leave off the front-end table on the side you present from, the left side, so that you have more room for your triangle.

The smaller the group, the more likely your setting will be in a conference room or in a training room with 10-foot or lower ceilings, limited lighting options, and less area for you to move. When you are faced with a lot of limitations, arrange the seats with more people facing one another. This shifts the focus more toward discussion and enables you to play the role of both lecturer and facilitator.

SEATING AND DISTANCE

The size of the text displayed should relate to the distance people are seated from the viewing screen. You learned about this earlier with the 8 to 1 rule. To recap, eight times the height of the visual (not the screen) is the maximum viewing distance to read 24-point text. If your visual is 6 feet high, people seated 48 feet away should be able to read text that is as small as 24 points in size.

Just for your reference, when you type a letter to someone, the text is usually 12-point size. The cell of a spreadsheet is about 10-point size. The pull-down menu bar on your computer screen (you know, File, Edit, View, and so forth) is about 8-point size. If you do the math, you can see that presenting software or demonstrating a Web site to an audience is going to be a lot harder than running a PowerPoint presentation. With the software program or Web page, you likely will be displaying 12-point type at best. If the point size is 12 rather than 24, the 8 to 1 rule becomes the 4 to 1 rule. This means everyone has to sit twice as close. Using a 6-foot-high image, people will have to sit no more than 24 feet from the visual (instead of 48 feet) in order to be able to read your screen. Unfortunately, when the room is set up, the hotel staff doesn't think about point size. Now you'll have to ask people in row 14 to move up to row 7.

Calculating the Distance

If you want a simple formula for calculating how far away a person can sit and still be able to read your information, use the letters T, V, and D. T is the type size, V is the height of the visual, and D is the maximum distance to sit. The formula is $(T/3)V=D$. (The type size T divided by 3, then multiplied by the visual height V equals the maximum seating distance D to read that type size.)

Find your smallest type on any visual you intend to display. Divide the point size by three. Multiply that by the height of your image. The result is how far away people can sit and still read your visual.

Try this example. The smallest type size in your presentation is 18 points, and your visual is 4 feet high. How many feet away can a person sit and still be able to read your image easily?

Why do type size and distance make a difference? Think about the number of people attending your presentation. When you know the maximum viewing distance, you can figure out if the room you plan to present in is big enough. In fact, the arrangement of the seats will make a difference as to how many people you can accommodate.

For example, using theater-style seating (no tables, just chairs), how can you figure out the number of people that can fit in the room? First, the typical space between rows—that is, from the back of one chair to the back of the chair in the next row—should be about three feet. This leaves enough room for people to pass by. But keep in mind that to display your image, the projection equipment will take up room in the front. The first row of chairs is usually set up a distance away from the screen, usually about 25% of the maximum seating distance from the visual. That means the audience can occupy only the space in the remaining 75% of the maximum distance.

Let's say you have a 6-foot-high image containing 24-point type, which allows a 48-foot maximum seating distance. That means the first 12 feet (one-fourth of 48) is cleared so that the projector can be set up to cast that six-foot-high image. You end up with only 36 feet of available depth for the audience. Because you need about three feet of space between rows, you now have room for about 12 rows of chairs.

Based on approximately 16 people across each row separated by a middle aisle, you have room for as many as 120 people, give or take a few.

Tip from

Tom Mucciolo

Set up one middle aisle and limit the width of any row on either side of the aisle to no more than 10 chairs. That way, no one needs to pass in front of more than five people to exit any row into the middle or side aisle.

Another way to set up the rows is to double the height of the visual. For example, if you have a 6-foot-high image, seat no more than 12 people per row. With a middle aisle, you'll have six chairs on each side.

Figure 26.4 is a section taken from the table "MediaNet Seating Calculations for Distance and Capacity." This chart is helpful in determining what changes you may have to make to the font sizes or the visual height in order to accommodate your audience. The rounded-off calculations allow for empty seats and extra rows here and there, but the general results are useful when planning your event. The entire table can be seen by visiting MediaNet's Web site at www.medianet-ny.com/seating.htm.

Figure 26.4
A section of MediaNet's seating table, showing calculations for visual heights of 6 to 10 feet and selected font sizes.

			Theatre-Style (Chairs only)			Classroom-Style (Tbls/Chrs)	
Visual Height (in feet)	Smallest Font (in Pt-size)	Distance to Last Row (in feet)	Total Rows to set	Max. People in each row	Seating Capacity (full rows)	Total Rows to set	Seating Capacity (40% of theatre)
6	12	24	4	12	48	1	19
6	18	36	8	12	96	3	38
6	24	48	12	12	144	4	58
6	32	64	17	12	204	6	82
6	38	76	21	12	252	7	101
6	44	88	25	12	300	8	120
6	48	96	28	12	336	9	134
7	12	28	5	14	70	2	28
7	18	42	9	14	126	3	50
7	24	56	14	14	196	5	78
7	32	75	20	14	280	7	112
7	38	89	25	14	350	8	140
7	44	103	30	14	420	10	168
7	48	112	33	14	462	11	185
8	12	32	5	16	80	2	32
8	18	48	11	16	176	4	70
8	24	64	16	16	256	5	102
8	32	85	23	16	368	8	147
8	38	101	28	16	448	9	179
8	44	117	34	16	544	11	218
8	48	128	37	16	592	12	237

MediaNet Seating Calculations for Distance and Capacity

When seating people classroom-style, the presence of tables reduces the available seating space. Typically, fewer than half the number of people seated theater style can be seated classroom style because you have about five to six feet of space between the rows of chairs to allow for the table.

For example, suppose you have an 8-foot-high image. If you use 6-foot-long tables and place two rows of tables on each side of a middle aisle, you'll probably end up with six people on each side or just 12 across (as opposed to 16 across in theater-style seating). Not only do you have fewer rows, but you have fewer people per row. When using classroom seating, estimate the capacity to be no more than 40% of theater-style seating to be safe.

Visibility from a distance and the seating arrangements are important considerations when you design your support visuals. If you can't get the room set up the way you want, you may have to change the appearance of some of your visuals. Of course, the more control you have over the room conditions, the fewer changes you'll need to make to your content.

Most presenters ignore the importance of the room. They take what they get when they get there and then wonder why the event failed. As a presenter, it is your job to provide a room layout diagram to a meeting planner, a hotel A/V group, or even a major presentation service in order to get what you want.

USING TECHNOLOGY

It seems any mention of technology is obsolete before you finish reading the sentence. However, you should be aware of some generalities when you use different devices, especially from a technical perspective. As a visual presenter, you should be adept at using different pieces of equipment, although you will probably get comfortable using one particular device for most of your presentation needs.

HANDLING PROJECTORS

If you recall, Chapter 23, "The Media—Designing Visual Support," covered the cost, convenience, and continuity issues related to overheads, 35mm slides, and electronic images. The traditional devices—overhead and slide projectors—are not difficult to work with from an operational standpoint. Typically, the big technical question is "How do you turn this thing on?" For electronic presentations, you have to know a bit more than the on/off switch when you work with the current crop of LCD (liquid crystal display) projectors.

→ For more information about projectors, **see** "Understanding Media Types" in Chapter 23.

PART

VII

CH

26

First the good news: These devices are getting easier and easier to set up, but until personal computers are a cinch to work with, these electronic projectors will carry a bit of intimidation along with them. Don't worry. If you haven't used one, chances are someone is available who has.

I don't want to get into a long list of specifications, except to tell you that the LCD projector connects directly to your PC. Depending on the features of your PC, the projected image may or may not need to be adjusted.

BRIGHTNESS

The brightness of the image is a big issue when you can't control the lighting in the room. You'll probably hear the word *lumens* when people talk of a projector's brightness. Lumens is a measure of brightness. The more lumens, the brighter the image. There's more to it than that, but that's why there are professionals who sell these things. Audiovisual companies (A/V dealers) are excellent sources for learning more about the unique features and benefits of electronic projectors.

In a room with only fluorescent lights, go for a projector with at least 500 lumens so that your image remains visible, even with the light spilling onto the screen. Of course, if you have less light hitting the screen, the image will look even better.

RESOLUTION

Think of resolution as the quality of the image. I like to use the comparison of a chain link fence, some chicken wire, and a screen on a door. The sizes of the holes are different in each. If you took a paint brush and painted the word "resolution" on the fence, the wire, and the screen, which would be easiest to read? It would be the screen, because the holes are closer and smaller, making the letters in the painted word appear less broken up and of higher quality. If you hear of 640×480 resolution, that's the chain link fence. 800×600 resolution is the chicken wire, and $1,024 \times 768$ is the screen door. The higher the resolution, the closer the holes, and the better the quality of the image, because the *pixels*, the little dots that make up the image, are closer together.

PORTABILITY

Naturally, if you don't have to carry anything to the presentation but your PC, then you don't need to be concerned about the portability of the projector. Such devices are getting lighter—most are around 10 pounds, and some are as light as 5 pounds. The benefit of bringing the device with you is that you can be confident of the image you will get. If you carry the light source to the event, you have more control of the display. I have made plenty of presentations when I did not have the quality image I was used to and had to overcompensate on my delivery to make up for the poorer image. A lighter projector means more likelihood of your taking it with you to the event.

MULTIPLE CONNECTIONS

Having options for more than one input and output is helpful, especially if you plan to use a variety of media, including video and audio. Some projectors even allow hookups for two computer sources. This can be helpful in an event with more than one presenter, each of whom has his own PC. The capability to connect a VCR, a video camera, or other device can add value and flexibility as well. In my full-day "Presenting Made Easy" seminar, I use my computer and play a videotape as well, using the same projector by simply switching sources when needed. Typically, to switch between different inputs, a press of a button on the projector is all that's required.

Note

When a projector enables multiple sources, it usually lets you set up each source independently. For example, when I switch from my PC to my video source, the video settings on the projector change. I can control volume, brightness, contrast, and so forth separately for each input because they are usually different.

Of course, not every piece of equipment works perfectly when connected to another piece of equipment, as may happen with some projector-to-computer hookups. Sometimes, one person's notebook PC works fine with a projector, but the next person's PC does not for a variety of reasons. Changing the settings on projectors varies among models and types, so it is best to arrive at your presentation early enough to make sure that everything works properly.

The worst moment in the world is when you start playing with menu options on the projector two minutes before the show is supposed to begin.

Many projectors have multiple outputs, as well. Outputs for video and audio can be valuable when presenting. For example, if you plan to use sound during your presentation, having an external audio feature on the projector is very helpful. When you have a larger group of people, the tiny speakers of a projector can't disperse sound evenly to everyone in the room. It sounds louder for those who sit closer. In some places such as in a hotel, you can connect the projector to the sound system used for your microphone, which is typically connected through the speakers in the ceiling. *House sound*, as it is called, distributes the audio evenly to the audience.

WORKING WITH LAPTOP PRESENTATIONS

Chances are, if you use an electronic projector, you are probably connecting a laptop or notebook computer to it. You'll have some limitations with laptop systems, but I don't want to get too technical on the subject. The good news is that the laptop is a fully functioning office, complete with backup information and tons of other stuff, literally at your fingertips. You need to know a few things about computers and projectors, especially when it comes to laptop presentations.

REMOTE CONTROL

No one who stands in front of a group of people should advance a PowerPoint presentation with the keyboard when a remote control offers you incredible freedom of movement and enhances your presentation skills accordingly. Consider using a two-button remote control that can advance your visuals while you stand inside your triangle and present.

Pro Presenter

Many types of remotes are available on the market right now, and although I normally avoid endorsing products, I've got to say that I've been using the same remote control for years. It's the perfect device for delivering linear electronic presentations. In fact, when I coach people, they are using it within seconds—that's how easy it is to control. It's called the Pro Presenter.

It's a flat, infrared wireless, handheld remote control for the PC or the Macintosh. The remote can be used with or without its software. It's the same size as a credit card, it fits snugly into the palm of your hand, and it operates from up to 35 feet away from your computer. It's a $99 wonder that frees you from ever touching the computer while you present. At the risk of sounding like I'm selling you something, visit MediaNet's Web site (www.medianet-ny.com) to learn more about this little product, which is manufactured by Varatouch Technology of California (www.varatouch.com).

Some remotes also have the capability to control the mouse pointer, as well. It's like having the left and right mouse buttons and the pointer all in your hand at the same time. The only thing to worry about is accidentally moving the mouse pointer while you present.

Some remotes work on an RF (radio frequency) signal rather than infrared. This means that you don't have to point at the receiver when you advance the visuals. Unfortunately, these remotes tend to be larger. When a remote cannot fit comfortably into the palm of your hand, it becomes more obvious that you are using one.

When you think of the amount of money invested in a computer and a projector—not to mention the presentation and your time to deliver it—the cost of adding a remote control is insignificant. Think of this: An inexpensive key can open the door to a top-of-the-line Chrysler. Buy a remote.

SIMULTANEOUS DISPLAY

This is a big advantage to any speaker, but particularly to a visual presenter. Think about overheads and slides for a minute. You have to turn your head back toward the screen just to glance at the information. If your visuals are busy, you end up doing this even more often. But a laptop offers you a unique advantage called *simultaneous display*. The image the audience sees on the big screen appears on the display of your PC at the same time. If this feature is not already set up in your PC, normally you can send the display signal to an auxiliary screen by pressing a combination of keys on your keyboard. On your notebook computer you might see a graphic symbol that looks like a PC and a screen on one of the function keys, usually F5. This is like a toggle that can be set in three positions. One keeps the image on your notebook screen; another sends the image out the VGA (monitor) port on the back and removes it from your notebook screen; the third setting sends the image out the back but leaves it on the notebook screen at the same time. This is called simultaneous display.

It's like a little TelePrompTer, except you don't have any speech to read. In fact, if your visuals are less busy, the text displayed on your notebook screen will be larger and should be readable from however far away from the computer you are standing as you present.

In addition, if you look back to Figure 26.3, you can see how your equipment (computer and projector) is centered in the front of the room. When you glance at your notebook screen, it will appear as though you are making eye contact with the section of the audience sitting beyond the table but still in your line of sight. It takes only a slight shift of your eyes downward to catch the information on the screen. Although some may notice the movement, it certainly is not as obvious as the complete look back to the screen done constantly with overheads and slides.

Depending on your computer and the projector, the simultaneous display option may not be available, however. This is a constantly evolving issue with both the computer and projector manufacturers, but in any case, what you need to be concerned about is this: In most cases, when the resolution of the projector is lower than the resolution setting on your PC, the projector compensates for the higher signal coming from your PC and drops bits of the image. This makes smaller text appear choppy. The solution is to lower the resolution setting on your PC to match the projector. However, with some computers, that's still not enough. You may have to disable the simultaneous display feature so that the projector can project a full and clear image at the lower resolution. This is not always the case, but you'll have to try it to be sure.

On the other hand, if the projector has a higher resolution than the computer, you should have no problem, for the most part, because the projector should be able to handle the lower-resolution signal coming from your computer.

TRANSITIONS

Electronic presentations allow the use of transition effects between visuals. Rather than use transitions randomly, you should consider the way the next image will appear to the audience. The most consistent approach is to try to use a transition that matches the eye movement pattern for the upcoming visual, not the current visual. In other words, transition effects are designed for the visual yet to appear, not for the visual already displayed.

For example, let's say you're displaying a text chart with several bullet points, followed by a horizontal bar chart and then a pie chart. You could use a "horizontal blinds" transition into the text chart because the lines of text are separated by horizontal space. Then you might use a "wipe right" transition from the text chart to the bar chart because the eye will be moving from left to right when the bar chart appears. Then, from the bar to the pie chart, a "box out" transition could be used. The circle of the pie centers the eye in the visual, and the transition opens from the center matching the circle.

Check the general geometric shapes in the next visual when planning a transition to assure a consistency in eye movement from one image to the next.

SCREENSAVERS, REMINDERS, AND NAVIGATION ISSUES

One of the things you should do with your laptop is turn off any screensavers you may have. If you stay on one visual too long and your screensaver comes on, it may knock out the signal going to the projector. The audience is left staring at a blue screen. Disable the screensaver in Windows and any timeout functions set in the computer itself. Your PC's diagnostics or setup screen will tell you if any screensavers are enabled.

Some contact-management programs offer reminders, such as alarms, that pop up when a task is due. When you present, don't load software that has task reminders, unless you want the audience to see just who it is you're having dinner with that night.

Finally, under Tools, Options in PowerPoint, select the View tab and make sure all three check boxes in the Slide Show area are unchecked. First, you don't want the pop-up menu to appear on the right mouse click. When you leave this box unchecked, your right mouse button will do what it is supposed to do—navigate the show backward one visual. If you need to navigate to different images or you need to get other help during the presentation, you can simply go to the keyboard and press F1, and the menu of choices will pop up. Second, you don't want the pop-up menu button to show in the corner of each visual as you present. Unless you have a remote mouse, you won't be able to click this transparent icon anyway. Third, you don't want to end your presentation with a blank slide, especially if you've been using a consistent background throughout. Instead, under the Slide Show menu, choose Set Up Show, and check the box Loop Continuously Until "Esc" so that your show loops back to the beginning. This causes your presentation to end with the same image you started with, if you so choose.

INCORPORATING MULTIMEDIA

Nothing you can do with a laptop computer—using animation, sound, video, or any special effects—even comes close to what you see in the movies. We are accustomed to seeing incredible special effects, and we have Spielberg and Lucas to thank for it. No one runs home from a business presentation saying, "Honey, you won't believe this, but at this presentation today—well, I don't know how—but the computer—well, it played music and a voice came out—a real voice!" It's hard to impress people with technology these days.

Although much has been said about multimedia, all I can add is this: Beware of multiMANIA. Multimania is the overuse of technology to the point that the audience is enamored by your special effects but can't remember the plot.

You should be concerned when you think about adding elements in your presentation that go beyond your delivery. For example, playing a video clip during your presentation introduces another character to the audience, another presence—basically, another messenger. This isn't wrong, any more than it's wrong to introduce another presenter. But elements that simulate or mimic real-life forms (speech, movement, real people in action) reach the audience in different ways than traditional visual content.

You need to understand the particulars of animation, sound, and video as unique multimedia elements and their effect on the audience.

ANIMATION

Animation is simply an object in action. However, it should never be text in action. Objects can move, but text should stand still. Take this test. Move this book up and down and try to read it. I rest my case. You can't read moving text until it stops or at least slows down enough for you to anchor on it. Ever try reading the weather warning as it crosses the bottom of your TV? You can't read each word as it appears from the far right; you have to wait for a few words to make it to the far left of the screen so you can anchor and read left to right.

Text should never move. All those transitions you picked with the animated bullet points—out. Just because a programmer can make it happen doesn't mean it's useful. Animated text lines can't be read until they stop. This means the only effect was the animation, the movement. If an action serves only itself, it is useless because the audience takes interest only in the action, not the information. Eventually, people will watch your text flying in from different points and begin to take bets on where the next line will enter from and when.

> **Note**
>
> If the text you are animating is part of a logo or is to be treated as a standalone item, then it is more like an object and probably contains very little of the *anchor-and-read* requirement. In those cases, you can animate the text object.

Objects can be animated, but apply a sense of logic. Don't have a clip art symbol of an airplane floating from the top of the visual downward. Airplanes don't do that—at least not more than once. Animated bars or moving lines showing a procedure can help the audience understand growth or flow and make the visual come alive to express an idea. Animation is not a bad thing as long as it is not overdone to the point that only the effect is noticed.

SOUND

The first sense you experienced was hearing. Before birth you could hear your mom's voice as she carried you from place to place. Sound is one of the most important senses throughout our lives and can dramatically affect our perceptions.

Sound can be either used or abused during a presentation. Typically, you might want to add sound at certain points to highlight a key phrase or to add value to some information.

The main thing is to be consistent with sound. The audience not only looks for anchors; they listen for them as well. Your voice becomes an anchor as people adjust to your volume, pitch, and tone. Other sounds placed in the presentation need justification and sometimes repetition to become anchored. Don't make a noise just because your software program has this great library of sounds that you feel compelled to use.

Sounds linked to elements on the visual are usually ineffective. Examples of these are the cash register sound linked to a symbol of money; the sound of applause signifying achievement; the shutter of a camera each time a photo of a person appears on the visual; and the worst of all sound effects—the typewriter sound linked to animated text and possibly to each letter on each text line. In all these cases, the sounds are one-time effects that can become phony or even obnoxious when repeated.

Don't get me wrong, sound can play a major role in the presentation if done right. Music is a good example of this. The movie *Jaws* wouldn't be the same without music. *The Omen* wouldn't be as scary. The nice thing about music, particularly instrumental music, is that you can talk over it, and the audience can blend your words with the background music. In addition, if the music track is long enough or loops continuously, the audience gets the benefit of repetition and will anchor to the music as it plays.

PART
VII
CH
26

Tip from *Tom Mucciolo*	Even if you don't incorporate music into the presentation, consider playing some tunes as people are coming into the room or perhaps as they leave.

You don't need to have the music clips stored on the computer; the files can be quite large. You can simply use your computer's CD-ROM drive (if you have one) or bring a portable CD player and connect it directly to the projector.

→ To see how to use sound effectively with the Nostalgia Theory, **see** "Knowing Particulars of the Audience" in Chapter 22, "The Message—Scripting the Concept."

For example, let's say you are giving a presentation in 1999 to an audience, the average age of which is 31. That means they were 15 years old in 1983. Michael Jackson's "Beat It" will be a more popular sound clip for this crowd than his 1970 tune "ABC," when the majority of those in this group were wearing diapers!

You get the idea. Continuity in sound is better than periodic or intermittent sound. You can process continual sound just like listening to the radio while driving a car. Hear a siren or horn beep (intermittent sounds), and your attention is immediately diverted.

VIDEO

Multimedia takes on a very different flavor when you incorporate video. The multimedia issues with video come in two flavors, full-screen and full-motion. The goal is to have both, but the technology you own may not enable either. Full-screen video is easy to envision. The video fills up the whole screen just like a TV. Many video clips in presentations today are half, one-third, or even one-quarter the size of the screen, depending on the computer system used to deliver the video.

Full-motion video is what you get when you watch TV—30 frames per second. That speed is fast enough for the images to appear lifelike, which is why TV is such a powerful medium. Much of the video shown through laptops is not full-motion; it is about half-motion or 15 frames per second. At times, especially during long computer or digitized video clips, you can get synchronization problems with voice and video after a while. That's when the video and voice get out of sync, and it looks like one of those foreign films with poor dubbing.

With most laptops, we sacrifice full-motion and full-screen for the sake of storage and speed. Naturally, the storage required for video is much greater than for still images or even clip art, for that matter. I won't go into the technical details of file sizes, but if you've ever loaded a video clip on your PC, you know that it takes up a lot of disk space. For example, a one-minute clip that plays in a window only half the size of your screen might be about 10 megabytes. Of course, one minute is a long time for a video clip when you consider that TV commercials average 15 to 30 seconds. Storage and speed are issues for video, and you should limit the length of the clips.

The goal is full-screen, full-motion video. Computer speeds are getting faster, so soon this will not be an issue. However, not everyone uses the latest technology, and I suspect it will be a few years before video is a breeze to watch through a PC in a presentation.

Regardless of speed, another issue with video concerns movement and direction. If your video clip is not full-screen, you may be including it as part of a visual. If the visual has text and the video clip shows something moving in one direction, make sure that direction matches the way the text reads. For example, a visual in English would have a left-to-right reading pattern. If your clip shows a car moving from right to left, you'll have an eye movement clash. Try to match the direction whenever possible.

IMAGE MAGNIFICATION

You may find times when your presence on stage is also reproduced on screen. This might happen if you present in a large venue where people are sitting so far back that they cannot get a good view of you or your expressions. *Image magnification* can be used to make you visible from a far distance. A separate screen is set up, a camera focuses on you, and the video signal is projected onto the big screen. The good news is that everyone can see you as if they were in the front row.

However, some problems can occur. Whenever a camera is used, you should be concerned about what the framed image looks like to the audience. Figure 26.5 shows how different the perspective is when the presenter is viewed from the audience and through the eye of the camera. The banner hanging behind the presenter looks fine when viewed from the audience, but the close-up shot framed by the camera clips some letters from the company name "Lawe Losetta, Inc.," showing only the last two letters of "Lawe" and the first four letters of "Losetta"; through the camera it reads "we Lose."

Figure 26.5
Be careful that camera cropping doesn't change your message.

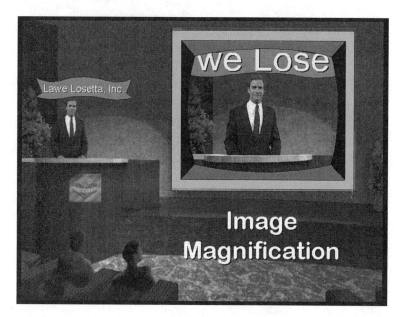

In Figure 26.6, the banner is hung vertically, and the framed image doesn't reveal any surprises. Always check the viewing angle when using a video camera to frame the presenter.

GLITCHES HAPPEN

It goes without saying that you should practice your presentation. In fact, the more multimedia effects you have planned, the greater the need for a technical run-through before the event. Sometimes (and usually at the worst moments), computers cause problems. Whether the video clip moves in a jerky motion or the sound effect doesn't play or the system just "locks up" for no apparent reason—the thing to remember is not to panic. We have all been there before, and it's not unusual for things to go wrong every so often.

If you know how to fix a problem, then fix it. At the same time, explain to your audience what you are doing. Don't just turn your back and say, "Pay no attention to that man behind the curtain!" The real issue is time. If you can fix it within three minutes, fine. If you think the problem will take longer to fix, give the audience an opportunity to take a short break.

Figure 26.6
Careful positioning
helps avoid image
magnification
problems.

For practice, run your presentation; somewhere in the middle of it, turn off or reset the computer. Time how long it takes to reboot your PC and get it back to the exact spot where you turned it off. If it takes more than three minutes, you'll know to give the audience a short break the instant you know you may have to reboot the computer during your presentation.

Overall, if you keep calm and collected during technical difficulties, you have a better chance of keeping the attention of the audience. Of course, the more command you have of the message and the more effective your delivery skills, the easier it will be for you to overcome any technical problem.

Remember that the technology carries only the speaker's support material. You are the speaker, and your delivery embodies the message. The audience will constantly look to you for guidance and direction. Never forget that *you* are in control.

TROUBLESHOOTING

SETTING A TIME AND PLACE

Do you have any advice for the best time and place to conduct a presentation?

Usually, a presentation happens as part of a meeting, seminar, or other type of planned event. Regardless of the size of the group, you have to consider the location and the calendar when planning the event. The bottom line is to develop a plan that captures your audience when they are most attentive. You can do this by conducting the event at the right location, on the right day of the week, and at the right time of day.

Regarding location, you should try to find a spot that contains the fewest distractions. This usually is offsite (not in your building). Most people, if close enough to their desks, will find opportunities to do a few work-related tasks and before they know it, the presentation is over. If you want the full attention of a group, keep them away from their desks by holding the event at a neutral spot (hotel or conference center) that is an easy drive but too far away to walk. You don't want people sneaking back to their desks at each break.

For timing, you should consider the best day of the work week for getting the most people to attend. Having conducted over 1,000 seminars, I can tell you that Tuesday is best, followed in order by Thursday, Wednesday, Friday, and, finally, Monday. I have met other presenters who agree with the order. If Tuesday is open for your next meeting, chances are more people will be available than on Monday. Check it out in your own environment and see if it's true for you.

Finally, consider the time of day. Early morning, between 9 a.m. and 11 a.m., seems to be the best time of day for getting the longest attention span from a group. One hour after lunch is the worst time of day because people are digesting. When you digest food, the blood goes from your head to your stomach, your eyes get heavier, and before you know it you doze off. The morning is better than the afternoon. In fact, in a sales presentation when your competitors are presenting on the same day, try to go first. Some say the last presentation is the only one remembered. In reality, it's the one the audience hopes will end most quickly. If you go first, you have the most attention from the group, and you become the tough act to follow.

INCORPORATING MUSIC AND VIDEO

If I want to use music or video in my presentations, do I need to be concerned with copyrights?

Copyrights protect intellectual properties. The rule I live by is simple: When in doubt, ask permission. However, you can use certain multimedia elements without infringing on someone's rights. For example, let's say you want to buy a CD-ROM that contained a collection of instrumental musical selections. If the CD packaging contains a statement such as "royalty-free" or "unlimited use," it doesn't mean there is no copyright. It means that you can probably use the selections in your presentations, and you won't have to pay a fee each time you use a clip. On the other hand, it doesn't mean you can repackage the selections on a new CD and sell it.

I have been at tradeshows, for example, where the movie *Top Gun* (with Tom Cruise) was playing in someone's booth. Without permission, this would be an illegal use of the movie, especially because it is being used in a selling process. The movie is entertaining, and the value of that entertainment brings people into the booth, at which point sales opportunities arise. Thus, the playing of the movie increases the prospects. The selling process is enhanced through the use of an intellectual property (the movie) with no payment (royalty) made to the property owner. A phone call to the copyright holder of the movie may be all that is needed to get permission to play the movie for one tradeshow without infringing on the copyright.

The same applies to popular music. If you want to play some songs from a CD during your presentation, perhaps as background filler while the audience is arriving, you should get permission to use the material.

Surely any point of law can be argued and interpreted in different ways. I have a lecture called "Multimedia vs. Multimania" in which I use several popular music tracks from different CDs. To be safe, I received permission from the copyright holders, and I even run credits at the end of the lecture to acknowledge the owners of the material. I suggest you research any use of copyrighted material and get permission, in writing if possible, to reduce the chances of a lawsuit.

CHAPTER 27

PRESENTING IN A VARIETY OF SETTINGS

In this chapter

by Tom Mucciolo

ADAPTING TO EVERYDAY ENVIRONMENTS

Not every performance takes place on the big stage. The majority of business presentations are done for smaller groups, and sometimes those talks take place in unique settings. You have to learn to adapt to different circumstances. The good news is that the skills we've been discussing translate well to the variety of situations you may encounter when delivering your message.

I always laugh when someone tells me, "Oh, the meetings I speak at are so informal that you don't really need great presentation skills to make your point." My response is, "I guess you don't need to wear clean clothes on those days, either." Don't underestimate the power of the moment. If the meeting really is unimportant, then your time is wasted. Do you really have that luxury? Given that the meeting is important, you want your voice to be heard and remembered. Presentation skills are universally adaptable to almost every circumstance in which you speak and someone else listens.

The goal is to use the same skills that work in a more controlled setting and apply them to the given environment. Most of your presentations are likely to take place close to your everyday work area. Believe it or not, these environments are the ones you prepare for the least and take the most for granted. At other times you may find yourself in a situation that challenges even the most basic of your skills. In fact, one of the biggest challenges will be in the way you use your skills in a highly visual setting, such as TV.

GETTING UP CLOSE AND PERSONAL

The most likely scenario you'll encounter is a presentation to a small group. I find that more than 80% of presentations are given to groups of fewer than 10 people, usually in a conference room setting. Typically, the fear factor is reduced when fewer people are in the room, so these up-close-and-personal situations are easier for most presenters. Perhaps that is what makes small group presentations more common. Another reason is probably scheduling: It's easier to convene a smaller group of people in a local setting than it is to gather a crowd for a larger event.

Regardless of how these situations develop, the common fallacy among presenters is that less formality exists when the group is smaller and people know one another. Be careful: Just because everyone knows one another doesn't mean your presentation has automatic impact. Remember that it gets more and more difficult to impress a person after the first date. When presenting in those informal settings, your skills must be better, especially if you think the formality is unnecessary.

Who can really define just what "formality" means in the context of a presentation? Moreover, who can say which presentations merit formality and which do not? Every presentation is formal in the sense that your skills must be as sharp as ever to make an impact with your message, and your goal is to maintain consistency of style in all presentation settings.

UNDERSTANDING THE CONFERENCE ROOM AND U-SHAPE

In Chapter 26, "Exploring Technicalities and Techniques," we discussed theater-style and classroom-style seating in relation to the room setup. The traditional conference room offers some important seating opportunities that are a bit different from the others. This is also true of another common room setup, the U shape. Both conference room and U-shape settings share the same seating dynamics. Because many conference room tables are longer than they are wide, most of the people at the table face one another. The same is true with the U shape.

Tip from
Tom Mucciolo

Increase the size of your triangle. You can give yourself more room to maneuver in the small group setting by moving or removing some seats. In the conference room, the first and possibly second seat immediately to your right can be eliminated. This makes your triangle longer (from the screen to the first available seat). When you have more space, your movements within the triangle are more distinct, and you can create more impact as you change positions during your presentation.

In a U shape, consider removing the first table on your right (the one closest to you) to create a larger space in which to move. The U shape starts to resemble a J shape when the first table is taken away.

If care is taken to arrange the seating of your "guests" properly, the results of your meeting may be more successful. As the presenter, you have three different audiences: There are people to your far side and your near side, as well as people seated straight ahead of you toward the middle. These three seating areas or positions are referred to as the power, input, and observer seats, respectively. Depending on where people sit, an interesting dynamic may be added to the discussion.

Note

I'm assuming that you are standing to the left of the screen, from an audience perspective. Even without a screen for visual support, you should still anchor to one side, preferably to the left, to maintain the same seating dynamics throughout the talk. Moving around to different sides is not recommended, because it disrupts the original perspectives of those in the audience.

POWER SEATS

Those who sit diagonally opposite you as you speak are in the *power seats*. Because these seats mirror the presenter, an implied power is given to those occupying those seats. Figure 27.1 shows the location of the power seats. In a typical conference room or U shape, these seats are grouped in the corner. Depending on the size of the table or the U shape, two or more people may occupy the power seats. Keep in mind that these people assume power whenever they make comments or interact in some way. Even though they are not standing when they speak, the dynamics of the room create the effect of the seating importance to the rest of the group simply because those in the power seats mirror you.

Figure 27.1
From the presenter's view, the power seats are diagonally opposite.

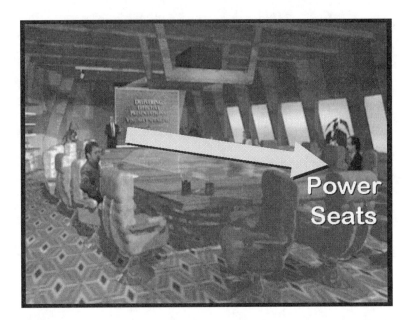

You can take most advantage of your rest and power positions with those occupying the power seats, because people in those seats tend to face you more than they face the other people in the room. In addition, you can stimulate more group interaction by directing your attention and targeting your gestures toward those in the power seats. Your efforts to include those opposite you will automatically spread the interest to either side, thereby including the entire group.

INPUT SEATS

As you present, the *input seats* are the ones along the far side of the conference table or U shape. Because you normally stand to the audience's left when you have visual support, the input seats are to your left. Figure 27.2 shows the location of those seats. Those sitting in the input seats have an unobstructed view of you, and they typically interact only when prompted. When they do interact, it is usually to provide input in the form of support information or to offer some type of agreement to a suggestion.

Those occupying the input seats will normally interact more often with the people sitting across from them. The constant challenge of conference room and U-shape seating is that many people in the room are distracted because they can see and interact with one another, which diminishes their attention to you. The input seats still offer a direct view of you and your support visuals (if any). These factors raise the importance of the input seats.

OBSERVER SEATS

The people sitting on the near side to you as you present are in the *observer seats*. Because you normally stand to the audience's left when you have visual support, the observer seats are to your right. Figure 27.3 shows the location of the observer seats. These are the worst seats in the house. People usually have to shift their chairs or lean over just to make eye contact with the presenter. More than likely, the people in these seats will have to give up the convenience of the table to position their chairs to see you as you speak. This means they lose a writing surface to take notes effectively, and they can't reach for the all-important coffee cup without making the effort obvious to the rest of the group.

Figure 27.2
From the presenter's view, the input seats are to the far side.

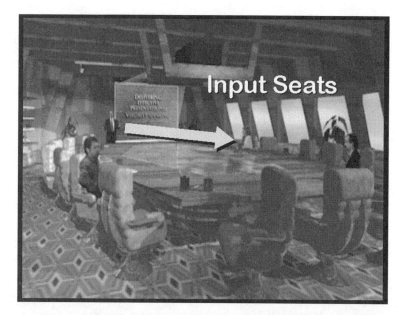

Figure 27.3
The observer seats are along the near side of the table, from the presenter's viewpoint.

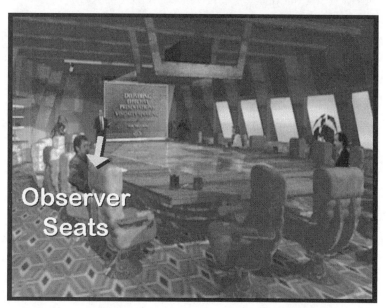

One of the main reasons these seats are referred to as "observer" seats is that the people in these seats tend to spend more time observing the group than they do the presenter. These people have to work harder just to see you in action, and this decreases their attentiveness to your message. If you're going to lose any of your conference room crowd, it will most likely be the observers.

PUTTING PEOPLE IN PLACE

It would be great if you could assign seats for people based on the power, input, and observer seating positions. As a meeting comes to order, people usually take seats on a first-come, first-served basis. There are exceptions to this, of course, but for the most part the seating in any presentation is left unplanned. You can balance the scales in your favor, however, by subtly forcing people to take certain seats.

For example, let's say you want to hold one of the power seats for a key person you expect at the presentation. Of course, you have no idea when he will arrive in relation to the others in the meeting. How can you increase the chances that the key person will occupy a power seat?

The strategy is simple, assuming you arrive in the room before anyone else. As soon as you can, place a folder or small stack of your papers on the table, right in front of the power seat that you want to hold from being taken. You could also use a briefcase or jacket on the chair itself, but a chair can be moved out of place more easily.

Then, as people come into the room, be ready to greet them at the door. This helps you spot when the key person approaches. As the room fills, there is less chance anyone will take the power seat you've held, because most people will assume the seat is already taken. People don't like to touch other people's stuff, unless of course no other place is left.

As soon as you greet the key person, you start a conversation as you both move into the room. If you are saying something of real value, the person will naturally follow you to keep listening. You casually meander to the open seat where your folder or papers are resting on the table. Just as you get there, you break the conversation and offer the seat while apologizing for having left your stuff on the table or chair. You also could plan a moment in the discussion when you need to refer to something in the folder. Either way, the excuse to remove your things makes the seat available. As you gather your papers, you pick up the conversation right where you left off, and the person will naturally take the seat as he continues listening.

Note

This is not to suggest that you will be more attentive to only one key person during your presentation. Instead, you must treat everyone the same. The difference is that the key person occupies a seat that offers the best opportunity for attention to your message. This seating strategy plays to your advantage only if you present with the same energy to everyone in the room without singling out any individual.

SEATING YOUR TEAM AND THEIR TEAM

Sometimes you may attend a presentation along with one or more people from your department or organization. These people are part of your presentation team, even though some or all of them may not present information. Teams are common in many of the sales forces I coach, especially those in financial services and real estate. The "seller-buyer" relationship is very clear when representatives of two companies meet.

That same relationship exists within organizations when several co-workers from one department present information to a team of workers from another department. One group is usually selling an idea, and the other group is asked to buy in. The seller-buyer relationship typically involves a persuasive argument.

I don't want to condense every possible presentation situation into a seller-buyer theme, but when a clear separation of duties exists within the group, some type of persuasive argument usually is being presented. Otherwise, what is the point of gathering members from diverse departments if not for consensus?

Regardless of why members of your team are involved, you can strategize a seating plan before everyone has taken their chairs in the room. Let's separate the teams by using the simple terms *their team* and *your team*. Figure 27.4 shows how you might seat some of the attendees at the meeting.

Figure 27.4
Try to have some of your team in the observer seats and some of their team in the power/input seats.

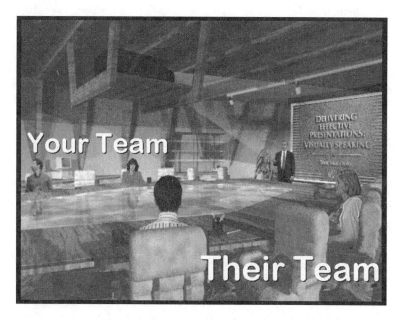

Obviously you want the power seats to be taken by members of their team, especially for a persuasive presentation. If you can identify key players from their team, try to get a few of them into the power seats. Following that, any of their team's subordinate decision makers or support staff should occupy some of the input seats. Naturally, you want your team to blend in, so use the remaining input seats for members of your team, specifically those who are not presenting at the meeting.

Finally, save some of the observer seats for your team, especially for those who will be presenting during the meeting. Then, when they are ready to speak, they've had the opportunity to glance at others during your presentation to notice key reactions, interest level, and so forth. Awareness of any details about the group's reactions to information is invaluable to each presenter. In addition, members of your team occupying the observer seats are probably familiar with your presentation. They don't need to be as attentive to your words at every moment.

Following the presentation, you should regroup with your team and discuss the behavior observed during the meeting. Someone might have noticed a perplexed look when a certain subject was covered. Another member of your team might have observed someone taking notes as soon as a specific chart was presented. The observers can also notice people nodding off; maybe the presentation is longer than it should be. In any event, the feedback from those in the observer seats can be helpful in preparing for your next presentation.

SIT-DOWN SCENARIOS

Let's scale down the setting to the times when you are just sitting down. In these meetings, typically in a conference room, you might spend a few minutes standing and giving a presentation and then sit to continue the discussion. The seating positions can still be used effectively.

Keep in mind that when seated, the position of your shoulders still controls the rest and power positions discussed in Chapter 22, "The Message—Scripting the Concept" (refer to Figure 22.3 for a visual example). When your shoulders match the shoulders of another person, you are in a power position in relation to that person (as he is with you). When your shoulders are at an angle to another person, you are in a rest position. Your goal is to be in a seat where the angles of your body can be used effectively with the greatest number of people in the room.

For example, avoid putting yourself in a center-seating situation at a conference room table. Take a look at Figure 27.5. Let's say that the man in the center of the group, at the head of the table, is leading the meeting. You might think he is in a power position in relation to the others on his right and left. However, he can take a power position only with the person directly opposite, at the other end of the table.

The seat at the head of the table is not as effective, unless you are facilitating a meeting rather than leading it. When facilitating, you represent a neutral position. This is similar to an arbitrator or mediator. If you are playing such a role, then consider a center-seating position in relation to the group.

If you want to lead and control a meeting, you have a better chance from one of the corner seats. Look at Figure 27.6. It's the same group of people, shown from a different position. The woman wearing the eyeglasses has a power seat in relation to the others at the table.

She is able to square her shoulders or angle them to many different people by swiveling her chair or shifting the upper part of her body.

Figure 27.5
The person at the head of the table is limited by his center position. He can create a power position with only one other person at the table, the one opposite him.

Figure 27.6
The woman wearing the eyeglasses occupies a power seat. The corner seats are the most effective in these conference room settings.

This strategy enables you to gain a wider perspective of the entire group. In addition, documents or other items will be easier to angle for view when you take one of the corner seats.

HANDLING ONE-TO-ONE SITUATIONS

What happens when you are faced with one or two people in the room with you? You can still have a seating strategy to help your message along. For one-to-one meetings, use your rest and power positions in the same way as you do in a conference room setting. The smaller the group, the easier it becomes to use body angles to your advantage.

CREATE ANGLES

The most common situation to avoid is one in which you are directly opposite the other person and your shoulders match each other. The goal is to avoid having your shoulders parallel to the other person in a "squared-off" position. Angling your body or your chair is the easiest way to avoid squaring off to the other person. Look at Figure 27.7. In the background of the photo you see two people standing and having a conversation. Because their shoulders match, they are both in a power position relative to each other. When two people square off like that, it's as if their bodies are yelling at one another. In the foreground of the same image, the two women are seated, but they are at angles to one another.

Figure 27.7
Communication is more effective when people are at angles to one another.

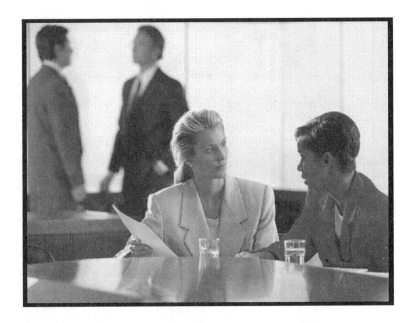

You can put yourself into an angled position in relation to another person in a number of ways. When seated, you can choose a corner of a table; if you are standing and someone else is sitting, you can lean on the edge of a desk (half-standing) and keep your shoulders angled to the seated person.

SHARE PERSPECTIVE

When two people look at something from completely different angles, they are not sharing a common perspective. This is not really a problem when the object is large enough to be seen from a distance, such as an image projected on a screen. If the object is meant for an audience of one, then perspective becomes an issue.

The most common object for one person to look at is a document. If you are opposite a person when you hand over a document, you immediately lose a common perspective. The person is looking down at the piece of paper, and you are looking at the same object upside-down. The perspective is different for each of you. It will be more difficult for you to point out specifics in the document from your perspective. You'll probably end up stretching your neck and rotating your head at some weird angle. Try to get the same perspective on the object as the other person.

Figure 27.8 shows a man standing next to a woman seated at a table. They share a common perspective of the document, which makes communication more effective. When people have the same point of view (literally) on something, the message is easier to convey and interpret.

Figure 27.8
By standing to the side, the man has the same perspective of the document as the woman.

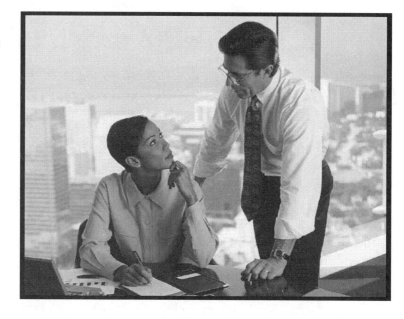

Once equal perspective is achieved regarding the document, the man can return to his original position at the other side of the table and continue the discussion, meeting, or presentation.

The same perspective can also be achieved when two people are sitting. In Figure 27.9, the two men have the same perspective in looking at the papers in front of them. It will be easy for one of them to point to information on the sheets if necessary to facilitate the discussion. Imagine how difficult it would be if one of them were standing opposite and looking over the top of the papers to point out something specific.

Figure 27.9
Two people sitting side by side share the same perspective when looking at documents.

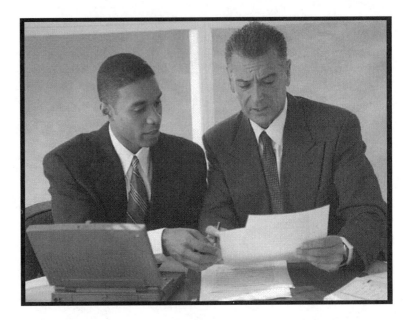

Tip from
Tom Mucciolo

Don't make your effort to get a common perspective so obvious that the other person wonders what you are doing. For example, if you are in a conference room with one other person and the table is long enough to hold 20 people, don't sit right next to the person. Instead, take a corner seat, if you can. Then, when you need to share a document, you can always get up and stand to the side of the person to point out information in the document.

SCAN THE EYES

A lot of information stored in your brain is in the form of pictures. These visual references are tucked away neatly in your brain waiting for retrieval. For example, if you think about your high school biology teacher, a visual image pops into your head, and you see that person in your mind's eye, so to speak. You even visualize situations that haven't happened. If I ask you to think about your own road to success, you create a little picture in your brain as you see yourself in some type of successful moment. Everyone uses visual references. When one of those references is retrieved, the eyes move in some direction to see the image in the brain.

Therefore, in many one-to-one situations, the eyes of the other person can offer you some interesting clues as to what he might be thinking. As an observer, you can scan the eye movement of a person whenever you say something thought provoking. To interpret the other person's reaction, however, you need to learn how he looks for the images he creates.

The easiest approach is to probe for a timeline. Figure 27.10 shows how you place an imaginary timeline in front of the person's face. The timeline is always from your point of view. Start with the assumption that the person's past is to your left, and his future is to your right.

Figure 27.10
When scanning the eyes of another person, place an imaginary timeline in front of him.

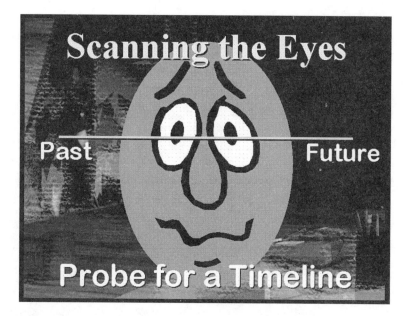

When you ask a question involving reflection or something in the past, the person normally shifts his eyes in one direction to look up the visual image of the experience. You can observe which direction the eyes travel as the person recalls the experience. Not everyone glances in the same direction to look up an image, but for most people, that direction is up and to the right. Whatever the direction, it represents the past. Figure 27.11 shows how a person's eyes might move when he reflects on a past experience. In this example, the direction of his eyes matches your timeline.

Figure 27.11
When a person reflects on the past, his eyes move in some direction.

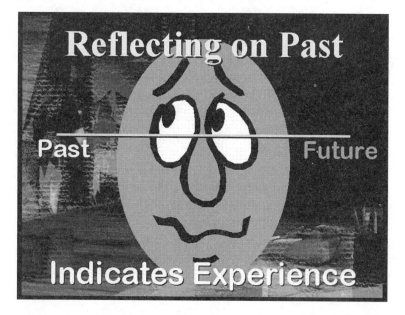

If his eyes shift the opposite way of your imaginary timeline, then reverse your timeline and realize that he looks up his past differently (to your right). You first have to notice how the person recalls past experiences to establish the end points of your timeline. Whatever the direction of his eyes, it represents the past on your timeline.

After you know the person's past, whenever you prompt a thought-provoking glance in the opposite direction, the person is likely indicating anticipation of something in the future. Figure 27.12 shows an established timeline with a glance to the person's left, indicating a vision of the future.

Figure 27.12
After a timeline is established and you know the person's past, a shift of his eyes in the opposite direction indicates anticipation.

I have always taken the position that, whenever a person paints a picture of his future, it is always positive, unless he has some specific reason to expect something negative to happen. Using the assumption that a person's view of the future is ultimately optimistic, a shift of a person's eyes to the "future" on the timeline you establish may be the most opportune moment for you to close the deal, so to speak. After all, if the person appears to be looking forward to using your product or service, take that eye movement as a hint and go for it. Close the deal, ask for the order, complete the call to action.

The eyes give other hints, as well. For example, if the person is staring directly at you and not shifting his eyes at all, there's a good chance that he is not listening. He is probably giving you the courtesy of direct eye contact, but he is probably drifting away in his thoughts. Break the eye contact and he will be attentive again.

WORKING IN REMOTE LOCATIONS

Not every presentation offers you the convenience of a roof over your head. In fact, sometimes you may find yourself presenting in harsh environments or in settings that make it nearly impossible to keep an audience attentive for more than a few minutes. Many business presentations take place in remote locations much different than the typical conference room. Let's take a look at some of these situations, including outdoor presentations, possible extreme or unusual conditions, and trade shows.

PRESENTING OUTDOORS

When someone talks about presenting "out in the field," don't be surprised if they are referring to a stretch of land that yields wheat. A number of companies have to conduct business in outdoor environments because of the nature of what they need to discuss or show. The reasons you might conduct a presentation outdoors are convenience and display. In some cases, you are forced to present yourself at the location of your listeners, thus making it convenient for your audience to evaluate your message. In other cases, you ask your audience to attend your presentation so that you can display some product that would be difficult to bring to the listeners.

For example, it is not unusual for a company that manufactures heavy construction equipment to demonstrate a large piece of machinery to a group of prospects outdoors. You won't find too many hotel ballrooms able to accommodate a 150-foot crane.

Naturally, there are many ways to show products in a presentation using photographs and line art. A picture of the crane or a schematic drawing of its unique functions can be inserted directly into a PowerPoint presentation. There is nothing wrong with this as a way to discuss features and benefits.

But the most effective way for someone to grasp the entire picture is to experience the real thing. If you were considering purchasing a building, you could look at photos or renderings, but you would benefit most by going to the location and walking through the space itself. It is during these moments that presenting outdoors takes place.

DEMONSTRATING LARGE OBJECTS

You're presenting outdoors, and you have a product to show or demonstrate. One of the first things to consider is the size of the object in relation to the group. Because you picked the outdoor venue for a reason, let's assume the object is bigger than you are. This being the case, you won't be able to pick it up and hold it. You can't pass it around for the group to examine. You won't even be able to move it without an obvious effort. This is no different than when you present visuals on a screen. You won't attempt to move the screen, and the good news is you don't have to. You can leave it stationary and use your own movement and gestures to refer to it.

The first thing you do with a large object is to anchor it for the audience. Leave it in the same spot for as long as you can while you present. This gives your audience a single perspective on a stationary object. If you need to change the viewing angle, decide if it is easier to reposition the object or reposition the audience by having them move in one direction or another.

For example, let's say your company manufactures cars, and you want to present the latest model to a group of car dealers who sell your products. You decide to hold the meeting at an outdoor venue, such as a racetrack, and you gather your group in an open space to show the vehicle. To make sure everyone can see, you have the group stand on a series of raised platforms with each row higher than the row in front. The long side of the car faces the group, and you describe features of the vehicle as you move slowly from one end of the car to the other. It doesn't matter which side you start from because there is nothing for the audience to read. Only when the visual content contains text do you have to anchor to the side of the visual where the reading normally starts.

The key to showing a large object is to create a linear path for the audience to follow. Don't move back and forth to different points. Try to plan your movements to navigate in as straight a line as possible from your starting to your ending point. This reduces distraction.

WALKING AND TALKING

Sometimes you may have to give your presentation as you lead your audience through a defined space. A number of businesses encounter these situations all the time. You can be selling real estate or conducting guided tours; the fact is that you are walking and talking with a group as you point out specific items. When the audience is moving, the dynamics of the presentation change in relation to the perspective.

Think about what happens when people are moving. They have to focus attention on where they are going before they even begin to concentrate on something else. This means that attention span is shorter when the group is moving. When the group is standing still, attention is greater. As a presenter, your goal is to make your key points at times when the group has stopped moving. The more you can control the movement of your audience, the more effectively you can direct their attention.

While you are moving, especially in situations where you are walking as you guide the group through a space, you must be aware of your ability to be heard. Each time you turn your face away from the group (perhaps to see where you're going), you have to speak louder for your voice to carry. In fact, anytime you are looking away and still speaking, try directing your voice toward a hard surface rather than a wide-open space. A hard surface reflects sound. This helps your voice bounce back in the direction of the listeners.

To help the group focus on objects more quickly, use vocal directions prior to describing the item. For example, if you are guiding a few people through a workspace in a building and you want to point out certain objects along the way, use phrases such as "to your left" or "along the floor to your immediate right" to indicate direction before a description.

When what you are describing is already in view, a person can relate to your description more attentively.

When walking and talking, you may also be gesturing toward things. Try to maintain a consistency with your gestures and with the direction you turn your body. Choose a repeating pattern such as using your right hand to gesture whenever your body turns to your right. The goal is to reduce distractions with a smaller variety of movements. Keep in mind the audience may be looking in three different places: at something you are pointing to, at where they are walking, or directly at you. You may be looking in three different places as well, depending on what you are doing at the moment. You can see how a moving presenter and moving audience limit the chance to establish anchors. At least a consistent pattern of movement will not add to the confusion.

DEALING WITH EXTREME CONDITIONS

Circumstances occur that may make it nearly impossible to conduct the presentation in the manner that you expect. I'm not talking about a projector bulb burning out. I'm talking about extreme conditions that test the limits of your ability to deliver the message. Think of an extreme condition as one that reduces your chances of either being seen, understood, or even heard by the audience. In each of these cases, the strategy is to focus your energy on the parts of the presentation that are of greatest importance to your audience.

Keep in mind that the components of communication involve your body, your voice, and your visual support. The audience concentrates on each of these elements while the message is being delivered. When one of those elements is restricted, the audience places more focus on the remaining elements to get the most from the message. Knowing this helps you put more emphasis on the more obvious components of the communication. Let's take a look at some extreme conditions that can hinder your efforts to deliver a message with impact.

DARK SHADOWS

When people can't see you, that's a problem. You already know how important it is for the audience to see your body and, more specifically, your face. Expressions help a listener understand your intent behind the message. Therefore, lighting is a critical element to your being seen by everyone. Poor lighting or no lighting at all can be a major obstacle in your effort to deliver your story with impact.

We already talked about lighting in Chapter 26, including some techniques to illuminate you as you speak. What happens when you end up presenting in the dark? Some people say that when there is very little light the audience falls asleep. That's a fallacy. People don't just fall asleep when the lights go down. After all, some of the most exciting moments in our lives happen in the dark. It's not the lack of light that puts people to sleep, it's lack of visible action.

→ To learn more about creative lighting techniques, **see** "Working with Lighting and Sound" in Chapter 26.

Because lack of visible action reduces attentiveness and interest, you need to work around poor lighting conditions as best you can. The best way to do this is to get your body in a position where it is most visible, closest to any available light source. In a very dark room, you already know that the greatest concentration of light will be on the screen displaying your visuals, so the screen is your closest light source. The amount of light bouncing off the screen determines how much of you the audience sees. Proximity to your screen or light source is the strategy to consider.

Under poor lighting conditions, you have to limit the movement in your triangle. You have to make your available space smaller and confined to those areas with the most light reflecting from the screen. Naturally, this forces you to use the back of your triangle, where the light is brighter from the screen.

Another thing you can consider is reversing your color scheme. I normally suggest a dark background and a bright foreground, but poor lighting conditions are not normal. You'll have to trade off some of the impact from your visuals to gain physical presence. If you use a lighter background and a darker foreground, you'll have more white (bright) light emanating from the screen. This gives you a better chance of being illuminated by the spillover of reflective light, especially as you get closer to your visual. You won't be so visible that people can see your facial expressions, but your gestures will make more sense even if the light from the screen casts you only as a silhouette for the audience to see.

From the audience's perspective, when your body language and facial expressions are less visible, the concentration of attention shifts more to the two components of your content: your voice and your visual support. From a vocal standpoint, realize that the audience can't see your mouth moving when you speak. This means you'll have to speak more slowly, enunciate your words better, and pause more often. Pretend you are in a phone conversation with your audience, where the greatest percentage of the message comes from your tone, not just from the words you say.

When referencing your visuals, use vocal directions. These are lead-in phrases such as "the second bar labeled 1999" or "the two largest slices on the right side of this pie chart." Actually, vocal directions help guide the eye in all presentation settings, not only when you find yourself in poor lighting conditions.

THE SOUNDS OF SILENCE

Sometimes the audience may have difficulty hearing you. Microphones are great tools for enabling people to hear your voice from a distance, but in many situations, a microphone is not available. Depending on the size of the space and the distance to the last row, making yourself heard might become a real challenge.

Part of the problem may be that you aren't speaking loud enough. In Chapter 24, "The Mechanics of Form—Developing External Presentation Skills," you learned several techniques to enhance your vocal delivery. However, even if you can raise the volume of your voice, it may create more problems than you think. For example, if you have to shout so that people in the back of the room can hear you, imagine the effect your voice has on the people in the front. As you examine the glaring evil stares of those whose eardrums have been ruptured, you will most likely begin to lower your voice. Of course, the people in the back will strain to hear you once again. You can easily see how distance creates a sound imbalance for your audience. What can you do?

→ For more information on vocal delivery techniques, **see** "Breathing Properly" in Chapter 24.

First find a volume level that is at least audible from the back, even though it is not at the level those people prefer. Because your words have less impact, you need to show more and say less. Remember that when a component of the communication is restricted, the remaining components draw more attention from the audience. If your voice is barely audible, then your gestures, your movements, and even your visuals are more apparent.

From a physical perspective, I'm not suggesting you run around flapping your arms to create more attention. You should emphasize your words with descriptive gestures by using virtual space more often to explain things. When your words are harder to hear, your actions speak that much louder and you'll have to "act out" your thoughts.

→ To learn more about virtual space, **see** "Using Virtual Space" in Chapter 25, "The Mechanics of Function—Developing Internal Presentation Skills."

Tip from
Tom Mucciolo

> Play a visual game like Charades in which you have to act out a phrase without speaking, or give directions to someone who doesn't speak your language. You also might simply spend a little time entertaining an infant. In each of these situations, you will have to rely more on your nonverbal skills to communicate a message completely.

Another way to compensate for your inability to be heard well is to add more visual support to your presentation. Naturally, you'll have to plan ahead for this because you can't create a whole bunch of extra visuals at the last minute. Additional content on the screen gives the audience a more visual reference for the words they may not hear. You can use builds and overlays to reveal information in stages so that the audience knows exactly where you are on a given visual. You can even create a series of additional images to support what normally might have been displayed as a single visual.

For example, suppose you have a map of the United States with three defined regions: west, central, and east. Under normal conditions you planned to cover information about all three regions without changing the visual. Because you are barely audible, you can help the audience through the topic by adding three more visuals, one for each region. On each of these subvisuals, you can add bulleted text to highlight some of the key points you are discussing. Even if it is difficult to hear everything you are saying, the audience is "reading" more of your visual content to get a better understanding of the message.

CULTURE SHOCK

In the growing world of global communication, it is not unusual to find yourself facing audience members who have trouble understanding you because they are less familiar with your language. Whether you present locally or abroad, you are likely to encounter language barriers with some people in your audience from time to time. In fact, you may present in another country where not only are your words difficult to understand, but your visual support is, too. When an audience views cultural differences as distractions, your presentation is less effective.

In these situations, your best bet is to put the majority of your effort into the physical delivery. After all, body language is universal; spoken language is not. You can test this theory at home. Find a TV station broadcasting in a language you barely understand. If you watch for a while, there will be enough visual clues and details for you to get some idea of what is happening. This is because you can see the action. Now, turn your back to the TV so you can't see the screen. Because you can't understand the words, notice how little information you can get. It's obvious that observable action is a big contributor toward understanding.

Your physical actions and your visual support play the major roles in overcoming language barriers when you present. Regarding your content, consider creating images that are more graphical. Embed more photographs in the backgrounds of your visuals. Use arrows, colors, and geometric shapes to help tell your story. Avoid showing too many text charts. In fact, numbers and other data-driven charts (bar, pie, line) may be easier for the audience to understand than heavy text-based visuals.

Your physical actions are important, but presenting in a foreign country can be challenging. Gestures and movements you make may be considered distracting, rude, or even offensive without you knowing it.

Tip from
Tom Mucciolo

You may want to investigate this reference regarding this topic: *Cross-Cultural Communication: A Practical Guide*, by Gregory Barnard.

You never know what certain actions might mean. The last thing you need is to accidentally scratch your right ear while your left elbow points at a 45-degree angle to the northwest corner of the room and, immediately, some military extremist in the middle of the crowd leaps up and declares that you've just insulted their leader. That's why it's always best to check with a resident about local customs and cultural issues.

DELIVERING TRADESHOW PRESENTATIONS

Many companies participate in tradeshows. Presentations at these events range from simple demonstrations to full-blown theatrical wonders. Regardless of all the hoopla and the hype, these events need to be planned and organized effectively.

The typical tradeshow involves people from a company standing on their feet about 10 hours a day for almost a week. During this time these brave souls are fielding questions, spouting theories, running for coffee, eating junk food, listening to arguments, shaking hands, smiling at strangers, reading badges, handing out literature, gathering business cards, and praying for the end of the show. Sound familiar?

Regardless of the excitement surrounding a tradeshow, the bottom line is that the interaction among participants is either from conversations or presentations. Conversations are the one-to-one spontaneous discussions with passersby and booth visitors. Presentations are more planned topics delivered several times a day to small groups of spectators, usually from a dedicated space inside the booth. You can spot these setups right away. Just look for a bunch of chairs facing a screen and maybe a sign displaying something like "The next presentation begins at" or words to that effect.

To get the most from your tradeshow event, you should understand the underlying objective or purpose behind every moment of your delivery, whether it is conversation or presentation. The reason people go to tradeshows is to see something new and different, something wonderful, something exciting, and something enlightening. Give people what they want, and they will remember you.

INFORMAL CONVERSATIONS

Earlier in this chapter we discussed one-to-one situations, and all the same rules apply to tradeshow conversations. The big difference between conference rooms and tradeshows is the underlying sense of urgency for both parties involved.

Naturally, you want to cover information quickly, and the listener wants to gather information quickly. At least you each agree on the result: quick, concise data. One of the informal studies we conducted at MediaNet was a random sample of tradeshow attendees to calculate the average stay at any booth location. We found the average stay to be 2 minutes and 14 seconds at those booths where the attendee actually stopped to have a conversation. During that time, the attendees focused attention mostly on items directly in view while they listened to the person talking with them. If you figure on people staying only a short time, then by all means, get to the point.

That's why conversations at tradeshows should be no more than short descriptions containing key words about the product or service on display. We call these brief phrases *sound bites* (or *bytes*, if you prefer). The sound bite should be a capsule summary of a somewhat lengthier statement that, given the extra time, you would have said. You should create a whole library of these little pieces of enlightening facts and then use them at the appropriate times during the conversation.

Sound bites are important for controlling the flow of traffic around you. Let's say you are standing in your booth and talking to one person about a new product that your company is introducing. You already know this person may walk away after a minute or two, so you use your strongest sound bites first. Your mention the top three features as soon you can. In the meantime, other people are passing by, eavesdropping, as they should. Before you know it, a new listener hearing a sound bite joins the small discussion. Now you have two people seeking enlightenment. You can't repeat the same features for the new person because the first listener gets no added value and probably walks away. You add a new sound bite and perhaps rephrase one of the original ones, as well. This keeps both listeners attentive a bit longer. The point is that you have to keep the enlightenment going in some small way as each new listener joins the group.

PART

VII

CH

27

After you run out of new things to say, you will begin to lose the people who have been there the longest. If you got two minutes out of them, you made a successful contact. Even though the person received only a brief impression, it gave him the choice of either moving on or seeking even more information from you or others in the booth.

One other interesting thing about conversations is the likelihood of joining one. In other words, most people would rather join an existing conversation than initiate one. Think about it. It is less work for you to approach two or more people engaged in open conversation than it is for you to approach someone and just start up a discussion from scratch. At a tradeshow, the more sound bites you have, the longer you can keep your first listener attentive. It follows that the longer a listener stays attentive, the greater the chances of another listener joining the existing conversation. As you continue, the crowd around you grows. Even from a distance, others will be attracted to see what is so interesting. Little do they know that it's just a bunch of really attractive sound bites.

PLANNED PRESENTATIONS

For many companies, the tradeshow venue includes a short presentation. Typically, these little shows are delivered a couple of times each day. They normally span 20 to 30 minutes, and the audience is usually seated in some theater-style arrangement. The presentation must be first and foremost entertaining. Second, the entertainment must directly relate to what your company does or sells, or else you can't make a lasting impression. That is why the magician at the tradeshow booth is a big waste of time, unless your product is truly magical. If the entertainment is simply to draw a crowd, how will you know who in the crowd is a potential customer?

Just follow the principle of "entertainment with direct relevance" to build a more effective tradeshow presentation. If you can provide an enlightening and entertaining experience, you will create a lasting impression with your audience.

The best way to provide a memorable show is to concentrate on a few logistics. First of all, rehearse the presentation so that you know it lasts the 20 or 30 minutes you plan for it to last. Second, be sure your visuals are extremely simple. Don't use a lot of text; use plenty of graphics and photos. Visual presentations attract people from a distance to get closer and keep those seated from being distracted by the constant activity in the surrounding area. If you are presenting software or a Web site or anything that requires a computer-looking interface, keep in mind that readability from a distance will be more difficult. It is best to concentrate on key features and benefits, rather than teaching unique details that are difficult for an easily distracted audience to grasp.

Regarding the position of your stage, try to face out to a cross-aisle. In other words, if you anchor your presentation area to a corner of your booth, perhaps you can be seen from two different aisles at the same time. This will increase the chances of attracting people walking from two different directions. When presenting, be sure your eye contact, your voice, and your gestures reach to the back of the group and beyond to increase the chances of others stopping to listen to your story.

Some of the most distracting elements at a tradeshow are light and noise. Without a canopy or enclosed space, the light from the exhibit hall can wash out your display screen. To offset this, your visuals should have a lot of contrast between backgrounds and foregrounds. When it comes to noise, expect a lot of it. Get used to the noises immediately around your booth. Sometimes you can detect a pattern from other presentations or activities. If your timing is good, you can make your key phrases heard at the least distracting moments.

Finally, be sure you get your captured audience to do something at the end of the presentation. You must get their contact information because they represent a more qualified opportunity. If the average person stays two minutes at a booth and some people sat for 20 minutes, you can safely assume they have greater interest—unless, of course, they only sat there to get a prize. In that case, you made the mistake of attracting the wrong people for the wrong reason at the wrong time.

Tradeshow interaction needs to be planned and practiced. Whether you are in a conversation or a presentation, if you focus on working around the distractions at a tradeshow, you can make the time spent on your feet worthwhile. The only thing that doesn't change is that after you work your first big show, you never look forward to working another one.

PICTURING YOURSELF ON TV

Before your career ends, you will most likely not be sending e-mail to people anymore. You will be seeing them, just like you see people on TV. It won't exactly be face-to-face, but it will be very close. One reason communication will have to be more visual is the fact that the baby boomers are past the age of 50. As our bodies get older, the dexterity in our fingers diminishes. As a maturing society, we will demand an easier way to converse electronically than using the verbal banter of e-mail messages. This evolution is inevitable. To prepare for the new age of visual communication, you need to have a better understanding of the following topics.

PLAYING TO THE CAMERA

Maybe you're already communicating on camera for occasional teleconferences, to produce videotapes, for image magnification at large conferences, or even when speaking to the media. When on camera, you need to reinforce your message using your voice, positioning, and movement.

VOICE

When you are on camera, you have to learn to relax and breathe normally. When you talk through a lens, even though you feel rushed and think you're speaking too slowly, fight the tendency to speed up. You must learn to phrase and pause naturally. Enunciate clearly and be careful to pronounce every syllable. When you're on camera, chances are you are wearing a small lapel microphone. These microphones are sensitive devices that pick up every sound in your voice. Be aware that certain consonants may cause problems. For example, the letter *P* can create a popping sound, and the letter *S* can cause a hissing sound. The microphone will pick up a lot of distracting sounds. Avoid mumbling, sniffing, clearing your throat, or using fillers (such as um, er, and so forth). Just be sure to keep all your comments directed at the camera. If you make a minor mistake, keep going. Don't add unnecessary information by apologizing or by whispering some short, frustrated phrase insulting yourself for not being perfect.

POSITIONING

Positioning yourself to the camera and your audience has as much to do with your physical presence as it does with your personal image. You just have to be yourself. Even though you are under the scrutiny of the camera, you should feel comfortable and act appropriately in everything you say and do. It's easy to forget this when you are alone in front of the lens without a live audience watching you. You need to present yourself as credible and confident.

Given the choice, standing is preferable to sitting because it is easier to breathe when standing. In addition, being on your feet tends to keep you more alert. Sitting may be necessary for longer sessions. Keep in mind that when the camera projects your image, any movements you make look much more pronounced to the viewer. When seated, choose a solid chair that doesn't swivel. If you wear a jacket, sit on the back hem and you'll actually sit up straighter. This also keeps your coat from bunching up in front. If you tilt your head slightly downward or slightly to one side every now and then, you will appear more relaxed.

Naturally, in well-planned environments, someone will play the role of stage manager or production director and make sure the set looks right. You need to be prepared for the local communication that becomes visual. But often, you'll be the one to play the role of producer, director, and actor, in much the same way that you play the role of publisher, editor, and author when you create your own e-mail messages. Before the cameras start rolling, check directly behind you. Pay attention to your backdrop. Is a disorganized bookshelf or a leftover lunch plate the image you want to portray? Assume the camera is always running and don't show or say anything that distracts from your message. Don't be distracted by items or other people in the room; you'll appear detached and uncertain.

MOVEMENT

Remember that we've been talking about the triangle since Chapter 24. The basic choreography used for stand-up presentations, whether in a large or a small setting, applies to working on camera, which is the smallest setting of all. The real difference between the environments is the proximity of the audience. In live situations you tend to be farther from the audience when you speak, and your movements need to be bigger to be seen from a greater distance. Through the camera, especially when the image is a close-up, the triangle is magnified for the viewer, and the movements need to be much smaller. You establish the triangle positions with a slight tilt of the head rather than full body movement. Take the basics of body movement and translate them to the sensitivity of the camera.

The three positions of the triangle are still used. You can establish intimacy with the audience by tilting your head forward. Technically, you are in the front of the triangle. You can create neutrality by not tilting your head at all, and you will be in the center of the triangle. You can tilt your head back to reach the back of the triangle and appear to present the larger view of the topic. On camera, the simple tilting of your head creates movement, inflection, meaning, and interest. Former U.S. President Ronald Reagan was a master at using subtle head movement to communicate his views. He was a film actor before he was politician. He knew how to take advantage of the camera.

You can also make adjustments in the angle of your body. Position your shoulders at a 45-degree angle to the camera to establish a rest position. By doing this, you can, when necessary, shift the upper part of your body and square off to the camera to evoke power and emphasis.

One of the other issues unique to the camera is the degree to which you exist in the frame. In a live event, your view of the presenter is a function of where you sit. Obviously the camera has the capability to zoom in or pull back to create a completely different view for the audience. That is why you need to know how close the camera is set at any particular moment. If you know your frame of reference, you can decide what movements, if any, are available to you. Depending on the camera setting, you may have to limit your expressions and gestures.

You'll have to learn to concentrate on both your topic and your movements. If you accidentally move out of the frame, those watching won't be able to see you. If you're operating the camera yourself, you will make the choice to change the zoom level or the camera angle. In many videoconferencing sessions, either you or someone sitting with you in the conference usually controls the camera. If someone else is controlling the camera, you should talk with that person in advance and discuss any movements you expect in which the camera will have to be adjusted. In fact, if your presentation hits a particularly emotional point, you may want to cue the camera to move to a close-up.

Unless the event is highly choreographed, chances are the camera will stay in a relatively fixed position and capture you from the waist up. In a videoconference, the equipment can usually be preset to certain angles, and many systems are voice activated so that the camera automatically shifts to the person speaking. As technology becomes more sophisticated, you will be less concerned about the technical aspects of the visual communication. For now, the camera angles and close-ups are controlled decisions. The timing of those decisions influences the viewer because the camera lens is the link between the presenter and the audience.

USING VIDEOCONFERENCING TECHNOLOGY

Technology is driving communication. The power of telecommunication and personal computers will soon have us all videoconferencing with the same ease and confidence that we currently use to pick up the phone. Video as the vehicle will be more the norm than the exception.

The current evolution in visual communication is toward videoconferencing, whether it is personal or group. When the videoconference is personal, it is conducted from your desktop. When a group delivers the session, it takes place in a larger setting such as a conference room. In either case, this technology is ever changing. Between the moment I write this and the time you read it, there will have been several changes to the systems available and already in use. Such is the nature of our fast-paced world. I don't want to talk a lot about features or limitations; instead, I want to cover the challenges posed by the nature of the technology itself.

The best way to explain videoconferencing is to think of it as combining the power of television with the intimacy of face-to-face communication, while bridging the gaps of distance, time, and relationships. How's that for a mouthful? It's important to understand the challenges of distance and time, especially to a growing world of visual creatures.

THE DISTANCE FACTOR

Face-to-face meetings require your physical presence. Although a lot can be accomplished through e-mail and voice, being in the presence of another person is the highest form of communication. Sometimes you have to travel to create a face-to-face meeting. When you think about attending meetings that require travel, distance influences your plans. For example, if you work in San Francisco and need to attend a meeting in Atlanta, you already know that much of your time will be spent traveling to and from the meeting. Typically, you'll try to arrange other appointments to help justify the trip, the expense, and the inconvenience of being away from the office for so long. However, if the meeting were on site you would not create additional activity with nearby departments just because you happen to be going all the way to the other side of the building. When travel distance is involved, the need to get other things accomplished while in the area becomes a priority.

As you plan your trip to Atlanta, you call two other contacts in the Atlanta vicinity, and you request a brief meeting because you plan to be in the area. The others may agree to meet with you more out of courtesy than real need. After all, they didn't call you, and they may not be as ready as you are to discuss things or make decisions. Some meetings are called because distance dictates the availability of one or more of the parties involved.

Videoconferencing tries to bridge the gap of distance while offering some of the benefits of face-to-face. It may be easier to coordinate mutually convenient schedules for a videoconference if all parties need to travel only a short walking distance to the visual meeting. You may be able to offer the other people two or three optional times, rather than let the airlines dictate the time and place for the event.

THE TIME FACTOR

Although convenience of scheduling is time related, the real factor here is length of time for a meeting. Today, most meetings that take place in company conference rooms are based around the convenience of the clock. Typically, conference room charts are filled with one-hour meetings, even though these meetings may not really need to be one hour. It is not feasible to schedule a 23-minute meeting, then an 18-minute meeting, and so on.

Our other forms of communication are much more to the minute, especially phone conversations. Even a telephone conference call among distant parties offers a start time, but rarely a stop time other than an approximation. Why? Because the parties involved are on private phones, separated from one another. If some of the people on the call are occupying a conference room to place the call, then the time for the call may be more limited to make the conference room available for others.

Today, videoconferencing equipment is not on everyone's desk as is a telephone or a personal computer. The availability of the technology from a time factor is still limited by appointment. However, when the technology is on each desktop, the length of meetings will be determined by the objectives of the conversation, not the availability of space.

Current videoconferencing technology has a higher connection time cost than a simple phone call. From an expense standpoint, companies need to limit the length of each call. This has a benefit because when you pay by the minute, you will likely make more prudent use of the time during a videoconference session than you might in a typical face-to-face meeting in the conference room.

THE RELATIONSHIP FACTOR

Many projects involve assembling a team of experts from within an organization or even across organizations. Too often, people in different departments, in different companies, and even in different cities don't have the time or resources to meet face-to-face, and yet they somehow are required to complete a task as a team. When face-to-face meetings are not possible, it is more difficult to get a group of diverse personalities to perform as a team.

A lot of our time during business communication is spent imagining what the people we haven't met really look like. Every moment we interact without seeing a person, we are communicating with our mental image of the person, which we create. This is a natural process. The beauty of face-to-face communication is the chance to meet and greet others. This is how relationships are formed. Relationships are a huge part of the team concept.

Videoconferencing gives separated parties the chance to see and hear others who may be brought together for only a short time to accomplish a task. Although everyone can't shake hands, at least they can avoid the task of imagining what the other people look like because they can see and interact through the technology of videoconferencing.

PART

VII

CH

27

THE POWER OF TELEVISION

Chances are that you grew up with television. How much money would you have if you were paid five dollars for each hour of TV you have watched in your life? If you averaged 20 hours a week and you've been watching TV for 20 years, you would have amassed more than $100,000 by now—and that's assuming you never put the money in an investment plan.

Regardless of how much TV you really do watch, no one can deny the influence of television over the generations of the past 25 years. Figure 27.13 summarizes the most obvious features of television that keep us glued endlessly to a variety of channels sometimes offering little content.

Figure 27.13
The major features of television are what really keep us entertained.

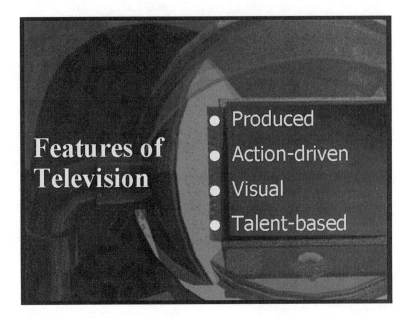

Television is a highly produced, action-driven medium. You thrive on visual images, and you have become highly critical of those writing, producing, and performing for television. Although you are comfortable with the medium as you watch the screen or talk into the lens of a home video camera, you have much higher expectations of those performing professionally on TV. It doesn't take a great stretch of the imagination to wonder what your expectations will be of those who communicate using videoconferencing technology. Maybe you won't expect TV personalities, but you might expect talent to be something better than what you have recorded on your home video camera.

From a business perspective, the power of television is used most often as a "store and forward" medium, rather than a real-time one. You may have been asked to view tapes in the workplace for training, informational, or motivational reasons. This is more private and mostly one sided—you are receiving information but not interacting. The good news is that these video productions are usually done well. They are produced using professional talent, and they are highly visual. You don't read a lot when experiencing video. We are content to use the medium of TV to serve our purposes both in business and at home. Until television is two-way and more interactive, it will continue to serve a much more passive and entertaining role in our daily lives.

THE BEAUTY OF FACE-TO-FACE

Television has its place in business as it does at home, but it can't compete when a situation requires a face-to-face encounter.

Figure 27.14 summarizes the aspects of face-to-face communication. The ability to engage in real-time conversation in the same room with another person is clearly important to all of us.

The whole interpersonal experience is very natural when it comes to using your five senses. Just the handshake as a greeting tells you so much about another person. A casual stroll past a freshly brewing pot of coffee can change the perspective of almost any conversation.

Figure 27.14
The attributes of face-to-face communication support the need for personal contact.

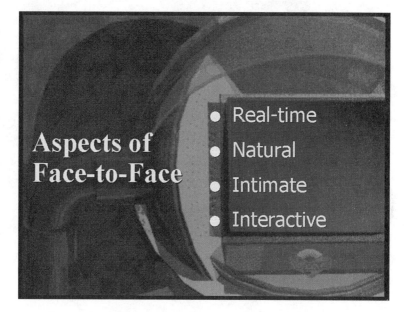

A heightened level of intimacy or closeness exists when people share face-to-face communication. The fact that people share the same moments at the same location allows them to cement a memory beyond what any other form of communication can offer. It's that closeness, that friendship, that helps develop business relationships over the course of time. Even the degree to which you can be truly interactive in a meeting makes you want to use the face-to-face process whenever you can. After all, you can tell right away if you need to change direction in a discussion or bring up additional data to support your point. In many cases, you know these things simply by being in the same space as the other person.

THE IDEAL COMMUNICATION CHANNEL

If any medium could harness the best of both television and face-to-face communication, it would be the ideal communication channel. Figure 27.15 shows the elements of the ultimate medium, if it really existed. Even at this stage in the development of this technology, videoconferencing possesses many of these attributes and comes close to being the ideal communication channel.

Videoconferencing is definitely action driven and highly visual. Videoconferencing happens in real-time, give or take a second for transmission of the signal. In addition, it's intimate and interactive.

PART
VII

CH
27

Figure 27.15
By combining the features of television and face-to-face, you can create the ideal communication channel.

However, of the eight elements of the ideal medium, videoconferencing falls short in some areas. Figure 27.16 shows where the technology misses, specifically in the areas of production, talent, and naturalness.

Figure 27.16
Although it offers a lot, videoconferencing falls short of the ideal communication channel.

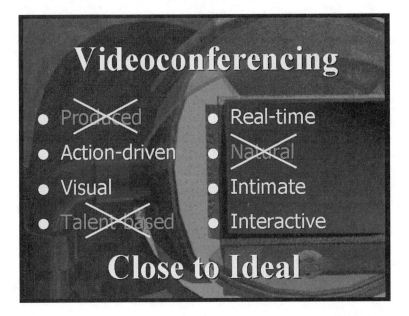

In terms of being produced and talent based, videoconferencing requires specific skills to make the event and the participants more effective. Acquiring these skills will put you on the fast track for decision making, problem solving, and getting noticed. You can't escape the eventual need to become a video communicator and screen-to-screen collaborator.

Regarding the technology enabling completely natural interaction, just like face-to-face, that kind of virtual reality is getting closer, but it is far from here. Let's take a look at what you can do to make videoconferencing look better produced and more talented than it is now.

THE PRODUCTION ASPECT

The only way to make videoconferencing more like TV is to create a simple production. Videoconferencing enables you to incorporate a few of television's powerful elements. The effectiveness of TV stems from its capability to tap emotions. The medium leaves little to the imagination as images, graphics, voices, and music provide every detail of the stories it tells. You can enhance the visual effectiveness of videoconferencing through your setting, screenplay, and special effects.

You can control the setting by enhancing the layout of the room where you conduct your conferences. Whether you are using personal or group videoconferencing, pay attention to the positioning of the equipment relative to the seating and doorways. In a group setup, the camera and codec (coding/decoding or compressing/decompressing) unit usually sit on top of the monitor to allow the most meaningful eye contact between the sites. Make sure the distance between the equipment and seats allows for a complete group shot, as well as appropriate close-up views of the individuals. The system's microphone should be equidistant from all participants and, if possible, positioned on a separate table to eliminate noises from shuffling and vibration. Doorways should enable people to enter and exit the room with minimal distraction in front of the camera.

Backdrops enable you to manipulate the audience's perception of you and your environment. The backdrops you see on television are chosen to provide details in the story being told. They are used to create an effect. This approach may be overkill for the business world, but remember that your image is everything; understanding the power of the visual image can give you an edge. For best results, choose a backdrop (or wall paint) that is about 17% gray. This ensures a flattering and smoothly transmitted backdrop.

The typical conference room is lit with fluorescent and incandescent lights. These are unflattering and provide little control. If you are creating a videoconferencing room, rely on professionals to design a lighting system that highlights each seat with quality lighting. If you will be conducting a lot of videoconferencing from your office, pay attention to how your face is lit and consider aiming a couple of spotlights at your chair.

When choosing the clothes you'll wear on camera, you need to consider both technical and personal image issues. From a technical standpoint, avoid white because it washes out the picture and reflects harshly to the viewers on the other side of the video transmission (also known as the "far side"). Also avoid narrow stripes and houndstooth prints because they tend to "vibrate" on the screen. Large prints and plaids tend to distract because there are more colors and patterns that need to be transmitted through the system. Your best choice is solid blue or gray, but make sure you don't become camouflaged by your background.

These colors evoke credibility and authority. Lavender and yellow are also good choices, but be careful with light pink because it tends to transmit as white, and it becomes too bright from the far side view.

Another way to make a videoconference appear more professionally "produced" is to write a screenplay. Like meetings, effective videoconferences require a bit of planning and a shared set of assumptions as to who does what and what rules are followed. The more the video-conference is structured around some type of plan, the better it will be for everyone.

An agenda is crucial and should be shared in advance with both parties so that the partici-pants can be prepared for the discussion and tasks at hand. The agenda should note any visual presentations and video that may be used and which site will be responsible for the delivery. In addition, be sure that both sites are equipped and prepared to use the videocon-ference technology. You don't want to waste valuable meeting time teaching people how to work with the equipment.

Decide who will be facilitating or leading the meeting and who at your site will be taking responsibility for the equipment and any media used. If you divide these responsibilities in advance, the meeting will run more smoothly, and if any troubleshooting is necessary, it can be addressed quickly. With the latest advancements in videoconferencing equipment, one person can easily manage to lead the discussion while controlling the technology through a simple remote, with a few touches of a button.

Before you begin, be sure the first-time users understand that there might be a slight delay in the audio transmission. Naturally, as the bandwidth increases, the transmission of audio and video signals will be closer to the broadcast levels we get with TV. For now, the equip-ment may have some limitations. Just let everyone know that their brains will adjust quickly to any sound delays and that, after a while, they will learn to pick up the cues of a video con-versation.

At the start, introduce everyone at each site. If someone has to leave in the middle of the conference and the camera doesn't make his departure apparent to the far side, be sure to let them know that someone left the room. In a face-to-face meeting this would not be neces-sary, but in a videoconference the only view you have to the other side is through the eye of the camera.

The fact that you have control of the camera can add value to the production aspect of the event. Your equipment probably enables the camera to pan and zoom, giving you a unique ability to change the perspective on the meeting. With a little practice (or a system that can program preset camera positions), you can bring the camera in close when you want to make an important point or pan the room for individual reactions.

In fact, some systems enable you to control the camera in your room as well as the one at the far side. You can pan around the room on the far side, zoom in on individuals as they speak, and pull back to view a group reaction. Just be aware that a picture-in-picture func-tion on the far side may enable them to see what you're seeing.

Your system may also enable you to incorporate an electronic presentation, videotape, or dataconferencing into your remote meeting. You can even audioconference outgoing and incoming phone calls if you need to access the expertise of a colleague. If you use these media, be sure that you rehearse the order and switching to ensure that you can move smoothly between the different devices. The power of these tools can be diminished when you begin fumbling with the technology. No matter how simple the equipment is to operate, take the time for a technical run-through.

Finally, keep in mind that a videoconference can also be videotaped for archival or review purposes. All it takes is a VCR connected to the videoconferencing system. Although the replay will include only the action from the far side, the audio will be two sided, similar to what it may have sounded like had you attended the meeting. The only thing you won't see is any interaction in the room on your side of the conference. Keep in mind that if your interactive sessions are archived, there will be compelling visual evidence available in case you change or need to defend your position on a particular topic. This is true of e-mail and voice mail messages, but a videotape is much more impressive. Of course, a videotape recording can be blessing or a curse, depending on the nature of the content.

Those are just some of the things you can consider if you want a videoconference to appear more like a TV production. This is not much different from the effort it takes to make an average presentation look extremely professional. The more you become aware of what to work on, the easier it becomes to accomplish the task.

BOOSTING YOUR TALENT

It goes without saying that a talent-based medium requires talent. The people embracing videoconferencing are developing a unique set of skills that is setting them apart as communicators. The skill set goes beyond the ability to write well and speak comfortably in public. This technology is quick, interactive, and intimate. It requires that you constantly assess what you are saying, how you are saying it, and how you look.

Earlier in this chapter we talked about playing to the camera, and a videoconference is a prime example of a situation in which your voice, positioning, and movement are most noticeable. Some other unique issues related to videoconferencing also come into play.

From a vocal standpoint, avoid the rudeness of side conversations. People may see you whispering but may not hear your comments. However, in negotiations, asides can be your ally. Many videoconferencing systems have a mute button on the microphone that enables you to pause the audio transmission temporarily. If you first get an agreement that both parties will be using this function to discuss items among themselves, negotiations can proceed more quickly. Just be aware that the video may still be running, allowing the other party to read your expressions and body language.

As I mentioned before, when you are using a system that has a slight audio delay, it's important to wait until an individual has completely finished a sentence before replying. Because we tend to interrupt each other a lot in normal conversation, many experts believe that the patience required by videoconferencing users may finally teach us to wait for the other person to finish. This more "formal" timing will actually put us in line with the communication styles of our European and Asian partners and could lead to more effective communication overall. Of course, when all systems are up to real-time broadcast quality speed (like telephones), there won't be any audio delays. Then we'll go back to stepping on each other's sentences again.

From a physical delivery perspective, facial expressions are critical to the communication process. By reading the face of the other party, you may be able to tell if he is confused or supportive, eager or bored, trustworthy or lying. Likewise, your face will communicate information about what you are thinking and feeling. Remember that even though you may not be the person speaking, you are still on camera and therefore are still communicating. Try to manage the messages you are sending through body language, and you will be much more effective.

Note

How to Read a Person Like a Book, by Gerald Nierenberg and Henry Calero (Pocket Books), offers some interesting insights into the role body language plays in interpersonal communication. Understanding nonverbal cues can be extremely useful in any small group environment, including a videoconference.

Eye contact is still a dilemma in videoconferencing. You can't make direct eye contact with the camera and the person on the screen simultaneously, unless you are sitting back far enough from the camera lens that you appear to be looking directly back at someone. Figures 27.17 and 27.18 demonstrate this issue. As I was typing this, I decided to take some quick photos of myself with the small digital camera attached to my PC. Imagine you are looking at me during a videoconference. Figure 28.17 shows how I appear to you when I look directly into the camera lens. Notice that I am looking right at you. Figure 28.18 shows how I appear to you if I look at your image on my end of the conference and my viewing screen is lower than the camera. The only reason you notice this is because I am so close to the camera. I would have to sit farther back from the camera to give you the appearance of direct eye contact as I look at your image on my screen.

That is why most videoconference systems use a 27-inch or 32-inch TV screen with the camera mounted on top of the set and the participants seated about 10 to 12 feet away. From that distance you really can't tell that the person you're looking at is really looking at your image on their screen, slightly below the camera lens. Of course, if the camera could be mounted in the middle of the TV screen, you would always appear to be looking into the lens regardless of how close you were to the screen.

If you were on TV, you would always be looking directly into the camera lens because it's still a one-way communication tool. This line-of-sight problem is most apparent in personal videoconferencing and close-up views. Until the technology is perfected (and many solutions are being researched), you must learn to look into the camera when speaking or adjust to any differences.

Figure 27.17
If I look straight into the camera lens mounted on top of my viewing screen, it appears that I am looking directly at you.

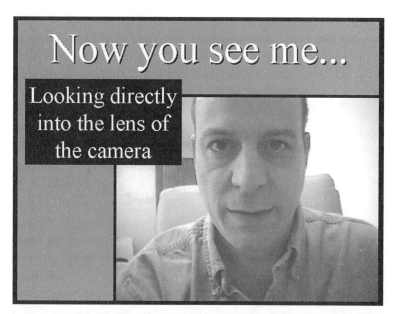

Now you see me...

Looking directly into the lens of the camera

Figure 27.18
I need to sit farther from the camera to make eye contact more direct.

Now you don't...

Looking at the video monitor to see the person

Look at Me When I Talk to You!

When you watch television, there is no reciprocal eye contact. The transmission of the signal is one way. As the viewer, you are not sending your image back to the person in the studio, so that person only has to look into the camera lens to know that eye contact is being made with you watching from home.

Unlike television, group and desktop videoconferencing systems today face the challenge of absolutely direct eye contact. Videoconferencing is interactive, and two-way communication means eye contact is important on both ends of the transmission. Because the lens is outside the viewing area of the screen, maintaining absolute eye-to-eye contact is impossible. To reduce this distraction, experts suggest reducing the angle by which the eyes are averted from the lens. Adjusting the distance people sit from the screen (TV or monitor) or using a smaller screen can help with direct eye contact problems.

As the screen size gets larger, you must increase the distance participants sit from the screen. The goal is to have the angle between the camera lens and the person's focal point (the spot focused on with the eyes) to be 10 degrees or less. Mount the camera on top of the monitor and center it. Be sure the monitor is at a height such that you're looking straight into the top third of the monitor when sitting. This reduces the angle that those on the other end (looking at you) have between your image and their camera lens.

To minimize the angle between your camera and the image of those you are looking at on your monitor, frame the shot of the other people so there is only a small amount of empty space above their heads. That way, your eyes have to drop down only a short distance when you look at them on your monitor, and it appears you are looking more directly into the camera lens.

Of course, the simplest way to know if your eye contact is a distraction is to ask those on the other end if it seems like you are looking directly at them or somewhat downward. If you appear to be looking down from their perspective, sit farther back from the monitor to reduce the distraction.

If you plan to move around at all, one way to stay within the frame of the camera is to test the camera positions in advance and plan your movement. If your videoconferencing equipment allows you to preset camera positions, you'll also be able to change from a wide shot to a close-up with the touch of a button.

Of course, real talent develops with experience. The more you use videoconferencing, the less your viewers notice the technology, and the more comfortable and natural you'll feel. As the technology becomes more common, you can share your expertise to introduce others to the power of the media. In the beginning, it might feel like the technology is controlling you, but eventually you will use videoconferencing with the ease with which you currently use your computer, fax machine, and phone.

NOT QUITE NATURAL

Although videoconferencing falls short of being the ideal communication channel, the efforts on your part concerning production and talent can bring the technology much closer to the ideal.

Current videoconferencing cannot duplicate the natural aspects of face-to-face communication. You still can't fill the coffee cup of the person at the far side. You can't smell cologne or shake hands. You can't see the subtle expression in his eyes or hear the faint pronunciation of his words. You can't casually notice the small actions of the group unless the camera picks them up for you. You can't do these things because you aren't there. This limitation of videoconferencing will never be overcome.

But technology advances as we speak, and perhaps, over the course of time, virtual reality will enable seamless workplaces that simulate very real and natural interaction among people. It is more likely that we will sacrifice the five senses for the sake of just two or three, rather than ignore videoconferencing as the new-age communication medium.

TROUBLESHOOTING

COVERING ALL THE BASES

Regardless of the setting, are there any general recommendations that you have for covering all the bases when preparing presentations?

Maybe the best way to approach this is to provide a presenter's checklist. These are some of the more important questions you might ask yourself when preparing for a presentation. Of course, not every question applies to every situation, but this is a pretty good list to check.

Presenter's Checklist:

- What is the topic of the presentation?
- How long is the presentation?
- What is the format: Lecture? Panel? Q&A?
- Do you need an outline of the presentation in advance of the event?
- What is the objective of the meeting? Call to action?
- When is the meeting scheduled? Date? Time?
- Where will the meeting be held? Directions?
- Is the event sponsored by an individual or an organization? Do they need to be recognized?
- Who will be attending?
- What is the anticipated size of the audience?
- What is the average age of the audience? Gender ratio?
- What cultural issues exist (language, customs, humor)?
- What is arranged for staging and A/V?
- Is the proper media (overhead, slide, or LCD projector) available?
- Is a microphone necessary and available?
- When are rehearsals and A/V checks scheduled?
- Will the meeting be videotaped or audiotaped?
- Is a speaker's lounge or ready room available?
- Will any other speakers be sharing the platform? Names? Topics?
- Who will be making introductions?
- What are the arrangements for housing and travel?
- What are the arrangements for hotel check out and return travel?
- Are any additional events planned onsite? Dress code?
- Can arrangements be made to sell/distribute support materials onsite?
- Will evaluation forms be used, and will results be available?

COPING WITH THE ELEMENTS OF NATURE

If you present outdoors and you still want to do a PowerPoint presentation, how do you cope with the elements of nature?

Sometimes presenting outdoors can involve the use of a screen and visual support. Assuming it's not inclement weather, lighting and sound become the major issues. Ambient (natural) light and background noises are controlled by nature when you present outdoors, so you have to cope with what nature provides you at the moment. I have found that most outdoor presentations that use visual support are linked to a greater outdoor activity or event. The presentation itself is not the main component of the day.

I remember designing a presentation for the president of a company to deliver at the company picnic. It was a short presentation supported by a few visuals. The visual content was required to help the president of the company remember everything.

The presentation took place inside a big tent, and all the sides of the tent were open, so there was a lot of light spilling into the space. With a lot of light hitting the screen, any dark backgrounds tended to wash out, and the related foreground elements were hard to see. The only way to create contrast was to reverse the normal design of the visuals. I had to consider lighter backgrounds and darker foreground elements. In fact, because the sun was shining so brightly, pure black and white ended up being my only choice for readability from a distance.

Another issue I had to deal with was sound. Because the sides of the tent were open, there were no walls for sound to bounce off. The microphone setup was adequate for the size of the space, but a number of background noises were drowning out the sound as I tested the microphone. It was breezy that day, and the wind was causing the hanging edges of the canvas tent to flap. Outside the tent, there were lots of kids running around playing games and making noise, as you would expect at a picnic.

Before the presentation started, I suggested to the president of the company that he invite some of the people standing at the back to move up along the sides. This created a "wall" of people in a sort of semicircle around those seated. The people-wall helped localize the sound by keeping it inside the tent. In addition, those standing reduced the amount of ambient light, giving the visuals higher contrast. The semicircle of people also cut down on the wind and the noise from outside the tent.

All in all, the outdoor presentation was easier to see and hear after coping with the elements of nature that seemed like huge obstacles from the beginning.

PART **VIII**

APPENDIXES

TROUBLESHOOTING POWERPOINT

In this appendix

DEALING WITH ERROR MESSAGES AND PROMPTS

Problems may arise with your PowerPoint presentation during the development, editing, printing, or saving process. The goal of this appendix is to give you some ideas of what to expect and how to handle these problems if and when they occur.

Many PowerPoint problems announce themselves in the form of an error message that appears when you attempt to issue a command or perform some task. Others are more subtle: The command you want to use is dimmed, or the graphic you want to rotate won't. Although it is frustrating when an error message occurs, it does give you more information about the nature and cause of the problem. Take advantage of this additional information, and react to it logically and cautiously. When an error message appears onscreen in PowerPoint or any application, read it carefully and make a written note of when it happened and what you were doing at the time.

Obviously, your first choice when dealing with any technical problem should be to consult this book's index to see if you can find a resolution. You should also consult PowerPoint's online help (press F1). If you can't find an answer, or the suggested solution doesn't work, here are some other ideas:

- **Try again**   As best as you can, attempt to perform the task again that resulted in the error message. If the process works with no problem, you might be out of the woods and can continue working. If the error appears again, you might want to find out what's going wrong before you continue to repeat the error-inducing procedure.

- **Get technical support**   If you work for a company or organization that provides a technical support staff, this is your best source of information after you've unsuccessfully tried to resolve the problem yourself. If you don't have access to an internal support staff, see what's available for online or phone support from Microsoft Product Support Services.

- **Research Microsoft's support site**   You'll find Microsoft Product Support Services at http://support.microsoft.com/directory/. This offers a knowledge base, FAQs, and other options for telephone and online support.

Note

If you need to show someone exactly what displays on your screen, use Print Screen. This key, located above your Insert key on a standard keyboard, might appear as PrtScn or Print Screen. Pressing this key takes a snapshot of your screen and places the image on your Clipboard. You can then paste the image into an e-mail message (to send to your company's technical staff) or WordPad document for printing. The image contains the exact message that appeared. Because what was going on in the background is clearly shown, the technical staff sees the error message in context.

RESOLVING PROBLEMS

Some problems you can solve yourself by determining the cause of the problem and eliminating any contributing factors. Most problems you encounter in PowerPoint will probably be memory related, even if you have a great deal of memory (RAM) on your computer. In addition, because PowerPoint is a graphical application and most of your slides contain several graphical elements (pictures, textures, and colors), printing and display can also be problem areas if your printer doesn't have enough memory or your video card isn't powerful enough.

When you consider solving a problem yourself, be honest with yourself—do you feel confident changing your computer's configuration? Are you comfortable with the Control Panel? If you begin tinkering in one dialog box or another, do you completely understand the nature and ramifications of all the changes and settings with which you're working? If the answers to these questions are not Yes on all counts, don't try to solve the problem on your own—call for help.

> **Note**
>
> If you want to try a possible solution on your own, try to exit without saving or choose File, Save As and save the file under a new name and restart PowerPoint. You might lose any work (in your original file) done since your last save, but if the last batch of changes was what caused your problem, you've also lost them!

DISPLAY PROBLEMS

Most display problems, if they occur suddenly, are memory related. Typical complaints include the following:

- Ghosts of previous slides or dialog boxes appear behind your current slide, or even on top of it.
- Text on your slides changes to a choppy, sans serif font.
- Graphics look incomplete, grainy or choppy, or as though a pattern is placed on top of them.
- Ornate graphics or background elements take a long time to refresh as you move from slide to slide.

If any of these problems occur, save your work and exit PowerPoint. If you have other programs running, shut them down, too. You should even consider restarting your computer to empty your memory and start with a clean slate. Most of the time, however, simply restarting PowerPoint resolves the problem.

If the problem is chronic, you might consider upgrading your video card to one that has more memory and is therefore capable of displaying and handling more complex graphic and multimedia content.

Note

If your slide's background or object fill colors appear in stripes or just don't look as smooth as you think they should, check your zoom level. Choosing 100% should smooth out the display, removing any distortion. You can also try viewing the offending slide in Slide Show view, which enables you to see the entire slide.

PRINTING PROBLEMS

Printing problems are generally related to your printer and are usually transient. Don't rush your computer in for repairs just because a print job doesn't come out as expected. Some common printing problems include the following:

- The whole page doesn't print; about a third or half-way through the page, the image appears to be chopped off.
- Text objects are missing.
- Nothing prints, or only a few pages of random characters and symbols print.

Most of the problems you'll encounter when printing will probably be due to a "confused" printer, one with too much input from too many people (if you're on a network) or too much data to handle in your particular presentation. If the same presentation with the same content printed fine before on the same printer, this is further evidence that the current environment—other printer traffic—is the culprit.

If you're on a network, contact your company's network administrator or technician. He might suggest printing the presentation at night or early in the morning before other workers come in and use the printer. If possible, direct your print job to another printer that is used by fewer people.

If you don't have the luxury of delaying your print job, you can always take the presentation on disk to a local printing and photocopying store. Many rent time on their computers, and you can print it out there.

To reduce the amount of information that your printer must handle for your presentation, try printing in black and white (use the Print dialog box setting).

If all quick-fix or workaround options fail or are inappropriate for your immediate needs, you can take a more direct approach and check your printer's settings. Each printer's settings are different, since they are based on the printer's specific capabilities, its connection to your printer or a network, and your system configuration. To access your printer's settings, choose Settings, Printers from the Start menu, and double-click the icon for the printer. The resulting dialog box will show you the current settings for your printer's connection to the computer, speed, resolution, and other options, again, depending on your printer. If you're working with someone else's computer (the computer on your desk at work, for example), it's a good idea to ask for assistance from a technical resource before making any changes.

You can also try changing or updating the driver for your printer to solve printing problems (equally unadvisable in a workplace where you're probably not supposed to do your own repairs). Check the manufacturer's Web site for the latest driver and download it. Install it by double-clicking the Add Printer icon in the Printers window. When asked, direct the installation program to the folder where you have stored the driver, and a new printer icon will appear, based on that driver file. Attempt your print job again, and if the previous driver was the culprit, your print job should be successful.

Troubleshooting Problems with PowerPoint Features

PowerPoint is loaded with effective and normally efficient tools to enhance your presentations and, most of the time, these features work perfectly. When they don't, however, they can truly be more trouble than they're worth. Before starting your next presentation, familiarize yourself with these situations and their resolutions:

- **AutoCorrect isn't correcting**   Be sure it's on. Choose Tools, AutoCorrect Options, and check to see that a check mark is next to Replace Text as You Type and any of the other AutoCorrect options that you want to use.

- **AutoCorrect is working when you don't want it to**   In your presentation for the law firm of Tidwell, Evans, and Havilland, you need to type TEH and not have it converted to THE. You don't want to remove the AutoCorrect entry from the list, and you don't want to turn off AutoCorrect altogether. What to do? Click the down arrow to the right of the AutoCorrect Options button (it's just beneath the corrected word) and choose Stop Automatically Correcting "teh."

- **Your hyperlinks don't work**   The most common cause of this problem is that the target file or Web location is no longer valid or has been moved. It's a good idea to maintain your links by checking them periodically, especially an intranet or Web pages on the Internet. If the hyperlink fails, right-click it and choose Edit Hyperlink from the shortcut menu. In the Edit Hyperlink dialog box that appears, you can enter a new hyperlink.

- **The speech and handwriting recognition tools won't work properly**   Remember that you need at least 128MB of memory for these powerful features to work (even though you might be able to access them with less).

- **Drag-and-drop editing doesn't work**   If you've ruled out that your mouse skills are the cause of the problem—not having text properly selected can often be the culprit—be sure that the drag-and-drop feature is turned on. Choose Tools, Options and, in the Edit tab, look for a check mark in the Drag-and-Drop Text Editing option. If it's not checked, click the option box.

Note

If your hyperlink works but takes a long time to get to the target Web site, the server on which the target resides may be busy. Try to reach the site later, or try during times of the day that are less likely to be busy, such as early in the morning or very late at night.

App

A

SLIDESHOW PROBLEMS

If you're having a problem with your slideshow, the problem is likely that the show is too slow or your animations don't work as expected. In the case of speed, your computer's memory might be the problem, or if you're using graphic files, if they were scanned at a high resolution (600 or 1200 dpi), this may slow down your show as well. To see if memory is the problem, close any other programs that aren't essential and restart PowerPoint. If the show is still too slow, and you are using graphic files in your presentation, consider rescanning it at a lower resolution (if you have access to the original artwork), or opening the file in a program, such as Paint Shop Pro or Photoshop, that enables you to edit and resave the image at a lower resolution.

If your animations aren't working as expected, try the obvious first. Go back to the slides and make sure your settings are correct. If they are, try deleting the offending object (a piece of clip art that doesn't fly in as desired or a title that doesn't appear at all during the show) and reinserting it. Then, reapply the animation effects. Years of using PowerPoint and helping hundreds of students create presentations has proven this method; although not technically elegant, it is the most effective and expeditious way to solve such problems.

> **Note**
>
> When any PowerPoint problem occurs in printing, running a slideshow, or editing your slides, try the Ask a Question box on the menu bar. Enter your question (or a keyword if you're in a hurry) and press Enter. If you type "Printing," for example, the topics that the Ask a Question box will find for you include "Troubleshoot printing."

RUNNING DETECT AND REPAIR

PowerPoint offers a feature called Detect and Repair that finds and fixes common system problems such as missing files and Registry settings (but not individual PowerPoint presentations). Select Help, Detect and Repair from the menu bar to open the Detect and Repair dialog box, shown in Figure A.1.

Figure A.1
Try Detect and Repair to resolve PowerPoint system problems.

You can restore your shortcuts while repairing or discard customized settings if you want. Click Start to run the process. PowerPoint may ask for your installation CD during this process, so it's a good idea to have it handy before you start. If Detect and Repair doesn't work, the next step is to uninstall Office and then reinstall it.

APPENDIX

B

USING POWERPOINT'S FOREIGN LANGUAGE CAPABILITIES

In this appendix

UNDERSTANDING POWERPOINT'S MULTIPLE LANGUAGE FEATURES

Office XP, including PowerPoint, includes many features that simplify creating multilingual documents and presentations. Some examples of these features are

- **A single worldwide executable**   This enables you to use one version of the application in multiple languages, including most European and Asian languages, as well as Arabic and Hebrew.

- **Independent language setup**   The MultiLanguage Pack offers independent setup for each language you want to enable, even though you can choose more than one language at a time during setup. This means that each language is treated as a separate product, letting you remove installed languages individually from the Control Panel.

- **Unicode support**   Unicode enables you to create documents in all languages installed on your operating system. This makes it easier to use an English-language version of PowerPoint, for example, to create presentations in multiple languages.

- **Language AutoDetect**   PowerPoint automatically detects the language you're using based on the keyboard and applies the appropriate proofing tools.

- **Multiple language editing**   PowerPoint enables the use of multiple languages in a single document, including the capability to check spelling and apply special formatting in the languages you enable.

- **Text editing in right-to-left languages**   If your system supports right-to-left languages, such as Arabic or Hebrew, PowerPoint displays these languages correctly and enables editing.

UNDERSTANDING THE MULTILANGUAGE PACK

The MultiLanguage Pack comes on separate CDs, not the one you use to install Office XP. Install one of the Language Pack CDs if you want to use multiple languages in PowerPoint.

Note

Even if you install the MultiLanguage Pack to enable multilingual features in Office XP, you still need to verify that your system supports the language you want to use. This varies depending on the language you want to use and the version of Windows you're using; check your operating system documentation for details on language support.

To do so, follow these steps:

1. Insert the MultiLanguage CD that contains your chosen language into your CD-ROM drive. The Microsoft Office MultiLanguage Pack Setup dialog box opens.

2. Check to accept the terms in the license agreement and click Next.

3. Select the language or languages you want to install (see Figure B.1) and click Next.

Figure B.1
Choose the language you want to install from a wide variety of choices.

APP
B

4. Choose the language in which you want to display menus, dialog boxes, and help as well as the default language of Office, shown in Figure B.2. Choices include one of your installed languages or automatic setup based on your system settings. When you're done with your selections, click Next.

Figure B.2
Another option is to have PowerPoint set your defaults based on system settings.

5. Choose Install Now to begin installation in the folder specified and click the Install button.

Office installs your selected languages; new features may be added to PowerPoint and other Office applications based on your language choice.

ENABLING MULTIPLE LANGUAGE EDITING

On the Enabled Languages tab of the Microsoft Office Language Settings dialog box, you can enable PowerPoint (and other Office applications) to edit additional languages. From the Start menu, choose Programs, Microsoft Office Tools, Microsoft Office Language Settings to open this dialog box, shown in Figure B.3.

Figure B.3
Enabling a language activates special menus and dialog boxes related to it.

> **Microsoft Office Language Settings**
>
> Enabled Languages | About Microsoft Office Language Settings
>
> Some applications have additional features, commands, and resources that make it easy to use other languages in your documents. Do you want to enable your applications to edit additional languages?
>
> Available languages:
> All scripts
>
> Bulgarian
> Catalan
> Cherokee   (limited suppor
> Chinese (Simplified)
>
> Add
> Remove
>
> Enabled languages:
> English (U.S.)
> French
> German
> Japanese
>
> Default version of Microsoft Office:
> English (U.S.)
>
> OK   Cancel

 Can't find the Microsoft Office Language Settings dialog box? See the "Troubleshooting" section at the end of the appendix.

Select the language in which you want to edit and click the Add button to add it to the Enabled Languages box. If you want to remove a language, select it in the Enabled Languages box and click the Remove button. When you click OK, additional features and commands are installed based on your language choices.

For example, if you enable editing in Japanese, new menu commands appear in PowerPoint such as Format, Line Break, which opens the Asian Line Break dialog box, shown in Figure B.4.

Figure B.4
You can specify how to set up line breaks in Asian languages.

> **Asian Line Break**
>
> Line break
> ☑ Use Asian rules for controlling first and last characters
> ☑ Allow Latin text to wrap in the middle of a word
> ☑ Allow hanging punctuation
>
> OK   Cancel   Preview   Typography...

Can't find the menu options you need? See the "Troubleshooting" section at the end of the appendix.

This dialog box enables you to set line break rules for Asian languages.

Note

Office doesn't automatically enable all languages for editing, in order to avoid adding unnecessary options. You must manually enable editing in any language in which you create a PowerPoint presentation.

Even if you enable editing in certain languages—such as many Asian, right-to-left, and Central European languages—you must also meet certain system requirements before you can truly edit in those languages. For example, for some languages you need to use Windows NT 5 to gain full support.

In other cases, you can simply install the appropriate keyboard layout to edit in a certain language. To do this, choose Settings, Control Panel from the Windows Start menu and double-click the Text Input Settings icon in the Control Panel dialog box. Figure B.5 shows the Text Input Settings dialog box, where you can set keyboard and other language-related input preferences.

Figure B.5
Adding keyboard layouts makes it easier to work in another language.

Note

> If you want to change the language of the user interface and online help, you need the Microsoft Office XP Multilingual User Interface Pack, which comes on a separate CD. If you've used a previous version of Office and are looking for the User Interface tab on the Microsoft Office Language Settings dialog box, you need to install this pack to view the tab. The MUI Pack includes translations for the user interface, online help, wizards, and templates, as well as proofing tools for spelling and grammar checks.

CHECKING SPELLING IN ANOTHER LANGUAGE

To check spelling in another language, follow these steps:

1. Select the text you want to spell-check.

2. Choose Tools, Language to open the Language dialog box, shown in Figure B.6.

Figure B.6
You can spell-check in multiple languages in PowerPoint.

3. In the scroll box under Mark Selected Text As, choose the language whose dictionary you want the spelling checker to use.

4. Click OK to close the dialog box.

5. Click the Spelling button on the Standard toolbar to check the spelling in the language.

Note

> You can change the language of the default dictionary by clicking the Default button in the Language dialog box. A prompt verifies that you want to change the default language for this and future presentations to the language you select.

REMOVING A LANGUAGE PACK

If you no longer want to work in another language and want to remove it (and its related menu options and dialog boxes) from Office, choose Start, Settings, Control Panel. Double-click the Add/Remove Programs icon and choose the specific Microsoft Office Language Pack you want to remove.

TROUBLESHOOTING

ADDING NEW MENU OPTIONS

I can't find the menu options to edit in a certain language.

You must enable a language for editing before you can view related menu options. To do so, choose Programs, Microsoft Office Tools, Microsoft Office Language Settings from the Start menu. Go to the Enables Languages tab in the Microsoft Office Language Settings dialog box to enable the language you want to use.

FINDING THE LANGUAGE SETTINGS DIALOG BOX

I can't find the Microsoft Office Language Settings dialog box, or I can find it but certain tabs don't appear.

You must install the Microsoft MultiLanguage Pack in order to view this dialog box and all its tabs.

INDEX

D